THE OLD TESTAMENT LIBRARY

Editorial Advisory Board

D0870067

A History of Israelite Religion in the Old Testament Period

A History of Israelite Religion in the Old Testament Period

Volume II: From the Exile to the Maccabees

Rainer Albertz

Westminster John Knox Press
Louisville, Kentucky

Translated by John Bowden from *Religionsgeschichte Israels in alttestamentlicher Zeit*, Das Alte Testament Deutsch, published 1992 by Vandenhoeck & Ruprecht, Göttingen

© Vandenhoeck & Ruprecht 1992

Translation © John Bowden 1994

First published 1994
by SCM Press Ltd,
26-30 Tottenham Road, London N1 4BZ

First American Edition 1994

Published in the U.S.A. by Westminster John Knox Press, 100 Witherspoon Street, Louisville, Kentucky 40202-1396

This book is printed on acid-free paper that meets the American National Standards Institute Z39.48 standard. ∞

PRINTED IN THE UNITED STATES OF AMERICA

00 01 02 03 — 10 9 8 7 6 5 4 3 2

Library of Congress Cataloging-in-Publication Data
(Revised for vol. 2)

Albertz, Rainer, date.
  A history of Israelite religion in the Old Testament.

  Includes bibliographical references.
  Contents: v. 1. From the beginnings to the end of the monarchy — v. 2. From the exile to the Maccabees.
  1. Judaism—History—To 70 A.D.   2. Bible.—O.T.—Theology.   3. Jews—History—To 70 A.D.   I. Title.
BM165.A4313 1994   296'.09'01   94-7424
ISBN 0-664-21846-6 (v. 1)
ISBN 0-664-21847-4 (v. 2)

Contents

4 The History of Israelite Religion in the Exilic Period 369

4.1 Sociological developments during the exile 370

4.11 The situation among those who remained in the
land 371
4.12 The situation in the Babylonian Gola 373
4.13 The situation in the Egyptian Gola 374
4.14 The basic features of the sociological development 374

4.2 The struggle over a theological interpretation of the
political catastrophe 375

4.21 Mourning in exilic worship 377
4.22 The conflict over the acceptance of the prophetic
opposition theology 379
4.23 The missionary work of enlightenment among the
people by the Jeremiah Deuteronomists 382
4.24 The struggle for a theological understanding of a
failed history 387

4.3 The support for Yahweh religion from family piety 399

4.31 The borrowings from personal piety 401
4.32 The reference back to the patriarchs 404
4.33 The family as a new vehicle for official Yahweh
religion 407

4.4 Towards a new beginning 411

4.41 'Deutero-Isaiah's' proclamation of salvation 414
4.42 The Ezekiel school's plan for reform 427

5 The History of Israelite Religion in the Post-Exilic
Period   437

5.1 Political and sociological developments in the Persian
period   443

5.2 The key experience of the failed restoration   450

5.21 The building of the temple and early post-exilic
prophecy of salvation   451
5.22 The fiasco of the prophecy of salvation and its
'eschatologizing'   454
5.23 The second temple   458

5.3 The struggle over the identity of the community   464

5.31 The canonization of the Torah and the Persian
imperial organization   466
5.32 The pre-priestly composition of the Pentateuch   471
5.33 The priestly composition of the Pentateuch   480

5.4 The social and religious split in the community   493

5.41 The social crisis of the fifth century   495
5.42 The ethical and religious split in the upper class   497
5.43 The formation of prophetic sects in the lower
class   503

5.5 The convergence of the religious strata and the split
in personal piety   507

5.51 The post-exilic convergence of personal piety and
official religion   508
5.52 'Theologized wisdom' as a personal theology of
the upper class   511
5.53 The 'piety of the poor' in lower-class circles   518

5.6 The Samaritans: a political and cultic split   523

5.61 The sources and the chronological framework   524
5.62 The sociological and historical context   529

6 A Prospect on the History of Religion in the Hellenistic
  Period 534

6.1 The sociological developments 534

6.2 The scribal ideal of a theocracy (Chronicles) 544

6.3 Torah piety 556

6.4 Late prophetic and apocalyptic theology of resistance 563

    6.41 Oppositional eschatological interpretation of
        history (Zech.9-14) 566
    6.42 An eschatological assurance of salvation from
        lower-class circles (Isa.24-27) 570
    6.43 Apocalyptic instructions for resistance 575

Notes 598

Abbreviations 672

Index of Biblical References 674

Subject Index 724

4. The History of Israelite Religion in the Exilic Period

Although – as has become evident – the transitions were historically quite fluid, the period of the exile, which is traditionally put between the years 587 and 539, marks a deep rift in the history of Israelite religion. With it the previous religion of Israel became involved in its most serious crisis, but in it the foundation stone for the most far-reaching renewal of this religion was also laid.[1]

We may wonder how it was possible for the religion of Israel not only to survive the loss of a state unity which for a long time was to prove final, but even to exploit it as an opportunity for its renewal. Here we must remember that its different levels and classes were affected quite differently by the national catastrophe: only official Yahweh religion was drawn deeply into the national suffering; if personal piety did not remain unaffected, it did remain largely intact. And it will prove that the latter not only made a quite vital contribution to the support of official religion which was now in crisis, but also representatively took over a whole series of its functions.[2]

But even within official religion not all classes were equally affected by the political disaster: with the destruction of the Jerusalem sanctuary and the downfall of the monarchy, old-style temple and kingship theology with their unconditional guarantees of salvation had totally failed. That means that there was a serious break only in the two lines of traditions which had first been added to official Yahweh religion with the monarchy. What had not failed was the Deuteronomic reform theology, which already at the end of the monarchy had considerably cut back temple and kingship theology and had brought them into a synthesis with traditions from the Yahweh religion of the pre-state period.[3] Certainly the loss of land as a result of deportations and emigrations also put deeply in question the exodus-settlement conception, which took up elements from before the state, but because of the link between the possession of the land and the law, this could still find a theological answer within Deuteronomic theology. So it is not surprising that the version of official Yahweh religion that had been maintained through the Deuteronomic synthesis became a decisive basis in the exile from which a majority of groups of theologians whom we may sum up as 'Deuteronomists' sought to master the crisis and formulate a new beginning.

Finally, the preaching and theology of the prophetic opposition groups was confirmed by the national catastrophe. Their announcement that Yahweh would not allow himself to be commandeered by either state or cult but would act against his people, who had forgotten all the ideals from the early period of Yahweh religion, had been bitterly fulfilled. Here the prophets of judgment gave the whole of society a key with which they could open up the enigma of their dark destiny and come to terms with it theologically. So it was the prophetic opposition theology, which in the pre-exilic period had been noticed only within small groups of religious outsiders or at the end also by groups of the political opposition,[4] that came to be accepted by the whole of society as part of its official theology – though only after tough struggles. It became the second decisive basis on which the crisis of official Yahweh religion could be coped with.

Thus the period of the exile led to a far-reaching realignment within official Yahweh religion and a revaluation of personal piety, to which previously little attention had been paid. This process was further favoured by a circumstance which was really rather more threatening: the wide-ranging dissolution of political and cultic institutions.

The downfall of the institutions of the temple cult and the monarchy led to a far-reaching break-up of the link between the currents of religious tradition and the institutions. This opened up an opportunity for priests, prophets, officials and other intellectuals who had lost their functions to converge in various religious pioneer groups modelled on the groups formed around the pre-exilic prophets of judgment,[5] who did theology without heed to existing institutions and power relationships, and only in relation to oral and written traditions. Informal groups of theologians centred on the prophets of judgment and their writings, on the priests and their traditions, and on Deuteronomy and the historical tradition were the typical tradents of official Yahweh religion in the period of the exile. Challenged by the crisis of their time, they engaged in broad literary activity, behind which we can penetrate only indirectly – since they remain anonymous. The consequence of this was a virtually explosive outburst of theology in the exilic period, though it harboured within itself the danger of a loss of reality and the splintering[6] of official Yahweh religion into divergent theological approaches. But these dangers were only to become fully visible in the subsequent early post-exilic period.

4.1 Sociological developments during the exile

N.Avigad, 'Seals of Exile', *IEJ* 15, 1965, 222-30; E.J.Bickerman, 'The Babylonian Captivity', in W.D.Davies and I.Finkelstein (eds.), *The Cambridge History of Judaism*, Vol.1, 1984, 324-58; G.Buccellati, 'Gli Israeliti di Palestina al tempo dell'esilio', *BeO* 2, 1960, 199-210; M.D.Coogan, 'Life in the Diaspora', *BA* 37,

1974, 6-12; I.Eph'al, 'On the Political and Social Organization of the Jews in the Babylonian Exile', *ZDMG* Suppl V, 1980, 106-12; J.N.Graham, *Palestine During the Period of Exile, 586-539 BC*, Diss.theol.Cardiff 1977; id., ' "Vinedressers and Plowmen". 2 Kings 25:12 and Jeremiah 52:16', *BA* 47, 1984, 55-8; B.Hartberger, '*An den Wassern von Babylon...' Psalm 137 auf dem Hintergrund vom Jeremia 51, der biblischen Edom-Traditionen und babylonischen Originalquellen*, BBB 63, 1986; E.Janssen, *Juda in der Exilszeit*, FRLANT 69, 1956; H.Kreissig, *Die sozialökonomische Situation in Juda zur Achämenidenzeit*, Schriften zur Geschichte und Kultur des alten Orients 7, 1963, 20-34; H.-P.Müller, 'Phönikien und Juda in der exilisch-nachexilischen Zeit', *WO* 7, 1970, 189-204; B.Porten, 'The Jews in Egypt', in W.D.Davies and L.Finkelstein (eds.), *The Cambridge History of Judaism*, Vol.I, 1984, 372-400; D.L.Smith, *The Religion of the Landless. The Social Context of the Babylonian Exile*, 1989; G.Wallis, *Die soziale Situation der Juden in Babylonien zur Achämenidenzeit aufgrund von fünfzig ausgewählten babylonischen Urkunden*, Diss.phil Berlin 1953 (typescript); R.Zadok, *The Jews in Babylonia during the Chaldean and Achaemenian Periods according to the Babylonian Sources*, Haifa 1979.

We have only very sketchy knowledge of historical and thus also sociological developments during the exilic period, since there are no direct sources apart for those for the period shortly after 587 (Jeremiah, Lamentations). The Chronistic history work makes it seem as if all Israel was deported and the land of Judah was uninhabited during the exile (II Chron.36.21), but this does not correspond to the historical facts. Even if we are unclear about the precise number of those exiled,[7] we can say with certainty that the deportations affected only a minority, above all the upper class; the majority of the population, above all the small landowners and the landless lower classes, remained in the land.[8] So in this period we have to consider the very different social conditions among those who remained in the land and the Babylonian and Egyptian Gola.

4.11 The situation among those who remained in the land

I have already discussed Gedaliah's failed reform.[9] The installation of the landless and refugees on the properties of the large landowners (Jer.39.10; 40.10) which had either been abandoned or even confiscated (Lam.5.2) indicates that it was in the interests of the Babylonian occupying power to consolidate the situation as soon as possible in the land which had been devastated by the war. The reports in Lamentations of extreme famine extending even to cannibalism in Jerusalem (Lam.1.11; 2.12,20; 4.4,10) and some interventions by the occupying power (5.11-13), probably on the one hand relate to local phenomena limited to a particular place and time, but on the other hand they show that the Babylonian policy of occupation could be judged quite differently by different groups of the population: what seemed to the poet of Lamentations, probably to be put among those of the upper class remaining behind, who formerly had a nationalistic attitude (cf.Lam.4.12,20), to be unjust appropriation (5.2), compulsory measures (5.12,13) and dishonour (5.16a) was welcomed by the small farmers who returned to the land more as fairness. At all events we can conclude from the slogan handed down in Ezek.11.15; 33.24 that the majority of those who remained in the land were positive about the division of property and even justified it theologically. For them the exile was Yahweh's judgment on the exploitation of the upper class and often even a *de facto* liberation from debt.

So we can assume that under the somewhat loose[10] Babylonian administration, despite occasional confrontations,[11] the land which had been devastated by the war soon recovered economically.[12] As the Babylonians did not import a foreign upper class, the people of Judah could evidently even develop a limited degree of self-government on the basis of elders (Lam.5.12), revitalizing institutions from before the time of the state. However, the place of the royal central authority was now taken by the provincial administration, to whom taxes were to be paid and for whom services were to be performed (Lam.5.12f.), as formerly for the Israelite king. To this degree little changed on the land for the majority of small farming families; domestically the situation seems even to have become easier for many.

The real threat from which the population of Judah had to suffer came from abroad, from the neighbouring small states which took advantage of the decline in the population of Judah and the quite weak Babylonian military presence to invade from all sides the territory in which Judah had settled and make their political and economic interests felt.[13] There is dispute as to when this process began.[14] But at the latest in the late exilic period the Negeb (Amos 1.11f.; Obad.19; Ezek.35.10; 36.5) and perhaps even already the southern part of the hill-country of Judah (cf. Jer.32.44) were lost to the Edomites, the Shephelah to the expansionist Phoenicians and Philistines (Obad.19; Ezek.26.2; 25.25) and Gilead to the Ammonites (Jer.49.1). In addition, there were military attacks on the civil population (Amos 1.9: slave raids by the Phoenicians; cf. Joel 4.6), in the face of which it was impossible to make good all the fortifications because of the degree to which they had been razed. Even Jerusalem was an open city at this time, and still in the early post-exilic period the Samarians attempted to prevent its rebuilding in order to keep down their old rivals in the south (Ezra 4.7-16). So it is no wonder that at this time the Samarian Sanballat, the Ammonite Tobias and the Arab Geshem had the say in Jerusalem (Neh.2.10,19). The military weakness and legal uncertainty in Judah at the time of the exile thus led to a constriction and a penetration of the area of Judahite settlement and to a constant confrontation with foreigners from the surrounding states, whose political and economic influence the people of Judah usually had to accept with clenched teeth, since they had no possibility of retaliation. Although they still lived in their own land, those who remained behind had to a large degree lost their territorial and social integrity.

4.12 *The situation in the Babylonian Gola*

For those who were deported, as opposed to those who remained in the land, the downfall of the state of Judah meant a deep social uprooting. They had lost not only their homes but also their land and a social status which was usually influential; often they had been torn from their clans or even families and as a rule were deprived of the solidarity provided by kinsfolk. And they had the bitter experience of seeing how quickly they were written off by the majority of the population which had remained behind and of being robbed of their property (Ezek.11.15; 33.24). The feeling of having been dragged off against their will kept high their hope of a return and of a revision of the facts of history.[15]

Difficulties over adaptation must initially have been considerable, as is shown by the ardent nationalistic religious hopes.[16] But when these were not realized, the exiles – following Jeremiah's advice (Jer.29) – evidently soon became integrated into Babylonian society[17] without giving up their ethnic or religious identity.[18]

This step was made easier by the Babylonian policy of settling the prisoners of war from individual countries as closed groups and granting them crown land.[19] Thus the exiles from Judah, too, were able to settle as a national group in various, sometimes abandoned, locations in the area of Nippur.[20] Perhaps they also formed associations (*ḫaṭru*), which were given crown land to work by the Babylonian state and paid for it by doing state service.[21] They lived in the locations in families (Ezra 2.59) or according to professional groups (Ezra 8.17); here Levites, priests and other former temple officials – despite their lack of function – formed their own groups (Ezra 2.36ff.). Alongside priests and prophets, elders took over functions of leadership (Jer.29.1; Ezek.7.1; 14.1; 20.1) and perhaps were even able to build up limited communal self-government.[22]

It looks as though after some initial difficulties the legal and economic situation was by no means oppressive for the exiles from Judah. The archive of the agricultural trading and credit house of Murashu from Nippur attests – though strictly speaking only for a later period (455-403) – that the people of Judah were legally fully integrated in Babylonia and got along quite normally in their businesses. Mostly they were in simple employment (farmers, shepherds, fishermen), but sometimes they could also rise to higher positions in the service of Persian masters (e.g. as irrigation experts). And as early post-exilic biblical texts indicate, some few found their way to the highest political offices (Sheshbazzar, Zerubbabel, Nehemiah, Ezra). Both the donation lists of this time (Ezra 2.69; 8.30) and the fact that only a limited number were prepared to return indicate that the majority of the Babylonian Gola had done very well for themselves in their businesses abroad.[23] Their needs were evidently primarily of a religious kind (Ps.137; Isa.40.27; 50.1f.).

The position of the Babylonian Gola, with its material and legal security, coupled with the intellectual potential of the former upper class and an orientation on their old homeland which they never gave up, explains why they in particular constantly provided important stimuli towards the renewal of Yahweh religion, during the exile and also beyond.

4.13 The situation in the Egyptian Gola

Unlike the Babylonian Gola, the Egyptian Gola did not arise as a result of compulsory deportation, but through voluntary emigration. Out of fear of Babylonian reprisals after the murder of Gedaliah a group consisting principally of soldiers preferred to seek their fortunes in Egypt – against the advice of Jeremiah (Jer.42f.). They settled in various places in Lower and Upper Egypt (Jer.44.1), and from the fact that three of these are known to be Egyptian garrison cities (Migdol, Daphne and Memphis) we can conclude that the group sought and made its living above all as soldiers in Egyptian service. Whether the later Jewish military colony in Elephantine (fourth century) also goes back to this group of emigrants is uncertain,[24] but it does bear witness to a similar social milieu. We can see from the texts which have survived from this colony that the Egyptian Gola became even more integrated socially into its host society than the Babylonian Gola, and that consequently it organized itself for an ongoing existence abroad – in worship too: the military colony had its own temple of Yahweh, which was founded before 525,[25] possibly still during the exile. This marked integration, combined with a more conservative religious self-sufficiency,[26] led to the Egyptian Gola largely dropping out of the theological renewal movement of the exilic period and therefore being seen by this in a negative light (cf. Jer.24.8; 44).

4.14 The basic features of the sociological development

Three principles can be extracted which govern the sociological developments of the exilic period, different though these are in detail:

1. The loss of statehood led to a dissolution of the state alliance which was part compulsory, part voluntary. The Israel of the exilic period consisted of at least three major groups in separate territories which were exposed to different historical developments, had different interests, and in part came into conflict over them. They were joined only by the loose bond of a common ethnic origin and a common religion. Thus the tendency towards splintering within various territorial groups (the tribes, the

northern and southern kingdoms) which was already recognizable in the pre-exilic period continued in an intensified way at a new level.

2. The loss of a central political authority led to the revival of decentralized forms of organization along kinship lines. In the Israel of the exilic period the family or the family association became the main social entity. Relics of tribal organization which had never been completely forgotten revived: the elders again became significant and took over limited local and political functions of leadership alongside priests and prophets.

3. The loss of the state alliance led to a penetration of group frontiers from outside. Above all in the Gola but increasingly in the homeland the Judaean families lived in constant contact or constant confrontation with members of other nationalities. On the one hand, as a result, membership of one's own group was no longer something to be taken for granted, but had to be proved time and again by the individual's decision. Here religious confession assumed greater significance as a guarantee of personal identity. Thus the Israel of the exilic period for the first time took on features of a community with a religious constitution. On the other hand the world of foreign religions which was present every day represented a constant challenge which had also to be overcome theologically. The constant fluctuation between universalist and abruptly particularistic theological approaches in the history of Israelite religion during the exilic period has to do with this new ambivalent fact of Israelite social history.[27]

4.2 The struggle over a theological interpretation of the political catastrophe

R.Albertz, 'Die Intentionen und Träger des Deuteronomistischen Geschichtswerks', in id., F.W.Golka and J.Kegler (eds.), *Schöpfung und Befreiung. FS C.Westermann*, 1989, 37-53; B.Albrektson, *Studies in the Text and Theology of the Book of Lamentations*, 1963; L.Bronner, 'Sacrificial Cult Among the Exiles in Egypt but not Babylon – Why?', *Dor le Dor* 9, 1980, 61-71; G.Brunet, *Les Lamentations contre Jérémie*, 1968; K.Galling, 'Erwägungen zur antiken Synagoge', *ZDPV* 72, 1956, 163-78; H.D.Hoffmann, *Reform und Reformen*, ATANT 66, 1980; J.Jeremias, 'Die Deutung der Gerichtsworte Michas in der Exilszeit', *ZAW* 83, 1971, 330ff.; id., 'Zur Eschatologie des Hoseabuches', in *Die Botschaft und die Boten, FS H.-W.Wolff*, 1981, 217-34; B.Johnson, 'Form and Message in Lamentations', *ZAW* 97, 1985, 58-73; K.Koch, 'Das Profetenschweigen des deuteronomistischen Geschichtswerkes', in *Die Botschaft und die Boten. FS.H.-W.Wolff*, 1981, 115-28; id., 'Die Rolle der hymnischen Abschnitte des Amosbuches', *ZAW* 86, 1974, 504-37; S.Kraus, *Synagogale Altertümer*, 1922 = 1966; J.D.Levenson, 'From Temple to Synagogue: I Kings 8', in *Traditions in Transformation. FS F.M.Cross*, 1981, 143-66; R.Liwak, *Überlieferungsgeschichtliche Probleme des Ezechielbuches*, Diss.theol.Bochum 1976; N.Lohfink, 'Welches Orakel gab den Davididen Dauer? Ein Textproblem in 2 Kön 8,19 und das Funktionieren der dynastischen Orakel im deuteronomistischen Geschichtswerk', in U.Struppe (ed.), *Studien zum Messiasbild im Alten Testament*, SBA 6, 1989, 127-54; E.W.Nicholson, *Preaching to the Exiles. A Study of the Prose Tradition in the Book of Jeremiah*, 1970; M.Noth, 'The Jerusalem Catastrophe of 587 BC and Its Significance for Israel' (1953), in *The Laws in the Pentateuch and Other Studies*, 1966, 260-80; id., *The Chronicler's History* (1943), JSOTS 50, 1987; K.-F.Pohlmann, *Studien zum Jeremiabuch*, FRLANT 118, 1978; G.von Rad, 'The Deuteronomic [sic = Deuteronomistic] Theology of History in I and II Kings' (1947), in *The Problem of the Hexateuch and Other Essays*, 1966, 205-21; W.Roth, 'Deuteronomistisches Geschichtswerk/Deuteronomistische Schule', *TRE* 8, 1981, 543-52; W.H.Schmidt, 'Die deuteronomistische Redaktion des Amosbuches', *ZAW* 77, 1965, 168-93; C.R.Seitz, 'The Crisis of Interpretation over the Meaning of Exile', *VT* 35, 1985, 78-97; W.Thiel, *Die deuteronomistische Redaktion von Jeremia 1-25*, WMANT 41, 1973; id., *Die deuteronomistische Redaktion von Jeremia 26-45*, WMANT 52, 1981; T.Veijola, 'Das Klagegebet in Literatur und Leben der Exilsgeneration', *VTS* 36, 1984, 286-307; H.E.von Waldow, 'The Origin of the Synagogue Reconsidered', in *From Faith to Faith. FS D.Müller*, 1979, 269-84; I.Willi-Plein, *Vorformen der Schriftexegese*, BZAW 123, 1971; H.Weippert, 'Das deuteronomistische Geschichtswerk', *ThR* 50, 1985, 213-49 (lit.!); H.W.Wolff, 'Das Kerygma des deuteronomistischen Geschichtswerkes', *Gesammelte Studien*, TB 22, 1964, 308-24; E.Zenger, 'Die deuteronomistische Interpretation der Rehabilitierung Jojachins', *BZ* NF 12, 1968, 16-30.

The political catastrophe of 587 was by no means as clear to the people of the time as it is to us, at our great historical distance. Rather, they experienced the collapse of their state – like the crisis ten years earlier – in very different ways and therefore could also interpret it differently. For Jeremiah and small groups of the reform party it meant liberation, relief and confirmation of their prognosis, and precisely for that reason they could recognize and acknowledge it as Yahweh's just judgment upon Judah (Jer.37.3-40.6). For the majority of those with a nationalistic religious orientation, however, who to the end had hoped for a miraculous deliverance, it represented total political failure and the collapse of their theological picture of the world. The city which they had regarded within the framework of Zion theology as being impregnable (Lam.4.12) had been conquered; the temple in which they had seen Yahweh himself as being present (2.1) had been devastated and desecrated by the heathen (1.10); and the king who had seemed to guarantee them life and security (4.20) had been executed or deported. We will not go far wrong in assuming that a feeling of dull despair spread among most of those who were deported and among those who remained behind in the ruins. They felt that they had been struck by an inexplicable blow of fate which put in question everything that had been handed down to them by priests, temple prophets and court theologians as the foundation of official belief in Yahweh. Where was the Yahweh enthroned on Zion, who was ruling the world with the help of his anointed? Had he not tangibly demonstrated his impotence in the face of the Babylonian gods (Isa.50.2), as the enemies had triumphed? Had not his promises, oaths and commitments been shown up as deception (Ps.77.9; 89.50)? Was he concerned about his people at all (Isa.40.27), or was Israel at an end (Ezek.37.11)?

But the Deuteronomic reform theology, too, had to ask itself critical questions. What had the whole reform of the cult achieved? Had not exclusive worship of Yahweh and its implementation even among the families proved to be a great error? Might it perhaps even have enraged other gods? At all events the wives of the people of Judah who fled to Egypt told Jeremiah in fury that all had gone well with their families as long as they had included the queen of heaven in their worship, and that disaster only broke in on them once they had given up worshipping her (Jer.44.17-19). So the collapse of the state could very well be interpreted as divine judgment on Josiah's reform. And the revival of syncretism, in particular at the level of family piety, which can be recognized in the exilic period,[1] belongs in this context. How the political catastrophe was to be interpreted theologically and what consequences were to be drawn from it had to be fought for in a lengthy process.

4.21 *Mourning in exilic worship*

One crucial point at which there was a struggle to find an appropriate way of dealing theologically with the political catastrophe was exilic worship.

As far as we can see, the main cult of the exilic period was predominantly lamentation. Even after the end of the exile it was still customary to commemorate the most important dates of the collapse of the state by holding four public liturgies of fasting (*ṣōm*) a year: the beginning of the siege in the tenth month, the breaching of the wall in the fourth month, the devastation of the temple and palace in the fifth month, and the murder of Gedaliah in the seventh month (Zech.7.2ff.; 8.18ff.). Thus this occasional form of worship, which even in the pre-exilic period was not necessarily tied to a holy place, became the element which supported the regular main cult in the exilic period.[2] It was probably held by those who remained behind on the devastated temple site; vegetable offerings and incense offerings could also be made there (Jer.41.5), but no animal offerings, since the site would have had to be cultically pure for them. Even if foreign lands were regarded as cultically unclean (I Sam.26.19; II Kings 5.17; Jer.5.19; Ps.137.4), services of lamentation were also possible among the exiles; these, too, were related to the destroyed sanctuary by the orientation of prayer on Jerusalem (I Kings 8.46-51). But despite this reference to the official cult-place, the main cult of the exilic period differed from that of the monarchy essentially in the fact that it was no longer under royal supervision. That made it more open, a forum to which the various groups could contribute their own theological ideas. This becomes evident among other things from the fact that alongside the normal genre of lamentation of the people (Pss.44; 60; 74[?]; 79; 89; Isa.51.9f.; 63.7-64.11; Lam.5) other genres were used in the ceremonies of popular lamentation, like free elegaic poems in the style of the lament for the dead (Lam.1; 2; 4), compositions mediating between the main cult and the subsidiary cult (Lam.3; Ps.102[3]), or even collections of prophetic judgments (e.g. Jer.8.4-10.25[*4]). Only through this greater institutional openness could the exilic liturgy become the place of theological clarification in the situation of political crisis.

Lamentations comprises a group of texts which illustrate the theological struggle among those who remained behind in the years immediately after the catastrophe. Before 587, the author[5] of these often skilfully composed poems[6] probably belonged in nationalistic religious circles.[7] That makes it all the more remarkable how in the texts, which swing between descriptive laments and lamentatory prayer, he distances himself a good deal from his former views and involves his fellow citizens in this learning process (Lam.2.18-22). In the long descriptive laments he indicates all the evil consequences of the war without sparing anything: his concern is that the distress should not be suppressed but accepted in all its harshness (Lam.1; 2.1-10; 4.1-11; 5.1-16a). Furthermore, he interprets the situation of distress by relating it to Yahweh in strictly theological terms: it was no blind stroke of destiny, nor ultimately the military power of Babylon, but Yahweh himself who destroyed Jerusalem, the temple and the monarchy (Lam.2.1-10; 4.11-16). And in deliberately taking up notions and formulations from Zion theology and kingship theology he is clearly seeking to show with unsparing openness how Yahweh in his wrath has himself shattered the foundations of this world of theological ideas: he has destroyed his throne on Zion (2.1); annulled the claim to world rule (1.1; 2.15) and the impregnability (4.12) of the city of God; rejected his sanctuary and its worship (2.6f.); and cast his kingship to the ground (2.2; 4.20; cf. Ps.89). With his political intervention against the state Yahweh has at the same time put deeply in question the correctness of these two important lines of official Yahweh religion, and has distanced himself from being falsely commandeered by theologians.

This theological insight leads the poet consistently to concede collective guilt: Yahweh is not to blame for the catastrophe but Jerusalem itself (Lam.1.18). It is God's judgment on its sins (1.5, 8, 22). And the poet is concerned that his fellow citizens should recognize this connection between judgment and guilt, should accept their guilt and confess it before God (5.16b). In detail this means, first, the concession of an erroneous foreign policy: the old seesaw policy between the great powers on which such great hopes were set to the end (4.17) had been sinful (5.6f.), and its devastating consequences now had to be borne.[8] Secondly, this meant the concession that there had been grave theological errors: the dominant official theology as advocated by priests and temple prophets had been wrong. Their guarantees and announcements of salvation had proved misleading, and in neglecting to disclose the faults of society they themselves had become sinners (2.14; 4.13). Instead of this the opposite position, that of the prophets of judgment, had proved itself (2.17).

We can still see from the texts what an effort it took the author of Lamentations to struggle through to this theological reorientation. He is in no way already in a position to accept all the accusations of the prophets of judgment; he only takes up their political charges and some of their religious ones, leaving out of account e.g. their social accusations and thus the whole sphere of misguided economic and social policies. And even his theological basis, from which he timidly develops a perspective of hope that Yahweh's eternal rule will not ultimately be affected by the catastrophe (5.19) and that Yahweh will not finally tolerate the scorn and triumph of his enemies over the collapse of Jerusalem (1.9, 21f.; 4.20ff.), moves only a little way beyond the traditional Zion theology. But at any rate here already in the early exilic period an important first step is taken towards accepting in worship the catastrophe that has been experienced as God's judgment, towards practising an acceptance of guilt and towards slowly finding a new theological orientation by accepting the prophetic proclamation of judgment. Further steps followed in the regular practice of exilic services of lamentation, even if we cannot follow in detail the learning process which was undergone by this mourning.[9]

4.22 The conflict over the acceptance of the prophetic opposition theology

The somewhat hesitant acceptance of the positions of the prophets of judgment by the poet of Lamentations indicates that general and complete acknowledgment of the proclamation of the prophets of judgment by no means followed automatically and at a stroke when their announcements came true. The rift opened up in the disputes between the parties before 587 was too great, the prophetic criticism too radical and their announcement of annihilation too total for that. The fact that even the utterly self-critical later Deuteronomistic history consistently refuses to mention even one of the prophets of judgment indicates what reservations had to be overcome at this point.[10] Thus to begin with it will have been only smaller groups which, driven by the national disaster, were concerned for a greater dissemination and acknowledgment of the prophetic message of judgment. There is evidence of this in the prophecy of Jeremiah, which was worked over by Baruch and other members of the reform party in such a way as to justify and propagate it (Jer.36; 37.3-43.7). The same thing was done for the prophecy of Ezekiel by a priestly reform group. But we can assume that on the basis of their experiences of the catastrophe, further groups of theologians gathered around the legacy of the prophets of judgment, read it, interpreted it and edited it, in order to gain some orientation for the future.

The struggle for the recognition of the prophets of judgment as the word of God which now pointed the way for the whole of the community went in two directions: on the one hand as the work of convincing people by the written and spoken word in the everyday life of society,[11] and on the other by launching writings of the prophets of judgment into worship. We have quite a number of indications in the prophetic books themselves that they have been used in worship.[12] Even if it cannot be proved in every instance that such cultic characteristics go right back to the worship of the exilic period, in general we can start from the assumption that shorter or longer writings by the prophets of judgment were read aloud in the exilic ceremonies of lamentation and sometimes also interpreted there. For at least part of the redactional work that can be recognized in the prophetic books, the formation of collections or updating and commenting on existing collections, can be shown plausibly to have arisen from such a cultic usage.[13]

On the whole this is an amazing process: originally the prophetic word of judgment was a form of the word of God which had been spoken in the everyday life of society. From that it had derived its provocative sharpness, and as a result it was naturally controversial, backed only by the theological claim of an outsider who felt himself to be driven by God. Now, however, the prophetic word was clothed in all the dignity of a cultic word of God which as such called for acceptance by the whole community assembled in worship. The only way in which we can understand this process is by supposing that during the course of the exile not only the traditional cultic experts (priests and singers) but also those groups which had gathered around the legacy of the prophets of judgment and were concerned for it to be handed down and disseminated, came to have some influence on the shaping of the liturgy. By seeing to it that the word of the prophet took on a new liturgical function, they made a considerable contribution towards communicating the prophetic theology of opposition in all its breadth to a wider public and as a result of constant liturgical reading gaining recognition for it as an ingredient of official Yahweh religion.

Unfortunately we can discover this process only indirectly from the history of the prophetic books, as we have no direct sources. I shall demonstrate it here by means of just two examples (Jer.8.4-10.25* and Amos 4.6-13).

The collection of sayings of Jeremiah,[14] which is itself already interspersed with many lamentations – lamentations of God (8.5a, 7), lamentations of the people (8.14, 19aβ) and of the city (10.19-21); summons to lament the dead (9.16-21); and lamentations of the prophet (8.18-23; 9.9) – culminates in a regular exilic lamentation of the people (10.23-25; cf.

Ps.79.6f.), and was therefore most probably created specially for a liturgy of lamentation. Using elements of sayings of Jeremiah in two sequences (8.4-23; 9.1-10, 22*), it represents the progressive realization of the divine judgment on Judah and Jerusalem. First it establishes the utterly incomprehensible refusal of the people to repent (8.4-6), which is explained by devastating examples of conceited self-righteousness (8.7-9) and social misdemeanours (8.10-12; 9.1-5, 7); then it indicates that Yahweh's effort to defer judgment by further testing (8.13; 9.6) went wrong, since the people's insight into their guilt came too late (8.14), so that the enemy invaded (8.16-17; 10.18-22); and finally it describes the terrified reaction of those concerned (8.15, 18-23; 9.19-21). Thus it is the aim of this collection once again to allow the exilic participants in worship to re-experience the course of the catastrophe – not, however, as they largely experienced it in historical reality but in the theological perspective of the prophecy of judgment. In so doing they are to learn that it is not Yahweh but they themselves who are to blame for the inexorable course of the disaster, and they must learn to mourn over their misconduct and unreadiness to repent. Only on the basis of this process of learning can they again turn to God in their lamentation (10.23-25), in order, conceding all their human fallibility and insignificance (10.23), to ask for the judgment to be limited in the face of the present threat from their enemies (10.24f.).

Another way of incorporating the prophecy of judgment into liturgy becomes clear from Amos 4.6-13. This is a liturgical text which has been reshaped for exilic worship and which was inserted into the collection of sayings of Amos.[15] It begins with a long divine accusation against the community at worship, which, taking up a series of curses (Deut.28.16ff.; Lev.26.14ff.), teaches them how Yahweh has time and again brought grave plagues upon Israel to move it to repentance, but has always come to grief on Israel's unreadiness to repent (4.6.1-11). Therefore nothing was left for Yahweh than to bring upon Egypt the total judgment which had been announced by Amos (4.12a[16]). In a regular liturgical appeal the community is now called on to prepare to meet this punitive God (4.12b); that means that in Amos's words of judgment (cf. Amos 1.2[17]) Yahweh appears in the cult in all his majesty. And the community responds to this divine encounter with a doxology (4.13), thereby explicitly acknowledging the God who punishes in his majesty – and with that also the Amos prophecy.

As becomes evident from these two examples, the groups of theologians who felt committed to preserving the heritage of the prophecy of judgment went very different ways in ensuring that the prophetic opposition theology was recognized in exilic worship. As a result of this the character of the main cult also changed. Now it took on markedly didactic features alongside its ritual features. Whereas the cultic element had in any case been suppressed by the circumstances of the time, the element of the word took on greater significance. Here already features of later synagogue worship become evident: in them the element of the word (the reading of scripture, confession, prayer) then came completely into the centre. Granted, because of our lack of sources we cannot discover precisely when this new form of worship came into being,[18] but we can probably say that the exilic service of lamentation is one of the roots from which synagogue worship developed.[19]

4.23 *The missionary work of enlightenment among the people by the Jeremiah Deuteronomists*

In the period of the exile there was a reception of the prophets outside the cult as well as with in it. We can also detect this in a wide-ranging literary activity within the history of the prophetic books.[20] Part of this can be assigned to the 'Deuteronomistic' strata of redaction.[21] And among these the Deuteronomistic redaction of the book of Jeremiah is the broadest and by far the most interesting.

Who were these Jeremiah Deuteronomists (JerD) who later in the exile (around 550[22]) devoted the whole of their literary and theological activity to preserving and disseminating the heritage of this last great figure from the prophets of judgment?

We should not imagine 'the Deuteronomists' as a single closed group. The Deuteronomists of the time of the exile – and the early post-exilic period – were more a theological current of the time which comprised very different groupings. The breadth of their dissemination and the power that they developed are quite simply connected with the fact that after the collapse of the official kingship and temple theology in the catastrophe of 587, with the exception of the prophets of judgment, Deuteronomic theology remained virtually the only expression of official Yahweh religion which was concerned to do theology seriously in the exilic period. Alongside it there was only the priestly reform theology which was developing in the wake of Ezekiel, but even this is not uninfluenced by the Deuteronomistic current of the time.[23] That means that as the exile continued, the Deuteronomic reform theology which in the late pre-exilic and early exilic period was still limited to specific groups of tradents became the most important theological basis on which very different informal groups of theologians could orientate and train their theological thought. And if we reflect that Deuteronomy itself already represents a large-scale theological synthesis, it is not surprising that the groups with a Deuteronomistic orientation – despite the degree to which they shared particular basic goals and a particular theological conceptuality – could arrive at very different approaches, depending on which lines of synthesis they emphasized and which they forced more into the background. So JerD was distinct from the Deuteronomistic groups which were concerned to rework the historical traditions, not only in principle in its assessment of the prophecy of judgment,[24] but also in its evaluation of the traditions of Zion and the monarchy and – even more importantly – of the social side of the Deuteronomic approach.[25] Here these theologians not only proved to be ready pupils of Jeremiah, but by their tendency also continued the direction of the reform of the Shaphanid Gedaliah, with its more markedly social and 'democratic' stamp.[26] So it is probable that JerD is the work of descendants of the Gedaliah reform wing of the second or third generation.[27]

The group of theologians with a Deuteronomistic orientation who edited the book of Jeremiah in no way limited their activity to literary work. Rather, there is a whole series of indications that what we find set down in writing in the book of Jeremiah goes back to efforts to enlighten by word of mouth those who remained behind,[28] of the second and third generations.[29] Thus among these texts there are brief judgment catechisms which in their play of question and answer explicitly seek to instruct hearers on the reasons for the historical catastrophe (Jer.5.19; 9.11-15; 16.10-13; 21.8f.; cf.7.13; 40.2f.). And a group of speeches put into Jeremiah's mouth (7.1-15; 22.1-5; 17.19-27: cf. 42.10-17; I Kings 9.1-9) can be understood as regular sermons which go back to the actual preaching practice of the group. They are all set in the gate, where according to ancient custom the legal assembly met; they are based on the 'text' of a prophetic saying which is interpreted, and they are all constructed according to the same scheme, an admonition with conditional promises of salvation and disaster, aimed at leading hearers away from false alternatives for action and towards correct ones. So here we have a form of non-cultic proclamation of the word which may have been another root of synagogue worship.[30] The practice and theology of the group is permeated with a marked pedagogical concern.[31] In highly stereotyped, simple and impressive language, it is concerned to instil into even the simplest of contemporaries that now – thirty years after the catastrophe – they really must learn from the mistakes of the past so that they understand the true cause of their distress, and reorientate themselves in such a way as to avoid further disaster and really embark on a new beginning. So we can indeed say that in JerD there is a popular missionary work of enlightenment. In adopting this course, those involved saw themselves following in the steps of the prophet Jeremiah.

This pedagogical aspect was now also the means by which JerD combined Deuteronomy and Jeremiah, and thus for the first time fully and systematically integrated the prophetic opposition theology into official Yahweh religion. Law and the prophets of judgment found a higher union in God's pedagogy; they were just two modes of the divine word (*dābār*),[32] with which God was to guide his people on the right way through history. In the view of JerD – which differs somewhat from the other Deuteronomistic groups[33] – Yahweh concluded his covenant with Israel on the very day of the exodus from Egypt (Jer.11.3f.,6f.; 31.32) and proclaimed his fundamental demands (7.22f.; 11.4, 7; cf. 31.32), i.e. the Decalogue and the Deuteronomic law (34.13f.). But – and here the views of Hosea and Jeremiah are made more radical[34] – Israel was already disobedient on this day and did not listen to God's voice or his word of guidance. So God sent it a chain of prophets throughout its history (7.25; 25.4; 26.5; 29.19; 35.15; 44.4; cf. 26.18), who indefatigably warned it against lapsing from him. Thus for JerD the prophets of judgment become preachers of repentance who have constantly summoned the people to repent (26.3; 36.3,7) and therefore to follow the Deuteronomic law (26.4; cf. 34.12f.).[35] Jeremiah was the last prophet in this chain. When his call to repentance went unheard (18.11), since the people of Judah attempted to silence him (11.9, 21; 18.18), the covenant was finally broken (11.10), and Yahweh was compelled to bring down on his people the disaster already threatened in Deuteronomy (Deut.28f.; cf. Jer.11.8).

It is in accordance with this postioning of Jeremiah in Deuteronomic theology that for a while he is made parallel to Moses (Jer.1.7b, 9,17 = Deut.18.18b) and by a fictitious process is even explicitly demonstrated to be the prophet envisaged by the Deuteronomic law of the prophet (Jer 26.16; cf. Deut.18.20). Beyond doubt this integration takes away something of the abrupt harshness of Jeremiah's accusations and the unconditional character of his announcement of judgment, but one cannot say that here JerD has totally distorted his proclamation. These theologians could not only refer to the fact that for a time Jeremiah himself had tried to convert the people,[36] but also take his announcements of disaster quite seriously for their own present and future. But unlike Jeremiah, in their new historical situation they also had to give their contemporaries a new perspective of hope. If it was now true that because of the misdemeanours which Jeremiah had shown up and that JerD not totally wrongly[37] interpreted as transgression of the Decalogue or the Deuteronomic law, Yahweh's judgment upon Judah had now dawned, then there was also hope that Yahweh would again turn to the people if they finally allowed themselves to be recalled by Jeremiah to observe the law. In reflecting on the connection which had become evident between their attitude to the words of the prophet and God's action in history, the theologians even thought that they could formulate a regular law about the divine government of the world which had universal validity far beyond Judah. At one time God planned salvation for a people; if this people then became disobedient and would not listen to the prophets' warning, then God could repent of the salvation and lead it to disaster. At another time God might plan disaster for a people, but if they heeded the warning of the prophets and converted, then God too could repent of the disaster (Jer.18.7-10; cf.1.10; 26.3,13,19; 36.3,7). Mindful of this divine pedagogy – thus JerD – everything depended on now finally, in the exile, listening to Jeremiah.

In the view of his Deuteronomistic interpreters, Jeremiah's main demand was that the first and second commandments should be observed. Apostasy from Yahweh, worship of strange gods and idolatry, were in their view the main reasons for the catastrophe (Jer.5.19; 9.13; 16.11; cf. 1.16b; 2.20b;

7.6,8; 11.10,17; 16.18; 19.13; 7.30; 32.34). In thus emphasizing so strongly the religious charge which Jeremiah had levelled above all in his early period,[38] JerD was probably not only corresponding to a postulate of Deuteronomic theology but in addition probably also feeling challenged to this by an acute state of disorder in its own present: the reviving syncretism of the exilic period. The theologians mention some of the details: worship of the queen of heaven (7.18f.; 44.15ff.); an abomination in the temple (7.30; 32.34); the 'Moloch sacrifice' at the Tophet (7.31; 19.5; 32.35); and star worship (8.2; 19.13; 32.29).

Even if these formulations sometimes sound very general and are directed against customs which had already found a way into Judah under the Assyrian expansion, leaving aside the difficulty of interpreting the abomination in the temple, they could be references to private syncretisms which were still quite acute under Babylonian rule. This can be demonstrated quite clearly in the case of family worship of the queen of heaven, which had its equivalent a century later in the worship of Anat-YHW among the Judaeans of Elephantine.[39] It not only corresponded to the custom of calling on a consort of Yahweh alongside Yahweh himself who was closer to everyday cares,[40] but is also explicitly explained in Jer.44.18f. by the view that the exclusive worship of Yahweh since Josiah's reform had proved a mistake. 'Star worship' on the roofs may remind us of Babylonian omen and conjuration rituals.[41] It is hard to judge how far the dedications of children ('Moloch sacrifices') were still actual practice.[42]

JerD regarded the syncretisms, which primarily flourished in the private sphere, as a serious threat. Here the theologians were not only guarding against an interpretation of the national catastrophe as punishment by gods neglected as a result of an exclusive Yahweh worship, but were also announcing a fearful continuation of the judgment unless everyone dissociated themselves from every possible form of syncretism (Jer.8.3; 19.12f.).

For important though religious self-purification may have been to JerD, these theologians – in contrast to the theologians of the Deuteronomistic history work – did not limit themselves to it. Here they also proved to be dutiful disciples of Jeremiah, in taking over his social accusations in full (7.1-15; 22.1-5) and combining them with the social legislation of Deuteronomy. They interpreted the revoking of the liberation of slaves (*deror*) when there was a pause in the siege in 588 (Jer.34) as a transgression of the Deuteronomic *shemitta* and slavery law (Deut.15.1ff., 12ff.) and maintained that here the members of the upper class were mostly to blame (34.19ff.; cf. 1.18; 2.26b.; 13.13; 32.32; 34.19; 44.21), with the result that they had been judged particularly harshly by God. For them apostasy and conversion also came about in the social sphere (34.14-17), and their slogan, 'Mend your ways and your actions' (7.3,5; 18.11; 26.13; 35.15; cf.15.5) embraced both religious and social obedience towards God. In the view of JerD, only if both intentions of the uncurtailed Deuteronomic reform plan could be realized in exilic Judahite society was there a chance of a new beginning.

With this plea for a religious and social renewal of Judah, the Deuteronomistic interpreters of Jeremiah were probably dissociating themselves from other hopes of salvation of which there is clear evidence in the early post-exilic period (Hag.1.3-11; 2.15-19), but which had probably already arisen again in the late exilic period: that it was only necessary to rebuild the temple and get the sacrifical cult going again to restore the safety and prosperity of the land. By contrast, JerD criticized false trust in the temple against which Jeremiah had already fought (7.4) and disputed in principle that the sacrificial cult had ever been an ingredient of God's original proclamation of his will (7.21f.; cf. Amos 5.25). For these theologians too – or for those who later interpreted them[43] – a functioning temple cult was probably part of the expected time of salvation (17.26), but only as its accompaniment, not as the basis on which it would be possible. In this connection it is striking that the JerD authors – in contrast to the Deuteronomistic history work[44] – know no election of Zion; Yahweh's relationship to it is sublimated in the extreme to a 'place over which Yahweh has called his name' (7.10, 11, 14, 30; 32.34; 34.15).[45]

The critical attitude of JerD to the temple is matched by restraint towards the monarchy. Unlike their colleagues responsible for the Deuteronomistic history work, these theologians did not pin their hopes on Jehoiachin's pardoning under Evil-merodach (II Kings 25.27-30). For them he remained the king rejected by Yahweh (Jer.22.24-30). In their view the monarchy was still under the same conditional promise or announcement of disaster as the whole people (22.1-5); it only had a chance if it reflected on its main task of securing justice for the weak. Certainly a restitution of the monarchy is expected in the new time of salvation (17.25; 23.4),[46] but nowhere is there any reference to the election of the king or a guarantee of the ongoing existence of the Davidic dynasty; this is cut back to the formula 'who sits on the throne of David' (22.2,4; 17.25).

The promises which the Deuteronomistic tradents of the Jeremiah tradition proclaimed to their contemporaries, at first cautiously and in part with reference to the prophets, and then increasingly openly, were essentially addressed neither to the temple nor to the monarchy but to the people. They were addressed on the one hand to the Babylonian Gola, whose return and resettlement in the land was forecast (Jer.24.6; 29.10-15; 30.3; 32.37,41), and on the other – though this is sometimes overlooked[47] – to those who had remained in the land and who, despite all the oppression from neighbouring peoples, are promised an eternal abode in the land (7.3, 7; 25.5b; 35.15), God's support against the Babylonian authorities (42.10-12), the resettlement of the lost territories in the south and south-west (32.42-44; cf. 17.26) and the normalization and safeguarding of life, including the monarchy and the cult (17.25; cf.23.4). Only the Egyptian Gola remained under God's judgment because of its high-handed decision to leave the land and because of its syncretism (24.8; 42-44). For JerD the crucial presupposition was that there should be a will to return obediently to Yahweh (7.3, 5ff.; 24.7b; 29.13,20).

The view of JerD was that the real shift to the new time of salvation could not be brought about by human efforts but only by Yahweh himself. In a remarkable piece of historical speculation these theologians calculated three generations (27.7) or seventy years (29.10) of Babylonian rule over the world, which Yahweh as creator of the world and lord of history had handed over to 'his servant' Nebuchadnezzar (27.5f.; 43.10). That is a rather longer span of time than Babylonian rule actually lasted,[48] but at any rate the JerD theologians saw themselves and their popular missionary activity as being in the last third (still around fifteen years) of it. They had to prepare the ground on which Yahweh would then build.

Now it is typical of the theology of the Deuteronomistic interpreters of Jeremiah that they put at the centre of their promise not some external features but the renewal of Israel's relationship with God. On the basis of his acts of forgiveness (31.34), Yahweh would make a new or eternal covenant with his people (31.31,33; 32.40) which would finally bring to fulfilment the close relationship between him and Israel originally intended in the exodus from Egypt (31.33; 32.28; cf. 7.23; 11.4; 24.7). And so that this new covenant would not immediately be broken again like the old one, this time God would root it directly in the hearts of the Israelites (31.33) or give them an obedient will and way of life in solidarity with it (32.39). Then finally even the demanding theological work of conviction and education to which the group now dedicated itself would become superfluous (31.34). Had this group of theologians proved right in their expectations, the history of Israelite religion would have come to an end here. But they were not; the theological struggle went on.

4.24 *The struggle for a theological understanding of a failed history*

It says much for the high value which history acquired in the religion of Israel from its beginning as the medium of divine action that in the crisis of the exile there was a large-scale theological revision of previous history. In the face of the threatening break in Israelite history the first consecutive account of history extending from the settlement of Israel to its exile came into being, the so-called Deuteronomistic History.

In 1947 Noth put forward the theory of a unitary Deuteronomistic history work (DtrG) extending from Deut.1 to II Kings 25; however, from the beginning of the 1960s the situation in scholarship has become increasingly diffuse: there is dispute today over both the literary unity of DtrG and the dating of it (see H.Weippert). It is certain that clear traces of growth can be recognized in DtrG, but no plausible hypothesis as to their origin can be framed either on the basis of a literary-critical model of strata (Smend, Veijola, Dietrich, Roth, etc.: DtrH, DtrP, DtrN) or by a block model (Cross, Nelson, H.Weippert, etc.). This is particularly the case with the theory of a still pre-exilic first version of DtrG which – ending with II Kings 23.25[49] – is said to have been a propaganda work for Josiah's religious policy.[50]

Given this situation, a more open traditio-historical model seems to me to make more sense,[51] one which explains the traces of growth in DtrG in terms of the ongoing literary work of a group and the slight conceptual differences in terms of a discussion within the group. There is no reason here to go back before the last date reported in 561 (II Kings 25.27) for the beginning of this process of discussion.[52]

But what kind of a group was it which in the years after 561 set out to write the national history of its own people in the light of the political catastrophe? Like JerD it had its most important theological basis in the Deuteronomic reform theology, but unlike these theologians it had a further theological pivot in the Jerusalem temple and kingship theology. The interest of the Deuteronomists (Dtr) in the construction and equipping of the Jerusalem temple (I Kings 6-8) and its destruction and plundering (II Kings 24.13f.; 25.13-17);[53] the undisguised way in which they elevated the claims to monopoly first realized under Josiah to a verdict of annihilation on the whole history of the northern kingdom (the building of Bethel = 'the sin of Jeroboam', I Kings 12.27ff.; 14.15f.; II Kings 17.21f.) and the high esteem in which they held David above all (like Moses, a servant of Yahweh, I Kings 11.32, 34, 36, 38; II Kings 8.19), but also some of his successors (Asa, Hezekiah, Josiah) suggests that they should be looked for among the groups which formerly had a nationalistic religious attitude. If we add to this the evident interest that the Deuteronomists have in the phenomeon of prophecy,[54] we can further suppose that these theologians were recruited from the Jerusalem priests[55] and temple prophets who had largely lost their occupations, and possibly also the elders.[56] On the basis of these considerations it will have been members of the ruling stratum of the Judahites who had remained at home[57] who undertook the task of working over the failed national history.

This sociological position could explain some distinctive features of the Deuteronomistic outline of history: the unique perspective of a 'historiography from above', according to which the kings decide on the weal and woe of the people; the one-sided restriction of the criterion for evaluation to the religious, ritual and cult-political level, and the remarkable circumstance that while the Deuteronomistic authors constantly introduce prophets who demonstrate the just and consistent action of Yahweh in history, they glibly pass over the radical prophets of judgment who had shaken the very foundations of official Yahweh religion.

This leads to a remarkable double perspective in DtrG which in the past has constantly prompted a search for literary-critical solutions but which can be better explained as a consequence of the process of theological discussion in the exile. On the one hand the Deuteronomists had learned from their reading of the prophets of judgment that the catastrophe of 587 was Yahweh's judgment as a consequence of Israel's ongoing disobedience. The history that they wrote attempted to verify this theory in detail from the course of history. It is one long confession of sin, which is meant to lead to the insight that it is not Yahweh but Israel who is to blame for the downfall of the state. On the other hand the Deuteronomistic authors dissociated themselves somewhat from the prophets of judgment, something that can be seen immediately if one compares their work with their historical reflections or the reflections that arose after them, which preached that the history of Israel had gone totally wrong from the start (Jer.3.6-11; 32.20-36; Ezek.16; 20; 23). Against such a sweeping view the Deuteronomists were concerned to limit and differentiate guilt and doom. Not everything in Israel's history was grey on grey; there were bright eras like the time of Joshua and the early monarchy. Nor was everything bad and perverse; there was the saving gift of the law, the election of the temple and the Davidic monarchy, and alongside periods of apostasy and judgment there were also continually periods of conversion, grace and salvation (Judg.2.10ff.; 10.6ff.; I Sam.7.3f.; II Kings 13.4; 14.25-27; 18-20; 22-23).

In addition to Deuteronomic theology, the positive aspects which the Deuteronomists advanced against a totally negative view of history like that of Ezekiel or JerD demonstrably drew on elements from the former official Jerusalem temple and kingship theology, now interpreted in Deuteronomic terms.[58] On the presupposition that they were originally connected with a nationalistic religious group, these elements could be seen as relics of former views which had continued despite the national catastrophe. Here we come upon an interesting learning process which the nationalistic religious party went through at the time of the exile: they had learned from the Deuteronomic theology to attach conditions to the unconditional promises of salvation in the kingship and temple theology, but shifted the synthesis of them which would have set pre-state religion above state religion one stage further in the direction of a stronger concern for kingship and temple theology. They had learned from the prophets of judgment to understand and accept the national catastrophe as Yahweh's judgment on the apostasy of Israel, but despite everything they attempted to preserve the shattered old basis of their former faith as a legacy of the failed history and bring it into play again as a potential hope for its continuation. If we compare the theological compromise made in DtrG with the sharp opposition to the prophets of judgment in the nationalistic religious party of the late pre-exilic period,[59] we can see just how far-reaching was the learning process required of them during the exile.

Here it is possible only to bring out some lines significant for the history of Israelite religion in the great historical work (Deut.1 – II Kings 25*) which was developed out of this lively discussion in constant controversy with the traditions that had been handed down.

The Deuteronomistic history begins with a great farewell speech in which Moses proclaims the Deuteronomic law to Israel shortly before the people move over into the cultivated land – with a retrospect on the events of the early period. Thus the Deuteronomists make clear from the beginning what in their theological conviction are the essential foundations for the existence of Israel: the miraculous experiences of rescue in the early period and the divine demands based on them which are set down in the 'law of Moses'. Moreover they make sure that the law which for Israel represents Yahweh's saving and demanding nearness accompanies the people through the further eras of its history. It is written out by Moses and handed over to the levitical priests and elders[60] for repeated preaching (Deut.31.9ff.), summarized on the stone tables of the Decalogue, brought to Canaan with signs and wonders which recall the crossing of the Sea of Reeds (Josh.3), and there written out again and proclaimed on Ebal (Josh. 8.30-35), in order finally to find its permanent place with the ark in the Jerusalem temple (I Kings 8.1,4,9). There, however, it was later to be forgotten, only to be rediscovered by Josiah (II Kings 22). The alternative futures held out by the Deuteronomic law, with blessing or curse, depending on whether the law is observed or transgressed (Deut.28), stand over the whole history of Israel.[61] The 'law of Moses' offers the norm by which for the Deuteronomists its further course will be decided.

However, if we look more closely we see that the Deuteronomists make only a section of the Deuteronomic law the criterion for their further account of history: first and foremost the prohibition against strange gods and images in the Decalogue (Deut.5.6-10),[62] then the law of centralization (Deut.12),[63] the prohibition of pagan practices like particular forms of manticism (Deut.18.10,14),[64] the dedication of children (Deut.18.10; cf.12.31)[65] and cultic prostitution.[66] Then there are the commandment relating to the ban in the Deuteronomic law of war (Deut.20.15-17; cf. 7.2),[67] and the prohibition of alliances and mixed marriages connected with it (Deut.7.2f.).[68] In other words, we have only those commandments and laws which sought to safeguard exclusive Yahweh worship, sharply setting it apart from pagan worship of God, commandments on which in the view of Deuteronomists the future of Israel was to be decided for better or worse. By contrast, they simply passed over all the social laws of Deuteronomy concerned with safeguarding the internal solidarity of the people of God. We may see the reason for this one-sidedness partly in the demands of the exilic period in which the Deuteronomists were working, in which syncretism was reviving and in which after the collapse of the unifying bond of the state the religious identity of the people of Judah was being threatened by arrangements and mixed marriages with the surrounding peoples and those which had infiltrated the community.[69]

But more probably here, too, we have the continuation of a development which was already making itself felt in the Jerusalem priesthood after the death of Josiah: the widespread lack of interest in the social side of the Deuteronomic reform once the cultic reform had been carried through.[70] This attitude is also typical of some of the priesthood in the early post-exilic period.[71] So the requirements of the time and some interests specific to their class combined to see that the Deuteronomists sketched out a history of Israel which is filled almost completely with defensive religious struggles and in which the social impulse of Yahweh religion, which continued to have a marked impact on the real course of history, was almost completely forced into the background.[72]

In addition to the gift of the law there is the saving gift of the land. Joshua conquered it by force of arms, observing the standards of the Deuteronomic law of war. In this period obedience to Yahweh was shown above all in unsparing implementation of the ban (Deut.20.15-17; cf. 7.2; Josh.6.18f., 21; 8.26; 10.28-33,39f., etc.), which is only once broken (Josh.7) or evaded by guile (Josh.9).[73] The martial policy of exterminating the other inhabitants of the land – fortunately purely theoretical – which the Deuteronomists project on to the early history of Israel is again born of a fear of cultural and religious swamping in the time of the exile. At the same time, in the oppressed situation of Judah they are concerned to make a powerful presentation of Yahweh to the peoples of the world (Josh.3.11,13; 4.24). With the granting of the conquered land all God's promises have been fulfilled (cf. Deut.28), especially the promise of land to the fathers (Josh.21.45; cf. 23.14); despite some small false steps, the Deuteronomists still saw this founding phase of Israel as a healthy period.

For the Deuteronomists the apostasy of Israel from Yahweh begins only after the death of Joshua (Josh.23.8). Two reasons are given for it: first, forgetfulness of the mighty acts of Yahweh (Judg.2.10,12; 8.34f.; cf. Deut.6.12ff.), and second, being led astray by other nations (Josh.23.7; Judg.2.2f.; 3.6; cf. Deut.7.1ff.). Joshua warns against the latter in his great farewell discourse (Josh.23). In order to explain it, various Deuteronomistic authors developed a somewhat complicated theory that Joshua had not yet conquered the whole land (Josh.13.1-6; 23.4f.; Judg.1; 3.3) and that therefore some peoples had been left behind to test Israel (Judg.2.21-23; 3.1-4). Therefore Israel is warned against mixed marriages and alliances (Josh.23.7; Judg.2.2; 3.6; cf. Deut.7.2f.). In the Deuteronomistic view the danger that Israel will be led astray by the surrounding nations to apostatize from Yahweh hangs like a sword over the whole history of Israel (Josh.23.12ff.). Again the anxiety about being swamped, characteristic of the exilic period, is evident.

But despite this great danger, the period of the judges, which follows the founding phase (Judg.2-I Sam.12), is still not a time of sheer apostasy. Rather, the Deuteronomists derive from the traditions about the charismatic wars of liberation in the period before the state the insight that there must constantly have been gracious interventions of Yahweh in this period and develop from this the theory of a constant wave movement of apostasy, threats from enemies, repentance and deliverance in the period of the judges (2.10-16, 18f.). The teaching that they want to give their exilic audience here is that there were phases in their own history when repentance (Judg.2.16), i.e. a resolute repudiation of syncretism (6.25-31), a confession of sin and a return to Yahweh in lamentation (6.25-31) and the sole worship of Yahweh, was possible (I Sam.7.3f.), and was met by Yahweh's intervention and deliverance (Judg.7; 11f.; I Sam.7.7f.).

The apostasy in this early phase of Israel's history is described in quite sweeping terms by the Deuteronomists, probably because they did not have any concrete information about it.[74] Israel had worshipped other gods (*'elōhīm 'aḥērīm*, Judg. 2.12, 17, 19; 10.13; I Sam.8.8), strange gods (*'elōhē hannēkār*, Judg.10.16; I Sam.7.3; cf. Josh 24.15), the gods of the peoples (Judg.2.3,12; 3.6) or the Amorites (Judg.6.10; cf. Josh.24.15) or other surrounding peoples (10.6). Certainly some names of gods are mentioned, namely Baal (Judg.2.11, 13; 3.7; 6.25,28,30-32; 8.33; 10.6,10; I Sam.7.4; 12.10), Astarte (Judg.2.13; 3.7[?]; 10.6; I Sam.7.4; 12.10) and Asherah (Judg.3.7; 6.25,28,30), but they are mostly already used in the plural,[75] are interchangeable (cf. I Sam.7.3f.), and thus stand simply for alien gods. One might at least ask whether with the way in which they frequently combine a male (Baal) and a female (Astarte, Ashera) deity the Deuteronomists do not want specifically to attack the old custom, especially widespread at the level of family piety, of worshipping a divine female consort alongside Yahweh,[76] which is still also evident in the exilic period.[77] Otherwise the sweeping charge of syncretism is more a theological theory than a real set of historical facts.

Now it is astonishing to see that the following period of the early monarchy (I Sam.13 -I Kings 10), which from the perspective of the history of religion was a heyday of official syncretism,[78] was evaluated by the Deuteronomists as a period of pure unfalsified faith in Yahweh. In their view, at the end of the period of the judges Israel made a great conversion to the exclusive worship of Yahweh (I Sam.7.3f.), and only the aging Solomon – again led astray by his foreign wives – apostatized from it (I Kings 11.1-13). In the whole intervening period, from Saul to the completion of the building of the temple, syncretism is not a theme for the Deuteronomists. This is all the more striking, since the tradition on which they worked provided a good deal of support for it.[79] This unique state of affairs can probably be explained only by the concern of the Deuteronomists to keep the saving gifts of the kingship and the Jerusalem temple away from the taint of syncretism, since these are as important to them as the law and the land. For them, the period under David and Solomon up to the completion of the building of the temple is a renewed time of salvation,

like the phase of the founding of Israel. It had become possible as a result
of the comprehensive conversion of Israel under Samuel; at its end, as in
Josh.21.45; 23.14, there is once again an explicit statement that the
promises of Yahweh have been fulfilled (I Kings 8.56).[80] The Deuteronomists manage to combine the two eras of salvation theologically by extending
the Deuteronomic promise of land. This was not just fulfilled by Israel
taking possession of the land; in addition, Yahweh promised Israel a resting
place (*mᵉnūḥā*) in which it could dwell secure from all the nations round
about (Deut.12.9,10; 25.19). However, Yawheh was not able to create this
resting place finally under Joshua (Josh.1.13,15; 21.44, 45; 23.21) but
only through the victories of David (II Sam.7.1,11), as Solomon gratefully
notes (I Kings 5.18; 8.56). So the Deuteronomists present the early
monarchy along the same lines as the saving early period of Israel and thus
make the kingship and temple theology a key ingredient of the exodus
theology (cf. I Kings 8.16-21).

Now the Deuteronomistic accounts of the introduction of the monarchy
in I Sam.8-12 do not seem to correspond with this assessment gained from
the survey of the whole era. Here the desire of Israel for a king is first
evaluated in a markedly negative way, as an incomprehensible assimilation
to the customs of the peoples (I Sam.8.5, 19); even worse, as the rejection
of Yahweh (8.7; 10.19), as a rejection of his saving power as the real
king of Israel (10.19; 12.12,17). And here this desire can be brought into
line with the syncretism which preceded it (8.8). However, if we look
closer, we can see that the Deuteronomists adopt these arguments which
come from the old opposition movements critical of the king only with
qualifications; the complicated argument also suggests that there were
critical discussions in the Deuteronomistic group about the need for the
institution of the monarchy. For remarkably, Yahweh reacts to this 'political
apostasy' of the people much more gently than to syncretism: he merely
has the people warned through Samuel, and finally accedes to its desires
(8.9), even electing (10.24) and appointing the king (12.13) himself. And
finally a request of Samuel removes even the last discord (12.20ff.). It is
the aim of this ambivalent view, first, also to subject the monarchy to the
conditions of the Deuteronomic law (12.20ff.; I Kings 2.1-4; 9.4f.) and by
way of warning point out that later it will even lead some of Israel astray
into apostasy (I Sam.12.21; cf. I Kings 11.1ff.). But this does not exclude
the possibility that the kingdom of God could be realized in full in the history
of Israel as a saving gift of Yahweh. In the view of the Deuteronomists this
happened above all in the kingship of David: he was chosen by Yahweh (I
Kings 8.16); he was utterly obedient to Yahweh and his law (I Kings 11.38;
14.8; 15.5);[81] in the further course of history the merits that he achieved
and the promise that rested on him (II Sam.7.14-16; I Kings 2.4; 8.25; 9.5)
could time and again mitigate the threat of judgment (I Kings 11.12f.) and
avert it (I Kings 15.4; II Kings 8.19). Despite all the threat that the

monarchy posed to Israel, in the Deuteronomistic view it was an essential saving ordinance of Yahweh, which not only fully realized the promise of the land but also proved time and again an effective counter to the threat of decline. It is therefore no coincidence that the Deuteronomists saw in the pardoning of Jehoiachin by Evil-merodach in 561, which they report at the end of their historical work, a first glimmer of hope that the curtailed history of Yahweh with his people would continue. For them the kingship theology as corrected by Deuteronomy contained an indispensable potential for hope.

What was true of the kingship with some reservations was even more true of the Jerusalem temple in the Deuteronomistic perspective: the building of it was explicitly approved by Yahweh (I Kings 8.18f.);[82] the decision to build it was shifted back to David, the king of salvation, and understood as a fulfilment of the Deuteronomic law of centralization (8.16; cf. Deut.12.8ff.). The building and above all the equipping of the temple are described at length (I Kings 6-7), and the Deuteronomists show a clear interest in the temple treasure throughout Israelite history.[83] The installation of the Zadokides as a priesthood well pleasing to God is explicitly reported and interpreted theologically (I Sam.2.27-36; I Kings 2.35). And the course followed by the ark until its move into the holy of holies in the temple is pursued in all its breadth (Josh.3f.; I Sam.4-6; II Sam.6). If we add all this together, the view so often expressed that the Deuteronomists had no interest in the Jerusalem cult[84] is quite untenable. That view arises from the misunderstanding that in I Kings 8 the temple is described above all as the place where prayer is heard. But this is only a historically-conditioned reduction of the cult by means of which the Deuteronomists register in their historical report the function that the destroyed temple had taken on as a place for liturgies of lamentation. None the less, for them it is the centre of all liturgical life, to which even the exiles continue to be related by the direction in which they pray (8.48). They explicitly refer back to the theologoumenon of the old Zion theology of the election of Jerusalem (I Kings 8.16; cf. vv.7, 29),[85] and for them this election is an essential element in later history – alongside the election of the king – which mitigates and wards off Yahweh's judgment on Judah (I Kings 11.13,32,36; 14.21; 15.4). However, the Deuteronomists made quite substantial corrections to the Zion theology along the lines of the Deuteronomic theology. The election of Zion no longer implies an unconditional guarantee of salvation; Yahweh's saving presence is communicated materially through the tables of the Decalogue in the ark (8.6ff.) and tied to the observance of the Deuteronomic law (I Kings 9.3,7b,8). So if Israel apostasizes, Yahweh can even destroy his own sanctuary (9.9). And the crude idea of a cultic presence of Yahweh in the temple is yet further sublimated in comparison with Deuteronomy: Yahweh really dwells in heaven (8.27), and has only set his name on the elect city.

Thus here he can be called on only in a special way (8.29ff.), and remains even if as a result of the destruction of the temple an intact cult is no longer possible (8.46ff.). Through these theological corrections it was possible for the Deuteronomists both to take account of the failure of the old Zion theology and also to maintain its claim to an eternal election (9.3) as a potential of hope for their present.

After the saving period of the early monarchy, the later monarchy, in the eyes of the Deuteronomists, is again a time of apostasy. Like Joshua in his farewell discourse (Josh.23), so Yahweh in his answer to the prayer at the dedication of the temple makes it unmistakably clear that not only the older saving gift of the land but also the new saving institutions of the monarchy and the temple are conditional upon obedience to the law (I Kings 9.1-9), thus already envisaging the possibility of their withdrawal. Nevertheless, in the view of the Deuteronomists the Israelite history of this period is by no means necessarily moving towards this threatened bad end. Rather, their concern is to identify quite different types of apostasy – in contrast to their treatment of the period of the judges,[86] to indicate their importance, and to differentiate between worse and better phases so as to be able to demonstrate in detail from the course of history how already before the great catastrophe larger or smaller national crises were connected with apostasy from Yahweh and in part could be overcome by resolute repentance.

In the view of the Deuteronomists the first great crisis, the detachment of the northern kingdom from the Davidic crown, was the direct consequence of the alien cults which the aging Solomon instituted for his foreign wives (I Kings 11.1-13). This already led to a far-reaching repeal of Nathan's promise to all Israel, as a result of which the rebel Jeroboam also received a similar-sounding promise of a dynasty (11.29-39). For the Deuteronomists, Nathan's promise continued in the history of the southern kingdom only in the reduced form of making David a 'lamp' before Yahweh in Jerusalem (the so-called *nīr* promise, I Kings 11.36; 15.4; II Kings 8.19),[87] granting the Davidides partial rule.

However, despite the promise of a dynasty and the initial divine protection (I Kings 12.24), in the Deuteronomistic view there was already decisive apostasy in the northern kingdom even under its first king Jeroboam, which had a disastrous effect on the whole of its further history: the cultic separation from Jerusalem by the building of the national sanctuaries of Bethel and Dan (I Kings 12.26-32). In the eyes of the Deuteronomists these were an offence against the Deuteronomic law of centralization (Deut.12) and thus 'worship on the high places'; because of the use of bull symbols in them they were a transgression of the prohibition of images (Deut.5.8f.), and thus idolatry (I Kings 14.8f.). It should be noted that for the Deuteronomists the 'sin of Jeroboam' which lies like a dark shadow over the whole history of the northern kingdom was not political apostasy but cultic apostasy, and was the cause of its turbulent course with repeated usurpations and changing dynasties, and finally its early collapse (722). Here we can clearly see the monopolistic claims of the Jerusalem priests in the Deuteronomistic group,[88] which they not only use to provide legitimation after the event for the destruction of the sanctuaries in the northern kingdom by Josiah (I Kings 13.2, 32; II Kings 23.15-20), but also continue to raise against the Samarians even in the exilic period.

In the Deuteronomistic view the apostasy in the history of the northern kingdom was further heightened when to the idolatrous worship of Yahweh was added an open cult of Baal, introduced by Ahab, who had been led astray by his foreign wife (I Kings 16.31ff.). In this view he was also responsible for the Aramaean crisis. Only Jehu brought an improvement, by exterminating the hated Baal cult root and branch (II Kings 10.18ff.); for his zeal he was granted the limited promise of a dynasty which once again gave the northern kingdom a degree of stability (II Kings 10.30). However, the insistence on cultic separation from Jerusalem prevented a real turn for the better (II Kings 10.29,31; cf. 3.2f.).[89] Moreover the Deuteronomists also attribute the repulse of the Aramaeans under Jehoahaz and Jeroboam II not to a conversion of the kings but to Yahweh's mercy, in analogy to the time of the judges (II Kings 13.4; 14.25-27). But in this way his punishment for the 'sin of Jeroboam', which had already been announced by Ahijah of Shilo in I Kings 14.8-16, could only be put off and not removed: it struck the northern kingdom in the conquest of Samaria in 722.

The long passage of historical reflection which the Deuteronomists add to this event (II Kings 17.7-23) once again lists all the crimes of the northern kingdom which led to its downfall.[90] The main blame is borne by king Jeroboam, who with his cultic policy directed against Jerusalem led Israel astray into sin (v.21-23), but Israel itself often went wrong. It could have known better, as Yahweh had incessantly summoned it to repentance and to obedience to his will (vv.13-15). The many prophets whom the Deuteronomists introduce above all in the history of the northern kingdom have not only the function of disclosing the justice of the divine action in history by their announcements of punishment which then come about consistently,[91] but also the task of time and again offering a chance of repentance through their accusations, admonitions and warnings.[92] In the Deuteronomistic view the history of the northern kingdom did not have to fail; it only failed because the prophetic admonitions to repentance were not heeded.

In adding to this summary register of sins yet another explicitly polemical survey of the further history of the former northern kingdom (II Kings 17.24-41), which in their view is characterized by a flourishing syncretism between worship of Yahweh and worship of the gods of the foreign peoples settled there, the Deuteronomists are pronouncing a sharp theological verdict on the Samarians who are their contemporaries in the exilic period. Here apostasy from Yahweh is continuing even after the arrival of the divine judgment; here even now the call of the prophets to repent and worship Yahweh exclusively has not been heard. In their view no new beginning to the history of Israel was therefore to be expected here.

Whereas according to the Deuteronomists the history of the northern kingdom which ends with this gloomy prognosis was governed totally by apostasy, the extent of which differed only by degrees, for the southern kingdom they outline a clearly different course of history, one of waves of apostasy and repentance. This recalls the Deuteronomistic picture of the period of the judges, except that, for the Deuteronomists, in the later monarchy the apostasy took place in cultic and ritual errors[93] and the conversion in more or less far-reaching cultic reforms.[94]

After Solomon had already lapsed into syncretism, the first wave of apostasy reached its peak under kings Rehoboam and Abijah: it consisted in the building of sanctuaries on the high places and the allowing of temple prostitution (I Kings 14.22ff.).[95] This was an offence against Deut.12; 23.18f. Where such provincial sanctuaries, termed 'high places', were still allowed before the building of the temple (I Kings 3.2f.), after the choice of Jerusalem as the central place of the cult (I Kings 8.16), they were seen by the Deuteronomists as the decisive error of the southern kingdom,[96] which was removed only provisionally in Hezekiah's cultic reform (II Kings 18.4) and finally in that of Josiah (II Kings 23.8). The Deuteronomists see the fact that Yahweh did not immediately respond to this terrible apostasy, comparable to the 'sin of Jeroboam', with a resolve to destroy the people, as a sign of the power of the promises resting on David and the Jerusalem temple (I Kings 14.21; 15.4f.). Yahweh limited his punishment to the invasion of Pharaoh Shoshenk (I Kings 14.25ff.). The Deuteronomists' explanation of the history of Judah, longer than that of the northern kingdom and on the whole peaceful, is that Yahweh's promises attached to the monarchy and the temple mitigated and limited his judgment on the apostasy of Judah.

In the Deuteronomistic view the situation improved somewhat under Asa and Jehosaphat, who removed idols and again abolished cultic prostitution (I Kings 15.12f.; 22.47); they could therefore again reinforce Judah militarily. But soon after that there was another deep division, when Baal worship from the North spilled over into Judah through Joram and Athaliah (II Kings 8.18; cf. II Kings 11.18). That nevertheless there was not a total judgment of Yahweh on the southern kingdom[97] was once again due to the *nîr* promise for the house of David and the bold intervention of a Jerusalem priest who renewed the exclusive worship of Yahweh and rescued the Davidic monarchy (II Kings 11.17f.).

This middle line was maintained by the following four kings: they preserved exclusive worship of Yahweh, but neglected to remove the cult on the high places (II Kings 12.4; 14.4; 15.4,35), and had to pay for this with dire personal fates.[98] After that things got worse again under Ahaz: not only did he himself engage in the cult of the high places, but by adopting the rite of the dedication of children he introduced an 'abomination of the nations' (II Kings 16.3f.), and purely to pander to the Assyrians he high-handedly intervened in the temple (16.10ff.). Therefore he also had to suffer the threat to Jerusalem in the Syro-Ephraimite war (16.5) and the loss of Elath to the Edomites (16.6). But this negative development is for the Deuteronomists only the dark background against which Hezekiah's reform of the cult (II Kings 18.4) is to stand out all the more brightly; this king, who for the first time since Asa is again evaluated as positively as David, for the first time did away with the fundamental evil of the sanctuaries on the high places and the last remnants of the cult of images in the temple (Nehushtan). So trusting in Yahweh – in contrast to the northern kingdom – he could experience the miraculous preservation of Jerusalem from the superior power of Assyria (18.9ff.).[99]

Up till now the Deuteronomistic history of the southern kingdom seems quite hopeful. Its message is that the reason for the crises in the past lay in apostasy from Yahweh, especially in the failure to concentrate Yahweh worship on the Jerusalem sanctuary. It also teaches that in the past, time and again it was possible to overcome these crises by a cultic reform along the lines of the Deuteronomic law, not least because the promises which rested on the Davidic kingship and the temple kept Yahweh from giving free rein to his wrath over the apostasy. Thus the correctness of the religious and cultic side of the Deuteronomic reform theology – supplemented by elements of kingship and temple theology – had been proved by history.

The great problem which the Deuteronomists faced was that it was difficult to back up this hopeful theological thesis from the actual course of events over the rest of the history of Judah. Despite everything, the state of Judah collapsed in a way comparable to the downfall of the northern kingdom, even though Josiah had undertaken a much more far-reaching reform of the cult. From this one could draw the much more obvious conclusion that the course of history had refuted Josiah's reform of the cult, and this conclusion was certainly drawn more frequently and more fundamentally in the exile than is attested to us in Jer.44.15ff. In order to take the ground from under such a conclusion and to salvage their thesis, the Deuteronomists pursued a twofold course to the end of their history. On the one hand they constructed an extremely negative development under Hezekiah's successor Manasseh (II Kings 21.2-9),[100] which brought down Yahweh's judgment on the southern kingdom (21.10-16); this judgment was postponed by Josiah (22.18-20), but it could no longer be annulled (23.26f.). And they shaped the report of Josiah's reform of the cult (II Kings 22.1-23.24) in such a way that it became the real goal and climax of the whole history of the southern kingdom; here not only are the errors of Manasseh corrected again, but all the cultic and ritual abuses which had happened in the history of Judah are abolished. According to this Deuteronomic conception all the partial reforms of the cult (Asa, Hezekiah, etc.) reach their goal in that of Josiah.[101]

What was the purpose of this approach? The answer becomes clear if once again we compare the Deuteronomistic conclusion to the history of the northern kingdom. The Deuteronomists concluded their reflections on this history in II Kings 17.7-23 by summing up there the sins of the northern kingdom which had led to its downfall. In antithesis to this, shortly before the end of the history of the southern kingdom, in a wide-ranging report of Josiah's reform of the cult they summed up all the cultic and ritual initiatives for repentance which were taken up in Judah. In doing this they wanted to maintain that only Judah took the right course in its history, a way which – as the preceding history demonstrates – led the way to a positive prognosis. Certainly the Deuteronomists cannot deny that the southern kingdom also came to a bad end, and they report this after the detailed account of the reform – though in a strikingly terse way (II Kings 23.31-25.26); however, for them this is only the consequence of a false development which, though bad, historically had narrow limits. It is more important for them to demonstrate that only the way indicated by the Deuteronomic reform of the cult, the consistent centralization of the cult of Yahweh on Jerusalem and the purification of Yahweh worship from pagan influences at all levels, offered the chance of a continuation of the history of Israel beyond national catastrophe. Thus in their great historical work the Deuteronomists are in no way concerned only to work out theologically the collapse of the state in 587; it is also essential to them to show their Judahite contemporaries what they believe to be the only true way out of the crisis, in the face of the popular syncretisms which are flourishing among them and the pre-Deuteronomic practice of the Samaritans, namely in an exclusive worship of Yahweh focussed on Jerusalem. In their view the decisive condition for a new beginning was not the comprehensive religious and social renewal of the people for which the JerD theologians were striving but the restoration of the Jerusalem state cult, the model for which had been shown by Josiah.

4.3 The support for Yahweh religion from family piety

R.Albertz, *Persönliche Frömmigkeit und offizielle Religion. Religionsinterner Pluralismus in Israel und Babylon*, CTM A9, 1978; N.-E.A.Andreasen, *The Old Testament Sabbath*, SBLDS 7, 1972; E.Blum, *Die Komposition der Vätergeschichte*, WMANT 57, 1984; F.Crüsemann, *Bewahrung der Freiheit*, KT 78, 1983; J.Döller, *Die Reinheits- und Speisegesetze des Alten Testaments in religionsgeschichtlicher*

Beleuchtung, ATA VII, 2.3, 1917; C.Hardmeier, 'Erzählen – Erzählung – Erzählgemeinschaft. Zur Rezeption von Abrahamerzählungen in der Exilsprophetie', *WuD* 16, 1981, 27-47; F.-L.Hossfeld, *Der Dekalog*, OBO 45, 1982; W.Kornfeld, 'Reine und unreine Tiere im Alten Testament', *Kairos* 6, 1965, 134-47; A.Lemaire, 'Le Sabbat à l'Époque royale Israélite', *RB* 80, 1973, 161-85; C.Levin, *Der Sturz der Königin Atalja*, SBS 105, 1982; R.Rendtorff, 'Speiseverbote. II. Im AT und Judentum', *RGG*³ VI, 1962, 231f.; G.Robinson, *The Origin and Development of the Old Testament Sabbath*, Diss.theol.Hamburg 1975; W.H.Schmidt, *Exodus. 1.Teilband: Exodus 1-6*, BK II/1, 1988; J.G.Schur, *Wesen und Motive der Beschneidung im Lichte alttestamentlicher Quellen und der Völkerkunde*, 1937; H.Wissmann et al., 'Beschneidung', *TRE* V, 1980, 714-24 (with bibliography).

The efforts of various groups of theologians to cope with and surmount the crisis which have been discussed so far were at the level of official religion; alongside them during the exile there was more of an underground development – and therefore often overlooked – towards an evaluation of personal piety which provided quite vital stimuli for the support and rescue of Yahweh religion under attack.[1] There are two reasons for this interesting historical shift between the two strata of religion: first, it is to be seen in terms of the sociological fact that despite the far-reaching dissolution of forms of political organization the family remained intact as the vehicle of personal piety in the exilic community of Judah – whether in Babylonia or in Palestine. Secondly, the piety which was cultivated in Judahite familes had been so far integrated into Yahwistic piety – lastly once again by the Deuteronomic reform movement[2] – that it could take over responsibility for the ongoing existence of this religion.[3] Nevertheless it had a religious structure of its own which gave it a certain independence from the official forms of Israelite religion and prevented it from being completely dragged down into the crisis of those forms.

Furthermore, we must be clear that the individual's relationship to God – in contrast to that of the people – was not constituted by history.[4] Its foundations lay, rather, at the personal level, so that it was rooted in a deep creaturely stratum of reality which in the end could not be touched by the vicissitudes of history, as long as the individual's life was not quenched. For the survivors after 587 this meant that their personal relationship to God was not necessarily mortally affected by a historical and political catastrophe of this extent. Certainly many people had to endure harsh personal fates, had lost their homeland and were mourning the loss of kinsfolk and friends. Certainly many were in mental torment as they wondered how it was possible that Yahweh seemed to have terminated his history with Israel by destroying all its historical institutions of salvation: the land, the monarchy and the temple (Ps.77.7-11). Nevertheless, they had come through all the turmoil and deprivation, and could see that alone as a sign of the support of their personal God and continue to complain in trust to their divine creator and father. Moreover, as soon as the situation had been consolidated again during the exile, children were being happily born, people were recovering from severe illness, the corn was growing again in the fields and the grapes were ripening, individuals had greater or lesser success at work, and whether at home or abroad found their own private happiness. That means that for the individual God's action in deliverance and blessing continued even after the national disaster. Yahweh may have turned away from Israel in wrath and have been quite unattainable for the people as a whole, but here, in the everyday realm of the family, he could again be experienced positively by the individual throughout the exile. So it is not surprising that from various sides attempts were made to utilize this treasury of personal experiences of God for an official Yahweh religion which was lying in agony. In parallel to that, the family itself increasingly took over representative religious functions for the people as a whole. The consequence of this was that during the exile the two levels of Israelite religion came even closer together, indeed overlapped.

4.31 *The borrowings from personal piety*

The first context of such recourse to the personal piety which was still intact was the exilic liturgy of lamentation. This is most clearly recognizable in the popular lament Isa.63.7-64.11, the basic material of which is certainly exilic. In this lament, alongside the traditional element of calling for God's intervention and a retrospect on God's former saving acts (63.11-14;[5] cf. Ps.80.9-12), there are two confessions of confidence expressed in the plural (Isa.63.16; 64.7) which really belong in the individual lament. The reason for this is clear. Quite evidently salvation history was no longer so obvious a basis for the community's relationship with God after the experiences of 587.[6] It therefore sought a new basis on which it could ground its hope that Yahweh would again accept it despite all the sins that divided it from him (64.4b-6). And it found this basis in the primal relationship of trust between the creator and his creature on which many also relied in their private prayers:

> Yet, Yahweh, you are our father;
> we are the clay, and you are our potter;
> we are all the work of your hand (Isa.64.8).

The relationship with the God of family piety, conceived of in analogy to the creaturely relationship between parent and child which is ultimately inalienable, is now to help people get over the deep shattering of Israel's relationship with God.[7] There is also a similar reliance on a personal relationship of trust in God in the prophetic liturgy Micah 7.10-20 (vv.7,8bβ, 9bf.).

The second context in which personal piety could serve to strengthen confidence in public was probably the exilic Toda festival. We may infer this from Lamentations 3, a text which represents a mixed form between the genres of the individual thanksgiving and the lament of the people – although there is already literary stylizing here.[8] While it had always been possible for an individual to give religious advice to a small circle of his guests on the basis of the experiences of suffering and deliverance which he had undergone,[9] in the exilic period evidently what were once family liturgies of thanksgiving could develop into ingredients of the occasional main cult in which someone who had been saved told his story in public to the whole community and combined this with some public instruction. Such an event can be traced in Lam.3.22-38, and it is no coincidence that its basis is once again the personal confession of trust (v.24). The person speaking here argues that only the fact that in his personal distress he put his trust in Yahweh and was not disappointed (vv.55ff.) tells against the lamentable thesis (Ps.77.8-10) that Yahweh's gracious acts are exhausted (Lam.3.22-24). Rather, his personal example shows that Yahweh will not be grieved for ever, nor is it his desire to be (vv.31-33). Therefore it is right and good to go on having a humble hope in God (vv.26,27-30) and not to run wild in protestation (vv.34-39). In this way an attempt is made to open up a perspective of hope for the community as a whole from the still ongoing intact personal relationship of individuals with God (vv.26,27-30) and to find a guideline for orientation.[10]

The third sphere in which events and notions of personal piety were taken up was the exilic prophecy of salvation. Here, where the venture was made to announce a new intervention by Yahweh beyond judgment in the face of long experiences of suffering and bitter disappointment, people felt the need to seek positive points of contact in the religious experience of their audience in order to overcome their mistrust and scepticism. So it is not surprising that these were found particularly in the sphere of family piety, where Yahweh's concern and nearness could still be experienced even during the exile.

This concern can be seen first from the fact that where the prophets of salvation go into the lamentations of their fellow citizens they are fond of stylizing these as individual laments (Isa.40.27; 49.14; Ezek.37.11), because such laments were familiar to them and had found a hearing in the exilic period. The transference of the original lament of the childless woman to Zion (Isa.49.21; 54.1-3) also belongs in this context, since from primeval times it had been a specifically feminine basic religious experience that Yahweh had continually heard this lament and given a child.[11] How the prophets could even derive the thought-world of their sayings about national salvation from the experiences of personal prayer and deliverance is clear from Ezekiel's famous vision of the revival of the dead bones (Ezek.37). This is spun out of a typical lament which is quoted in v.11:

Our bones are dried up,
and our hope is lost;
we are clean cut off (from life)[12] (Ezek.37.11).

And because the sick person was already caught in the jaws of death and experienced his or her salvation as deliverance from the power of death, in a vision Ezekiel depicts how the Israel of the exile was just a great pile of dead bones and is being revived by Yahweh. Moreover in describing the saving act of God in the image of the lifegiving spirit of the creator of humankind,[13] he again takes up the experience of personal piety that it is the creator of human beings who keeps his creature alive under the threat of death.

The concern to utilize personal experiences of deliverance for the proclamation of salvation to Israel can be seen, secondly, in the remarkable fact that the prophet Deutero-Isaiah makes use of the genre of the oracle of salvation to express the heart of his message (Isa.41.8-13,14-16; 43.1-4, 5-7; 44.1-5; cf. 54.4-6). In the oracle of salvation a positive answer from God could be communicated to a lamenting sufferer within a private penitential ceremony.[14] And Lam.3.57 attests that this had continued to be a current practice of personal piety even during the exile. Deutero-Isaiah took up this particular genre because it wanted to create a basis for trust in its incredible and sometimes even offensive proclamation of salvation out of the experiences of Yahweh's intervention in lesser family distress. Secondly, it was concerned to reinterpret the historical relationship of God to Israel in analogy to the individual's primal relationship of trust and to root it at a deeper, personal, creaturely level: Yahweh according to his purpose has created Israel, like every individual, 'from its mother's womb' (43.1; 44.2, 21, 24; 54.5; cf. 49.5). Just as he was with every individual (41.10; 43.5), took him or her by the hand (41.10) and helped them (41.9, 10, 13, 14; 44.2), so now he stands by his smitten people; and just as there is a close relationship of trust between each individual and his or her God, so now Yahweh persuades his people of the same personal trust: 'I am your God' and 'you are mine' (43.1; cf. 44.21).

Thirdly and finally, the activation of the experiential world of family religion can be recognized in the fact that in the exilic prophecy of salvation Yahweh's relationship to Israel is magnified and sometimes compared massively with personal family ties. Yahweh is not just addressed as the father who has created and cared for Israel (cf. Deut.32.6b; Isa.63.16; 64.7; Jer.3.4f., 19),[15] but is even compared to the mother who has carried her child Israel protectively in her arms since his birth (Isa.46.3f.), cannot forget him (49.15), and comforts him (66.13). For centuries there had been signs of a certain hesitation in official Israelite religion to call Yahweh father, probably partly because of the sexual connotations of the notion of father and probably also because this familiar family address hardly suited the historical experiences which Israel had had with its God. Yahweh was the God of Israel, its liberator, its lord and king, but not its father. Thus in pre-exilic times – with few exceptions[16] – the notion of father remained limited to God's relationship to the king.[17] The reservations against any form of feminine notions of God had been even stronger, and these finally made themselves felt in religious policy in the denunciation of all the so-called 'high places' with their traditional male-female symbolism expressed in the reforms of Hezekiah and Deuteronomy.[18]

However, things were different in the sphere of family piety. Here not only was the notion of father closely bound up with the notion of personal creator (Deut.32.6b,18; Jer.2.27; Isa.64.7; Mal.2.10), but the worship of a female deity alongside Yahweh as his consort was very popular.[19] Furthermore, personal piety orientated itself comprehensively on the parent-child relationship, and many elements contained more maternal features,[20] even when they are related to Yahweh as a 'male' God. If the prophets of salvation of the exilic period, while not finding room for a goddess alongside Yahweh, did introduce explicitly female traits of Yahweh into official religion, they were recognizing that the image of God sketched out in family religion was at least partially justified. In their view a one-sided male image of Yahweh was not capable of clarifying Yahweh's deep creaturely ties to Israel in a way which could make possible a new beginning beyond the collapse of salvation history. Just as naturally as a mother takes her crying child in her arms and comforts it, so Yahweh would also hear the laments of his people and take them to himself. The supportive, indeed corrective, function which family religion took on in the exile is evident here.

4.32 *The reference back to the patriarchs*

Another feature which belongs in the wider context of the broad influx of personal piety into the official religion of the exilic period is the often-noted phenomenon that it was in this period that the figures of the patriarchs and the traditions associated with them attained increased significance.[21] First of all there is a quite simple sociologial reason for this: since as a result of the loss of its state organization Israel had largely been reduced to a family basis, the patriarchal traditions which in the fiction of a genealogical model had sketched out the early history of Israel as a family history offered a welcome basis for identification. The Judahite families of the time of the exile who had become stateless could rediscover themselves in the patriarchs and their families. There were two further theological reasons. The first is again connected with the questioning of the other traditions of salvation history. Since the saving gifts of the land, the temple and the monarchy had proved fragile, Yahweh's action to the forefathers offered itself as the last historical basis which had not been detrimentally affected and on which it was possible to build. The second theological reason is connected with a pecularity of personal piety which had already been projected on to the fathers in an earlier phase of the tradition, namely the unconditional nature of the personal relationship with God:[22] the old promise of a son to Abraham (Gen.18) had already been unconditional, as had the promises of support and blessings experienced by Jacob (Gen.31.5,42; 27). And the promises of land to the patriarchs which were added later were also unconditional (13.14-16; 28.13f.). Since the patriarchs were not just individuals but always at the same time were represented as tribal ancestors of Israel, these divine promises which in essence drew on the experiential horizon of personal piety also applied to Israel as a whole. And as they were not dependent on any merits of the patriarchs, they could not be vitiated, no matter how badly Israel behaved. So unlike the largely conditional Deuteronomic promises,[23] which were annulled by Israel's sin, they offered a positive point of contact to which a national future hope could be fixed in the exilic period. The largely indestructible personal piety of official exilic theology could also show a way towards overcoming the theological crisis through the patriarchs.

This reference back to the patriarchs, which afforded some hope, was made in different contexts and had different functions: we can infer from Ezek.33.24 that already in the early exilic period those who remained at home had justified or defended their claims to possession of land to the deportees with reference to Abraham, to whom Yahweh had given the land.[24] And we can conclude from Isa.63.16 that it was customary in exilic popular laments to refer to the fatherhood of Abraham in order to move Yahweh to turn towards Abraham's descendants in the present.[25] This motif of trust was taken up in a positive way in the exilic prophecy of salvation: Deutero-Isaiah has Yahweh addressing exiled Israel as 'seed of Abraham' in an oracle of salvation and expressly calling it 'his friend' (Isa.41.8). God's renewed intervention on behalf of his defeated people thus has its basis in his quite especially close relationship to the patriarchs, whom he took up and called 'from the ends of the earth' (41.9). Thus the election of Israel was tied back to Abraham through the shattered history of exodus and settlement,[26] and Abraham's call was at the same time made the model for the expected recall of the exiles dispersed throughout the world. A further comforting aspect of the Abraham tradition comes into play with the disputation in Isa.51.1f.: the immense power of the divine blessing can be inferred from the fact that – in accordance with the conception of the genealogical model – the one family of Abraham called by Yahweh had increased to become the people of Israel. From this the small group of exiles could again derive hope of once again growing into a great people.

In addition to the brief references to the patriarchs in the exilic prophecy of salvation, another large-scale literary revision of the patriarchal tradition was undertaken during the exile.[27] In it the Israelite families of the time of the exile were presented with the patriarchal families of the early period as figures with whom they could identify in more than one way, as bearers of unconditional promises which had still not gone out of date and as models by which they could orientate themselves in their own time. Right at the beginning of the exilic patriarchal narrative Abraham is promised that Yahweh will make him 'a great people' (Gen.12.2.) and we are then shown how this promise is realized step by step (46.3), despite all difficulties, dangers and divisions (21.13,18). This account is directed against the anxieties of the scattered small groups of exiles that they were a minority and would be swamped by those around them. The further fact that the promises to the patriarchs are combined with a whole chain of divine commands to set out (Gen.12.1-3; 46.1-3; 31.11,13 are older), or prohibitions against emigration (26.2f.), indicates an attempt to counter the exilic temptation to settle down abroad or to emigrate. The exilic families are reminded of the land of Palestine as the living space assigned to them by God; the call of Abraham to break all his family ties (12.1) is virtually stylized as a model for the Babylonian Gola, who should be ready to return home. And when God even subjects Abraham to the extreme trial of once again sacrificing his promised son (Gen.22), we should perhaps keep in mind the sometimes sorely tried exilic contemporaries who at times had to believe in the promises of Yahweh even when these seemed maliciously to be destroying them.

Finally, Abraham is promised that he will become so impressive an embodiment of the blessing that 'all families' of the earth will want blessings in his name (Gen.12.2b,3).[28] This is said first of all to counter the widespread sense of inferiority among the exilic Israelites who feel that they have been made an example of by a curse and are suffering the mockery and scorn of all the other nations.[29] Nor does that exhaust the significance of this profound promise. For it takes up the old idea of the king as mediator of the blessing (Ps.72.17).[30] In the kingship theology this had been connected with the subjection of the nations. But there is no longer any mention of that in this exilic promise. Here, rather, it is hinted that a restored Israel will become the vehicle of a divine blessing at a family level, above the level of state power politics, in which 'all families of the earth', no matter to what state they may belong, will have a share. Here we have an indication of reflection on a universal positive function of Israel which had become possible in particular as a result of the dissolution of the state structure and which not least drew on the universal basic feature of personal piety.[31]

4.33 The family as a new vehicle for official Yahweh religion

Now in the exilic period not only did family piety become significant for all of society, but for the first time the family itself joined the ranks of those who handed on official religion. As the main form of social organization, it representatively assumed important functions which supported the identity of the people of Judah as a whole, in that old family customs took on a new confessional quality or earlier official cultic festivals were transformed into family rites. The former applies to circumcision and the various dietary customs; the latter to the hallowing of the sabbath and the feast of passover. Nothing makes clearer the prominent religous role which the family came to occupy after the exile than the fact that in the rather later priestly conception of history the covenant between Yahweh and Israel is not made with the people on Sinai, but with the family of Abraham (Gen.17).

The first family custom to develop into a confessional sign of membership of the people of Judah and its Yahweh religion after the dissolution of the state and territorial unity of Israel in the exile was circumcision. This development probably started from the Babylonian Gola. The authors of the Deuteronomistic history accorded circumcision an essential function – alongside the Passover – in Israel's becoming a people (Josh.5.2-9), and the P theologians even elevated it at a rather later date to the status of a sign of the covenant (Gen.17.10f.), which was to root Yahweh's covenant with Abraham in the flesh of each Israelite family.

Circumcision seems originally to have been an old apotropaic rite in connection with puberty or preparation for marriage (cf. Ex.4.25; Gen.34). This is suggested by Arab and Egyptian practice. This older custom also seems to be echoed in the circumcision of the ten-year-old Ishmael (Gen.17.25) and of the generation which grew up in the wilderness (Josh.5.2-9).[32] It was possibly only during the exile, when it became a confession, that it was detached from this context and associated with birth.[33] According to P it is to be performed on all male members of the family eight days after birth (Gen.17.12; 21.4; Lev.12.3). The inclusion of slaves and aliens (Gen.17.2f.) points to the family household as the community which handed down circumcision.

It was known in Israel that other peoples also practised circumcision (Jer.9.24f.: Egyptians, Arabs, Edomites, Moabites, Ammonites); only the Philistines had from of old been regarded as the uncircumcised (I Sam.18.25, etc.). Thus originally the rite was not at all suitable as a distinguishing mark for the people of Judah. That it could nevertheless take on such significance is probably to be explained from the fact that the Babylonian Gola saw it as an essential mark of differentiation from its environment, since circumcision was unusual in Mesopotamia. Moreover in the book of Ezekiel, which came into being in the Babylonian Gola, we can recognize a tendency to extend the mark of uncircumcision to all Israel's neighbours (28.10; 31.18; 32.19ff.). In the post-exilic period circumcision then became such a natural hallmark of Jewish faith that it was required as a presupposition of going over to Judaism (Judith 14.10; Esther 8.17 LXX).

Now since responsibility for performing the circumcision lay in the hands of the father of the family, individual families in fact bore the responsibility for ensuring the cohesion and ongoing existence of the people and religious community of Israel.

Alongside circumcision, during the exile the traditional dietary customs probably for the first time played a part in establishing identity, even if we know little about them in detail. Here too the development will have begun from the Babylonian exiles, who in a foreign land suddenly found that some of the dietary customs which they had previously taken for granted were a peculiarity of their people. Foreign lands (Amos 7.17) and also food abroad were regarded as potentially unclean (Hos.9.3; Ezek.4.13), so it was particularly important to observe the rules of cleanness in connection with the choice and preparation of food and in cases of doubt to lay down clear regulations (cf. the reflections in Dan.1.8-16). Even if many dietary customs and regulations go well back into the pre-exilic period (for example slaughtering, I Sam.14.32-34; Deut.12.23f.; 15.23), and their original significance largely escapes us,[34] it is probable that the detailed casuistry in the defining of clean and unclean animals to be found in Deut.14 and in an even more refined form in Lev.11 arose from this need in the exilic situation. This gave the exilic family an important mark of identity with the aid of which they could demonstrate in everyday life whether or not they still counted themselves among the people of Judah and held fast to their religious traditions.

In addition to these long-established family customs during the exile, the hallowing of the sabbath became a new and important form of the subsidiary family cult and from there developed into the decisive cultic confessional sign with which each week Judahite families could demonstrate their adherence to Yahweh religion (Ezek.20.12,20; cf. Ex.31.13,17).

The origin and history of the sabbath have still not been fully explained. However, there is much to suggest that in the pre-exilic period the sabbath was the Israelite new moon festival (II Kings 4.23; Isa.1.13; Hos.2.13; Amos 8.5).[35] As such it was celebrated regularly in the cult by the priests in the temple (Isa.1.13; Hos.2.13; II Kings 16.17f.; Lam.2.6) in a way – comparable to the *tamīd* sacrifice – which probably largely excluded the public.[36] This sabbath was significant for the population only to the degree that it was regarded as a favourable time for getting omens (II Kings 4.23) and – probably as with other temple feasts – trading on it was forbidden (Amos 8.5). Thus the pre-exilic sabbath was largely part of the official cult and had come to an end with the destruction of the Jerusalem temple (Lam.2.6).

Alongside this, in the pre-exilic period there had been a family custom of interrupting agricultural work every seven days for a day of rest. But this day was not called sabbath (in Ex.23.12; 34.21 only the verb *šābat* appears) and it had no direct cultic connotation. Rather, it was an old tabu custom which was probably originally connected with a hesitation to exploit working animals to their last breath.[37] In the Book of the Covenant it is also given a social purpose, that of allowing dependent workers in the family household, slaves and aliens, a period of relaxation.[38]

There is something to be said for Robinson's thesis[39] that the two institutions were combined in the exile.[40] The cultic functions of the former full moon festival which were lying fallow were transferred to the custom of a seven-day rest from work. The sabbath festival became the 'sabbath day' (*yōm haššabat*[41]) and was thus detached from the lunar cycle. The festival which was once limited to the official temple cult was opened up so that families everywhere could participate in it, and the rest from work on the seventh day as such thus took on cultic and religious dignity (Deut.5.12-15; cf. Ex.20.8-11).

However, even as a result of this transformation the sabbath had not completely lost its relationship to the temple cult. In the early post-exilic period it became a day on which particular cultic activities took place in the rebuilt temple (Ezek.46.1, 3, 6; Lev.23.3; Num.28.9), but these went on alongside the general hallowing of the sabbath.[42] The post-exilic sabbath is no longer a full moon festival[43] but a weekly festival (cf. Ezek.46.1), which the families can celebrate not only by resting from work but – to the degree that they live in Jerusalem and its environs – also by taking part in a festal assembly in the temple (Lev.23.3; cf. Ezek.46.9).

The cultic activities of the family had already been quite considerably curtailed by the centralization of the cult under Josiah.[44] They had once again been considerably reduced by the destruction of the temple and dispersion to distant lands. The harvest festivals could no longer be held and the offering of first-fruits could no longer be made. The complete lack of any link between family occupations and the cult created the need for a family festival which could be celebrated even under the conditions of the exile. This need was met by the transformation of the sabbath into a family celebration. As rest from work as such was given cultic dignity, the relationship between work and religion was made independent of all cultic installations and could be established generally everywhere, even in the unclean conditions of a foreign land.

Nevertheless, the introduction of this new family custom was evidently not a matter of course. With its admonitory tone and the lengthy reasons given for it, the extensive sabbath commandment, which was probably incorporated into the Decalogue only during the exile,[45] still clearly indicates that it was necessary to campaign among the fathers of families for the acceptance of this new institution. An earlier version can be found in Deut.5.12-15.[46] In its paraenetic framework (vv.12, 15b), it derives observance of the sabbath day from an express command of Yahweh. Then it cites the older regulation about a day of rest from Ex.23.12; 34.21 in order to change it at the decisive point: the seventh day is a 'sabbath for Yahweh, your God' (v.14);[47] that means that Yahweh can and should be worshipped by the observance of rest from work on the seventh day. The social function from Ex.23.12 is preserved and even emphasized: freedom from work for slaves and women servants is expressly put in the context of the liberation of Israel from Egypt (v.15, cf. Deut.15.15; 16.12). Taking up the social impulses of the Deuteronomic reform, here the ritually established rest from work is made a symbolic 'perception and practice of the status of freedom given by Yahweh'.[48] In thus refraining from the ultimate exploitation of their business resources and thus also accepting economic loss, the Israelites can show their gratitude to Yahweh, their liberator from Egypt, even without sacrifices.

The later version Ex.20.8-11 dispensed with this social connotation and justified the family sabbath regulation by means of the *otiositas dei* after God's completion of the creation of the world (cf. Gen.2.2f.).[49] Thus the sabbath day, more along the lines of Priestly theology, became an outflowing of the blessing of the creator (Ex.20.11) and in character came more to resemble other cultic festivals (cf. Isa.58.13; Neh.10.32). In the course of time the practice of resting from work took on the dignity of a confessional sign (*'ōt*) of the Israelite relationship with God (Ex.31.13,17) and became an expression of the eternal covenant (b^e*rīt 'ōlām*) between Yahweh and his people. As long as a family hallowed the sabbath day (*qdš*, piel),[50] it was visibly confessing Yahweh; in so far as it desecrated the sabbath (*hll*, piel),[51] it was recognizably turning away from him.[52] Thus the sabbath became the most important element of social control, which at the time of the exile could even help towards the cohesion of the people of Judah as a group by decentralizing it on a family level.

Alongside the sabbath, during the exile the passover became the most important element of the subsidiary family cult (cf. Josh.5.10-12; Ex.12.1-14, 43-50). In the course of the Deuteronomic reform the original family passover was combined with the feast of mazzoth and was thus transformed into an official pilgrimage festival.[53] It could no longer be celebrated as such after the destruction of the temple, least of all by the exiles living abroad. So during the exile a contrary development took place, in that the passover reverted to becoming a family festival which could be celebrated in individual homes rather than centrally. In the priestly passover legislation Ex.12, which already represents an advanced stage of this development, the father of the family is again responsible for organizing the passover (v.3). Only the slaughtering of the passover lambs still takes place communally (v.6); by contrast the passover meal proper is held in the family circle (vv.3f.,8ff., cf. 43ff.). The former mazzoth pilgrimage festival is simply attached to this family rite (vv.15-19) and thus loses its character as a cultic celebration of the grain harvest. But since the reference of the passover rite to the exodus from Egypt, probably made by the Deuteronomic reform, remained (vv.7ff., 12ff., 17), during the exile the families became the real vehicles of the official exodus theology, and they continued to remain important even when after the rebuilding of the temple it again became possible to celebrate the passover/mazzoth feast as a pilgrimage festival. Of course the main problems in such a decentralized family passover arose over regulating the nature of the participants and fixing a single date. So we see later legislation concerned with these problems (Ex.12.43-50; Num.9.1-14).[54] Thus the character of a quasi-official Israelite festival could be kept, even though responsibility for it lay with the family.

So during the exile in different ways the family became an important vehicle of the official religion of Israel. It did not lose this function again even after the restitution of the official temple worship in 515, and after the destruction of the second temple in 70 CE it again took on heightened significance. The impression made by Judaism of being markedly a family religion has its starting point here in the exile. But the family could asssume this representative function only because it was recognized by the Deuteronomic reform movement as an indispensable vehicle for religion, and since then had been prepared for by wave after wave of enlightening theological education.

4.4 Towards a new beginning

R.Albertz, 'Das Deuterojesaja-Buch als Fortschreibung der Jesaja-Prophetie', in E.Blum, C.Macholz, E.W.Stegemann (ed.), *Die Hebräische Bibel und ihre zweifache Nachgeschichte, FS Rendtorff*, 1990, 241-56; B.Albrektson, *History and the Gods. An Essay on the Idea of Historical Events as Divine Manifestation in the Ancient Near East and in Israel*, 1967; J.Begrich, 'Das priesterliche Heilsorakel', ZAW 52, 1934, 81-92 = *Gesammelte Studien zum Alten Testament*, TB 21, 1964, 217-31; W.A.M.Beuken, 'A Confession of God's Exclusivity by all Mankind. A Reappraisal of Is.45,18-25', *Bijdragen* 35, 1974, 335-56; J.Blenkinsopp, 'Second Isaiah – Prophet of Universalism', *JSOT* 41, 1988, 83-103; G.Braulik, 'Das Deuteronomium und die Geburt des Monotheismus', in E.Haag (ed.), *Gott, der einzige. Zur Entstehung des Monotheismus in Israel*, 1985, 115-59; B.Duhm, *Das Buch Jesaja*, HK III.1, ⁴1922 = 1968; R.D.Kuke, 'Punishment or Restoration? Another Look at the Levites of Ezekiel 44.6-16', *JSOT* 40, 1988, 61-81; H.Gese, *Der Verfassungsentwurf des Ezechiel (Kap.40-48). Traditionsgeschichtlich untersucht*, BhTh 25, 1957; B.Greenberg, 'The Design and Themes of Ezekiel's Program of Restoration', *Interp*. 38, 1964, 181-208; A.H.J.Gunneweg, *Leviten und Priester*, FRLANT 89, 1965; E.Haag (ed.), *Gott, der einzige. Zur Entstehung des Monotheismus in Israel*, 1985; H.Haag, *Der Gottesknecht bei Deuterojesaja*, EdF 233, 1985; H.-J. Hermisson, 'Voreiliger Abschied von den Gottesknechtsliedern', *ThR* 49, 1984, 209-22; D.E.Hollenberg, 'Nationalism and "the Nations" in Isaiah XL-LV', *VT* 19, 1969, 23-36; G.Lanczkowski, 'Iranische Religionen', *TRE* XVI, 1987, 247-58; B.Lang (ed.), *Der einzige Gott. Die Geburt des biblischen Monotheismus*, 1981; id., 'Die Jahwe-allein-Bewegung', in ibid., 47-83; id., 'Zur Entstehung des biblischen

Monotheismus', *ThQ* 166, 1986, 135-42; H.Leene, 'Universalism or Nationalism? Isaiah XLV 9-13 and its Context', *Bijdragen* 35, 1974, 109-34; B.Lindars, 'Ezekiel and Individual Responsibility', *VT* 15, 1965, 452-67; G.C.Macholz, 'Noch einmal: Planungen für den Wiederaufbau nach der Katastrophe von 587: Erwägungen zum Schlussteil des sogenannen "Verfassungsentwurfs des Hesekiel"', *VT* 19, 1969, 322-52; T.N.D.Mettinger, *A Farewell to the Servant Songs. A Critical Examination of an Exegetical Axiom*, 1983; id., 'In Search of a Hidden Structure: YHWH as King in Isaiah 40-55', *SEÅ* 51/52, 1986/87, 148-57; D.Michel, 'Deuterojesaja', *TRE* VIII, 1981, 510-30; id., 'Das Rätsel Deuterojesaja', *ThViat* 13, 1975/76, 115-32; O.Procksch, 'Fürst und Priester bei Hesekiel', *ZAW* 58, 1940/41, 99-133; A.Schenke, 'Saure Trauben ohne stumpfe Zähne', *Mélanges D.Barthélemy*, OBO 38, 1981, 449-70; A.Schoors, *Jesaja II*, De Boeken van het Oude Testament, 1973, 219-392; H.Vorländer, 'Der Monotheismus Israels als Antwort auf die Krise des Exils', in B.Lang, 84-113; H.E.von Waldow, *Anlass und Hintergrund der Verkündigung Deuterojesajas*, Diss.theol. Bonn 1953; M.Weippert, 'Die "Konfessionen" Deuterojesajas', in R.Albertz, F.W.Golka and J.Kegel (eds.), *Schöpfung und Befreiung*, FS C.Westermann, 1989, 104-15; J.Wellhausen, *Prolegomena to the History of Israel*, 1957; C.Westermann, *Isaiah 40-66* (ATD 1966), OTL 1969; id., *Prophetische Heilsworte im Alten Testament*, FRLANT 145, 1987; W.Zimmerli, *Ezekiel* (1979), Hermeneia (two vols), 1979, 1983; id., 'Planungen für den Wiederaufbau nach der Katastrophe von 587', *VT* 18, 1968, 229-55.

It seems natural to those of us who know the further course of the history of Israelite religion that the exile had to come to an end some time. However, this was by no means a matter of course to people at the time, for whom the future was still open. Certainly the practice of accepting guilt in the exilic liturgies, the reception of the message of the prophets of judgment in the general religious consciousness, the careful working over of the failed history and the supportive contributions of family piety created the presuppositions for overcoming the national crisis and made a vague hope for a continuation of the history of Israel possible. But all this in no way automatically pointed towards a new beginning.[1] Rather, it took a far-reaching change in the world political situation and quite powerful arguments in theological interpretation to set this new beginning going.

If we are to understand this, we must once again keep in mind the situation of those in exile. As far as we know, materially they were not in need; having been largely integrated into Babylonian society both socially and legally they had found a way of earning their livelihoods.[2] Their needs were primarily of a psychological and religious kind.

First of all their psychological distress. The exilic song Ps.137 bears witness to two things: first a deep home-sickness for Jerusalem, though after the long years this threatened to fade and therefore had to be kept alive artificially with self-cursing (vv.1-6); secondly, a dull feeling of impotence, a sense of not being able to do anything to change the political situation, which was vented in wild cries for vengeance against the alien power of Babylon and their brother people of Edom who profited from it (vv.7-9). According to Ezek.11.15; 33.24 the exiles had to accept passively that they, who had once been members of the upper class or had descended from it, were denied title to their property and thus also any claim to leadership by those who had remained at home. We can see from Ezek.33.10 how much, having learned in their worship to acknowledge their mistakes, they suffered under the excessive burden of their guilt and were utterly paralysed by it. And it seems that, as the sons and grandsons of those primarily responsible for the national catastrophe, they had their particular guilt pointed out in detail by the descendants of their former political opponents (Jer.36; 37ff.),[3] and it was deliberately made difficult for them to escape the guilt of their fathers (Ezek.18.2,19).[4] How great the undermining of their self-awareness, the irritation at their own social role and the guilt complex must have been among many exiles becomes evident from the fact that the prophet Ezekiel or his disciples engaged in regular pastoral work among them: they promised these people a restitution of their claim to possessions and leadership (Ezek.11.16-21), and in the form of personal conversion showed them a way in which they could avoid the burden of their fathers' guilt (Ezek.18).[5]

To the psychological distress was added religious distress, which intensifed as the exile went on: the eager expectations of an imminent return home[6] had long died and Yahweh had not intervened on behalf of Israel in more than a generation. He simply seemed to be passing over his people's right to live (Isa.40.27), to have parted company with them (50.1), and to have forgotten his city (49.14). Whereas the Babylonian gods, their images and symbols were borne through the streets in pompous processions to universal rejoicing (46.1f.), and publicly dominated society and world history, Yahweh apparently lacked the will or the power (50.2) to intervene in history. If the exiles could time and again trace in their private sphere the nearness of Yahweh,[7] in the sphere of political history over a long period he seemed to have moved so far from them that here they no longer expected anything of him. So most of them will have drawn the conclusion that national hopes should be set aside and they should seek their happiness in family life and advancement in their work.

If we take this psychological uncertainty and religious resignation among the exiles into account, we can understand how the majority of them did not notice, or looked with indifference on, the political shifts in power which were developing from the middle of the sixth century. If rival aristocratic families were fighting for control in distant Media; if with his victory at Ecbatana in 550 a Persian prince called Cyrus seized power and conquered the whole of Asia Minor in an impressive lightning campaign in 546, what had that to do with Yahweh and their own fate? Only a small prophetic group in the colony of exiles from Judah, concealed behind the designation 'Deutero-Isaiah', recognized that these political developments would represent a decisive new beginning, and they had to force through their theological interpretation of history against considerable resistance among their fellow-citizens.

4.41 'Deutero-Isaiah's' proclamation of salvation

It is hard to determine the sociological background of the group which raised its voice among the exiles in the last decade before the downfall of the Babylonian empire in 539. Their literary legacy, which is preserved in chapters 40-55 of the book of Isaiah, remains anonymous and – without any special introduction – purports to be a development of the preaching of the pre-exilic prophet of judgment. The term 'Deutero-Isaiah' which scholars have coined for them is a mere expedient.

But who lies behind this designation? Deutero-Isaiah shares its anonymity with the majority of exilic and post-exilic prophecy. To this degree it belongs in the further process of working over the tradition of the prophecy of judgment in terms of a prophecy of salvation, a process which begins in the period of the exile. This process, too, is largely obscure to us, but there are some indications that it was connected with the liturgical use of the writings of the prophets of judgment.[8] Perhaps cultic prophets proclaimed words of salvation[9] after the lamentation of the community which were subsequently incorporated into the prophetic books; or perhaps the legacy of the prophets of judgment was *a priori* provided with words of salvation so that it could be used in the liturgy,[10] in order to offer a hopeful perspective to the community after it had shown its penitence.

Deutero-Isaiah goes beyond these 'normal' commentaries by the prophecy of salvation, which in any case we cannot date any more precisely, in composing a whole book of prophecy of salvation and, unlike most of them, referring it to a specific contemporary occasion, the triumphant progress of the Persian king Cyrus in 550-539 (Isa.41.2; 44.28; 45.1-7,13; 46.11; 48.14). Certainly it has also been thought necessary to accept a cultic background for Deutero-Isaiah,[11] but the genres used, above all the numerous disputations, suggest more an activity outside the cult and contemporary preaching[12] than pure writing.[13]

However, the book of Deutero-Isaiah is remarkably ambiguous here: certainly elements of rhetorical units can still be recognized, which indicate contemporary preaching, but in the present text these are woven it into a carefully thought out major composition which presents a message with an emphatically theological perspective.[14] This state of the tradition, which in some respects recalls the book of Hosea, among other things supports the hypothesis put forward by Michel that there is not a single person but a whole 'prophetic school' behind this book.[15] Certainly in my view one can still talk of a prophet of salvation, Deutero-Isaiah, who shapes the quite distinctive poetic and emphatic language of the book, but he did not stand alone; he was the head of a group which discussed the content of his mesage with him, reflected on its theological presuppositions and consequences internally, and continued writing into the late post-exilic period.[16]

Since there is no biographical information, only the language and the theological traditions used can give an indirect indication of the context of this group. The remarkable mixture of sayings from psalms and prophets suggests that it was recruited from the descendants of non-priestly cult-personnel, i.e. above all the temple singers,[17] but probably also the cult prophets. The sovereign way in which it deals with all important religious traditions[18] suggests a profound theological education; the prominent place which the Zion tradition[19] occupies in its thought further points to the circle of those who formerly served in the Jerusalem temple. If that is the case, then we come close to formerly nationalistic groups,[20] though – as we shall see – their views are corrected and reinterpreted in totally new directions. This context is supported not least by the fact that the group attached itself to the Isaiah tradition in particular. And this had already served as a theological basis for the interpretation of history among groups with a nationalistic religious disposition[21] – in the form of a working over of the prophecy of salvation in the time of Josiah.[22]

So by 'Deutero-Isaiah' we can understand a group of theologians gathered round a master which came from circles of descendants of the temple singers and cult prophets of the Jerusalem temple with their nationalistic attitude, and was intensively concerned with the prophecy of Isaiah.

There is much to suggest that the group was inspired to its prophetic message by its study of scripture. The tradition of hymns which it cultivated saw Yahweh regularly as the lord of world history who humbles the mighty and exalts the lowly (Isa.40.23,29; cf. e.g. I Sam.2.4-8). It could learn from Isaiah that Yahweh rules world history according to a mysterious plan (Isa.5.19; 8.10; 14.24,26,27; 29.15; 30.1), giving his people periods of judgment and salvation (6.11; 8.17f.; 14.24-26), and even using foreign powers to implement his plan (5.25ff.; 10). Sensitized by this prior theological knowledge, in its reflections on where the hand of God could be recognized in its time the group was inspired to the surprising insight that Yahweh was at work in the spectacularly victorious course of the Persian king Cyrus. Yahweh had raised Cyrus up (41.2,25; 45.13), called him to execute his plan (44.28; 45.4f.; 46.1; 48.15), only for the sake of Israel (45.4), so that he could liberate his people from captivity in Babylon (43.14f.) and rebuild Jerusalem (45.13). With this insight the group felt, rather as Isaiah had done in ch.6, that it had been caught up into the heavenly council (40.1-8), where it was told that now the time of judgment once proclaimed (6.11) was finally past, the guilt of Jerusalem had been expiated (40.2; 44.22) and Yahweh would usher in a new period of salvation. And it saw itself called to communicate this message of salvation to its contemporaries in faith.

The Deutero-Isaiah group with its electrifying message of salvation largely came up against rejection among its resigned and privatizing fellow citizens. It describes them as being blind and deaf, people who neither want to see the signs of the time nor hear the word of God which interprets them (42.7,16, 18-20, 23; 43.8). That Yahweh should have commissioned in distant Media a foreign king who did not even know him (cf.45.5) to lead a great revolution in world politics solely because of a marginal colony of Jewish exiles sounded completely improbable; indeed it had all the official theological tradition against it. Yahweh might use foreign peoples and kings for his acts of judgment upon Israel, as the prophets had taught (Isa.10; Jer.27.6), but that he should choose a foreign king as his anointed (Isa.45.1) to save Israel had no support in the tradition. According to the Jerusalem kingship theology, only a member of the house of David could take on this function. Thus the message of the Deutero-Isaiah group was not only politically incredible but also theologically highly offensive. And one can suppose that – if the social context proposed above is correct – these theological counter-arguments were presented in particular by the circles of former temple servants with a nationalistic tradition, the circles from which the group itself came.

So the Deutero-Isaiah group was forced to defend its message in arguments and reflect on its theological presuppositions and consequences in relation to official Yahweh religion hitherto.

First of all it reminded its audience of the hymns of praise to God which had once resounded in the temple. Here Yahweh had been praised as the mighty creator of the world and lord of history. If these half-forgotten hymns of praise were really taken seriously, then the doubting objections to their message were unfounded: it was not the world powers but Yahweh who ruled world history in a sovereign way (Isa.40.12-17); it was not strange gods but Yahweh who sat in government (vv.18-24); it was not the Babylonian star gods but Yahweh who determined fate (vv.25-26). That meant that all the powers to which the small colony of exiles in Babylon saw themselves helplessly exposed disappeared before this universal power of Yahweh as a 'drop in the bucket', as weak creatures whom God could control at will. But if God as the creator of the world creates everything and rules the whole world without exception, then the appearance of Cyrus was necessarily on God's initiative (44.24-28). God could also call a foreign king to accomplish his will, and no mortal man – not even a theologian, however concerned – had the right to put a spoke in the wheel (cf. 45.9). In order to deprive their opponents of any possibility of evading their arguments, in describing the omnipotence of Yahweh the prophetic group even moved to a final statement which goes beyond the tradition: Yahweh is not only the one who creates light and salvation but also the one who creates darkness and disaster (45.8; Gen.1.2 differs); there is nothing that is not brought about by him.

Secondly, they picked up what their audience had been able to learn from the pre-exilic prophets of judgment: the purposefulness of the divine action in judgment. The national catastrophe had not hit Israel like a blind stroke of fate, but had been a consequence of its sin (42.24; 43.26-28). It would not have had to rush blindly to disaster had it observed the signs of the time and listened to the announcements of the prophets: but at that time it had proved to be blind and deaf (42.20-22). The Deutero-Isaiah group tried to disarm the counter-argument, which perhaps came from a circle of colleagues who had formerly had been in the service of the cult, namely that Yahweh's action in judgment was incalculable because it had afflicted Israel although Israel had worshipped Yahweh loyally in the cult, by a skilful reversal, taking up the pre-exilic criticism of the cult: Israel had not troubled itself for Yahweh in the cult (*'ābad* = serve) but had made trouble for Yahweh (*'ābad*, hiphil = make to serve) with its sins (42.20-22). The prophetic group believed that the reliability of Yahweh's action in history could in fact be proved from the failed history of Israel: Yahweh does not act arbitrarily, but announces the future and makes what he has announced happen (46.9f.; 48.3,5f., etc.). If this had already come true in the case of the prophets of judgment, the same would happen with the incredible announcement which the Deutero-Isaiah group felt called on to make. God would also reliably fulfil that; after all, formally it was in complete continuity with previous history and could therefore be relied on. However, in content – and the group did not tire of stressing this – the saving action of God which it had to announce was something quite new and unprecedented (42.9; 43.18f.; 48.6b-8). It could not simply be extrapolated from promises given formerly to Israel and be limited to that. So it would be a mistake to measure the group's message by what had formerly been customary and possible in theology and simply reject it because it went beyond that. To want to deny Yahweh the possibility of a completely new way of intervening on behalf of his people was ultimately to deny his power in history.

Now the awareness that it was proclaiming an exciting new message also led the Deutero-Isaiah group to reflect on the consequences of that message for the official Yahweh religion of its time, as a result of which this underwent persistent change. First of all – probably for the first time in the history of Israelite religion[23] – it arrived at the formulation of a consistent monotheism.

That external stimuli led the group to this, as has recently been conjectured again by Vorländer[24] and Lang,[25] is improbable. Certainly some tendencies to monolatry (cf. the inscription by an Assyrian from the eighth century on a statue, 'Trust in Nabu, not in another god', ARAB 1, 264) or 'monotheism' can be recognized in the late Babylonian period, but these either go quite different ways theologically (cf. the 'identification theology' which in the hymn SAHG 258f. identifies the parts of Ninurta's body with other gods) or in no way imply the denial of other gods, as in the case of the advancement of the cult of Nabu by the neo-Babylonian kings or of the cult of Sin by Nabonidus. The parallels to Zoroastrian religion go further: this in fact proclaimed around 600 a worship of Ahura Mazda ('wise lord') which excluded the traditional old Iranian polytheism. But not only does the chronological possibility of any influence remain questionable, since the notions of Zarathustra demonstrably first became officially effective only under Darius I (521-485), but considerable differences in content also remain. The abrupt dualism between Ahura Mazda and the 'evil Spirit' Angra Mainyu is virtually excluded by Isa.45.7,[26] and in Deutero-Isaiah monotheism is not grounded in the creation of the world as in Zarathustra (Yasna 44.3-5), though this has been asserted time and again (even by Vorländer[27]), but in Yahweh's power in history. So here we probably have a development within Israel.

Here too the starting point for the reflections is again clearly the raising up (Isa.41.2f.,25) or call (45.4) of Cyrus. If Yahweh was behind the meteoric rise of the Persian king, if Yahweh was overturning the power complex of the whole of the Near Eastern world in order to liberate his small people, and if finally Yahweh was also having his action in world history proclaimed by a group of prophets from Judah, so that there was no doubt as to the identity of the one who was acting, then Yahweh was the only God at work in history, and all the gods of the other nations had proved ineffective.

The Deutero-Isaiah group attempted to make it possible for their audience, who felt themselves to be the helpless pawns of the foreign nations and their gods, to visualize their exciting insight, by presenting imaginary judgment scenes in heaven (41.1-5,21-29; 43.8-13; 44.6-8; 45.20-5). In this trial Yahweh is both judge and plaintiff, and invites the nations and their gods to a formal legal process (41.1,21f.; 43.8; 44.7; 45.20). Who can lay claim to be God is to be clarified by a kind of verification procedure. The gods ought to be presenting their evidence, but they are silent (41.1,21f.; 45.21; cf.41.28). Only Yahweh has conclusive proof; this again lies in the purposefulness of his action in history: he has not only raised up Cyrus (41.2f.,25) and in connection with that announced salvation to Israel (41.27), but in general has been able to announce what is to come (41.22b,23a,26; 43.12; 44.7;45.21) and already did this in former times (44.7; 41.22a; 43.9), as Israel can attest (43.10, 12; 44.8). So the verdict can only be that the gods of the nations, who can demonstrate no such purposeful action in history, are of no account and indeed shameful (41.24), or 'empty wind' (*rūᵃḥ wātōhū*, 41.29). There is no God but Yahweh (44.6,8; 45.21), no saviour and rock on whom one can rely (43.11; 44.8; 45.21). As the first and the last he embraces all of world history (41.4; 43.10; 44.6; cf.48.12).

In these so-called 'judgment discourses against the nations', the monotheistic argument serves to dispel anxiety and to bring liberation. It begins from the polytheistic situation of competition in which the group of exiles from Judah live and under which they suffer. In the course of this the foreign gods who are apparently so influential dissolve into nothingness, and are unmasked as harmless spectres.[28] In contrast to the Deuteronomic and Deuteronomistic theologians, these theologians are not concerned to safeguard the sole worship of Yahweh by Israel. This is presupposed in Deutero-Isaiah.[29] Rather, the denial of all other gods serves to make it possible for the marginal group from Judah in their alien environment to have faith in a universal historical action on the part of their God. So the same argument also emerges in disputations with Israel (45.18; 46.9; 48.12). By their choice of form of discourse this group of authors also indicates at the same time that it is not seeking to give any 'objective' description of historical reality: the statement of monotheism remains a combative statement on the lips of Yahweh. Monotheism is 'reality' only in the heavenly world, with God himself.

This will become even clearer when we relate the main argument which the Deutero-Isaiah group adduces for Yahweh as sole God, namely that he is in a position to announce the future, to the historical fact that Babylonian religion in particular had a highly developed system of soothsaying and forecasting. That means that the Babylonian gods, too, constantly announced what would happen in the future; indeed, we can say that no king and no private person in Babylonia undertook any important action without first obtaining a divine prognosis of its outcome. The group also seems to have been aware of this fact (cf. Isa.44.25;[30] 47.12f.); to this degree – in historical terms – there was real rivalry. In this connection it must also be mentioned that Cyrus did not see himself called by Yahweh but by Marduk, to liberate Babylon from Nabonidus and repel his interventions in the cult of Marduk in favour of Sin (*TGI²*, 82f.). Whether the priesthood of Marduk who greeted him as liberator had prepared for his entrance by using oracles to this effect as propaganda we do not know,[31] but that is quite within the realm of the possible. In that case we would even have rivalry at the central point of Deutero-Isaiah's message.

So from the historical perspective we cannot deny that the Babylonian gods, too, were thought to have power in history;[32] I would see a difference from Yahweh only in the fact that their action usually related only to limited historical events or epochs[33] and the attempt was not made – as in Israel – to pursue a continuity of divine action through the whole of history in the reciprocal relationship of promise and fulfilment. Above all the positive religious reference to national catastrophes from which the Deutero-Isaiah group derived its insight into the purposefulness of Yahweh's action is absent from Babylonian-Assyrian religion. To this degree the argumentation in the judgment speeches represents a distinct way in which the action of Yahweh in history differed from that of other gods in the religious environment.

In its reflections on the action of Yahweh in universal history which they had to proclaim, the Deutero-Isaiah group was going one stage beyond the pure postulate of monotheism.[34] It arrived at the conclusion that the knowledge that Yahweh alone was God, which had already been demonstrated by judgment 'in heaven', would also take effect in history in the course of the work of salvation which Yahweh had set in motion with Cyrus. The calling of Cyrus focussed not only on the liberation of Israel

(45.4) but also on the fact that the king recognized Yahweh, the God of Israel, as the sole God (45.3,5), indeed ultimately on the fact that all the world recognized that there was no God but Yahweh (45.6).

The composition 44.24-48.22, which is shot through with statements that Yahweh alone is God (45.5f.,14,18,21,22; 46.9; 48.12; cf. 47.8,10), already begins to recognize something of the realization of this aim: the nations, who will be the witnesses to the universal saving work of Yahweh for his people (45.11-13), will come to Jerusalem and pay homage to Yahweh (45.14); those of the nations who have escaped will be invited to salvation (45.20-25), and the praise of the Israelites liberated from Babylon will go out to the ends of the earth (48.20). The downfall of the Babylonian empire is also depicted from this perspective of the establishment of monotheism: the Babylonian gods Bel and Nebo (i.e. Marduk and Nabû) fall (46.1f.), and with them the proud capital of Babylon (47). Significantly it falls because of its claim to absoluteness (vv.8,10), which is opposed to the monotheistic claim of Yahweh; with its self-certain, totalitarian claim to rule it has denied that Yahweh alone is God. Thus for the Deutero-Isaiah group monotheism, where it begins to establish itself in history, has two further characteristics. First, it has a tendency towards universalism: Yahweh is no longer just the national God of Israel (45.3), but becomes the God of the whole world, becomes 'God'.[35] And secondly, it has a tendency to be critical of domination: arrogant political rule is stripped of its power, and its victims are freed.

The second conclusion which the Deutero-Isaiah group saw itself compelled to draw from its message was an opening up of Yahweh religion towards universalism. If Yahweh commissioned an alien king to overthrow existing political power relationships, to rescue his small people from exile, then his saving activity could no longer be exclusively limited to Israel. Rather, in that case the question arose what would become of the other peoples and what form their relationship to Yahweh and to Israel would take.

However, at this point the group had quite special difficulties in detaching itself from long accustomed trains of thought and familiar patterns of religious conceptuality, especially since it had originated in the circles of those engaged in the service of the Jerusalem temple with their nationalistic disposition. For centuries the religion of Israel had been a national religion in which the frontiers of peoples or states also formed the natural religious frontiers.[36] In the light of the experiences of political and religious liberation from the early period, the salvation of Israel had always also been bound up with victory over opposing nations. In the Jerusalem kingship and Zion theology, which demonstrably had a great influence on the theological thought of the Deutero-Isaiah group, the radius of Yahweh's action had extended to the world of nations, but this divine rule over the world had here been conceivable only as the military subjection of the nations by Yahweh and Israel. The group would therefore have to change its character quite markedly if it were to get beyond the familiar pattern of 'salvation for Israel – disaster for the nations'. No wonder that different positions were put forward within the group specifically at this point.

It has frequently been recognized that different statements about the nations are made in the book of Deutero-Isaiah, which are difficult to reconcile.[37] Alongside statements which sound amazingly universalistic (45.20ff.; 42.4,6; 49.6; 51.4-6), and which envisage a kind of conversion of the nations, there are some terrifyingly nationalistic statements (45.14; 49.23,26) which further seem to presuppose that the nations will submit to Israel. Yet further passages speak of a military subjection of the nations – but not under Israel (!): these occur in the motif of 'Yahweh as lord of history' (40.14,15-17,20,23b-24), which is traditional in hymns; in the traditional motif of 'Yahweh as warrior', which recalls the early period (42.13; 49.22,25; 51.22f.); and where – along the lines of kingship theology – there is mention of Cyrus's task (41.2,5, 25; 45.1-3,13; 46.11; 48.14; cf.47); finally it can be said as consolation to Israel that it will overcome its powerful opponents (41.11f., 15f.). There is already a clear transformation of traditional notions from kingship theology and Zion theology where it is said that instead of paying tribute, the nations will bring the scattered exiles to Zion (43.3b; 45.14[?];49.22b-23). In addition to this there is another chain of notions which no longer has any military connotation, that the nations will become the witnesses of the saving work of Yahweh for Israel (40.5; 48.20; 49.7; 52.10) and will convert to Yahweh (45.6; 45.20-25; 51.4-6) or attach themselves to Israel (44.5f.; 55.5), and that Israel will assume a quite new function for the nations, that of being a witness to Yahweh (43.10-12; 44.8; 55.4), to give law and instruction to the nations (42.1-4; 51.5) and to become a light for the nations (42.6; 49.6; cf.49.8). In its suffering it has suffered vicariously for the sins of the nations (53.1ff.).[38] We do best to see this series of statements as an ongoing process of clarification within the prophetic group which, starting from the traditional theological notions from which the group derived, pressed forward to new limits, without completely reconciling them and systematizing them in a coherent system.

The best systematic description of the prophetic group's notion of universalism is a model of two concentric circles: the inner circle contains the relationship between Yahweh and Israel, the outer circle that between Yahweh or Israel and the nations. The event of the inner circle of course forms the centre: the central message of the group is that of the liberation of helpless Israel from the violence of the nations who hold it captive. As this is a process of political liberation, military power is necessarily involved, and Yahweh has commissioned the Persian king to break the political resistance of the powers which stand in the way of the liberation of Israel with military force (41.2,25; 45.1-3,13; 46.11; 48.14). That means that as long as Israel is the victim of alien powers, Yahweh intervenes with all his might on its side, casts down those in power (40.23f.) and compels the oppressors (49.22-26), very much along the lines of the old experiences of liberation (42.13).

But what was to become of the nations when Cyrus or Yahweh had broken the political resistance which stood in the way of the liberation of his people? That is the point where the prophetic group tentatively developed its notions about the outer circle of events. It addresses its decisive universal message (45.20-25) to 'the survivors of the nations' (v.20), i.e. those who have already experienced and survived the collapse of Babylonian world power. In the group's view, the many who were involved in Yahweh's world-wide work of liberation for his people could no longer simply be passed over theologically or be left to destruction, especially since as victims of political developments they would then find themselves in a similar situation to Israel before them. Here we should note that in Babylon the exiles from Judah lived in close proximity to members of other nationalities, cultivated business relations with them and may even have kept up friendships with them here and there. So quite simple interpersonal relationships may well also have forced the group to look for a new solution. The theological solution which they found was the expectation that Yahweh's world-wide work of liberation for Israel would not stop at the frontiers of his people but would also involve the wider circle of nations (45.18,22ff.; 55.5). What is important here is the course they thought that this process of opening up Yahweh religion would take. The new openness no longer comes about through political subjection, as in the old Jerusalem theology (Ps.47.4,10), but voluntarily and out of conviction: the great invitation goes out from Yahweh to members of the nations to turn to him and be saved by him (45.22). No one compels them to accept this invitation, but since they can be convinced by the work of liberation planned by Yahweh for Israel that Yahweh is the sole God and saviour (45.20-21), it is certain that they will recognize the uselessness of their gods and in the future turn once and for all to Yahweh, even if before they have rejected him (45.23-24). Because of the attractiveness of Israel's God, they will attach themselves to Israel (55.5), so that Yahweh will one day be given the universal recognition which is his due in the light of Israel's belief that he is the only God. Thus in the view of the group the opening up of Yahweh religion to universalism does not do away with Israel's particular relationship to God, but has this as its abiding presupposition.

The character of Israel and its function for the world of nations also change against the horizon of this universal perspective on the future. In the group's view Israel, too, must become open to the world of nations. On the one hand aliens can be accepted into communion with Israel through their religious confession of Yahweh (44.5). In this way, for the first time Israel takes on features of a community with a religious constitution, which, while not fundamentally putting its traditionally ethnic basis in question (45.25),[39] at least considerably relativizes it. On the other hand, Israel takes on a quite new religious function over against the world of nations which it could not perform as a purely national religion: Israel becomes the witness to Yahweh before the forum of the nations (43.10-12; 44.8; 55.4). It has to communicate to the nations the central insight that it has been able to learn itself from its history: that Yahweh is the only God and saviour (43.10f.).

The function of mediator between Yahweh and the nations which, in the group's view, Israel now takes on can be described in even more detail if we bring the so-called 'servant songs' into the interpretation.

From the time that Duhm wanted to separate out these texts (42.1-4 [,5-8]; 49.1-6; 50.4-9; 52.13-53.12) as a specific literary stratum, this has needed specific justification. Now Mettinger has shown convincingly that in compositional terms the texts are firmly incorporated into the structure of the book,[40] so that Duhm's separation of them becomes questionable. Thus in recent times there has been an increase in the number of those who entirely[41] or in part[42] understand the 'servant' mentioned in the text collectively and want to interpret it in terms of Israel. I largely agree with them.[43] In my view, however, 50.4-9(,10) is also to be applied to Deutero-Isaiah or his group of disciples.

The texts 42.1-4; 49.1-6; 52.13-53.12 are best understood as products of the ongoing reflection[44] of the group on the new role which accrues to Israel over against the nations: in 42.1-4 Israel is presented to the nations by God as the mediator who will bring them the law for which they are waiting (cf. 51.4f.). In 49.1-6, Israel itself then tells the people of its history with Yahweh, which is on the point of failure (v.4) when Yahweh announces that he is bringing it back to him, as had happened in the preaching of the prophetic group (v.5). But then Israel is given a universal commission by Yahweh:

> It is too light a thing that you should be my servant,
> to raise up the tribes of Jacob,
> and to restore the preserved of Israel,
> I will give you a a light to the nations,
> that my salvation may reach to the end of the earth (49.6).

The prophetic group recognized that it is not enough for Yahweh to save and bring back Israel. He wants his saving work to reach to the ends of the earth, and for this purpose Israel is given the decisive function of providing an orientation which will be a help to the peoples. Finally, in 52.13-53.12 the nations tell how the insignificant Israel, which they despise, and which had 'died' shamefully under the blows of Yahweh before God 'revived' it again, has suffered vicariously for their sins in order to bring them salvation.

Now all this is said in a very allusive and tentative way, and cannot be completely reconciled with the message of the group elsewhere.[45] However, here we can recognize a vigorous effort on the part of Israel to attach a positive function to the break-up of its state unity and its dispersion among the nations. Only by this destruction of the old iron limits to groups could Israel perform its missionary function in God's universal plan of salvation. Unlike the group which composed the Deuteronomic history, the Deutero-Isaiah group did not interpret the loss of state unity primarily as a threat to its own unity which had to be repelled, but as an opportunity for new missionary work on the part of Israel, to which it had to be open.

The third conclusion which the Deutero-Isaiah group drew from its message was that the fusion of divine and political power which had happened in pre-exilic kingship theology had to be dissolved.[46] The fact that Yahweh had called a foreign king to be his anointed (45.1-7) in order to free Israel refuted the thesis of Jerusalem kingship theology that he exercised his rule over the world through the political and military action of its Davidic kings (Ps.2). At this point, too, the group was compelled to come to grips with its theological heritage, and here too we need not be surprised that it never broke through to a completely coherent new concept. However, its members proved to be the ready disciples of their master Isaiah, who already in the eighth century had attacked the way in which Yahweh had been commandeered for the king's own political claims to power (Isa.31.1-3, etc.),[47] in seeking a solution in the direction of a separation.

The group still interpreted the political and military action of Cyrus very much along the lines of traditional kingship theology. Cyrus had been called by Yahweh to be his anointed, to carry out Yahweh's will (45.1-4; 44.28; 48.14). In his military conquests he could be sure of God's support (45.2f.). In particular by conquering Babylon (48.14f.) he was accomplishing Yahweh's plan in history for the salvation of his people. But the time in which once again Yahweh's power is fused with the political power of a ruler – albeit a foreign one (!) – is limited: it extends only until the fall of the Babylonian empire, which in its claim to absoluteness is opposed to God (47.8,10). For the time after that, Cyrus disappears completely from view.

The special feature here is that the prophetic group no longer promises Israel, freed by this powerful military political action, that its statehood will be restored. For the group, the Davidic king was not just temporarily displaced from his position by Cyrus, but no longer had any place at all in its view of the future. In its view Yahweh himself would lead the exiles home in a triumphal march through the wilderness and would directly assume royal rule on Zion (40.9-11; 52.7-12).

The theological concept of the kingly rule of God is of decisive significance for the Deutero-Isaiah group. Their whole book, chapters 40-52,[48] can and should be read from the perspective of the final victory of the final establishment of Yahweh's kingly rule over all the political resistance of the nations, and also over all Israel's anxieties and doubts.[49] In taking up this conception the group whole-heartedly adopted the thought-world of kingship and Zion theology (cf. Ps.47),[50] which had been its original context. But it turned it into a critical attitude to domination. That is already evident in the passages where it still uses the title 'king': here Yahweh is designated 'king of Jacob' (41.21) or 'Israel' (44.6) or as 'your king' (43.15). So here Yahweh is neither king of the gods (Ps.95.3) nor king of the nations (Ps.47.9), with all the imperial connotations of these titles, but king of Israel, as he is in the criticisms directed against the king in the early monarchy (I Sam.8.7; 12.12).[51] As the opponents of Davidic rule asserted at that time, so again in the exile the prophet's disciples came to recognize that Yahweh's kingly rule over Israel totally excludes a human kingship, i.e. the institutionalized concentration of political power.

The same tendency to be critical of domination is also evident if we ask what is excluded by the kingly rule of God in the book of Deutero-Isaiah. First to be excluded is any increase in the political power of Israel: much as the prophetic group can talk of the power of Yahweh and accentuate it further in their theological conception, they do not associate this with an increase in the political power of Israel. The old identification in the ancient Near Eastern kingship ideology that state power is a reflection of divine power is thus broken. Secondly, the military subjection of other nations by Israel is excluded: much as the group emphasizes the universality of Yahweh, this is not bound up with the notion that other nations are made subject to Israel. Israel has no part in the conquests of Cyrus. This position thus refutes the notion in kingship theology that the Israelite king secures the recognition of Yahweh in the world through the military subjection of other peoples (Ps.2.8-12).[52] It is not by chance that the Yahweh group (!) depicts the controversy with the nations and their gods not as a battle but as a legal dispute, in which Israel takes part only as a witness. The third thing to be excluded is Israel's rule over the world. Israel cannot derive any claim to rule over the world from Yahweh's monotheistic claim to be the only God. This refutes the claim to rule over the world which is part of the fixed inventory of ancient Near Eastern and also Israelite royal ideology (Ps.77.8-11).[53] Granted, it was not bound up with a monotheistic conception of God, but could equally well be made in a polytheistic context; however, it is clear that a much sharper and more inexorable imperialistic claim could have been drawn from the monotheistic thesis. The Deutero-Isaiah group evidently wanted to put a firm rein on this. Given the later campaigns of conquest under Christian auspices which were justified by the absolutist claim of monotheism, it is all the more important to point to the sociological fact that Israel made the break-through to monotheism in a situation of absolute political helplessness.

If we ask how the kingly rule of God is described positively in the book of Isaiah, we shall get only vague answers. The prophetic group leaves completely open the details of how Yahweh's power is to be exercised on Zion. Did it think of some human mediation,[54] or in its view had the potential of history been in principle exploded? One can only attempt to find some pointers. Thus the group seems to have had some inkling that the kingly rule of God is structurally different from the human political exercise of power: certainly in the situation of liberation it is still bound up with the collapse of totalitarian world power, but in the last resort it culminates in the liberation of the oppressed and the strengthening of the weak and those who have grown weary (40.29-31; 41.17; 42.22,etc.). Here the age-old experiences of liberation which had been there from the birth of Yahweh religion again make themselves felt. The departure from Babylon will be a new, even more wonderful, exodus (52.12; cf. Ex.12.11; Deut.16.3). In the time after it rule will be different and exercised in a different way: law will replace power (Isa.42.1-4); the Israel which is presented to the nations as the servant of Yahweh certainly still bears recognizable royal features,[55] but instead of subjecting the nations it will bring them law and instruction (*mišpāṭ, tōrā*). Moreover, this law will again not be the law of the stronger but the law which 'does not break a bruised reed' (v.3). There are distant echoes here of the powerful social impulse behind Israelite reform legislation[56] to protect the rights of the weak.

The transference of the Davidic covenant to Israel in Isa.55.3ff. goes in a similar direction. Instead of the house of David, Israel is appointed to the position of a crown pretender (*nāgīd*) and commander (*mᵉšawwē*) of nations. However, these titles no longer contain any claim to political rule over the world, but refer to Israel's office as witness (*'ed*) to the nations. Israel is not given any political authority for the world, but a moral and religious authority, in that it bears witness before the world to its God. The difference from political authority becomes clear from the fact that it does not exert any compulsion, but works only through conviction (cf. 45.22f.) and remains dependent on the voluntary assent of those who are addressed. Here, after bitter experiences of the misuse of God in the interest of exercising human power, the Deutero-Isaiah group breaks through to the insight that God's rule for others only becomes believably and convincingly visible when those who speak in God's name renounce any pressure and cease to seek their own advantage.

The mysterious song of the suffering servant Israel (Isa.52.13-53.12) goes one step further. The notion that Israel cannot bring salvation to the nations in its power, greatness and fame, but does so particularly in the phase of its absolute helplessness, seeks for the first time to attach a positive meaning in God's plan for history to Israel's loss of political power and is probably the most profound theological interpretation ever given to the sufferings of the exilic period.

4.42 *The Ezekiel school's plan for reform*

Alongside the Deutero-Isaiah group, which was probably recruited from the non-priestly personnel of the Jerusalem temple, from well on into the exilic period in the Babylonian Gola, a priestly reform group which had formed around the priest-prophet Ezekiel (who had been deported in 597, Ezek.1.3) and the writings he left behind increasingly made itself heard. But whereas the former group was still fully occupied in activating its resigned fellow-citizens to set out on a new beginning by preaching its great message of salvation and limited itself to a few hints about the new internal order, the Ezekiel group was intensively concerned in detail with the further question how, after the chance of a new beginning that it had been given, Israel was to organize itself so that the old mistakes of the pre-exilic period could not be repeated. The detailed sketch in which it successively developed its ideas for the time of rebuilding is to be found in Ezekiel 40-48.

Ezekiel's so-called 'draft constitution' (Ezek.40-48) can nowadays hardly still be attributed in its entirety to the prophet: it shows too many traces of a lengthy literary growth for that.[57] It is certainly possible that the formation of the tradition goes back to a vision of the aging Ezekiel in the year 573 (40.1) in which he saw the new temple as a fortified 'city' complex, lying in isolation on a hill (40.2), but the working out of this 'temple vision' is the product of scholarly work which gives the impression that its authors were sitting bent over a basic plan that was being worked out in more and more detail.[58] And in the wealth of texts which were added later the fiction of the vision is completely abandoned. On the other hand, as Greenberg has shown, the chapters all have a well thought out structure,[59] and despite some discrepancies[60] in terminology and content they display great conceptual coherence. Even texts which from a literary point of view seem to be insertions or appendices do not bring alternative concepts into play, but simply develop what was already implicit or hinted at in others. So Ezek.40-48 can be understood as the work of a closed group or school which developed its conception of the rebuilding sucessively over a period of one or two generations (573-520).[61]

Given the interest that this group has in the temple, its priestly origin is utterly beyond question. Indeed we can be even more specific and say that its members were probably Zadokides,[62] i.e. came from that priestly family which since Solomon had claimed the monopoly in the Jerusalem temple. In some ways it is astonishing that an impulse towards reform could emanate from this group in particular. Until 587 the Zadokides had been the ones who had handed on the Jerusalem state cult and had belonged to the hard core of the advocates of its temple and kingship theology.[63] Their status as royal officials had bound them closely to the Davidic royal house and had limited their theological interests completely to the preservation of the existing state. This basic conservatism did not exclude the possibility that parts of the Jerusalem priesthood had taken part in

Josiah's reform, which was supported by a broad coalition, since the centralization of the cult had also been concerned with their professional interests.[64] But at a very early stage this coalition had fallen apart again, probably not least because of the dispute over the question to what extent the country priests who had been put out of work had to be accepted into temple service in Jerusalem.[65] At any rate we found the focal point of the Jerusalem priesthood in the late pre-exilic period among the leaders of the nationalistic religious party.[66] Nor does that exclude the possibility that after the catastrophe, among others, members of the Jerusalem priesthood who had not been deported took part in working out the failed history in the Deuteronomistic history work and in so doing broke through to a critical estimation of certain developments in the cultic history of Jerusalem.[67] Here they continued to remain within the bounds of their accustomed presupposition that since David and Solomon the Israelite cult had been a royal state cult for which the monarchs bore the main responsibility.[68] Over against that, the really new element in Ezek.40-48 is that here for the first time in the history of Israelite religion a priestly group quite voluntarily and with its own distinctive voice engaged in discussion about reform. These people, the sons and grandsons of priests who had been deported and had lapsed from royal service, no longer wanted to remain the lackeys of a state cult which had met its end. Rather, freed from all worldly ties and considerations, they wanted to reflect on the quite distinctive professional priestly calling of their family as a basis on which they could make a specific contribution to the formation of a new Israelite society.

The Zadokide reform group was very probably stimulated by the prophet Ezekiel, who himself had been a priest (Ezek.1.3) and perhaps also a Zadokide, but was then led to dissociate himself sharply from his guild as a result of the vision he received at his call (22.26). His cultic accusation that the Jerusalem temple was unclean (8-11) and his social accusation that the kings, officials and the rich were using violence (21.30; 22.6, 25f., 27, 29f.; 34,2ff.) also left a deep mark on it.[69] However, the circle of Ezekiel's disciples does not seem to have been completely unanimous: the developments of his prophecies in 1-39 in the direction of a prophecy of salvation outline a far more traditional picture of the restoration of Israel along the lines of the great Davidic empire (Ezek.34.23f.; 37.22-25) than the reform political conception in Ezek.40-48.[70] Those who handed it down could evidently free themselves much more noticeably from their traditionally nationalistic ties than the authors of the other words of salvation. Nevertheless there are also common features.[71] Ezekiel 40-48 can best be understood as a critical and in part corrective reformulation of the more traditional expectations of salvation in the rest of the book. Here the critical reform wing of the pupils of Ezekiel derived its legitimation from a special vision of Ezekiel (40.1f.) and grounded the authority of its legislation – in contrast to the Deuteronomic-Deuteronomistic tradition – not on Moses but on the inspired prophets of old.

The starting point of the reflections of the Zadokide group on reform was the conception of the Jerusalem sanctuary as the throne of Yahweh in his glory (Ezek.43.7; cf. Isa.6.1ff.) and the basic priestly distinction between sacred and profane (42.20). If Ezekiel had seen the glory of Yahweh (*kᵉbōd yhwh*) departing from the profaned temple (8-11) and had accused the priests of obliterating the distinction between sacred and profane (22.26), then – the group concluded – the glory of Yahweh could return to his temple (43.1-12) and God could again take up his dwelling within Israel (37.26-28; 43.7,9) only if in future the Temple was protected from all profanation.

The whole of the temple vision Ezek.40.1-43.12 serves to demonstrate the architectural consequences of this theological postulate. The temple site is imagined as a sacred precinct with sides about 260 metres long clearly marked out by a boundary wall. Within it are three spheres of increasing holiness, which are marked out by their elevation and by further walls: seven steps lead up to the outer courtyard (40.22), another eight to the inner courtyard (40.31,34,37), and ten more to the temple building proper (40.49). Like the temple of Solomon, the newly conceived temple is also further sub-divided into three precincts of increasing holiness: the entrance hall (*'ūlām*), the main hall (*hēkal*) and the holy of holies (*qōdeš haqqodāšīm*, 40.48-41.4). The traditional triple protection of the holiness of the holy of holies is further duplicated at the front by three steps and at the rear protected against the profane outside world by a mighty construction (*binyān*, 41.12-15), 52 metres by 40 metres, which has no other function. Even more important than the walls are three doors which control access to the inner and outer courts (40.6-27). They are conceived of in analogy to Israelite city gates (three rooms and an antechamber), but in their measurements of 26 by 13 metres[72] they surpass the gates excavated at the fortified cities of Hazor, Megiddo and Gezer, and are even larger than the main hall of the temple (21 x 10.5m). The gate complexes give the temple the character of a regular fortress. While there may have been military reasons for such mighty gateways in the outside wall, they seem excessive for the wall between the outer and the inner forecourts. They can only be explained in terms of the theological programme of the priestly group, as making it possible for the priesthood to have complete control in all circumstances over access to the sacred temple precinct generally and to the inner precincts where the sacred actions were performed, possibly even without state help.[73] Never again will any unauthorized person be able to penetrate to the place of sacred action and become involved in the sphere of priestly tasks!

The heightened notion of holiness expressed in the building plan of the temple has a wealth of cultic, legal and political consequences: the sharp separation between inner and outer forecourt made a clear segregation of priests and laity possible. The sacrifices were offered only by the priests;

the laity were largely excluded from the official sacrificial cult and could follow its performance on festivals only from afar, as fleeting onlookers (46.8f.). The institutional independence of the priesthood was thus achieved at the high price of an almost complete exclusion of the laity from the cult – here the concept of the older Jerusalem state cult was perpetuated. Of course this inevitably caused difficulties at the private sacrifices (oaths, sacrificial meals, etc.). Here too the laity were not allowed any control over the preparatory sacrifical actions (the slaughtering and preparation of the animals), and this ultimately and consistently issued in the notion of two separate places for cooking the sacrifices: in the outer forecourt for the preparation of the lay sacrifice and in the inner precinct for the pure priestly sacrifice (46.19-24).[74]

In terms of the history of religion the consequences for the cultic personnel were even more momentous: the strict separation of the fore-courts as areas with different degrees of holiness called for a differentiation of the priesthood into two groups with different areas of responsibility. First of all the group thought more in terms of a functional division and distinguished those priests who looked after service at the altar (*mišmeret hammizbeᵃḥ*), i.e. the sacred cultic actions of the inner precincts, from those who looked after the 'service of the house' (*mišmeret habbayit*), i.e. all other less holy services in the temple sphere (40.45,46a). As the discussion continued further, however, the reformers of the cult resolved on a clear differentiation by groups: they laid exclusive claim for themselves, the Zadokide priests (40.46b; 43.19; 44.15f.; 48.11), not only to the service of the altar but to all cultic actions in the inner forecourt and in the temple building, and assigned the 'service of the house' to the 'Levites'. And they defined the latter more closely by limiting their activity to the outer forecourt: the 'Levites' served as doorkeepers, slaughtered the private lay sacrifices, and performed other services for the lay community (44.11). At the same time this group was excluded from anything to do with holy and most holy things, i.e. from priestly service proper (44.13).

Who are meant by the 'Levites'? The question is a controversial one for scholars, and how it is answered very much depends on how one imagines the pre-exilic history of priests and Levites, which is largely shrouded in darkness (see above, 58f.). As is well known, the 'classic' solution derives from Wellhausen: in his view the Levites of Ezek.44 are descendants of the country priests who had been put out of work by Josiah's centralization of the cult. Contrary to the intentions of Deut.18.6f., they did not succeed in gaining full access to service in the Jerusalem temple (II Kings 23.9), and Ezekiel merely puts 'a mantle of morality' over this logic of the facts. According to Wellhausen, 'Ezekiel' first introduced the distinction between priests and Levites, which P later then supposes 'always to have existed'.[75]

Gunneweg protested against this hypothesis: not only did he see the relations between P and Ezekiel as being more complex, but he raised doubts about a simple identification of the Levites with the descendants of the provincial priesthood. In his view the Levites were a special social class and by no means necesarily priests. And what he believed to be the old account of the special zeal of the Levites for Yahweh (Ex.32.25-29) was so important to him that he found it impossible to identify them with the 'priests on the high places' of II Kings 23.9; he therefore argued that the polemic of Ezek.44.10,12,13 was also completely theoretical. The Levites of Ezek.44 were thus groups of minor clergy who, as can also be recognized in P (Num.16ff.; 4.5ff.), wanted to extend their competence.[76]

Duke dissociates himself even further from Wellhausen's hypothesis: in his view the distinction between priests and Levites was old and existed prior to Ezekiel. Ezekiel 44.6-16 does not degrade the Levites, but refers to a restoration of their ancestral rights.[77]

However, some observations on Ezek.44.6-16 could disperse Gunneweg's suspicions, refute Duke and support Wellhausen's classical view. 1. The terse polemic and the terminology used in the description and delimitation of the spheres of tasks[78] make it probable that the relatively clear and natural separation between priests and Levites in P is still unknown to the authors of Ezek.44. They want to make a new and unprecedented division of cultic personnel. 2. A demotion of the group designated 'Levites' is clearly intended; otherwise v.13 would have no function in the argument and presupposes that the group claimed full priestly rights for itself.[79] 3. The substance of the polemic that at the time of the apostasy the 'Levites' had set themselves apart from Yahweh (44.10), had served idols and led Israel into sin (v.12), and thus lost their claim to priestly service, follows the same lines as II Kings 23.9, where they are denounced as 'priests of the high places'. So the charge was current among the Jerusalem priesthood,[80] but sometimes appears in the garb of Deuteronomist and sometimes in the garb of Ezekielian terminology. 4. The Zadokide group also begins from the Deuteronomic notion that all priests, including themselves, are Levites (43.19; 44.15). However – and this must be said much more clearly than Wellhausen does – this is an archaizing concept which has hardly anything to do with historical reality.[81] But in the light of this theory it is quite understandable that the Zadokides should have used the term 'Levite' to describe all non-Zadokide priests who had been associated with the Jerusalem temple as a result of the centralization of the cult under Josiah. In this way they allowed the rival group fighting for its rights its place among the cultic personnel, but at the same time demoted its members to the status of minor clergy.

The sub-division of the Jerusalem cultic personnel into (Zadokide) priests and Levites, who were to form a school in the post-exilic period,[82] thus probably goes back to the reform conception of the Ezekiel school. One can accuse the group of simply wanting to use this approach in a clever way to resolve in their favour an old dispute among the cultic personnel which had been smouldering since the reform of the cult under Josiah, before there was a new temple. However, we must note that behind it we can detect not only selfish motives, but at the same time a serious concern also to safeguard the sanctity of the temple in respect of cultic personnel and as far as practicable to exclude any possibility of impurity. If there was a desire not to expose the priests who performed the sacred action to the danger of lasting impurity, and also a desire that the more worldly activities in the temple should be carried out by people from outside, as had long hitherto been the case (44.6-9),[83] then the Levites were absolutely necessary for the practice of the cult. As servants of the cult with a lower degree of holiness they had once again to mediate between the laity and the priests, between the secular and the sacred.

The most far-reaching consequence which the disciples of Ezekiel drew from their heightened notion of holiness was the detachment of the cult from any state supervision. The new cult after the rebuilding of the temple was no longer to be a state cult of the kind that had existed previously since the days of David and Solomon. That was a first priority architecturally: the old Jerusalem temple had formed a single complex of buildings connected with the royal palace.[84] The reform disciples recognized that this fusion had led to an essential pollution of the temple, not only through the idolatrous worship of the kings, but also through their memorial stelae.[85] By these they had misused the temple to depict their own fame and advance state power (43.7b). The very proximity of the palace to the temple had been a profanation of the holy divine name (43.8). The consequence could only be that the temple should be physically quite separate from the royal palace.

Secondly, that had consequences for the legal position of the temple. The old Jerusalem sanctuary had been the possession of the king; David had seen to its consecration by bringing in the ark, and Solomon had decorated it with splendour.[86] However, the new temple was to be built by the Israelites (43.10ff.); it would no longer need royal legitimation, but would be consecrated by the entry of the glory of Yahweh itself (43.1-5); there was no longer any reference even to the ark as a symbol of divine presence.

Thirdly, this had consequences for the organization of the sacrificial cult. Whereas in the pre-exilic period the king had been responsible for providing the temple with sacrifices for the public cult, after the end of royal supervision the sacrifices now had to be provided by the whole people. Here it seems to have been the earlier view of the group that the tax for the sacrifices was to be paid directly to the temple (45.13-15); however, this was later revised to the degree that 45.16-17 decided to insert the king as an intermediate authority. In this way he was given a remnant of responsibility for sustaining the official sacrificial cult (45.17-46.15), but only as a mediator of the people.

Fourthly, the dissolution of the state cult compelled the group to reflect on a new way of providing for the priests. In the period before the exile the Jerusalem priests had been royal officials and had been provided for by the state.[87] In addition they were entitled to the portions of the sacrifices which were traditionally their due. But these alone were hardly enough, and moreover they were inappropriate for feeding the Levites, since the intention was to deprive them of their right to sacrifice. So in addition to extending the share of the sacrifices for the priests (44.28-31),[88] the disciples of Ezekiel conceived of a completely new kind of cultic offering (*t*ᵉ*rūmā*): a strip of land from tribal territory was to be assigned them, and from this the priests and Levites were each to be given an area of 25,000 x 10,000 ells, i.e. around 67 square kilometres (45.1-8; 48.8-14). The priests were to live on their part of the land and probably were also to be allowed to rear cattle (45.4);[89] the Levites were even to possess land (*'ᵃḥuzzā*) in their share and thus were to be allowed to engage in agriculture (45.5).[90] This latter measure went completely against the old levitical rule, which probably comes from the time when the Levites were an itinerant priestly association (Deut.18.1f.). That the reformers of the cult were prepared to set themselves so completely above this ancient principle in connection with the group of non-Zadokide priestly descendants whom they defined as Levites indicates not only that the group no longer had any connection with the old Levites but also that however much they demoted the Levites in the cult they were still concerned to guarantee the wherewithal to live. Not only did they claim the sole priestly rights for themselves; they were also prepared to bear the burden of the levitical rule in the future (44.28).[91] The new 'Levites', like all other Israelites, were to earn their own living.

The consistency with which the priestly reform group once again cut all ties with the state cult – even the comfortable ones – after 500 years of experience with it is quite amazing. They understood the downfall of the state cult in 587 as God's judgment on this form of worship and the compulsory 'dismissal' of their fathers and grandfathers from this state cult as liberation which they did not want to put at risk again. Certainly selfish professional considerations also played a part in their reflections, but these are not enough to explain the radical nature of their approach.

Those who are prepared to give up the familiar and indeed secure basis of their own professional existence to such a degree and to reflect on completely new possibilities for safeguarding it are driven by a higher power. The Protestant churches in Germany needed until 1919 to take a similar step – and then they were forced to it; and even now they do not dare to pursue to the end the course of a complete separation of church and state. The remarkable thing is that the disciples of Ezekiel arrived at precisely the same insight as the disciples of Deutero-Isaiah, but on completely different theological presuppositions, namely that the fusion of God with state power did damage to the divinity of Yahweh and therefore that the two had to be separated from each other. The potential of this God for opposition to domination was quite manifestly stronger than any involvement in schools and traditions of thought.

The abrupt break with the tradition of the state cult is matched in the political conception of the priestly reformers by a marked depotentiation of the king. Here too we can see a similar tendency to that in the Deutero-

Isaiah group. Certainly the Ezekiel group did not deny the king completely, as the Deutero-Isaiah group did, but – already under pressure from the nationalistic promises in the rest of the book of Ezekiel – [92] they granted a certain justification for his existence in the future Israel; however, his functions were markedly reduced by comparison with the monarchy of the pre-exilic period. This reduction already begins with his designation: the title 'king' (*melek*) is no longer used for the future king; it is replaced by the title *nāśī'*, which is usually translated 'prince' and in the period before the state could denote the tribal leader.[93] It continues in the absence in Ezek.40-48, in contrast to Ezek.34.23f.; 37.24f., of any reference to the Davidic origin of this leader.

If some attempt is evident here to go back beyond the time of the Davidic dynasty and take up the leading offices of the period before the state, this impression is confirmed by the way in which the reformers largely stripped the *nāśī'* of the sacrality of oriental kingship. While the kings since David and Solomon had as a matter of course also claimed the functions of priesthood by virtue of their divine sonship,[94] the reform priests wanted to deny them the right to sacrifice (46.2). The king was not allowed even to enter the inner forecourt at all (vv.2,8). Certainly he was still accorded some rights in worship, like the right to hold his private sacrificial meals in the walled outer east gate (44.3) or the privilege of approaching quite near to the official sacrificial ceremonies from the threshold of the inner east gate (46.2) – which remotely recalls the cultic mediation of sacral kingship -, but that does not alter the fact that in terms of cultic law he was counted among the laity. The future king is no longer to be the mediator of the cult but only the most senior representative of the lay community (46.10).[95]

The reform priests are also concerned to couple the desacralization of the monarchy with putting economic and political limits to it. In order finally to stem the insatiable consumption of land by the institution, which in the pre-exilic period had led to a marked exclusion of Israelite smallholders from the social structure by the creation of ever new crown estates and leaseholds, the reformers assigned the *nāśī'* a clearly defined ancestral possession (*'aḥuzzā*, 45.8a; *naḥᵃlā*, 46.16) in the strip of land marked out as an offering (*tᵉrūmā*) on both sides of the priestly land (45.7f.; 48.21). Royal grants of land were allowed only within this clearly demarcated territory, and land could be appropriated permanently only within the royal family, not by royal servants (46.16-18).[96] Through this typically priestly means of marking out territory the reforms attempted to nip in the bud the pernicious economic dynamic which had made a substantial contribution in the pre-exilic period to the oppression and dispossession of the traditional class of small farmers (45.8b,9).

Finally, the reformers planned to limit the centralization of political power by separating the capital from the royal domain. Since the conquest of Jerusalem by David the city had been the personal possession of the royal house and its central power base.[97] By contrast, the view of the reformers was that the new capital should be established in a distinctive territory outside the royal land, south of the land of the priests and Levites, and should belong to all the tribes of Israel together (45.6; 48.15-18). Separated by some ten kilometres from the temple, which lay in the priestly territory, the city was to be a purely secular centre of administration and was no longer to be run by royal officials but by workers from all the Israelite tribes. These were to derive their livelihood from the land surrounding the city (about 26 square kilometres, 48.18), so that taxes would not be needed to support them. With its twelve gates, which bore the names of the twelve tribes of Israel, the city was once again to represent in microcosm the unity of Israel (48.3-34). And the new name of the city, 'Yahweh shamma' ('Yahweh is there', v.35), was no longer meant in the sense of the old Zion theology, namely as an indication that Yahweh dwelt in the royal sanctuary and represented the power of the state, but indicated that he was present in the midst of the people[98] and occupied the supreme position of power in the face of all human attempts to grasp it.

However, for the disciples of Ezekiel the territorial and institutional separation of the monarchy from the temple was only part of further reflections on a comprehensive new distribution of the land (47.13-48.29). In assigning an equally wide strip of land west of the Jordan[99] in a highly schematic way to all the tribes, they were evidently going by an ideal image of Israel from the time before the state, which had an egalitarian social structure. According to the notions of the group, Israel was to tribalize itself again; all the tribes were to be of the same size and were to receive an equal portion of land as an inalienable ancestral inheritance (*naḥᵃlā*, 47.13f.).[100] All differences in the size of properties which had become so dangerous in the period of the monarchy were to be levelled down again; no portion was to surpass that of others, and possible differences in the fertility of the land were to be equalized by the temple in a miraculous way – the wilderness of Judah is a particularly obvious example here.[101] The equal distribution of property is no longer to be infringed by any royal grants of land (46.16-18), nor is it to be upset by any high taxation. Since all other functionaries (except priests) could provide for themselves, in accordance with the economic principle of the pre-state period, there was no need at all for a state tax. That left only the cultic offerings, in particular what was needed for the official sacrificial cult. However, compared, say with the tithes, the taxes called for in 45.13-15 represented a far-reaching reduction.[102] Finally, the last remaining social problem, that of the landless strangers (*gērīm*), was solved by integrating them completely into the new order of landholding (47.22f.). All families were to have equal rights, and were to be able to continue their occupations freely, unburdened by state intervention, as in the period before the state.

If we survey the political and social side of the draft reform, we can only be amazed at how serious an attempt is made here, in the planning of the new beginning after the exile, to revise the erroneous social developments of the period of the state and again take up the ideals of freedom from the pre-state period. Granted, the reformers did not deny the central institutions which had accrued to Israel during the monarchy and to which even its priestly family owed its prominent position: the monarchy and the capital, not to mention the central sanctuary. But they did reflect on how they could so separate and reorder this religious and political conglomerate of power with the help of their priestly pattern of thought and their hierarchical sacred precincts that these institutions could be integrated without any damage into the tribal social structure. And the amazing thing about this new order is that the marked emphasis on the temple at the expense of the monarchy and the capital was not matched by any political claim to power on the part of the priesthood. The priestly group was not calling for any church state for itself; it limited its monopolistic claim to cultic interests and allowed other authorities in the secular sphere. Rather, its aim was for the central sanctuary to have a prominent place in society and for the decentralized political powers of the people to be reinforced, with a view to their liberation from the oppression of the royal central authority and the safeguarding of their economic equality. Thus for the reformers, the battle for the liberation of the cult from state supervision and for the social liberation of the people from an unjust social structure went hand in hand. In this connection, in completely changed circumstances room was made once again for the age-old impulse towards liberation characteristic of Yahweh religion in the pre-state period. That is the abiding significance of this revolutionary outline of a radically new beginning, even if little attention was paid to it when the rebuilding was actually begun.[103]

5. The History of Israelite Religion in the Post-Exilic Period

J.Blenkinsopp, 'Interpretation and Tendency to Sectarianism: An Aspect of the Second Temple History', in E.P.Sanders (ed.), *Jewish and Christian Self-Definition* II, 1981, 1-26; E.Blum, *Studien zur Komposition des Pentateuch*, BZAW 189, 1990; F.Crüsemann, 'Israel in der Perserzeit. Eine Skizze in Auseinandersetzung mit Max Weber', in W.Schluchter (ed.), *Max Webers Sicht des antiken Christentums*, 1985, 205-32; P.D.Hanson, *The Dawn of Apocalyptic. The Historical and Sociological Roots of Jewish Apocalyptic Eschatology*, [2]1979; id., 'Israelite Religion in the Early Postexilic Period', in *Ancient Israelite Religion. FS F.M.Cross*, 1987, 485-508; H.D.Mantel, 'The Dichotomy of Judaism during the Second Temple', *HUCA* 44, 1973, 55-87; O.Plöger, *Theocracy and Eschatology*, 1968; O.H.Steck, 'Das Problem theologischer Strömungen in nachexilischer Zeit', *EvTh* 28, 1969, 182-200; id., 'Strömungen theologischer Tradition im Alten Israel' (1978), in id., *Wahrnehmungen Gottes im Alten Testament*, TB 1970, 1982, 291-317.

The post-exilic period is treated in a niggardly way in current accounts of the history of Israelite religion.[1] This is not just because of the sparseness of the historical source material, which makes it possible to get a closer look only at the beginning (538-400)[2] and the end (c.200-150)[3] of this long stretch of time covered by the Old Testament writings – and then one with a tendentious colouring. Nor is the reason just the difficulty of dating many of the texts of this period even approximately.[4] It is also – at least – the consequence of a deep-seated dogmatic Christian view, which sees the church as the goal of the history of Israelite religion, and therefore likes to go straight from the lofty heights of Deutero-Isaiah – perhaps through late prophecy and apocalyptic[5] – to the New Testament. In this approach the religion of 'late Judaism' degenerates into legalism and ritualism. The account which follows is also affected by the difficulties of the situation with the sources, but may do more justice to this period.

More recent research, which at many points has prompted critical questions about the customary early dating of many biblical texts,[6] shows increasingly clearly that the post-exilic period, and especially the early post-exilic period (538-400), was one of the most productive eras in the history of Israelite religion. In the face of the challenge posed by the opportunity and the problems of rebuilding, at this time the foundations were laid which were normatively to shape later Jewish and Christian religion; at this time the course towards canonization was taken in the creation of a universally binding holy scripture; at this time the temple came to occupy the centre of religious life and became the central symbol of wide-ranging hopes; and at this time a horizon of eschatological expectation arose which increasingly clearly went beyond the limits of political history and human existence.

The liveliness of the theological discourse, particularly in the post-exilic period, is evident from a multiplicity of 'theological currents' which scholars have long detected in the texts of this period. Deuteronomistic, Priestly, Chronistic, wisdom, prophetic and psalms traditions clearly stand side by side and over against one another and often cross. Their variety is so great that even now it is difficult to give them their due place in the history of Israelite religion and the social history of the community.

Plöger's bipolar model has had great influence.[7] He sees the whole history of post-exilic religion as dominated by the opposition of two great currents of tradition: the theocratic tradition, which finds expression above all in the Priestly Writing but also in Chronicles, and which was handed down by the official circles of the post-exilic restoration; and the eschatological tradition of late prophetic texts (Joel 3f.; Zech.12-14; Isa.24-27), which is developed by small conventicles. These can be seen as forerunners of the Hasidim mentioned in the books of Maccabees (*Asidaioi*, I Macc.2.42; 7.13; II Macc.14.6), which according to Plöger were those who handed on the apocalyptic book of Daniel.

Although this model has been widely accepted and has many variations,[8] it is much too simple to be an appropriate description of the multiplicity of historical developments in Israelite religion. It takes no notice of important lines of tradition like the Deuteronomistic and the Wisdom traditions.

Steck has therefore attempted to extend Plöger's basic model and to differentiate it historically.[9] To the theocratic position he assigns not only the Priestly Writing but also the Nehemiah memorandum, the Haggai redaction, the Jerusalem cult tradition and the wisdom currents. For this tradition the shift towards salvation took place at the rebuilding of the temple. By contrast, he sees the eschatological position, which still awaited this shift in the future, as represented not only by the late prophetic current but also by the 'Deuteronomistic current'. However, in Steck's view this simple contrast is not all; it has many connections: he regards the formation of the canon as a theocratic reception of the Deuteronomistic historical tradition. And he argues that the Chronistic history work played a similar part in the process of integration. Moreover, in the late-Persian, Hellenistic period the prophetic current opened up to the Jerusalem cultic tradition (Isa.24-27; Joel 3f.; Deutero- and Trito-Isaiah), while on the other hand the wisdom tradition opened up to the prophetic current (Sirach). Finally, in the Seleucid period there was the 'anti-Hellenistic coalition' of the Hasidaeans in which the eschatological current issued in apocalyptic under the guidance of the wisdom tradition.

This complex 'diagram of currents' beyond doubt does more justice to the many levels to be found in the texts, even if a series of inconsistencies remains.[10] To give only one example, how do we explain the fact that Nehemiah, whom Steck makes an exponent of the theocratic tradition, quite evidently shares the Deuteronomistic view of history, in his prayer (Neh.1.5-11) and elsewhere (13.26)? Moreover Steck almost completely refrains from giving his 'currents' and mixtures a sociological context and does not attempt to demonstrate their plausibility.[11]

By contrast, Crüsemann was concerned to couple the historical development of religion in the early post-exilic period closely with sociological data. He rightly challenges the existence of a theocracy for the Persian period and differs from Plöger in developing a tripolar model:[12] starting from the evidence in the Nehemiah memorial (Neh.5.; 6.7,14), he reconstructs three groups. The mass of lowly free farmers forms a strong middle group. It has support from circles of the Gola (Nehemiah), and according to Crüsemann is firmly allied with the priesthood. This coalition stands behind the formation of the Pentateuch, which on the one hand offers a compromise between the interests of the priests and farmers in debt, but on the other hand takes account of the situation of the Gola even in its narrative parts (especially the patriarchal history). In Crüsemann's view the Torah, established with Persian support, is deliberately unprophetic. Alongside this stands a second group, the local aristocracy. This group does not submit to the social laws of the ethics of brotherhood but with its wisdom theology develops an ethic which by-passes the Torah. It has an anti-eschatological attitude and is open to aliens and other peoples (Job, Jonah). The third group is difficult to fix; it consists of prophetic conventicles who opposed the compromise which the two other groups had made with Persian power with its eschatological expectations of a political and social upheaval. This group was perhaps recruited from parts of the landless lower class and the intellectuals.

Crüsemann's model stands on a much firmer footing than that of Steck. Nevertheless, it, too, still seems too crude: Crüsemann himself already suggested that 'parts of the more senior priesthood' went along with the aristocracy.[13] And so we find members of the highest priestly circles in particular among the opponents of Nehemiah (13.10ff.). Thus there can only have been parts of the priesthood who according to Lev.19; 25 were concerned to protect the lowly farmers.[14] On the other hand, Nehemiah clearly belongs to the aristocracy, part of whom in turn according to Job 29.12ff.; 31.13ff. felt close ties with the 'brotherhood ethic' and fought unselfishly against the impoverishment of the small farmers.[15] Here, too, then we must reckon with a division of the upper class into at least two different groups. Finally we should ask whether wisdom theology lies on the same level as the official foundation of faith, the Torah. At any rate Nehemiah, who recognizes a commitment to the Torah in the public interest (Neh.5.13.4ff.), evidently moves along the lines of pious wisdom in his private prayers.[16] According to the model of internal religious pluralism which I am using, one would thus have to put the wisdom theology on the level of personal piety. So my own sketch will attempt to refine the conception presented by Crüsemann in the direction of the three questions that have been raised.

The splintering of official Yahweh religion into rival traditions or conceptions, which becomes so striking in the post-exilic period, can best be understood as a late consequence of the collaspe of the state and cultic institutions in 587. In the exilic period official Yahweh religion lost its institutional support. In the exile it had been handed down – leaving aside the families who helped to fill the gaps – by informal groups of theologians who had developed their theological conceptions more or less freely and more or less theoretically.[17] At the level of official Yahweh religion, in the early post-exilic period at least three rival schemes were available which fought for influence in the reshaping of the Jewish community: Deutero-nomistic theology in its different genres (DtrG, JerD), the priestly reform theology (the Ezekiel school) and the exilic prophecy of salvation (the Deutero-Isaiah school, etc.). But these could only find a partial basis in the newly created institutions: Deuteronomistic theology perhaps in the lay college and priestly reform theology in the priestly college of the self-administration of Judah,[18] the prophecy of salvation only for a short time in the framework of the rebuilding of the temple (Haggai, Zechariah). They remained limited to parties or more or less small groups of activists who had to canvass for the realization of their theological conceptions within their particular contexts or among the population. The reasons for this are to be sought in two directions: first, all exilic schemes had a utopian potential – Deutero-Isaiah in particular, but also Ezek.40-48, JerD and even DtrG – which in the constrained political and harsh economic conditions of the early post-exilic period could only be realized to a minute degree. So in this form they could not become common property, but had to be selected from or adapted. And secondly, none of the groups of tradents had the political power to carry through its particular conception in the face of the others as the sole official religion of Yahweh, since a restitution of the monarchy was impossible. They were largely dependent on convincing and forming a consensus between the different interests. So in the post-exilic period we shall have to distinguish between the different institutions (council of elders, priestly college) and social strata (aristocracy, small farmers, landless); between the minority formed by the authentic tradents of the official theologies and the majority made up of the more or less half-hearted fellow travellers or even opponents.

The splintering inherited from the exilic period now set in motion two opposite movements in the further development of official Yahweh religion: integration and disintegration. The most important example of integration is the formation of the canon. The Torah, created in the fifth century probably under Persian pressure, is a compromise between the adherents of Deuteronomistic theology and those of priestly theology, which was to secure the religious identity and legal basis of the community of Judah along the lines of the two dominant groups. Here for the first time a written document was created which was to be the norm for official Yahweh religion – albeit in the form of a tense, agitated dialogue. The most important consequence of the development of this norm was that kingship theology was largely excluded[19] and prophecy was recognized only within the framework marked out by the law. At the end of the fourth and beginning of the third centuries the Chronistic history was a further example of an integrative concept which once again gave an important place in the official view of history to the Davidic kingship from a cultic perspective and to a 'tamed' prophecy. Only as a result of this far-reaching attempt at integration did that part of DtrG (Joshua – II Kings) which covers the monarchy find general recognition in the course of the canonization of the prophets in the third century.

The most important example of disintegration is closely connected with this. After the far-reaching fiasco suffered by exilic and early post-exilic prophecy,[20] the prophecy which had enjoyed broad official recognition in the exile and during the rebuilding of the temple (Haggai, Zechariah) was again forced into the role of opposition theology in marginal social groups for reasons of political opportunism and the economic interests of the normative groups. Whereas it was completely passed over by the priestly reform party (cf. P), it was acknowledged to a limited degree – along the lines of the Deuteronomistic revisions of the prophets – by the laicist Deuteronomistic party.[21] Banished to the periphery of society, in study, exegesis and reinterpretation of earlier prophecies these small groups arrived at the conception of an eschatological action of God which would overthrow the world and society. Here elements of kingship and temple theology for the first time took on a revolutionary, subversive function in an eschatological mutation. Suppressed because of their political explosiveness, these revolutionary expectations came to be generally accepted as an indispensable part of official Yahweh religion only in the second half of the third century (the prophetic canon). In the religious wars of the second century, in the new guise of an apocalyptic theology of resistance, for a short time they once again took on central public significance, soon afterwards to disappear rapidly beyond the fringes of society.

A further characteristic of the post-exilic period is the continuing development of the convergence of official religion and family piety which began in the exilic period. Since there was still virtually no trace of any action by Yahweh in history because of ongoing political dependence on the great powers, official religion increasingly resorted to the relationship of creaturely trust characteristic of personal piety.[22] On the other hand, the controversies within official religion had an effect on personal piety.[23] For example, among the groups who quite deliberately submitted to the Torah as 'the pious', the canonization of the Torah produced a regular Torah piety in which the law became a guarantee of the personal relationship of trust in God (e.g. Ps.119).

In connection with this convergence, in the post-exilic period there was a theologizing and a splintering of personal piety. From the 'pious', committed part of the upper class which in its way of life had gone by wisdom maxims since the time of the monarchy, there developed a regular personal wisdom theology, so-called 'theologized wisdom', especially as this is expressed in Proverbs 1-9 and the book of Job. By contrast, in the lower class, on the basis of the lamentations and thanksgivings, there

Official religion   Personal piety

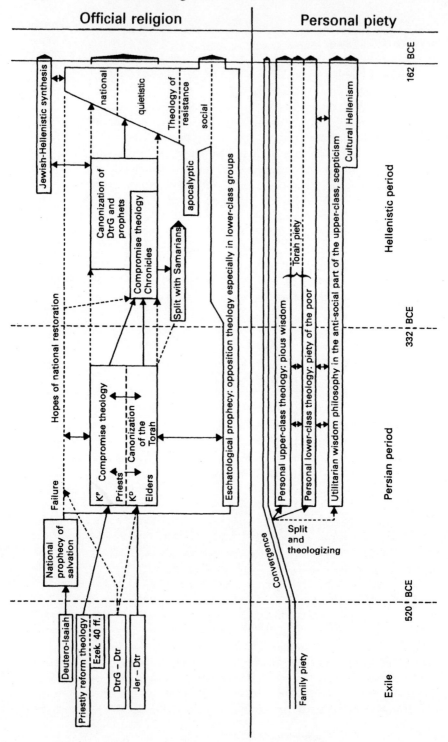

developed an explicit piety of the poor in which groups brought the eschatological potential of expectation to bear in their personal relationship with God, directing it against that part of the upper class (i.e. the wicked) which oppressed them (cf. Pss.9f.; 12; 22, etc.). But in the late post-exilic period a counter-movement can also be recognized here. The collecting of the psalms or the formation of the third part of the canon indicates a concern to give the different types of piety the same rights within Yahweh religion. Thus the dialectic of splintering and union so typical of the post-exilic period continued at the level of the religion of the small groups.

5.1 Political and sociological developments in the Persian period

N.Avigad, 'Bullae and Seals from a Post-exilic Judean Archive', *Qedem* 4, 1976; J.Blenkinsopp, *A History of Prophecy in Israel*, 1984; F.M.Cross, 'A Reconstruction of Judean Restoration', *JBL* 94, 1975, 4-18; F.Crüsemann, 'Geschichte Israels als Geschichte der Bibel', in E.Lessing (ed.), *Die Bibel. Das Alte Testament in Bilder erzählt*, 1987, 133-70; K.Galling, *Studien zur Geschichte Israels im persischen Zeitalter*, 1964; E.L.Grabbe, 'The Jewish Theocracy from Cyrus to Titus. A Programmatic Essay', *JSOT* 37, 1987, 117-24; K.Koch, 'Weltordnung und Reichsidee im alten Iran', in id. and P.Frey, *Reichsidee und Reichsorganisation im Persenreich*, OBO 55, 1984, 45-116; H.Kreissig, *Die sozialökonomische Situation in Juda zur Achämenidenzeit*, Schriften zur Geschichte und Kultur des Alten Orients 7, 1973; E.Meyer, *Die Enstehung des Judentums*, 1896/97 = 1987, esp. 13off.; E.M.Meyers, 'The Persian Period of Judean Restoration. From Zerubbabel to Nehemiah', in *Ancient Israelite Religion. FS F.M.Cross*, 1987, 309-21; J.Nikel, *Die Wiederherstellung des jüdischen Gemeinwesens nach dem Exil*, 1900; A.F.Rainey, 'The Satrapy Beyond the River', *Australian Journal of Biblical Archeology* 1, 1969, 51-78; W.Schottroff, 'Zur Sozialgeschichte Israels in der Perserzeit', *VuF* 27, 1981; id., 'Arbeit und sozialer Konflikt im nachexilischen Juda', in id. and L.Schottroff (eds.), *Mitarbeiter der Schöpfung*, 1983, 104-18; E.Stern, 'The Archaeology of Persian Palestine', in W.D.Davies and L.Finkelstein (eds.), *The Cambridge History of Judaism*, I, 1984, 88-114; id., 'The Persian Empire and the Political and Social History of Palestine in the Persian Period', in ibid., 70-87; S.Talmon, 'Jüdische Sektenbildung in der Frühzeit der Periode des Zweiten Tempels', in W.Schluchter (ed.), *Max Webers Sicht des antiken Judentums*, 1985, 233-80; H.C.M.Vogt, *Studien zur nachexilischen Gemeinde in Esra-Nehemiah*, 1966; J.P.Weinberg, 'Das Beït 'Abōt im 6.-4. Jh. vor unserer Zeit', *VT* 23, 1973, 400-14; id., 'Die Agrarverhältnisse in der Bürger-Tempel-Gemeinde der Achämenidenzeit', in J.Harmatta and G.Komoroczy (eds.), *Wirtschaft und Gesellschaft im Alten Vorderasien*, 1976, 473-86; id., 'Demographische Notizen zur Geschichte des nachexilischen Gemeinde in Juda', *Klio* 54, 1972, 45-59.

The remarkable dialectic of splintering and integration in the history of Israelite religion in the post-exilic era is directly connected with the political and sociological developments of the Persian period. The decisive factor here is that Israel did not achieve any restoration of the state[1] along the pre-exilic pattern, but under the pressure of political circumstances found its way to a new form of community which was more orientated on pre-state structures.

Now this fact was not *a priori* inevitable, but was the consequence of Persian imperial policy and internal controversies and decisions. For the Judaeans in Babylonia and Palestine the conquest of Babylon by Cyrus in 539 did not bring the triumphant turning point which the Deutero-Isaiah group had announced, but only a change of overlords. However, it did bring a turning point, in that in order to safeguard their rule, the Persians embarked on a different policy towards the subject peoples of their empire from that of the Babylonians and Assyrians: it was no longer aimed at suppression but at respecting and even furthering cultural and religious identity. The Persians dispensed with deportations and saw to the restitution of local cults.[2] So it is not improbable that in the very first year of his reign Cyrus decreed the restoration of the plundered temple vesels and commissioned a delegation under the leadership of Sheshbazzar[3] to take them back to Jerusalem (Ezra 1.7-11). Possibly he also already authorized the rebuilding of the temple with state support (Ezra 6.1-5) and in principle raised the possibility of a return of the exiles.[4]

Thus for the Judaeans in Babylonia and Palestine the decisive question arose whether or not to accept this very limited chance for a shared new beginning which had been offered to them by Persian imperial policy. And the eighteen years that it took for a start on rebuilding the temple make it probable that for most people a positive answer was by no means obvious.[5] On the one hand there were political hesitations: the groups with a marked nationalistic orientation (for example those around DtrG and Ezekiel) will have asked whether the price of being permanently loyal to the Persian authorities in such a deal was not too high. And on the other hand there were economic constraints; given the wretched economic situation (cf. Hag.1.6, 9-11; Zech .8.10) in Palestine, for many exiles their occupational chances will have seemed far more attractive in Babylonia. Moreover, among those who remained at home the prospect of the return of a large number of exiles who wanted to enforce their ancestral rights to property will hardly have caused great outbursts of enthusiasm.

There are several reasons for the fact that nevertheless, after long discussions, probably at the beginning of 520 a majority decided to venture the risky chance of a new beginning and for the first time formed a major wave of returnees.[6] The three revolts which plagued Babylonia from the spring of 522 to the autumn of 521 and the tight organization of the empire that Darius I (521-486) introduced after they had been put down made the decision much easier for many undecided exiles. Moreover, by virtue of his interest in permanently pacifying the problematical western flank of his empire and the way to Egypt Darius met the concerns of those with nationalistic inclinations by putting Zerubbabel of the house of David, a nephew of Jehoiachin, in charge of the work of rebuilding.[7] Nevertheless, only some of the exiles were involved in this enterprise. A large part of the Gola remained in Babylon, even though theoretically they were in favour of the return, and the Egyptian Gola remained completely aloof.[8] That means that it proved impossible to overcome the territorial splintering of Israel brought about by the collapse of the state. Given the conditions under which it began, the community in Judah which was to be created anew could at best be the focal point of various centres, but never the focal point of the whole.[9]

The building of the temple, which began in difficult conditions, at the same time manifested the instability of the compromise made with the Persians. It sparked off glowing expectations of a revolution in world history and a national restoration which attached themselves to Zerubbabel of the house of David.[10] The situation seemed so dangerous to the Persians that the satrap Tatnai paid a personal visit to Jerusalem to sort things out (Ezra 5.3-17). While he allowed the rebuilding after consultations with the court (6.1-15), this was probably only on condition that Zerubbabel was withdrawn[11] and that the dangerous prophetic movements were stopped or controlled effectively.[12] The displacement of eschatological prophecy beyond the fringe of society goes back to this near-fiasco.

The groups which after rebuilding the temple (520-515) went on to rebuild the community in conscious loyalty to the Persians were, first, those elements of the priesthood concerned to construct a cult for which they themselves were responsible, outside the grasp of royal supervision (cf. Ezek.40ff.), and, secondly, those of the lay leaders who – like the group of officials around Gedaliah – for the want of a monarchy of their own saw the chance of achieving a 'democratic' self-administration (cf. JerD).[13] But although this coalition had things under control throughout the Persian period, its political option was by no means undisputed; at the time of the rebellions which had been shaking the Persian empire since the death of Darius I in 486[14] it must constantly have had to fight against the nationalistic efforts at rebellion which kept flaring up: the accusation against the Judaeans mentioned in Ezra 4.6, which was made to Xerxes (486-465), probably belongs in the context of the Habasha revolts in Egypt (486). Two petitions from the Samarian provincial administration to Artaxerxes (465-424) could prevent the people of Jerusalem from restoring the fortifications of their city (Ezra 4.7, 8-23) in the wake of the Egyptian Inarus rebellion (460-454). Even if we regard some of the wild accusations made by the Samaritans against the 'ever-rebellious Jerusalem' (vv.12f.,15) as exaggerated denunciation of a neighbouring province which feared its influence, the charges were not completely plucked out of thin air, since the Persian government reacted with violence. In all probability they indicate that in Judah the nationalistic forces were threatening to gain the upper hand politically and, following the well-tried pattern of the pre-exilic seesaw policy, were attempting with Egyptian help to shake off the yoke of the Persian power, which the Greek wars had proved to be fragile. In all probability the missions of Nehemiah (444-432) and Ezra (398?)[15] were connected with rebel movements.[16] They are to be seen as skilful ploys by the Persian government to strengthen the pro-Persian coalition which had come under pressure by means of the collaboration of senior Jewish officials from the Gola and by making concessions in the direction of autonomy for Judah in order to guarantee a new loyalty to the Persian empire. As Persian governor, Nehemiah may have claimed credit for himself and the pro-Persian coalition for the successful rebuilding of the walls and thus the elevation of Judah to a province with equal rights.[17] But even he had to protect himself against being commandeered by nationalistic prophets who wanted to proclaim him king (Neh.6.6-14). As Persian secretary for Jewish affairs (Ezra 7.12), Ezra was given the full authorization of the Persian crown to apply the laws of the Pentateuch to all Judaeans of the satrapy of 'Abar Nahara (v.25).[18] Only in this way did the new form of social organization under Persian supervision, which renounced any restoration of the state, probably come to be generally recognized.

But how was the organization of the new community of Judah created? At the latest after Nehemiah, but probably already earlier,[19] it was headed by the Persian governor (*peḥā*, Neh.2.7,9; Ezra 8.36), who could be Jewish or Persian[20] and was subordinate to the satrap of 'Abar Nahara (Transeuphratene). Together with his family (Neh.4.17; 5.10,14) and a team of officials who in the time of Nehemiah consisted of 150 persons, mostly Jewish nobility, but also some foreigners (*seḡānīm*, 'officials', 2.16; 4.8,13; 5.7,17; Ezra 9.29),[21] he formed the Persian provincial administration. This extended down to individual localities through the presidents (*śārīm*) of the nine administrative regions (*pelek*, Neh.3.9ff.). The military posts were limited to a few positions of leadership (Neh.2.9; 7.2). A special tax had to be levied from the province to finance the court of the governor and his administration (5.14,18).

Below the Persian administrative apparatus came Jewish self-government. At the upper level this consisted of two leading bodies: a 'council of elders' and a priestly college which had to advise the governor in his decisions.[22] The members of the lay body are called *ḥōrīm*, 'prominent men, nobles' in the Nehemiah memorandum (Neh.2.16; 4.8,13; 5.7; 7.5; 6.17; 13.17); they are to be identified with the 'elders of Judah' (*śābē yehūdāyē*, Ezra 5.5,9; 6.7,8,14), responsible in the Aramaic source of the book of Ezra for building the temple; in the terminology of the author of Ezra/Nehemiah they are called 'heads of the fathers' (houses)' (*rā'šē hā'ābōt*, Ezra 2.68; 4.2, 3; 8.1; Neh.8.13; 11.13, etc.). So these are the most prominent leaders of the clans (*bēt 'ābōt*, Ezra 2.59 = Neh.7.61, etc.) which were newly created in the course of the return and incorporation;[23]

every family which wanted to belong to the community had to be registered in one of these clans (Neh.7.5).[24] The priestly college consisted of members of the priests, Levites and other temple personnel under the leadership of the high priest, and was similarly organized by *bēt 'ābōt* (Neh.2.16; 3.1; 12.1-7; 13.4,28; Ezra 2.36ff. 61f.).[25] Below these two governing bodies stood the popular assembly (*qāhāl*, Ezra 10.1,12; Neh.5.7,13), which was summoned every now and then when important decisions were due.

The structure of the Jewish self-administration clearly borrows from models from the period before the state: apart from the college of priests, the council of elders and the popular assembly are parallel to the assembly of elders and arms-bearing men.[26] Indeed, if we imagine the head of the Persian administration replaced by a king and his officials, the ordering of state and tribal bodies completely meets the desire for a 'constitutional monarchy' which was already in the minds of those groups which were critical of the king in Absalom's rebellion[27] and in the minds of the Deuteronomic reform party.[28] We can even say that the regular ordering of the population in clan alliances (*bēt 'ābōt*) is an attempt at an artificial restoration of the social structure of the pre-state period, something also envisaged – in an even more radical form – by the reformers of the Ezekiel school.[29] Thus elements of the tribal ideals of freedom which were never wholly forgotten broke through again in the organization of post-exilic society. And it is quite understandable that here those groups which were concerned for reform believed that under the Persian aegis those rights of co-determination for which people had been fighting against their own monarchy for a long time were being realized. They were ready to pay the price of alien rule in order to achieve this.

However, this very fine organizational model had a decided flaw. Despite great efforts which will be mentioned later,[30] it was impossible to revive artificially the equality and solidarity of pre-exilic society. There was no going back on the social differentiations which had arisen in society under the monarchy. On the contrary, they became even more marked under the pressure of the rigorous Persian taxation policy, which in contrast to the Persian religious policy was anything but tolerant.[31] Whereas the poorer families of smallholders were driven further and further into misery under this burden, which became even greater in the fifth century as a result of the disastrous wars of the Persians against the Greeks, the richer families of larger estate holders profited from developing trade and the business of making loans.[32] The result of this social gulf was that in the college of elders and priests the families from the upper classes set the tone, while the popular assembly, which had had supreme authority in decision-making in the pre-state period, deteriorated into a purely executive organ; the poorer families in the clans could only assent to what the richer members had already decided (cf. Neh.10.29ff.). That means that Jewish self-administration came close to oligarchy, in which above all the propertied families set the tone. Certainly some of the aristocracy voted against this development and attempted to keep the general well-being in mind, but from the perspective of the lower class, who were becoming increasingly poor and losing their influence, it inevitably looked as if many rich people had renounced solidarity with them and had gone into Persian service on the side of their oppressors as lackeys who profited from the situation, or even tax-collectors. In the tense social conditions of the community of Judah the intrinsically 'tolerant' ruling practice of the Persians, who made as much use as possible of members of subject people in their rule, thus giving them some possibility of co-determination, led to a far-reaching conflict of loyalty in the upper class and to a sharp opposition of fronts in society. The relative autonomy which the social experiment granted to the Jewish community under Persian rule could be purchased only at the high price of a social and religious polarization.[33]

Here we come up against a remarkable dialectic at the sociological level. On the one hand it proved possible to develop an expressly integrative form of social organization which accorded all groups a degree of political involvement, of a kind that had not existed since the pre-state period. On the other hand, the political framework of political and especially economic dependence on the power of Persia and the split in social structure associated with it unleashed strong forces of disintegration which drove large parts of the population into a social abyss and constantly threatened the community.

However, the whole span of the religious dialectic connected with this first becomes clear when we ask in conclusion: what criteria defined the unity and identity of the new community of Judah? How is it to be classified sociologically?

At this point there is great uncertainty among scholars which frequently distorts assessments of the history of Israelite religion after the exile.

Since Josephus it has become customary to designate the post-exilic community of Judah a 'theocracy'.[34] The correct insight in this view is that here for the first time in the history of Israel the priesthood forms an independent power factor. But at least for the Persian period there is no question of a dominant priestly rule. The priestly college was only one governing body alongside the council of elders, and while the temple was an important unifying symbol, temple power and the temple economy were not decisive factors.[35] To this degree the model of the 'temple community' put forward by Blenkinsopp in a comparison with Ionian cities[36] needs critical examination. Here the model of the 'citizen-temple community' with which Weinberg operates seems more appropriate, since it gives an important place to the lay element.[37]

Alongside this, the view is often put forward that in contrast to the people of Israel in the pre-exilic period, post-exilic Israel was a religious community or a cult community.[38] For example, Donner defines it as a 'theocratic' community under the law, which, while it still understood itself as a community linked by blood, in fact decided membership through 'submission to the "law" as the making known of Yahweh's will'.[39] Crüsemann vigorously opposed such a use of the term community: he not only points out that the post-exilic community has clear political features (its own governor, its own territory, its own legislation and a – limited – right to its own coinage), but even draws the opposite conclusion from the fight against mixed marriages, 'that it is not loyalty to the law which is decisive for membership but only kinship and affinity. Membership is not regulated "voluntarily", but ethnically.'[40]

We have to grant to Crüsemann that the term community barely does justice to the political character and emphatically tribal organization of Judah. Nevertheless the term indicates an important characteristic in which post-exilic Israel differed from pre-exilic Israel and which is important for understanding the religious splintering which took place. Thus Talmon has pointed out in connection with the formation of sects in the Hellenistic period that the 'status of a "confessional faith community"' after the returns was in no way given up again but '*mutatis mutandis* was taken up into the new social model of Judaism'. In his view, in the early Persian period a 'symbiosis of faith community and nation' developed. 'From this time on the Jewish people formed itself into communities which accentuated its historical and religious heritage in different ways.'[41]

The special feature of the post-exilic community of Judah was that it was by no means defined merely ethnically, politically and territorially, but also in a markedly religious way. The emphatically ethnic definition of membership which was becoming established on the one hand indicates that the political institutions and territorial limits which in the period of the state had quite naturally guaranteed the national identity of Israel had evidently lost their clarity; foreigners were included in the provincial administration,[42] and even after the establishment of an independent province, the territorial limits did not fully correspond with the areas of Jewish settlement.[43] Secondly, even ethnic belonging was no longer something that could be taken for granted. On the one hand, as is indicated not least by the problem of mixed marriages, it had to be actively proved by decision and confession: anyone who did not observe the resolutions of the self-administrative body was threatened with exclusion (Ezra 10.8; Neh.13.28).[44] On the other hand, foreigners could also join the community (Ezra 6.21; Neh.10.29).[45] Certainly the broad missionary openness to society envisaged by the prophecy of Deutero-Isaiah (45.20ff.; cf. Zech.2.15) did not come about, but following it there were groups which were discontented with the more restrictive practice of admission (Isa.56.3-8).

Now the fact that the post-exilic community of Judah also had features of a community with a religious consitution must have had considerable effects on the social and religious discussions of its members; whereas in the pre-exilic period the conflicts, for all their sharpenss, were always limited by the fact that those involved were beyond question members of

one and the same people or state, now it was possible for a group sweepingly
to deny others membership of the community and to make the claim that
it was the 'true' Israel. Thus the social and religious conflicts became much
more tense and could put in question the very cohesion of the community.
This explains on the one hand why in the post-exilic period there could be
divisions, and conventicles and sects could form. From this we can also see
why an integrating compromise had to be found, by the progressive
formation of a canon which would prevent the parties in conflict from
drifting apart completely.

5.2 The key experience of the failed restoration

W.A.M.Beuken, *Haggai-Sacharja 1-8. Studien zur Überlieferung der frühnachex-
ilischen Prophetie*, 1967; K.Beyse, *Serubbabel und die Königserwartungen der
Propheten Haggai und Sacharja*, Diss.theol.Halle 1968; E.J.Bickerman, 'En marge
de l'écriture II. La seconde année de Darius', *RB* 88, 1981, 23-8; T.A.Busink, *Der
Tempel von Jerusalem* II, 1980; D.J.A.Clines, 'The Evidence for an Autumnal New
Year in Pre-exilic Israel Reconsidered', *JBL* 93, 1974, 22-40; M.Dunand, 'Byblos,
Sidon, Jérusalem. Monuments apparentés des temps achémenides', *VTS* 18, 1969,
64-70; B.Janowski, *Sühne als Heilsgeschehen*, WMANT 55, 1982; U.Kellermann,
Messias und Gesetz. Grundlinien einer alttestamentlichen Heilserwartung, BSt 61,
1971; N.Kiuchi, *The Purification Offering in the Priestly Literature*, JSOT.S 56,
1987; K.Koch, 'Sühne und Sündenvergebung um die Wende von der exilischen zur
nachexilischen Zeit', *EvTh* 26, 1966, 217-38; H.J.Kraus, 'Die ausgebliebene
Endtheophanie', *ZAW* 78, 1966, 317-32; J.Maier, 'Tempel und Tempelkult', in
id. and J.Schreiner, *Literatur und Religion des Frühjudentums*, 1973, 317-89;
R.A.Mason, 'The Purpose of the "Editorial Framework" of the Book of Haggai',
VT 27, 1977, 413-21; C.L. and E.M.Meyers, *Haggai, Zechariah 1-8*, AncB 25B,
1987; R.Rendtorff, *Studien zur Geschichte des Opfers im alten Israel*, WMANT
24, 1967; K.H.Rengstorf, 'Erwägungen zur Frage des Landbesitzes des Zweiten
Tempel in Judäa und seiner Verwaltung', *Bibel und Qumran, FS H.Bardtke*, 1968,
156-76; G.Sauer, 'Serubbabel in der Sicht Haggais und Sacharjas', in *Das ferne
und das nahe Wort. FS L.Rost*, BZAW 105, 1970, 199-207; W.Schottroff, 'Das
Jahr der Gnade Jahwes (Jes.61.1-11)', in id. and L.Schottroff, *Wer ist unser Gott?*,
1986, 122-36; E.Schürer, *Geschichte des jüdischen Volkes im Zeitalter Jesu Christi*
II, ⁴1907 = 1970; O.H.Steck, 'Der Grundtext in Jesaja 60 und sein Aufbau', *ZTK*
83, 1986, 261-96; id. 'Zu Haggai 1, 2-11', *ZAW* 83, 1979, 355-78; G.Wallis, 'Gott
und seine Gemeinde', *ThZ* 27, 1970, 182-200; L.Waterman, 'The Camouflaged
Purge of Three Messianic Conspirators', *JNES* 13, 1954, 73-8; H.W.Wolff,
Dodekapropheten 6. Haggai, BK XIV/6, 1986; E.Zenger, 'Israels Suche nach
einem neuen Selbstverständnis zu Beginn der Perserzeit', *BiKi* 39, 1984, 123-35;
W.Zimmerli, 'Das Gnadenjahr des Herrn', *Archäologie und Altes Testament, FS
K.Galling*, 1970, 321-332.

The book of Ezra (chs.1-6) suggests that the development of the early post-exilic period purposefully and necessarily ran towards the building of the temple – which was only held up by malicious neighbours – and that further considerations of a restoration of the state had not been discussed at all. However, this view can hardly be historically accurate, since while the Persian imperial policy offered an opportunity for restoration above all in the cultic sphere, the horizon of expectation which had been sketched out, above all by the exilic prophecy of salvation, went far beyond that – regardless of whether the rebuilding was imagined in more conservative terms as a restoration of the Davidic empire,[1] more progressively as the establishment of a 'tribal society' with a monarchy stripped of its power and priestly self-administration (Ezek.40-48), or even in a utopian way as the rise of a moral and religious centre of the world under direct divine guidance (Isa.40-55). And the weakness which the Persian empire had shown through the chain of revolts from the last year of Cambyses (the Gaumata rebellion in 522) to the third year of the usurper Darius (Elam, Scythians, 520/19)[2] shows that such wide-ranging expectations were not completely without foundation. So the people of the time were by no means certain in which direction things would develop.

5.21 The building of the temple and early post-exilic prophecy of salvation

The reason why nevertheless, shortly after the arrival of a major group of returnees, the rebuilding of the temple could be put in hand as the first measure of restoration is that it was based on a broad coalition of interests which could be created in the late summer of 520 (Hag.1.1). The priesthood, for whom the rebuilding of the temple was the necessary presupposition of employment and a livelihood and the realization of its plans for self-administration was of course the most interested party. However, the pragmatic politicians around the governor Zerubbabel were also interested, wanting to make the most of the opportunity offered them by the Persian imperial policy. But this set of interests would not in itself have been enough to accord the building of the temple absolute priority, for there were substantial reasons against it. The economic situation in Judah was disastrous because of the long years of political instability and a period of drought (Hag.1.6,9,10f.; 2.16; Zech.8.10). The reintegration of those who had returned caused considerable problems: property claims made against those who had remained behind had to be fought through the courts and created further social tensions (Zech.5.1-4); homes had to be planned and built to house those who had returned (Hag.1.9). This means that the wider population were fully occupied with securing their own livelihoods. In addition there were theological objections to building the temple: all the signs in this bleak time told against the view that the favourable time vouchsafed by God for such an enterprise had already come (Hag.1.2). And had not Jeremiah, in the view of his Deuteronomistic interpreters, warned against putting false trust in the temple, and instead of this called on the people first to bring about just social conditions in society (Jer.7.1-15)? Thus the groups of those who had remained in the land who were influenced by JerD in particular would have accorded priority to a just solution to the social problems over the building of the temple.[3]

There was a change in public opinion only when the pragmatic political interests in building the temple were combined with the utopian potential which the prophets Haggai and Zechariah contributed to the discussion, partly taking up the prophecy of salvation. Both succeeded in motivating not only the political and priestly leaders but also the wider population (Hag.1.2-11), despite all external difficulties, to set to work on the rebuilding and carry it through despite some disappointments (Hag.2.3-9; Zech.4.6aβ-10). Thus for a short time prophecy became a direct influence in politics, to a degree which it had not attained previously in Israel and was not to achieve subsequently. The only problem was that with the concrete act of rebuilding the temple the prophets Haggai and Zechariah aroused much more far-reaching hopes of restoration,[4] which in the prevailing political conditions quickly proved a dangerous illusion and almost endangered the whole enterprise.

In detail, the proclamation and thought-worlds of the two prophets were quite different: Haggai, who in a lively discussion style aimed at the real breakthrough and emerged during the first three months of the building of the temple (29.8 – 18.12.520),[5] probably came from the circles of the former court prophets and moved in the realm of conservative nationalistic ideas; for him the temple was above all the guarantee of blessing, and he indefatigably pointed out to his fellow-citizens that their bleak economic situation was a consequence of the fact that the temple was lying in ruins (Hag.1.2-9); it would only change if the rebuilding was begun (2.15-19; cf. Zech.8.9,12). In addition to the people, the other party mainly responsible for rebuilding the temple – very much along the line of the pre-exilic state cult – was Zerubbabel of the house of David (2.4),[6] to whom he promised Yahweh's unconditional support (2.4b,5b). So it is no coincidence that with the conclusion of the rebuilding of the temple Haggai proclaimed a complete restoration of the Davidic kingdom (Hag.2.23) which would explicitly mark the repeal of the divine verdict of rejection on Jehoiachin (Jer.22.24-26). He expected a world-shaking intervention on the part of Yahweh, which would not only cause the peoples to bring their riches to Jerusalem, to adorn with splendour the now impoverished temple (2.6-9), but would also totally reverse the present political conditions (2.21f.), so that Zerubbabel could enter into his office as a 'signet ring', i.e. the one mandated by Yahweh on earth, very much along the lines of the earlier kingship theology.

Zechariah, who appeared rather later (beginning of 519 to end of 518), also cherished the expectation of an imminent[7] upheaval which Yahweh would bring about in the world of nations as the universal 'Lord of the whole earth' (Zech.4.14; 6.5). His prophecy had a marked visionary stamp: he saw the divine messengers who had announced to Yahweh that politically all was quiet in the world (1.7-17) already storming on their horses to all points of the compass (6.1-8), and four smiths who cast down 'the horns of the nations' (2.1-4). In contrast to Haggai, Zechariah, who like Ezekiel came from a priestly family, was more markedly influenced by the new ideas of restoration which had been developed by the Deutero-Isaiah and Ezekiel schools. In line with the former he proclaimed that Yahweh would return to Jerusalem when his sanctuary had been rebuilt (2.16), and would put the great city, after its restoration, under the protection of his glory (2.5-9). In line with the latter he developed the picture of a dyarchy of the high priest and the king, who, as the two figures anointed by God ('the sons of oil'), would see to his rule over the world (4.1-6aα + 10aβ-14). Indeed, Zechariah even undertook – at least symbolically – a coronation of the high priest Joshua and the Davidide Zerubbabel[8] in keeping with this vision, proclaiming their harmonious rule (6.9-14).[9] However, evidently things went wrong.[10] In addition, he thought that the troublesome disputes over property which were still burdening the life of society would be set aside (5.1-4), and that all the evil and godlessness would be removed from society and transported to Babylon (5.5-11). Still, for Zechariah this whole fundamental change in Jerusalem, both internally and externally, was not aimed at the annihilation of the nations, but – again in line with the prophecy of Deutero-Isaiah – was so that they would turn to Zion and be converted to Yahweh (6.8[11]; 2.15; cf. 8.20-22,23).

We may confidently conjecture that the prophecy of Haggai and Zechariah, who with the rebuilding of the temple in different ways announced a restoration of the Davidic monarchy or the rise of Jerusalem to become a world centre ruled by a priest-king, kindled a powerful mood of national excitement. Not only did they inspire those circles which had a traditional nationalistic approach; they also infected many of those who initially had been sceptical about the whole enterprise. The widespread mood of nationalistic excitement can be seen from the fact that for his symbolic coronation Zechariah was even sent a major gift of precious metal from the groups in the Gola (Zech.6.9ff.). By contrast, the pragmatic politicians among the priesthood and the elders found themselves caught between two stools: on the one hand they needed the nationalistic excitement to mobilize all forces for the rebuilding of the temple, and on the other they still had to raise the tricky question how long the Persian empire would stand by and watch this activity if the rule of Darius were to prove stable. Of course Zerubbabel, the Persian governor who was a member of the house of David, found himself in a particularly difficult conflict of loyalties: if he did not want to put his loyalty to the Persian king at risk in the interest of the whole community, he had to resist the temptation of yielding to the messianic projections which Haggai and Zechariah applied to him; but on the other hand, he could not disappoint the expectations of large areas of the population too much. A correction which Zechariah had to make to his prophecy probably derives from his refusal to go on playing the dangerous game. After Zerubbabel clearly distanced himself from the symbolic anointing, Zechariah transferred the coronation solely to the high priest Joshua (6.11), and saw the one whom he was defending against now unfathomable accusations and to whom he promised the supervision of the temple (3.1-7) as at the same time a substitute for the future king (3.8b). Possibly because of this adaptation to reality which had now become necessary, Zechariah already had to argue against doubts about the legitimacy of his prophecy (2.13b, 15b; 4.9b; 6.15aβ).

5.22 The fiasco of the prophecy of salvation and its 'eschatologizing'

The prophecies of Haggai and Zechariah were not fulfilled. The rebuilding of the temple which they helped to set in motion did not usher in the great miraculous turning point. The expected upheaval in world politics did not come about; at the latest by 518 Darius was sitting firmly in the saddle and a downfall of the Persian empire was no longer conceivable. Probably the Persians, who had an excellent grapevine for news, already intervened through their satrap Tatnai before the rebuilding of the temple was complete[12] and put an end to the nationalistic pressures in Judah. That Haggai, Zechariah and Zerubbabel all suddenly disappeared from the scene and that none of them seems to have survived to see the dedication of the temple in 515 is probably a result of the Persian intervention. The high-flying nationalistic hopes had collapsed at a stroke. Certainly the people of Judah received permission from Darius to rebuild the temple, but the fact that there is no contemporary tradition whatsoever about the dedication of the temple, which had been so ardently desired,[13] strongly suggests that this rebuilding was accompanied with experiences which tended, rather, to be depressing.

The fiasco of the early post-exilic prophecy of salvation had far-reaching consequences. Now that it had become clear that not only this prophecy, but with it the great promises of the exilic prophecy of salvation, had remained unfulfilled, prophecy as a whole, which had gained general recognition only in the exilic period, once again became deeply discredited among a major part of the population. There were three consequences of this: prophecy was corrected to tone it down; it was marginalized socially; and it was increasingly 'eschatologized'. The most impressive example of the corrections made to tone it down is provided by the books of Haggai and Zechariah themselves. The books have undergone two different redactions: the first stratum of redaction (Hag.1.1-3*,13-15; 2.1-2,4*, 10,20 and Zech.8.9-13[14]), which uses a remarkable mixture of Deuteronomistic and Priestly language,[15] transforms the book of Haggai into a 'chronicle of the temple'. It shifts the emphasis on to the part of Haggai's prophecy which was either realized, namely the rebuilding of the temple (Hag.1.13-15), or not clearly refuted, namely the improvement of economic conditions (2.15-17; Zech.8.12), and completely marginalizes the unfulfilled designation 'king' as a possible perspective for a distant future. In this way it attempts to rescue the activating impulse of Haggai from the bitter disappointments for the further work of rebuilding (Zech.8.9,13; cf. Hag.1.4f.), without taking over its politically dangerous implications. The perspective of hope is cut back to the obvious and indispensable transformation of Judah from being an accused and despised part of the family of nations to being one that is blessed and respected (Zech.8.13).

The second stratum of redaction (Hag.2.5a; Zech.1.1-6; 6.15b; 7.1-8,19[16]) clearly speaks a Deuteronomistic language and strongly recalls JerD in its theological intentions. It combines the promise that God would be with the people, which Haggai gave unconditionally, with the law (Hag.2.5a), and made the whole prophecy of Zechariah conditional on the demand for repentance (Zech.1.3). It puts Zechariah in the context of the history of the pre-exilic prophecy of judgment (7.4-14), and derives from it the criterion by which its prophecy must be understood: social relationships must be restored and social justice must be realized before the salvation proclaimed by Zechariah can come. So here the disappointed national hopes are transmuted – in a way typical of Yahweh religion – into a serious social appeal.

If we attempt to discuss these strata of redaction in sociological terms, we will do best to think, first, of the pragmatic political wing of the coalition which, on the basis of the Persian intervention and the failure of the great nationalistic hopes, exercised control in the community of Judah: the institutions of the council of elders and the college of priests which were then developing.[17]

We will also come across the laity of the council of elders in the development of the Pentateuch, as adherents of Deuteronomistic theology;[18] the attitude of a critical sympathy with prophecy (attachment to the law of Moses) recognizable there fully corresponds to the second stratum of redaction in Haggai and Zechariah. Certainly, as we can see from P, the majority of the priestly college were still opposed to prophecy, but they had to be interested in Haggai and Zechariah because of the significance that they had attached to the temple and the high priest. Moreover, collaboration between the two bodies is a good explanation of the mixture of Deuteronomistic and priestly language in the first stratum of redaction.

If this assumption is correct, then in the redactions of Haggai and Zechariah we would have the first example of the way in which, after the failure of the attempts at national restoration, a majority of lay and priestly leaders favourable to Persia took responsibility for the consolidation of the community of Judah under alien rule. The compromise that they aimed at is typical: whether under pressure from Persia or out of their own insight, on the one hand they corrected the prophetic spokesmen of the nationalist hopes for restoration, curbed them with the law, and banished their failed prophecies to a distant future. On the other hand, they attempted to divert the unfulfilled potential of hope to existing practical political possibilities, active co-operation in the rebuilding (Zech.8.9-13) and the creation of a social climate governed by a social contract (8.16f.,19b).

The two other consequences of the fiasco of early post-exilic prophecy, the marginalization and 'eschatologizing', are already evident in the book of Zechariah,[19] but are even clearer in the book of Trito-Isaiah (Isa.55-66). What is beyond question its oldest nucleus, Isa.60-62, probably to be dated to the time after 515,[20] is impressive evidence that there was a group in Judah which even after the fiasco unswervingly held firm to the great promises of the Deutero-Isaiah circle that had remained unfulfilled and adapted them for the future. But the form and language of this prophecy already indicate the changes which had taken place in the meantime: the group makes use of remarkably vague metaphorical language,[21] which is arrived at from scriptural exegesis of the texts of Deutero-Isaiah and militates far more than the latter against any specific application. There are none of the formulae (messenger formula, etc.) which point to a situation of proclamation; who speaks and who is spoken to remain vague.[22] All this points to internal discussion within a small marginal group which does not enjoy any public respect and which has largely lost all connections with historical and political reality.

The prophecy of the Deutero-Isaiah group had already often broken out of the scribal theological circle by going beyond the bounds of what could be realized in history, but had always been focussed on a specific upheaval in world politics. Once its great promise that Yahweh would establish his universal kingship over all the world visibly on Zion (52.7-10) had finally been left unfulfilled with the failure of Haggai and Zechariah, the prophecy of the post-exilic period largely lost any reference to concrete political events, and the expectation of the great reversal to be brought about by God, still unfulfilled, continually bordered on a distant future extending to the end of history. We can term this process 'eschatologizing'.[23]

However, here it is important to be clear that we can speak of eschatology in the strict sense (= the doctrine of the last things) only at the end of this development, in apocalyptic. For only in the book of Daniel do we find for the first time a clear idea that previous political history is coming to an end, to be followed by a completely new era (Dan.2.28; 8.17,19; 11.45, etc.). The term 'eschatology' can only be used with a pinch of salt for all the other late prophetic writings, if the intention is to indicate a tendency.[24]

The content of the process of eschatologizing can also be demonstrated from Isa.60-62. It becomes evident from 62.1-7 how much the followers of the Deutero-Isaiah group suffered from the fact that the great turning point of salvation for Zion had not materialized. They could persist in their expectation only at the price of detaching themselves from concrete political history. They expected a mighty theophany of Yahweh, who would shine out in his glory over Zion in the darkness of the world of nations (60.1-3). This epiphany would then spark off a great pilgrimage of the nations in which the nations would bring the exiles (vv.4-9) and their treasures (60.5-6,9,11b, cf.16; 61.6) in order to adorn Jerusalem and its temple miraculously (60.7,13) and glorify Yahweh (60.6,9). The nations would help in the building of Jerusalem (v.10), and even the descendants of the former oppressors would recognize that it was the city of God (v.14). This painting in splendid colours, taking up Isa.49.13ff. and Ps.72, is very reminiscent of the simpler expectations in Hag.2.6-9, but it leaves historical reality even further behind to the degree that – very much along the lines of the prophecy of Deutero-Isaiah – it does not presuppose any violent upheaval among the world powers but a voluntary change of consciousness. It is in accordance with this that internally, too – again along the lines of Deutero-Isaiah – there is no longer any expectation of a restitution of royal or priestly rule as with Haggai and Zechariah. Rather, this prophecy transferred royal status to the city of Jerusalem (61.1;[25] 62.3) and priestly dignity to the whole people (81.6; 62.12). This prophecy had a specific reference to political reality as experienced and endured only to the degree that it formulated the salvation which it promised predominantly as economic liberation (61.1, $d^e r\bar{o}r$, cf.62.8f.) or restitution (61.7f.), thus probably indicating the burdens of tribute and taxation under which Israel had to suffer from the Assyrian period to the contemporary rule of the Persians.[26] In contrast to this, the group thought that after the great transformation the nations would work for the economy of Israel while Israel – visibly blessed (61.3,9) – performed priestly service for them.

Thus the prophecy of salvation in the Trito-Isaiah group – like the prophecy of judgment in the pre-exilic period – again was an opposition theology. It did not just accept the political and economic facts of early post-exilic society, but put them fundamentally in question by projecting an alternative picture for the time after the great upheaval. However, this fundamental change brought in by God could no longer be attached to any real historical development. That was what made this prophecy so suspect in the eyes of the majority of the population during the early post-exilic phase of rebuilding. Only when, as the Persian period advanced, the society of Judah split apart socially, did eschatologized prophecy take on renewed significance, above all for the de-classed lower class.[27]

5.23 The second temple

The only visible success of the mood of national exaltation had been the temple, which it was possible to dedicate after five years of rebuilding (520-515). Even though all the expectations associated with it were far from having been realized, it and the cult which was being established in it had such an essential role above all for the community in Judah, but also for the Diaspora, that we must pay special attention to it.

The second temple was not a completely new building, but was erected on the ruins of the temple of Solomon. The existing holy place developed its own emphasis, and the limited means available did not allow more far-reaching solutions, so that a complete separation of temple and city as had been contemplated in the Ezekiel school was unthinkable. In its division, too, the new temple site largely followed the Solomonic model. The temple building was subdivided into three areas with different degrees of holiness: the holy of holies (*d^{e}bīr*), the main holy place (*hēkal*)[28] and the vestibule (*'ūlām*). In front of this was the court of the priests with the altar of burnt offering and in front of that – separated by a barrier – was the forecourt of the Israelites, from which later yet another part was marked off which women could enter; all round this was a forecourt which all could enter, created by an artificial mound of earth.[29]

The differences from the first temple were only a matter of a few details – though these were not unimportant. After the loss of the ark and the cherubic throne (Jer.3.16), the holy of holies evidently remained completely empty.[30] In place of the wooden cube marked off by leaved doors there was a curtain (*pārōket*, Ex.26.31; II Chron.3.14);[31] before it in the middle of the *hēkal* was a wooden incense altar covered with gold leaf (Ex.30.1-10; 37.25-29);[32] on the left side a seven-branched lampstand (*m^{e}nōrā*, Ex.27.20f.; 30.7-8; Lev.24.1-4; Num.8.1-4; II Chron.13.11) which replaced the ten lampstands of Solomon's temple; and on the right side the table for the showbread (Ex.25.23-30; 37.10-16; Lev.24.5-9).[33] The very way in which the temple was equipped already shows a shift of cultic significance in favour of the *hēkal*:[34] almost the whole of the regular and occasional main cult took place here – apart for the altar of burnt offering, which was outside; by contrast the holy of holies was entered only once a year, on the 'feast of atonement', by the high priest.

According to Busink, the façade of the temple was probably more markedly influenced by Babylonian models: it extended beyond the additions made to both sides, and the vestibule was less deep, so that it was possible for the public to have a full view of the priests entering and leaving through the door of the *hēkal*, hung with a further curtain (Sir.50.5;

II Macc.1.23f.; Aristeas 86).[35] The new extensions probably went the full height of the *hēkal* (II Chron.3.8), which was perhaps given an upper story. Thus in appearance the temple building lost the characteristics of the antae temple.[36]

Another change was the mighty altar of burnt offering (II Chron.4.1, c.10 x 10 x 5m),[37] which could only be approached by a ramp on the south side and which dominated the court of the priests. Its size is probably connected not only with a further development of and increase in sacrificial offerings, but also with the abolition of all the subsidiary altars in the outer forecourt, so that all the sacrificial gifts, including those for the private cult, were concentrated on this one altar. One effect of this concentration, which in the subsequent period brought the official cult even closer to the family cult, was that it proved impossible to make the sharp separation between the inner and outer forecourt which the disciples of Ezekiel had had in mind to safeguard its holiness;[38] the laity had to be allowed to enter the court of the priests at any rate to perform some rites of their private sacrifices (laying on of hands, slaughtering, cf. Lev.1-7).[39] The persistent resistance of the laity to being completely excluded from the cult (cf. Num.16ff.) thus made it impossible to achieve a complete architectural separation between the inner and outer courtyards: in the Herodian temple the barrier consisted only of a stone lattice half a metre high (*BJ* V, 226), and at times there does not seem to have been one at all.[40] As the population was also very much involved in the regular official cult (*tāmīd*) – which later was even governed by regulations – the cultic practice at the second temple had more populist features than the Jerusalem cult in the pre-exilic period. An attempt was made to counter the resultant danger of possible cultic uncleanness by an annual cleansing of the sanctuary. The institutionalization of the Day of Atonement (Lev.16) can at least also be explained from the need to balance the relatively open practice of the cult desired by the laity with the degree of holiness postulated by the reform priesthood, which had increased since the exile.

As for the legal status of the temple, the priesthood very soon succeeded in pushing through its demand for self-administration over a relatively wide area. The architectural fusion of temple and palace was abandoned, as the disciples of Ezekiel had wanted.[41] However, the administrative separation did not completely succeed: the post-exilic Jerusalem cult was still a state cult in so far as the Persian king had contributed part of the building costs (Ezra 6.4), and also continued to make contributions to support the regular sacrificial cult (6.8-10; 7.21-23).[42] In return, the foreign authorities asked for sacrifices and intercessions for the life of the royal family and for the ongoing existence of the empire (6.10; 7.23). Moreover those who were associated with the temple enjoyed exemption from taxes (7.24). But at a local level the Jerusalem cult no longer had the features of a state cult. When Nehemiah intervened in the cult (Neh.13.1ff.), he did so less in his function as Persian governor than in his role as representative of the lay wing, which felt itself responsible for the observance of the cultic laws.

Normally the administration of the temple and the supervision of the cult were in the hands of the priestly college under the leadership of the high priest (*kōhēn gādōl*).[43] The development of the office of the Jerusalem high priest which had already existed in the pre-exilic temple (*kōhēn rō'š*, II Kings 25.18) into the new concept of the high priest with which the reformed priesthood had evidently already returned from exile (Hag.1.1; Zech.3.1) is usually understood as an attempt permanently to occupy and perform the role which the king had played in the cult with a member of the priesthood. The form of his institution (anointing)[44] and his adornment (turban, breastplate, girdle)[45] evidently quite deliberately resorted to royal elements. But he was also subject to intensified priestly conditions of holiness (Lev.21.10-13) and therefore was the only one who had the privilege of entering the holy of holies (Ex.19.20-24; Lev.16), and performed the liturgy on festivals (sabbath, annual festivals) and in particular on the Day of Atonement. In accordance with the organization of the priesthood by families, the office was open only to members of the Zadokide family of Joshua (the sons of Eleasar). Because of this emphasis on his cult-political functions, with which wider political functions were associated in the Hellenistic era, and also because of his own aristocratic interests, the high priest later often came into conflict with priests and laity concerned for reform (Neh.13.28).[46]

The plans for reform developed by the Ezekiel school which had been aimed at a differentiation of priests and Levites[47] could be carried through in respect of the other clergy. However, the large number of 4,289 priests compared with the small number of 74 Levites in the list of inhabitants from the years after 520 (Ezra 2/Neh.7) is evidence that to begin with only a few non-Zadokide priests were prepared to exercise their calling in the new sanctuary under these worsened conditions. Still, in the course of time the Levites constantly increased in number and were also able to improve their position, e.g. by assuming the function of temple singers.[48] Because there were so many of them, the priests were first divided into twenty-one or twenty-two divisions (*mišmārōt*, Neh.10.3-9; 12.1-7), later into twenty-four (I Chron. 24.7-18); these performed their services by rotation. The non-priestly temple personnel consisted of singers, gatekeepers (temple police) and temple slaves (Ezra 2.41ff.; 7.24).

Such a self-administered cult, freed from the clutches of the state, could of course only be organized if its finances were secure. The contributions of the Persian government covered only part of what was needed, and if the temple was not to return to the state domain[49] under which it had suffered in pre-exilic times, support had to be guaranteed in another way. That the second temple was widely accepted as a self-administered communal institution is indicated by the way in which the population of Judah was prepared without any recognizable opposition to assume quite considerable economic burdens voluntarily (!) in order to support it.[50] For the first time since the period before the state the public cult was again an institution of the whole community, indeed a symbol of the unity of Israel, and to this end people were ready to go to the limits of the tolerable to share financial responsibility for it.

The reform party consisting of the disciples of Ezekiel had wanted to provide for priests and Levites not only by increasing their portions of the sacrifices (Ezek.44.28-30) but also by assigning temple land to them (45.1-8), and resorted to the 'prince' for collecting the offerings for the permanent sacrificial cult (45.13-17). But there was no prince, and even the reform idea that the temple personnel should largely live off their own land was impossible to achieve in the prevailing economic circumstances. Moreover there were theological objections to this (the old levitical rule that they should not possess land, Deut.18.1). So the priestly reform party who are represented by the letter P took the course of a drastic increase in the portions of the sacrifice and the raising of direct taxes.

The conception of P was that the priests should receive the greater part of the sin, guilt and food offerings and also the twelve showbreads each week (Num.18.9; cf. Lev.2.3; 7.9; 5.14; 6.18f.; 7.6f.; 24.5-9).[51] These offerings were regarded as most holy and had to be consumed in the sanctuary. In addition to this the priests also had considerably larger portions of the private meal offerings,[52] which could also be consumed at home by the priestly family, and the skin from the burnt offering (Lev.7.8). However, only the serving priests profited from these shares in the sacrifice, i.e. everyone twice a year and at the annual festivals. So further levies and taxes were added, which were distributed to all priests: the best of the grain, wine and oil (Num.18.12; Neh.10.38),[53] the firstfruits (Num.18.13; Neh.10.36), with substitute payments for human firstborn and unclean animals (5 shekels), and offerings of leaven (Num.15.17-21) and free-will offerings or 'what is banned' (Num.18.14).

According to the reformers, the Levites, who were excluded from the sacrifical cult, were to be fed directly from a new tax, the tithe of what was produced from the land (Num.18.20-32; Neh.10.38, cf. 13.10-13). Of this, they had in turn to pay a tithe to the priests.[54] To support the permanent official cult, a money tax at first of a third of a shekel (Neh.10.33f.) and later of half a shekel (Ex.30.11-16, cf. Matt.17.24) was levied, and in addition deliveries of wood were requisitioned by rotation from the *bēt 'ābōt* (Neh.10.35; 13.31). On top of this there were voluntary offerings and gifts.

In the later development, in which these new priestly regulations were combined with the earlier Deuteronomistic regulations, the cultic offerings swelled to around a third of the total income, with the state taxes on top of that. As a result, the temple developed into the most important economic factor in the community of Judah.

The expense of the official sacrificial cult had hardly diminished since the time of the state cult: quite the contrary. Indeed at some points we can even note marked increases: whereas in the eighth century the daily *tāmīd* cult still consisted of a morning burnt offering and an evening meal offering (II Kings 16.15; cf. I Kings 18.29,36), the priestly reformers developed this into two burnt offerings which – according to the general priestly systematization (Num.15.1-16) – as with all animal offerings were to be combined with offerings of food and drink (Ex.29.38-42; Num.28.3-8; I Chron.16.40, etc.). In addition there was the daily food offering made by the high priest (Lev.6.12-16). Here the *tāmīd* cult was developed into regular liturgies in which the population was involved. In addition to the external service at the altar of burnt offering there was the internal service in the *hēkāl* at the incense altar (Ex.30.7-8), the lampstand (Lev.24.1-4; Ex.27.20f.) and the table for the showbread (Ex.25.30; Lev.24.5-9). According to the Mishnah Tamid, the morning *tāmīd* was combined with the recitation of the Shema, a benediction, the Decalogue and the Aaronic blessing. Choirs of Levites sang their hymns, and at the priests' trumpet signal the people prostrated themselves in worship.

On festivals there were more or less further sacrifices. Thus for example on the sabbath, which along with the traditional new moon festival was again celebrated at the sanctuary (Num.28.11-15),[55] the offering amounted to an additional *tāmīd* sacrifice (Num.28.9f). The sacrificial cult was particularly expensive on the traditional annual festivals, the feasts of passover and mazzoth, the feasts of weeks and tabernacles, the latter being the climax (Num.28.16-25,26-31; 29.12-34). Two new festivals were inserted in the festival calendar before the feast of tabernacles (the fifteenth to twenty-first days of the seventh month): the new year festival on the first day of the seventh month, perhaps under Babylonian influence,[56] and the Day of Atonement on the tenth day of the seventh month (Lev.23.23-25,26-32).

The latter denotes a new element in post-exilic worship which permanently changed in comparison to pre-exilic worship, in both the public and the private spheres: an emphasis on the function of the cult in making atonement. It was the decisive means by which the reform priesthood reacted to the traumatic experience of a national catastrophe which had happened despite a functioning cult and which it offered to the community for averting the danger of a possible repetition. The ritual of the Day of Atonement had two functions. First, it was to purify the sanctuary from 'infection' from all the impurities and sins of the laity and priests and thus consecrate it once again for the cult of atonement in the new year (Lev.16.16, 18f.,33), and secondly it was to make atonement for the sins of the high priest – as a representative of the priesthood – and the people (vv.17, 20-22,24f.,33). Here two rituals were combined: taking up more popular conceptions, the sins of Israel were transferred to a scapegoat and eliminated from the community by sending it into the wilderness (16.7-9,20-22,26). In the real theological conception of the reformed priests, purification and atonement were achieved by the high priest when, in analogy to the scapegoat ritual, he sprinkled a few drops of blood in the direction of the place of God's presence (*kapporet*) in the holy of holies (16.14f.). Here it is the encounter with the holiness of God, combined with the notion of the offering of life represented by the blood of the sacrificed animal (cf. Lev.17.11), which brings atonement.[57]

Hand in hand with this periodical atonement for sanctuary and people went the propagation and dissemination of the *ḥaṭṭā't*, i.e. the 'sin offering', or better 'atoning offering', by the reform priesthood.[58]

Originally the *ḥaṭṭā't* was a blood rite to consecrate the altar or sanctuary. It is not certain how far it goes back into the pre-exilic period (it is absent, e.g. from II Kings 16.10ff.). It is attested for the first time with this significance by the Ezekiel school (Ezek.23.18-27), and there are also echoes of it in this sense in the P tradition (Ex.29.36f.; 30.10; Lev.18.5; 16.16,18). Originally probably a single act, it was made into an annual or semi-annual rite by the disciples of Ezekiel (Ezek.45.18-20 on the first day of the first month/the seventh day of the first month, or the first day of the seventh month in LXX), and thus became a forerunner of the later Day of Atonement. In addition to this, already in the pre-exilic period sacrifices could make atonement for human beings: this is probably the function of the burnt offering (*'ōlā*) in the framework of the ceremony of the lamentation of the people at the level of official religion and the so-called 'guilt offering' (*'āšām*), a rite of reparation for sacral transgressions committed unknowingly at the level of family religion.[59] The P reformers extended the *ḥaṭṭā't* blood rite related to sacred objects to make atonement for human beings and transformed it into a sacrifice by having the fat of the entrails burnt on the altar in analogy to the meal offering (Lev.4.8ff.).

Two different kinds of *ḥaṭṭā't* are to be distinguished here. If the high priest or the whole community unwittingly transgressed in a way which affected the public, the blood rite had to be performed within the sanctuary (smearing the altar of incense, sprinkling the curtain before the holy of holies, Lev.4.1-12,13-21); in this kind of sacrifice, in accordance with the older ritual of purging sacred objects the flesh of the animal was burnt outside the sanctuary and thus destroyed (6.23; cf. 26.27). In the case of an unwitting transgression by an individual, however, the blood rite needed to be performed only at the external altar of burnt offering (Lev.4.27-35) and the flesh of the animal was destined to be consumed by the priests (6.19).[60]

Now since the reform priesthood established the sin offering not only for the consecration of priests and Levites (Ex.29; Lev.8; Num.8) and on the Day of Atonement (Lev.6), but also in succession at all the annual feasts (Num.28.15,22; 29.5,11,16ff.; 23.19, cf. already Ezek.45.18-25), it set the whole official cult of the year in the perspective of an ongoing prophylactic atonement. Furthermore, by connecting it with frequent rites of purification from everyday life, as in the case of uncleanness caused through birth, emission of semen, menstruation and 'leprosy' (Lev.12; 15.14), the priesthood made deep inroads into family piety. The joyful meal offering which had previously predominated in the cultic life of the family (*zebaḥ, zebaḥ hattōdā*) was forced out (Lev.3; 7.11-21,28-34) in favour of the earnest sin offering (*ḥaṭṭāʾt*) prompted by unwitting transgressions or made in order to regain cultic purity. The first consequence of this was an increasing ritualization of personal life, which became dependent on the atoning institution of the temple, at any rate in the case of the population of Judah who lived in close proximity to it. The second consequence was even more far-reaching in the subsequent period: the implanting of a deep and sometimes anxious consciousness of sin in the personal piety of the individual which had previously been completely alien.[61]

Thus the new cult of the second temple had far-reaching consequences both for the further development of official Yahweh religion and for personal piety. However – and this must also be emphasized in conclusion – it no longer formed the only kind of worship: alongside it there developed prototypes of synagogue worship, at the centre of which there was no longer sacrifice but the reading of scripture.

5.3 The struggle over the identity of the community

F.Ahuis, *Autorität im Umbruch. Ein formgeschichtlicher Beitrag zur Klärung der literarischen Schichtung und der zeitgeschichtlichen Bezüge von Nu 16 und 17. Mit ein Ausblick auf die Diskussion um die Ämter der Kirche*, CTMA 13, 1983; E.Blum, *Die Komposition der Vätergeschichte*, WMANT 57, 1984; id., *Studien zur Komposition des Pentateuch*, BZAW 189, 1990; D.J.A.Clines, 'Nehemiah 10 as an Example of Early Jewish Biblical Exegesis', *JSOT* 21, 1981, 111-17; F.Crüsemann, 'Das "portative Vaterland". Struktur und Genese des alttestamentlichen Kanons', in A. and J.Assmann (eds.), *Kanon und Zensur* II, 1987, 63-79; id. 'Der Pentateuch als Tora. Prolegomena zur Interpretation seiner Endgestalt', *EvTh* 49, 1989, 250-67; id., 'Die Eigenständigkeit der Urgeschichte. Ein Beitrag zur Diskussion um den "Jahwisten"', in J.Jeremias and L.Perlitt (eds.), *Die Botschaft und die Boten. FS H.W.Wolff*, 1981, 11-29; K.Elliger, 'Sinn und Ursprung der priesterlichen Geschichtserzählung' (1952), in *Kleine Scriften zum Alten Testament*, TB 32, 1966, 174-98; P.Frei, 'Zentralgewalt und Lokalautonomie im Achämenidenreich', in id. and K.Koch, *Reichsidee und Reichsorganisation im Perserreich*, OBO 55, 1984, 9-43; T.E.Fretheim, 'The Priestly Document; Anti-Temple?', *VT* 18, 1968, 313-29; V.Fritz, 'Das Geschichtsverständnis der Priesterschrift', *ZTK* 84,

1987, 426-387; id., *Tempel und Zelt. Studien zum Tempelbau in Israel und zum Zeltheiligtum der Priesterschrift*, WMANT 47, 1977; U.Kellermann, 'Erwägungen zum Esragesetz', *ZAW* 80, 1968, 373-85; K.Koch, 'Die Eigenart der priesterlichen Sinaigesetzgebung', *ZTK* 55, 1968, 36-51; id., *Die Priesterschrift von Exodus 25 bis Leviticus 16. Eine überlieferungsgeschichtliche und literarkritische Untersuchung*, FRLANT 71, 1959; A.Kuschke, 'Die Lagervorstellung der priesterschriftliches Erzählung', *ZAW* 63, 1951, 74-105; N.Lohfink, 'Die Abänderung der Theologie des priesterlichen Geschichtswerkes im Segen des Heiligkeitsgesetzes. Zu Lev.26.9, 11-13', in *Wort und Geschichte*, FS K.Elliger, AOAT 18, 1973, 129-36; id., 'Die Priesterschrift und die Geschichte', *VTS* 29, 1979, 189-225; J.Magonet, 'The Korah Rebellion', *JSOT* 24, 1982, 3-25; T.N.D.Mettinger, *The Dethronement of Sabaoth. Studies in the Shem and Kabod Theologies*, CB.OT 18, 1982; M.Noth, *Numbers* (ATD 7, 1966), OTL 1968; G. von Rad, 'Die Theologie der Priesterschrift' (1934 extract), *Gesammelte Studien* II, TB 48, 1979, 165-88; M.Rose, *Deuteronomist und Jahwist. Untersuchungen zu den Berührungspunkten beider Literaturwerke*, ATANT 67, 1981; E.Ruprecht, 'Exodus 24,9-11 als Beispiel lebendiger Erzähltradition aus der Zeit des babylonischen Exils', in R.Albertz et al., *Werden und Wirken des Alten Testaments. FS C.Westermann*, 1980, 138-73; id., 'Stellung und Bedeutung der Erzählung vom Mannawunder (Ex 16) im Aufbau der Priesterschrift', *ZAW* 86, 1974, 269-307; M.Saebø, 'Priestertheologie und Priesterschrift. Zur Eigenart der priesterlichen Schicht im Pentateuch', *VTS* 32, 1981, 357-74; H.-C.Schmitt, 'Redaktion des Pentateuch im Geiste der Prophetie', *VT* 32, 1982, 170-89; R.Schmitt, *Zelt und Lade als Thema alttestamentlicher Wissenschaft*, 1972; V.Wagner, 'Zur Existenz des sogenannten "Heiligkeitsgesetzes"', *ZAW* 86, 1974, 307-16; P.Weimar, 'Struktur und Komposition der priesterschriftlichen Geschichtsdarstellung', *BN* 23, 1984, 81-134: 24, 1984, 138-62; C.Westermann, 'Die Herrlichkeit Gottes in der Priesterschrift' (1971), in *Forschung am Alten Testament* II, TB 55, 1974, 115-37; id., 'Genesis 17 und die Bedeutung von *berit*' (1976), *Erträge der Forschung am Alten Testament* III, TB 73, 1984, 66-78; E.Zenger, *Gottes Bogen in den Wolken. Untersuchungen zur Komposition und Theologie der priesterschriftliche Urgeschichte*, SBS 112, 1983.

Important though the rebuilding of the Jerusalem temple was for the consolidation of the community of Judah, by itself it was incapable of securing the cohesion and future of post-exilic Israel in the precarious political situation after the failure to restore the national state. Not only did it largely by-pass the Diaspora groups, which – apart from occasional pilgrimages by individuals – could not take part in its cult and had to limit themselves to providing material support,[1] but – after all the prophetic criticism of the cult and the Deuteronomic/Deuteronomistic revisions of the temple theology which had been made in the meantime – it had long since ceased to meet the theological demands which broad areas of the population were making on official Yahweh religion and its realization in society. A broader and more far-reaching theological foundation was needed to provide religious and social cohesion despite all the divergent group interests, even without territorial and state unity.

The course adopted in the early post-exilic period was the canonization of the Pentateuch. In other words, a foundation history of Israel was set down in writing and was established as an obligatory basis for all Israelite groups. In thus putting not the temple but a book at the centre of official Yahweh religion, people were accepting the decision already made by the Deuteronomic reform movement when, in order to legitimate its concern for reform in the face of the monarchy, temple and society of its time, it referred back to the authority of Moses and the shared religious experiences of the early period of Israel.[2] The 'lawbook of Moses' (Josh.8.31; 23.6; II Kings 14.6), which for a short period had already been binding state law under Josiah[3] and which afterwards was held in high respect at least among the Deuteronomistic groups, was now to be developed and made the universally binding foundation for all social groups.

5.31 *The canonization of the Torah and the Persian imperial organization*

Traditionally the canonization of the Pentateuch is associated with the mission of Ezra, which according to Ezra 7.1-8 took place in the seventh year of Artaxerxes, i.e. 458 or 398.[4] According to the Aramaic text of Ezra 7.11-26, which has the style of a confirmatory document sent by the Persian king, Ezra, who is called 'priest' and 'scribe' of the law of the God of heaven (v.12), is explicitly authorized by the Persian court among other things to make researches in Judah and Jerusalem on the basis of the law of his God which he has in his hand (v.14, cf.25), to appoint judges for all Jews in the province of Transeuphratene and to instruct the ignorant in the law (v.25), to ensure that the law is observed, and if need be to implement it by imposing legal penalties (v.26).

However, it was impossible to make much use of this text in connection with the question of canonization as long as scholars limited themselves to the hotly disputed question of what the 'law of God' was which Ezra 'brought' from Babylonia, whether it was the Pentateuch, the Priestly Writing or some other legal corpus.[5] For Ezra 7.11f. certainly does not mean that Ezra introduced to Judah a law which had previously been unknown there – with the consequence that the whole process of canonization would sink into the *terra incognita* of the Babylonian Diaspora – but quite explicitly already presupposes the knowledge of this law among the Jews of the western province of the empire (v.25). According to vv.25f. the task of Ezra is, rather, to secure full legal recognition in all Jewish communities of the province of Transeuphratene of this divine law, which was widely known but evidently not yet properly understood by all Jews, or practised in a careless way by them, and to see that it was implemented properly. Not only does Ezra receive a commission to this effect from the Persian crown, but he is also given decisive support by the crown over its implementation, support which gives Jewish law the status of a royal law[6] and backs up its proper execution with all the authority of the Persian state (v.26).

Now in a completely different direction this unique procedure gives us a key to understanding the process of canonization. Even if the so-called Ezra decree is hardly authentic in the form which has been handed down to us,[7] it nevertheless reflects a Persian legal practice which can also be demonstrated from other sources and which Frei calls 'imperial authorization'.[8] Thus for example a stele from Lycia for the period around 360 attests that a decision of the community of Xanthus about the establishment of a cult of the Persian satrap in office was published, adopted as a law of the people (line 19), and thus declared to be locally valid imperial Persian law.[9] According to the evidence of a Demotic papyrus from the time of the Ptolemies, Darius I is said to have authorized a commission of Egyptian specialists to carry out a codification of valid Egyptian law.[10] And finally, the so-called Passover Letter from Elephantine (AP 21) contains a decree of Darius II from the year 419/18, the content of which is probably detailed regulations for celebrating the passover, which are mentioned after a brief gap in the text.[11] In all these texts we can see the interest of the Persian administration in offering state support and at the same time controlling the local legal practice of subject peoples – also and indeed especially in connection with their cultic interests. By including local norms in imperial legislation for the nations within the Persian empire, the institution of imperial authorization offered legal security[12] and in exchange gave the Persian central authority the possibility of exercising effective control over the bodies involved in its self-administration, to ensure that their legislation did not go against imperial interests. Here we have a constitutional means, amazing for its time, of securing the loyalty of foreign subjects by reinforcing their cultural and religious identity.

If we include the process of the canonization of the Torah in these political conditions, which Blum was the first to do to a large extent,[13] then we can understand much more clearly the motivations, mechanisms and tradents involved. The imperial authorization offered the Jewish people a unique chance of claiming the support of the Persian imperial organization in securing its cultural and religious identity. But it could only seize this chance if it finally formulated a text which was binding on all its members, and which it could present to the Persian authorities for approval and authorization. Here the Jewish groups exposed themselves to the pressure of agreeing on a common text, i.e. of finding a compromise tolerable to the majority, over and above all internal differences of opinion and quarrels.

Thus Jewish and Persian interests coincided in the canonization of a universally binding foundation document: the interest of the Jewish authorities in securing and stabilizing the identity of their own national group and the Persian interest in a unifying norm for the life of its Jewish subjects which limited their internal controversies, excluded anti-Persian influences where they had existed in the past,[14] and guaranteed its permanent loyalty to the Persian crown. It is impossible to discover from which side the process of canonization was initiated, whether on the initiative of the Jewish authorities or as a result of prompting or gentle pressure from the Persians, but it is probable that the two sides supplemented each other and worked together in a way which is described with basic accuracy in Ezra 7.11-26.

The question is, of course, which Jewish groups pressed forward the process of canonization. According to the discussion on the Pentateuch so far, which has been carried on largely at a purely literary level, it often seems as if these were writers or redactors who were working more or less privately for themselves.[15] However, the political conditions which have been outlined make such a view quite improbable. This was an official project of the community of Judah, and we must assume that it was carried out by groups which held positions of public responsibility in that community. Only those groups are worth closer consideration which decided for loyal collaboration with the Persians. That reduces the circle of possible candidates to the anti-nationalistic parties in both Jewish self-administrative bodies: the council of elders and the priestly college, which had taken on the leadership here after the failure of the national restitution.[16] Of course these also had their supporters in the Diaspora, who could make contact with the central Persian administration in Susa.[17] With a touch of imagination one could suppose that these majority parties in the council of elders and the priestly college each appointed a commission of professional theologians and entrusted it with working out a foundation document for Israel on the basis of existing traditions which could command an internal majority and at the same time was a suitable model for the central Persian authorites.

This scenario, inferred from political and sociological conditions, must of course be correlated with the insights which we have gained from the literary history of the Pentateuch if it is to have any heuristic value. Here the difficulty arises that in view of the discussion which has now broken out again over the Pentateuch we are further than ever from arriving at a consensus at this point.

However, despite these controversies it is possible to formulate at least two relatively undisputed insights which fit well into the scenario that I have outlined. 1. The present Pentateuch is a compromise text between priestly and non-priestly traditional material. 2. The texts assigned to the so-called 'Priestly Writing', which in turn shows traces of a lengthy growth, come, at least to a considerable extent, from the early post-exilic period.[18]

The main problem is the non-priestly texts. The classical literary theory of their origin reckoned that they were composed relatively early, explaining them as a combination of two narrative works, the 'Yahwist' from the tenth/ninth century and the 'Elohist' from the eight century (JE), a combination which is said to have taken place before Deuteronomy (end of the seventh century). According to this hypothesis the pre-priestly Pentateuch would essentially have come into being during the pre-exilic period. But the hypothesis is already weakened by the fact that a large number of texts which display unmistakable Deuteronomic or Deuteronomistic linguistic characteristics, and some of which came to play quite essential functions in the composition as a whole, must be said to be later additions.[19]

In the more recent past, therefore, on the basis of a variety of approaches, the view has developed that the proportion of exilic and early post-exilic texts in the pre-priestly Pentateuch must be put very much higher.[20] In my view Blum has developed the most convincing model for its formation.[21] According to him the pre-priestly Pentateuch, which for the first time embraced the history of the foundation of Israel from the departure of Abraham to the death of Moses, was first decisively worked out and given its theological stamp in the early post-exilic period. Certainly it often worked over older tradition and connected it together redactionally, but over wide stretches its conceptions were so thoroughly new that it is impossible to detect early stages in the text.[22] Blum uses the siglum K^D for this early post-exilic composition, since on the one hand it was conceived as an extension backwards of the Deuteronomic history,[23] and on the other it partly speaks a language influenced by the Deuteronomists and takes up many Deuteronomic and Deuteronomistic notions.[24] But in addition he emphasizes the unmistakable differences betweeh K^D and Deuteronomy and the Deuteronomists.[25] According to Blum this first composition orientated on Deuteronomy and the Deuteronomists was then subjected to a comprehensive priestly revision (K^P); some even later smaller supplements in turn again indicate a Deuteronomistic[26] or mixed priestly/Deuteronomistic language.[27]

The traditio-historical model of the origin of the Pentateuch presented by Blum fits seamlessly into the scenario developed above and allows us to refine it further, The pre-priestly composition K^D can well be connected with the council of elders or the lay commission formed from it. First, it accords the elders a quite special significance and dignity.[28] Secondly, its sometimes Deuteronomistic language and Deuteronomic/Deuteronomistic world of ideas corresponds with the observation that from the time of the Deuteronomic reform movement[29] the theologians who had developed and handed down this Deuteronomistic theology were sometimes exclusively (JerD)[30] and sometimes essentially (DtrG)[31] lay. It will prove[32] that both theologically and politically, K^D belongs more with the trend represented by JerD (the Shaphan family, the descendants of the party of reform officials), but it is quite possible and indeed probable that many people from the trend with a stronger nationalistic orientation on the state cult which was represented by DtrG reorientated themselves on the new majority in the council of elders. The language and content of K^D in any case tells against the assumption of an unbroken personal continuity with the preceding Deuteronomistic groupings. This is a new body with a new task, and a partial overlap in personnel is enough to explain the traditio-historical connections.

It is clear from the history of the tradition that the leading laity were politically the first to seize the chance offered them by the Persian imperial authorization. That is not surprising, since in the self-administration of Judah they were immediately confronted with the task of securing the survival of the community under Persian rule.

The priestly composition K[P] which follows with some delay can easily be connected with the priestly college or the commission of priestly theologians formed from it.[33] Challenged by the first conception of the lay theologians, which deliberately took hardly any cultic and priestly interests into account, with their composition, which fluctuates between being a revision and a new conception, they introduced their professional priestly interests and thus developed a counter-model orientated on the sanctuary within the pre-existing framework of the 'Torah of Moses'.

The juxtaposition, opposition and also interweaving of the two Pentateuchal compositions can be sufficiently explained from the juxtaposition of two rival groups of tradents who had different, indeed contrary, views of what could make up and preserve the identity of Israel, but which were nevertheless bound together in the same responsibility through the two leading bodies in the self-administration of Judah and were under pressure from the Persian authorities to find a compromise acceptable to both sides.

In conclusion, the question must once again be raised of the period of the canonization and the role of Ezra's mission in it. For traditio-historical reasons we can already assume that it was a lengthy process which probably took place in several stages. The *terminus a quo* can be set with some certainty as the dedication of the temple in 515, and the *terminus ad quem* is at the latest the fourth century.[34] But we may probably follow Blum in shifting the lower time limit back to the middle of the fifth century, since with his mission Nehemiah (444-432) already presupposes Deuteronomistic and priestly precepts of the Pentateuch as valid norms to be taken for granted.[35] So the working out of the Pentateuch can be dated more closely to the end of the sixth and beginning of the fifth centuries. If we follow this dating, then Ezra's mission fits into the closing stage of the process of canonization, especially if we prefer the later dating for him.[36] Strictly speaking, Ezra 7.26 does not provide imperial authorization but presupposes that it has already been given. Ezra's mission is evidence of how the Persian crown fulfilled the obligations which it had taken on with the authorization of the Pentaeuch and of how it was prepared to back this recognition with all its authority.[37]

5.32 The pre-priestly composition of the Pentateuch

When the secular leading body in the self-administration of Judah resolved to seize the chance offered by Persian policy and commission the working out of a basic document to which all the Jews in the empire would be committed, the lay theologians involved faced a task whch was far from simple. They had to decide what the identity of Israel was that they had to safeguard, and this meant above all deciding what elements of official Yahweh religion which had accumulated and competed in a long history were central and indispensable and which were not. Was the religion of Israel in essence a historical religion or a cult religion? Was it a state religion or a prophetic religion? In the conflict of opinions in the early post-exilic period there was a need to take a position, to choose between possible options and assess them. Was Israel to define itself from the liberation traditions of the early period or were the salvation traditions of the state, kingship and Zion theology still indispensable, as the nationalist groups thought? Where was Israel's relationship to God ultimately to be decided, in the functioning of the temple cult, as argued by the priesthood which was becoming stronger, or in the shaping of social relationships? And what was to become of the wide-ranging perspectives on the future which had been sketched out by the exilic and early post-exilic prophecy of salvation, but which had seemed to have failed so lamentably:[38] were they to be discarded completely because of their dangerous political explosiveness or were at least some of their approaches to be integrated?

Against the background of such a theological debate the pre-priestly Pentateuch can be understood as a stimulating theological position which on the one hand drew clear dividing lines and made clear assessments and on the other was concerned for integration and compromise.[39]

The most important preliminary decision taken by the lay theologians was their resolve to write a history of the early period of Israel and its foundation. They did not choose the form of a prophetic vision of the future, of the kind presented by the priestly disciples of Ezekiel (Ezek.40-48), nor, as might have been much more natural for them, did they continue the Deuteronomistic history down to their day, for example showing along the same lines how the promise of David and Zion had newly been confirmed and how the cult and society were to be shaped according to the model of the earlier royal reforms.[40] Rather, they took the course that the Deuteronomic reform theologians had already taken before them: back to the beginnings. If the Deuteronomic theologians had put their reform legislation at the end of the early history of Israel and referred to the preceding foundation history of Israel only in reflections and comments,[41] the early post-exilic theologians now wanted to develop this foundation history in full, supplement the Deuteronomic legislation and root it still more broadly in history. With this extension of the Deuteronomic structure of the Torah in a historical direction they gave an even more important place in Yahweh religion to religious experiences of history than these had in any case already had in the Deuteronomic/Deuteronomistic tradition. In concentrating here wholly on the historical experiences of the early period of Israel, they shifted the focus of the history which in DtrG had been on the saving institutions of the state (David, temple) right back to the experiences of salvation in the pre-state period. Israel had not first assumed its essential character under David and Solomon, but already under Moses, as a result of its liberation and the covenant with its God Yahweh on Sinai. This fundamental theological decision corresponds to the political decision which the majority party in the Jewish self-administrative bodies had taken after the failure of the restoration of the state: that in the rebuilding of the community they would not go by the monarchy but deliberately by the pre-state period.

We can get a first view of the content of what the lay theologians planned to say in their foundation history of Israel by asking what it contains and what it lacks.

There is no creation story in the pre-priestly Pentateuch: it begins with the calling of Abraham from Babylonia (Gen.12).[42] By resolving not to include the traditions of earliest times, which were certainly to hand[43] in their basic document, the lay theologians decidedly wanted to write a history of *Israel* and here gave preference to the isolationist tendencies of the Deuteronomic/Deuteronomistic tradition: in their view Israel had to reflect on itself in order to prove its identity; it did not find its controlling factor in missionary openness to the world of nations, as the Deutero-Isaiah group had envisaged. Certainly for these theologians, too, Yahweh was the sole God and Lord of all the world (Ex.19.5), but this was only the background to his wonderful acts to Israel (Ex.7.17; 8.6,18; 9.14,29) and Israel's incomparable privileged position in the world of nations (Ex.33.16; 34.10; Num.14.14); by contrast, any positive function of Israel for the nations is hinted at only as a future perspective (Gen.12.3; Ex.19.6). It therefore looks as if the authors of the D composition quite deliberately wanted to cut back again the elements of a theology of creation and a universalist theology which had advanced to the centre of Yahweh religion during the exile, in order not to undermine their battle against a tendency to dissolve the Jewish people as a group by assimilation (the prohibition against mixed marriages in Gen.24; Ex.34.15f.; Deut.7.2f.; cf. Ezra 10; Neh.13.23ff.).[44]

A connection between the patriarchal history and the history of the people was first made at the level of the D composition (Gen.50.24; Ex.1.6,8; 3.6,15f.) with the history of the people. With their decision to accept into their basic document the patriarchal traditions which had become increasingly important in the conditions of the exile, the lay theologians for the first time declared that personal piety was a recognized part of official Yahweh religion. They thus on the one hand made room for a Yahweh piety of the kind that could also be lived out in the conditions of the Diaspora, and on the other strengthened further the tendency which could already be recognized in the exile to make the patriarchs the models for those who had returned (Gen.12.7; 15.7; 28.15).

The question of the end of the D composition is more complicated, probably because at this point the views of the group of authors, who came above all from the various Deuteronomistic groups, diverged widely. Given the theology of DtrG, the foundation history should really have run up to Josiah's reform, or at least to the completion of the building of the temple by Solomon. And it may be that representatives of this Deuteronomistic wing with a more markedly nationalistic stamp also argued in this direction. At all events the D composition was made in such a way that it fitted seamlessly before DtrG.[45] There are probably two reasons why the opinion became established within the group of authors that only the first part of DtrG containing the Deuteronomic law would be included in their own composition and the foundation history of Israel would end with the death of Moses.[46] On the one hand a foundation document which ended with the establishment of an Israelite kingdom would never have had a chance of being recognized and authorized by the Persians, and on the other there were also those among the Deuteronomistic groupings (e.g. JerD) who – at least under the conditions of their day – certainly did not want a kingship of their own,[47] but were glad finally to be able to realize their ideal of a strong 'democratic' form of rule under Persian auspices.[48] And this trend will have won through in the council of elders – already backed up by the power of the facts. Probably in a later phase of the process of canonization an attempt at a compromise was made once again, at least to incorporate the book of Joshua into the foundation history (Gen.33.19; 50.25, 26b; Ex.13.19; Josh.24)[49] and thus at any rate to underline the territorial claims of the Jewish people to Palestine. However, given the martial tendency to extermination in the Deuteronomistic Joshua tradition, this will hardly have met with approval from the Persian authorities, whose interest must have been in a peaceful cohabitation of peoples. The foundation history of Israel was broken off with the death of Moses, and thus the future and how Yahweh's promises of land rooted there would finally be realized was left open.[50] Even more, the monarchy was excluded from the foundation history of Israel, and thus from official Yahweh religion. The Deuteronomic law of the king (Deut.17.14-17) had completely marginalized the kingship theology which had formerly been so dominant by setting a critical limit to it; now this theology was almost completely passed over by the D composition in the rest of the Pentateuch:[51] only in the enigmatic words of Balaam the seer (Num.24.17ff.) is an allusion to it left at a hidden point, which is perhaps meant to indicate a possibility in the distant future. The tendency of Yahweh religion to be critical of domination thus won another victory, and this time for good.[52]

Further important shifts of accent which the lay theologians wanted to make in official Yahweh religion become visible if we investigate its view of the relationship between God and Israel. These are the miraculous history of deliverance, the law, the land, and Moses as 'super-prophet'. While the first three elements accord with Deuteronomic theology, the fourth clearly goes beyond it.[53] Here we have an element which derives from a current controversy with early post-exilic prophecy. Of course particularly if we note the historical situation, we must be struck by the complete retreat of temple, cult and priesthood.[54] We shall investigate this in due course.

For the authors of the D composition, the existence of Israel rested on a twofold historical foundation: the promise to the patriarchs and the liberation of Israel from Egypt. But the fact that they back up the divine promises with miraculous signs to endorse them (Gen.15.5; 4.1-18), stylize the promise of land to the patriarchs as a solemn oath (Gen.15.7ff.),[55] and make the problem of faith a dominant theme in their account (Gen.15.6; Ex.4.1-8.31; 14.31; 19.9; Num.14.11) shows clearly how much the historical action of Yahweh has lost significance and credibility for them and for their contemporaries. In their presentation of the old religious tradition of liberation they are no longer interested in the political process, like older accounts of it,[56] but in the wonderful mighty acts of Yahweh[57] which gave the action of God in history during the period of the foundation of Israel a clarity[58] that was now so grievously missed.

With these promises and wonders Yahweh had firmly bound himself to Israel (*berīt*, Gen.15.18) and singled it out from all nations (Ex.19.4; 34.10). This initially one-sided tie developed on Sinai into a reciprocal relationship between Israel and God (*berit*, Ex.19.5). Whereas with this view the authors were still moving along the lines of the Deuteronomic/Deuteronomistic theology of the covenant,[59] when it came to describing this relationship with God they introduced new accents: Deuteronomic theology had said that Israel had been chosen by Yahweh's elective action of salvation to be a special, i.e. holy, people (*'am qādōš*, Deut.7.6; 14.2,21; 26.19; 28.9). Its late heirs took over this description (*gōy qādōš*, Ex.19.6), but understood it literally as a special religious consecration which all Israel had received from God: the covenant with Yahweh qualified Israel as a 'kingdom of priests' (*mamleket kōhᵃnīm*, Ex.19.6), and in accordance with this description it was also sealed formally with a priestly consecration (Ex.24.3-8).[60] In content, this initial relationship between God and Israel was characterized by the quite special nearness of Yahweh and the willingness of the people, who often spontaneously with one voice committed themselves to be obedient to all God's commandments (Ex.19.8; 24.3,7). And it found its fulfilment in the first worship on Sinai, in which the seventy elders of the people are put on almost the same footing of Moses as representatives of the people, hold a sacrificial meal before Yahweh without any cultic mediator, and are allowed to look on the God of Israel (Ex.24.1,9-11).

What is the intention of this unique account? In the Deuteronomic revision of the Sinai tradition everything had culminated in the gift of the commandments and laws (Decalogue, Deuteronomic law, Deut.5; 12ff.). The authors of the D composition also adopted this view: they were probably the ones who introduced the Decalogue into the Sinai pericope on the model of Deut.5 (Ex.20.1-17);[61] and by leaving in place the Book of the Covenant (Ex.20.22-23.19),[62] which had probably been anchored in its position much earlier, they created a deliberate parallel with the structure of Deuteronomy and made room in the canon alongside the Deuteronomic law for further legislation which came from the beginnings of the reform movement.[63] This last action was probably taken also with the aim of restoring to the foreground the social side of the reform legislation[64] which had been neglected in parts of the Deuteronomic movement.[65]

Now the Sinai theophany really and originally culminated in the foundation of the cult.[66] Nor did the authors of the D composition, unlike their Deuteronomic predecessors, want to suppress this element completely from the context. So as a concession to the rebuilt temple they took up the cultic focus of the Sinai tradition but gave it a new significance which was critical of the cult. First, in their view the cultic worship of God (Ex.24.9-11) was fundamentally subordinate to obedience to the law, and the covenant committed Israel in the first place to serving God in everyday life (24.3-7). Secondly, they insisted that worship in the cult was initially a matter for the whole people. Here Israel did not yet need priests, but everyone had priestly qualities as members of the holy people (19.6). The young people could offer sacrifices (Ex.24.5) and the elders could hold a sacrificial meal in God's immediate presence (vv.9-11). Now that meant that in the people of God which was marked out by such a close relationship with God there should really be no fundamental division between laity and priests; in principle the laity too had competence in the cult and could also have their say in cultic matters.[67] So the changes made by the D composition to the Sinai tradition are not least a protest of political lay leaders against the efforts of the priesthood to deny them competence in cultic matters.

However, in the opinion of the lay theologians the close and untroubled relationship with God which existed at the beginning did not last. Israel experienced its 'fall', apostatized from Yahweh, destroyed its relationship with God and so put its existence at risk (Ex.32.1-10). Certainly by his great dedication Moses succeeded in reducing total annihilation to a judgment of purging (Ex.32.28-34), and persuaded Yahweh not to distance himself from his people (Ex.33.1,3,5f.,12-17), so that he renewed the covenant (Ex.34.1-10,28). However, from then on a rift ran through the relationship between God and Israel which excluded the earlier immediacy; from now on Israel was and remained a 'stubborn people' (Ex.32.9; 33.3,5; 34.9); proximity to God could be dangerous to it (33.5), and it was only Yahweh's fidelity to his promises to the patriarchs (Ex.32.13; 33.1; cf. Num.14.16, 23), his long-sufferingness which outweighed his anger (Ex.34.6-7; Num.14.18) and the mercy which he showed to Moses (Ex.33.17; 34.9) that led to the continuation of his history with his people. Beyond doubt, by this account the authors of the D composition wanted paradigmatically to root a theological interpretation of the crisis of the exile and the new beginning that had been granted in the foundation history of Israel itself.[68]

Now it is interesting to see how in the view of the lay theologians the first cultic institutions only grew out of this crisis in the relationship between God and Israel: these were the levitical priests (Ex.32.26-29) and the tent of meeting ('*ōhel mō'ēd*, Ex.33.7-11). However, their functions remain quite limited: the selection of the Levites by Moses is countered by his accusations against Aaron (Ex.32.21-24). The use in a foundation history of Israel[69] of material which so compromised Aaron, whom the post-exilic reformed priesthood had chosen as its ancestor,[70] can only be understood as a malicious warning by the lay theologians to the priests of their time that without Moses and therefore without the authority of the law, even the priesthood was not in a position to prevent the apostasy of the people. So it was not the priests and their cultic rites which brought expiation for Israel (Ex.32.30) in its deepest crisis but only Moses and his intercession (Ex.32.7-13; 32.30-32; 34.6-7,9; Num.14.13-19).

In the view of the lay theologians the tent of meeting was not a holy place in the sense that the permanent cult had taken place in it, but a place of meeting 'outside the camp' (Ex.33.7a). Here, despite the disruption to the relationship with God and the distance from the mountain of God, Yahweh could communicate with Moses (Ex.33.7-11; Num.11.16-17, 24-29; 12.4-10). Thus it tended to institutionalize more the prophetic inspiration than the sacrificial cult.

So the tendency of the pre-priestly Pentateuch to criticize the cult is quite evident. That also explains why the Levites and the tent appear as it were by chance (Ex.32.26; 33.7) and their installation is not attributed to instructions from God.[71] It was quite evidently an intention of the lay theologians in their foundation history of Israel to deny the newly-established institutions of the temple and priesthood any direct theological legitimation.[72] Precisely because this became increasingly significant in the religious life of their time, in their writing they went against the power of the facts and sought at all events to prevent Yahweh religion drifting in the direction of a cult religion.

A second controversy which the lay theologians were entering into in the composition of their foundation history of Israel centred on the theme of the land. As we know, the majority of the Diaspora Jews could not make up their minds to return home, as they were living well in a foreign land and felt that the economic risk of giving up everything and starting again in their old homeland was too high.[73] This evidently led to a debate as to whether Yahweh was powerful enough to smoothe out the way to the land for his people (Num.14.16). Alongside that, those who had taken the risk of returning, trusting in the great prophetic promises,[74] lamented bitterly that the newly founded Jewish community did not have enough people to maintain the old claims to land against foreigners (Gen.15.2f.).[75] Given the circumstances which they found in Judah, they simply felt cheated of their reward by Yahweh (v.1). Such and similar doubts may have led the theologians of Judah to accord the land a central position in official Yahweh religion. Since they too were politically responsible for seeing that the new community of Judah did not waste away, they must have had an interest in the return of as many people as possible. Therefore on the one hand they developed the promise of land to Abraham into a regular 'covenant making' of Yahweh (Gen.15.9-12,17-21) in which God himself in a vision performed the oath in a rite which otherwise human beings performed before him (cf.Jer.34.18f.). What they want to tell the vacillating Diaspora Jews here is that in particular the promise of the land was an expression of Yahweh's firm commitment to Israel; it was and is a firm basis, if not indeed the firmest basis, of the relationship with God.[76] After all, it was what helped to overcome the deepest crisis in Israel after its apostasy from Yahweh (Ex.32.13), and Yahweh still counted it as valid even when he himself wanted to withdraw from his people (33.1,3). So it could absolutely be relied on.

On the other hand the lay theologians warned their brothers in the Diaspora through the story of the spies (Num.14.11-24,25b) of what had already happened in the early period of Israel to those who had refused to enter the land. They had had to go back into the wilderness and were for ever excluded from salvation in the land (vv.23,25b). They made it clear that a refusal to enter the land out of anxiety and lack of faith (v.11) was contempt of God (vv.11-23), which in their view endangered Israel's existence and its relationship with God (vv.12,15).[77] By making the episode of the spies the second great crisis experienced by Israel after its apostasy from Yahweh (Ex.32-34) through the way in which they stylized it in their revision, they showed the great importance that they attached to the problems of the return. Certainly one could also worship Yahweh in the Diaspora, but for them a refusal to accept the promise of the land in faith came near to a transgression of the first commandment.[78]

A third controversy in which the lay theologians engaged in their foundation history of Israel turned on the theme of prophecy. Unlike their priestly colleagues, they were sympathetic and understanding towards prophecy.[79] Not only could they use patterns of prophetic speech in their work,[80] but they were demonstrably also inspired by the contents of the promise in early post-exilic prophecy of salvation: for example, the ideal definition of Israel as a 'kingdom of priests' recalls notions which were developed within the early eschatological prophecy of the book of Trito-Isaiah (Isa.61.6; cf. 62.12; 66.20), and the desire for the gift of prophecy to the whole people (Num.11.29) recalls Joel.3.1f. However, that the authors of the pre-priestly Pentateuch quite deliberately wanted to accord a place in official Yahweh religion to the phenomenon of prohecy is evident above all from their picture of Moses: according to their account Moses was called like a prophet (Ex.3.1-4,12,16),[81] was the bearer of a prophetic spirit (Num.11.17ff.) and like the prophets interceded for the people (Ex.32.7-13; Num.14.13-19, etc.). Finally, they related his direct conversations with God explicitly to prophetic forms of revelation (Num.12.6-8; Deut.34.10).

All these positive borrowings from prophecy are not surprising when we recall the interest that the exilic Deuteronomistic groups had show in the prophets and their literary legacy.[82] There are even some indications that descendants of the group of reform officials who took responsibility for the Deuteronomistic redaction of the book of Jeremiah were also represented in the lay 'canon commission' and indeed even perhaps had a leading influence here.[83]

However, despite all their sympathy for prophecy, the members of the commission could not simply write it a blank cheque. After all, with its expectations far transcending historical reality prophecy had put in question the precarious compromise with the Persians and thus severely endangered the whole new social experiment.[84] So theologians who were working on behalf of the self-administrative body which owed its existence to the good will of the Persians must have been very concerned to domesticate the somewhat dangerous phenomenon of prophecy in official Yahweh religion.[85]

To do this they took a threefold course. First they banished utopian elements of early post-exilic prophecy to a lost primal condition of Israel (Ex.19-24) or a distant future (Num.11.29).[86] Secondly, they developed Moses into an incomparable 'super-prophet' whose face-to-face contact with God put all prophetic revelations in the shade (Ex.33.7-11; 34.29; Num.12.6-8). Certainly Yahweh also spoke with and through the prophets (Num.12.2,6), but he only communicated through an intermediary; prophetic words of God were therefore enigmatic and needed interpretation (v.6). By contrast only the words of Moses, his commandments and instructions, were lucid and clear words of God. Thus all prophetic sayings had to be measured by them. The aim of this whole construction was to make primarily the law, but also Moses' political instructions, the criterion for all prophecy.

Thirdly and finally the authors developed the notion of a succession of the prophetic spirit from Moses to the seventy elders (Num.11.11f., 14-17, 24b-30). They expanded the old story by saying that in order to relieve Moses of the burden of leading a people which was constantly rebellious (11.11f.; cf. 12.7) Yahweh himself had from the tent of meeting given a share in the spirit which was on Moses to seventy men[87] who had proved themselves as 'elders of the people and its leaders',[88] so that they were caught up in lasting[89] prophetic ecstasy (11.17, 25). In this way the prophetic inspiration was attached to an office of leadership in succession to Moses, and the leading political body of elders claimed prophetic competence for itself.

The interest of this single delegation of officials is clear throughout the pre-priestly Pentateuch:[90] here the council of elders which for other reasons we have already envisaged as those who carried out or commissioned this work give themselves theological legitimation in the foundation history of Israel. In its task of leadership, standing in the succession of the 'super-prophet' Moses, this body understood itself to have prophetic inspiration. So it could claim theological as well as political competence, judge the prophets, point out their limitations and finally also decide on the appearance of official Yahweh religion.

Now in the D account, the claiming of the spirit of Moses for the leading political body is not wholly exclusive. Taking up earlier notions of the infectious character of prophetic ecstasy (I Sam.10.10-12; 19.18-24), it is said that far from the tent of meeting, two people were inspired with the spirit of Moses who did not have the title of elders, although they were among those who were 'written down', i.e. those who had been chosen in some way by Moses (Num.11.26). Simply by virtue of the unique circumstance that these marginal figures are even named (Eldad and Medad), it has long been conjectured[91] that there must be some concrete background to the scene. Did the authors of the pre-priestly Pentateuch here erect a concealed literary memorial to themselves?

On grounds of practicability alone I conjectured above[92] that the council of elders was not directly behind the D composition but had entrusted this work to a theological commission. Could Eldad and Medad possibly be code names for this commission on the canon? Not only would the juxtaposition of the seventy elders and two persons endowed with the spirit in a special way in Num.11.25f. fit that, but so would the argument over competence which follows in vv.27-29: when Moses hears of the inspiration of Eldad and Medad, Joshua attempts to persuade him to put 'fetters' (*kālā'*, v.28) on them. He expresses the opinion that theological competence must be limited to the council of elders, who are to submit themselves to the commission without question. In rejecting Joshua's view and explicitly confirming the inspiration of Eldad and Medad (v.29), the commission on the canon could be safeguarding its own quite independent theological competence over against the leading political body on the basis of the foundation history of Israel.

Only for the distant future is the possibility offered in Num.11.29 – in accordance with the 'democratic' conception of the people of Yahweh which also governs the rest of the D composition – that the institutional control of prophecy will cease when Yahweh gives his spirit to all, and thus the whole people of God will become prophets, just as originally it had been a 'kingdom of priests' (Ex.19.6).

5.33 The priestly composition of the Pentateuch

If the pre-priestly composition of the Pentateuch was not least a response to the challenge of the rebuilding of the temple, the priestly composition is in turn a response to the challenge of the lay theological Torah. A normative basic document of official Yahweh religion which accorded so little room to the most basic professional interests of the priesthood, indeed which attempted to point out the problems of the cultic renaissance which they had been promoting, inevitably provoked a counter-reaction from the leading body of priests. Here we need not suppose that there was any great interval of time between the two compositions of the Pentateuch. There are some indications that they even arose contemporaneously.[93] In other words, we must suppose that there are beginnings of the priestly tradition in the D conception and that its conceptions were at least known to the lay theologians, while conversely the priests already knew of decisions by the lay theologians when they were developing their conception and finally working it out in the detailed D composition. We will not be far wrong in reckoning on much toing and froing in theological discussion between the two theological commissions before the Pentateuch finally emerged as a compromise work which was acceptable to both.

If we begin from the assumption of a lively theological discussion of this kind, it becomes easier to understand why despite all the difference in detail which will be mentioned later, the priestly theologians agreed with the lay theologians on fundamental matters. They accepted the model of the Deuteronomic 'Torah of Moses', in other words the fundamental orientation on conditions before the state; the juxtaposition of law and history; the towering authority of Moses which they did not put in doubt at any point, despite their concern to push Aaron, as ancestor of the priests, into the foreground of the foundation history; and in addition the ark with the tables of the Decalogue as the central symbol of the presence of God in the holy of holies;[94] the notion of the covenant and the covenant formula, etc.[95] In other words, the two groups of authors shared a relatively broad common theological basis. This came about predominantly because the lay theologians were able to persuade their priestly colleagues to accept their ideas; however, there was also traffic in the other direction.[96]

Even more important than the common theological basis, however, were parallel social and political interests which bound the lay and priestly groups together. As representatives of the Jewish self-administration the priestly theologians were quite naturally interested in the land and those who returned, but perhaps not quite so keenly as the lay theologians of the council of elders.[97] The priestly theologians had no interest in the monarchy either, because its absence was the presupposition for their newly acquired autonomy. Their hostility to the monarchy was even harsher and more final than that of the lay theologians.[98] And finally the priestly theologians, too, were concerned to abolish the social tensions and achieve more solidarity in society in order to benefit the impoverished small farmers.[99] If they were the ones[100] who attempted to develop the Deuteronomic reform model of a regular remission of debts (*shemitta*, Deut.15.1-11) into a detailed social programme (year of jubilee, Lev.25.8ff.), then it becomes clear how at this point there was more than a chance overlapping of interests. Rather, in social commitment to the protection of the weak groups in the population the concerns of the leading priests and laity came together in a common political aim. With their agreed basic document, among other things the majority parties in the council of elders and the priestly college wanted to introduce a far-reaching social renewal of the community.[101]

These shared political and social interests which existed despite differing theological emphases will have made the marked interventions of the priestly theologians in the draft canon produced by the lay theologians easier for the latter to bear. On the other hand, it could not have been in the interests of the reform priests to push their notions so far into the background that collaboration with the leading laity was endangered. Both groups wanted to create a new form of community without its own king under Persian rule, and both wanted a social revolution in order to protect the weak; so they had to come to a compromise over the normative foundation history of Israel if the social experiment was to have any lasting prospects of success.[102]

We can understand against this background the remarkable form of the priestly composition as a frozen dialogue which in part confirms, enlarges, corrects and even contests the D composition, but allows the positions that it rejects to stand as equally possible and legitimate perspectives.

The pattern of interests and the capacity for cooperation documented by the priestly Pentateuch once again raise the question of the sociological context of its tradents. We should certainly not imagine the priesthood of the early post-exilic period as a homogenous group. There were aristocratic families in it who were more interested in increasing their political influence than in the success of the social experiment in Judah and therefore made pacts with foreigners instead of being concerned about the well-being and ordering of the community. We find these groups, which extended up into the family of the high priest, among the opponents of the lay reformer Nehemiah,[103] and they cannot be considered as those which handed down the Pentateuch. Probably we should look for the latter more among the poorer priestly families; this is suggested by their solidarity with the traditional families of small farmers which is indicated by the priestly legislation of the Pentateuch. We may also assume from their language and ideas that they formed a branch of the reform priesthood[104] which had developed in the Babylonian exile from the disciples of Ezekiel and had returned with those who came back in 520, finally to put their ideas into practice with the building up of the community of Judah. Their relative poverty was perhaps directly connected with their status as returnees. The fact that they could make themselves so strongly felt in the Pentateuch suggests that they had a majority in the priestly college. But they were evidently not so strong that they could claim all priests for their reform aims; they also had half-hearted fellow-travellers and even opponents among the influential aristocratic priestly familes. Thus the priestly Pentateuch also has the character of a *draft* reform which represents not simply the view of the priesthood but only those of a strong reform party in it which had to accept curtailments to the realization of its conception.[105]

Within this draft we can recognize traces of a lengthy growth and slightly different accents which in turn indicate a process of discussion within the group of tradents. But they are not marked enough to put the unity of the group in question. So we can confidently dispense with a distinction of different strata within the priestly texts on which in any case scholars have not arrived at any clear conclusion.[106]

Of course it was the most important concern of the reform priesthood to root the temple and the cult as absolutely necessary elements of official Yahweh religion in the normative foundation history of Israel.[107] This arose from their vital professional interest, and they could doubtless also count on the support of their internal opponents here. Therefore they developed the Sinai accounts into a comprehensive description of the foundation of cultic worship: in their view the theophany of Yahweh on Sinai (Ex.24.15b-18) led to detailed instructions from Yahweh about the building of the sanctuary (25.1-31.17), which were consistently carried out in 35.1-39.43. After the installation and dedication of the sanctuary (40.1-35), Yahweh gave the instructions for the offering of the sacrifices (Lev.1-7);[108] and after the priests had been consecrated (Lev.8; cf. Ex.29) the first worship could finally be offered (Lev.9). Here the purpose of the priestly authors was not just to derive the whole practice of the cult from divine instructions but also explicitly to emphasize its cultic legitimation by God himself. The glory of Yahweh (*keḇôd yhwh*) which had appeared to Moses on Sinai (Ex.24.16b) itself consecrated the sanctuary (40.34f.) and itself kindled the first sacrifice (Lev.9.23f.); in this way, on the basis of the instructions of Yahweh to Moses, once the temple and the sacrificial cult had been created they were explicitly recognized and accepted by Yahweh as valid.[109]

The first line of argument in this account is clear: it was directed against the tendency of the lay theologians to state that cultic worship was secondary to obedience to the commandments within the relationship of Israel to God[110] and to marginalize the cultic institutions as emergency ordinances which had only come into being after its apostasy. By contrast the priestly account was meant to free the temple cult of any odium of apostasy[111] and restore it to the heart of the Israelite relationship with God; certainly the priestly theologians did not go so far as simply to replace the service of God in everyday life with cultic worship; they left the commandments and laws in the prominent place claimed by the lay theologians. However, they wanted to accord the cult at least the same theological status as the law;[112] indeed in their own world of ideas the laws intended to safeguard the purity and righteousness of the community (Lev.11-26) were even secondary to cultic worship (Lev.9). By arranging the cultic legislation in the D composition in such a way that it in fact framed their account of the 'fall' of Israel, they wanted to indicate what in their view the cult could do for Israel and why it was so indispensable: it could create atonement for the people, which was constantly threatened with apostasy, and by ritual maintain the close relationship with God which was originally established by Yahweh. The regular cult could guarantee Yahweh's nearness to his people, his 'dwelling in the midst of the Israelites' (Ex.29.42-26), and regular or occasional rites of atonement could effectively stem crises in the relationship with God.[113]

The second line of argument of those laying down the foundation of the priestly cult is more controversial. Scholars have often wanted to suppose that the portable nature of the sanctuary depicted in Ex.25ff. and its identification with the 'tent of meeting' in the Priestly texts implies a more or less critical conception of the cult: P wanted to replace the massive static conception of the dwelling or enthronement of Yahweh on Zion in the Jerusalem cult with a dynamic notion in which God is beyond human control, and encounters his people now and again in the sanctuary.[114] But that such theories stem more from Protestant desires than the texts is already shown by the fact that the designations 'tent of meeting' (*'ōhel mō'ēd*)[115] and 'dwelling' (*miškān*)[116] are used in juxtaposition without any recognizable difference, and alongside them there is at the same time talk of both Yahweh's 'meeting' (*yā'ad*, niphal)[117] and 'dwelling' (*šākan*);[118] even the portable sanctuary knows areas of different degrees of holiness (the holy of holies, the holy place and the forecourt).[119] And if polemic against binding Yahweh to a holy place is already relatively improbable, the problem disappears completely once we recognize that the priestly theologians distinguish between a normal constant presence of Yahweh *in* the holy of holies[120] and a demonstrative appearance of the glory visible to all people *above* or *before* the temple on special occasions.[121] It can certainly be said that the priestly reform theologians sublimated the notion of the presence of God to an extreme degree,[122] but this does not mean that they wanted to challenge it in principle.[123]

We come closer to the concerns of the reform priests if we note that they stripped the official picture of God of any royal features: they avoid the predicate Yahweh Sabaoth and thus the idea of a God-king who reigns above his heavenly hosts.[124] Instead of this, for them Yahweh came near to his people in his glory (*kābōd*).[125] In their view Yahweh was no longer enthroned (*yāšab*) in the temple on the cherubic throne in the midst of his court (Isa.6.1ff.), but dwelt in the midst of his people (Ex.25.8; 29.45) by appearing and encountering them (Ex.25.22; 30.6,36; Lev.16.2) over the covering of the ark (*kapporet*).[126]

From this changed notion of God we can already recognize the two most important characteristics of the reform priests' conception of the cult: their hostility to the king and their close connection with the people. Their polemic is not directed against the idea of the holiness of the Jerusalem temple but against its former organization as a state cult and the world of ideas assocated with it. Even in the late-exilic period those who handed down DtrG can imagine a renewal of the Jerusalem cult solely along the lines of the royal state cult,[127] and we may certainly assume that even after the failure of the restoration of the state there were circles – even among the priests[128] – who wanted this solution. Against this the party of reform priests resolutely set their new option of a self-administered priesthood and a cult offered by the whole people. Their whole conception of the foundation of the central sanctuary already in the pre-state period can be understood as a deliberate alternative to the development of Jerusalem into a central state temple by David, Solomon and Josiah (II Sam.7; I Kings 6-8; II Kings 23). They were concerned finally to liberate the official cult of Yahweh from its state ties and to remedy its alienation from the people.

Many details of the legend of the priestly sanctuary in Exod.25-Lev.9 fit this double aim: on the one hand the reform priests took up the old portable oracle tent (*'ōhel mō'ēd*) of the early period, but developed it in analogy to the Jerusalem temple[129] and – differing from the lay theologians – gave it the character of a permanent cult place 'within the camp'.[130] On the other hand they reduced its equipment to cultic objects from the time before the state.[131] Here it is particularly significant that they dispensed with the giant cherubic throne which had filled the holy of holies in the temple of Solomon. Instead of this, in an archaizing way they again gave the ark heightened significance[132] and built an addition (*kapporet*) to it as the symbolic place of the presence of Yahweh,[133] which was flanked by two cherubs reduced to small guardian figures.[134]

If in this way the holy of holies had already been stripped of any royal symbolism, the reform priests attributed the initiative towards the building of the temple not to the king but to Yahweh and Moses (Ex.25.1ff.; 40.33).

Nor did royal architects work on it, but craftsmen from the people endowed with grace by God (31.1-11; 35.30-36.7), under the leadership and supervision of Moses (40.1-33). Finally, it was again not the king who financed the building but the whole people, which voluntarily gave it rich gifts (35.4-29; 36.3-6; 38.21ff.; Num.7.1ff.) and supported the craftsmen in every possible way (Ex.36.2f.). There is no doubt that in their description of the foundation of the cult the reform priests were concerned to make the building of the sanctuary a work of all Israel (39.42) and to shift the concern for its existence from the king, making the whole community responsible for it. This purpose is also served by the introduction of the temple tax (30.11-16) and finally also by the census (Num.1; 26) as the foundation for the taxation (Ex.28.25f.). As they made clear in their arrangement of the camp in Num.2, the sanctuary and not the king is to be the centre of society: their 'democratic' conception of the cult and their notion of Yahweh's dwelling in the midst of the Israelites, who are divided into tribes or 'fathers' houses', is here demonstrated in an ideal way.

What was true of the sanctuary was also of course to apply to the cultic personnel. It was no longer to be royal officials who served as priests in the sanctuary but 'Aaron and his sons' who on the instructions of Yahweh were consecrated to priestly service 'from the midst of the Israelites' (Ex.28.1ff.). It is not completely certain whether the reform priests projected the office of high priest *a priori* with the intention of filling the king's role of sacral leadership by a priest; be this as it may, as the development of the high priest's adornments shows (Ex.28; 29), this was the issue in the subsequent period.[135] It is no longer the king but the priests under the leadership of the high priest who are to be responsible for the administration of the sanctuary (29.44). Finally, according to the description given by the reform priests, the priestly self-administration is rounded off by the subordination of the Levites, who in support of the priests are to see more to the practical services in the sanctuary (Num.1.48-54; 3f.). For them these were not, as for the disciples of Ezekiel, demoted priests,[136] but – very much along the lines of their conception of a cult close to the people – 'gifts' from the Israelites to Yahweh (Num.3.9; 8.16,19; 18.6f.), with which they redeemed their firstborn (Num.3.12,40-49; 8.16).

We could suppose that the reform priesthood could count on the understanding of at least part of the lay theologians with a Deuteronomistic orientation for their conception of a cult opposed to the monarchy and close to the people. Here both reform groups came together in their concern to establish a self-administered community without royal supervision. However, conflicts inevitably broke out over how far the priestly self-administration of the cult should go and whether it excluded the collaboration of the laity.

For all their concern that the former state cult should be opened up to the people, the reform priesthood were necessarily interested in a clear distinction between priests and Levites for a strengthening of cultic self-administration. In a very traditional way[137] they based the need for this on the dangerous potential of the holy, which excluded any unauthorized dealing with it (Lev.10). What was new, by contrast, was the seriousness with which the reform priesthood took responsibility for a proper performance of the sacred actions by the priesthood. As they indicated immediately after the successful first offering of worship, even a slight deviation from the divinely willed rite could put even the priesthood in deadly danger (Lev.10.1-3): God impressed on Aaron and his sons that they would pay for any transgression against the sanctuary with their lives (Num.18.1); in their view the privilege of being a priest carried a great responsibility with it.

So it was not striving for power but concern for the ongoing existence of the community that made the priests insist that any unauthorized person (*zār*[138]) should be kept away from the holy. The reform priests gave an ideal description of their view of the relationship between priests and Levites in the way in which they ordered the camp: here priests and Levites were to form an inner ring around the central sanctuary (Num.1.50-53; 3.38[139]), around which the tribes of Israel had to camp in another, outer, ring (Num.2). In this way the cult personnel took on the function of a protective wall between the sanctuary and the laity which was carefully to prevent any unauthorized contact with the holy and to ward off any blow of wrath[140] that they might provoke. The disciples of Ezekiel had still been thinking of thick walls and mighty gates to perform this function.[141] The fact that the reform priests – probably out of consideration for the laity – either would not or could not implement such an abrupt architectural sealing off of the sanctuary means that they had to be concerned to achieve the same end by a sharp demarcation between groups of persons and a clear distribution of competences. Therefore it was a concern of theirs to lay down precisely the actions of laity and priests in sacrifices (Lev.1ff.); for that reason they constantly made new attempts to regulate in detail the competences of priests and Levites (Num.3.1-3; 4.1-33; 8.5-22). In their view only a careful separation and ordering of priests, Levites and laity could make certain that the cult brought atonement and blessing for the whole community.

However, the priestly composition in Num.16-18 shows just how controversial this distribution of competences between priests and laity on the one hand and priests and Levites on the other must have been in the early post-exilic period.[142] Here the reform priesthood took up the older tradition of the rebellion of Dathan and Abiram against Moses,[143] transforming it – so to speak as a priestly pendant to Ex.32-34 – into a comprehensive scenario of crisis in order to give expression to the priestly privileges.[144]

The crisis began when 250 leading representatives of the laity, who are entitled 'princes' (*nāsī*) and 'chosen' (*qārī*'), assembled against Moses and Aaron and fundamentally put priestly privilege in question:

> You have gone too far!
> For all the congregation are holy,
> every one of them,
> and Yahweh is among them.
> Why then do you exalt yourselves above the assembly of Yahweh? (Num.16.3)

The theological arguments which the lay leaders advance here to challenge the claim that the priest alone is competent in the cult in substance correspond precisely to the conception of Israel as a holy people and 'kingdom of priests' presented by the lay theologians in their Pentateuch composition (Ex.19.5f.). So it is probable that at this point in the priestly composition we have an explicit reflection of the real points of dispute between the two groups involved in handing down the Pentateuch (the council of elders and the priestly college). Here it is interesting that the lay representatives also allude to a theologoumenon of the priest theologians, namely that also according to their conception of the sanctuary Yahweh dwells in the midst of the people (Ex.25.8; 29.45; Lev.26.11). The lay leaders also held the priests to the 'democratic' openness of worship which they, too, wanted in order to demonstrate to them with a concept of holiness understood in Deuteronomic terms that an exclusive claim to holiness leading to a subordination of the laity to the priests was inconsistent with this. If Israel had at least potentially been singled out by Yahweh and given holy status, then the priests could not claim such a status for themselves alone. The laity too had to be allowed competence in the cult.

In making Moses yield to these laicistic claims (Num.16.4), the reform priests probably wanted to indicate that they utterly respected the view of their reform colleagues in the council of elders.[145] They did not want simply to throw out the theological postulate of the lay theologians but to present a genuine matter of dispute to God for a decision. A divine verdict (ordeal) was to declare who had been chosen by Yahweh to approach the holy place (v.5) and therefore who had the necessary holiness to perform the cult (v.7). However – as their lay colleagues attempted to make clear through the tradition of Dathan and Abiram (vv.27-34) – this could only have a negative outcome (v.35; cf. Lev.10.2).

The disputes with the group of Levites around Korah which the reform priests connected with this were carried on in a much more direct and much harsher way; their claim to full priestly office (*kᵉhunna*, Num.16.10) was described as ingratitude over their selection (v.9) and was expressly rejected and punished by an appearance of the glory of Yahweh (vv.19-24). Only the intercession of Moses and Aaron could prevent the revolt of the Levites from dragging down the whole community into the abyss (v.22). A degree of restraint on the part of the priests towards the Levites can be recognized only to the degree that they deliberately left open the fate of their ancestor Korah in this divine judgment (v.32b).

It says much for the rigour of the controversies that even by the priests' own account the conflict with the divine verdict was not yet settled, but continued to escalate. In this new phase of the crisis it was the 'whole community of the Israelites' (Num.17.6) which rebelled against Moses and Aaron. In other words, after the failure of the council of elders the popular assembly of the people also protested, as the basic body of Jewish self-administration, an action which makes it clear what broad social support the lay leaders had in their battle against priestly privileges.

Here again the charge levelled by the whole community against Moses and Aaron was firmly based on the theology of the people of God in the D composition inspired by Deuteronomy;

'You have killed the people of Yahweh!' (Num.17.6)[146]

That means that by provoking a divine judgment to justify its privileges, the priesthood had lightly set itself above Israel's special status as people of God, and had endangered its existence.

The reform priests who took their priestly responsibility so seriously would not and could not ignore such a charge, which the priesthood even forced through, insisting that they alone were competent in the cult. So they thought up a didactic story which vividly showed that a denial of priestly privilege would necessarily put the very existence of Israel at risk; in their view Yahweh could respond to such a charge only with a verdict of total annihilation (17.7b-10). The plague which emanated from Yahweh was already taking its course and would have totally annihilated Israel had not Aaron made atonement for the people from the sanctuary and stemmed the catastrophe (vv.11-15). That means that the priests wanted to demonstrate to their own generation and future generations of laity that only when the cult was performed by those people chosen and consecrated by God for it[147] could the sanctuary develop its function of bringing salvation to the community. And once the laity had seen the danger posed to them from a cult which was not administered by the priesthood (17.27f.), the responsibility of priests and levites for the sanctuary and its hierarchy of personnel would again be confirmed by Yahweh (Num.18.1ff.). The inclusion of Num.16-18 in the foundation history of Israel was meant to teach that only when this division between the competence of priests and Levites was no longer being shaken could danger to Israel be avoided (18.4f.,7).

In thinking that it had to insist that for the general well-being that it alone had competence in the cult, the reform priesthood came up against the lay theologians to the degree that it no longer regarded the cultic and ritual ordinances as more or less internal professional knowledge on which the priests only had to rule internally, but resolved to publish them and fix them in the foundation document of Israel. In this way it also allowed the lay leaders to control the observance of cultic regulations and to take on indirect responsibility for the orderly performance of the cult. From the way in which they even subjected their own way of life to public control (Lev.21.1-22.16) it becomes clear that in their battle for the self-administration of the cult the reform priests were not – or at least not primarily – motivated by a selfish desire for power but by a concern for a real renewal of the cult from top to bottom. It was not just the laity who had to behave in accordance with the holiness of God (Lev.19f.); so did the priests and the high priest, who had to submit to quite special rules of cleanness (21.1-23). Not only did the laity have to see to the orderly peformance of their sacrifices (19.5-8; 22.17-25), but the priests also had to ensure that their parts of the sacrifices were dealt with in an orderly way (22.1-16). The interweaving of the laws for laity and priests in particular in the priestly legislation in Lev.17-26 is a clear indication that the reform priesthood was just as prepared as the laity was to submit itself to a generally binding norm. The priests recognized that for all the difference in their spheres of competence, laity and priests together bore responsibility for a renewal of the community. In addition, a readiness for compromise can also be seen in the ethical qualification of the concept of holiness in Ex.31.13; Lev.11.44f.; 19ff. Whether the lay theologians defined Israel as a whole as a 'holy people' or the priests insisted on their quite special holiness, both had the task of proving their 'holiness' by obeying the commands of the holy God Yahweh and progressing along the way of their holiness (Lev.19.2; 20.7f., 26; 22.9,31f.).

The vital interest of the priest theologians in the temple cult also led at another point to a marked expansion and revision of the lay-theological Pentateuch composition: in the creation stories, and therefore in the question of the foundation of the Israelite relationship with God.[148]

For the lay theologians influenced by Deuteronomy and the Deuteronomists the Israelite relationship with God was exclusively grounded in history. They had made their foundation history begin with the exodus of Abraham from Babylon (Gen.12) and continued it with the exodus of Israel from Egypt (Ex.3ff.). Their sole concern had been to bring out the particular privileged history of Yahweh with Israel, and – probably to exclude any efforts at assimilation – they had completely bracketted off the level of the theology of creation.[149]

The priestly theologians could only partially accept this conception of the foundation history. For them, too, the relationship between God and Israel was in principle grounded in history (Gen.17; Ex.6), although for them this history had been determined more by one-sided divine decrees than by an open interplay between Yahweh and Israel.[150] But they could not accept a limitation either to history or to the particular relationship with God; after all, the older Zion theology had always been universal,[151] and preaching about the creator of the world and mythical notions of primal times (the battle with chaos) had played a role in it which could not be ignored.[152] So it is no coincidence that it was priestly theologians who incorporated the creation and primal history into the foundation document of Israel, using an earlier composition about primal times (Gen.1-11).[153]

Earlier Babylonian and Canaanite myths lay behind this priestly conception: in Enuma Elish, Marduk's battle with chaos and his creation of the world issues in the building of the temple of Marduk, Esangelia, in Babylon.[154] And in the Baal-Yam cycle the victory of Baal over the rebellious sea was probably followed by the building of his palace on the mountain of God in Ugarit.[155] So in the priestly composition, too, the creation of the world and the building of the temple were to serve as foundation pillars; that is why the priestly theologians took some effort to make the two basic data of their foundation history parallel.[156] But in contrast to their religious models they did not shift the building of the temple into mythical primal time, but on the contrary brought the creation of the world into history. They made the mythical-other-worldly primal time a part of history, a part of universal history into which the history of Israel was also to be fitted, by putting the primal history before the history of Israel. In so doing, on the one hand they helped themselves to lead the basic historical character of the religion of Israel to a new victory, and on the other they gave Israel's historical relationship with God in the official foundation document a broader and deeper foundation in the theology of creation.

Many of the characteristic elements of the priestly composition can be understood from this concern to relate the universal creaturely dimension of the relationship with God to the particular historical relationship between God and Israel. First there is the system of dating which embraces creation, primal times, the patriarchal history and the history of the people, by means of which the priestly theologians made the various Pentateuchal traditions into a unilinear historical development with every possible kind of symbolic numerical cross-reference and accent.[157] Then there is the consequence of the progressive revelations of the divine name, starting from the universal creator God (*'elōhīm*), through the El-Shaddai of the forefathers (Gen.17.1), to Yahweh the God of the people of Israel (Ex.6.2f.), who in the end comes near to his people in the cult in the form of the *kᵉbōd yhwh* (Ex.25.1ff.). And finally there is the juxtaposition of a universal covenant of God with all humankind and all creation (the Noah covenant, Gen.9) as the outer circle surrounding the inner circle of the covenant of Yahweh with the patriarch Abraham that constituted Israel's special relationship with God (Gen.17). With all these regular 'historical' systematizations the priestly theologians wanted to show how the religion of Israel was part of a deeper religion of humanity rooted in creatureliness, and how this in turn found fulfilment in the special relationship of Israel with its God.

This twofold aspect of the theological arrangement also connects up with a whole series of motifs in the priestly composition: the blessing of the creator and the command to increase (Gen.1.28; 9.1,7), which was realized for all of humanity in the procreation of the first human beings (Gen.5) and their expansion and branching out into peoples (Gen.10), became especially efficacious for Israel in the promise of increase to the patriarchs (Gen.17.2,6,16; 18.2; 35.11; 48.3f.; cf. 47.27) and in the growth of Israel into a people (Ex.1.7).[158] It thus formed a basis of a hope that the small scattered groups of their own people would also not die out. The creator's command about culture, that people were to fill the earth and subject it to themselves (Gen.1.28), which had been universally realized in the advance of culture (Gen.4.1ff.) and in the formation of states (Gen.10f.), became especially efficacious for Israel in the promise of the land (Gen.17.8; 28.4; 35.12; 48.4; Ex.6.4)[159] and formed a basis for the hope that despite its dispersion, Israel would one day again be able to settle fully on its land. The rhythm of God's creative work had already brought for all humankind the alternation of working time and liturgical festivals (2.1-3). This found a concrete form of blessing specifically for Israel at the end of each working week in the sabbath rest (Ex.16.25f.; 20.11), and again took shape in the building and dedication of the sanctuary (Ex.31.12-17).[160] Israel also shared in all these saving institutions of the creator, but at the same time these promises and institutions of Yahweh had special content for Israel and indeed were surpassed there. Yahweh's special intervention in Israel was based on the intervention of the creator in the whole world and for all human beings.

As the priestly theologians indicated, however, now the principle of analogy and surpassing applied not only to different elements of the relationship with God but also to the relationship with God itself.[161] This relationship was made possible by the resolve of the creator to create human beings in his own image (Gen.1.26). By this special intervention of the creator among humankind, men and women became partners of God, were in a special relationship with God, set apart from all other creatures. This honoured position of being in God's image was something which all human beings had, nor was it lost (Gen.5.1ff.), and it laid the foundation for the special protection of human life (9.6). And in the ideal early period before the flood, the relationship of human beings to God could be so close and direct that it is said of Enoch and Noah that they 'walked with God' (*hithallek 'et 'elōhīm*, 5.22, 24; 6.9).

But this originally close communion of God with human beings was deeply disrupted. The creator, who in Gen.1.31 still sees his work as being 'very good', had to note in Gen.6.12 the violence and corruption of all earthly creatures. So he harshly distanced himself from his creation and had the water of chaos break in again (6.13,17). That he nevertheless did not totally separate himself from his creation was due to his special relationship with Noah. Certainly the creator again allied himself to his creation by making a covenant with Noah and 'all flesh' which imposed on him the condition that he would not destroy the world again (9.8ff.), but this remained a more distant relationship to a destroyed creation in which the violence among creatures could only channelled in a rough and ready way. There could no longer be a direct communion with God.[162]

The special relationship which Yahweh had built up with Israel was interpreted by the priestly theologians as God's concern to make possible again a new proximity within the damaged relationship of the creator to his world. The first step on this way was the covenant of El-Shaddai with Abraham through which God permanently bound himself to Israel in order to be God to him and his descendants after him (Gen.17.7). The second step followed with the exodus of Israel from Egypt, when Yahweh disclosed his full identity to Moses and promised that he would take Israel to himself as his people and be their God (Ex.6.3,7). The third step finally followed with the foundation of the sanctuary, when God resolved to dwell amongst the Israelites and thus be their God in an unprecedented immediacy (Ex.25.8; 29.45f.). Thus the Israelite temple cult was what made possible an unprecedented nearness to God under the conditions of a disrupted relationship between God and his world. The presence of Yahweh in the temple and the encounters with God which it made possible were at least a partial overcoming of the distance between the creator and his creation. In the cult of Israel the primal will of the creator for community with his creatures had come to its provisional goal.[163]

The priestly theologians indicated a fourth step for the future which went even beyond this: if Israel observed God's cultic ordinances and in accordance with God's commandments was concerned for purity and justice in everyday life, there was a possibility of overcoming the deep disruption of creation at least within the sphere of Israel, doing away with violence and restoring the original blessing and peace of God's creation (Lev.26.3-10)[164] and the original direct communion with God. Then God himself would walk in the midst of Israel (*hithallek betōk*) and Yahweh would be Israel's God and Israel his people with no distance between them (Lev.26.12).

Thus the orientation of official Yahweh religion on the temple cult as the centre of the relationship with God which the Priestly theologians undertook with their composition of the Pentateuch was not aimed – as might be assumed – at narrowing down the Israelite relationship with God or even at retreating from the world. Rather, the concentration on the cult made it possible for Yahweh religion to be open to the universal breadth of creation. In the view of the reform priesthood the special position of Israel might not find its goal solely in cultural and religious segregation, as might seem to be the case in the lay theological draft of the Pentateuch. The reform priests, too, regarded such a demarcation as necessary at many points in order to further and preserve the holiness of Israel (Lev.18.1-5,24-30; 20.22-27), but for them this did not yet exhaust the identity of Israel; rather, they introduced the perspective that Israel's privileged relationship with God has a positive function for the whole world[165] as a symbolic realization of the communion with God initially intended by God for all human beings and the whole world. In their view Israel had a mission for the world, and as all the world was God's creation, it could also take part in this world without a permanent bad conscience.

Thus the priestly conception made it easier for the scattered Jewish minorities to live in the multicultural and multireligious world of the Persian empire. It offered a viable theological basis for a constructive collaboration with the Persians, something which was certainly also welcomed by the lay leaders who were willing to co-operate, as their Deuteronomic/Deuteronomistic theological tradition did not have anything comparable to offer at this point. So the priest theologians made a not inconsiderable contribution towards ensuring that the enterprise of creating for the Jews in the Persian empire, in collaboration with the Persian government,[166] a normative basic religious and legal basic document, backed up by the law, would really succeed.

5.4 The social and religious split in the community

R.Albertz, 'Der sozialgeschichtliche Hintergrund des Hiobbuches und der "Babylonischen Theodizee"', in J.Jeremias and L.Perlitt (eds.), *Die Botschaft und die Boten. FS H.W.Wolff*, 1981, 349-72; id., 'Die "Antrittspredigt" Jesu im Lukasevangelium auf ihrem alttestamentlichen Hintergrund', ZNW 74, 1983, 182-206; W.A.M.Beuken, 'Isa 56:9-57:13 – An Example of Isaianic Legacy of Trito-Isaiah', in *Tradition and Re-Interpretation in Jewish and Early Christian Literature. FS C.H.Lebram*, Studia Post-Biblica 36, 1986, 48-64; W.Beyerlin, *Der 52. Psalm. Studien zu seiner Einordnung*, BWANT 111, 1980; H.Bolkestein, *Wohltätigkeit und Armenpflege im vorchristlichen Altertum*, 1939 = 1969; F.Crüsemann, 'Hiob und Kohelet. Ein Beitrag zum Verständnis des Hiobbuches', in R.Albertz et al. (eds.), *Werden und Wirken des Alten Testaments, FS C.Westermann*, 1980, 323-93; W.Golka, 'Die Flecken des Leoparden. Biblische und afrikanische Weisheit im Sprichwort', in R.Albertz, F.W.Golka and J.Kegler (eds.), *Schöpfung und Befreiung, FS C.Westermann*, 1989, 149-65; A.H.J.Gunneweg, *Nehemia*, KAT XIX/2, 1987; A.E.Hill, 'Dating the Book of Malachi: A Linguistic Re-examination', in *The Word of the Lord Shall Go Forth, FS D.N.Freedman*, 1983, 77-89; H.Irsigler, *Psalm 73 – Monolog eines Weisen*, Arbeiten zu Text und Sprache im Alten Testament 20, 1984; O.Keel, *Feinde und Gottesleugner*, SBM 7, 1969; C.A.Keller, 'Zum Vergeltungsglauben im Proverbienbuch', in H.Donner et al. (eds.), *Beiträge zur Alttestamentlichen Theologie. FS W.Zimmerli*, 1977, 223-8; H.G.Kippenberg, *Religion und Klassenbildung im antiken Judäa*, SUNT 1978; H.Koenen, *Ethik und*

Eschatologie im Tritojesajabuch, WMANT 62, 1990; H.Kreissig, *Die sozialökono-mische Situation in Juda zur Achämenidenzeit*, Schriften zur Geschichte und Kultur des Alten Orients 7, 1973; B.Lang, *Die weisheitliche Lehrrede*, SBS 54, 1972; S.Mowinckel, 'Psalms and Wisdom', *VTS* 3, 1955, 204-24; P.A.Munch, 'Das Problem des Reichtums in den Psalmen 37, 49, 73', *ZAW* 55, 1937, 36-46; R.E.Murphey, 'A Consideration of the Classification "Wisdom Psalms"', *VTS* 9, 1963, 156-67; K.Pauritsch, *Die neue Gemeinde. Gott sammelt Ausgestossene und Arme (Jes 56-66)*, AnBib 47, 1971; L.G.Perdue, *Wisdom and Cult*, SBL Dissertation Series 30, 1977; W.Rudolph, *Esra und Nehemia*, HAT I, 2, 1949; L.Ruppert, *Der leidende Gerechte*, 1972; id., *Der leidende Gerechte und seine Feinde. Eine Wortfelduntersuchung*, 1973; W.Schottroff, 'Arbeit und Sozialer Konflikt im nachexilischen Juda', in id. and L.Schottroff (eds.), *Mitarbeiter der Schöpfung*, 1983, 104-8; M.Schwantes, *Das Recht der Armen*, BET 4, 1977; K.Schwarzwäller, *Die Feinde des Individuums in den Psalmen* (2 vols), Diss.theol. (typescript), Hamburg 1963; R.B.Y.Scott, 'Wise and Foolish, Righteous and Wicked', *VTS* 23, 1972, 146-65; U.Skladny, *Die älteren Spruchsammlungen in Israel*, 1962; O.H.Steck, *Befreite Heimkehr*, SBS 121, 1985; id., 'Beobachtungen zu Jesaja 56-59', *BZ* NF 31, 1987, 228-46; C.Westermann, 'Struktur und Geschichte der Klage im Alten Testament' (1954), *Forschung am Alten Testament* I, TB 24, 1964, 266-308; id., 'Weisheit im Sprichwort' (1971), *Forschung am Alten Testament* II, TB 55, 1974, 149-61.

The great effort at integration which is represented by the first move towards forming a canon was not a complete success. Certainly the reform coalition of leading laity and priests succeeded in safeguarding the position of Judaism in the Persian empire both externally, by working out a basic religious document and having it authorized by the Persian authorities, and internally, by achieving a consensus over many questions of self-understanding, lifestyle and political or cultic organization – though this was not without its tensions; however, they did not succeed in preventing social divisions in the community.

The conflict to be found here can perhaps be clarified by Isa.58.1-4, a text which is to be dated between 515 and 450.[1] The community laments that Yahweh does not heed its fast liturgies (v.3), and a prophetic voice accepts that the people have had a concern for religious and cultic observance (v.2). It seeks Yahweh daily, wants to be near to him, wants to know what way of life God demands, wants not to neglect his law and to do justice. This could suggest that the efforts of the reform coalition at a religious and cultic renewal of society were really bearing fruit and meeting with widespread consent. Nevertheless in the economic and social sphere society looked quite different, as the prophetic voice indicates in its accusation (v.4). Here people went about their business even on public fast days; here people were not afraid even to use physical force to take pledges[2] from debtors in arrears. So a harsh, heedless business practice stood in blatant contradiction to the widely accepted desire for religious renewal.[3]

Since there was a consensus over social legislation along the lines of the

Deuteronomic 'brotherhood ethic' among the two groups which handed down the Pentateuch,[4] the only probable interpretation of this situation is that the economic interests, structures and pressures were too strong for the ideal of Yahweh religion from the early period of Israel to be able to break through them, no matter how impressively it was formulated. The fascination of the religious symbol of liberation was not enough to win everyone over to an economic and social restructuring of society and to overcome the division of society into rich and poor which had grown up in the period of the state. On the contrary, from the latest after the middle of the fifth century, the new community of Judah which had been founded with so many hopes slipped into a deep social crisis which persistently governed the whole of subsequent post-exilic social and religious history. After it, the relatively broad social consensus which the process of canonization had initially brought was shattered.

5.41 The social crisis of the fifth century

The social crisis in the community of Judah became manifest at the beginning of the second half of the fifth century. What probably sparked off the severe social conflict was the additional taxation needed for rebuilding the walls, which Nehemiah imposed on the people of Judah in 444 in the form of forced labour (Neh.3). However, the real causes were probably structural, and we may assume that the conflict had already been simmering for a while.[5]

In Neh.5.1-5 Nehemiah gives us a lively report of an outcry made to him as governor (5.1) by the humblest people against Jewish 'nobles and officials' (5.7).[6] Three groups are mentioned: there was a group which complained that it had to mortgage[7] its children for credit simply to get the bare means of survival (v.2). Then there was a second group which complained that it was having to mortgage its fields, vineyards and houses to get grain – probably both for food and for seed – in the famine (v.3). And there was a third group which had to mortgage its fields and make its children slaves to borrow money to pay the 'king's tax' (*middat hammelek*, vv.4-5).

Even if the details of how the different groups are to be related to one another are not completely clear,[8] the structural mechanisms of the crisis are: all the groups were caught in the mill of the harsh ancient law of credit, which allowed the creditor to seize the property and the family of the debtor (enjoying the benefits of their produce) if they were unable to pay. Whether they were now already landless (v.2) or still had a smallholding (vv.3-5), because of this law of credit the poorer strata of the population were driven into increasing poverty and had to hand over their children, i.e. their workforce, to their creditors as slaves; they had to give them the lion's share of the produce of their fields and vineyards and themselves worked only as leaseholders or as slaves on their former property – that is, if they and their children were not driven out and sold into slavery abroad.[9]

These are the same economic mechanisms which already in the late monarchy had led to an impoverishment of the traditional stratum of small farmers. As then, so now, individual periods of drought and the failure of harvests were enough to endanger the existence of small farmers whose businesses were backed with only a small amount of capital. In addition, now in the early post-exilic period there was a further heavy burden: after the financial reform of Darius the taxes for the Persian king (v.4) had to be paid in silver coin, at a level fixed in advance for individual provinces without heed to the actual yields of harvests.[10] As the province of Judah had no silver of its own, the money could be raised only by selling natural products. But for this a surplus production was necessary, and the smallholding which had traditionally aimed at self-sufficiency was not tailored to that. That meant that in the face of this new burden[11] the small farmers had to cut things to the bone simply to get by, and it only took very slight additional difficulties like failures in the harvest or conscription for building the walls to upset their precarious situation over a broad front. It was the well-founded fear of being inexorably dragged down in the undertow of the annihilation of their businesses and the destruction of their families which drove a large part of the population of Judah to protest to the governor about their treatment by their 'Jewish brothers'(5.1,5).

The complaint of the small farmers to Nehemiah was successful: he angrily rebuked their creditors, the 'nobles and officials', in public before the popular assembly for their anti-social conduct (Neh.5.6f.) and imposed a general remission of debt on them (vv.10-12).[12] At first that will have brought relief to the small farmers and once again kept the social peace. But it was not a long-term solution to the structural crisis; the process of impoverishment among the small farmers continued, as is attested by a wealth of evidence from later in the Persian period (second half of the fifth century and first half of the fourth).[13]

In Isa.58.4 the practice of dispossession by force had already been castigated, and Mal.3.5 criticizes the oppression of day labourers and the eviction of widows and orphans, i.e. the landless groups of the population right at the bottom end of the social scale. While this evidence probably still dates from the time before Nehemiah,[14] the book of Job seems to document the advanced process of social erosion in the subsequent decades.[15] At the time of the poet of the book of Job day-labourers and slaves are evidently already so widespread a phenomenon that he can use them as a comparison for the human lot (Job.7.2-3; 14.6). The merciless seizing of pledges from impoverished 'brothers' for no real reason is common practice (22.6); these people are rushed before the court (29.17), robbed of their houses, and their meagre existence is shattered (20.19). Moreover, how far the social decline of many of the small farmers had already gone can be seen from the fact that in the book of Job the traditional terms *'ebyōn*, 'poor'; *'ānī*, 'wretched';

and *dal*, 'humble', which in the eighth century had still denoted the small farmers who, while poorer than the great landowners had their own property, are used side by side with references to the landless widows and orphans.[16] That means that by this time, for the most part those so designated have already sunk to the level of notorious recipients of alms who need the beneficence of the rich to survive.[17] The new term *'ōbēd*, 'perishing',[18] used in parallel in the book of Job to denote the impoverishment, also points in the same direction.

A quite similar picture of social conditions also emerges from a whole series of texts in the prophets and psalms which probably belong in the same period of time (Isa.29.17-24; 35.1f.; 58.5-9a; 59.1-21; Pss.37; 94; 109, etc.). The poorer strata of the population are brought to court regardless of their rights (Isa.29.21; Ps.37.32f.; 94.21; 109.2f), are trodden down (Ps.94.5), broken (Isa.58.6), deliberately finished off (Isa.29.20; Ps.37.7,12,14,32; 94.6) and driven into slavery for debt (Isa.58.6). Hunger, nakedness, homelessness and beggary become a social phenomenon which can no longer be overlooked (Isa.58.7; Job 22.6f.; 31.16-20). Isaiah 59.13-15a paints the gloomy picture of a society in which lies, violence and injustice have driven out all the positive values like truth, honesty and justice.

Though the date and content[19] of some of the evidence may be doubted, as a whole, given the breadth of its distribution, it indicates that the conflict attested in Neh.5 was no episode, but a far-reaching and long-lasting social crisis which shook post-exilic Judah to the core.[20] The creeping decline of increasing numbers of the population, which at time became acute, to a level below the minimum needs of existence, grew into an abuse which could no longer be overlooked by anyone who held a position of responsibility in the community.

5.42 The ethical and religious split in the upper class

The social crisis of the fifth century represented a powerful ethical and religious challenge for the whole community, but above all for its upper class. After all, it was above all the rich and influential families who held positions of responsibility in the Jewish self-administrative bodies or in the service of local Persian administration,[21] and they were the ones who according to Neh.5.7 emerged as creditors and derived economic advantage from the crisis. Thus the upper class found itself in a conflict of interests between its public duty to see to the welfare of the whole community and its private economic interests; moreover, it found itself in a crisis of loyalty: was it to give priority to confidential collaboration with the Persian authorities or to the well-being of the community of Judah?

It looks as if the majority of the upper class was not morally up to this conflict. Its leaders were agreed only that the political framework which had caused the social crisis should not be shaken. In the given circumstances of the harsh Persian policy of taxation, to abolish the Persian king's tax or even to fight for a reduction in it was not only a delusion but would have led to forfeiting the benevolence of the great power, which was beyond question needed to secure the law and religion of the community. But how could such a political option be communicated to the poorer members of the people who were suffering under this tax?

This tricky conflict of loyalty gave additional sharpness to the conflict of interests: if the loyalty of the leading upper-class families had inevitably already seemed doubtful to an increasingly impoverished lower class, was it possible to go on using in a clever and unsentimental way the rights offered by the ancient law of credit in order to extend one's own estate, to get cheap labour from the small farmers who had been degraded to leaseholders, slaves or day-labourers, and to profit from the trade which derived from this enforced surplus production? According to Neh.5 there were many members of the upper class who answered these questions in the affirmative, and who decided on loyal collaboration with the Persians and their own advantage – which in any case was the simplest solution. They denied that they bore any personal responsibility for the structural crisis and probably regarded it as a transitory problem which would solve itself as the small farmers and their businesses collapsed. They felt that the regulatory mechanisms in their own legal tradition, like the obligation to ransom, which was meant to be a counterbalance to taxation, asked too much of them (Job 6.22f.); and if there was no alternative, well, a remission of debt might be proclaimed in God's name (Neh.5.12).

It says more for the social impulse within Yahweh religion that some of the upper class were not content with such a simple solution to the conflict of loyalty and interests and such a crude reaction to the social crisis. In Nehemiah's own account this part is represented by himself and his family; but we will not go far wrong in assuming that his supporters also included members of the reform coalition in the self-administrative bodies, though their majority began to crumble in the conditions of the crisis. Like Nehemiah, despite their loyalty to the Persians they felt obliged to show solidarity with their brothers as these became poorer.[22] For them, as for him, the obligation to redeem those in debt imposed by the Pentateuch was binding law (Neh.5.8; cf. Lev.25.47ff.), and they were agreed with him in attempting to follow the Deuteronomic legislation in imposing on society a regular remission of debt so that it became more than just a single occasion (Neh.10.32). While they did not succeed in really putting a stop to the pernicious process of social erosion, for religious reasons they were ready personally to renounce some of their claims to property (Neh.5.9,15) and voluntarily to use their riches and their social position to alleviate the social distress (Job 31.13-34,38-40; Isa.58.6-7). Here, if it was a matter of defending the rights of the small farmers in court (Job.29.14-17; Isa.29.21), they were not afraid of open conflict with their anti-social colleagues. Indeed they even entered into theological dispute with them on a broad front.

Thus the social crisis split the upper class of Judah into two camps, one which used it shrewdly and unsentimentally to its own advantage and was not very bothered about the social damage that it caused, and one which showed solidarity with brothers who were becoming poorer and at considerable financial sacrifice sought to protect them. So the dividing line was over the question of social commitment, i.e. once again over the question of how binding the social reform legislation of Yahweh religion was.[23]

If already in the days of Jeremiah the attempt at a religious control of social conduct had contributed to an intensification of the conflict within the upper class,[24] so in the post-exilic period it inevitably intensified once again, since both the Deuteronomic and the priestly social legislation had become part of the normative religious foundation document of Judaism. For the members of the pious upper class who felt completely committed to the ethic of solidarity in the Pentateuch, the cool calculation and lack of concern which had been shown up among other of its members could only be regarded as a departure from the religious consensus of Yahweh religion which they therefore had to censure vigorously. Thus – taking up Jeremiah[25] – they attached to these others the hostile stereotype of the *rāšāʿ*, the wicked and godless person. In so doing they wanted to make it unmistakably clear to their aristocratic colleagues, with whom socially they had much in common, that with their anti-social behaviour they had put themselves outside any relationship with God and the community of Israel. In so doing they elevated social solidarity to the status of a confessional question by which allegiance to Yahweh had to be decided in the face of the social crisis.

The problem of the sharp contrast between wicked and righteous which runs through very different areas of texts (prophets, psalms, Proverbs, Job) in the Persian period has often been discussed by scholars, but so far nothing like a convincing explanation has been found.[26] Since the wicked in particular have not been successfully identified,[27] the general tendency nowadays is to resort to the view that they are a wisdom antitype used to illustrate negative patterns of behaviour or problems in the doctrine of retribution.[28] But broad distribution of the term tells against limiting it to wisdom,[29] and the evidence that this contrast is typically Israelite tells against describing it as a universal human 'anti-ideal'.[30] Here there need be no dispute that the picture of the wicked person has typical features of a hostile stereotype. But even such a stereotype is not random, and some features of the wicked man are not simply typical. Thus, for example, the wicked man is always rich;[31] according to Job 21.28 he is one of the aristocrats (*nᵉdībīm*), has grown fat,[32] and his business is still prospering.[33] But he makes his riches his God,[34] and is therefore heedless ('man of the elbow', Job 22.8), and his wickedness consists above all in a deeply anti-social attitude in that he maltreats the weak, destroys their livelihood and seizes their possessions.[35] In addition, he refuses alms to those who are completely impoverished.[36] Nevertheless he enjoys great social respect, because hardly anyone dares to criticize him.[37] And because his economic position is secure, he thinks that he is no longer dependent on God and can scorn his commandments.[38] All these are by no means universal human features, but are typical descriptions of a particular social group and a particular social conflict. Since Jeremiah had attached the epithet *rāšā'* (Jer.5.26) to the anti-social large landowner, whose real existence no one disputes, it seems likely that the wicked man should be identified with the anti-social part of the upper class which was developing during the social crisis of the Persian period. Here, of course, we must take into account the fact that these are not objective descriptions, but deliberate, partisan, devastating characterizations which could also include generally hostile features.[39]

The social context of the righteous (*ṣaddīq*) or the pious (*ḥāsīd*) is less clear: he can be either rich[40] or poor.[41] But this ambiguity, too, has its roots in the social crisis of the fifth century. It arises out of the common front which the socially-committed upper class and the impoverished lower class took up against the 'wicked'. The image of the pious rich which is presented above all by the book of Job is very precise:[42] the Job of the dialogue poem is a once rich and respected member of the city aristocracy (Job 29.6ff.; 30.15, *nᵉdībā*), just like the wicked man. But what distinguishes him from the latter is above all his social conduct: he uses his high position in society to rescue the poor, who are in process of being attacked by the wicked (29.17), and is therefore called 'father of the poor' (29.16). And he uses his great wealth generously to support the distressed groups of the population with alms (31.16ff.). As a rich man, he too has slaves and leaseholders, but he respects their right to life (31.13-15,39). The pious rich man is thus the precise opposite of the wicked man, and in what is surely a typical way reflects that part of the upper class who were in solidarity with the poor.

The image of the pious poor man, who is usually depicted only as the victim of the wicked, is less sharp.[43] The reason for this is probably that the majority of these descriptions do not come from the persons concerned but from the perspective of the pious upper class.[44] But despite this element of vagueness, this third type completes the scenario, which precisely corresponds to a situation of social crisis (divided upper class, lower class which is becoming increasingly poor).

If the antithesis between the wicked man and the pious man which runs through so many post-exilic texts has its starting point in the social crisis of the fifth century, then the theological dispute being fought out in it can be described much more precisely.

As far as we can see, the dispute was predominantly carried on at two levels: by a part of the aristocracy who were in solidarity with the poor against their colleagues who were not, and by groups of the lower class against their aristocratic oppressors, but also at times against their supporters.[45] However, for the most part we know only one side of these controversies. There are no texts in which the so-called 'wicked' are authentically allowed to speak for themselves.[46] This is on the one hand certainly connected with the selectivity of the tradition, and shows that despite all the oppression, the reform coalition could in the end maintain its leadership in public opinion. On the other hand the aristocrats who were making the most of their economic advantage did not need to offer any further defence, since in formal legal terms they were in the right and had facts on their side. Precisely because they adapted to economic pressures and argued for purely rational perspectives without any 'false' sentimentality, they were successful, were able to enlarge their properties and improve their social position.[47] Were they not, as otherwise loyal members of the Yahweh community, being visibly blessed and justified by God? The theological dispute and the sharpness with which it was waged become understandable only if we assume that the attitude of the so called 'wicked' was in reality convincing and attractive.

The battle waged by those aristocrats who accepted the obligations of Yahweh religion to show solidarity had therefore to be on two fronts: first, externally, against the seductive position of the 'wicked'; and secondly, internally, to keep their own supporters in line.

Externally they developed a wide-ranging propaganda campaign to stem the influence of their opponents in society. They already began with school education: they inserted into the collections of proverbs used above all by the children of the upper class in learning to read and write a whole series of proverbs about the wicked and the pious,[48] in order to give adolescents a black-and-white picture of the two social alternatives between which they had to choose. Here they did not weary of branding the apparently so rational behaviour of the wicked as what it was in their eyes: injustice and godlessness.[49] And in line with the pattern of retribution customary in the wisdom tradition, but also widespread elsewhere, they gave their children warnings of where in their view such a false option must inevitably lead: to rapid and fearful disaster.[50] It has already frequently been noted that the proverbs about the wicked and the pious, which occur over and over again, keep stating in an almost incantatory undertone how evil the wicked man is and what a fearful fate he is going to meet.[51] This can be explained from the purpose of the 'pious' upper class to immunize the children of the well-to-do as early as possible against the option of not showing solidarity which was presented to them by many of their parents.

At the same time the aristocrats also attempted in worship to win over the adults to their position and show up their opponents' position as dangerous godlessness. They pointed out clearly that the reason why Yahweh did not react visibly to the community in liturgies of fasting and why the great dawn of salvation had still not come was because in the social crisis Yahweh wanted a quite different kind of fasting (Isa.58.5):[52] he wanted the rich to forego some of their possessions, release those whom they had enslaved for debt, clothe and cherish the impoverished, and not avoid their obligation to show solidarity (vv.6f.); then Yahweh would bring his great promises true at least in individual life (vv.8, 9a).[53]

In addition they composed regular didactic psalms in order to challenge the position of the wicked publicly in the temple (Pss.37; 49; 52; 62; 73; 94; 112).⁵⁴ Here, with pedagogical skill, they left room for the doubts which the manifest success of the wicked prompted among the pious (37.1; 49.6f.; 73.2ff.; 94.20f.) and conceded the seductive fascination that they exercised (62.4f.; 94.15ff.). They then went on to show up the good fortune of the wicked as a mirage which would soon fade (37.9,10,15,21, etc.; 49.14ff.; 73.18ff.) and the self-confidence which they paraded as an illusion (94.6ff.). In rhetorical dramatizations they regularly made room for their opponents to speak (52.3-7;⁵⁵ 62.4f.; 94.8-11) in order to persuade them to see the impossibility of their conduct. And the theological argument came to a climax in the claim that those who, like the wicked, in fact put their own riches in place of God (Ps.49.7; 52.9)⁵⁶ and exploited the weak to their own advantage (Ps.94.5-6) were placing themselves outside the relationship between Israel and God and outside the people of God (94.5,14f.⁵⁷). So they called on the community to distance itself publicly from such an attitude and such people by no longer putting its trust in riches and doubtful gain, but only in Yahweh (Ps.62.9-11). Thus they assured themselves that the pious who directed their conduct by the law and generously shared their riches with the poor (Ps.112.4,5,9) would be immeasurably blessed by Yahweh (vv.2f.,7,9).

Alongside this, the pious part of the upper class developed a wealth of pastoral activity within its group (Job 4.3-5). This was necessary not only because the public success of those aristocrats who showed no solidarity with the rest of the people was a lasting source of doubt and seduction (Pss.73.2ff.; 62.4f.; 94.16ff.) which might have enticed some others into doing the same. It was therefore necessary to give theological reassurance to those who had not taken this course. In addition, for the pious aristocrats there was the very much worse tribulation that despite – or probably even because of – their considerable show of solidarity they had to accept material losses, fall behind their craftier colleagues in building up their income, and indeed – as a result of incalculable blows of fate – might themselves even run the risk of social decline. This social process can be reconstructed with some degree of probability from the book of Job:⁵⁸ after all, Job represents a pious aristocrat who as a result of blows of fate or sickness has lost everything – his possessions, his high social position and his family – so that in social isolation (Job 10.13. 15) he falls below the level of even his lowliest servant (Job 30.1f.) – even though the solidarity he had shown with the poor had been exemplary.

The distress caused here to the pious aristocrats was above all theological: the bitter insight that their resolute hold on the religious ethic of solidarity and their unceasing and active commitment to the increasingly impoverished members of the community had quite evidently not paid off. Thus the problem of theodicy arose for them in full force. The whole of the book of Job can be seen as one long pastoral scheme seeking to cope with this difficult problem within the group.[59] But theologically it moves entirely on the level of personal piety and theology, and must therefore be treated in connection with them at a later stage.[60] Here I would simply point out that the pious aristocracy held out no prospect of a great intervention by Yahweh which would overturn society and which could also serve their needs. Their critical attitude to the excited expectations of eschatological prophecy,[61] which indeed was also expressed in the Pentaeuch,[62] becomes quite clear from the lack of any prophetic perspective on the future in the book of Job.[63]

5.43 The formation of prophetic sects in the lower class

It goes without saying that the small farmers who increasingly found themselves caught in the vortex of indebtedness and dispossession experienced the social crisis in quite a different way from the two camps in the upper class. What for the rich was a profitable business or a problem of social ethics was for the poor a massive existential threat. The more it became clear to them that they had to pay the bill for collaboration with the Persians which their leading class had run up, the more the suspicion must have dawned on them that all their aristocrats were collaborators to whom the favour of the occupying forces and their own advantage were more important than the anxiety and distress of their poor fellow-countrymen (Job.22.8).[64] Certainly they were able to distinguish between those who exploited their distress shamelessly and those who attempted to support them. And as the example of Neh.5 shows, political collaboration with the pious part of the upper class could bring an improvement in their situation. But in the face of the structural crisis, all the alms were like drops of water on a hot stone, and general mistrust was deep-seated. Could one trust one of those up there who claimed to be showing solidarity but at the same time were exacting the hated king's tax from them on behalf of the Persian government?

So we can start from the assumption that the social crisis led to a feeling of deep alienation and hopelessness among the lower class who were affected by it. And only in that way can we understand how circles formed among it which now also set themselves apart in religious terms and eagerly turned towards the only religious tradition which offered them any potential for hope after the failure of official Yahweh religion, namely eschatological prophecy.

Scholars have already made many conjectures about the process as such,[65] but it is hard to document from the texts with any certainty, since the late prophetic texts are even more difficult to date than the 'wisdom texts' which were used above to describe the position of the 'pious' upper class. So I shall base my account in what follows only on some texts which it is at least possible to date to well on in the

Persian period and which in both terminology and content probably point towards the social crisis. These are Mal.2.17; 3.5; 3.13-21; Isa.29.17-24; 56.9-57.21.[66] For the development of a specific personal piety among the lower class see below, 518ff.

A first step in the formation of a prophetic conventicle seems to me to be attested by the prophecy of Malachi, which still belongs in the initial phase of the social crisis – to be dated around 480. Malachi was still addressing the whole community, but he offered a special perspective of hope (vv.16-21) in particular to those who were suffering from the savage conditions in it (Mal.2.17; 3.14f.), and not least under the inexorable process of social repression (3.5): the wicked who thought that they could set themselves above Yahweh's commandments, i.e. also and particularly above his social commandments, and now still seemed to be triumphing, would be annihilated by Yahweh (v.19), while the 'sun of righteousness' would dawn on the righteous who really served him (v.20). Those who inevitably suffered under the upper class with its lack of solidarity would one day be able to leap around freely like fatted calves and trample on those who had formerly tormented them (v.21).

If the exilic and early post-exilic prophecy had still announced a saving intervention by Yahweh which in principle was for all Israel, under the pressure of the social crisis a simultaneous partial prophecy of salvation and judgment became typical. As Malachi recognized, in this crisis Yahweh's saving intervention could only be on behalf of some, the pious and the victims; their brazen adversaries and exploiters would necessarily be excluded from future salvation. Indeed, a judgment on the oppressors was the presupposition for the liberation of the oppressed.

We clearly find ourselves one stage further on in Isa.56.9-57.21.[67] This composition is already clearly formulated from the perspective of the small farmers and their increasing impoverishment (57.1). It is an example of the way in which circles from the lower class seized on the prophetic tradition, both the exilic/early post-exilic prophecy of salvation (57.15-19) and the pre-exilic prophecy of judgment (57.3-11) and developed and rewrote it for use in their conflict with the upper class (56.9-12; 57.3-5) and their own assurance of salvation (57.13b.; 57.14ff.).

The text unfolds the whole panorama of social conflict;[68] in Isa.56.9-12 complaints are made against the leaders, who are said not to notice in their blind greed (v.10f.) and intoxication (v.12) that they have invited strangers who are devouring the produce of the land (v.9). The consequences are described in a lamentation in 57.1f: the righteous (*haṣṣaddīq*) is snatched away without anyone taking any notice. Here the lower-class circles gave an amazingly clear-sighted analysis of the reasons for their impoverishment: the harsh Persian policy of taxation was impoverishing the land and their own selfish leaders were not doing anything about it.

In Isa.57.3-5 there are again accusations against leaders who among other things are polemically entitled 'children of transgression' and 'offspring of deceit'. These are probably in particular that part of the upper class which did not show solidarity, which even delighted in the downfall of the righteous (v.4). In still levelling against them the old accusation of worship on the high places and 'child sacrifice', the lower-class circle were probably wanting to point out their lustful, homicidal godlessness.

In Isa.57.6-11 the city of Jerusalem is accused with images of religious and political 'wantonness' that we know from the proclamation of Jeremiah and Ezekiel.[69] With this reference to the earlier prophecy of judgment, the lower-class circles were putting co-operation with the Persians on the same level as the self-destructive policy of currying favour with the great powers in the pre-exilic period. This was certainly a one-sided and partly unjust judgment, since the responsible part of the upper class at any rate was concerned to safeguard Jewish identity;[70] however, from the perspective of the lower class it was quite understandable, because this policy in fact destroyed the very foundations of their existence.

If hitherto the contemporary situation was being analysed in the light of earlier prophecy, and the guilty and their victims were being named, in 57.12-21 the text goes over to an announcement of the future. It is again two-sided: only the impoverished poor (57.1) who can only survive at all through trust in God will take possession of the land and of Jerusalem (57.13b);[71] only the shattered and humiliated victims of the present social development (57.15) will benefit from the great eschatological promise of peace (vv.16-19); unjust Jerusalem will be destroyed (vv.12f.), and the wicked will be excluded from divine peace (vv.20f.).

It is striking that the blind and selfish leaders of Isa.56.9-12 are not identified with the wicked. Those addressed are thus probably those in positions of political responsibility,[72] who in 57.14 are called on finally to remove the 'offence', so that the salvation already announced by the Deutero-Isaiah group (cf. Isa.40.1ff.) and ardently expected in the early post-exilic period (Isa.62.10) will finally come to 'his people'. In the present context the latter can only be a reference to the 'pious' impoverished lower class. Evidently the prophetic circles hoped that they could still persuade parts of the upper class finally to put an end to the policy of collaboration which was so disastrous for them.

The third text, Isa.29.17-24,[73] clearly comes from a lower-class circle with a prophetic orientation (v.19), but it goes one step further than Isa.56.9ff., as the social fronts have visibly hardened further. The ones speaking here who call themselves 'the poorest of men' (*'ebyōnē 'ādām*) no longer expect that any of their leaders can make any contribution towards removing their misery, but they reassure themselves in the hope that God alone will very soon bring about a great upheaval in nature and society, in which the lofty will be brought low and the lowly raised up

(29.17).[74] Then their oppressors who cynically and wickedly bring them down in the courts will disappear at a stroke (vv.20f.) and they will be able to rejoice in God in exuberant joy (v.19). Whether the part of the upper class which is not showing solidarity is still part of the people of God and whether it still has any share in future salvation has long since ceased to be an issue here. For the lower-class group whose voice can be heard here, it clearly represented the enemies of the community,[75] who must be removed by God. They, the poor and oppressed, claimed for themselves that they were the real pious (*ʿanāwīm*, v.19), the real Israel (v.22).[76] We can see how here a special piety of the poor developed from the social crisis; it was to be an important strand of Yahweh religion from early Judaism up to the New Testament. It was born of the protest of the victims who refused to accept as God-given the humiliating economic pressures which cast them to the ground, and it gave those who were robbed of their rights and their dignity a new dignity with a religious foundation.

Now in the text alongside the wicked rich and the pious poor there is mention of a third group of people who are called 'deaf and blind'[77] in v.18 and 'erring and murmuring' in v.24. They are to be led by the social revolution which Yahweh introduces (v.18) to true knowledge (v.24) or the right understanding of scripture (v.18). There is something to be said for supposing that this group represents that part of the upper class which was showing solidarity and which, as we know, was demonstrably reserved in the face of eschatological prophecy.[78] Despite all the compassion they showed to the impoverished small farmers, these upper-class supporters regarded the latter's prophetic expectations of an upheaval as politically dangerous and socially inopportune. And a divine intervention which would make the leaders the lowliest would also deprive them of their social privileges. So their concern was reform and not revolution. Whether they went so far as to pour scorn on and mock the excited expectations of the prophetic conventicle among the lower class, as Isa.66.5 indicates, is uncertain,[79] but at all events – simply with an eye to the Persians – they must have had an interest in forcing those who had revolutionary expectations of an overthrow right to the margin of the official community.

If this identification is right, then Isa.29.18-24 indicates that there was a theological dispute over the interpretation and evaluation of the prophetic heritage between the lower-class circles and their aristocratic patrons. The former attempted to convince the latter by means of the prophetic writings that the shift towards salvation already promised by the disciples of Deutero-Isaiah would have to come very soon and would do away with the social crisis at a stroke. And the latter struggled to recognize such an exegesis and allow it some theological relevance for the present. At any rate in the canonization of the Pentateuch they had deliberately allowed eschatological prophecy only as a distant future horizon,[80] and imposed the controls of the law and the political leadership on it.[81] So the lower-class circles could only hope that Yahweh himself would justify them and their prophetic theology by intervening, and would teach a lesson to their rich friends with their Torah or wisdom theology which, while well-meaning, did not go anything like far enough. Only when the rich recognized that Yahweh would completely do away with the unjust economic and social structures and completely take the side of the poor and the humble could they too, as the rich, unite with the community of the poor in the hallowing of God's name (v.23).[82]

Finally, note must be taken of the positive effect on the history of Israelite religion of all the social and theological problems into which the social crisis of the fifth century hurled the community of Judah. First of all, they meant that the question of the theological legitimation of riches and property was raised at the level of official Yahweh religion with a sharpness unparalleled in an ancient religion. The Jewish pattern of almsgiving, which was so exemplary in the Hellenistic and Roman world, has its origin here.[83] Secondly, they ensured that despite all the political and cultic religious consolidation of early Judaism, the impulse of Yahweh religion towards social revolution was not lost but, taken up and developed in lower-class religious groups, could time and again develop its dynamics anew.[84]

5.5 The convergence of the religious strata and the split in personal piety

R.Albertz, 'The Sage and Pious Wisdom in the Book of Job: The Friend's Perspective', in J.G.Gammie and L.G.Perdue (eds.), *The Sage in Israel and the Ancient Near East*, 243-61; J.Becker, *Israel deutet seine Psalmen*, SBS 18, 1966; W.Beyerlin, *Werden und Wesen des 107. Psalms*, BZAW 153, 1979; H.Birkeland, '*ānī and 'ānāw in den Psalmen*, SNVAO 1932, 4, 1933; J.Botterweck, '*ebyōn*', TWAT I, 1973, 28-43; A.Causse, *Les 'pauvres' d'Israel*, 1922; E.S.Gerstenberger, '*ānāh*', TWAT VI, 1989, 247-70; id., 'Psalm 12: Gott hilft den Unterdrückten', in B.Jendorff and G.Schmalenberg (eds.), *Anwalt des Menschen*, 1983, 83-104; R.Gordis, 'The Social Background of Wisdom Literature', HUCA 18, 1944, 160-97; id., *Poets, Prophets and Sages*, 1971; H.Gunkel, *Die Psalmen*, HK II/2, [5]1968; J.Jeremias, *Kultprophetie und Gerichtsverkündigung in der späten Königszeit*, WMANT 35, 1970; H.W.Jüngling, *Der Tod der Götter. Eine Untersuchung zu Psalm 82*, SBS 38, 1969; H.J.Kraus, *Psalms 1-59*, *Psalms 60-150*, [2]1992, 1993; A.Kuschke, 'Arm und reich im Alten Testament mit besonderer Berücksichtigung der nachexilischen Zeit', ZAW 57, 1939, 31-57; C.van Leeuwen, *Le développement du sens social en Israël avant l'ère chrétienne*, SSN 1, 1955; N.Lohfink, 'Von der "Anawim Partei" zur "Kirche der Armen". Die bibelwissenschaftlich Ahnentafel eines Hauptbegriffs der "Theologie der Befreiung"', Bibl 67, 1986, 153-75; J.Maier, *Die Texte vom Toten Meer* II, 1960; B.V.Malchow, 'Social Justice in Wisdom Literature', *Biblical Theology Bulletin* 12, 1982, 120-4; W.McKane, *Proverbs*,

OTL, 1972; D.Michel, 'Armut II, AT', *TRE* IV, 1979, 72-6; H.-P.Müller, *Hiob und seine Freunde. Traditionsgeschichtliches zum Verständnis des Hiobbuches*, ThSt 103, 1970; P.A.Munch, 'Einige Bemerkungen zu *ʿanīyyīm* und *rᵉšaʿīm* in den Psalmen', *MO* 30, 1936, 12-36; J.D.Pleins, 'Poverty in the Social World of the Wise', *JSOT* 37, 1987, 612-78; J.van der Ploeg, 'Les pauvres d'Israël et leur piété', *OTS* 7, 1950, 236-70; H.D.Preuss, *Einführung in die alttestamentliche Weisheitsliteratur*, UT 383, 1987; G.von Rad, *Wisdom in Israel*, 1972; A.Rahlfs, *ʿani und ʿanaw in den Psalmen*, 1892; F.Stolz, *Psalmen im nachkultischen Raum*, TS 129, 1987; G.H.Wittenberg, 'The Situational Context of Statements Concerning Poverty and Wealth in the Book of Proverbs', *Scriptura* 21, 1987, 1-23.

The developments undergone by personal piety in the post-exilic period are connected with the social form and socio-religious crisis of the community of Judah. The small size of the community, its reduced statehood and the structure of its political and religious organizations, which aimed at the broadest possible participation of the family associations, considerably narrowed the gap between the larger and smaller groups in comparison to pre-exilic times. In addition there was the new liturgical structure of the synagogue communities, combining elements from the subsidiary cult and the main cult; starting from the Diaspora, this had an influence back on the homeland and became increasingly influential in further historical development. The convergence of personal piety and official religion which had begun in the exilic period could thus continue and be consolidated. This led on the one hand to the development of a 'community theology' which drew strongly on the experiences of personal piety and on the other hand on a regular theologizing of personal piety.

Alongside the mutual convergence of personal piety and official religion a further development can be recognized: the social and religious split experienced by the community of Judah in the economic crisis of the second half of the Persian period robbed personal piety of its former 'innocence'. As 'personal theology' it was dragged into the conflicts between the groups and thus split. Alongside more general forms which still continued, in the post-exilic period for the first time we can see class-specific types of personal piety: the theologized wisdom of the pious upper class and the piety of the poor in lower-class circles with a religious orientation.

5.51 The post-exilic convergence of personal piety and official religion

That in the post-exilic period the strata of religion which had largely been separate in pre-exilic times combined more closely with each other is indicated above all by the numerous overlaps of formulae and motives between the individual and collective genres in the psalms.[1]

In a series of individual laments there are petitions for Israel or Zion;[2] the history of the people is incorporated into some[3] or the personal vow of praise is extended to the community.[4] The confession of confidence on the part of the individual is offered as a basis for the trust of the community;[5] and in some individual laments the difference between personal enemies and the adversaries of Israel becomes blurred.[6] Alongside this, in some songs of thanksgiving it is possible to recognize an extension of the private Toda community to the whole liturgical community.[7]

Such a striking mixture of forms and motives can first be explained from a purely spatial convergence of their settings: simply because the area of settlement in Judah was so small, we can conjecture that both the petitionary ceremony in the family circle and the Toda ceremony in the circle of relatives and friends moved to the Jerusalem temple in the post-exilic period. So quite naturally there were already many points of contact with the community as a whole or with other groups in the community.

But this explanation is probably not enough; further social psychological and theological reasons can be identified. Because of their shared experiences of the difficulty of rebuilding the temple, and participation in governing the community through the bodies involved in its self-administration, many families of the post-exilic period felt far more responsible for the existence of the people as a whole and involved in it than say during the monarchy. So in their private cultic ceremonies they showed more signs of solidarity with Israel, included petitions for Israel, Zion or the pious in their personal petitions for deliverance,[8] related their trust and hope in God to past experiences of the people which gave them strength (Ps.22.5f.) or the promises for Israel in the future which were still outstanding (Ps.102.13-23), and gave their personal experience of deliverance a significance for the wider community which strengthened its trust (Ps.22.23-32; 69.31,33-36). Precisely because the solidarity of society was deeply threatened after the social crisis from the middle of the fifth century on, such indications of theological solidarity performed an important function in personal rituals which supported the existence of the community as a whole. In the face of the manifest lack of solidarity on the part of some of the upper class, they took on a confessional character, but under the pressure of the controversies were increasingly limited to the pious part of the community.[9]

Other manifestations of the mixture of genres can be explained from the fact that it was customary to use individual psalms in liturgies of the community or groups from the community.[10] Israel could also rediscover itself in the fate of the individual sufferer, his tribulation, his being threatened by the enemy and his trust.[11] Such a paradigmatic transference was made possible by the fact not only that both the post-exilic community of Judah and even more the Diaspora communities were sociologically much closer to the small family group and in religious terms much closer to the individual's experiential horizon, but also that it stemmed from the oppressive theological problem that history as the horizon of the experience of divine action, which had provided the central basis for official Yahweh religion since its beginnings, was almost completely ruled out in the post-exilic situation. With the best will in the world, no historical intervention of Yahweh could be recognized in the historical constellation in which the weal and woe of the small province of Judah and even more the scattered Diaspora communities were dependent on the political decisions of the remote Persian imperial government in Susa. So it is all too understandable that in the post-exilic main cult, as already in the exile,[12] there was increased recourse to the piety of the small groups, which offered a treasury of living experiences of God even in a time which was poor in salvation.

In addition to simple transferences, this borrowing also led to 'mixed genres' which I would like to call community intercessions[13] and community hymns of praise.[14] They differ from the earlier genres of the main cult, the lamentation of the people and the hymn, in almost completely lacking a historical dimension.[15] This is replaced by generalized personal religious experiences and confessions of trust: for example, the poet of Ps.107 presents to the post-exilic community (v.2f.) experiences of salvation stylized in a didactic way (vv.4-32), which different groups in it could have had time and again, in order to show it that the grace of God which changes nature and society (vv.33-42), of which the Deutero-Isaiah group had once spoken (Isa.41.18; 42.15; 44.27; 50.2), was also effective in the present social crisis (vv.40-42).[16] The poet of Psalm 13 refers back to the elemental experiences of healing from sickness (vv.3-5) in order to praise the groundless, overflowing mercy shown to his sinful and insignificant community (vv.8-18), with which God's universal kingly rule was already dawning (v.19).[17] And the poet of Psalm 90 gains from this confident confession that over countless generations Yahweh has been the refuge of many Israelites (vv.1f.) a basis of trust for asking Yahweh to intervene visibly on behalf of his community, despite the experience of lasting divine anger and human insignificance.[18]

All these community psalms have a strongly reflective character. They do not just use the personal piety of the members of the community in the public interest, but also want to think it through theologically and purge it. The authors of these psalms enquire behind the piety which has long been taken for granted, and reflect on the foundations of the largely unconditional divine concern for the individual. And by inscribing the insight into the sinfulness of Israel and the justification of divine anger deriving from the history of official Yahweh religion anew on the individual's relationship with God,[19] they give the direct intervention of God the character of a miraculous unmerited act of grace for his insignificant, sinful creature. Certainly the author of Ps.103 is still aware of the massively creaturely basis for this concern of God's ('as a father has mercy on his children', v.13), but according to his insight it is an utterly inexplicable gracious divine condescension extending over a tremendous gulf (vv.11-12). In this way he wants to make clear to the community that it certainly cannot take for granted that the positive experiences of God in personal piety are possible despite the mountain of sins with which Israel is burdened; it is a great miracle (vv.8-10). So this divine mercy is no longer directed generally to everyone, but only to the real members of the community (vv.11, 13), who keep God's covenant and take God's commandments seriously (v.18). The wicked are excluded from it.[20] The theologizing of personal piety in community theology thus leads to the limitation and ethical conditioning of what was originally a universal and unconditional personal experience of God.

The theologizing of personal piety at the level of community theology very probably goes back to the individual's world of religious conceptions and practical piety. The distance between God and human beings in personal prayer also increases; the individual's own feeling of sinfulness spreads.[21] The confession of sins and the forgiveness of sins, which only played a subordinate role in earlier personal piety, now also become the regular presupposition for the saving intervention of the personal God on behalf of those commended to his protection.[22] Alongside this, under the pressure of social and religious controversies the close relationship of trust with the personal God ceases to be something which is taken for granted. That sense of being safe with God in the distress of death, which knows no alternative, now often became a deliberate decision for Yahweh differing from the options which the wicked seductively offered.[23] In accordance with this, in many prayer formulae the accusation against the enemy which had originally expressed a threat from demonic powers[24] is transformed into an accusation against the wicked.[25] We may leave aside here the question how far the sometimes massive threats which arose as a result really accorded with the facts. But they are at least an indication of the anxieties and tribulations which were caused for many members of the community by the social and religious split in it. In their practice of prayer, individuals saw themselves caught up in the social conflict and challenged to prove their piety in it.

Alongside these general changes which personal piety underwent as the early post-exilic period continued, at around the same time there were two class-specific phenomena which are even more directly connected with the social split in the community of Judah: 'theologized wisdom' as a personal theology of the upper class, and the piety of the poor which spread from the religious circles in the lower class.

5.52 'Theologized wisdom' as a personal theology of the upper class

We find the specific personal piety of that part of the upper class of Judah who showed solidarity with the poor above all in the book of Job and

Prov.1-9, which are generally classified as 'theological or theologized wisdom'.[26]

That 'theologized wisdom' represents a late stage of the Israelite wisdom tradition has been largely recognized in scholarship,[27] and in the meantime many exegetes have argued that it must be attributed to an educated upper class.[28] However, there is a lack of clarity over its sociological context. If we understand wisdom generally and theologized wisdom in particular as one of the streams of tradition which could be set alongside the official theological traditions, for example the Pentateuchal and prophetic traditions,[29] then it is impossible to see why even in its theologized form it never refers to the salvation history of Israel and the proclamation of the prophets. One is then compelled to think in terms of 'wisdom circles' who even in the post-exilic period did their theology quite separately from the tradents of the official religious tradition.[30] But that is almost unimaginable, simply because post-exilic Judah was so small.

The model of internal religious pluralism makes a solution of the problem possible. If we assign theologized wisdom to the stratum of personal piety, then it does not appear as a rival to the official religious tradition of Israel, but lies on quite a different line. The lack of any reference to the salvation history of Israel is then explained simply from the fact this history never played a major role at this level of the history of Israel.[31] And a social model becomes conceivable in which the same leading groups of laity and priests who in their professional function were involved in the shaping and establishment of official Yahweh religion depended on a pious wisdom theology in their private, everyday sphere of life. Thus the quest for some isolated wisdom circles becomes superfluous.

Such a setting is also supported by the course of the history of the wisdom tradition as a whole; however, that can only be hinted at here, without going into scholarly controversies.

Already at the earliest stage of popular wisdom, wisdom had been connected with life in families and villages. The proverb was meant to help individuals to get along in their everyday life. Nor do things change fundamentally at the next stage, that of 'court wisdom', when wisdom, starting from the royal court, is practised and taught professionally, and becomes the educational ideal of well-to-do urban circles. Certainly its sphere widened and now also related to city trade and commerce, and to a small degree also to parts of public life, for example in dealings with the court.[32] However, it remained a kind of private philosophy of life. It had the function of safeguarding the social position, reputation, prosperity, happiness and success of the members of the upper class against all possible dangers in life (Prov.14.13).

At least up to the late monarchy, the relationship with God did not play an essential role in this philosophy, and was only expressed, if at all, in connection with inexplicable limit experiences.[33] So the early stages of the wisdom tradition did not need to be an element in this history of Israelite religion.[34] If we investigate the factors which set in motion the theologizing of wisdom, we are referred in particular to the social crisis of the eighth and seventh centuries, which unmistakably revealed the problems of sheer utilitarianism intrinsic to this philosophy of the upper class. The way in which riches are made a problem and revalued in a series of proverbs is an indication of this;[35] so too is the emergence of massive social admonitions[36] which counter other sober, shrewd business maxims.[37] If we also take into account the observation that Deuteronomy, the document of the great reform movement at the end of the seventh century, was demonstrably influenced by wisdom (see above, 202), and that its social laws converge with the social concern of such proverbs, we can conjecture that it was groups of the upper class becoming aware of their social responsibility which set in motion the theological and ethical questioning behind wisdom. If these considerations are correct, then the process of the theologizing of wisdom can be understood in terms of the concern of such well-to-do and educated circles in creating for their private sphere a philosophy of life which better matched the intensified moral demands to which they saw themselves exposed in public life. Whatever the details of this process, which we find essentially completed in Prov.1-9 and the book of Job, in the light of this prehistory it is not surprising that it gave rise to a species of personal piety.[38] However, this was a markedly reflective, rationalized form of personal piety of a kind that I would prefer to term 'personal theology'.

The normal form of wisdom theology which governed the thought and action of the pious upper class can best be seen in the speeches of the friends of Job. It is characterized by a quite remarkable synthesis of the educational ideal in wisdom and personal piety, which is best expressed in Eliphaz's comforting question to Job:

Is not your piety (*yir'ā*) your confidence (*kesel*) and your hope (*tiqwā*)... the perfection (*tōm*) of your way of life?[39]

The background to this question is the confession of confidence expressed in the lament of the individual.[40] But if there it was God himself in whom the one who lamented put his trust in his distress, here it is 'piety' and 'perfect way of life'. Now it would be a gross misunderstanding of the concerns of the pious upper class to suppose that they simply wanted to replace God by their own merits. Eliphaz seeks to comfort Job by saying that through his great merits he has created an additional, certain basis on which he can ground his trust in God. He is no poor wretch who is solely dependent on the grace of God, but has something to point to. Nor is he a wicked man who has made his possessions his God (Job 8.13-15; 31.24-28) and avoided his moral and social obligations (31.5ff.). So on the basis of his high moral qualifications he can hope that God will hear his prayer (Job 8.5f.; 22.30).

So this wisdom theology had a twofold concern: on the one hand it wanted to anchor wisdom practice in the heart of the individual's relationship to God, the relationship of trust in God, and thus 'ethicize' personal piety, i.e. make it the basis for a high degree of ethical responsibility. On the other hand it wanted to give a deeper theological foundation and direction to the naive belief in retribution from earlier wisdom: the wisdom maxim that it pays to do good became the optimistic trust that God will reward true piety, and in particular unselfish action for the weak.

These two developments, the ethical permeation of personal piety and the theological permeation of the wisdom way of life, were meant to ward off two dangers which were always virulent in upper-class circles: the danger that personal piety and a rational, shrewd way of life would completely part company and the danger of 'cheap' grace which arose especially where a rich man claimed for himself the unconditional relationship of trust in God which was characteristic of traditional personal piety and misused it to provide a religious support for his merciless behaviour. The so-called wicked had then succumbed to both dangers (Job 8.13-15; 20.19f.). So we must allow that this personal wisdom theology has deep moral earnestness. However, it shows its class-specific limitations in the fact that the demonstrable services which it puts at the centre of the personal relationship with God presuppose considerable possessions and social influence.

Now the book of Job as a whole bears witness that this personal theology of the upper class underwent a serious crisis. The reason for this is not its 'hardening into dogma', as is constantly asserted, but the severity of the crisis which shook the community of Judah in the second half of the fifth century.[41] In particular the most zealous advocates of this theology, who like Job lived up to their high claims and wanted to prevent the mass impoverishment of the small farmers by the unselfish commitment of all their possessions and their social influence (Job 29.16f.; 31.16ff.), saw that their sacrifice was not paying off, that God was not rewarding them, but that on the contrary they were being overtaken by others of their class who tried to derive personal advantage from the crisis and simply denied that they had any personal religious responsibility; they were even in danger of social decline (30.1, 15). The optimistic promises of their personal theology and the bitter social experiences that they underwent became hopelessly incompatible. And as a result of this inexplicable contradiction, like Job, not a few fell victim to deep religious torment, doubted the righteousness of God and despaired over the meaning of their life.

Now it says much for the strength and flexibility of this personal theology that on the basis of it members of the pious upper class undertook broad pastoral activity among their desperate colleagues.[42] The most impressive literary expression of this is the book of Job itself.

The author of the narrative framework (Job 1.1-2.13...42.7-17*)[43] attempted to explain the suffering of the aristocrats who were now in distress by the legendary example of the rich and pious Job, who lost everything, interpreting this as a testing of their piety by God. By means of the heavenly accuser he showed them that a piety which insists too directly on just retribution of one's own merits becomes degraded to a mere transaction (Job 1.9). The desperate question about the utility of piety which was raging because of the unashamed good fortune of the wicked among them (Mal.3.14f.; Ps.73.13) should not to be put in such a form. Instead of this, by means of the exemplary conduct of Job, he presented a higher form of piety to them, which was in the position at least for a while to dispense with any calculations. Such a form of piety, he promised them, would later be rewarded even more richly by God (42.12-17). In making Job renounce wild accusations and protests as he endured the divine testing[44] and instead of this still praise God in his social decline and physical decay (1.21; 2.10), the author of the narrative framework points out a way far beyond the Israelite practice of piety which had been customary and possible hitherto.[45] The wisdom ideal of the person who remains silent and under control shifts into a new ideal of a piety of humble surrender to God, which is to be imitated by an aristocracy tried by suffering.

Demanding though this pastoral conception was, in the way in which it simply tried to push severe and incomprehensible suffering on one side in both rational and religious terms, it was asking too much of those concerned. So the author of the Job poem (Job 3-27; 29-31; 38-42.6) developed an alternative pastoral concept in which he gave a good deal of room to the lament and protest of the person afflicted and explicitly contrasted the situation with pastoral teaching. Certainly he had no illusions about the success of such a theological argument: the 'dialogue of comfort' fails, the pious doctrine of the friends simply rebounds against the severity of Job's suffering, and no intellectual solution to the problem of theodicy is achieved. But by the open debate which he allowed, the poet of Job gave his readers the possibility of working through their suffering. And here many may have found new forms of expression and a mitigation of their dull despair simply through the highly poetic stylization of their battles of faith.

The poet of Job introduced the arguments based on personal wisdom theology into the debate above all through Job's friends; this allowed him to distance himself to some degree from the issue. The friends, too, reject the question of the utility of piety as irrelevant, since it implies the impossible notion that human beings can do God some good through their merits (Job 22.3f.). Then they keep on emphasizing at length that the good fortune of the wicked will not last long and that they must soon suffer a terrible fate in keeping with their anti-social behaviour.[46] However, the author of Job shows up this crude doctrine of retribution as a theoretical postulate which could easily be rejected by Job on the basis of actual social reality (Job 21). But this theoretical postulate, in line with the notions of retirbution in wisdom, strengthened the purpose of the pious upper class not to tolerate the unjust conditions which they had to experience.

The friends in the dialogue poem also interpret the suffering of the pious as an educational measure on the part of God, by means of which he wants to lead Job further along the way of his piety.[47] Therefore it is all-important to accept the chastisement of God humbly and with a readiness to learn.[48] Only then is there a justified hope that this suffering, like any other educational measure, will have its limits and be used by God.[49] Thus an attempt was quite obviously made by the advocates of pious wisdom theology to cope with the oppressive failure of their philosophy of life with a pedagogizing of the relationship with God.

As in the narrative framework, which completely devalues the prayer of lamentation (1.22), the friends distinguish between illegitimate and legitimate prayer. The wild accusation, which, as in the case of Job, heaps upon God the whole contradictory nature of his action is compared with the behaviour of the fool who is finally brought down by his unpleasantness and zeal (Job 5.2-5).[50] It destroys true piety, a concern for God, and therefore cannot be allowed (Job 15.4). And as Job will not desist, his pious friends simply rank him with the wicked (15.5f.). For broad circles of the pious upper class, the only legitimate prayer was evidently the humble prayer which trustingly commits its cause to God,[51] a view which the author of Job himself cannot share without qualification.

Finally, the friends refer to the insight into the creaturely sinfulness and insignificance of human beings, which separates them so much from God.[52] This is meant to exclude any thought of making a claim against God. However great the merits of human beings may be, they are never enough before God to make them appear pure and just (Job 4.17). Now such an argument was in quite blatant contradiction to the otherwise optimistic educational ideal of personal wisdom theology. For if thought through consistently, it made all the ethical efforts which were its concern ultimately insignificant. The fact that those who handed it down nevertheless introduced this insight[53] shows how flexible they were when it was a matter of guarding against false conclusions which might be drawn from their ethicizing of the personal relationship with God. At all events they wanted to prevent anyone from their circles from thinking that he could claim from God a just reward for his merits, as Job then goes on to do (Job 13; 31.35-37).

The pastoral concern of the poet of Job is now made explicit in the way in which he makes his hero undergo a development, although the theological arguments from pious wisdom do not convince him. At the beginning, in ch.3, Job has the attitude of a potential suicide: he wants to throw away his life and abandon God. But then he turns to God again (7.11ff.), his will to live revives (10), and in the end he once again fights for his happiness (29.2ff.) and struggles with God for the recognition of his great merit (31). With such a description the poet of Job without doubt wanted to call his readers back from their bitterness at life and restore them to an affirmative attitude. However, he now describes this process of regaining health in a way which indicates that Job, who begins from the expectation of reward characteristic of personal wisdom theology (29.18-20), goes so far as to think that he has a legal claim to his happiness and can so to speak call God to witness to his merits (Job 13; 31.35-37). But in so doing he transcends his creatureliness and is personally shown his limitations by God in a great disputation. In the end Job submits and repents of his former complaints (42.1-6). Such an account should probably be understood simply as a critical warning that the poet of Job wanted to give to his readers: disappointed and embittered though they might be, and much as they might feel unjustly treated by God, they could not overturn the whole divine rule of the world to gain due recognition for their struggle for true piety and social justice before God. If they were to abolish injustice in society where the wicked triumph and thus put an end to the way in which they were unjustly taken advantage of, they would have to take over rule of the world in place of God (40.8-14), and they were quite incapable of that. They had to go on living with injustice.

Thus the poet of Job could not offer his disappointed colleagues any solution. The eschatological expectation of a great social revolution in which God himself would do away with the blatant injustice in society was not something that, as a member of the upper classes, he entertained. Here we can see the class-specific limitation of his wisdom theology. But against the modest horizon of personal relationships with God he was breaking new ground which was later to become an element in eschatological hopes. At three points in the dialogue (Job 14.13-17; 16.8-21; 19.23-27a) he made Job tentatively formulate a confident hope that God, who now encountered him still as an enemy, would once again turn to him after his death. Even in the realm of the dead God would long for him, his creature (14.15); even after the dissolution of his body he would see God (19.26), and then in heaven there would be a witness to intercede for him, to present his case to God (16.19,21). Then he would have the recognition by God which was now denied him.

Here we see how for the first time in the history of Israelite religion, under the pressure of the massive experiences of injustice in the second half of the Persian period, the primeval creaturely relationship of trust of individuals in their creator, coupled with a new struggle for God's righteousness, transcended the limits of death. It was first of all the members of an upper class, seeing themselves deceived over the success of their unselfish self-sacrifice for a pious personal way of life and justice in society, who in their theological permeation of personal piety found their way to the recognition that death simply could not be the end of their personal relationship with God. Once again God had to intervene in a way which would bring his love and righteousness to fulfilment.[54]

5.53 The 'piety of the poor' in lower-class circles

In all probability, the social split in the community of Judah in the second half of the fifth century, after first beginnings in the late pre-exilic period,[55] also led to the formation of a special personal piety in the impoverished lower class, to the so-called 'piety of the poor'. That is already indicated by the frequent occurrence in the Psalms of the terms *'ebyōn*, 'poor' (28 times); *'ānī/'ānāw*, 'oppressed, wretched, humble' (38 times); and *dal*, 'insignificant, poor' (5 times). However, in terms of text and content it is hard to differentiate this 'piety of the poor' clearly from the 'normal' personal piety of the post-exilic period, and therefore there is some dispute about it among scholars.

Lohfink has recently provided a useful and critical survey of research,[56] which can be referred to for details. In his view, the sweeping hypotheses from the end of the last century and the beginning of this, which seek to see the poor as a special 'party' (Graetz, Loeb, Renau, Rahlfs and in part Munch), have largely been refuted by the critical examinations of Birkeland, Kuschke and van der Ploeg; however, he does not think that the last word has been said about the striking evidence in the Psalms, and for that refers to the more recent approaches by Gerstenberger[57] and Stolz.[58]

The most important problems over which scholars argue may be briefly sketched out here. First of all there is the semantic problem whether the terms mentioned above are to be understood 'literally' in the Psalms, i.e. whether they have a social connotation. That is indisputably the case where the poor as a group are the object of the concern of the king (Ps.72.2,4,12,13), the rich (Ps.112.9) or God (Ps.113.7), but these passages have nothing to do with a special piety of the poor. Things become difficult where an individual presents himself to God as 'wretched and poor', etc. (Ps.40.18 = 70.6; 86.1; 109.22; cf. 25.16; 69.30) in order to move him to intervene. Here only the general need for help could be addressed; and as here sometimes self-designations as the 'pious' occur in parallel,[59] one might also interpret them as an expression of pious self-abasement.[60] But the evidence that in most of these texts those who lament see their distress caused by persecution and injustice (40.15 = 70.2; 69.27; 86.14; 109.16) tells against such a generalizing and spiritualizing interpretation. The religious connotation cannot be denied, but it also includes the social connotation.

The second problem is whether the terms mentioned above are designations of parties, or better groups, and if so, to which group they refer. Here we must agree with Birkeland that the self-predications of the suppliant in the singular ('I am wretched and poor') primarily denote an acute situation of distress and do not denote membership of a group.[61] But in a series of passages, the one who laments attaches himself to a group which can be called *'anāwīm*, 'wretched' (Pss.10.12; 22.27; 34.3; 69.33), or *ṣaddīqīm*, 'righteous' (Ps.140.14), and *dōr'šē yhwh*, 'those who seek Yahweh' (Ps.22.27; 69.33). Here we get the impression that we have a group designation.[62] But who is meant by this and other plural terms? In a series of passages this is certainly Israel as a whole (Ps.74.19,21; 147.6; 149.4), but this is questionable at other points (Ps.22.27[63]; 69.33) and completely ruled out where the 'poor' are victims of political enemies at home (Pss.10.9,12,17; 35.10; 140.13; 12.6; 14.6; 82.3; cf. Jer.20.13). Here what is meant is a group within Israel which at the same time understands itself as a social victim of the wicked and as the community of the pious (Pss.9.11; 70.6; 69.33f.,37; 140.14; 12.2; 75.11). In Ps.35.20 it is called the 'silent in the land'.

The third problem relates to the genre and the criteria for separating out the 'psalms of the poor'. The terms for the poor are scattered widely over the Psalter and its genres.[64] That appears first to tell against the existence of a special piety of the poor, unless one wants to resort to the sweeping verdict of Causse that the whole Psalter was composed by the poor for the poor.[65] But the present evidence indicates an accumulation of the terms mentioned above in the genres of the lament and thanksgiving of the individual,[66] eschatological hymns of praise[67] and cult-prophetic psalms.[68] By contrast, their occurrence is sporadic in the genres of the lamentation of the people (Ps.74.19, 21), the hymn (107.41; 113.7; 147.6; 149) and the song of Zion (Pss.76.10; 132.15),[69] which are specific to the main cult. This evidence could suggest that the piety of the poor was more at home in the genres of the subsidiary cult and could later move into other genres as it was adapted by the community as a whole, and influenced its official theology. The assumption of such a subsequent expansion could also explain how piety specific to a particular group could find a place in the Psalter.

In view of this somewhat diffuse evidence, in the reconstruction of the piety of the religious circles in the lower class it is worth beginning from those texts which 1. belong in the genres of the subsidiary cult; 2. have singular or plural group designations (poor, righteous, etc.); 3. make reference to a social conflict; and 4. have elements of eschatological prophecy.[70] So I begin from the following texts: Pss.9/10; 35; 69; 70; 109; 140 and the prophetic liturgies Pss.12; 14; 75; 82.[71]

If the pious upper class already had to cope theologically with the problem of falling behind aristocratic colleagues who demonstrated no solidarity, the lower class which had been driven into poverty by the latter saw itself confronted with even greater attacks on its faith. It found itself exposed to the brutal, merciless and persistent attack of a group (Ps.10.2-11; 12.2-5; 109.2-5, 12, 16) which, although made up of influential and 'loyal' members of the community, did not care what God would say (Ps.10.4,11,13; 14.1,4) and cynically displayed its self-assurance (10.6; 75.5). The question of the lower class was: how could Yahweh tolerate this blasphemy (10.13)? Must he not finally intervene on their behalf and against the wicked for the sake of his divinity (109.20f.)?

Thus in lower-class circles, too, the question of God's righteousness arose, but from quite a different perspective from that of the pious upper-class group. Their members had no merits to which they could refer;[72] they had only their wretched and oppressed existence, which they therefore never tired of presenting to God in order to touch him.[73] They had no claim to deliverance except the fact that Yahweh, the God of liberation, would be denying himself if in the long term he kept on overlooking the crying of the poor, so time and again they anticipated his ultimate mercy on the oppressed in eschatological songs of praise.[74] And for them a settlement with the wicked was not just a theoretical but a deeply existential problem. The wicked had to be annihilated, so that they could be freed and again be able to rejoice in God.[75]

On the last two points the piety of these groups also differed clearly from 'normal' personal piety. God's concern for the poor no longer derived simply from a bond between the personal creator and his creature, but from the centuries of the old official historical experience of Yahweh, that he frees the oppressed. And deliverance was no longer simply a matter for the merciful God; God had to use his whole power as judge and king of the world (Pss.9.8f.; 10.16; 75.3; 82.1) if the self-glorifying violence of the wicked was to be broken. Because the deliverance of the impoverished lower class had a political dimension, the lower-class circles had to refer back to elements of official Yahweh religion in order to give appropriate religious expression to their expectations. Thus the piety of the poor, too, played a part in the general theologizing of personal piety.

There is a whole series of indications that the lower-class religious circles had their own worship apart from the temple cult, whether in their homes or in synagogues. This worship evidently in part attached itself to the ceremonies of the subsidiary cult: thus in Pss.9/10 we find the thanksgiving of an individual (vv.2,5,14f.) which serves as the basis for the assurance of salvation (vv.6,10,11,16f.,18-20; 10.16-18) in the lamentation ceremony of a group of the poor (10.7-15). And Pss.35; 69; 109; 140 represent individual lamentations in which individuals and the group assure one another of salvation despite all the oppression (35.9f.; 70.5; 69.7,33-37; 109.30f.). Through the deliverance of the individual member, all Yahweh's followers are to have grounds for rejoicing (35.27f.), and on the basis of the theological certainty of the group that Yahweh will intervene for its rights, the individual is assured of being heard (140.13). The general convergence of personal piety and community theology typical of the post-exilic period took on an even more intensive reciprocal form and a clear pastoral function in the religious group of the lower class.

Alongside this, in these groups there was very probably also a quite specific form of liturgical assurance of salvation: a cult-prophetic proclamation of salvation and judgment.[76] For example, Ps.12 begins with a cry for help and a descriptive lament about the desolate social situation of the group (vv.2-3) which strongly recalls Isa.57.1f.[77] The pious and faithful are perishing, while the wicked (cf.v.9) demonstrate their arrogance and power with lying and deception (v.5). Therefore the group expresses to Yahweh its desire for the final extermination (vv.4f.) of the wicked with their arrogant talk, which does it violence (v.6a). Thereupon a single voice from the group, whether that of a regular cultic prophet or a prophetically gifted member of the community, utters a word of God to the effect that 'because the poor are despoiled, because the needy groan', Yahweh will really intervene to bring salvation to the victims of the wicked (v.6). After this comforting promise, the group as a whole[78] expresses its confidence in Yahweh's word and protection, even if the wicked still triumph in the present (vv.7-9). Similar words of God which anticipate the liberation of the poor and judgment upon the wicked also occur in Pss.14.5f.;[79] 75.3-9; 82.1-7. They are all connected with the liturgy[80] and can all be understood as a dramatic form of the assurance of salvation which was practised in the worship of the religious circle in the lower class.

We can only conjecture the place and time of such 'community worship'. Occasional polemic against sacrifices (Pss.40.7-9; 69.32) could indicate that it did not take place in the Jerusalem temple; the connections with private ceremonies of lamentation and thanksgiving suggest more of a casual occasion; the liturgical 'prophetic' proclamation could also have been a constant. These were probably pure liturgies of the word which will have taken place in the homes or meeting places of the religious groups from the lower class.[81]

If it was the most important function of the personal theology of the pious upper class to salvage the ethical responsibility of the group from all disappointments in the social crisis, the most important task of the piety of the poor which was developed and practised in the lower-class communities was to restore dignity and hope to the oppressed victims of the social crisis.

This purpose was served, first, by the petitions and wishes directed against their oppressors,[82] which in their uncompromising harshness and sometimes wild fantasies of vengeance[83] nowadays terrify many delicate bourgeois Christian spirits. Here the dull fury and desperate sense of impotence among those who had been robbed of their rights and trampled on made itself felt; here their concerted will to resist, their refusal to be content with their hopeless situation, found words to express itself.

The purpose was served, secondly, by their keen eschatological expectations of a great divine judgment[84] which would punish the wicked rich and bring justice to the poor (9.20; 12.6; 14.5). In part they imagined this as a universal judgment which would affect not only the wicked but also the nations or the whole earth (Pss.9.8f.,20; 82.8); this universalization of the perspectives of judgment, which is particularly striking in Pss.9f.,[85] is to be explained from the fact that for the lower-class circles the political dependence of Judah on the Persians and their exploitation by the upper-class collaborators were closely connected (cf. Isa.56.9ff.).[86] But in part they also envisaged an individual judgment in which the wicked would be blotted out of the Book of Life (Ps.69.29; cf. Mal.3.16).[87] In any case they hoped that with such a judgment Yahweh would totally reverse the present political and social conditions of domination (Ps.75.8), banish the hated occupiers from Judah (Ps.10.16), break the power of those who were exploiting them (75.11) and give the land as a heritage solely to them and their descendants (69.37). Yahweh would overthrow all the divine powers which now supported the oppression of the poor (Ps.82.2-7) and establish his kingly rule on earth (10.16). Then the poor and oppressed would finally secure their rights and there would be an end to all violent human rule on earth (10.18). By incorporating the whole of this horizon of eschatological expectation on which they were working in their exegesis of the prophets into their personal piety, the religious circles in the lower class were creating the possibility of holding fast to their personal God even in their extreme, chronic distress. The unjust social conditions which largely excluded them from the personal protection and blessing of God would not last; Yahweh himself would reverse them, and again become a 'citadel for the oppressed' (Ps.9.10), in accord with the age-old experiences of personal piety.[88]

Thirdly, the self-understanding of the religious circles in the lower class, that precisely because of their wretchedness they were the ones who were really pious, served to assert and stabilize their human dignity. This function explains why the social terms for 'poor' took on a religious undertone in the piety of the poor.[89] What is meant here is not a religious transfiguration of poverty,[90] but religious compensation for a social lack. The groups which thought the wretched situation of their class through theologically were not content with being forced to the margin of society, despised, forgotten and at best noticed as the recipients of alms. No, their impoverishment was not a sign that they had been abandoned and despised by God,[91] as the current theological view had it. Rather, Yahweh, the God of liberation, was particularly close to them, the poor (Ps.35.10; 140.13), and although they did not have many sacrifices and offerings to contribute to the praise of Yahweh since they could only lay their miserable existence at Yahweh's feet[92] in order to expect deliverance and a future from him (Ps.10.14), they were the real pious (*ḥᵃsīdīm*;[93] *ṣaddīqīm*;[94] *'ᵉmūnīm*[95]).

As they understood things, they were not on the periphery of the community but formed its core; they claimed – above all over against the wicked – to be the real people of God (Ps.14.4). That gave them the power to assert themselves within the community of Judah despite their social marginalization, indeed even to gain influence over the community as a whole with their piety of the poor.[96] The fact that it was possible in the religion of Israel for the socially oppressed groups to make their personal piety the means of their liberating self-assertion once again shows in miniature what an impulse towards liberation it contained.

Moreover in the later history of Israelite religion the piety of the poor constantly helped religious outsider groups to formulate their will to resist against the dominant social circles and their official theology.[97]

5.6 The Samaritans: a political and cultic split

A.Alt, 'Die Rolle Samarias bei der Entstehung des Judentums' (1934), *Kleine Schriften* II, 316-37; id., 'Zur Geschichte der Grenze zwischen Judäa und Samaria' (1935), ibid., 346-63; A.Büchler, 'La Relation de Josèphe concernant Alexandre le Grand', *REJ* 36, 1988, 126; R.J.Coggins, *Samaritans and Jews. The Origins of Samaritanism Reconsidered*, 1975; F.M.Cross, 'Aspects of Samaritan and Jewish History in Late Persian and Hellenistic times', *HTR* 59, 1966, 201-11; id., 'Papyri of the Fourth Century BC from Daliyeh', in D.N.Friedman and J.C.Greenfield, *New Directions in Biblical Archaeology*, 1969, 41-62; A.D.Crown, 'The Samaritan Diaspora', in id., *The Samaritans*, 1989, 195-217; F.Dexinger, 'Limits of Tolerance in Judaism. The Samaritan Example', in E.P.Sanders (ed.), *Jewish and Christian Self-Definition*, II, 1982, 88-114; R.Egger, *Josephus Flavius und die Samaritaner*, NTOA 4, 1986; A.H.J.Gunneweg, *Esra*, KAT XIX, 1, 1985; H.G. Kippenberg, *Garizim und Synagoge. Traditionsgeschichtliche Untersuchungen zur Samaritanischen Religion der aramäischen Periode*, RGVV 30, 1971; Y.Magen, 'A Fortified Town of the Hellenistic Period on Mount Gerizim' (in Hebrew), *Qad.* 19, 1986, 91-101; J.A.Montgomery, *The Samaritans. The Earliest Jewish Sect. Their History, Theology, and Literature*, 1907; M.Mor, 'Samaritan History. 1. The Hellenistic and Hasmonean Period', in A.D.Crown (ed.), *The Samaritans*, 1989, 135-77; J.D.Purvis, *The Samaritan Pentateuch and the Origin of the Samaritan Sect*, HSM 2, 1968; H.H.Rowley, 'Sanballat and the Samaritan Temple' (1955f.), in id., *Man and His God*, 1963, 246-76; id., 'The Samaritan Schism in Legend and History', in B.W.Anderson et al. (ed.), *Israel's Prophetic Heritage. FS J.Muilenburg*, 1962, 208-22; S.Talmon, 'Biblische Überlieferungen zur Frühgeschichte der Samaritaner' (1973), in id., *Gesellschaft und Literatur in der Hebräischen Bibel, Gesammelte Aufsätze* I, 1988, 132-51; G.E.Wright, *Shechem. The Biography of a Biblical City*, 1965; E.Würthwein, *Die Bücher der Könige. 1 Kön 17 – 2 Kön 25*, ATD 11.2, 1984.

The so-called 'Samaritan schism' is usually regarded as the 'classical' example of the religious split in post-exilic Israel.[1] This is probably above all connected with the fact that – leaving aside Christianity – the split caused by the Samaritans was the only split in the ancient history of the religion of Israel which is still manifest in the present. However – from the perspective of the history of religion – it was by no means an extraordinary phenomenon in the Old Testament period as a whole, and played more of a subordinate role in the development of religious history. Indeed it has to be said that the theological controversy which ultimately led to the split has left so few clear traces in the Old Testament writings[2] that to the present day scholars have found its chronological, social and religious setting strikingly diffuse.

5.61 *The sources and the chronological framework*

One discrepancy in present scholarship is striking: whereas a majority particularly of exegetical scholars begin as a matter of course from a conflict between Jews and Samaritans from the time of the first great waves of returns from the exile (520 BCE) and interpret texts like II Kings 17.24-41; Ezra 4.1-5.7ff. on this basis,[3] in particular more recent scholars who are attempting to make a historical reconstruction of the specific history of the Samaritans are increasingly firmly denying that these texts have anything to do with the later religious community of this name and are dating its constitution and separation later and later: at the earliest with the building of the sanctuary on Gerizim in the late Persian or early Hellenistic period (c.330),[4] and more likely in the second century BCE in connection with the destruction of the temple on Gerizim by John Hyrcanus (128),[5] or even only in the Christian period.[6]

If we ask in amazement how such a discrepancy is possible, then – alongside some difficulties over subject matter, which are caused by the lack of sources – we come up against the different perspectives adopted by scholars in evaluating the sources: if the texts mentioned above are interpreted in terms of their predominantly pro-Judahite tendency, then for example one can see in the characterization of the inhabitants of Samaria as alien syncretists (II Kings 17.24-4a) a polemically exaggerated but basically accurate description of the Samaritans, who had not shared in the religious purging undergone by the groups in the exile but persisted in the 'pre-exilic mode of faith'.[7] However, for those who look at the Samaritans in terms of their later development and reflect that they took over the Torah with its utterly monotheistic focus, understood themselves later as painstaking 'guardians of the law',[8] and did not give the least indication that syncretism was a particular danger for them,[9] a historical derivation of II Kings 17.24ff. becomes quite meaningless.[10] Certainly in the Christian period the characterization of II Kings 17.24ff. was applied by Josephus and then by the rabbis to the Samaritans, as a result of which the rabbis could describe them in a more or less derogatory way, following v.24, as Cuthites,[11] but this already presupposed final exclusion from the Israelite people and comes at the end rather than the beginning of the development.[12] But if the reference of the texts which are to be taken into account for an early theological controversy is no longer obviously to the Samaritans, then what they say must once again be examined carefully.

The wording of the polemical description in II Kings 17.24-41 of conditions in what was formerly the northern kingdom after its conquest by the Assyrians in 722 does not refer to the Samaritans. The term *haššōmᵉrīm*, 'the Samarians' (v.29), to which an appeal is frequently made,[13] denotes the earlier Israelite population which in the view of the Deuteronomists (vv.6, 23) was deported in its entirety to Assyria.[14] Their sanctuaries, which from the perspective of Jerusalem were illegitimate ('houses on the high places', vv.9,32), especially Bethel (v.28), were again used by the groups of people newly settled by the king of Assyria from Babylon, Cuthah, Avva, Hamath and Sepharvaim, who worshipped their national gods in them but at the same time – instructed about a legendary plague of lions by a priest of Yahweh who had been ordered back – worshipped Yahweh the God of the land (vv.30-33). So the first part of the text (vv.24-34a) is clearly about the foreign upper class of the city, and not about Israelites and their syncretism, especially in Bethel, nor about Shechem and Gerizim. Even in terms of subject-matter, those who later became the Samaritans cannot be meant here.[15]

But to what else can the polemic of the text be related? Of course the answer depends on its dating. Now the author certainly wants to depict religious developments which in his view took place after the time of the Assyrians (seventh century); however, as the formulation in v.34a, 'until that day', shows, he is indicating that in his view these still determine the situation of the former northern kingdom up to his own day. If we assume that the text is part of DtrG, this is most probably well on into the exile (c. 560 BCE). Authors who want to relate the text to the controversy with the 'Samaritans' or their predecessors are forced to regard it as an insertion into DtrG. They want to regard it as a theological legitimation of the exclusion of the 'Samaritans' from the rebuilding of the temple (520-15) which Ezra 4.1-5; Hag.2.10-14 indicate.[16] In that case this would in fact be a reference to a first theological break. But the references in this text to II Kings 17 are by no means as narrow as is often assumed.[17] There is no trace in II Kings 17.24-34a of the problem of the people of Samaria taking part in the cult in Jerusalem; rather, the issue is that of separation from them and their cults. So I would understand the text as a still-exilic dispute of the DtrG group fixated on Jerusalem with the official cult of Samaria. Their own readership in Judah is to be urgently warned against taking part in the Yahweh cult of Bethel, which had evidently been re-established during the exile after the destruction of the sanctuary by Josiah.[18] Even if the cult was no longer practised in Jerusalem, for people of Judah loyal to Yahweh the Bethel cult could not be a way out: in the view of the Deuteronomists it was a syncretistic cult of alien peoples along the line of the 'sin of Jeroboam'.[19]

Now II Kings 17.24ff. is not all of a piece. As the resumption of v.34a in v.40 shows, 17.34b-40 is a clear addition.[20] In this section people from Samaria are accused of not worshipping Yahweh at all and not keeping the commandments which Yahweh gave to the 'sons of Jacob' when he made a covenant with them and led them up out of Egypt (vv.34b-36). They are called on not to forget these saving acts and commandments, and to worship Yahweh alone and no other gods. Then he would deliver them out of the hand of their enemies (v.37-39). Those reminded here of the special salvation history of Israel can only be Israelites who remained behind in the land, although the change of subject is not marked clearly.[21] They are called on to abandon the syncretism of the alien upper class, which in practice means that they are invited to come to the Yahweh cult in Jerusalem. Certainly the accusation is made in v.40 that they did not accept this invitation,[22] but this addition proves to be part of a new wooing of the Israelite part of the mixed population of Samaria, which no longer existed in the original Deuteronomistic polemic aimed at segregation (vv.6, 23f.). This altered perspective in fact indicates a new situation of the early post-exilic period. After the Jerusalem temple had been rebuilt, it was evidently in the interest of leading circles of the community of Judah to win over as many descendants of the former population of the northern kingdom to it. This is in fact an event which is important for the prehistory of the Samaritans.

Now such an exegesis of II Kings 17.24ff. does not support but relativizes the report of the exclusion of the people of Samaria from the rebuilding of the temple (Ezra 4.1-5). If this is not completely a Chronistic construction which is meant to give an explanation of the chronological gap between the edict of Cyrus (538) and the beginning of the rebuilding (520), and is projecting forward the manifest split at the end of the fourth century, then the 'enemies of Judah and Benjamin' primarily once again mean the foreign upper class (4.1f.).[23] We cannot completely rule out their having had an interest in at least becoming involved in the establishment of a new cult place in their province. But even if this should have been the case, here we have a controversy over cult politics, and even the Chronistic author does not offer theological reasons for the rejection of participation, but has the people of Judah referring to the edict of Cyrus (v.3).

Moreover the earlier examples which the Chronicler cites as proof of the constant enmity of the people of Samaria (Ezra 4.6, 7-22) are all of a political kind: as is well known, they are not about the temple at all but about the building of the wall. The same goes for Sanballat's attempts at sabotage to which Nehemiah was exposed (Neh.2.10,19; 3.33; 4.1; 6.2,5,12,14). So at all these points we have an expression of the Samarian concern to safeguard its influence over the consolidation of community of Judah and to do as much as possible to prevent the establishment of an independent province within the Samarian sphere of interest. There is therefore much to be said for Alt's thesis that the starting point of the Samaritan schism was a political conflict.[24]

Now the note in Neh.13.28 adds yet a further element. A son of the high priest Jehoiada, who had married a daughter of Sanballat, governor of Samaria, was expelled from the community of Judah by Nehemiah. Of course this was first of all a political measure aimed at preventing the governor of Samaria from having any influence on the Jerusalem cult. But it is also an indication of a fundamental religious conflict aimed, like the prohibition of mixed marriages, at safeguarding the ethnic basis of the community. Was it to be interpreted widely, as the high-priestly family probably thought, and not applied to adherents of Yahweh from Samaria, of which Sanballat was one,[25] or was it to be interpreted very narrowly so as to exclude marriages with all those who could not clearly prove their Judahite identity?[26] For Nehemiah Sanballat was clearly a foreigner (*n^{e}kar*, 13.30). Thus problems of the definition of Israelite identity in an ethnically mixed milieu further intensified the political conflicts.

There is no biblical evidence for the first step in the Samaritan schism, as the tradition of the history of Judah breaks off at the beginning of the fifth century. We are dependent on Josephus's account to fill this gap (*Antt.* XI, 302-47). According to Josephus it was again a disputed 'mixed marriage' which set things moving:

In the time of Darius III (338-331) the governor of Samaria, Sanballat, is said to have married his daughter Nikaso to Manasseh, the brother of the high priest Jaddua (302f.); he had been given the choice by the 'elders of Judah' of either divorcing her or giving up the priestly office so as not to set a bad example for those to come (306-308). When Manasseh posed his dilemma to his father-in-law, the latter promised him that he would seek permission from Darius to build a temple on Mount Gerizim in which he could function as high priest; he would then take over Sanballat's governorship after the latter's death. Thereupon Manasseh went over to Sanballat, and 'many priests and Israelites who were entangled in such marriages' went over to him and were endowed by Sanballat with gold, land and homes (310-312). The plan with Darius did not work out, because Darius was unexpectedly defeated at Issus by the Macedonians, but when Alexander invaded Syria and laid siege to Tyre, Sanballat seized his opportunity, submitted to Alexander as a loyal vassal, offered him 8,000 soldiers, and asked permission for his son-in-law to build the temple (313, 317a + 320b-322). Here he referred both to the wish of many of his fellow-countrymen (*homoethneis*) to have a temple in his sphere of rule and also to the political advantage of 'dividing the power of the Jews' (322-323). Thereupon Alexander gave his assent, and Sanballat used all his forces to complete the building of the temple as quickly as possible and install Manasseh as high priest (324); he died nine months later (325a).[27]

Josephus's account has often been doubted.[28] But at least the most important information is to some extent confirmed externally: the existence of a temple on Gerizim as a centre of the Samaritans is presupposed in II Macc.6.2 for the beginning of the second century and is also attested in inscriptions.[29] The excavations which Magen has recently carried out on Gerizim – after initial frustration[30] – have now also provided archaeological evidence of a great Hellenistic temple at the highest point of the mountain.[31] The evidence that the city of Shechem (Tell Balata), which was abandoned between 480 and 330, was again fortified at the end of the fourth century, and reached a new heyday around 300, points to the time of Alexander.[32]

And since the seal impressions and papyri from *wadi ed-Daliyeh* have shown that in addition to Sanballat in the time of Nehemiah there was a second governor of the same name in the early fourth century and that the office was inherited within the family, the attestation of a further governor named Sanballat at the time of Alexander has ceased to be a curiosity.[33]

Certainly some inconsistencies remain in Josephus' account,[34] which probably indicate that he used several sources, and we can ask whether a period of only nine months for the building of the temple is realistic. Should we not think in terms of forerunners of the sanctuary as early as the end of the Persian period, and attribute the prominent role played by Alexander to the interest of the later Samaritans in creating just as famous an ancestor for their temple as the Persian king Cyrus, who could be referred to in connection with the Jerusalem temple?[35] But good reasons can be given for the haste, and the legitimation by Alexander could also mark a real shift from Persian to Macedonian religious policy.[36] Certainly Josephus describes the event too much from a personal, family perspective, in keeping with the tastes of his time; but he at least indicates that behind this there was more than the generous fancy of a loving father and the ambition of his priestly son-in-law: according to his account, too, the founding of the temple was a religious and cult-political decision in which the state interests of the governor in the cultic consolidation of his province and the interests of groups in Samaria loyal to Yahweh in having a cult centre of their own that was above suspicion coincided with the interests of influential priests and laity in Jerusalem (cf. especially *Antt.* XI, 312, 322). From all that we know of the formation of the community in Judah,[37] too, such a coalition of interests is quite credible, even if we have no sources[38] to make clear the motivation of those concerned.

The cultic split and development of the Samarian community around Gerizim was still far from being a final schism. While the Chronistic work from the third century on the one hand already presupposes a certain detachment from the rivals in Samaria with its limitation of the 'true' salvation history to the southern kingdom, the Babylonian Gola and the community of Judah, passing over the history of the North almost completely, on the other hand it is still full of appeals to the brethren in the North aimed at winning over as many of them as possible to the Jerusalem sanctuary.[39] In the confusions of the Syrian wars at the end of the third century the two communities probably took different political lines,[40] but both partly yielded to the pressure of Hellenization and then had to suffer equally under the rabid religious policy of Antiochus IV Epiphanes (II Macc.5.23; 6.2). More serious differences probably emerged only when the Zadokide priesthood was displaced from high-priestly office by the Hasmonaeans (152 BCE); this must have made the new priesthood seem illegitimate to the cult community in Samaria, which had a legitimate Zadokide line. But in the end it was probably only John Hyrcanus's violent

Judaizing policy, which robbed the Samarian community of its cultic and political centre by the destruction of the temples of Gerizim (128 BCE) and Shechem (107 BCE), that led to the rival model to the community of Judah in Samaria becoming the religious community of the Samaritans.[41] The independent religious history of the Samaritans in the strict sense thus begins outside the period of time covered by the writings of the Old Testament.

5.62 The sociological and historical context

If we attempt to fit the sources indicated above into the reconstruction of the history of Israelite religion so far, we can develop the following scenario. Whereas evidently still during the exile the official cult of Yahweh which had continued without interruption on the territory of the former northern kingdom had a considerable attraction for the population of Judah, even though it was affected by the syncretisms of an alien upper class, so that the leading group of Deuteronomists felt led to issue sharp polemic (II Kings 17.24-34a), the situation changed fundamentally when under the leadership of those who returned from exile the people of Judah rebuilt the Jerusalem temple. Now it was those faithful to Yahweh in the Israelite lower classes of the province of Samaria who were attracted by the Jerusalem temple (II Kings 17.34b-40). And we will probably not go wrong in supposing that many of them, at least from the regions bordering on the North, streamed to Jerusalem as pilgrims on the great annual festivals in order to take part in the official cult there (cf. Ezra 6.21).

That was no problem as long as the territory of Judah was still part of the province of Samaria and its political structures had not been firmly fixed. Only once did the striving of the South for political independence provoke the resistance of the leading class in Samaria (Ezra 4.6, 7-22; Neh.4-6), and it will hardly have had a detrimental effect on the intellectual and cultic connection of the adherents of Yahweh from the North with Jerusalem. The problems only began when the political structures of the community of Judah hardened and finally led to the establishment of an independent province of Judah.[42]

In the structure and organization of their community, those who returned to Judah had had considerable recourse to tribal and ethnic structures to protect it from the threat of being swamped. All members had to prove that they belonged to 'Judah and Benjamin', and had to be registered in one of its *bēt 'ābōt*.[43] This system succeeded in achieving the social and political integration of the people of Judah who had remained in the land with the majority of the population who were in fact living around Jerusalem, but it left out the adherents of Yahweh of northern origin. They could take part in the Jerusalem cult, were to make offerings to it and to live in accordance with the Torah which had been laid down by the key bodies in the community, but they had no rights whatsoever in shaping it. The clan organizational structure excluded them from the self-administrative bodies. They had no more rights than Diaspora Jews, who lived as guests in Jerusalem a few times in their lives. This legal discrimination againt the adherents of Yahweh in Samaria is probably an essential factor in the later cultic split.

Now in the tribally organized social structure there was only one way of gaining political and cultic influence from outside: to marry into a recognized family of Judah. And this way was evidently taken often, not only by aristocrats like Tobias (Neh.6.16-18; 13.4) and Sanballat (13.28; cf. *Antt.*XI, 302f.), who married straight into the family of the high priest, but also by the less influential (*Antt.* XI, 312). And it was precisely at this point that a theological dispute now broke out within the community of Judah: were such marriages with non-Judahite Israelite adherents of Yahweh permissible, or were they illegitimate mixed marriages like those with foreigners (Neh.13.28; *Antt.* XI, 306-9)? We can understand the vigour with which this question was fought over only if we note that the issue here was the political and theological definition of the community. Was it defined primarily in theological terms, and did it therefore have to allow the influence of all the adherents of Yahweh in the former people of Israel, or was it primarily political, and did it have to defend the independence of Judah? The fact that there are accounts of marriages in particular between the high-priestly families and adherents of Yahweh in Samaria (Neh.13.28; *Antt.* XI, 306-9) is not to be regarded as aristocratic laxity but as a serious theological option for a greater Israelite community which included all the Yahweh worshippers of the region. By contrast, the politician Nehemiah fought for a solution limited to Judah; he saw the community exposed by such openness to uncontrollable external influences which endangered its existence. The fact that this political calculation aimed at self-assertion prevailed against wider-ranging solutions which would have met the theological claim better is a further reason why the Samarian adherents of Yahweh founded their own community at the end of the century.

Under Nehemiah, the narrow ethnic demarcation of the community of Judah consistently issued in the establishment of a province of Judah independent of Samaria. This made the situation of the Samarian adherents of Yahweh really precarious; they no longer had a cultic centre of their own within the frontiers of their province.[44] The situation was all the more intolerable since in the meantime the adherents of Yahweh – strengthened by the restoration of Judah – had become more than marginal groups in the Samarian community; if even the family of the governor Sanballat, which had held office without interruption from the end of the fifth century to the end of the Persian period, was part of them or stood close to them, then they must have found support among the ruling class of Samaria. The question of a regular official Yahweh cult for its increased following in the province of Samaria thus became a state matter.

It seems as though Sanballat I at the end of the fifth century and Sanballat III in the second half of the fourth century had attempted to provide an amicable solution to the problem in conjunction with those priestly circles in Jerusalem whose attitude was more open by marrying their daughters to members of the high-priestly family. In this way the governor of Samaria had gained official influence over the Jerusalem cult and Jerusalem had been able to function as a central cult place for the two provinces. But both times the attempt failed; priests who were ready for co-operation were driven out of office (Neh.13.28; *Antt.* XI, 309ff.). Only after the failure of these attempts did Sanballat III finally conclude that he should give the Yahweh worshippers in his province a cult centre of their own (Antt.XI, 310ff.).

We may ask why Sanballat I had not drawn this consequence immediately after the expulsion of his son-in-law by Nehemiah. Here we must first of all probably assume that the leaders of the community of Judah had put up bitter resistance to the establishment of a rival sanctuary to Jerusalem and had used all their contacts with the Persian imperial government to stop the governor of Samaria's plan. Certainly the Persians clearly did not completely share the rigorous standpoint of the people of Judah that in accordance with Josiah's reform of the cult there should be only one temple of Yahweh, as is attested by their assent to the rebuilding of the Elephantine sanctuary.[45] But to allow a rival sanctuary close by and thus put at risk the loyalty of their subjects in Judah could have destabilized the endangered western flank of their empire, and that was certainly not in their interests.[46]

Secondly, we may probably suppose that the Samarian worship of Yahweh which, as their adoption of the Pentateuch shows, fully endorsed the renewal that Yahweh religion had undergone in the post-exilic period, had considerable theological problems in legitimating the building of a separate cult centre. Not only the power of the facts but also the whole Zion theology, almost all the prophetic writings and the concentrated Deuteronomic and Deuteronomistic tradition were against this. After all, the Deuteronomistic history had clearly attached to the Jerusalem temple the sanctuary which according to Deuteronomy Yahweh was to choose (I Kings 8.16).[47]

Now in this theological dilemma the canonization of the Pentateuch came to the help of the Samarians. For the separation of this from the Deuteronomistic history at Joshua 1 and the elevation of only the section from Genesis to Deuteronomy as the foundation history of all those loyal to Yahweh had not decided in a theologically binding way the question of which sanctuary Yahweh had chosen. In accordance with the fiction of the age-old Torah of Moses, the name of Jerusalem had not been mentioned in Deuteronomy,[48] and indeed did not appear in the Pentateuch at all.[49]

Instead, there was explicit mention of cultic actions of Moses on Ebal (Deut.27.4)[50] and Gerizim (27.11f.), and the patriarchs had already founded holy places in Bethel (Gen.28.10-20) and Shechem (12.6; 33.18ff.; 35.4). That means that with just as much, if not more, justification, one could read out of the newly-created foundation document of Yahweh religion which had been given Persian authority that the sanctuary chosen by God had to lie in the province of Samaria. And as the old cult centre of Bethel had been made unclean by a syncretistic cult, and moreover in the meantime had come to be part of the province of Judah, a new foundation on Gerizim was the only possibility.

These or similar considerations may have long been in the minds of the population of Samaria who were loyal to Yahweh, and it needed only an occasion to put them into practice. This occasion was presented by the international situation, when the victorious progress of Alexander from 334 announced a new constellation of power in the Near East and suggested to the Samaritans that the Persians could be persuaded to make cultic concessions (*Antt.* XI, 311, 135f.), and at home when the council of elders in Judah once again scuppered an attempt at agreement between Sanballat III on the one hand and the high priest and part of the nobility of Judah on the other (*Antt.*XI, 302-9). Now the governor of Samaria seized the chance of winning over the duped brother of the high priest and with him a member of the legitimate Zadokide priesthood to the plan for a Samarian cult centre (310f.). And by generous material support he suceeded in wooing over a large group of priests and laity who – as their marriages with Israelite women from Samaria showed – had long since fallen out with the majority over the latter's attempts at narrow demarcation. They were to help him to build around Shechem a partially autonomous community of the kind that had long existed in the province of Judah (312).[51] We may conjecture that these renegades from Judah in no way saw themselves as apostates;[52] they did not deny the Deuteronomic law of centralization (Deut.12) but only disputed that a perpetual political claim to a monopoly of the cult by Jerusalem could be derived from it. They probably thought that they were interpreting the spirit of this law in keeping with the time if they helped their Samarian brothers to build in their province a cultic and political centre which would made it possible for them to safeguard a pure Yahweh cult and a life in accordance with the Torah in a mixed religious environment.

When the Persian empire collapsed with unexpected speed, the wise tactician Sanballat III seized his opportunity: he voluntarily submitted to his new overlord, Alexander, put troops at his disposal for his campaign of conquest, and negotiated with him for his approval for the building of the temple on Gerizim (*Antt.* XI, 321f.), Alexander not yet being bound by any promises to the Jews. This was also in the best Macedonian interests, since it assured Alexander of the loyalty of a majority of the population of

Samaria and drove a wedge into the Jewish religious group which limited the influence of the people of Judah.

However, this splitting of the official Yahweh cult into two rival political centres by no means amounted to a final break. Among the population of Samaria and Judah who were loyal to Yahweh, whether in Palestine or in the Diaspora, for two hundred years it was a quite open question from which of the two sanctuaries one took one's guidelines, to which one paid one's temple taxes and other offerings, and in which cult one participated.[53] In other respects people lived in close proximity,[54] read the same holy scripture and observed the same Torah. It was only the restitution of the state of Judaea under the Hasmonaean kings which gave the monopolistic religious and cultic claim of Jerusalem the intolerance which abruptly cut off a quite possible development of Judah into a network of several cultic and local political centres.[55] A decentralization of the offical Yahweh cult was possible only at the level of synagogue worship and synagogue communities.

6. A Prospect on the History of Religion in the Hellenistic Period

The Hellenistic era (332-64 BCE) forms yet another separate division within the long post-exilic period. The change of supremacy from the Persians to the Greeks not only brought a whole series of political, economic and social changes for post-exilic Israel, but also introduced a fundamental new cultural orientation: Israel became part of the Hellenistic world which brought together East and West. To this extent this era needs separate treatment.

However, in terms of religion the Hellenistic period is a transitional period. During it on the one hand we have a continuation of developments which had already begun in the Persian period, like the dialectic between splintering and forming a consensus which is manifest, for example, in the formation of apocalyptic and the canonization of the historical and prophetic books. On the other hand there are new developments like the rise of a Hellenistic Diaspora Judaism which is very aware of itself or the attempt at a restoration of the state and, following it, the formation of new opposition groups of scribes and those with eschatological orientations (Pharisees, Qumran sect), which ushered in the religious history of Judaism and Christianity.

A history of Israelite religion which has taken on the task of covering the period of the writings of the Old Testament must discuss this era to the extent that Old Testament developments to some degree come to a conclusion in it. However, it would be too much to ask that all the developments which were to become important in the subsequent period should be treated in detail. For these the reader is referred to accounts of Judaism and histories of the New Testament period and its religion.

6.1 The sociological developments

E.Bickermann, *Der Gott der Makkabäer*, 1937; L.H.Feldman, 'How Much Hellenism in Jewish Palestine?', *HUCA* 57, 1986, 83-111; J.Goldstein, 'Jewish Acceptance and Rejection of Hellenism', in E.P.Sanders and A.I.Baumgarten, *Jewish and Christian Self-Definition* II, 1981, 64-87, 318-26; A.H.J.Gunneweg, *Geschichte Israels bis Bar Kochba*, TW 2, ⁶1989; M.Hengel, *Judaism and Hellenism*, 1974; J.Kampen, *The Hasideans and the Origin of Pharisaism. A Study in* 1 *and 2 Maccabees*, Septuagint and Cognate Studies 24, 1988; H.G.Kippenberg, *Religion und Klassenbildung im antiken Judäa*, SUNT 14, 1978; id. and G.A.Wevers, *Textbuch zur neutestamentliche Zeitgeschichte*, NTD Ergänzungsreihe 8, 1979; J.Maier, *Geschichte der jüdische Religion*, 1972; H.D.Mantel, 'The Development of the Oral Law during the Second Temple Period', in M.Avi-Yona and Z.Baras, 'Society and Religion in the Second Temple Period', in *The World History of the Jewish People* I, 8, 1977, 41-65; O.Plöger, *Theocracy and Eschatology*, 1968; S.Safrai, *Das jüdische Volk im Zeitalter des Zweiten Tempels*, Information Judentum I, ²1980; P.Schäfer, 'The Hellenistic and Maccabaean Periods', in J.H.Hayes and J.M.Miller (eds.), *Israelite and Judaean History*, 1977, 539-604; M.Stern, 'Die Zeit des Zweiten Tempels', in H.Ben-Sasson, *Geschichte des jüdischen Volkes*, I, 1978, 29-373; id., *Greek and Latin Authors on Jews and Judaism* (three vols), 1974-1984; E.Täubler, 'Jerusalem 201-199 BCE. On the History of a Messianic Movement', *JQR* 37, 1946/47, 1-30, 125-37, 249-63, V.Tcherikover, *Hellenistic Civilization and the Jews*, 1961 = 1982; id. and A.Fuks, *Corpus Papyrorum Judaicorum* (three vols), 1957-64.

Politically, the transition from Persian to Greek supremacy at first did not bring any far-reaching changes for Judaea. After the turbulent phase of the wars of the Diadochi (321-301 BCE), in which the Jewish population of Palestine, too, experienced all the harshness of the superior Macedonian war machine,[1] Judaea finally became part of the empire of the Ptolemies and experienced a phase of political stability and economic prosperity which lasted almost a century (300-c.220 BCE). Certainly the Ptolemies firmly incorporated the former Persian province of Judaea into their centralistic administrative and economic system, but they probably granted it a partially autonomous status, 'to live in accordance with ancestral laws'.[2] This included both the recognition of the Torah as a locally valid law and limited self-administration.

The social form of organization of the community of Judah which had developed in the Persian period[3] existed with slight changes up to the early Seleucid period (175 BCE): at the top was the high priest; in the middle were the two leading bodies of the elders (*gerousia*)[4] and the priests (*to koinon ton hieron*);[5] and at the lowest level was the popular assembly (*ekklesia, demos*).[6] However, as already in the second half of the Persian period, because of the social split in the community the latter had lost influence and was able to regain it only for the intermediate phase of the Maccabaean fight for freedom (168-142 BCE).[7]

It was an innovation that the Ptolemies refrained from installing a governor in Judaea.[8] This led to the high priest becoming a political representative of the community to the king (*prostates*),[9] extending his function of leadership from the priestly college to the council of elders, and now also taking over the political leadership (Sirach 50.1-4). Moreover he had control of the temple treasury and thus fiscal autonomy – though this was strictly supervised by the Ptolemies.[10] So only in the Hellenistic period did a hierocracy or theocracy form, which, if one ignores the sharp economic control exercised by Ptolemaean government, could give the Judaeans the feeling that they had regained something of the splendour of the former monarchy.[11]

However, the more time went on, the more the shift of power in favour of the high priest provoked the resistance of the economically influential aristocratic families. As early as the middle of the third century, Joseph, the offspring of the rich Transjordanian Tobiads, challenged the *prostasia* and thus the fiscal autonomy of the high priest Onias II.[12] And it is no coincidence that the complete disintegration of the community in the Maccabaean period began with the attack of the emancipated Hellenistic aristocracy on the high-priestly office:[13] in 175 BCE, under pressure from them, Onias III was replaced by his brother Jason, and three years later Jason was expelled and replaced by Menelaus. A hereditary office of rule, restricted to the Zadokide line, stood in the way of the economic and power interests of the aristocracy; if it could not be completely abolished, then they could degrade it into a venial state office which could be occupied as they thought fit (II Macc.4.7f., 24).

The social rift in the community also continued from the Persian into the Hellenistic period. The Greek historian Hecataeus of Abdera already notes from the time around 300 BCE that although the sale of portions of land had originally been forbidden among the Jews, some of them had made such purchases out of a desire for domination and would exploit those without means.[14] And both Koheleth during the third century and Jesus Sirach at the beginning of the second report a constant destructive oppression of the poor by the rich.[15] The danger of slavery for debt was so threatening that the Ptolemies even enacted laws to guard against it.[16] A new acute threat, especially for the impoverished members of the population, was being sold into slavery abroad (Joel 4.6f.). Palestine became a land which exported slaves to meet the needs of the Graeco-Roman world.[17]

Here we should note that under the Ptolemies Palestine experienced a considerable economic boom. The Zeno papyri give the impression of hectic economic activity for the period around 260 BCE.[18] The aim of the Ptolemaean kings, who regarded their state territory as crown property along the lines of the Pharaonic state economy, was to derive as high a profit as possible from the land. To this end they also imposed strict centralistic economic and financial administration on their province of 'Syria-Phoenicia'. Along the lines of Greek domestic housekeeping, their supreme official in Alexandria (*dioketes*) supervised virtually all economic processes right down to the smallest village, from agricultural production through trade to taxation, by means of a host of local financial officials (*oikonomoi*) and central agents. The growing of productive crops (wheat, olives, vines) which brought more profit was encouraged; agricultural methods were improved (terracing, artificial irrigation) in order to increase the yield of the land. Trade was encouraged by an extension of the coinage system, and a wide-ranging system of taxation which went far beyond Persian tribute saw to it that the tax income of the region multiplied in comparison with Persian times.[19]

We can begin by assuming that Judaea, too, profited from this general economic boom. And it may be that the marked growth in population experienced by the Jewish people in the Hellenistic period is connected with these generally improved living conditions. The small settlement area of Judah became too cramped, and many Jews emigrated and went about their business in numerous regions of Palestine, and also in the new Greek cities like Ptolemais (Acco), Jaffa, Scythopolis (Beth-shean) and above all Alexandria.[20]

However, the rich aristocratic families especially profited from the economic boom. The flourishing Ptolemaean state economy offered them improved chances of agricultural production and trade. In addition there was the completely new possibility offered by the system of 'state tax leasing',[21] with which the Ptolemaean state utilized the local aristocrats' interest in profit. Taxes, tolls and every possible kind of levy were leased by the state to the person who offered the highest sum; for this he received the privilege of levying the taxes on his own responsibility on behalf of the state financial administration: everything that he collected above the sum agreed was his profit.

The most striking example of how readily the aristocracy of Judah fell in with this new refined system of exploitation is the Tobiad Joseph. According to the account in the Tobiad romance (*Antt.* XII, 160-236), he succeeded in securing a royal tax lease for the whole province for twenty-two years (c.240-218) by doubling the amount to be raised. Granted, we are only told how he collected the increased tax heedlessly and sometimes by armed force in the face of the furious population of Greek cities (181ff.), and it is claimed that he shared his wealth with his Jewish compatriots (224).[22] But this is quite certainly crude apologetic, and we can confidently assume that he also fleeced his own countrymen in a similar way and that the unimaginable wealth flowed into the pockets of his family (184) and a small group of aristocrats. So the institution of tax leasing not only deepened the social rift in the community of Judah as compared with Persian times but also stoked up considerable aggression in the lower class against those aristocrats who, like Joseph, allowed themselves to be drawn right into the oppressive system of the foreign power and in addition derived their own personal profit from it.

Social tensions were further intensified in comparison with the Persian period because a cultural split was now added to the social split. The groups of aristocrats who greedily seized the opportunities offered them by the Ptolemaean and later Seleucid economic system also welcomed the

Hellenistic life-style. Granted, initially this cultural openness for the most part involved only external things like learning Greek, the use of Greek names, Greek clothing and taking part in festivals and entertainments offered by the refined Hellenistic culture. Jewish religious identity was taken for granted and was not yet fundamentally put in question, even if people could at times use polytheistic forms of greeting in business correspondence with Greek partners.[23] But from the perspective of the lower class in city and country, who hardly came into contact with Greek culture in Judaea,[24] it must have seemed as if they were being exploited by a clique which not only did not care about the solidarity required by the Torah, but also increasingly drifting off into a suspect un-Jewish life-style that was alien to them. As a result of this cultural reshaping, the chronic class contrast developed such a potential for conflict that it only needed an occasion to turn it into a civil war.

Now even in the Hellenistic period the upper class by no means formed a single block. Rather, the split which took place in the second half of the Persian period into a 'pious' and an 'impious' part continued. As the example of Jesus Sirach shows, by no means all the leading class had gone over to Hellenistic economic practice and life-style; there were also rich and respected members of the community of Judah who deliberately remained faithful to ancestral traditions and wanted to show solidarity with the poorer and more conservative levels of society.[25]

There was a power struggle between the two groups for a majority in the self-administrative bodies. Whereas towards the end of the period of the Ptolemies (before 200) the cultural and economic pressure of the 'Hellenists', led by the Tobiads, was evidently already so great that there were violent riots against the Ptolemies inspired by apocalyptic (Dan.11.14),[26] at the beginning of Seleucid supremacy (198-180), the conservatives under the leadership of the high priest Simon II the Just once again succeeded in gaining a majority and renewing the religious and cultural independence of the community, until after 175 the 'Hellenists' again seized power and provoked a bloody religious war.

It emerges from this that even the parties were not united: there were moderate 'Hellenists' who began their primarily political reform plans with Jason (175-172 BCE), and there were extremists who with Menelaus wanted completely to level out the special cultural and religious position of Judaism (172-162). It was even more important that the conservative party, too, did not form a single block. Among its members there seem to have been quite a number who were prepared to tolerate certain Hellenistic modernizations.[27] Here the hard core was formed by a special religious group who called themselves *hasidaioi* (Aramaic *ḥᵃsīdayyā'*; Hebrew *ḥᵃsīdīm*), 'the pious' (I Macc.2.42; 7.12ff.; II Macc.14.6).

The discussion of the *ḥᵃsīdīm* is impossible to survey[28] and can only be hinted at here. There is no dispute over whether it was a fixed group; that is indicated by the transcription of the name of the group in the Greek text of the books of Maccabees and the description of it as *synagoge*, 'assembly, group' (I Macc.2.42). But there is a dispute as to its social and religious context. Whereas Plöger[29] and Hengel[30] see the Hasidim as a pietistic conventicle which was in opposition to the 'official' Judaism embodied by the priestly hierarchy and the rich lay aristocracy,[31] and is to be assigned more to the lower class, Tcherikover has interpreted it as the 'scribal class' concerned for the exegesis of the Torah which under Simon II the Just rose to become a leading intellectual and theological group.[32] He has recently been supported by Kampen, who has indicated the probability that the Hasidim are to be regarded as forerunners of the Pharisees.[33] His most important findings are as follows. I Macc.2.29-41 is to be distinguished from the mention of the Hasidaeans in 2.42, thus cutting the links which Hengel and others have made with the Essenes and the Qumran sect. The descriptions of the Hasidim as *ischyroi dynamei apo Israel*,[34] I Macc.2.42 and the *protoi*[35] in 7.13 are to be interpreted as statements about their social status, 'leading citizens devoted to the law'.[36] The 'group (*synagoge*) of scribes' mentioned in I Macc.7.12 has to be identified with the Hasidaeans of 7.13.[37] The identification of Maccabeans and Hasidim which II Macc.14.16 makes in contrast to I Maccabees presupposes that the latter must have belonged among the 'leading religious personalities'.[38] Now Kampen thinks that his social placing of the Hasidim would also tell against the claim made by Plöger, Hengel and others that they were the ones who handed down apocalyptic;[39] however, this need by no means be the case: Daniel and I Enoch can very well be explained against the background of scribal groups.[40]

If the Hasidim are an influential group of scribes, then for the first time we encounter a new group of tradents of official Yahweh religion. The edict of Antiochus III (197 BCE) also attests that the 'temple scribes' had become a separate professional group among the Jewish leaders alongside the priests and temple singers in the Hellenistic period.[41] We have already conjectured scribal groups for the Persian period, who were active, for example, in the canonization of the Pentateuch on behalf of the council of elders and the priestly college.[42] Alongside this there were also famous individual scribal personalities like Ezra, whom the Persian government employed in connection with its imperial organization.[43] So we are to suppose that in the late Persian and early Hellenistic period a regular profession of scribes developed from such forerunners; they had the task not only of seeing to the transmission and elaboration of religious documents but also of expounding and giving a binding interpretation of the Torah of Moses, which had become canonical.[44] Thus by profession they were already familiar with the care of the 'ancestral tradition'. The fact that under Simon the Just a number of scribes from this professional group combined into a religious circle who explicitly designated themselves 'the pious' can only be understood to mean that it wanted to live out among its members and propagate to the public a loyal, voluntary surrender to the law (I Macc.2.42) in the face of the attractive Hellenistic alternative.

As such, it could give backing to the pious part of the upper class in resisting the economic and cultural blandishments to which the 'Hellenists' were so readily open.

To this religious split in the upper class was added a political one which the incipient conflicts made completely unavoidable. As in the pre-exilic period and in contrast to the Persian period, in the Hellenistic period Judaea again got caught up in the field of tension between rival great powers, the kingdom of the Ptolemies in the south and of the Seleucids in the north. As soon as the balance of power between these two poles became unstable – as it in fact did, with the exception of the period of the Diadochi, after the accession of Antiochus III (221 BCE) – the internal political conflicts came to be combined with opposing options in foreign policy and gave them additional sharpness. Here the upper-class parties kept changing in a bewildering way. After 221, the promoters of Hellenization, the Tobiad family, who had so long been active as instruments of the Ptolemaean taxation authorities, put their money on the Seleucids. So did the high priest Simon the Just and the pious after 200, in the hope of introducing new reflection on Jewish identity with Seleucid help. In disillusionment, Simon's son Onias III moved back from the Seleucids to the Ptolemies. Onias's brother Jason, who displaced him, initially carried through his Hellenistic reform with the help of the Seleucids, but went over to the Ptolemies' camp when he was driven out by the radical Hellenists. To the conservative lower class in the country these bewildering partisan struggles inevitably suggested that here the clique of leaders in the city was playing its egotistic game with the foreign powers heedless of the common good. In addition to the cultural alienation of part of the upper class, the partisan political struggles contributed to deepening the social rift further.

The political, social, cultural and religious conflict which had been stoked up for so long exploded with great force in the Maccabean wars, the first armed social rebellion since the days of Rehoboam, and the first Israelite war for more than 400 years.

The catalyst was a quite external one, a party-political dispute between the pro-Ptoemaean high priest (Onias III) and the pro-Seleucid Hellenistic wing of the aristocracy. But more was at stake: the intention to integrate Judaism not only politically and economically but also culturally and religiously into the Hellenistic world.

Only the basic structures of the conflict can be described here.[45] It had three phases. It began with a political reform, continued as a religious and cultural struggle and ended in a war of liberation for the restoration of the nation.

When the Hellenistically inclined aristocrats negotiated permission from Antiochus IV to establish a polis named Antiochia in Jerusalem on the Greek model, with a gymnasium and ephebeion (II Macc.4.7-10), their main aim was to secure their economic interests. They wanted to obtain for Jerusalem the trading privileges possessed by the Hellenistic cities and to link the community of Judah into the international economic and cultural network of the Hellenistic world, thus doing away with all the obstacles to trade which hindered them in their economic development. But there were also further interests of a domestic political kind: citizenship of the new polis was bound up with a very costly education in gymnasium and ephebeion; in practice it ruled out the lower class of the city and forced the conservative part of the aristocracy who did not want to be subject to it out of the self-administrative body. Thus the political Hellenization of Jerusalem was an administrative cementing of the social and religious division in the society of Judah.[46] Now clearly the 'Hellenists' were dominant in its self-administrative bodies, and their tiresome critics in the upper and lower class were robbed of their voting rights in the coup.

Since Persian times, the functions of the leading bodies made up of laity and priests under the leadership of the high priest had also included religious and cultic legislation or interpretation of the law. Thus behind the political reform measures there was probably also a Hellenist intention to gain sole influence over these – by suppressing the conservative scribes (Hasidim). Initially the Hellenists were probably not concerned in any way to put in question the authority of the Torah of Moses, but simply to do away with the interpretation which had been put on it in the minority situation of the Persian period since Nehemiah and Ezra. This sometimes introduced deep demarcations, for example by prohibiting trade on the sabbath (Neh.13.15-22), imposing prohibitions on food which made it almost impossible to have a meal with foreigners, or interpreting rigidly the laws about mixed marriages (Ezra 10). As a result of the growth in population, the Jewish people had long ceased to be a minority whose existence and identity had to be anxiously protected; indeed, it could be asked whether all these protective laws were not now out of date. Furthermore, the majority of the Jewish people had long lived in close contact with the Gentiles outside the frontiers of the province of Judah, in many places in Palestine and the Diaspora; a mitigation of the rules about separation could only unburden their trading and way of life and contribute to demolishing the resentment in their pagan environment. It must be conceded that the Hellenists were also concerned, in the changed situation of the Hellenistic period, to create a more appropriate and safer foundation for Judaism.[47]

The reason why this reform under Jason nevertheless met with no success was that the 'Hellenists' discredited the plan, which was worth taking quite seriously, by their aristocratic power interests, excluded the majority of those concerned from the religious discussion, and did not have the patience to work step by step towards a new consensus. This is evident from the fact that only three years later a more radical wing of the Hellenists took things in hand and exchanged Jason for Menelaus (II Macc.4.23-25), evidently because the changes were not going ahead fast enough for them (172 BCE). This now introduced the second turbulent phase of the social revolt and religious war.

The way in which the radical Hellenists exploited the temple treasure for their power interests (II Macc.4.30-39) and boycotted their critics in the council of elders (4.43-49) must have made even the well-disposed doubt whether this group still had the well-being of the whole community in mind. And so when the first unrest in the city (4.39-42) and conditions resembling civil war between moderate and radical Hellenists (5.1-7) provoked Antiochus IX to brutal massacres in the city in 169 and 168, and the radical Hellenists did nothing to moderate him, but continued with their power struggle, in the eyes of the majority of the population the reform had been discredited before it had really begun. And when in 167 BCE the radical reforms even used the power of the Seleucid state in a kind of shock therapy on the population to eliminate all the rites of the Jewish tradition which separated them from the Hellenistic environment[48] and incorporate the official Jerusalem Yahweh cult into the religious thought-world of Hellenism,[49] open rebellion broke out.

The rebels, made up of members of the lower class who had fled from Jerusalem and the impoverished country population, gathered under the military leadership of a lowly priestly family in the surrounding countryside, the Maccabees (II Macc.5.27; I Macc.2.29,43). It was important that they also secured the support of the nucleus of the pious upper class, the Hasidim (4.24). Having been displaced from their position as influential scribes by the Hellenists, the Hasidim gave the rebels not only the social recognition and theological legitimation that they needed, but also their religious slogan. With the Hasidim, the rebels could understand their wars against the Seleucids and their fight for social liberation against the hated aristocracy as 'zeal for the law and the covenant' (I Macc.2.27; cf.3.21). This theological legitimation first gave the rebel movement its breadth of influence and its persuasiveness. It first gave the 'little folk in the land' the awareness that they were fighting for a just cause, for the existence of their Jewish religion and identity and against being swamped by 'Greek customs'. Their adversaries and exploiters were not to be regarded as reformers but as the godless (I Macc.3.8), who, since they were disregarding all Jewish solidarity, could confidently be massacred and dispossessed (I Macc.6.24).

The unexpected military successes of the rebels under Judas Maccabaeus (I Macc.3f.) made the radical Hellenists ensconced in the fortress of Jerusalem (the Acra) and their Seleucid sponsors yield three years later; the brutal edict on religion was repealed in March 164, to rob the rebels of their religious motivation (II Macc.11.27-33). But the freedom fight had long since taken on a dynamic of its own. Judas not only seized Jerusalem, purified the temple of all Hellenistic influences and on 14.12.164 BCE restored the official Yahweh cult (I Macc.4.36-61), but immediately went on to fight against the neighbouring peoples in order to protect the numerous Jewish communities outside Judaea from the attacks of the Syrian population (5f). Thus began the third phase of the war, which issued in a restoration of the nation.

However, now the rebel coalition fell out over this extension of the war aims. When the Seleucids offered a compromise peace in 162 BCE, abolished the constituion of the polis, again recognized Jewish customs (II Macc.11.22-26) and in Alcimus presented a moderate Hellenistic high priest, the Hasidim decided to enter into peace negotiations (I Macc.7.12ff.).[50] The restoration of the partially autonomous community which had existed since Persian times was evidently enough for these pious scribes. In their eyes, in view of the traditions of their own religion which were massively critical of domination, it was the appropriate social form for providing the necessary freedom for the practice of Jewish life and faith. However, the new elite of the Maccabean leaders no longer wanted to share the power. Fully aware of the military strength that they had recently experienced, their view was that the Jewish population of Palestine, which had grown far beyond the frontiers of Judaea, could only be protected by the re-establishment of an autonomous Jewish state.

However, the state option for which the Maccabees fought against the disintegrating power of the Seleucid kingdom was not in a position to resolve the social, cultural and religious conflicts which had led to the rebellion and to create a new social consensus. Certainly liberation from the oppressive burden of Seleucid taxation in 142 BCE was greeted with jubilation (I Macc.13.36-41), but the rulers lacked the power permanently to do away with the chronic social split by means of a wide-ranging economic reform.[51] Certainly it was possible to extend the territory of the state to the frontiers of the great empire of David, but only at the price of a problematic fusion of religion and state power; their own forcible Hellenization, which had been successfully prevented, was now replaced by the forcible Judaizing of other nations by the state (*Antt*. XIII, 257f.). The seizure by the Maccabees of the high-priestly office (I Macc.10.15-21; 14.41), which had traditionally been held by the Zadokide line, provoked the splitting off of the Qumran sect under the leadership of Zadokide priests; and the combination of the high-priestly office with the posts of commander, ruler (14.47) and finally king drove the Pharisees, as successors to the pious scribes (Hasidim), into opposition (*Antt*. XIII, 288-292) and led to the disintegration of the leading religious elite (Sadducees- Pharisees, *Antt*. XIII, 293-89).[52]

The Hasmonaean rulers were very soon behaving like typical Hellenistic and oriental potentates who would not even shrink from murder in their families and bloody acts of terror against their own population. The traditional self-administrative bodies were robbed of their power and ordinary people were driven into resistance. So it is not surprising that at the end of the Hellenistic era the aristocracy and people asked the Romans for help against their own leaders: it had been the purpose of their freedom fight 'that no king should perform the business of state, but that the high priest should stand over (*prohistemi*) the people. But these (i.e. the Hasmonaeans) would rule by violation of the ancestral laws and unlawfully enslave the citizens.'[53] Thus at the end of the Old Testament era of the history of Israel it remained an open question what form of political and social organization Israel would have to adopt really to do justice to the claims of its religious tradition of liberation.

6.2 The scribal ideal of a theocracy (Chronicles)

P.R.Ackroyd, 'History and Theology in the Writings of the Chronicler', *CTM* 38, 1967, 501-15; id., 'The Theology of the Chronicler', *LexTQ* 8, 1973, 101-16; R.L.Braun, 'A Reconsideration of the Chronicler's Attitude toward the North', *JBL* 96, 1977, 59-62; id., 'Chronicles, Ezra and Nehemiah', in J.A.Emerton (ed.), *Studies in the Historical Books of the Old Testament*, VTS 30, 1979, 52-64; H.Gese, 'Zur Geschichte der Kultsänger am zweiten Tempel' (1963), in id., *Vom Sinai zum Zion*, BEvTh 64, 1974 = 1984, 147-58; A.H.J.Gunneweg, *Esra*, KAT XIX, 1, 1985; S.Japhet, *The Ideology of the Book of Chronicles and Its Place in Biblical Thought*, BATAJ 9, 1989; id., 'The Supposed Common Authorship of Chronicles and Ezra-Nehemiah Investigated Anew', *VT* 18, 1968, 330-71; W.Johnstone, 'Chronicles, Canons and Contexts', *Aberdeen University Review* 169, 1983, 1-18; id., 'Guilt and Atonement: The Theme of 1 and 2 Chronicles', in J.D.Martin and P.R.Davies (eds.), *A Word in Season, FS McKane*, JSOTS 42, 1986, 113-38; J.Kegler, 'Das Zurücktreten der Exodustradition in den Chronikbücher', in R.Albertz, F.W.Golka and J.Kehler (eds.), *Schöpfung und Befreiung, FS C.Wester-mann*, 1989, 54-64; R.Mosis, *Untersuchungen zur Theologie des Chronistischen Geschichtswerkes*, FTS 92, 1973; J.M.Myers, *I and II Chronicles*, The Anchor Bible, 1965; J.D.Newsome, 'Toward a New Understanding of the Chronicler and his Purposes', *JBL* 94, 1975, 201-17; M.Oeming, *Das wahre Israel. Die "genealogische Vorhalle" I Chr 1-9*, BWANT 128, 1990; G.von Rad, *Die Geschichtsbild des chronistischen Werkes*, BWANT 54, 1930; id., 'The Levitical Sermon in I and II Chronicles' (1934), in *The Problem of the Hexateuch and Other Essays*, 1966, 267-81; W.Rudolph, *Chronikbücher*, HAT 1, 21, 1955; D.Talshir, 'A Reinvestigation of the Linguistic Relationship between Chronicles and Ezra-Nehemiah', *VT* 38, 1988, 165-93; P.Welten, 'Geschichte und Geschichtsdarstellung in den Chronikbüchern', in *Textgemäss. FS E. Würthwein*, 1979, 169-83; C.Wester-mann, 'Die Begriffe für Fragen und Suchen im Alten Testament' (1960), *Forschung am Alten Testament* II, 1974, 162-90; T.Willi, *Die Chronik als Auslegung. Untersuchung zur literarischen Gestaltung der historischen Überlieferung*, FRLANT 106, 1972; H.G.M.Williamson, 'Eschatology in Chronicles', *TynB* 28, 1977, 115-54; id., *Israel in the Book of Chronicles*, 1977; id., 'The Dynastic Oracle in the Book of Chronicles', *Isaac Leo Seeligmann Volume*, Vol.III, 1983, 305-18; id., 'The Origins of the Twenty-Four Priestly Courses. A Study of 1 Chronicles

XXIII-XXVII', in J.A.Emerton (ed.), *Studies in the Historical Books of the Old Testament*, VTS 30, 1979, 251-68.

It is in keeping with the far-reaching sociological continuity of the community of Judah despite the change of political supremacies that there is hardly any record of the transition to the Hellenistic period in the Old Testament writings. There are only a few references to it in the late-prophetic tradition, and these are not undisputed;[1] but remarkably, they are completely absent where one would expect them most, in the latest historical tradition of the Old Testament, the Chronicler's history.

The question how this is to be interpreted will be decided primarily by the dating of the books of Chronicles and Ezra/Nehemiah. In current discussion this varies betwen 520 and 200 BCE,[2] though there are good reasons for limiting the *terminus post quem* to 400.[3] Because of the lack of Hellenistic references, many scholars decide to put the books in the late Persian period (400-332 BCE).[4] However, such a solution causes chronological problems.

The discussion over whether Chronicles and Ezra/Nehemiah belong together, which for a long time seemed not to be in question, makes it appear increasingly improbable that the so-called Chronistic history was conceived at a stroke.[5] The solution which is emerging is that Ezra/Nehemiah is earlier than Chronicles,[6] though they both come from the same milieu.[7] But simply because of manifest historical obscurities in the course of events in the fifth century recorded by the author of Ezra and Nehemiah,[8] it is to be assumed that some interval of time separates these books from the events they describe (say around 350 BCE); in that case the time left for the composition of Chronicles, which indicates a lengthy process of literary growth,[9] before Alexander's campaign is hardly sufficient. So I join those authors who put Chronicles in the early Hellenistic period (330–250 BCE);[10] thus for me Ezra/Nehemiah belong before, but Chronicles after, the cult-political separation of the Samarians.

But however the problem of dating may be resolved, it remains striking that the account of the post-exilic history of the community of Judah in Ezra/Nehemiah was not continued into the Hellenistic period. The only interpretation of this can be that for its leading groups the political events of their time had no theological relevance whatsoever.

If the great external upheaval in world politics may have given the prophetic circles in the lower class new nourishment for their expectation of God's last great intervention,[11] to judge from Ezra/Nehemiah and Chronicles it was rather the small events internal to Israel which occupied the leading circles of the community of Judah in the late Persian and early Hellenistic period: above all the intensification of the theological claims of the Samarians and their final split from the cult.[12] The process put in question the legitimacy of the community of Judah which had previously been taken for granted; it challenged the assertion of Judah's claim to religious and cultic leadership and therefore called for the provision of a new theological foundation.

If the dating adopted above is correct, the controversy had two phases. The claim of the Samarians to equal religious and cultic co-determination in the late-Persian period[13] is given a blunt and unyielding answer by the historical outline of Ezra/Nehemiah: with his description of the post-exilic period the author pointed out in detail that only the community of Judah was the legitimate successor to the old Israel. Only its members were descendants of the Babylonian Gola, had suffered the judgment of Yahweh and therefore again stood under his promise (Ezra.1.2-4); only they – organized into their fixed clan alliances (*bēt 'ābōt*) – could demonstrate beyond doubt their genealogical connection with the 'tribes' of Judah and Benjamin and had carefully protected themselves against mixing with the 'peoples of the lands'.[14] Only they had received the commission from Cyrus to rebuild the temple (Ezra.1.3; 4.3; 5.13), and in the temple vessels they still possessed a direct continuity with the pre-exilic cult (Ezra 1.7; 5.14f.; 6.5). And only they had consistently observed the Torah of Moses (Neh.8-10). By contrast, the author of Ezra/Nehmiah depicted the Samarians as the arch-enemies of the community of Judah from the beginning (Ezra 4; Neh.3; 6). These people of doubtful descent (Ezra 4.2,10) had constantly and meanly undermined the work of rebuilding in Judah (Ezra 4.3), so their right to have a say in community matters (Neh.3ff.) had always rightly been rejected, and this would also be the case in the future.

Now if the Samarians gave up their efforts at co-operation and in the early Hellenistic period decided to create for themselves a rival model to the community of Judah on and around Gerizim, it was no longer enough for Judah simply to take its stand on its post-exilic history. For the Samarians in their enterprise were in all probability referring to the Pentateuch and could provide themselves with good credentials from the canonized version of the early history of Israel.[15] So in the second phase of the controversy, pre-exilic history had to be struggled with in order to rescue the claims of Judah, to be, if not the sole representative of Israel, at least its leader. This process took place at the beginning of the third century with the creation of the Chronistic history.

The main problem for the authors of this work was that the Jerusalem temple and the Davidic kingdom on which Judah's claim to leadership was theologically based did not appear explicitly in the canonized foundation history of Israel.[16] Since this foundation history could no longer be changed at random, their only way out was to elevate the early monarchy in which the Davidic kingship and the Jerusalem cult were established to be a necessary ingredient of the foundation history of Israel. So they used almost half of their work (I Chron.11-II Chron.9) to describe this period,[17] gave it a compelling slant, ending in the building of the temple and the establishment of the Jerusalem cult, and made it directly continuous with the pre-state foundation history. Not only the ark of the covenant of the pre-priestly composition but also the wilderness sanctuary of the priestly composition, which according to the Chronistic view had survived in Gibeon,[18] were brought into the Jerusalem temple (I Chron.13; 15f.; II Chron.5.5). Correspondingly, David was designated a second Moses, who, like Moses on Sinai, received from God the revelation of a model for building the temple,[19] and, following him and supplementing him, regulated the whole cult down to details.[20] According to the Chroniclers' account, God's action of election in the early period continued with compelling logic down to the early monarchy, through the tribe of Judah and the family of Jesse (I Chron.28.4; cf.5.2), to David the founder of the cult and the dynasty and Solomon who built the temple (28.4-6,10). Furthermore Yahweh had tangibly confirmed the site of the Jerusalem temple (I Chron.21.26ff.; II Chron.7.1-3), and chosen the city, the temple and its legitimate priesthood.[21]

The evaluation of the time of David and Solomon as the goal and climax of the Israelite foundation history with which the authors of Chronicles reacted to the challenge from Samaria amounted to no less than a revision of the canon. In their view, the decision taken in the Persian period, in the interest of opposition to domination and enthusiasm and with a view to the emancipation of the priesthood, to end the foundation history of Israel with the death of Moses and thus largely exclude the old theology of kingship and the state cult from official Yahweh religion,[22] needed revision. They felt that the canon should be urgently enlarged, that the historical tradition of DtrG which had been cut out, and also the prophetic writings which brought out the special Jerusalem traditions of salvation, should be accorded their due place in official theology. And with their work the Chronistic historians wanted to indicate the direction in which this could come about. So the Samarian split provoked a new effort at integration within the community of Judah aimed at extending the consensus over the foundations of the offical religion of Israel beyond the framework created by the Torah.

One characteristic of Chronicles which has been noted in different ways, but the significance of which has not yet been fully assessed, is to be understood against this background: its concern to offer the broadest possible synthesis of the different religious traditions of Israel.

The first synthesis for which the authors of Chronicles were concerned was that of the Torah and DtrG. If they wanted to secure the recognition of DtrG as canonical they had to demonstrate that its traditions were fully in accord with the norms of the canonical tradition of the law, provided that they were interpreted correctly. So in their new interpretation they constantly related the historical tradition of the state of Judah to the 'law of Yawheh' (*tōrat yhwh*)[23] or the 'law of Moses' (*tōrat mōše*)[24] and constantly emphasized that the ordinances of the kings of Judah and the cultic celebrations in Jerusalem were performed 'as it is written'.[25] They changed the text of DtrG to bring it into line with regulations in the Torah,[26] and they reinterpreted its traditions on the basis of the Torah. No wonder that, for example, the first attempt of David to bring the ark to Jerusalem had failed (II Sam.6-11); that was because it had not been done according to the law (*kammišpāṭ*, I Chron.15.13); immediately the divine ordinance that the Levites had to bear the ark (Deut.10.8) was observed (I Chron.15.2ff.,15), the enterprise succeeded (15.26).

Now DtrG had already been related to 'the Torah'; but at the time when it was composed the 'Torah' was still Deuteronomy. One task that the Chronistic historians faced was therefore to make not only Deuteronomic but also priestly regulations valid in the historical tradition, for example in respect of cultic personnel (distinction between priests and Levites),[27] sacrificial practice[28] and the dating of festivals.[29] Indeed, they faced the even more difficult task of reconciling divergent regulations in the Deuteronomic and Priestly traditions which stood side by side in the Torah. How they did that is shown, for example, by their detailed exposition of Josiah's passover (II Kings 23.21; II Chron.35.1-19). As ordained in Deut.16.1-8, the passover was a pilgrimage festival at the central sanctuary and was brought close to the meal offering (*zebaḥ*); but as the priestly legislation in Ex.12 had referred back to the custom of the family passover, they compromised by saying that both the cult personnel and the laity had to sacrifice and consume the passover by family divisions (II Chron.35.4,12). And by the form of preparation that they described ('boiling in the fire', 35.13) they wanted to satisfy the regulations of both Deut.16.7 ('boil') and Ex.12.8f. ('roast in the fire').[30]

Simply because of the 'dialogical character' of the Torah, reference to it could no longer be flatly mechanical, but presupposed exegesis. In addition the actual cultic conditions of the post-exilic period had to be taken into account,[31] and finally the Chronistic historians also had their own, prospective reform interests in view, for example extending the functions of the Levites.[32] The divergences in Chronicles from 'P' and Deuteronomy which are constantly emphasized by scholars take too little account of the possibilities of the interpretation of the Torah and merely distort the manifest concern of the Chronistic historians to present a history of Israel following the rules of the canonical Torah.

But the Chronistic historians set themselves the most difficult task of exegesis in the two central themes, which had brought DtrG into discredit with the promoters of the canonization of the Torah: the kingship and the state cult. DtrG had already shifted the Deuteronomic synthesis of Yahweh religion from the pre-state to the state traditions of salvation by putting alongside the foundation time of Moses and Joshua with the saving gifts of the law and the land a foundation period of David and Solomon in which Israel had been given the saving gifts of kingship and temple.[33] The

Chronistic historians were also keenly interested in precisely these saving gifts of the state because they alone were the foundation of a leadership claim by Judah. Because of the pressure towards legitimation put on them by the rival Samarian model, they had to shift the weight even further from the Yahweh traditions of the early period to those of the period of the foundation of the state. This meant that they deliberately allowed the exodus to fade[34] and distorted the pre-state period into a chaotic time without proper worship and instruction in the law (II Chron.15.3-6). Nevertheless, they could not avoid the fact that the fathers of the Pentateuch had clearly decided against the state cult option of DtrG and against the monarchical form of rule.[35] In the view of the founders of the Pentateuch the official cult had to be the responsibility of the whole people, to be administered autonomously by the priests,[36] and the elders, not an autocratic sacral kinship, were to rule the people.[37] So the Chronistic historians had to devote a good deal of effort to making room for the emanicipatory 'democratic' concerns of the Torah within DtrG.

As already in the first process of canonization, this resulted in a compromise: for theological reasons the Chronistic historians could not of course start from the fact that the Jerusalem temple had been the work of the kings David and Solomon, who had been chosen by God; on the contrary, in the interests of legitimating as much as possible of the whole post-exilic cultic practice by these kings who had been endowed with grace, Chronicles had considerably to extend their cult-political functions.[38] Nevertheless the Chronistic historians were concerned to set narrow limits to the sacrality of the king, to give the laity as much part as possible in cult-political decisions and to preserve the autonomy of the cultic personnel. So in their view, while the king might sacrifice, as in DtrG, he could not enter the temple building (II Chron.23.6; 26.18). David summoned the people and all its leaders to plan the building of the temple (I Chron.28.1)[39] and asked them to support his son Solomon (29.1ff.). The temple was therefore also only partly financed by the king and to a large extent, along the lines of the Priestly stratum of the Pentateuch (Ex.25.3-8; 35.4-29), by voluntary gifts from the people (I Chron.29.1-9,14,17); the same also went for the upkeep of the temple (II Chron.24.6f.; adoption of the temple tax from Ex.30.12ff.; Neh.10.33f.) and the sacrificial gifts (II Chron.30.24; 35.7-9). Similarly, while the king had the right to instruct cultic personnel, the priests and Levites were no longer simply royal officials,[40] but received provisions from the people which they administered themselves (II Chron.31.4ff., following Num.18). In other words, in the Chronistic historians' view, while the Jerusalem cult was to be associated with the Davidic royal house to give it theological legitimation, the old mistake of the royal state cult with its fusion of throne and altar and its alienation from the people would be avoided.

The compromise which the authors of Chronicles offered over the

Davidic monarchy took a similar form. Certainly they could not and would not dispense with the theological legitimation of the Davidic kingship and the guarantee of its eternal existence (I Chron.17; 22.10; II Chron.6.16; 7.17f.; 13.5; 21.7; 23.3), since Judah's claim to leadership[41] and its continuity[42] depended on that. But they qualified quite considerably the massive statements of the Nathan promise that the king was the son of God, derived from the kingship ideology of the ancient Near East, by limiting these to Solomon (I Chron.17.11ff.; 22.10; 28.6), in order to describe God's quite extraordinary condescension to the builder of the temple. In other respects they interpreted the special nearness of the kings to God functionally, by making the Davidides executive organs of the kingly rule of Yahweh over Israel[43] (I Chron.17.14; 28.5; 29.23; II Chron.9.8; 13.8). In this way they could deny their brothers in the North the legitimation of their independent state (II Chron. 13.5,8) without having to surround their own kings with a supra-terrestrial aura. On the contrary, as a mere executive organ of the theocracy, the monarchy made room for the involvement of the people and its leaders in government. So throughout their work, the Chroniclers tried to draw the sympathetic picture of a human kingship, close to the people: the kings sought contact with the people, constantly summoned popular assemblies,[44] regularly took counsel with the leaders of the people,[45] avoided all dynastic quarrels (I Chron.29.20ff.; II Chron.11.22f.), and were almost touchingly concerned for the religious,[46] cultic,[47] legal[48] and political[49] well-being of the whole people. All the negative experiences of oppression and misuse of power which Israel had had with this institution were almost completely suppressed.[50] In other words, by resorting to the old ideal of the 'constitutional monarchy' that had never been realized, but which left room for Israel's drive towards freedom and its claim to self-determination, the Chronistic historians attempted to achieve a consensus over the Davidic kingship without lapsing into the error of the old kingship theology, that of ideologically exalting state power by fusing it with divine power.

The second synthesis with which the authors of Chronicles were concerned emerges in the deliberate inclusion of prophecy. They not only often introduced prophets in their account[51] and put forward the view that the whole historical tradition of DtrG is predominantly based on the portrayal of prophetic witnesses of the time,[52] but often alluded to phrases from the prophetic writings in their historical account.[53] Behind this there probably lay the intent of once again according prophecy a greater role in official Yahweh religion than the fathers of the Torah wanted to allow because of their fear of enthusiasm:[54] 'Believe in his (Yahweh's) prophets, and you will succeed,' they make Jehoshaphat say to the oppressed people of Judah (II Chron.20.20). But what the Chronistic historians allowed in was by no means the whole spectrum of prophecy; both the harsh unconditional prophecy of judgment[55] and the radiant unconditional prophecy of sal-

vation[56] are absent from their work. Instead of this they gave preference to
the conditional prophecy of judgment and salvation: in their understanding the prophets admonished and warned, seeking to stimulate the people
to a right relationship with God. So it was no coincidence that they above
all took up two conditional promises from the classical prophetic books,

II Chron.20.20: Believe in Yahweh, your God, and you will be established
(Isa.7.9);
II Chron.15.2: 'If you seek him, he will be found by you' (Jer.29.13f.),[57]

and time and again demonstrated the validity of these promises in their
history.[58] In so doing they wanted to demonstrate that, properly understood, prophecy was very useful for the orientation of Israel in history. For
the Chronistic historians the word of prophecy was an indispensable
guarantee that Yahweh remained faithful to his Israel – and even more to
his special Judah – as long as the people always constantly returned to him.
   The third synthesis made by the Chronistic historians was their incorporation of the Jerusalem psalm tradition into their work. Not only were they
interested in the cultic songs and cultic singers,[59] but sometimes they even
wove quotations from the Psalms into their text (I Chron.16.7-36[60]), by
means of which they gave above all the liturgical praise of the Jerusalem
cult,

II Chron.20.21: Give thanks to Yahweh, for his steadfast love endures for ever,

the function of supporting their whole history.[61] To show that in the end
Yahweh's grace endures for ever is one of the purposes of the Chronistic
account of history. In addition, it can be shown that they orientated their
whole account from the accession of David to the building of the temple
on Psalm 132, with its distinctive interlocking of kingship and Zion
theology, a psalm which is quoted at the end of Solomon's prayer of
dedication for the temple (II Chron.6.41f.; cf.I Chron.28.2).[62] In this way
the authors of Chronicles wanted to show that – rightly interpreted – the
cultic and the historical realities were ultimately identical. The history of
Israel was transcended and taken up into the Jerusalem cult: in the cult its
central period of salvation is liturgically present. And the reality of the
saving nearness of God celebrated and sung in the Jerusalem cult could be
proved in detail by the course of the history of Israel provided that one
accepted that its centre lay in the South.
   Finally, the fourth synthesis of the Chronistic historians was an intensified
incorporation of personal piety into their presentation of official Yahweh
religion. Challenged by the new situation of cultic rivalry which made it
necessary for all Yahweh worshippers to take a personal decision over
their orientation, the authors of Chronicles evidently had a vital interest

in not leaving the religious bond to the Judaean manifestation of Yahweh religon in external nomistic or ritual features but rooting it deeply in personal religious feeling and thinking. Only in that way can we understand how, going beyond DtrG, they emphasized the close personal bond between the king or the people and 'its God' Yahweh,[63] which was typical of personal piety at all times. So it is also not surprising that in Chronicles in particular there is a greater accumulation of the designation of Yahweh as 'God of the fathers'[64] than anywhere else but in the 'family religion' of Genesis.[65] Yahweh is said to have been present to the Israelites in both South and North as the family friend, known for generations. And finally, that helps us to understand why in Chronicles more frequently than elsewhere there is reference to the primal religious experience of God's 'being with', his personal support for each individual.[66]

The authors most frequently denote the positive relationship with God with the phrase 'seek God' (*dāraš*,[67] *biqqeš*[68]). They evidently wanted to use this term, which originally belonged in private enquiry of God,[69] and then was generalized into a term of prayer,[70] to create an overarching concept which was to embrace both all 'external' cult-political measures like the building of the temple,[71] the abolition of syncretistic cults[72] and the establishment of the Torah,[73] and also inner conversion to God in prayer[74] and obedience.[75] Everything that Israel undertook towards God was to be supported by a deep and honest turning to God, so these authors never wearied of emphasizing that true 'seeking of God' had to happen with 'all the heart, and all the mind and all the will'.[76] Furthermore, seeking God had to be supported by deep trust in God[77] and spring from a deeply humble attitude.[78] Here it strongly recalls the ideal of piety in the book of Job,[79] and we may conjecture that the Chronistic historians took their guidelines from a similarly attractive personal theology of their time.

Now the personal theology of the post-exilic period with its marked ethical stamp which we know not least from the book of Job was governed by an intense belief in recompense.[80] So it is probable that the distinctive theological perspective of Chronicles, which unlike that of DtrG is concerned to demonstrate a precise accord between human behaviour and divine recompense in the life of each individual king,[81] similarly draws on personal piety. In the view of the Chronistic historians there was no immutable doom hanging over the history of Israel, as could seem to be the case for wide stretches of it according to DtrG,[82] but each king, each generation, and ultimately each individual had the possibility of shaping his or its own destiny positively by turning in honesty from idolatry,[83] faithlessness[84] and arrogance[85] to God. Just as an ultimately inalienable grace of God had always been typical of personal piety, so the Chronistic historians argued for a view of history in which Yahweh's goodness stood open anew to each and every generation if only they were concerned for it. In this conviction, for them personal faith, the history of the promise of

David and Zion, the proclamation of the prophets and the legacy of the Psalms agreed: it was never 'too late' for Israel; everyone, including the brethren in the North with their centuries-long history of error, was still invited to Jerusalem to Yahweh's salvation.[86]

Who could have written this synthesis, which, while wide-ranging, was amazingly clear theologically in its result? We would do best to look at the class of scribes which was establishing itself in the late-Persian/Hellenistic period.[87] As their work shows, the authors were not only deeply familiar with the whole religious literature of Israel but also knew the business of interpreting and assimilating different positions, and in their studies had adopted a style of language which teemed with allusions to and quotations and passages from other writings (a musing style).[88]

This context seems to go against the current view of scholars who want to derive Chronicles from the circle of Levites or levitical singers.[89] Now the work undoubtedly has sympathy for the Levites[90] and is even concerned to extend their cultic competence.[91] But we would certainly be wrong to see this as the main interest of the work. Alongside it we can also recognize a concern to safeguard the right of the lay leaders to speak not only on political and legal but also on religious and cultic matters.[92] The only group which is treated somewhat unlovingly is that of the priests, though their position of cultic leadership is not challenged.[93] So the interests of the work, which embrace both laity and cultic personnel, suggest rather that the authors should be sought in a group which cut straight across the traditional divisions. The scribes are such a group. It is quite possible that they were recruited both from educated Levites and from the laity.

Sociologially, we do best to put these scribal authors of Chronicles in the middle class. That would explain not only their sympathy with the lowlier cultic personnel but also their explicit need for harmony, typical of members of the middle class of all ages. The bright picture of an ideal theocracy in which the king addresses his subjects as 'my brothers' (I Chron.28.2) and in which the people gathers in solidarity around its king and its temple excludes all social conflicts.[94] The authors act as though Israel were a social unity and, by turning to God in Jerusalem, could also become a great political unity, although – as we know – it was torn apart by social and religious trench warfare. The only indication given by the authors that there were quite considerable social problems in rejoicing before God in solidarity[95] is that they begin with great sacrificial gifts from the king and the leading families, so that all can take part in the cultic festivals.[96] Otherwise the scribes deliberately covered over the social question which had so torn apart the upper class in the Persian period. Probably they were seeking to maintain good relationships with their two parties, the 'pious' and the 'wicked'. They offered all three leading forces of Judah a new religious consensus with a specifically Judaean stamp which was to unite them in a defensive war against their Samarian rivals, and therefore they deliberately put all internal divisions in the background. By contrast, the lower-class groups with their suffering and their ardent expectations of an imminent removal of unjust social structures were left outside.

If we attempt once again in conclusion to evaluate the tendencies of Chronicles from this sociological background, the following picture emerges:

1. Chronicles has a clearly anti-Samarian orientation.[97] The recent tendency to dispute this[98] overlooks how deeply the orientation governs the plan and theology of the whole work. Granted, the theological syntheses are not exclusively governed by it, but they can also essentially be understood from it. The fact that the Chronistic scribes maintain a concept of all Israel,[99] with a positive attitude towards the population of the northern kingdom even in the time of the divided kingdoms,[100] and with a warm welcome to the brethren in the North after the downfall of the northern kingdom,[101] and that they even hint again under Hezekiah and Josiah at the vision of a united kingdom, does not tell against this.[102] For all this merely underlined Judah's claim to leadership; and once the cultic split had taken place, this was the only way to win back to the cult of Jerusalem as many as possible of the Israelites in the North who had orientated themselves on Gerizim. The situation of open rivalry which had arisen from 330 on compelled a revision of the tendency to abrupt segregation which is still evident in the books of Ezra and Nehemiah.

2. Chronicles has a deliberately uneschatological bias. The scribes certainly had an interest in making more room for the prophetic writings in official Yahwism because these writings contained much that could give an orientation in history. But for all their concern to create a new consensus within Judah, they were not ready to accord a place to the eschatological expectations of upheaval current among the lower class. Indeed, we can ask whether it was not one intention of the integration of the prophetic writings to challenge the use of them in eschatological circles and to counter the interpretations of them in terms of social revolution with an integration which was also acceptable to the upper class. One did not have to wait for the distant future and the result of a social upheaval for God to allow himself to be found, or Israel to receive a reward for its tribulation (Jer.29.13f.; 31.16); that could already be experienced now as a consequence of pious dedication to God in the cult.[103] Even now Yahweh could grant Israel rest in its threatened situation,[104] provided that Israel remained loyal to its Torah and cult. In the view of the scribes, the eschatological exegesis of the prophets by lower-class circles simply proved superfluous.

In their opposition to the Samarians, the Chronistic historians had to achieve a theological rehabilitation of the Davidides and the promise that rested on them. Nevertheless, they avoided giving their work a messianic horizon of expectation.[105] For the Chronistic historians the theocracy was once and for all realized in the Jerusalem cult founded and ordered by the Davidides and the political self-administration that had been achieved. Whether there would once again be a complete political restoration under a Davidide, which the favourable context of the early Hellenistic period could encourage, they deliberately left open.[106]

3. Chronicles is probably deliberately a-Hellenistic. Apart from some details of military technology[107] it does not display any kind of Hellenistic influence. Now Judaea hardly had very intensive contacts with Hellenism in the early Hellenistic period. But if we take into account the fact that Hellenistic culture and thought had already been streaming into Palestine since the late Persian period, we must probably see this restraint as a deliberate decision. The lasting appeals to seek the familiar God of the fathers with all one's heart, and to depart from all pagan influences, can be understood as a warning to preserve Jewish identity in the face of modern Hellenistic seductions. And the emphasis on divine recompense following free human decision could also be understood as a counter-model to Hellenistic belief in fate (*moira*). At the same time, we could also understand the idealized description of the Davidic king movingly concerned for his people as a counterpart to the behaviour of the remote Hellenistic rulers. But the Chronistic scribes had no interest in a real controversy with the new cultural surroundings; their education and training, focussed entirely on their own Israelite tradition, probably did not allow any alternative to sealing themselves off.

The most important consequences of Chronicles probably lie more in the literary than in the historical sphere. The propaganda which it developed was not enough to heal the cultic breach with the Samaritans. However, this interpretative and integrating form of literature which combined into a unity almost all the religious traditions in the Old Testament that had hitherto been separate found a following.[108] The combination of the Pentateuch and DtrG brought about a reconciliation between the pre-state saving traditions of Israel and those of the state while preserving the 'democratic' ideal of the former; together with the integration of prophecy it prevented the connection between the distant foundation period of Moses and the Torah and the historical present from being lost. And both prepared the way for the canonization of the historical and prophetic traditions. The marked integration of the Psalms tradition and personal piety protected early Judaism – in complete contrast to some prejudiced Christian views – from ritualistic externalization and spiritual dessication.

We can see the national restitution of Judah under the Hasmonaeans in the second century as being a remote political effect of Chronicles. Granted, this did not have Davidic legitimation, but it did prepare the way for a revival of the monarchy.

It was certainly a great defect that Chronicles had nothing to say about the social problems which were such a heavy burden on the community of Judah in the Hellenistic period as well. No social obligations were laid on the rehabilitated monarchy; the desire for a recognition of the prophets in the canon was not combined with an acceptance of their social criticism; nor was any attention drawn to the social laws of the Torah. Instead of this, the scribal theologians masked the notorious social problems from their superiors with pious zeal. This lack of courage in the face of the upper class and lack of sensitivity to the suffering of the lower class in the last great Old Testament synthesis of Israelite religion was to have devastating consequences for subsequent history. It contributed virtually nothing towards making the leading circles of Judaea sensitive to the rising social conflict which exploded with bloodshed in the Maccabean period.

6.3 Torah piety

Y.Amir, 'Psalm 119 als Zeugnis eines proto-rabbinischen Judentums', in id., *Studien zum antiken Judentum*, BEAJ 2, 1985, 1-34; A.Deissler, *Psalm 119 (118) und seine Theologie*, MThS 1, 11, 1955; I.Fischer, 'Psalm 19 – Ursprüngliche Einheit oder Komposition?', *BN* 21, 1983, 16-25; M.H.Fishbane, *Text and Texture*, 1979, 84-90; H.Gese, 'Die Einheit von Ps 19', in *Verifikationen, FS G.Ebeling*, 1982, 1-10; H.Gunkel, *Die Psalmen*, HK II, 2, [4]1929 = 1968; H.J.Kraus, 'Freude am Gesetz. Ein Beitrag zu den Psalmen 1; 19B und 119', *EvTh* 10, 1950/51, 337-51; id., *Psalms 1-59, Psalms 60-150*, 1992, 1993; id., 'Zum Gesetzesverständnis der nachprophetischen Zeit', in id., *Biblisch-theologische Aufsätze*, 1972, 179-94; J.D.Levenson, 'The Source of Torah: Psalm 119 and the Modes of Revelation in Second Temple Judaism', in *Ancient Israelite Religion, FS F.M.Cross*, 1987, 559-74; J.M.Mays, 'The Place of the Tora-Psalms in the Psalter', *JBL* 106, 1987, 3-12; A.Meinhold, 'Überlegungen zur Theologie des 19.Psalms', *ZTK* 79, 1982, 119-36; M.Noth, 'The Laws in the Pentateuch' (1940), in *The Laws in the Pentateuch and Other Essays*, 1966, 1-59; N.Sarna, 'Psalm XIX and the Near Eastern Sun-God Literature', *Fourth World Congress of Jewish Studies*, Vol.I, 1967, 171-5; H.W.Wolff, 'Psalm 1', *EvTh* 9, 1949/50, 385-94.

In the early Hellenistic period, in which pressure was felt to achieve a comprehensive theological synthesis at the level of official religion in order to meet the challenge posed by the Samarian separation and the first contacts with the Greek world culture, a new type of personal theology came into being, probably at the level of personal piety, which in its turn represents a wide-ranging emphatically Jewish synthesis. This is so-called 'Torah piety', of the kind that can be seen above all in Psalms 1; 19 and 119. If Chronicles had integrated many elements of personal piety in its presentation of the official history and theology of Israel, this new type of piety borrowed from a central element of the official religion of Israel by seeking to incorporate the Torah, created around a century before, which

essentially constituted Israel's identity, into each individual's personal
relationship with God.

Of course a precise dating of Pss.1; 19; 119 is impossible, but Deissler in
particular, after carefully weighing up linguistic and traditio-historical arguments
and arguments in terms of content[1] has indicated the probability of a dating for
Ps.119 in the first half of the third century. A similar dating is also considered
for Pss.1 and 19.[2] Psalms 19 and 119 in particular belong together linguistically
and thematically.[3] And both in turn seem to be at some distance in time and content
from the Chronistic history in its two stages. Like Ezra/Nehemiah the author of
Ps.19 quotes earlier sources, in vv.1-8 parts of a Canaanite creation hymn and an
Egyptian hymn to the sun,[4] and like Chronicles, Ps.119 stands out for its numerous
allusions to earlier Israelite literature (the musing style).[5] Finally, both agree in a
small but important linguistic innovation: only in Ezra 7.1; I Chron.28.8 and
Ps.119.45,94,155 is the verb *dāraš*, 'seek, research', which formerly denoted
enquiry of God and then religious devotion to God, related in the Old Testament
to the law. These agreements suggest that Torah piety similarly originated in scribal
circles.[6]

Now doubts have been expressed time and again whether the Torah of Yahweh
(*tōrat yhwh*, or *tōrā* with suffix) praised in the three Psalms denotes the canonized
Pentateuch.[7] However, such doubts are inappropriate. Certainly there is never any
mention of the Torah of Moses; certainly its character as scripture is never
emphasized particularly; and certainly some of the synonyms used for the Torah
go beyond the nomistic content of the Torah.[8] But God's Torah – in contrast to the
synonyms – is spoken of only in the singular: that indicates an already technical
usage. One can look at it (*nābaṭ*,[9] *šā'ā*[10]), reflect on (*śi'ḥ*[11]) and meditate on it (*hāgā*,
Ps.1.2, literally 'murmur'); so it is already fixed before the eyes. And of course the
Pentateuch contains not only laws but also promises and announcements of
judgment; the concept of Torah must therefore have a considerable span. Nor does
the fact that the author of Ps.119 often refers to prophets and wisdom writings tell
against the canonical understanding of the Torah; rather, it corresponds to the
tendency which can also be recognized in Chronicles to arrive at a synthesis of all
the religious writings.[12] Nor can the prominent references to the Deuteronomic/
Deuteronomistic strand of tradition in the Pentateuch be occasion for thinking of
a different Torah of Yahweh from the canonical one.[13] First of all, references to the
priestly strand are not completely absent,[14] and secondly, there had ceased to be a
pre-priestly Pentateuch, at the latest after Nehemiah.[15] Nor can it be concluded
from the fact that essential elements of the Pentateuch like the Deuteronomic/
Deuteronomistic and the Priestly notions of the covenant are passed over in the
Torah psalms that the Torah has been made absolute and detached from
the foundation history of Israel.[16] The lack is simply explained by the sociological
difference between official religion and personal piety: the functions of the Torah
of Yahweh related to the people as a whole simply play no part as a basis for the
personal relationship to God. The dehistoricized character of the Torah with an
individualistic focus[17] in the psalms mentioned is a consequence of internal religious
pluralism, and is no argument against its being identified with the canonical
foundation document of the same name.

The concern of those who promoted this new personal theology becomes clearest where they transferred to the Torah expressions of prayer language which in current personal piety were applied to God:[18] in their view not only God but God's Torah are to be the objects of the trust (Ps.119.42), the faith (v.66) and the hope (vv.43,74,81,114,137) of individuals. They are attentively to study it (v.30, cf. Ps.16.8), ardently to long for it (119.82,123), indeed raise their hands to it in supplication (v.48), and to ask God not to hide it (instead of 'his face', Ps.27.9, etc.) from them (119.19). The Torah is to be the basis on which individuals trust, confessing the certainty of their relationship with God (119.67,94,98,105,111,125); it is to be the guideline by which they can pray for their rescue by God ('Yahweh, teach me according to your ordinance', v.149).[19] Indeed, the advocates of this piety attributed not only to Yahweh but also to the Torah itself the power to give help and new life (19.8; 119.5, 144, 175). And so they also completely transformed the vow of praise into talk about following God's Torah and constantly being concerned with it (119.17,88,117,134,145,146), and set praise of the Torah (19.8-12; 119.171, etc.) alongside praise of God.

Now to suppose that the authors of the Torah psalms wanted to displace God by the Torah would certainly be a misunderstanding. On the contrary! Their interest was rather to intensify the personal relationship with God through the Torah and describe it in a new way: in their view the Torah was to be the medium through which the exchange between individuals and their God had to run. By anchoring the Torah at the heart of each individual's quite personal relationship to God, they wanted to offer people a material basis outside themselves on which they could ground their trust in God. In their view, God came very close to each individual not only in subjective feeling but also in 'Holy Scripture'. So everyone could come to close to God in a much more certain way, provided that they directed all their feeling, thought and action by scripture.[20]

Moreover, the centre of this new 'Bible piety' lay in the construction of a strongly emotional bond between the individual and scripture. Its promoters never grew tired of emphasizing their love for the Torah ('āhab, Ps.119.47,97,113,119,127,140,163,165,167), their joy (śīś, vv.14, 162; śāmaḥ, Ps.19.9) and their delight in it (śā'a, hitpalpael and noun, Ps.119.16,24,47,70,77,92,143,174; ḥepeṣ, Ps.1.2, verb, Ps.119.35), indeed their almost erotic longing for it (yā'ab, Ps.119.131; ṭā'ab and noun, vv.20,40,174; dābaq, v.31, cf. Gen.2.24). But in their view even religious reverence towards it was appropriate (119.120,161). In both, conscious dedication to God was to be symbolically visible to others and possible for everyone to experience for themselves.[21]

In the view of the promoters of this new piety, this emotional reference to scripture was to take shape in the life of each individual in two ways: in 'doing the Torah' and 'learning the Torah'.[22]

Here the more traditional possibility was the rooting of an ethical practice in a personal relationship with God. Here the authors took up the concerns whch had already governed the Deuteronomic reform movement[23] and which had also been pursued in personal wisdom theology.[24] A new development in comparison with the former was the individualizing focus which attributed responsibility for the obedience of faith completely to the individual and no longer wanted to be dependent on obligations of the popular community ('covenants'). What was new in comparison with the latter was on the one hand the normative exclusiveness of the ethical orientation: it was important not only to translate general ideals of piety from wisdom theology like the fear of God and a perfect way of life (cf. Job 41.6) into ethics, but to follow the existing regulations of the Torah of Moses.[25] On the other hand, the advocates of the new piety were no longer concerned, as the tradents of pious wisdom had been, to implement quite specific, e.g. social, modes of behaviour in the face of specific social challenges, but with a constant fundamental orientation of the individual on God's commandments: all individual decisions were to fit together into the way of life indicated by Yahweh's Torah.[26] For them, the Torah formed a way (Ps.119.14,27,32,33,35) which was clear to everyone and for which it was possible for the pious to decide (v.30), in which they could walk (vv.3,32,45) and not err from it (v.110), with God's guidance and illumination (vv.5, 27, 37, 105).

Alongside this generalized and individualized ethical practice the advocates of the Torah piety set a new *praxis pietatis*, an intensive pre-occupation with scripture. In their view the Torah was to be the object of constant contemplation (*nābaṭ*, Ps.119,6,15,18; *šāʿā*, v.117), penetrating research (*dāraš*, vv.45,94; cf. v.155[27]), intensive reflection (*śrḥ*, vv.15,23,27,48,78,148, noun vv.97,99), understanding (*yādaʿ*, vv.79,125,152) and learning (*lāmad*, vv.7,71,73). Evidently they already had the idea of regular 'meditation exercises' which were to be performed regularly day (vv.97,164) and night (vv.147f.). They probably took the form of a meditative reading half-aloud (*hāgā*, Ps.1.2). They thought that such a regular spiritual concern with scripture would give individuals a completely new basis for their personal relationship with God: in the study of scripture God would give them revelation (*gālā*, Ps.119.18), illumination ('*ōr*, hiphil, Ps.19.9; 119.30), true teaching (*lāmad*, piel, 119.12,26,64,66,68,108,124,135,171) and right understanding (*bīn*, hiphil, vv.27,34,73,125,130,144,169), provided that they prayed for it with all their hearts. In their discovery of constantly new references in the text God would open their eyes to the wonder (v.18) and boundless breadth (v.96) of the world of the Torah, give them a glimpse of its clarity (v.140), harmony (v.147) and truth ('*emet*, vv.142,151,160), so that they could only be amazed and praise God and his Torah (vv.129,164,171). Thus in addition to the sphere of normal everyday experience, in the study of scripture a new horizon of religious experience was opened up to individuals which was open to them even if they traced little of God elsewhere. And if here predominantly the side of the divine word of scripture was made the focal point of the religious insight that brought about life (v.50) and salvation (vv.75,144,172), this was very much in line with the primarily supportive function that personal piety had always had for the individual. From such immersion in study of the Torah individuals should and could gain direct divine strengthening and guidance for their lives.

What was the relationship between the new Torah piety, the basic features of which have just been described, and the preceding types of personal piety? The first thing to strike us is the way in which there are references to theologized wisdom, which since the fifth century had been the personal piety of the pious upper class. Alongside numerous overlaps in language and formulae,[28] both agree in a concern to root the ethical responsibility of the individual deeply in the personal relationship with God;[29] both understand suffering as a pedagogical measure on God's part,[30] expect God's individual recompense for the individual,[31] and propagate an attitude of humble piety.[32] We may infer from Ps.119.90f. that the author of the psalm had had a training in wisdom and thus had probably himself been one of the adherents of personal wisdom theology before he turned to Torah piety. Thus there is something to be said for regarding this as a development of the type of piety cultivated especially in the upper class.

However, the Torah piety is also not wholly unrelated to the piety of the poor which was cultivated especially in lower-class circles. Certainly the authors of the Torah psalms did not call themselves the poor (*'ebyōn, 'ānī,* etc.),[33] but like the latter they did feel themselves exposed to the direct attack of the influential wicked who tried to put them off their piety (Ps.19.14; 119.78), oppress them (vv.121f.,134) and annihilate them (vv.87,95). And so – in contrast to the pious upper class – they shared the expectation of the poor that Yahweh would soon have to intervene to put an end to the machinations of the godless rich (v.126, cf.84).

Thus Torah piety occupies a kind of intermediate position in relation to the earlier class-specific types of piety. This insight has consequences not only for its sociological setting but also for a more precise estimation of its intention in the religious discourse of the early Hellenistic period.

The simplest sociological consequence is probably to look for the adherents of Torah piety in a group which ran counter to the notorious split in the society of Judah between upper and lower classes. If in addition we note the central role they accorded to a concern with scripture, then we will most likely have to think of a group among the scribes. This conclusion is supported by the learned techique of exegesis in Ps.119, the presentation of both poems as so to speak 'intellectual sacrifices' (Ps.19; 119.108) and the excessively developed form of the acrostic of Ps.119. Accordingly, in contrast to wisdom theology and the piety of the poor, personal Torah theology was a development of personal piety not so much specific to a class as specific to a profession, in which scribal professional practice had attained the status of a new *praxis pietatis*. This intermediate sociological position of the group of scribal tradents is best explained by the assumption that while their members had had a wisdom education (Ps.119.90f.), through it they had come into close contact with members of the upper class and as a result shared many of their convictions; however, by descent they could come from quite different strata and their profession did not necessarily assure their rise in society.[34] They belonged among the educated, and therefore, like many aristocrats, among the intellectual leaders, but they were to be assigned more to the middle class in terms of income and social influence.

Now the social function of Torah piety can be described even more precisely in terms of this sociological determination of the group of tradents. The Torah scholars wanted, first, by incorporating the Torah indissolubly into personal piety, in accord with their position in the middle of society, to offer to the pious at all levels of a socially riven society a bond to unite them which would overcome all the class-specific distinctions of personal faith. And secondly, in this way they wanted to provide a clear theological criterion by which they could also set themselves apart from their adversaries through their quite personal practice of faith.

Both aspects of the aim can be demonstrated in detail, especially in Ps.119. Over long stretches its author is concerned to take up the notions and values above all of pious wisdom and redefine them in terms of his Torah theology. In his view, the only 'perfect of the way' (*tᵉmîmē derek*), as the pious aristocrats understood themselves to be (cf. Prov.11.20; Job 4.6), are those who 'walk in the Torah of Yahweh' (Ps.119.1), and the only ones who 'fear Yahweh' (Prov.1.7; Job 4.6) are those who 'follow Yahweh's ordinances' (Ps.119.63). He replaces the 'way of wisdom' (*derek ḥokmā*, Prov.4.11) with the way of God's commandments (Ps.119.27,32,33,35), and that of paternal instruction (Prov.6.23) with the guidance of God's word (Ps.119.105). He denies that wisdom has the mediating role in revelation which had been attributed to it in wisdom speculation (Prov.8), since in his view this role is played by the eternal word of Yahweh which was present at creation, and the world exists only in relation to the dispositions of the Torah which follow from it (Ps.119.89-91; cf. 19.1-5). In other words, the poet is constantly concerned to convince the adherents of personal wisdom theology with which he knows that he has bonds of friendship (119.63,74) that the orientation of their piety on universal human ethical and religious maxims is not enough; rather, their personal notions of faith will only come to fulfilment when they are focussed solely on the tradition of Israelite commandments and history. At the same time he also occasionally referred to notions from the piety of the poor, and its conviction that Yahweh is near to the humble with his grace, and will impose his judgment on the powerful wicked; this conviction was for the first time given a secure basis on the promises of the Torah and its announcements of judgment.[35]

Now what is striking in this pattern of argument aimed at a consensus is that the author of Ps.119 avoided any substantive discussion of where true obedience to the commandment lay in the face of the challenges of his time. Indeed this was difficult, given the different interests of the groups addressed. He contented himself with a concern to achieve the fundamental acceptance of an orientation on the Torah. His purpose was to create a distinctive Jewish personal theology and practice of piety which could unite all those who took their faith seriously beyond social and territorial barriers. To achieve that, he deliberately accepted a loss of ethical concreteness.

Where this plan for integration creates barriers becomes evident in the way in which the author of Ps.119 continually rules out the wicked (vv.53,113,136,139,158). There is no doubt that the references here, as already in the social controversies of the fifth and fourth centuries, are to the anti-social business activities of groups in the upper class.[36] But in Ps.119, strikingly, it is not so much social misconduct of which the scribe accuses them as wanton failure to observe the Torah (vv.21,53,85,118,126,136,139,150,155,158). For him, a personal bond with the Torah was the dividing line which clearly separated the pious from the wicked, and his own emotional concern for scripture was a demonstrative confessional act against the hated social group (vv.51ff.,61,69f.,78,87,95,100,139).

Beyond doubt such theologizing further hardened the fronts in the social conflict. The aristocrats who took no heed of social responsibility were not only subjected to social scorn with the general taunt of being wicked (*rāšā'*), but were also set apart in religious terms as standing outside the canonical consensus. Since there was nothing more to discuss, there were two clear ways that could be taken, that of the pious of the Torah and that of the despisers of the Torah, and by the choice of their practice of piety all individuals had to decide firmly which one to take (Ps.1; 119.29f.). Such a black-and-white religious picture of society, insisted on by the Torah scholars, was of course a provocation. And we can ask whether the enmity to which the author of Ps.119 saw himself exposed did not derive from acts of vengeance by the rich who were being attacked and felt that they were denigrated by such a theological view.

Nevertheless, there is no overlooking the fact that Torah piety – whether conscious or unconscious – also contributed towards sublimating the social conflict in religious terms. According to the pious scribes, it was no longer the scandalous social abuses which posed the real challenge to personal piety but what in their eyes was a scandalous lack of religious solidarity (Ps.119.136,139).[37] In contrast even to the adherents of personal wisdom theology in the fifth and fourth centuries, the Torah scholars of the third century evidently no longer saw any possibility of remedying the social abuses which had been consolidated over the centuries by religiously motivated, heightened social involvement.[38] From this perspective, the meditative immersion in the Torah which they propagated was also to some degree substitute religious satisfaction and a flight from reality.

So we have to say that unlike their colleagues who created Chronicles, the pious Torah scholars did not simply cover over the seething social conflict in the community of Judah in an idealistic way, but like them they did not make a very active contribution towards a solution to it either.[39] The contribution towards the future made by the Torah piety which they created certainly lay in its religious function of integration. Since with it the widespread personal piety which had originally been international was for the first time in the history of Israelite religion transformed into a specifically Jewish theology, a common basis had now been found at a family level as well on which all Jews who took their faith seriously could unite and by means of which they could also maintain their identity in an alien environment. From now on 'Holy Scripture' became the common axis for both the religion of the people and private religion. The distinctive and demanding personal theology and practice of piety in Judaism that required every lay person to be a 'mini-theologian', which we find fully developed in the rabbinic period, had its starting point here.

6.4 Late prophetic and apocalyptic theology of resistance

R.Albertz, *Der Gott des Daniel. Untersuchungen zu Dan 4-6 in der Septuagintafassung sowie zur Komposition und Theologie des aramäischen Danielbuches*, SBS 131, 1988; R.Bartelmus, *Heroentum in Israel und seiner Umwelt*, ATANT 65, 1979; K.Beyer, *Die aramäischen Texte vom Toten Meer samt den Inschriften aus Palästina, dem Testament Levis aus der Kairoer Genisa, der Fastenrolle und den alten talmudischen Zitaten*, 1984; J.J.Collins, *The Apocalyptic Vision of the Book of Daniel*, HSM 16, 1977; K.Ellinger, 'Ein Zeugnis aus der jüdische Gemeinde im Alexanderjahr 332 v.Chr.', ZAW 62, 1950, 63-115; H.Gese, 'Anfang und Ende der Apokalyptik dargestellt am Sacharjabuch' (1972), in id., *Vom Sinai zum Sion*, BEvTh 64, 1984, 202-30; id., 'Nachtrag: Die Deutung der Hirtenallegorie Sach 11,4ff.', ibid., 231-8; P.D.Hanson, *The Dawn of Apocalyptic. The Historical and Sociological Roots of Jewish Apocalyptic Eschatology*, [2]1979; D.Hellholm (ed.), *Apocalypticism in the Mediterranean World and the Near East*, 1983; A.Hultgaard, 'Das Judentum in der hellenistisch-römischen Zeit und die iranische Religion – ein religionsgeschichtliches Problem', ANRW II, 19.1, 1979, 512-90; O.Kaiser, *Isaiah 13-39* (ATD [2]1976), OTL, [2]1980; K.Koch, 'Vom prophetischen zum apokalyptischen Visionsbericht', in D.Hellholm (ed.), see above, 413-46; id., 'Die Sabbatstruktur der Geschichte', ZAW 95, 1983, 403-30; id., *Das Buch Daniel*, EdF 144, 1980;

H.S.Kvanvig, *Roots of Apocalyptic. The Mesopotamian Background of the Enoch Figure and the Son of Man*, WMANT 61, 1988; P.Lampe, 'Die Apokalyptiker – Ihre Situationen und ihr Handeln', in U.Luz (ed.), *Eschatologie und Friedenshandeln*, SBS 101, 1981, 59-114; J.C.H.Lebram, 'The Piety of Jewish Apocalyptists', in D.Hellholm (ed.), see above, 171-210; id., 'Apokalyptik und Hellenismus im Buche Daniel', *VT* 20, 1970, 503-24; J.T.Milik, *The Books of Enoch. Aramaic Fragments of Qumran Cave 4*, 1976; K.Müller, 'Die Ansätze der Apokalyptik', in J.Maier and J.Schreiner (eds.), *Literatur und Religion des frühen Judentums*, 1973, 31-42; G.W.E.Nickelsburg, 'Apocalyptic and Myth in I Enoch 6-11', *JBL* 96, 1977, 388-405; id., 'Riches, the Rich and God's Judgment in I Enoch 93-105 and the Gospel according to Luke', *NTS* 25, 1978, 324-4; id., 'Social Aspects of Palestinian Jewish Apocalypticism', in D.Hellholm (ed.), see above, 641-54; id., 'The Apocalyptic Message of I Enoch 92-105', *CBQ* 39, 1977, 309-28; P.von der Osten-Sacken, *Die Apokalyptik in ihrem Verhältnis zu Prophetie und Weisheit*, TEH NS 157, 1969; O.Plöger, *Theocracy and Eschatology*, 1968; G. von Rad, *Old Testament Theology* II, 1965; M.Saebø, *Sacharja 9-14*, WMANT 34, 1969; J.Schreiner, 'Die apokalyptische Bewegung', in id. and J.Maier (eds.), *Literatur und Religion desfrühen Judentums*, 1973, 214-53; H.Stegemann, 'Die Bedeutung der Qumranfunde für die Erforschung der Apokalyptik', in D.Hellholm (ed.), see above, 495-530; S.Uhlig, *Das äthiopische Henochbuch*, JSHRZ V, 6, 1984; M.-T.Wacker, *Weltordnung und Gericht. Studien zu 1 Henoch 22*, Forschung zur Bibel 45, 1982; H.Wildberger, *Jesaja. 2. Teilband: Jes 13-27*, BK X/2, 1978; I.Willi-Plein, *Prophetie am Ende. Untersuchungen zu Sach 9-14*, BBB 92, 1974; R.R.Wilson, 'From Prophecy to Apocalyptic. Reflections on the Shape of Israelite Religion', *Semeia* 21, 1982, 79-95.

It says much for the revolutionary force intrinsic to Yahweh religion from its beginnings that among those who handed it down were circles which were not content with the harmonizing syntheses which Chronicles offered for the sphere of official religion and the possibilities of retreat which Torah piety offered for the sphere of the private practice of faith, but, challenged by the sometimes painful political contradictions in the reality of Hellenistic Israel, at home and abroad, developed a new apocalyptic theology of resistance. With the at first tentative and then almost pedantic formulation of a broad complex of eschatological ideas of the total end of world history hitherto and a redemption in another world they made a decisive contribution towards preserving the religion of Israel from succumbing to the Hellenistic pressure to adapt, and gave it a new, second centre alongside the Torah. This development of Yahweh religion from a historical religion of liberation to an eschatological religion of redemption may be regarded as the most important change brought by the Hellenistic era.

Though this process is by and large undisputed, it is difficult to provide a detailed historical, traditio-historical and sociological context for it. For on the one hand many beginnings of the development can already be recognized in the 'eschatological' prophecy of the Persian period, indeed can be traced back to the exilic prophecy of salvation and the pre-exilic prophecy of judgment. On the other hand, the so-called apocalyptic writings which emerge at the latest from the end of the third century (I Enoch, Daniel) are formally and in terms of content such independent entities that they cannot simply be understood as a continuation of later prophecy. The endless discussion among scholars as to whether apocalyptic is still to be regarded as a child of prophecy or whether it is not rather a child of wisdom[1] marks this dilemma. The provisional conclusion that has been drawn is that certain formal elements (e.g. the description of visions,[2] interpreting angels,[3] coded accounts of history[4] and many individual motifs (e.g. the battle of the nations,[5] the theophany of judgment,[6] the revelation of the kingly rule of God[7]) have been taken from the prophetic tradition but cannot be called essential marks of apocalyptic writings.[8] The vague extension of the term 'apocalyptic' to cover prophecy already in Persian times, now usual in some quarters,[9] merely conceals the differences in content.

The problem becomes more acute in that the texts discovered in Qumran, above all those of the Enoch cycle,[10] have clearly shown that the beginning of the formation of the apocalyptic tradition is not the Maccabaean crisis (175 BCE), as had been thought on the basis of the book of Daniel, for a long time regarded as the earliest apocalypse. Rather, the oldest parts of the book of Enoch go back into the third century and indeed possibly to the end of the fourth.[11] And – as will emerge – the Aramaic book of Daniel was already an apocalyptic book from the end of the third century. But this also makes it chronologically impossible to understand the apocalyptic writings as a continuation of later prophecy, since the canon of the prophets was closed towards the end of the third century.[12] Rather, we must reckon that the latest parts of the prophetic writings (Zech.9-14; Isa.24-27) arose partly in parallel to the earliest apocalyptic writings.[13] Hence the assumption of a unilinear development is almost ruled out.

That in turn poses the problem of the sociological setting of the group of tradents. The differences in content and the chronological overlaps make it seem unadvisable to seek the tradents of later eschatological prophecy and early apocalyptic in one and the same social group, as Plöger, Hanson and others[14] did. Plöger's bipolar model of theocracy and marginalized 'prophetic conventicles' had already proved to be too sweeping for the early post-exilic period.[15] Rather, it emerged that only after the failure of the prophecy of Haggai and Zechariah, which had found broad acceptance in society, was the overflowing exilic prophecy of salvation forced into outsider groups, where it underwent an increasing 'eschatologizing'.[16] The formation of a prophetic conventicle in the lower class could then be demonstrated in the social conflict of the late Persian period (from the middle of the fifth century).[17] It seemed probable that essential parts of post-exilic prophecy, above all those which focus on judgment for the wicked and the liberation of the poor, could be derived from these lower-class circles.[18] And the same can be said at any rate for the later prophetic tradition of the Hellenistic period (Isa.24-27).[19]

However, such a derivation cannot be considered for the apocalyptic literature, because the theme of social conflict plays no role at all in it until its second main phase (up to 160 BCE). This theme was only partly incorporated into it after the establishment of Hasmonaean rule (thus especially I Enoch 92-105).[20] Now the presentation of Enoch as 'scribe of righteousness' (*grammateus tes dikaiosynes,*

I Enoch 12.4; 15.1; cf.12.3) or Daniel as a member of the 'truly wise' (*maśkīlīm*, Dan.12.3, 10) most probably indicates groups of scribes, and the learned diction of the apocalypses also fits this well. Other texts standing near to the apocalypses suggest priests as tradents (4QAmram; Jubilees; 1QM 1[21]). So there is everything to be said for supposing that unlike parts of the late prophetic tradition which came from lower-class circles with a prophetic orientation, the new type of apocalyptic literature was created by members of a stratum of intellectual leaders,[22] albeit ones who were in marked opposition to the Hellenizing part of the upper class and in solidarity with the impoverished conservative population of city and country. Such a sociological context not only explains the difference in content and parallelism in time between eschatological prophecy and apocalyptic, but also defines its positive relationship: apocalyptic is a scribal working out of eschatological prophecy. With it, intellectuals took up expectations for the future which had previously been developed or handed down above all in marginal groups and lower-class circles, and transposed them into new teaching on the course and necessary end of world history which had been carefully reflected on and systematized. By this quasi-scholarly presentation, they gave eschatological expectations which had hitherto been marginalized an enormous penetrative power in the anti-Hellenistic and anti-Hasmonaean rebel movements and a broad social influence which they had never had before. That is the only explanation of the way in which eschatology could become a widely accepted element of official Jewish and later also the Christian religion, even even if most apocalyptic writings later fell into discredit again.[23]

The following account cannot possibly survey all the texts which might possibly be relevant, the dating of which is sometimes also disputed. For late-prophetic texts it is limited to Zech.9-11 and Isa.24-27, and for apocalyptic literature it is concentrated above all on Ethiopian Enoch (= I Enoch) and Daniel.

6.41 *Oppositional eschatological interpretation of history (Zech.9-14)*

Though the leading circles of the community of Judah attached little importance to the collapse of Persian supremacy and the establishment of Macedonian supremacy, in prophetically orientated groups the upheaval in world politics seemed to be watched with ardent expectations and bitter disappointments. At any rate, the formation of a prophetic tradition which it sparked off can be seen with some probability in the books of Deutero- and Trito-Zechariah.

That Zech.9ff. belongs in the Hellenistic period is shown by the mention of the 'sons of Jawan' (= Greece) in 9.13.[24] Moreover, the hypothesis put forward by Elliger, namely that Alexander's campaign of 332 BCE underlies the saying about the nations in Zech.9.1-8, still has a good deal to be said for it. Zechariah 11.15 also marks a change of rule, probably that from the Persians to the Greeks;[25] Zech.10.11 seems already to presuppose the break-up of Alexander's empire after 323. So the dating of at least the book Deutero-Zechariah, Zech.9-11, in the early Hellenistic period is relatively certain.[26] The book of Trito-Zechariah (12-14) cannot be dated with certainty, but -- as the many links with Zech.9-11 show[27] -- it was probably composed from the start as a continuation of Deutero-Zechariah.[28] It will belong to the end of the fourth or the beginning of the third century.

Zechariah 9[29] still wholly breathes the atmosphere of tense expectations of salvation which the prophetic group had about the upheaval in world politics. Having for two hundred years under stable Persian rule evidently bidden farewell to history, Yahweh now finally seemed to be intervening again (9.8; cf. v.12), to usher in the overthrow of the world powers of which the prophet Zechariah had spoken in 519 (cf. 4.10) and which had been so long desired. In the view of the group, it had been a word of Yahweh which had set in motion the triumphant progress of Alexander to Syria-Palestine (9.1ff.), and Alexander's crushing of the small states of Phoenicia and Philistia showed the might with which God broke the pride of the political powers (9.3f.,5f.). It was thought that God would also proceed against the power of Greece in the same way (9.13), and defeat it in a great epiphany (9.14) to liberate his people Israel (9.11f.) and with it all those who similarly had been the victims of alien political rule (9.7). Then God would establish his kingdom of peace (9.10) in which all could enjoy his blessing undisturbed (9.17) without fear of threat (9.8).

The way in which the group envisaged the dawn of the rule of God shows that they were fully in the prophetic tradition with its criticism of domination, especially that of Isaiah and Deutero-Isaiah, and therefore attempted to combine various ideas from it in a concrete way: Yahweh's kingly rule ultimately establishes itself in the face of all human political power, as in Deutero-Isaiah, even if it makes use of a great power for an intermediary phase.[30] It is itself of quite a different quality from human power. To make this clear, in Zech.9.9 the group combined the cry of joy over the advent of the divine king on Zion (Isa.52.7) with the notion of a Davidic king of salvation of the kind that had been developed e.g. in Isa.11. But it depicted this human king who represents divine rule even more consistently than in Isa.11 as a complete antitype to the usual political potentates: not only does he come without power and glory, but he himself is a victim of the exercise of political power hitherto, wretched (*'ānī*) and pious (*ṣaddīq*). He is one who himself – like the oppressed pious – was in need of God's deliverance (*nōšā'*). Therefore the rule which he exercises in the name of God will also be different from all human rule known hitherto:[31] he will disarm his own people and set up his universal realm of peace, not through military subjection but simply through the word (9.10). With this concretizing of the kingly rule of Yahweh the prophetic group found its way through to a utopia of political rule based on conviction and consensus which recalls earlier utopias like Isa.2.2-4 and 42.1-4. However, a new element was that it positively introduced its own experiences as a victim of political domination into the utopia: only those who like it had helplessly suffered the whole oppressive mechanism of political power would be able to exercise non-violent rule on behalf of God. We will also rediscover a similar utopia fundamentally critical of domination in apocalyptic garb, in the Aramaic book of Daniel.[32]

However, the prophetic group had the experience that its great hopes associated with Alexander's campaign were not fulfilled; on the contrary, the never-ending wars of the Diadochi which caused Palestine such bitter suffering between 321 and 301 confronted them vividly with the whole inhuman absurdity of the human exercise of power. So in the extension of its prophecy in Zech.10 and 11 we see the group concerned to revise its prophecy of salvation and seek the reasons why the kingdom of God did not come. It concluded that Yahweh first had to annihilate all political holders of power ('shepherds'), both the new Greek potentates (10.3,11; 11.1f.) and their collaborators from Judah (10.3; 11.3,17),[33] before he could liberate Israel with the help of the masses of its people who were now still oppressed and being led astray (10.3-5; cf. v.2). And it identified as the reason why salvation failed to come a complete lack of religious orientation among its own people, for which it put the blame on its ruling class (10.1-2). The group believed that the great salvation for Israel was possible only through a new future judgment which would above all affect the leading elite abroad and at home, one which, in other words, would be both universal and selective.[34] Moreeover universality and selectivity would be characteristics of apocalyptic notions of judgment.[35]

Finally, the prophetic group attempted to interpret its bitter disappointment over the result of the shift in world politics in terms of a theology of history (Zech.11.4-16). However, it did this in allegorical symbolic action which is so cryptic that it has yet to be interpreted in a completely convincing way; evidently it was intended only for use within the group and could presuppose knowledge among the hearers of the time that we no longer have.[36] Still, at least it is clear that after the mission of a first shepherd has failed (vv.4-14), Yahweh commissions a second shepherd who will rule in such a 'crazy' way that he negates all that makes a good regent: he will not be concerned for the weak, and will plunder and torment the rich (vv.15f.; cf. Ezek.34.3f.,16).[37]

If such an interpretation in terms of contemporary history is correct, then the first shepherd commissioned by Yahweh is either the Persian kingdom or the whole sequence of oriental empires from the Assyrians and Babylonians to the Persians.[38] This commissioning, too, was already a sign of the wrath of God, as a result of which he withdrew his mercy from the nations (Zech.11.4: 'battle of the sheep') and abandoned them to the whim of their potentates (v.6). Nevertheless, this rule was still backed by a remnant of divine grace in that in it Yahweh had made a covenant with all peoples (v.10) which united them in 'grace' and 'union' (v.7). When Yahweh then became sated with the oriental kingdoms and destroyed the

Persian empire (v.8-10), 'the traffickers who were watching me', i.e. probably the leading class of Judah,[39] recognized clearly that the prophetic word of God had brought this about (v.11; cf. 9.1). But despite this demonstration of the credibility of their message, the tradents of this word of God,[40] the marginalized eschatological groups of prophets, in no way received due recognition from the religious and political leaders of Judah but were fobbed off with a 'slave's reward' (11.12). Because of this lack of respect Yahweh also withdrew the last remnant of grace from his rule of the world: he made the 'brotherhood between Judah and Israel' collapse (v.14).

If this interpretation is correct, then Zech.11.4-16 points to a deep dissent between the political and religious leaders of the community of Judah and the groups orientated on the eschatological prophets. The latter clashed with the former over what the theological assessment of the past, the present and the future required: whereas the Chronistic history had understood Persian rule, which at any rate had given Israel the Torah, as an expression of God's gracious concern (Ezra.1.1ff.), the prophetic group saw it as the expression of a wrath which had only been assuaged a little. If Chronicles sought to understand any historical present as a time in which Yahweh's everlasting grace was in principle open to Israel, provided that Israel proved itself, the prophetic group regarded the present as a chance of salvation which had been finally forfeited. And if on the basis of the saving gift of the temple Chronicles confidently looked toward the future and perhaps even expected from the Hellenistic period a restoration of Davidic rule, the prophetic group saw Israel facing a new time of judgment under a foreign rule more brutal than any yet. It saw the cultic split with the Samarians, who also rejected the prophetic hopes of union which it had put forward (Zech.9.13; 10.6f.; cf. Ezek.37.15ff.), as a sign of judgment, whereas the leading circles of Judah which stood behind Chronicles saw it only as an infringement of their claim to leadership which could be remedied with the right theological propaganda.[41] The nub of the argument was the official recognition of eschatological prophecy. The scribal authors of Chronicles had certainly attempted to give prophecy a greater status in official Yahweh religion, but they only allowed it to the degree that it seemed useful for everyday guidance.[42] They had deliberately excluded eschatological prophecy. Such a failure to take note of eschatological prophecy in the decisive hour of the upheaval in world politics and the ongoing marginalization of its tradents was the decisive reason why the prophetic opposition group behind Deutero-Zechariah believed that the great chance of the coming of the kingdom of God had been forfeited.

The cryptic allegorical description of the divine rule of the world with a sequence of deteriorating world empires, the beginnings of which are present in Zech.11.4-16, is taken up and developed systematically by the apocalyptic authors.[43]

The book of Deutero-Zechariah ended with sharp imprecations on the leaders of Judah (Zech.11.17), but at a later point it was expanded again to make the whole work end in salvation. The authors of Trito-Zechariah followed in the footsteps of their preccecessors to the degree that their starting point was that there must first be a settling of internal conflicts[44] and a removal of uncleanness[45] before Yahweh could establish his universal kingdom in Jerusalem (14.5b,9). For that, Yahweh would subject his people to a harsh judgment of purification (Zech.13.7-9) which, going beyond the leading class, would also exterminate two-thirds of the people (vv.7f.). For Israel the day of Yahweh would in no way be a day of triumph but would first be a day of judgment (14.1).[46] The onslaught of the nations on Zion would certainly not be stopped by God at the beginning, as the traditional Zion theology wanted to make people believe,[47] but would first strike Jerusalem with all its force: the city would be conquered and plundered, and half its population deported (14.2). Thus there would not be an unbroken development leading to the promised salvation, as might have been expected in line with the exilic and early post-exilic prophecy of salvation; first Israel would have to undergo Yahweh's harsh judgment, like the nations. It was even intimated that this would be associated with a civil war between Judah and Jerusalem (14.14).[48] With such an emphasis on the aspect of judgment in the ultimate deliverance to be expected, the Trito-Zechariah group prepared for the apocalyptic notion of the 'terrors of the end-time'.[49]

6.42 An eschatological assurance of salvation from lower-class circles (Isa.24-27)

Unlike Zech.9ff., the second late-prophetic formation of tradition, the so-called 'Isaiah Apocalypse' (Isa.24-27), was not sparked off by a great historical event but arose entirely out of the theological reflections of a group. So it is more difficult to date than Deutero-Zechariah, though easier to put into a sociological context.

For a long time scholars have thought that they could understand the chapters about the destruction of an unnamed city, mentioned in Isa.24.10-12; 25.2,12; 26.5; 27.10, as the reflection of a historical event, and thus be able to date it. Events considered have included the capture of Babylon by Cyrus in 539, Xerxes in 485 or Alexander in 331; the destruction of a Moabite city (cf.25.10bff.), say Dibon, in 270; or even the fall of Carthage in 146, the Jerusalem Acra in 141 or Samaria in 107 BCE. But the quite manifest randomness of the identifications only proves the impossibility of drawing any historical conclusions. So there is much to be said for the view put forward by Plöger[50] and Kaiser[51] that the thought is not of the annihilation of a particular city but of urban life generally. Unlike 9.1-8, the description of the catastrophe in Isa.24 lacks any historical details; instead of this it has dimensions of primal history (for 24.1, cf. Gen.11.9; for 24.18b, Gen.7.11) and in part seems to have been spun out of earlier prophetic announcements of judgment (cf. on 24.4; Hos.4.3); i.e., evidently the authors did not envisage any acute political threat.

Now if we add to this the observation that Isa.24.2 presupposes a society in which the priests occupy a clear position of leadership over the laity, which as far as we know was first the case in the Hellenistic period, and further take into account that some details of the idea of the future have parallels in the apocalyptic literature,[52] there is something to be said for a dating in the Ptolemaic period, which before 221 granted Palestine a lengthy period of peace.

The chapters show traces of literary growth, though so far no generally convincing literary-critical solution has been found.[53] It is clear that 24.21-23 and 25.6-10a form a later stratum and that ch.27 has a rather special position.[54] But the formation of the tradition at least of chs.24-26 – apart from some small possible additions[55] – seems to have taken place in the same milieu.[56] So it is inadvisable to extend its time-span over more than a few generations: I think it most probable that the chapters were written between 300 and 221.

The sociological context at least of chs.24-26 is quite clear; in contrast to Zech.9-14 we find all the terminology developed in the social conflict of the Persian period with its contrast between 'righteous' (*ṣaddîq*, Isa.24.16; 26.7) and 'wicked' (*rāšā*, 26.10; cf. 'faithless', 24.16; 'ruthless', 25.2,5[57]) or 'poor' (*'ebyōn*, 25.4; *'ānî*, 26.6; *dal*, 25.4; 26.6) and 'oppressor' (*'arîṣ*, 25.4f.), which we found both in the proclamation and the piety of lower-class circles orientated on prophecy.[58] The assumption that such circles are also to be seen as the tradents of Isa.24-26 (27) has much to be said for it.

The distress which the group of tradents of Isa.24-26 suffered and from which it developed its eschatological hopes becomes clear from the lament (26.7-18), which may go back to its liturgical practice. First of all there was its real distress: it was dominated by lords, native and foreign potentates, where really Yahweh alone should be its lord (26.13).[59] Secondly, and even more oppressively, there was its theological distress: Yahweh's great judgment on its opponents to which it looked forward (v.8) still failed to come. The wicked who oppressed it could twist the law further without having to take note of the compelling power of Yahweh; they could refuse to take any heed at all of Yahweh's hand already raised to strike (vv.10bf.). Were their exploiters to find grace without finally learning righteousness and solidarity (*ṣedeq*) under the compulsion of God (v.10a)? And thirdly, there was the distress resulting from the two distresses already mentioned: the political and theological impotence of the group. Its members attempted with their constant prayers finally to force Yaweh to intervene, but they did not achieve anything. They could not win any victories on earth or bring down their over-powerful opponents (vv.16-18).[60] So theirs was an impotent suffering over the fact that Yahweh took no steps against the injustice that they had to suffer, and that formed the existential background to their eschatological expectations.

The observation that, for the group, political enemies at home and abroad quite clearly correspond is important for understanding these expectations. In Isa.26.9f., in parallel to the wicked man (*rāšāʿ*) there is mention of the inhabitants of the earth (*yōšᵉbē tebel*, cf. v.18). We came up against the unique parallelizing of the wicked and the nations earlier, in the piety of the poor (Ps.9.6, etc.).[61] This was clearly a characteristic perspective of the lower class, which coincided with the fact that that part of the upper class of Judah which was showing no solidarity collaborated more or less openly with the foreign power. The lower-class group behind Isa.24-27 generalized and universalized the conflict within Judah one step further: it saw itself delivered over to a world of evil enemies as a small, lost group. From its perspective the inhabitants of the earth seemed in general to be apostate (24.5) and faithless (24.16); they had desecrated the earth with their misdeeds to such an extent that even this seemed sinful to them (24.20). This totally negative view of the world was probably connected with the marked international economic and cultural interweaving of the Hellenistic world into which the upper class of Judah were increasingly allowing themselves to be incorporated. And the fact that 'Israel' as an entity was largely absent from this view[62] and a small group of the pious saw themselves as being face to face with a corrupt world reflects the loss of social and cultural solidarity in the society of Judah which no longer provided in any way for those forced into a situation of distress. The individualizing universalism which moreover is also partly typical of apocalyptic literature[63] originally derived from the perspective of oppressed marginal groups as victims, as we can see from Isa.24ff.

In the light of the lament in Isa.26.7-18, the whole eschatological scenario which is flicked through in Isa.24-27 can be understood as an assurance of salvation within the group, offered in a whole variety of new approaches. The members of the religious circle in the lower class were evidently not prepared to be content with their lasting situation of oppression, but despite lasting experiences of disappointment and helplessness built up a counter-liturgical world by singing and reciting texts in which their great hope had already been fulfilled (cf.Isa.25.9f.). That explains the interweaving of prophetic and liturgical genres[64] and the preponderance of verb-forms in the perfect.[65]

The eschatological expectations of the group have a universal and an individual perspective. The first is marked above all by the fact that the dawn of salvation is preceded by a more total and universal act of judgment on the part of God than had ever previously been conceived of in the prophetic tradition: the group thought that Yahweh would make the whole earth desolate and depopulate it (Isa.24.1,6). And to depict the extent of the destruction for the first time they also had recourse to the categories of primal history; since the covenant with Noah had been broken by the inhbabitants of the earth (24.5), Yahweh too would withdraw his guarantee of the earth's existence (Gen.8.21f.; 9.11f.) and bring a new flood on the earth (Isa.24.18b; cf. Gen.7.11). The whole civilized world of human beings would sink into chaos,[66] and humankind would again be scattered as it had been once after its failure to build the tower of Babel (24.1b *pūṣ*, hiphil, cf. Gen.11.9).

Now this hope of judgment, virtually amounting to the end of the world, had a clear function for the lower-class group, as a critique of society and civilization: the judgment would above all affect 'the heights' of the population of the earth (24.4).[67] All social differences in its society, split as it was between priests and laity, masters and slaves, creditors and debtors, would be levelled out: the rich masters under whom they suffered would lose all their social privileges (24.2). The whole life of the city with its carefree, joyful delights, cherished above all by its upper class (cf.25.5) would come to grief (24.7-12). How marked the aversion of the group was to city culture is shown by the fact that along with the destruction of the earth (24.19f.) they could rejoice in the destruction of 'the city' as an act of their liberation (25.2; 26.5; cf.25.12). To the group, the towering city with its fortifications and 'palaces of the wicked' (25.2) was a model of blasphemy (cf. *zēdīm*) and violent oppression (cf. *'ārīṣīm*, 25.5). Only if it fell, along with its godless inhabitants, would the poor again be able to experience the protection of God in their need (25.4). And the group happily depicted how the wretched would trample down the city with their own feet (26.6).

What was the social background to this unique interweaving of a critique of society and civilization? Alongside the notorious conflict between city and country, which stemmed from the fact that the great landowners resided in their city houses and indulged in their life of luxury while the small farmers dependent on them spent their life far away in the villages, we must also take into account the new developments of the Hellenistic period, which gave a powerful impetus to city culture in Syria-Palestine and made the cities centres of Hellenistic culture. Certainly we do not have foundations of any Hellenistic cities in the sphere of Judah, and even in Jerusalem Hellenistic culture took some time to spread.[68] However, the lower-class groups which lived on the land must have felt that they were surrounded by a city culture suspect to them, which formed the starting point for their oppression. So I would see the cultural transformation undergone by the social conflict in the Hellenistic period,[69] from which the Maccabaean revolt then derived a good deal of its potential for conflict, as being responsible for the remarkable notion of judgment in Isa.24-27.

Initially the notions of the group centred on a universal abolition of the upper class of the city and a social liberation of the poor, who as the true pious would be received into a totally new city which Yahweh would build (Isa.26.1-3). Rather later, though, its eschatological expectations of judgment and salvation were developed more strongly in the direction of world politics and cosmology. On the day of judgment Yahweh would visit 'the kings of the earth' and imprison them for a long time until their final condemnation, before he entered into his royal rule on Zion (24.21-23). Coupled with this there would be a judgment on the 'host of heaven, in heaven', probably meaning stars or the gods or angels standing behind them, who guided the destiny of the kings and their peoples.[70] With this unique notion – perhaps stimulated by Bablyonian astrology, which was becoming popular in the Hellenistic period – they probably meant simply to indicate that supernatural powers stood behind the earthly powers under which they had to suffer. The wickedness of the powerful reached to heaven; therefore it was no use for them simply to fall: they had to be imprisoned permanently if Yahweh's rule was to come into being. This projection of the political and social conflict on to a cosmological and mythical level, which is only hinted at here, was then to find a following in apocalyptic literature.[71]

By contrast, the way in which the lower-class group elaborated the traditional eschatological expectation of the establishment of the reign of Yahweh on Zion (Isa.15.6-8; cf. Isa.52.7) can again be explained far better from its situation of social distress. Taking up the theme of the pilgrimage of the nations, it imagined that Yahweh would prepare a lavish banquest on Mount Zion for the oppressed of all the peoples, who would finally be liberated from the power of their taskmasters;[72] he would take from them all their mourning garb [73] and lovingly, like a mother, wipe away all their tears. Then finally the shame which his tiny people of the pious had had to endure so long on earth would be removed. That is the language of people for whom hunger, suffering and tears alone are a constant everyday experience. That is the language of people who have learned from their decades of oppression that there should be a world-wide human solidarity of all who suffer, which extends further than the frontiers between the nations.

It says much for the marked pastoral impulse which dominated the theological work of the prophetic lower-class circle that in developing a universal eschatological panorama it did not keep to a general assurance of salvation but also developed individual eschatological notions which could comfort any of its members. These were the notions of the resurrection of the dead (26.19) and the ultimate permanent abolition of death (25.8aα).[74]

The tentative and pictorial formulas of Isa.26.19 also indicate that in its liturgical assurances of salvation, at this point the group was venturing on to new ground. This was a confession of confidence which was formulated by the leader of the group[75] in the face of its painful experience of helpless waiting for the great intervention of God in judgment. He answered the doubt as to how they and those of their number who had died trusting in God would ever achieve the dawn of salvation which was so long delayed with the assurance that the bodies of the pious would awaken once again from the dust, rise and live,[76] to share in the joy of those who had been liberated. So we do not yet have a 'general resurrection of the dead' of the kind that we are later to find in the book of Daniel (Dan.12.2), but a resurrection of the pious poor, who had been denied salvation by God in their miserable lives. On the basis of this certainty of not being excluded from the eschatological dawn of salvation they were able confidently to survive the time of wrath still to come, no matter what might happen to them personally (Isa.26.20f.).

The hope of individual resurrection was also incorporated – in a generalized pespective – into God's universal work of liberation (Isa.25.8aα); the group arrived at the conviction that after the dawn of salvation not only all suffering but also death would be removed as the last power to separate from God. The constant threat of death which was now strangling the life of each individual would no longer be able to trouble joyful communion with God. So the budding resurrection faith in Isa.24ff. is an expression of the concentrated spiritual will to resist on the part of oppressed people who were not content with their hopeless personal perspectives on life.

6.43 Apocalyptic instructions for resistance

As I have indicated above,[77] the literature of late prophetic opposition from the lower class was not continued directly in apocalyptic. Rather, the formation of the tradition of apocalyptic literature took place independently, and initially in parallel to it – its content probably related to prophetic eschatology. Certainly today we are still a long way from being able to illuminate its beginnings and its course in every detail, but at least some important phases of the development can be reconstructed. The most important approach to it is provided by the tradition history of the two earliest works of apocalyptic literature, the book of Enoch and the book of Daniel.

The origin of the mighty compendium of the Ethiopian book of Enoch (I Enoch) with its 108 chapters spans at least a quarter of a millennium (from around the middle of the third to the end of the first century BCE). We can give a firm date only to the 'Book of Dream Visions' (I Enoch 83-90), the 'Animal Apocalypse' in which denotes Israelite history up to the battles of Judas Maccabaeus, and therefore must have been composed before his death in 160 BCE. As this already presupposes the story of the fall and punishment of apostate angels (86-88) which is reported in I Enoch 6-11 (16), the 'Book of the Watchers' (I Enoch 1-36) must be older, though how much so is not completely certain. Since the fragmentary Qumran manuscript 4QEnᵃ, which for palaeographical and philological reasons is to be dated to the time around 170 BCE, at any rate attests the Aramaic text of I Enoch 1-11, the complicated history of the origin of the 'Book of Watchers' must have been completed at least up to ch.19 by then,[78] and probably even further, so that its beginning goes back into the third century. How far, however, cannot be determined with certainty. Kvanvig[79] and Nicklesburg would want to go back to the time of the Diadoche, i.e. even to the end of the fourth century (before 301) for its undisputed earliest part, I Enoch 6-11; however, the latter also considers an alternative dating in the time of Antiochus III (after 221).[80] But since the chapters already indicate some knowledge of Greek mythology, as Nickelsburg himself works out, a later dating is more probable, and since economic rather than military oppression is in the foreground (I Enoch 7.3; cf.10.18), we need not necessarily assume a time when Palestine was caught up in war. So I would prefer to put the earliest nucleus of the book of Enoch around the middle of the third century. This nucleus was probably worked over at a very early stage (Azazel stratum, I Enoch 7.1b; 8.1-3; 9.6f.,8b; 10.4-8),[81] and in a series of stages was given an apocalyptic framework (I Enoch 1-5 + 12-19) which was then expanded once again (20-36, Enoch's second heavenly journey). This process of tradition may have occupied the second half of the third century and perhaps extended into the beginning of the second century.

In all probability the 'Book of Heavenly Luminaries' (I Enoch 72-82) similarly goes back to the third century, but still in Qumran it forms a separate – very much more extensive – scroll and does not belong directly to the apocalyptic Enoch literature. The 'Epistle of Enoch' (I Enoch 92-105), which also contains the so-called 'Apocalypse of Weeks' (I Enoch 93.1-10 + 91.11-17), comes from a later phase of the controversy under the Hasmonaeans (beginning of the second century).[82] By contrast, the 'Similitudes of Enoch' (I Enoch 37-71) are not contained in the Enoch writings from Qumran and probably come from a later time. So they are not considered here.

The tradition history of the book of Daniel was comparatively shorter. In its present mixed Aramaic/Hebrew form it was composed at the time of the Maccabaean revolt before the dedication of the temple (164 BCE), probably in 165 BCE. It was preceded by the Aramaic book of Daniel (2-7*),[83] which, contrary to widespread view, was also an apocalyptic book and, like the Aramaic 'Book of the Watchers' (I Enoch 1-19/36), comes from the end of the third century. Here, as I have attempted to demonstrate elsewhere,[84] it contains an eschatologically orientated Greek collection of conversion stories from the Egyptian Diaspora (Dan 4-6* LXX), which probably arose in the first half of the third century.

This produces the following approximate chronology for early apocalyptic literature:

Preliminary phase (third century to c.221): Ptolemaean rule to the accession of Antiochus III.
    Collection of Greek Daniel narratives (Dan.4-6* LXX)
    Narrative of the fall of the angels (I Enoch 6-11 including the Azazel revision).
First main phase (v.221-200): riots against the Ptolemies (Dan.11.14)
    'Book of the Watchers' (I Enoch 1-19/36)
    Aramaic book of Daniel (Dan.2-7*)

Second main phase (176-160): Maccabaean revolt
  'Animal Apocalypse' (I Enoch 85-90)
  Hebrew book of Daniel (Dan 1-12)
  Subsequent phase (c.110-75): anti-Hasmonaean rebellions
  'Epistle of Enoch' including the 'Apocalypse of Weeks' (I Enoch 91-105).[85]

It becomes clear above all in the preliminary phase of the formation of apocalyptic tradition how markedly this differed both materially and formally from the late prophetic lines of tradition. The Greek narrative collection Dan 4-6 LXX, which connected together three individual stories about Daniel, the legendary wise interpreter of dreams and sage court official, from the Babylonian Diaspora of the late Persian period,[86] probably had an eschatological perspective, but in contrast to the prophecy of Deutero- and Trito-Isaiah which arose at about the same time this was quite predominantly optimistic; its author, who probably came from the upper class of the Alexandrian Diaspora, saw the developing Greek ecumene – probably encouraged by the liberal religious policy of Ptolemy II Philadelphus (285-246 BCE) – as a great opportunity for Jewish mission.[87] Using Nebuchadnezzar as an example, he wanted to demonstrate that God himself could turn this ruler who destroyed the temple into an adherent and defender of Jewish religion if only he was guided by a wise Jewish interpreter of dreams (Dan.4 LXX). Certainly there were constant set-backs, as he made clear by the example of Belshazzar, so that a world ruler lapsed from the true God and turned blasphemously to pagan idolatry, with the result that God also deprived him of his rule (Dan.5 LXX), but these were not irreversible, as he showed by the example of Darius (Dan.6 LXX). Despite the intrigues of malicious minions which brought pious and loyal Jewish officials into discredit, with God's help there was time and again the opportunity to convert the ruler of the world and create a form of political rule in which pious Jews even occupied leading posts in government.

The ultimate conversion of all peoples to Yahweh had in fact also been the perspective of the eschatological prophecy along the lines of the Deutero-Isaiah group.[88] But in contrast to Zech.9-14, in the view of the Diaspora theologians this would not come about through a terrifying judgment of Yahweh which annihilated all present rulers, but through the brave witness of pious Jews in pagan service, by converting the ruler and reforming his government from within.[89] The upper-class perspective of the author of the Greek Daniel narratives becomes evident above all from the fact that he depicts the universal extension of worship of Yahweh as a mission from above, in that the converted ruler of the world enacted protective laws in favour of Jewish faith and accorded these the status of a state religion (Dan.4.37A,B; 6.26-28 LXX). In his eyes the Hellenistic ruler of the world was Yahweh's instrument for achieving universal recognition.

Certainly time and again there were points of conflict, like the Hellenistic ruler cult (Dan.6.8f., LXX), but these could be survived if Jewish officials in the service of the Ptolemies at the same time remained loyal both to Yawheh and to their king. Fundamentally in his eyes Greek alien rule could be reformed; it just needed wise and loyal members of the Jewish upper class to guide it in the right way.

The author of I Enoch 6-11* could not share this optimistic assessment of Hellenistic rule in the pre-apocalyptic Daniel tradition. In his view this rule caused economic exploitation (7.3), injustice, violence and blood (9.1,9; 10.15) which devastated existence, and this dire evil was directly linked with the self-deification of the Hellenistic rulers. To explain the true grounds for this destructive rule and its future, on the basis of the Torah he created a mythical didactic narrative. A small piece of the mythological hero tradition had been included in Gen.6.1-4 to illustrate the corruption of human beings before the flood. The author of I Enoch 6-11* took up these hints from the Torah (6.1f.,7.2), and countered the religious claim of Hellenistic rulers to be divine incarnations[90] by connecting it with the old tradition of a sexual union between angels and human women. But in contrast to the Greek hero tradition,[91] for him – further developing the critical tendency of Torah – it was the evil action of apostate angels which tore the structure of the world apart (6.3-6). So the children of this union (the giants, according to Gen.6.4) could only destroy the whole creation: they devoured everything, first human achievements, then themselves, and finally the animals (I Enoch 7.3-5).

If in late prophetic texts the idea had emerged that there were heavenly powers behind the political rulers (Isa.24.21), the author of I Enoch 6-11 showed by means of a clear mythological explanatory model how political power had come to be so destructive and demonic. His mythological information about the world of angels, which took up and systematized the belief in angels and demons that was suppressed in official Yahweh religion but grew increasingly virulent among ordinary people, clearly aims to enlighten and teach his audience.

The continuation of the Genesis narrative gave the author of I Enoch.6-11 the possibility of writing about not only the origin but also the future of Hellenistic power, which had been recognized as demonic: at the request of the archangels who bear to him the complaint of human beings annihilated by the giants (7.6; 8.4; 9.1-10), God resolves to destroy by a flood the whole world which has been thus put out of joint (10.2b). God commands the archangels to make the giants destroy themselves in internecine battles (10.9, 12), to imprison the rebellious angels until the final judgment (10.12,14), and announce to Noah the imminent end of the world, so that Noah can save himself from the judgment of the flood and afterwards the 'planting of truth' (neṣbat qušṭā', cf. Isa.60.21; 61.3), i.e. the eschatological Israel of the just, can arise.[92] This Israel will then be able to live in a world of righteousness and blessing in which each will cultivate his field without fear of being exploited (10.16b-11.2). Finally, all human beings will join with Israel in the universal praise of God (10.21).

Throughout this second part of his account the author of I Enoch 6-11 follows the notions of eschatological prophecy, that salvation for Israel and all humankind can be created only by a great judgment of God on the present world which does away with all unjust political authorities. This judgment is similarly heightened in a mythological way; the fallen angels are imprisoned and preserved for the final judgment, which will bring them eternal torment. But here too this is merely giving shape to hints which also already appeared in late-prophetic texts (Isa.24.22).[93]

The most important difference is that the recourse to the story of the flood puts the eschatological expectations in a clear and compelling sequence. Certainly, already at some points in the late prophetic texts we found parallels to the future judgment with the flood (Isa.24.18b). But the author of I Enoch 6-11 for the first time shaped this into a thoroughgoing typology of primal time and end time. In his view the chain of events in primal time of original corruption, universal judgment and the rescue of the righteous which was related by the creation stories was as it were modelled on the eschatological future event.

With this notion he succeeded, first, in giving the future a clearer structure than had been possible for eschatological prophecy: the divine decree in the flood story brings the corrupt present world age to a clear end (*qēṣ*, Gen.6.13), so that everything that then follows was qualified as 'end time':[94] for example the expected great judgment is the 'final judgment' (I Enoch 10.14, *qēṣ dīnā' rabbā*).[95] And secondly, in this way he succeeded in plausibly demonstrating a necessary decline from the present time to the end time, thus indicating to his readers where they were in the course of history, namely where the end of the world resolved on by God is being revealed to them as once it was to Noah (Gen.6.13; I Enoch 10.2). In other words, they are at the dawn of the end time. Here the author sought to back up the 'synchronization'[96] of his historical present with the course of the world age by describing the annihilation of the giants which he announced as a mutual extermination (10.9,12) in which anyone could recognize the battles of the Diadochi and the never-ending chain of Syrian wars.

Now the definition of the end time as the goal of world history and the synchronization of the present in the course of this history proved to be two essential elements of apocalyptic. Here at the beginning of the Enoch tradition they emerged as the result of a typologizing interpretation of scripture, which at this early stage was still largely supported by the authority of the Torah itself and did not need additional revelations of famous wise men. They served to structure the manifold eschatological expectations of the prophetic tradition, permeate them rationally and make it possible to teach them as 'knowledge of the future'. As well as mythologizing, the apocalypticizing too had a recognizably pedagogical interest. The author of I Enoch 6-11 wants to make it possible for his audience to see rationally that the deification of power, violence and economic exploitation in the Hellenistic rule of the world must necessarily soon come to an end.

His way of working and the aim of his early-apocalyptic didactic narrative indicate clearly that the author of I Enoch 6-11 is a scribe. His quite different estimate of political rule from that of the author of the Greek Daniel legends indicates that he is not one of the upper-class collaborators but belongs to an opposition circle which – possibly working in Galilee, far from the capital[97] – showed solidarity with the victims of Ptolemaic economic policy and was active among them, enlightening and teaching.

The early-apocalyptic narrative of the fall of the angels was then worked over once again in the same milieu with the introduction of a second chief angel, Azazel, who revealed to human beings 'heavenly mysteries of primal times' (I Enoch 9.6), i.e. the technique of forging weapons, jewellery, cosmetics and all kinds of magical and mantic practices, and thus led them astray into violence and godlessness (7.1; 8.1-3; 9.6f.). Thus criticism of the political power was extended to cultural criticism; here alongside Hellenistic military techniques and the Hellenistic culture of luxury, conjuration and soothsaying, especially astrology, which was again being disseminated from Babylonia, are envisaged. Now as Nickelsburg and others have indicated, the Azazel revision has clear echoes of the Prometheus tradition.[98] In other words, the Jewish scholars who were working on the development of the apocalyptic picture of the world were not at all afraid to use foreign, here specifically Greek, mythological material in their fight against Hellenistic culture. They wanted to offer to their audience, which was increasingly exposed to the influence of foreign culture, a modern integrative conception to prevent it turning away from Jewish culture. In this openness they were basically distinct from their conservative colleagues, who for example in Chronicles thought that they had deliberately to barricade themselves against all the influences of alien culture.

The expansionary policy of Antiochus III which led to the Fourth (221-217) and Fifth Syrian Wars (202-197) put an end to the long period of peace in Judaea and dragged it into the quarrels between Seleucids and Ptolemies. The advanced Hellenization of part of the upper class of Judah, the vigorous partisan struggle between its wings and the ruinous consequences of the harsh taxation policy of the Tobiads led to an increasing polarization of society and to such a heated climate among the impoverished population of city and country that in 200 BCE there was a revolt against the Ptolemies which was demonstrably backed by apocalyptic expectations of the end (cf.Dan.11.14). The economic distress and the internal and external political situation had evidently intensified for those concerned to such a degree that they thought that the end of the world had come. Yahweh would be passing judgment on the mighty of this world, and they felt that they should help in the long-desired overthrow by force of arms.

The political upheaval in 221 therefore introduced the first main phase of apocalyptic literature, in the first fully developed apocalypses, the 'Book of the Watchers' (I Enoch 1-10/36) and the Aramaic book of Daniel (Dan.2-7*). Despite many common features each has a very different character and a different intention.

The learned circle centred on the Enoch tradition involved itself above all in the internal argument between those loyal to Yahweh (Enoch 1.1, 'Elect true/righteous', *bahīrayyā qašiṭayyā*) and the Hellenizing members of the upper class (Enoch 1.1; 5.7, 'sinners/wicked'). As the latter evidently refused to attach any significance to the eschatological notions of judgment with which the pious threatened them, the pious composed an apocalypse to demonstrate that the wicked would be judged and to what form the judgment would take.

Virtually all the pecularities of form and content in I Enoch 1-19/36 as compared with I Enoch 6-11 can be explained from its concern to bolster conviction. First, form: the 'Book of the Watchers' was first stylized as the testament of the 'truthful man' Enoch for the future (I Enoch 1.2; cf.19.3). We do not know whether the choice of this figure from before the flood simply arose from a reference to the story of the angelic marriages and the flood or whether he was suggested for other reasons.[99] However, the deliberate pseudonymity quite clearly served to provide credentials: the disputed knowledge about the future is to be presented as age-old truth from the mouth of a man to whom the Torah already attributed a special nearness to God and access to the heavenly sphere (Gen.5.24). The stylizing of the whole work as a report of visions (I Enoch 1.2; 13.8; 14.1ff.; 19.3) and transportations (17.1ff.; 21.1ff.) performs the same function of providing authorizations, taking up the relevant prophetic traditions.[100] Such special credentials as revealed 'heavenly knowledge' were necessary because the learned formulation of the apocalyptic picture of the world which was to give convincing plausibility to the judgment on the wicked went far beyond the Torah, and therefore could be disputed even by loyal Jews.

The new focus of the 'Book of the Watchers' emerges even more clearly from the way in which its content is shaped: very much in line with eschatological prophecy (Micah 1.3; Isa.26.21), the book begins with the announcement of the universal epiphany of God in judgment (I Enoch 1.3ff.) and then applies this immediately to the wicked (1.9). The wicked are described as those who have spoken 'great and hard words' about God (1.9; cf. 5.4). The reference is certainly to the apostate 'Hellenists'; what is criticized is not their political or social misconduct but the blasphemous statements with which they slandered Jewish traditions and turned to the apparently superior Greek culture.

There follows a lengthy admonition of Enoch to the wicked (I Enoch 2.5) which warns the Hellenists that with their apostasy they are falling out of the eternal world order (5.4) and thus are incurring eternal damnation (5.5f.). Whereas Yahweh has made peace with the 'truthful' and will save them in the final judgment (1.8), 'the wicked will have no peace' (5.4; cf.Isa.48.22; 57.21), i.e. will finally be excluded from the future salvation for the righteous (I Enoch 5.7-9).

This introductory section redirects the criticism which in the early apocalyptic didactic narrative I Enoch 6-11 was still directed against the Hellenist rulers or foreign culture towards internal opponents and once again sets existing tradition against an apocalyptic horizon as a quasi-historical exemplary narrative. We may see the fact that the authors of the 'Book of the Watchers' abandoned the direct identification of flood and last judgment made in I Enoch 6-11 as a concession to their opponents, now within Judaism, who could demonstrate very easily that the Torah knows only of a flood judgment in the past. In order to derive their opponents of this possible recourse, the authors distinguished between the events in primal times and those in the end time, but sought to prove that there was a necessary parallelism betwen the two: they made Enoch reveal that the spirits of the giants who perished in the judgment in primal times would continue to work until the time of the final judgment (I Enoch 15.8ff.), and as demons do much damage and lead many astray into wicked actions (15.11; 16.1,3; 19.1). Thus according to this construction the present apostates were directly linked to the primal fall of angels which was shaking the world and therefore everything that God had already resolved in primal times about the apostate angels and their offspring would also happen to them in the final judgment (19.1).

The authors added to the story of the fall of the angels, which they took over, a visionary report of Enoch (I Enoch.12-16) about how he was commissioned to be the messenger of judgment for the fallen angels and thus the witness to the final judgment authorized by divine revelation. Thus they combined the figure of Enoch with the tradition that they had received, and made sure that it was credible and valid for the present. In their account, Enoch had been quite prepared to intercede with God for the fallen angels at their request, but was told by God himself that there could be no forgiveness for this apostasy which was shaking the world. In so doing they wanted to demonstrate to their opponents the inevitability of the judgment which also threatened them and at the same time relieve themselves of the charge of primitive feelings of vengeance. The Hellenizing apostates were deluded in thinking that they could still attain forgiveness through cultic atonement or the intercession of the pious. And if they thought that they could dismiss the threats of judgment on them as laughable tirades of hatred from inferior enemies, then they were suffering under an illusion.

The authors ended their apocalypse with another report of Enoch about his visionary heavenly journey (I Enoch 17-19) which they detailed successively in a second travel account (20-36). Here their purpose was above all to extend the Israelite world-view to such an extent, by borrowing from the mythical cosmology of the surrounding world,[101] that the eschatological hopes for the future could find a 'geographical place' in it. In its anti-mythical tendency, official Yahweh religion had been markedly more restrained about cosmological speculations, and in its opposition to the cult of the dead had accepted only very rudimentary notions of the underworld. So it was easy for the opponents of the eschatological groups to doubt their expectations simply because there was no place for these expectations in the traditional Israelite picture of the world. The authors of the 'Book of Watchers' wanted to take the ground from under these doubts: Enoch, who by heavenly guidance had reached the limits of the world and the depths of the underworld, had already seen the place of the final judgment (26f.),[102] the place of torment for the apostate angels and the wicked (19.1f.,22), and the place of joy for the righteous (25) and had gained the necessary information about them. So in their view there was no escape, and in addition the Greek mythology to which the Hellenists felt drawn had similar notions.[103]

Setting the events of the end time geographically in a quasi-objective world of the beyond also gave the authors the possibility of making the notion of judgment more concrete and differentiating it. In their view the underworld was divided into three parts (22.9), in order to segregate human beings from immediately after death until the final judgment: whereas the spirits of the righteous could already drink from the 'clear water of life', the spirits of the wicked, whose judgment had not taken place already during their lifetimes, would be kept apart immediately after death for torment until the last judgment (v.10f.) The wicked who had already been punished would have a slightly easier lot: they would no longer be punished in the final judgment, but would not take part in the resurrection of the righteous[104] either (vv.12f.).[105] A just balance would not be introduced first in the final judgment but already directly after death. But in this way they already changed Sheol for the wicked into a kind of hell.

Thus the 'Book of the Watchers' was primarily meant as an ultimatum to the Hellenists as the clashes intensified at the end of the third century. They were not to deceive themselves! God's eternal goodness was not open to them at any time, as they might perhaps have been able to conclude from the optimistic theology of Chronicles.[106] It could be too late, and they would fall into the inevitable torments of hell after death and eternal pain after the final judgment unless they immediately broke with the demonic temptation which had been shaking the world since primal times. Only secondarily did the 'Book of the Watchers' seek to communicate to those loyal to Yahweh – probably more the educated among them – the certainty that God's judgment on this whole perverse world would open up a miraculous saving future to them (I Enoch 1.8; 5.7,9; 10.16b-11.2; 25.4-7).

In contrast to I Enoch 1-36, the second apocalypse from this span of time has no place for the dispute with the Hellenists within Judaism. The Aramaic book of Daniel (Dan.2-7*) focusses wholly on the theme of alien political powers which are making increasingly aggressive gestures, and primarily addresses its victims, to give them comfort and courage to resist. The reason why this author leaves the problem of the Jewish collaborators completely on one side may be that in the view of the lower-class group for which he was writing the Hellenizing part of the upper class in any case no longer belonged to the people of God, of which the group regarded itself as the pious nucleus ('saints of the Most High', Dan.7.18,22,27). The fact that its language is simpler than that of Enoch and it is more restrained in the use of foreign mythological material may be connected with this other audience.

The reason why the author took up the collection of Daniel stories in particular, which he knew from the Alexandrian Diaspora, to serve his purpose of providing clarification about the turbulent world-political situation for pious groups which were unsure of themselves and had been forced on the defensive, was probably that here a famous Jewish sage and interpreter of dreams had come up against a series of world rulers. The effects of political rule of the world on pious Jews could be demonstrated from this material, and its hero offered points of contact for apocalyptic instruction. Nevertheless, given the depressing experiences of his time the author of the Aramaic book would not and could not share any longer the optimistic estimation of the foreign power in this Greek collection with its upper-class perspective. So he subjected the Daniel tradition that he had to profound changes.[107]

He prefaced the collection with the martyr legend of the 'three men in the fiery furnace' (Dan.3), which hitherto had been circulating independently, using it to demonstrate the self-divinizing claim of the Hellenistic state power with which pious Jews necessarily came into conflict and which they had to resist. Then he transformed the story of Daniel in the lions' den' (Dan.6), which in the Greek version had only been about the limited intrigue of minor officials, into a showpiece of totalitarian state power which could no longer tolerate the religious loyalty of pious Jews, but was shown its limits by the decision of Daniel to take the way to martyrdom in trust in God. In his view a state power which made such absolutist gestures no longer offered any possibility of collaboration, and the hope of the pious upper class to reform it from within by collaboration was a dangerous illusion. In his view, all that was left was for pious Jews to offer resistance to the violent pressure of the Hellenistic state towards assimilation, in loyal allegiance to the ancestral tradition, even to the point of martyrdom.

The narrative composition thus framed by martyr legends was ultimately focussed on a new theological perspective on the future: it almost completely removed the statements about a conversion of world rulers which had formed the eschatological horizon of expectation of the Greek collection[108] and replaced it with its new general theme of the unstoppable establishment of the kingly rule of God (Dan.3.31-33; 4.31f.; 6.26-28; cf.5.21).[109] In so doing, it not only parted company with the hope cherished by leading circles, of winning over foreign rulers to Jewish belief, but also rejected all their moves towards reform which made a change for the better dependent on the benevolence of the alien powers. No, in its view God would himself impose his rule, not with but against the political world powers: by humiliating the power-crazy king Nebuchadnezzar (4.27) to the level of a beast, God was compelling him to acknowledge with praise the divine kingly rule (4.31bf.). Only in this way did he grant a limited existence to the Babylonian world empire. In casting down Belshazzar, who refused to recognize him, with wicked blasphemy (5.21), he was demonstrating that he could establish his rule against a world empire, however powerful. And by exploding the claim of the empire of the Medes to power with the rescue of Daniel from the lions' den, he compelled Darius, the ruler of the world, to subject himself voluntarily to the eternal and universal divine kingly rule. Thus the theologoumenon of the kingly rule of God gave the author of the Aramaic book of Daniel a potential critique of rule on the basis of which he could fundamentally put in question the legitimacy and existence of the world powers in the face of depressing experiences with the Hellenistic empires.

For the author, the Daniel stories thus reworked as a critique of domination (3-6) formed the historical basis for his apocalyptic teachings, which he put as a framework round them (Dan.2; 7*). The expectation that Yahweh would establish his kingly reign on Zion had always played a major role in eschatological prophecy since the announcement of Deutero-Isaiah had remained fulfilled (Isa.52.7), and later prophetic opposition and lower-class circles had come to believe that along with this rulers would be stripped of their power (Zech.9.1-10; 10.3; 14.3, 9; Isa.24.21-23). The author of the Aramaic book of Daniel took up these eschatological expectations – though without reference to Zion[110] – and made them an apocalyptic theory of history legitimated by the authority of Daniel as a pre-eminent interpreter of dreams. This was to demonstrate to his audience the need for an imminent establishment of the kingly rule of God: resorting to the idea of the four world empires, which was originally Iranian,[111] but then taken over and developed by the Greeks,[112] and which he combined with another idea of four world ages of declining quality, similarly mediated through Iran and Greece, he created the theory of a totality of eastern world empires which had sunk to their absolute nadir and end with the present Greek rule. He impressively depicted the unity and seqence of the four world empires in the dream version of Dan.2.31ff. as a giant statue; its parts, from the golden head of the Babylonian government to the half-iron, half-clay feet of the Seleucid-Ptolemaic government, were to symbolize the ongoing coarsening and ultimate fragility of political rule. Since the last, Greek rule of the world had developed such a potential for destruction that it 'broke in pieces and shattered all things' (2.40; cf. 7.7abα), what he wanted to suggest to his audience was that there could be no further decline. Completely of its own accord a chunk of rock would break off, hit the fragile feet of the statue, and shatter it (2.34); the kingly rule of God must almost of necessity 'break in pieces all these kingdoms' (2.44), i.e. annihilate the whole system of political rule and itself make the final breakthrough. The author of the Aramaic book of Daniel backed up the view expressed in I Enoch 6-11 by the scribal primal time/end time typology that world history so far had come to its necessary end (cf.2.28), which the present generation would experience shortly, with a no less learned apocalyptic theory of history.

Now the author did not limit himself to demonstrating the eschatological establishment of the kingly rule of God in the face of the whole rotten system of world power; he also wanted to lift the veil of mystery a little for his audience, to show the positive characteristics of this rule in contrast to previous expressions of political power. He did this tentatively in the secret vision of Daniel at the end of his book (Dan.7): after the four terrible beasts which had arisen from the stormy sea and trampled down and devoured everything had been judged and destroyed by God, Daniel suddenly sees in the bright world of God 'one like a man' (*kᵉbar 'ᵉnāš*) appear, to whom the kingly rule of God is given (7.13f.). This 'son of man' is identified with the 'saints of the Most High' in the interpretation (v.18).

What is meant by this mysterious symbolism?[113] There is much to suggest that as yet no individual mediator figure is meant as in the later texts.[114] In the imagery of Dan.7, the 'one in human form' first of all simply represents the human as opposed to the inhuman beasts. That means that the author of the Aramaic book of Daniel wants to indicate that the kingly rule of God will have profoundly human features, in contrast to the bestial and destructive rule of previous world empires. In that case, however, the 'saints of the Most High' cannot simply mean angels, as some scholars assume,[115] especially as there is mention of the 'people of the saints of the Most High' in v.28.[116] In all probability the author was thinking of the community of the pious who had previously been the victims of totalitarian state power.[117] He evidently expected that they, who on the basis of their own long experience of impotence and suffering had learned to see through the inhuman self-divinization of political power and to resist its seduction, were in a position to become bearers of a quite new form of political rule which 'raises up all who are bowed down'.[118]

Thus the Aramaic book of Daniel is a political apocalypse through and through. It not only denied all legitimation to alien Hellenistic power but also propagated a positive political utopia: rule would very soon pass to the groups which had previously been victims of the political system. It gave a clear call to pious Jews to resist the state power's claim to absoluteness and totality not by violence but by a demonstrative refusal to the point of martyrdom (Dan.3; 6). So the Aramaic book of Daniel will have made a quite considerable contribution towards creating a deliberate will to resist the Hellenistic pressure to assimilate, above all in the lower class, which was suffering especially under foreign rule. We do not know whether it also provoked the violent revolt against the Ptolemaeans in 200; but at least it created the climate in which such a rebellion was possible at all.

The failure of the rebellion (Dan.11.14), and the initially hopeful arrangement with the new Seleucid overlords (the decree of Antiochus II in 197 BCE) which made another conservative restoration under the high priest Simon probable, once again led to the decline of the apocalyptic movement. It only reformed when from 175 on, provoked by the Hellenistic reforms, the community of Judah slid into a religious and cultural battle which under conditions akin to civil war escalated in the religous edict of Antiochus IV in 167, and issued in the Maccabaean struggle for liberation.[119]

The dramatic events introduced the second main phase of the formation of the apocalyptic tradition. The fact that this was predominantly[120] expressed not in the formulation of completely new writings but in updating earlier apocalypses (Dan.1 + 8-12; I Enoch 85-90) indicates a certain continuity of tradents. If behind the 'Book of the Watchers' (I Enoch 1-36) and the Aramaic book of Daniel (Dan.2-7*) we conjectured a variety of groups of scribal tradents who had become involved in the controversy with the Hellenists or the activation of the oppressed pious before 200, it seems likely that we should also envisage scribal opposition groups as those who developed these works in the Maccabaean period. We have direct evidence of one such group in the Hasidim, who in my view were an influential religious alliance of scribes (I Macc.2.42; 7.12f.) who allied themselves with the Maccabees at the height of the crisis in 167 BCE, but who after the Seleucids had come round in 162 at least partially distanced themselves from the Maccabees again.[121] Now if we assume that at least some tradents of the earlier apocalyptic tradition or its descendants were among the Hasidim, the continuity of the new formation of the tradition is understandable, and there is much to be said for the old theory that the Hasidim are to be regarded as the tradents of the Maccabaean apocalyptic movement.[122] However, two corrections need to be made to this theory. First, they are by no means a marginal religious group, as has often been thought, but a nucleus of the pious religious leading class. And secondly, we must assume either a broad spectrum of political options among them, or in addition to them other scribal groups with apocalyptic orientations, since, as we have seen,[123] the Enochite 'Animal Apocalypse' (I Enoch 85-90) and the Hebrew book of Daniel advanced virtually opposed positions: the first propagated active participation in armed struggle, the latter passive suffering as martyrs. So I would assume that under the pressure of events there was a split between the pious scribes as a result of which some (those behind the 'Animal Apocalypse') joined the Maccabees while others (those behind the Hebrew book of Daniel) joined the radical religious opposition groups said in I Macc.2.29-38 to have fled into the desert and allowed themselves to be slaughtered on the sabbath in pious self-sacrifice.[124]

For the militant wing of the Hasidim, the violent revolt under the leadership of Judas Maccabaeus was the decisive act which ushered in the end time; the author of the 'Animal Apocalypse' (I Enoch 85-90) described his historical situation like this. When 'they began to open their eyes and see', i.e. brought eschatological speculation and teaching to the centre of their work, the pious scribes ('the lambs', as the apocalypse[125] cryptically calls them) first of all completely failed. Their cry was not heard by the sheep, i.e. Israel; on the contrary, Israel proved completely deaf and blind (90.6f.). Indeed they even had to watch one of the lambs, probably the high priest Onias II, who was the most important leader of the pious, being snatched away by the devouring Seleucid ravens (v.8). This experience of failure could well relate to the first period of the apocalyptic movement before 200, in which the Enoch apocalyptists had fought vigorously against the Hellenists.[126] As their successors had to concede in retrospect, this battle had remained unsuccessful. After the hopeful period of restoration, the Hellenizing upper-class party, which cared not a jot for eschatological warnings, triumphed, as was made clear by the deposition of Onias III in 175 and his eventual murder in 170 BCE. On the contrary, when the Hasidim resorted to violence against the Hellenistic structures of the community, they were removed with the help of alien Seleucid power (v.91).

It was the 'great horn', Judas Maccabaeus, who in the estimation of the Hasidim brought about the decisive change. Under his leadership apocalyptic teaching was widely recognized among the mass of the population and became the political force which provided solidarity for and motivated the rebel movement (vv.9bf.). At any rate it changed some of the people from sheep, who silently tolerated everything, to goats, who were ready to protest and resist (v.11b). Certainly the Maccabaean revolt provoked rabid retaliation from the foreign power (v.11a), but now that had no effect (v.12).

The author of the 'Animal Apocalypse' could only understand the surprising military successes which Judas Maccabaeus achieved as caused by the intervention of Yahweh himself – through the mediation of the archangel Michael – in the battle on the side of the rebels (v.14). Yahweh was there to pour out his wrath on the alien powers and their Jewish collaborators ('sheep of the field', vv.15f.). In his view this could only be understood as a herald of the great final judgment which Yahweh would initiate against the foreign power and all its enemies (v.17). He saw the Maccabaean war of liberation as leading straight into the great eschatological battle in which Israel would drive all its enemies to flight, with its God at its side (vv.18f.).

Thus I Enoch 90.6-19 is evidence that the Hasidim who allied themselves with the Maccabees developed a martial apocalyptic propaganda among the rebels. Although the Maccabees themselves did not have an apocalyptic orientation, as I Maccabees shows, but used the old tradition of the Yahweh war[127] as their credentials, they were evidently quite ready – at least in the initial phase – for the influential scribes to carry on their work of apocalyptic enlightenment among troops and supporters and thus contribute to raising morale in the struggle. But the text also makes it clear why some of the Hasidim decided to join the armed rebel movement: this offered them the opportunity to overcome the lack of success in their work of theological enlightenment hitherto and to transform their defeat by the Hellenists into a victory. They hoped that the Maccabees would make a decisive contribution here towards a fulfilment of their eschatological expectations. It is obvious that this coalition of interests could only last until it became clear beyond doubt that the Maccabees were only interested in securing their own interests in power.

The political and military reorientation of apocalyptic instruction which, as we shall see,[128] was hotly disputed among the pious scribes, made unavoidable a revision of the Enoch tradition which would legitimate it; the simple primal time/end time typology of the earlier strata was no longer enough, for a Judaean war of liberation could hardly be justified by its universal horizon. So the author fitted into the universal framework (85.3-89.9 + 90.20-37) a survey of the whole history of Israel (89.10-90.19) giving rise to a sketch of the whole of world history which Enoch is said to have seen in advance (85.2-3a; 90.39-41).[129] The author worked out that the basic pattern of this world history was violence and oppression: this already began with Cain and Abel (85.4ff.), continued with the giants before the flood (86.5)[130] and the oppression of Israel in Egypt (89.15ff.), and finally issued in oppressive alien rule lasting from the exiling of the northern and southern kingdoms to the present (89.55-90.17). Under Greek rule the violence and exploitation once again intensified extremely (90.2,4,17). The decisive insight that the author wanted to communicate was that throughout its history Israel had usually been the victim of unjustified violence. Granted, the long period of alien rule had been punishment for Israel's apostasy (89.51, 54), but the foreign rulers – or their heavenly leaders[131] – had arbitrarily taken the decimation and exploitation of Israel far beyond Yahweh's ordinance (89.69,74; 90.2,4,8,11). So they had to be called to account by God, and throughout history the archangel Gabriel had scrupulously to note these transgressions for the final judgment (89.62f.; 90.17,22,25). But as the victim of overwhelming oppression Israel had the right to bring down its oppressors. This had been prefigured initially by Saul and David in the one long period of salvation, the early monarchy (89.3,4, 48), and has was now taking place in the Maccabaean war of liberation (90.12). And just as God had already come to the help of the oppressed and lamenting Israelites in Egypt ('a sheep among the wolves', 89.13-27), so now he supported the oppressed rebels (90.13f.). The apocalyptic presentation of the history of Israel thus served totally to legitimate active resistance; if Yahweh and Israel had already collaborated in earlier eras to free the people of God from oppression, then the Maccabaean freedom fight, too, was a necessary ingredient of the eschatological process of liberation.[132]

However, not only the nature of the resistance but also the particpation of the pious scribes in it needed to be justified. The author did this positively by connecting liberations which had already taken place with the 'teaching of mysteries' (Noah, 89.1) and the 'opening of the eyes' (Samuel, 89.41) that the Hasidim now claimed for themselves (90.6,9f.), and he did it negatively by defining the apostasy of Israel not only as departure from the Torah (89.32) but also as a blindness or being blinded towards divine revelations (89.31-33) and the disclosures of the prophets (89.51-54,74) which had continued down to the failure to heed the apocalyptic teaching of the Hasidim (90.7). Now if rejection of the revelation of the future had been the cause and sign of judgment in the past (89.54ff.,74), then the wide acceptance of apocalyptic teaching which the Hasidim experienced among the rebels (90.9f.) could only be the sign of a new dawn of salvation. It becomes clear that it was the pressure towards legitimation of their own role which first led part of the apocalyptists to define themselves as successors to the prophets.

Finally, the militant wing of the Hasidim had to explain what role they would accord the temple in the eschatological process of liberation. There was probably a dispute among the pious generally and the rebels in particular over the aim of the war: was it above all about the conquest and restitution of the violated temple, or was it about more, the removal of foreign rule and the power of the Hellenists? In uniquely – in contrast to the Hebrew Book of Daniel – making no reference at all to the desecration of the temple under Antiochus IV,[133] the author of the 'Animal Apocalypse' is clearly arguing for the latter alternative. He clearly wanted to define the revolt as a political battle of liberation. He justified this view by saying that in his belief Yahweh had already left the first temple with the exile (89.56; cf. Ezek.8-11), and that from the very beginning the second temple had been 'polluted and impure' (I Enoch 89.73). Thus the Hellenistic rededication of the temple had not created a new situation which now had to be remedied. Rather, God himself would do away with the desecrated temple – after liberation had been achieved (90.17-19) and final judgment had been passed on all the rebellious powers, including the apostate upper class (90.20-26) – and build in its place a new temple, in which he would again be present (90.27-29). In the view of the pious scribes it would be a mistake now to put the temple at the centre of the revolts, as the pious priests wanted to do.[134]

Thus the whole course of the 'Animal Apocalypse' can well be explained as a committed attitude of the politically active wing of the Hasidim within the Maccabaean rebel movement.

That such a functionalizing of apocalyptic instruction for active political and military resistance came up against resistance in the circle of the pious scribes is shown by the Hebrew book of Daniel. Its author, who probably came from the quietistic wing of the Hasidim or another radical religious group of scribes, vehemently opposed the assessment of his activist colleagues that the Maccabean war of liberation would usher in the eschatological turning point. In his view the armed rebellion had no significance whatsoever for the eschatological drama; it was apparently only a 'small help' for the Hasidim, who thought that with the help of the Maccabees they could win over the broad masses of the people to their apocalyptic teaching (Dan.11.34a), but would find only a doubtful following among people who in truth were pursuing quite other aims (v.34b). It all had nothing to do with the final battle; there was still an interval before the end (v.35); Antiochus must still pursue his godless course to a culmination (vv.36-39); he still had to come to a fall in a further arrogant war (vv.40-45) and then all alone the archangel Michael would save Israel from yet further unspeakable distress (12.1).

In the view of the Daniel apocalyptist the serious crisis in the present provoked by Antiochus and his Jewish collaborators was more a time of religious testing. And in his view this testing also and in particular included the apocalyptic teachers (*maśkīlīm*, 11.33,35; 12.3,10).[135] Certainly the 'teachers of the people' would communicate to many apocalyptic instruction (11.3a) which would put them in a position to resist the temptation of apostasy to Hellenism (11.32), but they themselves would run the risk of 'stumbling' (*kāšal*, niphal) under the pressure of the confusions of the civil war, i.e. of lapsing from the true teaching[136] and not doing justice to their mission 'to lead many to righteousness' (12.3). In the view of the apocalyptist of Daniel, the militant Hasidim, who staked their cards on the Maccabees, had quite evidently succumbed to this danger; in their uncertainty they had made themselves leaders of a doubtful following

(11.34). But in his view the danger to all apocalyptic teachers which was becoming manifest in their conduct should serve to bring about a purifying separation among these before the end (11.35). Only those teachers who resisted the seduction to political activism and limited themselves to inciting others to attain salvation through the last judgment would be raised up in splendour after the eschatological turning point (12.3). The apocalyptist of Daniel thus opted for purely religious, verbal and non-violent resistance, and he canvassed among his colleagues on the quietistic wing of the Hasidim for understanding the turbulent present as the decisive test which would decide on whether or not they participated in the final salvation (12.10).

Many individual features of his work make clear to us that the author of the Hebrew book of Daniel – despite the same anti-Hellenistic attitude – attempted to stand apart from those colleagues who were voting for military resistance, and how he did so.

First of all there is his striking attitude to the apocalyptic movement under Antiochus III. He sharply attacked the violent revolt against the Ptolemies in 200 (Dan.11.14). For him, those involved in it were simply 'robbers' (*parīṣīm*) whose erroneous view was that they could bring in the fulfilment of the apocalyptic 'vision' by force. For him, the failure of this movement was therefore not – as for the authors of the 'Animal Apocalypse' – a depressing defeat (I Enoch 90.6f.) but a necessary consequence.

Given such a decidedly negative attitude to the preceding phase of apocalyptic, the inclusion of the Aramaic book of Daniel, which had sketched out a completely political utopia, can be understood only as an attempt to correct and neutralize it. By prefixing it with Dan.1, the Hebrew author immediately put in the foreground the indidivual-ethical aspect which was his concern: he made Daniel and his companions the model of Jews faithful to the law who refused to assimilate to the pagan environment and self-consciously observed the Jewish food laws. Read through these 'spectacles', the martyr legends (Dan.3; 6) of the Aramaic book could now be understood as a call to purely religious resistance. And he sought to neutralize the political implications of the Aramaic Daniel utopia by adding two further apocalyptic visions in parallel to Dan.7 (Dan.8; 10-12) which on the one hand emphasized that it was only God's heavenly powers which guide world history (10.13,20f.) and which without any human violence (8.25) would put an end to the last blasphemous foreign power (11.40-45; 12.1), and on the other hand replaced the political theme of the kingly rule of God with a purely individual eschatology (12.2f.). He replaced the eschatological realization of a humane rule by the pious with the perspective of the resurrection, after which those who had proved themselves in the time of tribulation would enter into eternal life, while all the rest would succumb to eternal damnation (v.2). The strikingly narrow and individualistically constricted horizon of salvation in the Hebrew book of Daniel compared with the original Aramaic work and even more I Enoch is the expression of a deliberate intent to take the ground from any political speculations about the future.

Secondly, there is the presentation of I Enoch 89f., which is clearly different from the world history of the apocalyptist of Daniel. Not only does it leave out the whole pre-exilic history of Israel to avoid over-hasty political parallels, but it does not even set the period of alien rule in the perspective of the ongoing oppression of Israel. For the author, the fall of the Persian empire, the establishment of Macedonian rule and the ups and downs of the Seleucid and Ptolemaic potentates (Dan.8.2ff.; 11.2bff.) had nothing to do with the history of Israel at all. For him, everything was the consequence of ongoing heavenly battles among the angels of the nations which the perceptive pious, knowing full well that Michael, the strongest prince of the angels, was on their side (10.21), could allow to pass in front of them from the perspective of an onlooker. Only under Antiochus IV was a dramatic threat posed to Judah (11.28f.), but here it was not political oppression or economic exploitation that stood in the foreground, but above all Antiochus's blasphemous attack on Yahweh and his sanctuary (7.26; 8.11f.,25; 11.31). That means that while the apocalyptist of Daniel probably took from his Aramaic basis the charge of hybris against alien powers, he no longer saw this hybris as being the state's absoluteness and totalitarian claim, but specifically its failure to observe the religious and cultic order.[137] The marked concentration on the desecration of the temple which distinguishes the Hebrew apocalypse of Daniel from the 'Animal Apocalypse' is thus connected with the de-politicizing programme of its author.[138] He wanted to make clear to his audience that the real controversy was taking place not in the political but in the religious sphere. It was not the depravity of political rule as such, as the author of the Aramaic book of Daniel thought, but in particular the wicked challenge to all the godly, which would lead Yahweh to put an end to world history.

Thirdly and finally there is the remarkable numerical speculation peculiar to the Hebrew book of Daniel. Certainly the Aramaic book of Daniel[139] and even more markedly the 'Animal Apocalypse' attempted to periodize world history[140] in order to make the imminent eschatological turning-point plausible. However, the author of the Hebrew book went far beyond that by attempting to fix the time up to the 'end of wrath' (8.19) numerically. Here the prophecy of Jeremiah (29.10; 25.11f.) gave him the exegetical basis that the time of judgment on Jerusalem would last 70 years (Dan.2), which he interpreted as 70 weeks of years (= 490 years) and thus could relate to his present. He did not manage a quite exact synchronization through this exegesis, as the many attempts to identify the symbolic periodization of Dan.9.24-27 with historical dates adequately demonstrate,[141] but he did succeed in realizing a twofold concern. First of all he wanted to maintain that the time up to the eschatological dawn of salvation had been fixed firmly by God in advance (Dan.9.24). For him the end as a fixed date[142] was something that had been decided (*neḥᵉraṣā*, 9.26f.; 11.36), and no human being could either accelerate it (cf. Dan.11.14) or prevent it by his intervention. That not only made all the political and military activities of the rebel movement insignificant, but also showed to be exegetically false the notion of the militant Hasidim that the revolt would lead without a break into the eschatological battle (I Enoch 90.18f.). Secondly, he attempted to calculate and fix the time of the tribulation under Antiochus IV. Since he saw the last week of years as dawning with the deposition (175 BCE) or murder (170) of Onias III (9.26), and some years had already passed before Antiochus IV's religious edict (167), he concluded that the duration of the tribulation would be a further period of around three and a half years (9.27; 7.25; 12.7).[143] Now this dating clearly has a pastoral function: it was meant to assure the pious who keep asking 'How long?' (8.13; 12.6f.) that the time of trial ordained for them (cf.12.12) would not be endless. And such comfort was needed above all by the groups who were passively resisting and simply suffering as helpless victims of the civil war. For the active resistance fighters who thought that they could bring in the end of oppression themselves, this temptation did not arise. So the attempts at dating peculiar to the book of Daniel, which gave the eschatological turning point expected by most opposition groups much more the character of an end to the world that could be fixed,[144] can be explained in terms of the quietistic attitude of those who made them.

The theological struggle which became visible between the Hebrew book of Daniel and I Enoch 85-90 makes it clear that the dispute over the proper way to assess the painful present and the right alternatives of action for the future was fought out in the Maccabaean period essentially on the ground of apocalyptic theology. For a short time in the years between 167 and 162 BCE apocalyptic gained a dominant role in official Yahweh religion, so that from this time on it spread in quite different groups and forms of literature.[145]

However, very soon the apocalyptic movement again lost its dominant social influence. Certainly the expectation of the book of Daniel that the worst time of tribulation, the desecration of the temple and the persecution of the pious, would be over in around three or four years was fulfilled; it was possible to purify the temple from its Hellenistic accretions (164) and the Seleucids gave in.[146] But the great eschatological turning-point did not come. Resigned over the progress of political events and put in question by the radical religious wing of the resistance, some of the militant Hasidim withdrew from the Maccabaean fight for freedom and accepted a peace offer from the Seleucids in order at least to safeguard the partial autonomy they had regained (162 BCE). The resistance movement split apart, and it proved that while apocalyptic theology had been very well suited to motivate active and passive resistance against a political power, it did not have sufficient elements of a political utopia to play an active part in shaping a new beginning for society.

The build-up of the Hasmonaean state by the Maccabees took place without any recognizable influence from the groups which handed down apocalyptic; and its rulers very soon turned into Hellenistic potentates, as though there had never been the inexorable critique of state power in apocalyptic. The scribes orientated on apocalyptic were again forced to the periphery of society. But it is moving to see that despite all the disappointments they did not give up, but fought against the new mechanisms of oppression in Hasmonaean society: the social exploitation and social declassing of the lower class by the rich urban upper class. In the subsequent phase of the Maccabaean revolt, as the 'Epistle of Enoch' (I Enoch 92-105) attests, apocalyptic became a theology of social resistance, just as a part of the late prophetic tradition already had.[147]

The Ethiopic text of I Enoch 91-105 is somewhat disordered, but it can now be reconstructed with the aid of the Aramaic fragments from Qumran: I Enoch 91.1-10, 18f. is probably a subsequent, second, introduction which incorporated the 'Epistle of Enoch' into the book of Enoch as a whole. The 'letter' which Enoch gave to his son Methusaleh for posterity originally began with I Enoch 92.1-5. Then followed the 'Ten Weeks' Apocalypse' (93.1-10 + 91.11-17), which is clearly a separate entity that has been quoted. However, it is probably not essentially older than the rest of the letter.[148] On the basis of this apocalyptic instruction, after a general introduction (93.11-14) there follow extensive paraeneses (94-104) and a closing admonition to the tradents of the Enoch tradition (105). The whole Epistle is commonly dated to the beginning of the first century BCE.[149] The presentation of Enoch as a 'scribe' (92.1) and the remarkable mixture of prophetic-apocalyptic and wisdom tradition[150] again indicate a scribal origin.

The author of the 'Epistle of Enoch' saw himself confronted once again in the Hasmonaean society of his time with that social crisis that we know all too well, which had split the community of Judah from the middle of the fifth century. A group of the rich was heedlessly increasing its possessions at the cost of the poorer strata of the population[151] and putting its life of luxury on show unrestrainedly (I Enoch 96.5f.; 97.7f.; 98.2f.), heedless of the Torah's demands for solidarity (99.1) One can put it even more sharply and say that these rich who showed no solidarity were open to alien cultural and religious influences (99.7,14; 104.9), were supported by their own Hasmonaean dynasty (103.14f.) and propagated their life-style in literary form through their own writings (104.10).

In this social and religious conflict the author of the 'Epistle of Enoch' clearly took the side of the oppressed and conservative religious lower class. He sought to strengthen their powers of resistance in suffering and tribulation by reinforcing the insight that God would quite certainly make good the unjust world order in the future and see to just recompense in each individual life.

For this he first of all used apocalyptic instruction, the 'Ten Weeks' Apocalypse' (I Enoch 93.1-10 + 91.11-17), which extended the world-historical panorama of the Enoch tradition on the one hand – like the 'Book of the Watchers' – to the conflict within Judaism between the wicked and the just, and on the other – as in the 'Animal Apocalypse' – to the material of political conflict: 'lies and violence' already prevailed before the flood (93.4), but neither the judgment of the flood not the gift of Torah and temple (vv.6f.) had been able to prevent their revival, so that injustice and lies reached a new climax in the seventh era of the world, i.e. throughout the post-exilic period up to the author's day (93.9f.; 91.11). But it was clear to the author of the apocalypse that from now on world history could no longer continue in this way, but must take a turn for the better simply from the fact that at the end of the seventh era of the world, 'witnesses of truth' (*šᵃhedē qošeṭ*) had appeared in Israel to whom 'sevenfold wisdom and knowledge had been given' (93.10). In other words, the existence of the apocalyptic movement, which for the first time could explain the course and goal of world history, was an indication of an imminent change for the better. Its instruction about the imminent annihilation of the wicked and its fight against injustice and lies (93.10; 91.11) itself set the revolution in motion. So the eighth era of the world would be a time of truth and justice, in which the oppressed pious would violently break the domination of the wicked (91.12) and possessions would be gained only in an honest and just way (91.13). The ninth era of the world would then bring the end of the wicked (91.14), until finally in the tenth era the last judgment would be made on them, so that all human beings did only goodness and truth (91.15,17).

We get the impression that the 'Ten Weeks' Apocalypse' wanted to take acount of the disappointing failure of the great eschatological turning point to materialize, which undermined the credibility of apocalyptic theology, by extending the eschatological events in a long process which progressed stage by stage. If the setting of the duration of a week at 490 years, the probability of which has been demonstrated by Koch,[152] is correct, then the author was expecting the final judgment only around the time of the late Middle Ages. It was also important to the author of the 'Epistle of Enoch' to open up the perspective of time which gave the pious a share in reshaping the world with a view to its new creation, because that gave renewed room for ethical action.

Secondly, the author of the 'Epistle of Enoch' referred to the notion of the resurrection of the just (9.2; 103.4; cf. 91.10; Isa.26.19), which had played only a minor role in the preceding Enoch tradition (cf. I Enoch 22.12f.), in order to assure the pious of their personal participation in eschatological salvation. Each individual pious person could be certain that his dead kith and kin (102.4-103.4), and he himself, if he did not live to see the eschatological development towards salvation, would quite certainly receive after death a just recompense for the happiness which had been denied him in his life. Thus the resurrection hope was given the task of neutralizing the delay of salvation and making the personal hope of life dependent on the actual course of world history. Now individual eschatology became the basis of the relationship to God in the community of the pious, for which universal-historical eschatology simply formed the universal goal.

On this twofold basis, thirdly, the author of the 'Epistle of Enoch' developed for the first time an ethic with an eschatological orientation. The majority of his work consists of cries of woe about the wicked, whose social and religious misconduct is described in detail and who are confronted vividly with the future judgment which they are facing.[153] The recitation of these cries of woe in the community of the pious already anticipates the eschatological judgment in the present, deprives the lack of solidarity shown by the rich of its legiitmation and frees the poor from their anxiety and their feeling of helplessness towards their all-powerful oppressors. In the shared anticipation of judgment in the beyond the pious could now already now build up with words a counter-world in which God's justice comes fully into play.

In addition there runs through the 'Epistle of Enoch' a chain of words which calls the pious to hope (I Enoch 96.1; 104.2,4); to faith (97.1); to an abandonment of fear (95.3; 96.3; 102.4), mourning (102.5) and despondency (104.6); and to joy (105.2), combined with references to the salvation of the pious or judgment on the wicked. With this summons the author tries to activate the will to resist of the poor who are sinking into the lethargy of suffering, so that they are not crushed by their oppressors, do not make pacts with them (104.6), but constantly maintain their righteous way of life even in distress, and do not abandon their eschatological hope (104.3). After all, they have been chosen by God to share with him in breaking the violence of the oppressors once and for all (95.3; 96.1; 98.12; cf. 91.12).

Apocalyptic as a theology of social resistance was widely disseminated in early Judaism among the poor strata of the population, which extends as far as the Jesus movement.[154] With its easily understandable eschatological horizon of ideas (resurrection, judgment after death), it created a new form of piety of the poor within which there was a marked force for social revolution. That in the end even learned apocalyptic advanced to cover social themes is certainly no coincidence in the history of a religion which began with the experience of the liberation of oppressed conscript labourers.

2 Notes

4 The History of Israelite Religion in the Exilic Period

1. Here is the justification for the custom of no longer speaking of the religion of Israel for the period after the exile but of Judaism or early Judaism. However, this does not do justice to the continuity that there is – above all in the self-understanding of the biblical tradents.

2. See below, 225ff.

3. See above, 238f.

4. Cf. also the preaching of Jeremiah, especially after 597; see above, 239f.

5. See above, 172f.

6. This splintering has a forerunner in the partisan battle of the late pre-exilic period – which was still related to institutions (see above, 237f.)

7. Cf. the divergent numbers in II Kings 24.14,16; Jer.53.28-30, and Donner, *Geschichte* II, 371f. Kreissig, *Juda*, 22, calculates 15,600 deportees.

8. Cf. Janssen, *Juda*, 39ff.; Kreissig, *Juda*, 34, calculates around 60,000 inhabitants.

9. See above, 241f.

10. Apparently Judah was not a separate Babylonian province but administered from Samaria.

11. Cf. the renewed deportation in 582 according to Jer.52.30, which was probably preceded by yet another revolt.

12. This is rightly stressed by Kreissig, *Juda*, 26f., also with references to archaeological evidence, cf. also Buccelati, 'Israeliti', and Avigad, 'Seals'.

13. Cf. the verdict of Müller, *Phönikien*, 206: 'The constriction of Judah by its neighbours, of which the Phoenician immigration is only one example, had a more persistent influence on its exilic and post-exilic history than the hurt inflicted on it by the great powers.'

14. Cf. Hartberger, 'An den Wassern...', 198ff.

15. We may possibly also understand in the light of this basic mood the decision of the Babylonian Gola, unlike the Egyptian Gola, not to organize its cult permanently abroad by the building of a temple; there were probably also tendencies in this direction within it, but they were abruptly rejected by the Ezekiel circle (cf. Ezek.20.32 and for the problem Bronner, 'Sacrificial Cult' [4.2], 69-71).

16. See above, 237f.

17. The pardoning of Jehoiachin at the court of Evil-merodach in 562 reported in II Kings 25.27-30 presupposes co-operation between the Judahite colony and the Babylonian state. So the change took place at the latest in the second generation.

18. For the slight syncretisms which are evident in personal nomenclature see 98f. above. But they are clearly less than in the Egyptian Gola.

19. Cf. Bickerman, 'Captivity', 344ff.

20. There is mention of five localities in the Bible: Tel-abib, Tel-harsha, Tel-melah, Cherub'addan-immer and Casiphia (Ezek.3.15; Ezra 2.59; Neh.7.61; Ezra 8.17). The Murashu tablets attest that there were Judahites in 28 of the 200 settlements named.

21. Thus the attractive conjecture in Bickerman, 'Captivity', 345f., even if his extrapolation into the Babylonian era of circumstances first attested in the Persian period remains vulnerable, cf. Wallis, *Soziale Situation*, 194f.

22. Cf. Bickerman, 'Captivity', 349f. Eph'al, 'Organization', 100, refers to a cuneiform legal document from 529 which mentions an 'assembly of the elders of Egypt' in Babylon, probably with legal functions. Perhaps the Judahite colony was allowed a similar institution.

23. Josephus, *Antt.* XI.9, explicitly gives the desire of the exiles to hold on to their property as a reason for the delay in returning.

24. The Letter of Aristeas (v.13) associates the first Jewish mercenaries in Egypt with a Nubian campaign of Psammetichus. If we take this to be Psammetichus II, we arrive at 591, i.e. still in the period of the last pre-exilic anti-Babylonian rebel movement, when Zedekiah was seeking a military alliance with Egypt. That would fit the situation quite well and could explain why in 587 Johanan could believe that he and his troops would find better living conditions in Egypt. By contrast Porten, *Jews*, 378f., envisages an emigration under Psammetichus I at the time of king Manasseh.

25. See AP 30.13, TGI², 86.

26. Porten has shown that the YHW cult in Elephantine has more conservative features, orientated on the time of the monarchy (*Jews*, 385), and that contrary to views which are often expressed, the syncretism there is held within check and limited to the sphere of personal piety (AP 44: appeal to Anat-YHW in an oath, cf. the queen of heaven in Jer.44.15ff.), see below, 385. The more detailed information which is given in AP 30 to the governor of Judaea about the YHW cult indicates that the Elephantine colony only turned to Jerusalem in a specific crisis, and before that does not seem to have had more intensive contact with it.

27. Cf. Müller, 'Phönikien', 203.

4.2 *The struggle over a theological interpretation of the political catastrophe*

1. Jer.7.31; 8.2; 19.13; 44.15ff. (cf. the Elephantine papyri); Ezek.13.17-23; 14.1-11; Isa.57.3-13; 65.3-5,11; 66.17; perhaps Ezek. 8.14ff. is also already to be interpreted in this context, see above, 233.

2. In addition there were also occasional fast liturgies for particular reasons, cf. Ezra 8.21, 23.

3. See below, 509.

4. See below, 380f.

5. Whether Lam.1-5 all come from the same author (thus Johnson, 'Form and Message', 72) may be left open here; this seems to me certain for Lam.2 and 4; I think that Lam.3 is later, see below, 401f.

6. Lamentations 1-4 are acrostics; probably they were originally composed for private purposes but were soon used in the public cult.

7. Cf. the numerous references to Zion and kingship theology, sometimes in the form of quotations (Lam.1.1; 2.1,6f.,15,20; 4.12; 5.19; 2.2; 4.20; cf. Ps.99.5; 132.7; 110.1; Ezek.15.13; Ps.48.3,14) and Albrektson, *Studies*. It is not surprising after Josiah's reform of the cult that references to Deuteronomy can also be recognized (e.g. Lam.1.10, cf. Deut.23.2ff.); Deuteronomy was also accepted by the nationalistic religious party, see above, 240; given Lam.2.14,17, the view of Brunet, *Lamentations*, that Lamentations is opposed to Jeremiah certainly goes too far.

8. In the text Assyria stands for the power of Mesopotamia generally; here the poet takes up the political charge of the prophets Hosea and Jeremiah (cf. Hos.5.12-14; 7.11f.; Jer.2.18, 36f.) and indicates that there was also a concern to secure economic advantages.

9. It is difficult to date and locate the psalms of lamentation Pss.44; 60; 74 (?); 79; 89; Isa.63.7-64.11, which are probably exilic. The prose passages which Veijola, 'Klagegebet', claims for the exilic period (I Sam.23.10-11a; Judg.6.13; Josh 7.6-9) are even more difficult to locate. But at least we can see that the last two focus on the contradiction between Yahweh's promise and the real crisis; the combination of individual and collective perspectives is also typical of the exilic liturgy of lamentation, see below, 401ff.

10. Cf. Koch, 'Profetenschweigen'; in his view it is in particular the unconditional character of the prophetic announcement of judgment which contradicted the Deuteronomistic understanding of the word of God (127f.).

11. See below, 381ff.

12. Isa.2.6aα; 8.8b,10,24-26; 30.18-26; 33; Jer.10.25 = Ps.79.6f.; Amos 4.13; 5.8f.; 9.5f.; cf.1.2; Micah 4.5,7b; 7.7,8-10 etc.

13. Cf. e.g. Isa.1.2-20; Jer.8.4-10.25*; Amos 4.6-13; 5.1-17; the addition of prophecies of salvation to the prophets of judgment is probably also connected with this usage, see below, 414.

14. The tradition Jer.8.10aβ-12, a duplicate to 6.13-15, shows that this was a collection independent of Jer.2-6*; it did not yet include Jer.9.11-15,22-25; 10.1-16.

15. H.-W.Wolff, *Joel and Amos* (3.6), 111, 208ff., assigned the text to a 'Bethel interpretation of the time of Josiah', but a later dating remains more plausible, cf. Koch, 'Rolle', 536. It is certainly no coincidence that this is attached to a prophetic saying about the cult (Amos 4.4f.).

16. That is probably how we are to understand the sweeping reference of the *kō*.

17. This so-called 'motto' represents the Amos prophecy as a theophany of Yahweh from Zion in judgment.

18. The exilic and early post-exilic passages cited for this (Ezek.11.16b; Jer.52.13; Isa.56.7; Ps.74.7f.; Ezra 8.15-20) are unclear; the first certain evidence for a synagogue is an inscription from Egypt in the third century BCE; for discussion cf. Kraus, *Altertümer*; Galling, 'Erwägungen'; Waldow, 'Origin'.

19. Cf. the reading of the prophets alongside the reading of the Torah in early synagogue worship, Luke 4.16; Acts 13.15.

20. Thus e.g. Willi-Plein, *Vorformen*; Jeremias, 'Deutung'; id., 'Zur Eschatologie', etc.

21. Thus in the books of Amos and Micah; close to them also Isa.1.2-20; cf. Schmidt, 'Redaktion'; Thiel, *Redaktion* I and II.

22. Cf. Jer.27.7; 29.10 and Thiel, *Redaktion* II, 114.

23. Cf. the echoes of Deuteronomistic language which have constantly also been discovered in the book of Ezekiel; cf. Liwak, *Probleme*, 205ff.; the view of Deuteronomism proposed here is a simple explanation of this remarkable fact.

24. Apart from Isaiah (II Kings 18-20), reinterpreted in terms of a prophecy of salvation, there is not a single mention of the classical prophets of judgment in the Deuteronomistic history.

25. See below, 392f., 393f.

26. See above, 241f.

27. Cf. already the considerations of Lohfink, 'Kurzgeschichte' (3.8), 333ff., in this direction. The relatively slight difference in language and content between the Jeremiah narratives that celebrate the Shaphanids (e.g. Jer.36) and the Deuteronomistic redaction (cf. vv.3,7,31 and Nicholson, *Preaching*, 38ff.) could suggest a continuous line of tradition; like the Shaphanids, the theologians of JerD probably have a fundamentally pro-Babylonian orientation (cf. Jer.27.5ff.; 28.14; 42.11; 43.10): their critical attitude to the *'am hā'āreṣ* (1.18; 34.19; 44.21) could be explained from the splintering of the latter in the late pre-exilic period (see above, 234) and need not necessarily be an argument against this.

28. For locating JerD in Judah see the arguments brought together by Thiel, *Redaktion* II, 113; that would be a simple explanation of the remarkable lapse into addressing those who remained behind in Jer.29.19. Nicholson's location of them in the Babylonian Gola (*Preaching*, 116ff.) is quite improbable, because his main argument (127), namely the negative judgment on those who remained behind in Jer.24.8; 29.16-19, remains limited to the time before 587, cf. 32.15ff.; 42.10-12.

29. Cf. Thiel, *Redaktion* I, 290ff.; II, 107ff.

30. Cf. von Waldow, 'Origin', 273ff., and comparable post-exilic collections like Neh.8.

31. Cf. the constant charge that in the past Israel had not listened to God's instructions and had 'accepted no discipline' (*lāqaḥ mūsār*, Jer.7.28; 17.23; 32.33; 35.13; cf. with *lāmad*, piel, 'instruct', Jer.32.33); according to this conception the time of theological instruction will stop only with the new covenant (Jer.31.34).

32. The sympathy between prophetic sayings and the 'words of the covenant' becomes clearest in Jer.11.1-14,17; cf. Jer.7.23, etc.; in addition the theologians of JerD use the terms *qōl*, 'voice', 7.23; 9.12; 11.4, 7; 32.23 and *tōrā*, 'instruction', 9.12; 16.11; 26.4; 32.23 for the promulgation of the law; these are similarly used for the prophetic word (cf. 42.6; 44.23).

33. According to Deut.4.44ff., the proclamation of the Decalogue and the making of the covenant took place on Horeb, the proclamation of Deuteronomy shortly before the crossing of the Jordan, but cf. also Deut.29.24; I Kings 8.21.

34. According to Hos.9.10; 13.6 and Jer.2.7b, the apostasy began with the settlement, so also JerD in 32.23.

35. Similarly also in DtrG II Kings 17.13f.; cf. Judg.6.7-10, but without reference to the prophets of judgment.

36. Jer.3.12, 22; 4.1,3,14; 5.1-3; 6.8-27; 8.4-6.

37. The single freeing of slaves (*dᵉrōr*) in Jer.34 was rather different from the remission of slavery for debt or the *shemitta*, the regulations for which are given in Deut.15.12-18, 1-11; nevertheless, even if their annulment was not according to the letter of this social legislation, it was in its spirit.

38. Cf. Jer.2.5-8,11,13,17,19,20,23f.,27f.,32; 3.1,2; 18.13-15.

39. Cf. AP 44; Porten, 'Jews' (4.1), 393, has shown that it is probable that the title *nbt pt*, 'mistress of heaven', borne by Anat in Egypt, is identical with the Semitic 'queen of heaven'. Under this name she also had a temple in Syene.

40. See above, 86.

41. See above, 193f.

42. On the one hand from the interpretation of it as regular child sacrifice (Jer.19.5-9) one could already infer a certain distance from actual practice; on the other, it still seems to have been an acute danger for the Holiness Code (Lev.20.1-5; 18.21), which is probably early post-exilic.

43. With its sabbath theme, Jer.17.19-27 could also belong in the early post-exilic period, cf. e.g. Neh.13.15-22.

44. Cf. Josh.9.27; I Kings 8.16, 44; 11.13,32,36; 14.21; II Kings 21.7; 23.27; see 394f. below.

45. In the Deuteronomistic history only I Kings 8.43; elsewhere more crudely with *śim*, 'put', I Kings 11.36; 14.21; II Kings 21.4, 7; 23.27, or *hyh*, 'be', I Kings 8.16-29.

46. Remarkably in Jer.17.25; 22.2,4, 'his officials' (*śārīm*, *ʿabādīm*) are also mentioned along with the king. Is this an indication of hope for a change of the kingship into a 'constitutional' monarchy, as was cherished after the time of Josiah by the reform wing of officaldom, especially by the Shaphanids (cf. Gedaliah)?

47. Thus e.g. by Nicholson, *Preaching*, 127; Pohlmann, *Studien*, 186, etc.; the verdicts on those who remained at home (Jer.24.8; 29.16-18) are limited to the time before the fall of Jerusalem.

48. Reckoning from Nebuchadnezzar's accession in 605, one would arrive at 535.

49. II Kings 23.25 is by no means a clear conclusion, and with its assessment of Josiah presupposes a survey of the period of the monarchy which has come to an end, cf. 18.5.

50. Thus Nelson, 'Double Redaction', 119ff., following Cross; cf. H.Weippert, 'Geschichtswerk', 237ff.

51. Hoffmann, *Reform*, 15ff. also takes this line.

52. Cf. the divergent dates within the advocates of the strata model in H.Weippert, 'Geschichtswerk', 232ff., all of which rest on quite uncertain literary divisions in the closing chapter of DtrG. Over against this, Zenger has demonstrated that the report of Jehoiachin's rehabilitation in 561 (II Kings 25.27-30) is firmly rooted in the closing part and is its climax ('Rehabilitierung', 28f.). Historically it could well have been the catalyst for the composition of DtrG.

53. Cf. already Josh.6.19, 24 and then II Sam.8.11f.; I Kings 7.51; 14.25-28; 15.18f.; II Kings 11.10; the bronze and gold utensils, I Kings 7.13-47, 48-50, which Solomon prepared for the temple; II Kings 24.13f.; 25.13-17 again go in the reverse direction. In addition there are further reports about the different elements in the Jerusalem temple cult (II Kings 12; 16.8,16ff.; 22f.).

54. Cf. Deut 34.10; Judg.6.7-10; II Sam.12; I Kings 11.29-39; 12.22-24; 13; 14.1-18; 17-21; 22; II Kings 1; 2-6; 8.7-15; 9; 13.14-21; 14.25-28; 17.13f.; 19f.; 21.10-15; 22.14-20.

55. The 'levitical' priests, behind which, according to Deuteronomic terminology, stand the Jerusalem priests (see above, 219ff.), take over important functions in DtrG; alongside Moses they commit the people to the Deuteronomic law (Deut.27.9f.; cf. Josh.8.33); alongside the elders they receive its written version from Moses (Deut.31.9) for proclamation at worship and are the ones who carry the ark (Josh.3.3; 8.33); sometimes they are simply called 'priests' (Josh.3.6ff.; 4.3ff.; 6.4ff.; I Kings 8.3ff.). We are also to understand in this connection the charge in I Kings 12.31 that Jeroboam did not appoint 'levitical priests'. I Sam.2.35 even contains an explicit divine election of the Zadokide priests of Jerusalem. Regardless of the difficulty of establishing that the Levites were a separate group in the pre-exilic period, the thesis renewed by Roth, 'Geschichtswerk', 547, that the authors of DtrG were 'Levites orientated on the Jerusalem temple' overlooks the fact that the 'Levites' in DtrG have hardly any function (Deut.27.14; I Sam.6.15), and that their participation in cultic functions alongside the priests (Josh.3.3; I Kings 8.4; II Sam.15.24) is secondary in the text. After I Kings 12 there are no Levites or levitical priests at all in DtrG, but only priests, sometimes in a prominent role (cf. II Kings 11; 22).

56. In Deut.31.9; I Kings 8.1, etc. the elders are also given important functions. The 'two faces' of DtrG, which have become a problem for scholars since the interpretations by von Rad and Wolff, can easily be explained by such a sociological location of its circle of authors, cf. Albertz, 'Intentionen', 37-40, 46-50.

57. The arguments used by Noth, *The Deuteronomistic History*, 79ff., for locating the authors in Judah still have much to be said for them, cf. also Janssen, *Juda* (4.1), 16-18, against a location in the Babylonian Diaspora, thus e.g. Roth, 'Geschichtswerk', 545, etc.

58. For the election of Zion cf. Pss.76.3; 132.13; for that of the king, Pss.47.5; 89.4,20; for the notion that Yahweh is preparing a lamp for the king cf. I Kings 11.36; 15.4; II Kings 8.19, cf. Ps.132.17; II Sam.21.17.

59. See above, 237ff.

60. I.e. the groups of which those who composed DtrG feel themselves to be the representatives.

61. In Deut.29.15-27; 31.16ff. there is already an anticipatory hint of the negative outcome; in 30.1-10 a new beginning in the exile on the basis of repentance.

62. Josh.23.7f.; Judg.2.11 passim; I Kings 9.6,9; 11.7f.; 14.8f.; 16.30f.; II Kings 21.3-7 etc.

63. I Kings 11.7; 12.31f.; 14.23; 15.14; 22.44; II Kings 12.4; 15.4, 35; 16.4; 18.4; 21.3; 23.8.

64. I Sam.15.23; 28.3ff.; II Kings 9.22; 17.17; 21.6; 23.24.

65. II Kings 16.3; 17.17,31; 21.6; 23.10.

66. I Kings 14.24; 15.12; 22.47; II Kings 23.7.

67. Josh. 6.17f.,21; 7.10ff.; 8.26f.; 9.3ff.; 10.28ff.; cf. I Sam.15.9ff.

68. Josh. 9.6ff.; 23.7,12; Judg.2.2; 3.6; cf. I Kings 11.3f.; 16.31; II Kings 8.18.

69. See above, 371f.

70. See above, 234.

71. See below, 481.

72. Social transgressions appear almost only in traditions which have been incorporated, like I Sam.8.11ff.; I Kings 12; 21; granted, there is limited condemnation of David's adultery in what may be (though this is by no means certain) a

Deuteronomistic insertion II Sam.11.27b-12.15a, but in the overall framework of DtrG it remains a sin (cf. I Kings 15.5). The only king who is accused of social as well as religious and cultic transgressions is Manasseh (II Kings 21.16).

73. Circumcision and passover are explicitly performed in Josh.5.3-9,10-12, as family rites of the exilic period which were important to the Deuteronomists.

74. The Deuteronomists infer a concrete syncretism only in Judg 8.33, from the Shechem tradition Judg.9.4, 46 (El- or Baal- bᵉrīt).

75. Baal in the singular occurs only in the scene Judg.6.25-32 which is spun out of the name Jerubbaal and in 8.33. The singular in 2.13 alongside the plural 'aštārōt is strange and perhaps a textual error.

76. See above, 86f.

77. See above, 385f.

78. See above, 132f.

79. See the teraphim of Michal (I Sam.19.13,16; negatively II Kings 23.24), Saul's necromancy (I Sam.28; are vv. 3b,9, Deuteronomistic corrections?), and Solomon's 'cult of the high places' in Gibeon (I Kings 3.2ff.).

80. The parallel adoption of the theme of mixed marriages in Josh.23 and I Kings 11 also shows that the time of Joshua and the early monarchy are to be undertood as foundation epochs of salvation.

81. II Sam.12 and I Kings 15.5 show that this theological postulate gained from a kingship theology interpreted in Deuteronomic terms was difficult to bring into line with the picture of David in the earlier tradition.

82. And here in the Deuteronomistic account of Solomon's building of the temple the syncretistic prehistory of the Jerusalem temple is quite deliberately suppressed, see above 129f.; the rejection of the building of a temple in principle in II Sam.7.4-8 probably derives from the early post-exilic discussion, see 451f. below.

83. Cf. Josh.6.19,24; II Sam.8.11f.; I Kings 7.13-47,48-50, 51; 14.25-38; 15.15; II Kings 12.18f.; 16.8; 24.13f.; 25.13-17.

84. Thus Noth, *Deuteronomic History*, 92ff.; Wolff, 'Kerygma', 321f.; and in a weakened form also Hoffmann, *Reform*, 24.

85. This would be even more evident if II Chron. 6.5f. rather than I Kings 8.16f. were the original text; the somewhat unbalanced alternative in I Kings 8.16 could be explained by homoioteleuton.

86. The sweeping charge of syncretism occurs only rarely in summary accusations or demands: I Kings 9.6,9; 11.2,4, 10; 14.8f.,15; II Kings 17.7,12,15,34-41; 21.21; otherwise concrete accusations predominate in the books of Kings.

87. Thus Lohfink, 'Orakel', 150f., though according to him only for his Dtr1; however, for the questionable nature of the literary-critical division of DtrG see Albertz, 'Intentionen', 40.

88. Cf. the charge that Jeroboam appointed a non-levitical, i.e. non-Jerusalemite priesthood at his national sanctuaries (I Kings 12.31). So it is only consistent that the Deuteronomists should denounce all priests active outside Jerusalem as 'priests of the high places', both in the northern kingdom (I Kings 13.33) or the province of Samaria (II Kings 17.32) and in the southern kingdom (II Kings 23.8f.), and that they do not want to allow the latter – contrary to Deut.18.6f. – to sacrifice in Jerusalem; cf. the even stricter Zadokide view in Ezek.43.19; 44.15.

89. Also an Ashera image which Jehoahaz is said to have set up in Samaria, cf. II Kings 13.6.

90. For the worship of other gods, II Kings 17.7,12,15 cf. I Kings 14.8f.; 16.13,26; and I Kings 21.26; for the cult of Baal in II Kings 17.16 cf. I Kings 16.31; 22.54; for the Ashera cult II Kings 17.16, cf I Kings 16.33; II Kings 13.6; for the cult on the high places II Kings 17.9-11, cf. I Kings 12.31; II Kings 23.15; for the cult of images II Kings 17.16; cf. I Kings 12.28,32; 14.8f.; II Kings 10.29. The last two charges are also intended by the phrase 'walking in the sin of Jeroboam' (II Kings 17.22), which runs through the whole history. Only the charges of worshipping the host of heaven (v.16), the dedication of children and mantic practices (v.17) are not covered by the historical account; elsewhere they are levelled only in the history of the southern kingdom against Ahaz and Manasseh (II Kings 16.3f.; 21.3f.,6): this may be because the accusation in II Kings 17.7ff. was later extended to Judah (II Kings 17.13, 19).

91. Cf. the prophetic announcements with indications of fulfilment: I Kings 13 – II Kings 23.16-18; I Kings 14.10 – I Kings 15.29; I Kings 16.1ff.- 16.12; I Kings 21.21f. – 21.27-29; II Kings 1.6-17; II Kings 20.17-24.13; II Kings 21.10ff.-24.3.

92. Cf. the prophetic accusations which lead to repentance (II Sam.12; I Kings 21) or are thrown to the winds (I Kings 13).

93. These are various cults of foreign gods (limited to Solomon, Joram-Athaliah and Manasseh-Amon), the cult on the high places, cultic prostitution, mantic practices and 'child sacrifice'.

94. In defining the call to repentance as the kerygma of DtrG ('Kerygma', 321f.), Wolff has indeed rightly recognized the main interest of his authors, but he has overlooked the fact that for the Deuteronomists in the time of the monarchy this repentance does not just take place as in the early period (Judg.2.16; I Sam.12.19; cf. I Kings 8.47) in prayer but also in concrete cult-political and ritual measures and remains limited to Judah and Jerusalem as an open possibility.

95. According to MT, Judah as a whole is responsible for the apostasy; according to LXX, Rehoboam.

96. Cf. n.63.

97. In II Kings 8.20ff., the Deuteronomists attribute only the loss of Edom to this apostasy.

98. Joaz and Amaziah became the victims of attacks; Azariah was smitten with leprosy; Jotham was attacked by the Syro-Ephraimite coalition.

99. The fact that the Deuteronomists incorporate into their work in II Kings 18-20 the pamphlet of the nationalistic religious party against Jeremiah and the reform party from the last months before the fall of Jerusalem (see above, 239f.) also fits in with locating them at this particular point of the spectrum.

100. There is something to be said for supposing that these accusations are highly exaggerated and that the syncretistic developments under Manasseh extended more to the sphere of personal piety (Assyrian omens and conjurations, the Aramaean custom of the dedication of children, and so on, see above 192f.).

101. For the destruction of the vessels used in worship of Baal, Ashera and the host of heaven, II Kings 23.4, cf. 21.3f.; for the abolition of foreign manticism and star omens, 23.5,24, cf. 21.6; for the removal of the image of Ashera, 23.6, cf. 21.3; for the abolition of cultic prostitution, 23.7; cf. I Kings 22.47; 15.12; 14.24; for the abolition of the cult of the high places, cf. II Kings 21.3f. passim; for the abolition of the dedication of children on the Tophet, 23.10, cf. 21.6; 16.3; for

the destruction of the roof altars, 23.11f.; cf. 21.4f.; for the abolition of Solomon's foreign cults 23.13f.; cf. I Kings 11.5-7.

4.3 The support for Yahweh religion from family piety

1. For details see Albertz, *Frömmigkeit*, 178-90.
2. See above, 210f.
3. One of the peculiarities of Israelite as opposed to, say, Babylonian religion is the relative proximity of the two strata of religion (cf. Albertz, *Frömmigkeit*, 158ff.); such an adoption of functions would have been inconceivable in the latter.
4. See above, 97.
5. The introductory praise in 63.7-10 is probably an addition, influenced by the Deuteronomists, in the style of post-exilic penitential prayers (cf.Neh.9).
6. Cf. the question form in v.11; v.10 even takes Israel's apostasy into account.
7. The second confession of confidence in 63.16 goes beyond the fatherhood of Abraham by mentioning the fatherhood of God; it very probably presupposes the exilic custom of referring to the patriarchs (see below, 404ff.) behind which yet further questions are asked with a reference to the creative action of God.
8. The hymn of thanksgiving includes vv.1-21, a retrospect on the lament; the confession of confidence (vv.22-23); and the accusation against the enemy (vv.52-54). Verses 55-63 are the report of the deliverance; there are elements of the popular lament in vv.40-47, and of the lament over the destroyed city in vv.48-51. Both lines are probably meant to converge in the closing petition of vv.64-6, for details see Albertz, *Frömmigkeit*, 184f.
9. Cf. Ps.32.8ff.; 34.5ff.; 40.5ff. etc.
10. A similar intent can also be recognized in the lamentation Ps.130, but this perhaps already belongs to the post-exilic period; the references to the history of the people in the individual laments (Pss.102.14-23; 69.35-37; 25.22; 51.20; 59.6b, 9b, 12, 14) also belong here.
10. See above, 101.
12. These motives occur in connection with individuals, e.g. in Ps.102.4; Job 14.19; Lam.3.54.
13. Cf. the twofold action of creation and giving of life in Gen.2.7; however, Ezekiel does not call the breath of life *n^e šāmā* but *rū^a h*, which really denotes the liveliness which revives with the healing of the sick person.
14. See above, 100f.
15. Cf. Ps.68.6; 103.13 and Ps.27.10; Mal.2.10; polemically related to strange family gods, Jer.2.27.
16. Jer.2.27; 3.4f.,19; alongside this see also the notion of Israel as Yahweh's son (Hos.2.1; 11.1; Isa.1.2; Ex.4.22f.).
17. Thus II Sam.7.14; Ps.2.7; 89.27; I Chron.17.13; 22.10; 28.6.
18. See above, 87, 180ff., 206ff.
19. See above, 86f., 193f.
20. Cf. e.g. the widespread notion in the individual lament of being safe with Yahweh (*ḥāsā*, Ps.7.2; 11.1; 16.1; 25.20; 31.2; 57.2; 71.1; 141.8), as an anxious child feels safe in its mother's arms. Remarkably, wherever Yahweh is called father,

what stands in the foreground is not his 'fatherly' strictness but his almost 'motherly' concern.

21. Apart from the adoption of the Jacob tradition in Hos.12.3ff. there is no reference back to the patriarchs in pre-exilic prophecy: for a thorough study see Hardmeier, 'Erzählen'.

22. See above, 212f.

23. See e.g. the conditional promises of blessing in Deut.7.12ff.; 11.8ff.; 28.

24. This claim was vehemently contradicted by the exiled prophet Ezekiel, cf. 11.14-21.

25. The critical exaggeration here presupposes such a theological argument.

26. In Deuteronomic theology the notion of election had been tied to the exodus, cf. Deut.7.6f., and above, 229.

27. Here I am referring to the results of Blum, *Komposition*, 297ff., which I regard as being essentially convincing.

28. I agree with Blum, *Komposition*, 350ff., that the *niphal* of *brk* in Gen.12.3b is to be understood in this sense, in the light of the *hithpael* forms in Gen.22.18; 26.4; Ps.72.17; Jer.4.2 (cf. Gen.48.20). But I feel that his conclusion that the focus is only on Abraham as the one who has been 'blessed in exemplary fashion' and not on the theme 'blessing for others' is too exaggerated. For in wishing blessings for themselves in the name of Abraham, the 'families of the earth' are in fact sharing in his blessing.

29. Cf. Jer.24.9; Zech.8.13, etc.

30. The promise of a 'great name', in Gen.12.2; cf. also II Sam.7.9; 8.13; I Kings 1.46; Ps.72.17, also comes from the kingship theology.

31. See above, 98.

32. The origin and function of circumcision are still disputed, cf. the surveys in Wissmann, 'Beschneidung', 714-24, and Schmidt, *Exodus*, 220ff.

33. Wellhausen, *Prolegomena*, 340, had already conjectured that Ex.4.24-26 was meant to legitimate the transition to the circumcision of infants. However, one must get rid of the presupposition that this is an old text; it simply uses old motives in a very allusive way.

34. For earlier attempts at explanation cf. Döller, *Reinheits- und Speisegesetze*, 168ff. The thesis which has recently become current, that the dietary prohibitions originally had the function of marking a separation from alien cults, has been rejected with good arguments by Kornfeld, 'Reine und unreine Tiere', 135f., but his attempt to find a common category for the unclean animals ('hostility to life by virtue of their habits or spheres of life, 146) clearly comes up against limits (e.g. in the case of the ass) and probably moves too quickly from the subsequent systematization to an originally unitary principle of selection.

35. Thus, taking up an old theory of Meinhold's, now the majority of more recent scholars, cf. Lemaire, 'Sabbat', 162ff.; Robinson, *Origin*, 29ff.; Levin, *Sturz*, 39; Crüsemann, *Bewahrung*, 55; Hossfeld, *Dekalog*, 251.

36. This has to be concluded from the fact that the celebration of the full and new moons is absent from the old festival calendars in Ex.23.14-17; 34.18,22-24; Deut.16.1-17; only in the late post-exilic festival calendar Lev.23.3 did the sabbath festival also find a place.

37. Cf. also the rest for ox (*šōr*) and ass (*ḥᵃmōr*) mentioned in first place in Ex.23.12; the ox was used for ploughing (Deut.22.10) and threshing (Deut.25.4),

the ass for ploughing (Deut.22.10), riding (Gen.22.3) and as a beast of burden (Gen.42.26).

38. As a second purpose in Ex.23.12, which on 185f. above is derived from Hezekiah's reform.

39. Robinson, *Origin*, 314ff.

40. The combination is still clearly recognizable from the circumstantial formulation of the Decalogue commandments in Deut. 5.12-15; Ex.20.8-11; for its exilic origin cf. Hossfeld, *Dekalog*, 247ff.

41. Thus for the first time Deut.5.12,15 and later in Ex.20.8,11; Ezek.46.1,4,12; Jer.17.21ff.; Neh.10.32; 13.15ff.; Ex.35.3; Num.15.32.

42. This is overlooked by Andreasen, *Sabbath*, 235ff., who vastly underestimates the changes which the sabbath underwent in the exilic period. By contrast, in wanting to put the development of the sabbath into a weekly day of rest only in the early post-exilic period, Lemaire, 'Sabbat', 181ff., and Levin, *Sturz*, 41f. (quite apart from some questionable literary judgments) overlook the fact that after the rebuilding of the temple there was no occasion for changing the old full moon festival.

43. Even if the parallelism 'sabbath and new moon' was dragged on into a later period as a literary fossil (cf. Ezek.45.16; 46.1,3; Isa.66.23).

44. See above, 210f.

45. Cf. Hossfeld, *Dekalog*, 33-57, 247-52; by way of a qualification of his view that the commandment Deut.5.12-15 is of Deuteronomistic origin it should be observed that it can hardly come from the authors of DtrG since – as has been demonstrated – these were not interested in the social side of the Deuteronomic reform. Rather, groups like JerD with a social orientation should be considered.

46. The evidence has been collected by Hossfeld, *Dekalog*, 33-57.

47. Cf. Ex.20.10; Lev.23.3; similarly Ex.31.15; the formula comes from the Deuteronomic designation of the annual feasts (Deut.16.1,10, cf.15); it almost becomes a replacement for them.

48. Thus Crüsemann, *Bewahrung*, 58.

49. The social and purely cultic orientation of the sabbath commandment reflects the different reception of the Deuteronomic reform by JerD and DtrG. The mixed form of Deuteronomic and priestly language in Ex.20.8-11 could indicate that these versions of the sabbath commandment were framed by priestly groups in succession to DtrG in the early post-exilic period (cf. also the echoes of Neh.9.6).

50. For *qdš*, piel, cf. Deut.5.12; Ex.20.8; Ezek.20.20; 44.24; Jer.17.22; Neh.13.22.

51. For *hll* piel cf. Ezek.20.13,16,21,24; 22.8: Neh.13.17.

52. There is a further accentuation of the sabbath rest in Ex.35.2f.; Num.15.32-36.

53. See above, 214: cf. also the literature mentioned there.

54. The Passover Letter from Elephantine, AP 21, is possibly also about the date; cf. also the private enquiry on an ostracon: 'Tell me when you will hold the passover.' Cf. A.H.Sayes, *PSBA* 33, 1911, 183 lines 8f.

4.4 *Towards a new beginning*

1. The history of the Babylonian Gola could certainly have taken the same course as that of the Jewish military colony of Elephantine.

2. See below, 373f.

3. Cf. the striking detail in the narratives with their mention of the names of those involved in the clashes with Jeremiah. These only make sense if they are regarded as an attempt by the reform officials to identify their nationalistic opponents as the main culprits in the catastrophe and at the same time to exonerate themselves.

4. Schenker, 'Saure Trauben', 456ff., has convincingly demonstrated that contrary to the predominant view, the floating saying Ezek.18.2 (cf. Jer.31.29f.) cannot be understood as bitter ironic criticism of God's justice: in v.19 Ezekiel's conversation partners rather insist on the principle that even the righteous son must bear his father's guilt. If we take seriously the reference in v.2, that the proverb was current particularly 'in the land of Israel', i.e. among those who remained behind (cf.12.22; 11.15; 33.24), then it may be being used here with some satisfaction to justify the ongoing hard lot of the next generation of exiles.

5. Ezekiel 18 is often seen as the breakthrough from a collective to an individual understanding of guilt. But first of all it is not about collective guilt generally, but about the ongoing effect of guilt in the chain of generations (vv.5-19, cf. Deut.5.9; Num.14.18), and secondly – after the replacement of blood vengeance – the legal understanding of guilt was for a long time individual (cf. Deut.24.16). The special feature of Ezekiel's argument is that he applies this individual category of guilt from sacral law in a context of moral and historical guilt and thus breaks with this.

6. See above, 238.

7. See above, 400.

8. Cf. now Westermann, *Heilsworte*, 208ff..

9. Cf. e.g. Pss.60; 85; Jer.14.

10. Cf. the conclusion of the book of Amos and its promise of salvation (9.11-15) or the contrast between Micah's sharp word of judgment against Jerusalem (3.9-12) and the great description of salvation in 4.1-5, in which Jerusalem rises to become the centre of a universal realm of peace.

11. Thus for example von Waldow, *Anlass*, 89, 101f., who wants to derive the genre of the oracle of salvation used in Deutero-Isaiah directly from the exilic festivals of popular lamentation.

12. The observation of Begrich, 'Heilsorakel', 225ff., that the oracle of salvation is an answer to the lament of the individual and that it is already present in Deutero-Isaiah in a transferred form is still valid.

13. Thus e.g. Duhm, *Jesaja*, 287, and some others following him.

14. The great composition 40.1-52.12 presents the liberation of Israel wholly from the perspective of God, of the establishment of his kingly rule in the face of resistance from the nations and the doubts of Israel (cf. the framework 40.3-5, 9-11; 52.7-10); the question of the composition of the book has not yet finally been answered in detail.

15. Michel, *Rätsel*, 130-2; cf. id., *Deuterojesaja*, 519-21, 527.

16. The book shows clear traces of growth, cf. the successive 'conclusions'

48.20-21; 52.11-12; 55.8-13; 62.10-12, which extend as far as so-called 'Trito-Isaiah'.

17. Thus the stimulating conjecture of Westermann, *Isaiah*, 8.

18. It knows traditions of the creation of the world (40.22b, 26, 28; 44.24b; 45.6f., etc.) and of human beings (43.1; 49.5; 42.5; 45.12, etc.), of the primal history (51.9f.; 54.9), the patriarchal history (41.8f.; 43.27; 51.1f.; cf. 49.8), the exodus (43.16f.; 51.9f.; 52.12) and the kingship (55.3-5; cf. 42.1) and temple (51.13,15; 52.7f.) theology.

19. As well as the passages mentioned above cf. 40.2.9-11; 41.27; 44.26, 28; 45.13; 46.13 and the whole second part of the book, 49.14ff., in which Zion stands in the centre.

20. See above, 237.

21. See above, 239ff. and Albertz, 'Deuterojesaja-Buch', 253f.

22. I.e. the 'Assur redaction' which H.Barth has worked out, see above, 240.

23. The only examples which should perhaps be put rather earlier (Deut.4.35,39; II Sam.7.22; I Kings 8.60) belong to the Deuteronomistic tradition: thus Braulik, *Deuteronomium*, 153, conversely Vorländer, 'Monotheismus', 95f.

24. Vorländer, 'Monotheismus', 103-60.

25. Lang, 'Entstehung', 139, is rather more restrained.

26. Thus rightly also Lanczkowski, *Iranische Religionen*, 251. He also shows that polytheistic elements from ancient Iranian religion soon surfaced again in Achaemenid religion.

27. Vorländer, 'Monotheismus', 107f.; the only examples in which the monotheistic self-predication appears together with the predication of the creation of the world are 45.7,18; but here the one is not concluded from the other, but both are used in parallel against objections. The argument is rather a demonstration of the sole divinity of Yahweh from his power in history (cf. 41.4; 44.6; 45.21,22; 43.10-12; 44.8; 46.9f.). It appears as a presupposition of his action in creation and history in 48.12f.

28. Cf. the polemic against idols (40.19; 41.6f.; 44.9-20; 45.20b; 46.6f.), which sarcastically identifies the gods with the figures of them made by craftsman; however, these texts are probably later insertions into Deutero-Isaiah.

29. Israel is to bear witness that Yahweh alone is God (43.10-12; 44.8), even if as a blind and deaf people (45.8) it is not to be fully in a position to do so; for Deutero-Isaiah the problem is not apostasy to other gods but the lack of trust in Yahweh's intervention (cf.44.21f.).

30. If the difficult *baddīm* in 44.25 is a misreading of *bārīm*, the group even knew the most frequent Babylonian designation of experts in omens (*barū*) and used it as a loanword.

31. Unfortunately there are too many gaps in the lampoon of the priests of Marduk against Nabonidus (*ANET*, 312-13). Still, signs are mentioned in col.IV.10 in a fragmentary context.

32. Cf. Albrektson, *History and the Gods*.

33. Cf. e.g. the theological interpretations of the rise of the old Babylonian kingdom in the prologue of Codex Hammurabi (*TUAT* I.1, 40ff.) or the Gutaean invasion in the Naram-Sin legend (*AnSt* 5, 1955, 93-113; 6, 1956, 163f.)

34. The two phases are expressed in the composition of the book by putting almost all the 'judgment discourses against the nations' *before* the Cyrus oracle

(41.1-5, 21-29; 43.8-13; 44.6-8); in the only text after the oracle (45.20-25), the judgment discourse is transformed into an invitation to the nations to salvation.

35. The name Yahweh turns into an appellative in the monotheistic self-predications: 'I am Yahweh (= God) and no other' (Isa.45.5); it is no coincidence that in 45.21 and 46.9 it is replaced by *'el*, 'God'; cf also the use of *'el* in 40.18; 42.5; 43.10,12; 45.14.

36. Exceptions are Jethro (Ex.18.1-12) and Naaman (II Kings 5); here, too, the missionary shaping of these narratives can be followed first in the exilic period.

37. Cf. Hollenberg, 'Nationalism', 23ff., and the authors to whom he refers. Whereas some authors like Schoors want to deny Deutero-Isaiah any universalism, Beuken, Leene and Blenkinsopp are concerned to provide a balanced definition of the relationshp between particularity and universality.

38. For the collective interpretation of the 'Servant Songs' see below, 423.

39. With its insistence on the 'seed of Israel' (*zera' yiśrā'el*) the disputed verse 44.25, which is often regarded as a corrective addition to the universal perspective of vv.22-24, seems to me to be seeking to emphasize the abiding significance of the biological and ethnic basis of the people of God.

40. Mettinger, 'Farewell', 19-28; since 40.4-9 (10f.), as Mettinger himself observes (28), remains outside the compositional element of the system of references, this text is to be extracted from the group and interpreted differently.

41. Thus Mettinger, 'Farewell', 29-46; there is a good survey of research in Haag, *Gottesknecht*, 138ff.

42. Thus M.Weippert, 'Konfessionen', 109f., the third-person songs 42.1-4; 52f.; by contrast he sees the first-person texts 49.1-6; 50.4-9 as 'confessions' of Deutero-Isaiah (110-12).

43. For detailed reasons see Mettinger, 'Farewell', who, details apart, is not shaken by the verbose refutation by Hermisson, 'Abschied'.

44. However, in the form of a fictitious dramatization typical of Deutero-Isaiah. Its position in the composition suggests that the text originated in successive stages: 49.1-13 after the first conclusion in 48.20f. forms the bracket to the 'Zion part' 49.14-52.12, which was added later. 52.13-53.12 comes after the second conclusion 52.10-12 and stems from a further extension of the book.

45. The most important difference is that in 40.2; 42.24; 43.24-28 the sin of Israel is regarded as the cause of its humiliation in exile, whereas 53.9 emphasizes Israel's innocence in its humiliation. But both the former passages are about the verdict of God, so 53.9 is an evaluation from the perspective of the nations, who become conscious of their great sins.

46. See above, 116ff.

47. See above, 167ff.

48. Cf. the parallel between the start (40.1-5, 9-11) and the arrival (52.7-10) of the divine king in the framework. Granted, the term *melek* occurs only at 52.7, but the substance can be found in the notion of the shepherd (40.11), the processional street and the glory (*kābōd*) of Yahweh (40.5; cf.42.8,12).

49. Cf. also Mettinger, 'Hidden Structure', 148ff., even if the structure of chaos-battle, royal proclamation and building of the temple (Enuma Elish, Baal-Yam myth) is perhaps further in the background than he thinks.

50. See above, 133f.

51. See above, 133.

52. See above, 119.

53. See above, 120.

54. Isaiah 2.1-4 seems to envisage a prophetic communication of Yahweh's word and instruction (for *tōrā* cf. Isa.5.24; 30.9).

55. Cf. the echoes of Ps.89.4,18,22; I Sam.9.16; II Sam.6.21.

56. See above, 421, 423.

57. Cf. Gese, 'Verfassungsentwurf', the results of which have been taken over in modified form by Zimmerli in his commentary, see Ezekiel II, 547ff. However, I would not speak of 'strata' but of stages of editing.

58. Thus vividly, Zimmerli, *Ezekiel* II, 547, etc.; almost all measures of height are absent from the 'guidance vision' Ezek.40.1-37, 47-49; 41.1-4 (5-15a); 42.15-20; 43.1-11 (12); 44.1-2.

59. Greenberg, 'Design', 189ff.; he sees the material as being arranged from three perspectives: 1. Ezek.40.1-43.12, vision of the future temple; 2. Ezek.44.1-46.24, 'goings in and out', rules for access to the temple and activities in it; 3. Ezek.47.13-48.35, distribution of the land to the people. 43.13-17 and 47.1-11 serve as transitions. However, it is probably going too far to deny any literary growth on the basis of this apt insight (181ff.).

60. Thus e.g. in respect of the division of the priesthood and its functions (cf. 40.45, 46a; 42.13 alongside 40.46b; 43.19; 44.9-16; 48.11), the sacrificial gifts (cf.43.13-15 with vv.16-17) and the qualification of the portions of land (cf. 45.3f. with 48.10).

61. The *terminus ad quem* is the mention of a high priest in Zech.3.1,8 who is still absent from the sketch in Ezek.40ff.; as P already presupposes him (Aaron, but the title first comes in Lev.21.10; Num.35.25ff.), the priestly composition of the Pentateuch is generally to be put later than Ezek.40-48.

62. Cf. 40.46b; 43.19; 44.15f.; 48.11; as Gese's 'Zadokide stratum' is firmly tied into the whole composition by 44.1-5 (cf. the thematic words 'goings in and out', v.5), we can hardly attribute it to another group of tradents.

63. See above, 116f., 129f.

64. See above, 202.

65. See above, 222.

66. See above, 237.

67. See above, 388.

68. See above, 398f.

69. See above, 238.

70. In contrast to Ezek.1-39, Ezek.40-48 avoids the title king (*melek*) for the future ruler and does not connect him with the house of David. Ezekiel 21.31 could have been the starting point for the more critical view of the king.

71. E.g. the all Israel conception, cf. Ezek.37.15-28 with 47.13ff.

72. The full breadth is to be imagined as being even greater, since the 25 ells of the text (c.13m) only gives the inner dimension of the gate rooms. The Solomonic city gates measure 20.3 x 18m in Hazor, 20.3m x 17.5m in Megiddo and 19m x 16.2m in Gezer.

73. As Greenberg, 'Design', 194ff., has shown, the whole section 44.1-46.24 is a discussion of the control of access.

74. This radical solution did not win through: the sacrificial *tōrōt* of Lev.1-13 again foresee laity participating in the preparation of the sacrifice.

75. Wellhausen, *Prolegomena*, 121-6, 145ff.: 124.

76. Cf. Gunneweg, *Leviten*, 81, 118ff., 188-203; Haran, *Temples*, 107, similarly rejects Ezek.44 as ideological.

77. Duke, 'Punishment', 62ff.

78. Against Gunneweg, *Leviten*, 192, who concludes from the supposedly technical use of the term *mišmeret* ('service') that the 'Zadokide stratum' knows a special levitical office with such a designation, as is attested in P. But first, the text in no way refers the term only to the Levites (v.14), but also to the priests (v.15), the foreign cultic personnel (v.8b) and even to the Israelites generally (v.8a); and secondly, apart from v.14, in which it takes up 40.45, it uses it for past cultic services, and where it is describing the future tasks of both groups it uses completely untechnical, vague formulae (vv.11,13,15bf.). So we must distinguish between the undeniable fact that *mišmeret* is a priestly technical term which is used by the authors of Ezek.44 and the question whether Ezek.44 already contains a fully-fashioned notion of the different areas of tasks: the latter is certainly not the case. The specific association of *mišmeret* with levitical service in P is a later specialization. Numbers 18.5; 3.38 show that the broader sense of *mišmeret* was still present in the P tradition.

79. So it is not just a matter of preserving or extending levitical rights as in the dispute with the Kohathites (Num.4.5ff.), as Gunneweg, *Leviten*, 203, would have it. In reducing vv.13f. to a 'general summary of the role of the Levites', Duke, 'Punishment', 70, overlooks the polemical function of negated statements. His attempt to shift the blame for idolatry not on to the Levites but on to the Israelites is certainly original, but comes to grief on vv.10 and 12.

80. For the assumption that there were also Jerusalem priests among the authors of DtrG see above, 388; Gunneweg's objections to such a combination of Deut.18.6-8 and II Kings 23.9 (*Leviten*, 120) rest on the assumption that the Deuteronomic and Deuteronomistic groups of tradents are identical, which is not the case. He himself feels (*Leviten*, 203 n.1) that the lack of the (polemical!) Deuteronomistic conceptuality of II Kings 23.9 in Ezek.44 is still no argument against supposing that the same thing is meant on both occasions.

81. See above, 220f.; it seems to me to be a methodological weakness of Gunneweg's reconstruction that he does not distinguish clearly enough between historical development and theological theory. Dependence on the Deuteronomic conception is clearly evident in the use of the term 'levitical priests' (*hakkoh°nīm hall°wiyyīm*, Ezek.43.19; 44.15) for the Jerusalem priesthood (Deut.17.9,18; 18.1; 24.8; 27.9); the fact that this is lacking in P again simply shows that here the distinction between priests and Levites is already being much more taken for granted.

82. Cf. the priestly composition of the Pentateuch and the Chronistic history, which begin from this distinction but indicate an ongoing dispute over the demarcation of competences. In general it can be said that the Levites succeeded in largely revising the abrupt declassing of Ezek.44, see below, 485, 548.

83. We might think, say, of the Gibeonite hewers of wood and drawers of water in Josh.9.23 and of the *n°tinīm* ('temple slaves') or 'slaves of Solomon', Ezra 2.43-58; the further use of the latter also remained disputed in the post-exilic cult (cf. Ezra 7.24; 8.20, 'servants of the Levites'; by contrast P in Num.3.9; 8.19, takes the line of Ezek.44).

84. See above, 128.

85. In Ezek.43.7,9 *peger* does not mean 'corpse' but 'stele', cf. *KBL*³, 861bf.

86. See above, 129f.

87. See above, 128.

88. Thus for example the priests are also assigned the firstfruits of plants, going even further than the sacrificial portions for the priests in P, Num.18.8-19.

89. Read according to the usual construction of the text *ūmigraš leʿmiqnē*, cf. LXX and Josh.14.4; 21.2.

90. Read with LXX *ʿārīm lašābet*. This provision for the Levites could not be realized; in Num.18.25-32 it is regulated through the tithes.

91. However, the decisive negative has dropped out of the text, possibly because the divergence from 45.4 was felt.

92. Cf. Ezek.34.23f.; 37.22-25; only 21.30-32 is more critical; here the titles *melek* and *nāśīʾ* stand side by side.

93. See above, 74.

94. See above, 120f.

95. To this degree the free will offerings of the *nāśīʾ* were also accorded a certain public status (46.12). One really cannot say that the *nāśīʾ* has a central position in Ezek.40-48, as Procksch, 'Fürst', 115ff. and Gese, 'Verfassungsentwurf', 122f., thought; Zimmerli, 'Planungen', 243ff., and Macholz, 'Planungen' 342f., have a more appropriate assessment.

96. There is provision for an annulment of all loans in the year of release (*šeʿnat haddeʿrōr*), Ezek.46.17. Thus the Ezekiel disciples already seem to have envisaged a similar institution to what was later developed in Lev.25.8ff. under the concept of the 'year of jubilee' (*šeʿnat hayyōbel*, 25.13, etc.; the term *deʿrōr* also appears in v.10). On the other hand, Lev.25 presupposes the new division of the land in Ezek.47.13ff. Here for the first time close connections can be seen between Ezek.40-48 and parts of the P tradition.

97. See above, 110.

98. The notion of a universal presence of God among the Israelites alongside a specifically cultic presence can also already be found in Ezek.37.27; granted the relationship between the two notions is not explained, but we must begin from the view of the reform priests, for whom the cultic presence was primary. We could see behind 48.35 a revival of the conception of Jerusalem as city of God (Ps.46.5), but it should be noted that the capital of Ezek.48 no longer lies on Mount Zion.

99. The description of the frontiers in 47.15-20 on the one hand extends the territory towards Phoenicia and on the other limits it to the land west of the Jordan (cf. Num.34; similarly also the patriarchal tradition); this notion is probably orientated on the frontiers of the Egyptian province of Canaan in the second millennium.

100. 47.13b 'Joseph "two" parts' is clearly a gloss aimed at reconciling Ezek.47.13ff. with Josh 17.14ff.; cf. Zimmerli, *Ezekiel* II, 527. The only gradation made between the tribes relates to their proximity to or distance from the sanctuary; the tribes descending from the tribal mothers are in the centre, and those descending from the maidservants are put on the periphery. In order to bring Judah as close as possible to the sanctuary, against the tradition it is put north of the *teʿrūmā*, whereas the second most important tribe of the southern kingdom, Benjamin, is put south of it; for details see Macholz, *Planungen*, 333f., who in passing corrects Zimmerli's

exegesis (*Ezekiel* II, 536) that the priestly land with the temple must have lain on the north side of the *tᵉrūmā*.

101. In the vision of the temple spring in Ezek.47 a view widespread in the history of Israel's religion that streams of blessing go forth from the temple into the land around is significantly focussed on the function of social compensation.

102. The level of the offerings is only 1.7% of barley and wheat, 1% of oil and 0.5% of sheep and goats.

103. Significantly, almost only specifically priestly interests have won through – though with some deletions – e.g. the division of the clergy into priests and Levites; the self-administration of the temple through the clergy; and the priestly claim to direct the fortunes of the community alongside the lay body. We can probably see a revival of the structures of tribal organization in early post-exilic Judah, but this did not produce a balanced society along the lines of the pre-state ideal of equality. Since the principle that clergy and administration provided for themselves could not be established, the ideal of freedom also dropped out; on the contrary, the burden of taxes grew considerably.

5 The History of Israelite Religion in the Post-Exilic Period

1. Fohrer devotes about a sixth of his book *Israelite Religion* to this period of 400 years; that is about a third of the space he needs to describe the monarchy, which is approximately the same length of time. The disproportion is even worse in Ringgren and Schmidt.

2. Ezra; Nehemiah; Haggai; Zechariah 1-8.

3. I and II Maccabees; Daniel.

4. This is particularly true of the late prophetic texts Isa.56-66; Zech.9-14; Joel; Isa.24-27, and also of Proverbs, Job, Koheleth and Chronicles. Moreover Ringgren, *Israelite Religion*, 297ff., makes things easier for himself by making a thematic survey.

5. Cf. Schmidt, *Faith*, 251ff.; from the whole exilic (!) and post-exilic period only apocalyptic interests him!

6. That is particularly true of the more recent discussion of the Pentateuch; cf. the most recent outline by Blum, *Komposition* (see above 4.3), 392ff., 461ff., and id., *Studien*, 357. In it a large part of the texts which are traditionally assigned to the Pentateuch source J from the tenth and ninth centuries slip into the early post-exilic period (first half of the fifth century: 'pre-priestly composition Kᴾ').

7. Plöger, *Theocracy and Eschatology*, esp. 106ff.

8. Cf. Mantel, 'Dichotomy'; Hanson, *Dawn*; id., 'Religion', etc. In the case of Hanson we also have the questionable early dating of the Albright school; for criticism cf. Blenkinsopp, 'Interpretation', 13; Crüsemann, 'Israel', 212f.

9. The report follows Steck's more recent account, 'Strömungen', 310-15; cf. especially the diagram on 314.

10. E.g. Haggai and Zechariah have no place in the model, as they represent a perspective related to the temple ('theocracy'). The assignment of the Deuteronomistic tradition to 'eschatology' remains difficult, since as Deut.18.9-20; 34.10f. show, it has more of a critical relationship to prophecy; cf. also Num.11f. and

Blum, *Studien*, 194ff., and the Deuteronomistic framework in the book of Proto-Zechariah (Zech.1.1-6; 7.4-14; 8.14-18).

11. Most of the time Steck refrains from investigating the groups of tradents, and sometimes he assigns representatives of the alternative positions to one and the same group (thus 310, Deutero-Isaiah, and 311f., the 'wisdom current' of the temple singers).

12. Crüsemann, 'Israel', 212-21.

13. Crüsemann wants to derive the coalition from Neh.5.12 ('Israel', 213), but this is hardly possible, because here the priests only take the oath, and thus appear in the conflict as unpartisan, thus rightly Blum, *Studien*, 359. Here Blum has already pointed out that the Pentateuch is not a compromise in the sense that the priests and small farmers each protect their interests (thus Crüsemann, 'Israel', 215). Rather, social commands for protection appear particularly in the priestly texts. Thus in the Pentateuch we find a priestly reform group which has an eye not only to its own interests but also to social considerations.

14. See below, 480f.

15. Against Crüsemann's statement in 'Israel', 220.

16. The quite natural notion of retribution in Neh.5.19; 13.14,22,31 recalls Job 29.18f. and the view of Job's friends about prayer, cf. Job 5.8ff.; 22.21ff.

17. See above, 370f.

18. See below, 446.

19. The only references to a future (!) kingdom are to be found in the Balaam saying of Num.24.17ff.

20. See below, 451ff.

21. See the corrective redactions of the books of Haggai and Zechariah, above n.10.

22. Cf. Ps.33.20,22; 90; 123; 126.

23. Thus in the confession of trust which draws a dividing line, Pss.115.9 par 62.6-8; 94, cf. Albertz, *Frömmigkeit*, 190ff., and below, 508.

5.1 Political and sociological developments in the Persian period

1. So the term 'restoration' which is often used to describe early post-exilic history is questionable; thus rightly Crüsemann, 'Geschichte', 163.

2. Cf. Donner, *Geschichte*, 393ff.; for the theological background to this polemic see Koch, 'Weltordnung', 55ff.

3. The manifest failure of his mission and the slightness of the impression that it has left behind in the memory (cf. Ezra 5.14,16) rather tell against identifying him with Shenazzar of the house of David (I Chron.3.18); perhaps he was a Babylonian and therefore did not gain acceptance.

4. For the problems connected with the 'edict of Cyrus' see Galling, *Studien*, 61ff.

5. The author of Ezra/Nehemiah attributes the hesitation solely to the resistance of neighbouring peoples, especially the Samarians (Ezra 4.4ff.); however, this clearly derives from later apologetic and can hardly have been the decisive reason.

6. That the list Ezra 2/Neh.7, which gives the high figure of 42,360 persons,

names only those returning home, is a Chronistic interpretation; this is a listing of the total population from the time before Nehemiah; cf. Galling, *Studien*, 88, and Weinberg, 'Demographische Notizen', 51f.

7. If Avigad is right in his dating of the inscriptions which are evidence of further governors (*peḥā*), then there is much to indicate that Zerubbabel was not only 'commissioner of repatriation' (thus again Donner, *Geschichte*, 411, following Alt) but was also appointed governor of the sub-province of Judah.

8. The fact that the Jewish mercenaries of Elephantine were already building their own temple before the time of Cambyses (530-522, cf. AP 30.13; TGI², 86) indicates that Cyrus's victory over Babylon did not mark a turning point in their history and that they played no part whatsoever in the discussion about rebuilding.

9. Talmon, 'Sektenbildung', 247ff., has worked out 'multicentrism' as a characteristic of the exilic/post-exilic period.

10. See below, 405ff.

11. I still regard this as the most plausible interpretation of his enigmatic disappearance (cf. Zech.6.10-15). The fact that the book of Ezra and its Aramaic source consistently suppress his title *peḥā* or omit the name where the title occurs (Ezra 6.7) and instead of this emphasize the leading function of the elders in the building of the temple (5.3ff.) is a deliberate obliteration of his role as a messianic identification figure (cf. Hag.2.20-23; Zech.4.1-6,10b-14).

12. Cf. the relativizing redactions which Haggai and Zech.1-8 have undergone. The fact that the two prophets do not seem to have lived to see the completion of the temple building suggests violent action against them. In the anti-eschatological book of Ezra there is again silence over the reason for Tatnai's intervention (5.3ff.).

13. See above, 241f., 386.

14. Cf. Rainey, 'Satrapy', 57ff.; Stern, 'Empire', 72ff. Meyers, 'Period', 510f., 514ff., even reckons with a dramatic political destabilization of the south-western part of the empire from 486 on.

15. The dating of Ezra's mission is a permanent crux of Old Testament research; cf. Donner, *Geschichte*, 419. I regard a dating in the seventh year of Artaxerxes II (404-358) as the more probable solution (Ezra 7.8).

16. In 448 the rebellion of Megabyzus shook the satrapy; in 404 Egypt was able to regain its independence for sixty years and extended its rule beyond the coasts of Palestine.

17. Thus the classical view of Alt, which Stern, 'Archeology', 82f., has supported by an evaluation of the stamp seals.

18. See below, 466f.

19. Cf. Neh.5.15; Mal.1.8; Ezra 6.7; Hag.1.1 etc., and the seals and coins which attest four further Jewish holders of the office.

20. Thus probably the Bagohi/Bagoas mentioned in AP 30.1; but cf. also the Jewish clan of Bigwai, Ezra 2.2.

21. In Neh.10.1 they are called *śārîm*. Meyer, 'Entstehung', 132ff., had not distinguished between *seḡānîm* and *ḥōrîm* and as a result caused some confusion; cf. Vogt, *Studien*, 107f., and even Schottroff, 'Arbeit', 121f. But that the *seḡānîm* are subordinate to the governor not only follows from the Babylonian title for the official (*šaknu*, cf. Jer.51.23; Ezek.23.6), but is clear in Neh.5.17 and moreover finds support from the Daliye papyri, cf. Stern, 'Archaeology', 81.

22. The 'triple star' of governor, council of elders and priestly college is confirmed

by the forms of address in AP 30 (TGI², 84ff.). In line 1 the letter mentions the governor of Judah, and in lines 18f. – as those addressed by an earlier document – 'the high priest Jehohanan and his colleagues, the priests in Jerusalem', and 'Ostanes, the brother of Anani and the leading men among the Jews' (*ḥōrē yᵉhūdāyē*), cf. already Galling, *Studien*, 162f. It is not the *sᵉgānīm* but the *ḥōrīm* who are to be regarded as the forerunners of the *gerousia* (Josephus, *Antt.* XII, 3.3). By contrast, the Sanhedrin is more a kind of 'committee' made up from the two colleges (Matt.16.21, etc.).

23. Cf. in Neh.4.7 the traditional expression *mišpāḥōt* = 'clans'.

24. As a basic work on this see Weinberg, 'Beīt 'Abōt', esp. 412ff. The novelty of this institution is evident from the fact that the *bēt 'abōt* are identified partly with the families (Ex.12.3), partly with earlier clans (Num.26.2; 34.14), and partly with the earlier tribes (Num.1.4; 7.2; 17.17, 21).

25. Cf. AP 30.18.

26. See above, 73f.

27. See above, 122ff.

28. See above, 227ff.

29. See above, 435.

30. See below, 499.

31. Stern, 'Archeology', 113, has drawn attention to this discrepancy in Persian policy.

32. For this division in the social structure cf. Neh.5; Isa.58.1-4,6f. and in detail below, 494ff. H.Weippert, *Palästina*, 706ff., has drawn attention to the ambiguity of the small finds in the Persian period: indigenous utensils are less developed than those of Iron Age II, whereas luxury goods experience a detectable boom. She interprets the latter in terms of 'the orientation of the provincial upper class on the standards of the capital'. This evidence thus seems to indicate a marked social differentiation.

33. Cf. the typical contrast between the wicked and the righteous, which runs through many post-exilic texts (Proverbs, Job; Psalms; Malachi; Isaiah 50-66).

34. *Contra Apionem* 2, 165f., and recently again Grabbe, *Theocracy*, 123; in 119 he even speaks of a temple state.

35. Between the sixth and the fourth centuries the Jerusalem temple possessed no land, nor did it have an economy of its own, cf. Kriessig, *Sozialökonomische Situation*, 86; Weinberg, 'Agrarverhältnisse', 484.

36. Blenkinsopp, *History*, 227f.

37. Unfortunately Weinberg's basic article on this is written in Russian and is not accessible to me. In his German publication Weinberg already begins from the model without giving reasons for it. At any rate there are hints in agricultural conditions, 473; 484f. However, the parallels from the Near East and Greece mentioned here differ so fundamentally from conditions in Judah in respect of temple land and the economy of the temple that the comparison becomes questionable.

38. Cf. Weber's classical statement: 'Jewry was a purely religious congregational association' (*Judaism*, 374). I myself used the term congregation earlier, albeit with considerable qualifications (*Frömmigkeit*, 90f.; cf. esp. n.171). [This discussion of Gernan terminology is very difficult for English-speakers, whose the vocabulary is much more limited. The author prefers 'Gemeinwesen' to 'Gemeinde', and uses it

throughout, but in English there is only the one word 'community' to serve for both without being impossibly pedantic. Tr.]

39. Donner, *Geschichte*, 431.

40. Crüsemann, 'Israel' (see 5.0), 208-11: 209f.; I completely agree with Crüseman that Weber's concept of the congregation, which he contrasts to the political grouping, cannot be applied to the post-exilic Jewish community. But in my view he goes one step too far in 226 n.49 in not allowing it 'in any conceivable variant'; in the end the term *qāhāl*, 'congregation', in Ezra/Nehemiah is also used to denote the community (Ezra 2.64 = Neh.7.66; 8.17; Ezra 10.8). Cf. below the moderate statement by Talmon.

41. Talmon, 'Sektenbildung', 252f., correcting Max Weber.

42. Cf. Neh.5.17.

43. The surveys of L.Y.Rahmani in the Adullam region and M.Kochavi in the hill-country of Judah have disclosed lines of forts from the Persian period which correspond with the descriptions of the boundaries in Ezra 2.21-35; Neh.7.25-38; 3.2-32; 12.28f. and also the distribution of the *yᵉhūd* stamps, cf. Stern, 'Empire', 86. This indicates a relatively clear territorial demarcation of the province. But on the one hand there seem to have been isolated Jewish settlements outside it (cf. Neh.11.25-35; Ezra.7.25), and on the other, on the basis of the lists of Ezra 2/ Neh.7; Neh.11.4-22, the shifts within the *bēt 'ābōt* and the places mentioned, Weinberg, 'Demographische Notizen', 51ff., has shown the probability that the community of Judah only successively grew from 20% to 70% of the population of the province between the end of the sixth century and the middle of the fifth century.

44. The extension of the prohibition against mixed marriages to the Samarians, who ethnically at least were in part still descendants of Israelites, makes it clear that the ethnic means of exclusion and limitation certainly did not just follow biological lines but also political and religious ones.

45. Here it is ultimately a matter of indifference whether the author of Ezra and Nehemiah, for whom in principle the community is made up solely of those who returned from the Gola, is thinking of the people of Judah who remained behind or real foreigners; at least he knows the possibility of a voluntary increase on religious grounds. The rise of new *bēt 'ābōt* which is attested by Neh.3 in comparison with Ezra 2/Neh.7 suggests that successive new members were incorporated into the tribal system of the community, cf. Weinberg, 'Beīt 'Abōt', 411f.

5.2 The key experience of the failed restoration

1. Cf. Amos 9.11-15; Micah 5.1ff.; Ezek.34; 36f.; Jer.23.1-6; in a weaker form in JerD 17.19-27; 32.36-44.

2. Cf. Darius's Behistun inscription, *TUAT* I/4, 419-50; for the problem of dating see Wolff, *Haggai*, 54ff.

3. It is difficult to make out what specific arguments lie behind Hag.1.2. Steck, 'Haggai', 373ff., sees here confirmation of his thesis, which he has stated in different ways, that for the 'old Judaeans shaped by the Deuteronomists' the judgment of 587 was still persisting; however, this is questionable (cf. only II Kings 25.27-30; Jer.29.10-14). Wallis and others think that in the background they can make out a

rejection of the rebuilding of the temple in principle, as this appears in Isa.66.1-2 ('Gott', 193ff.), but this text is very probably later. Wolff, *Haggai*, 24, conjectures purely economic reasons. Zenger, 'Israels Suche', 129, indicates that the issue could be the priority of the social question.

4. It can be said, as Meyers, 'Persian Period', 512ff. (see above, 5.1), has recently argued, that Haggai and Zechariah advocate an anti-nationalist policy of adaptation only if one takes no account of the explosive political nature of statements like Hag.2.20-23; Zech.6.9-14.

5. For this customary dating cf. Wolff, *Haggai*, 54. Alongside it, attempts are constantly made to put Haggai in the year of the great rebellions (521) by counting the time from the accession of Darius on 29.9.522 to 13.4.521 not as an accession year but as the first year of his reign (Waterman, 'Purge', 76; Bickerman, 'La seconde année', 23ff.); this would make his hopes of an upheaval more understandable. But even then it remains difficult to make a connection with the historical dates, and at least the dating of Zech 1.7 would clearly be too late (see Waterman, 78).

6. The naming of Joshua in 2.4 goes back to the redactors.

7. If in his lamentation in 1.12 Zechariah is taking up the seventy years from Jer.25.11; 29.10, then – if we count from 587/6 – he seems to be expecting an intervention of Yahweh around the year 517-16, i.e. within a space of two or three years.

8. Beyse, *Serubbabel*, 83ff., and Kellermann, *Messias*, 59f., have indicated the probability that the coronation was not just of Zerubbabel but of the two of them. We already find comparable dyarchic notions in Jer.33.17f., 22.

9. Thus clearly in v.13 LXX. MT alters the text along the lines of the later political claims of the high priest.

10. Cf. the preservation of the one crown (thus LXX, MT two crowns) in the temple as a memorial (v.14) and the mutilation of the text in v.11.

11. The formulation of 6.8 that Yahweh will settle 'his spirit' on the North is ambiguous: $r\bar{u}^a\dot{h}$ here can mean both anger (Ezek.5.13) and the activating spirit (Zech.4.6) of God.

12. See above, 445.

13. Thus rightly Waterman, 'Purge', 78; the generalized report of the dedication in Ezra 6.16-18 is composed to such a degree in Chronistic diction that it was probably supplemented by the author of Ezra because his Aramaic original did not say enough about it.

14. Cf. the framework in Hag.1.10f.; 2.4, 18f., which is often noted, e.g. by Beuken, *Haggai*, 166f.; the second framework which stands alongside it between Zech.1.1-6 and 8.14-17.19b gives me cause to differ somewhat from Beuken et al. in assuming two redactions.

15. Thus aptly Mason, 'Purpose', 414ff., correcting Beuken, who in his linguistic comparison is too fixated on the Chronistic tradition.

16. It strikes me that the whole shaping of the composition in connection with the question of fasting (Zech.7.1-3 + 8.18,19a) is the work of the Deuteronomistic reaction which emerges in 7.4-14; 8.14-17,19b.

17. If the assignment of the redaction(s) to a 'milieu with a Chronistic orientation' made by Beuken, *Haggai*, 331, etc., is right only in tendency and is by no means compelling, there is no reason for removing it far from the prophets in time; thus

also Mason, 'Purpose', 421, and Wolff, *Haggai*, 4. However, I would think in terms of the years after 515.

18. See below, 469f.

19. Thus in 1.17; 8.20-23, and later in chs.9-11; 12-14.

20. Thus with good reasons Steck, 'Grundtext', 267 n.31, etc.; Westermann, *Isaiah*, 295f. (see above 4.4) still differs, wanting to date the earliest strata of Isa.56-66 in the period between 537 and 520.

21. Cf. Zimmerli, ' "Gnadenjahr"', 322f.; Schottroff's 'quest for a clear understanding of the text' ('Jahr der Gnade', 132ff.) comes up against a clear limit and can only be read out of a context which is by no means certain.

22. In ch.60 Zion is addressed by the group; after vv.10f., ch.61 evidently adresses Zion itself (vv.7-9 are a reflection of Yahweh on Zion) and not the prophet 'Trito-Isaiah'; in ch. 62 an individual is again addressing Zion.

23. Cf. Fohrer, *Religion*, 345ff.; he puts the beginning of eschatology with Deutero-Isaiah (335-7).

24. Cf. the critical objections of Westermann, *Heilsworte* (see above, 4.4), 207.

25. Cf. the gift of the spirit and anointing in I Sam.16.13; II Sam.23.1-7, if the 'I' who is speaking is to be assumed to be Zion, in analogy to vv.10f.

26. Because of the term $d^e r \bar{o} r$, and in the context of Isa.58, Schottroff, 'Jahr der Gnade', also thinks of freedom from taxation within Israel, but this is clearly not meant in the narrower context of chs.60-62 (61.5f.,7f.; 62.8f.), which is again evidence that this prophecy resists a literal interpretation.

27. See below, 502f.

28. Neh.6.10.

29. Cf. the reconstruction by Busink, *Tempel*, 81ff.: remains of the supporting wall of the outer courtyard from the Persian period have been preserved in the present-day Haram east wall, cf. Dunand, 'Byblos', 64-70 pl.I, A-B; II, C-D. For what follows see the surveys by Maier, 'Tempel', 371-90, and Schürer, *Geschichte*, esp.277-63.

30. Thus Josephus, *BJ* V, 219; that would mean that the notions of P in Ex.25.10-22; 37.1-9 are still orientated on the temple of Solomon and that the *kapporet* (Luther, 'mercy seat') must be understood more as a symbolic place of the presence of God; cf. Janowski, *Sühne*, 280ff., esp.347f.

31. Cf. Josephus, *BJ* V, 219; *Antt.* XIV, 72.

32. Cf. I Macc.1.21; 4.49; *BJ* V, 216.

33. Cf. I Macc.1.22; 4.49.

34. Similarly Busink, *Tempel*, 821.

35. Ibid., 811ff.

36. See above, 130.

37. The measurements for the Herodian altar are even larger, cf. Josephus, *BJ* V, 225; Middot III, 1-4.

38. See above, 428f.

39. Cf. Kelim 5.8.

40. Thus evidently after 300, cf. Busink, *Tempel*, 827ff.; in the Seleucid period the high priest Alcimus, who went over to Hellenism, had the barrier torn down, to the indignation of the pious (I Macc.9.54; *Antt.*XII, 413f.); however, Alexander Jannaeus (103-76) with his Sadducaean orientation again strengthened it against the hostile mass (*Antt.*XIII, 373).

41. The citadel in the temple mentioned in Neh.2.8; 7.2 was probably not to supervise the temple but to protect the vulnerable northern flank.

42. This also applied to the Hellenistic and Roman period, cf. Schürer, *Geschichte*, 360ff.

43. Further officials and authorities in the temple administration developed from this in time, cf. Schürer, *Geschichte*, 318ff.

44. Cf. Lev.4.3,5,16; 6.15; 8.12; 21.12.

45. The turban, *miṣnepet* (Ex.28.4), is elsewhere attested only for the *nāśî'*, Ezek.30f.; the breastplate (*ḥošen*, Ex.28.15ff.) adorned with precious stones recalls the pectoral which was found in a middle Bronze Age royal tomb in Byblos; the girdle (*'abnet*, 28.39) was regarded as a mark of the royal official (Isa.22.21). The royal 'flower' (*ṣîṣ*) on the turban is probably to be compared with the royal diadem (*nēzer*), Ps.132.18.

46. Cf. the sympathy which later high priests in particular showed to Hellenism.

47. See above, 429ff.

48. Cf. Ezra 8.18f.; Neh.11.18; the figure of 38,000 mentioned in I Chron.23.3 is certainly much exaggerated, but bears witness to the heightened self-awareness.

49. That the second temple was endowed with former royal domains (thus Rengstorf, 'Erwägungen') is a very vague conjecture.

50. This fact is overlooked in the somewhat malicious descriptions of the priestly income in Maier, *Tempel*, 374f., and Schürer, *Geschichte*, 297ff.

51. The first two types of sacrifice, which make up an increasing proportion of all sacrifices, are new in this form, see below, 463f.; apart from the public sin offerings which were burned outside the sanctuary, in practice the priests received all these sacrifices; only the fat of the entrails was burned (Lev.4.27-35; 6.19). The food offerings were increased by being required as an accompaniment to any animal sacrifice (Num.15.1-16).

52. Namely the breast and the loin (Lev.7.30-34; 10.14f.) instead of the shoulder, the cheeks and the stomach (Deut.18.3); later the Deuteronomic parts were required from profane slaughterings.

53. Later set at between a fortieth and a sixtieth of the crop.

54. In Deuteronomy the tithe was consumed for two years by the worshippers themselves and in the third year used to provide for the poor (Deut.14.22-29). The poor at that time included the unemployed country priests whom Deuteronomy calls Levites, see above, 219ff. The reservation of the whole tithe for the newly created class of Levites (*clerus minor*) is very much in line with the existing legal tradition.

55. See above, 408f.

56. For the difficult problem of the calendar see Clines, 'Evidence'.

57. Cf. Janowski, *Sühne*, 347ff., 242ff.

58. For a fundamental study see Rendtorff, *Opfer*, 199-234.

59. Ibid., 233f.; to make a detailed differentiation between *ḥaṭṭā't* and *'āšām* in Lev.5 is difficult. The claim by Koch, 'Sühne', 219ff., that the forgiveness of sins by God played no part in the pre-exilic cult is certainly an exaggeration. Janowski, *Sühne*, 360, seeks to show that the dedicatory and atoning function of the *ḥaṭṭā't* go together, but he completely leaves aside the question of the development of the cult.

60. According to this conception of sin, deliberate transgression could not be made good, but was to be avenged by exclusion from the community (Num.15.30f.).

61. Cf. Albertz, *Frömmigkeit*, 70f.

5.3 The struggle for the identity of the community

1. Cf. the gifts of the Babylonian Diaspora for the temple which are often mentioned (Zech.6.10f.; Ezra 1.6; 2.68f.; 7.15f.; 8.33); these probably indicate an existing custom, even if in part they are a Chronistic construction.

2. See above, 205f.

3. Cf. II Kings 23.1-13 and above, 205.

4. Depending on whether Artaxerxes I or Artaxerxes II is meant.

5. For the discussion, which is virtually impossible to survey, see just the collection by Kellerman, 'Esragesetz', 373-9.

6. Verse 26 mentions 'the law of your God' and 'the law of the king', linking them with a copula; but as no other royal law is mentioned in the text, the same law must be meant on both occasions, so that the copula is to be understood explicatively.

7. Cf. the Chronistic phrases and notions which Gunneweg, 'Esra', 129ff., has pointed out.

8. Frei, 'Zentralgewalt', 13ff.

9. Cf.Frei, 'Zentralgewalt', 12-14; Blum, *Pentateuch*, 346.

10. Frei, 'Zentralgewalt', 14f.; Blum, *Pentateuch*, 346f.

11. Thus Frei, 'Zentralgewalt', 15f., with good arguments against the doubts expressed by scholars. He fills in the gap in line 4 as follows: 'I have given orders that you, Arsames, shall convey to the Jewish garrison' (32 n.31).

12. Cf. the reflections of the proverbial permanence of codified Persian law in Esther 1.19; Dan.6.9, though this is already caricatured in Dan.6.15f. by exaggerating it to the point of immutability.

13. Blum, *Pentateuch*, 345-60; cf. also now Crüsemann, 'Pentateuch', 256ff.

14. See above, 453f.

15. Cf. the remarkable fact that the current introductions treat the question of the origin of the Old Testament canon quite separately from their account of the history of its redaction.

16. Cf. the way in which the redactions of the books of Haggai and Zechariah tone things down, above, 455f.; an anti-nationalistic tendency will also emerge as a characteristic feature of the Pentateuch, see below, 471f., 480f. By making this connection I think I can provide a plausible solution to the conjectural questions raised by Blum, *Pentateuch*, 344, esp.n.39, and 358f., which are still vague.

17. Its most prominent representatives are Nehemiah and Ezra; there is no occasion to conclude from the activity, especially of the latter, that the process of canonization was essentially prompted or even carried out by the Babylonian Diaspora; according to Neh.1, messages went to and fro between Jerusalem and Susa, so that everything points to close collaboration. The fact that even the Jewish

colony in Elephantine did not grant the two leading organs of self-administration in Judah the competence to decide on its cultic matters (AP 30) completely rules out the possibility that in such an important matter as imperial authorization these were not taken into account by the Persian.

18. Even if we follow many scholars in assuming that the oldest parts of the Priestly Writing (P^G) belong in the late exilic period, we arrive at the early post-exilic period for the mass of cultic law and legal material, cf. the discussion in Lohfink, 'Priesterschrift', 201.

19. Cf. simply Gen.15; Ex.3.1-4,18; 13; 19.3-9; 32.7-14; 34; Num.14.11-23, etc.

20. It is quite impossible to discuss the rapidly growing literature here; the reader is referred to the surveys in Blum, *Komposition*, 461ff., and *Pentateuch*, 1ff.; one example of the new redaction-critical hypotheses which reckon with a late, even post-priestly 'Yahwist', is Schmitt, 'Redaktion'.

21. Unlike Schmitt and others, Blum pursues a consistently traditio-historical approach, following Rendtorff. He worked it out first on Gen.12-50 in his dissertation *Die Komposition der Vätergeschichte* and extended it to Exodus-Numbers in his Habilitationsschrift *Studien zur Komposition des Pentateuch*.

22. Blum, *Pentateuch*, 9-218, esp. 208ff.; cf. also the small corrections made to his first book, 288. For the dating cf. already *Komposition*, 392-6.

23. Cf. already Rose, *Deuteronomist*, 321ff.; Blum, *Pentateuch*, puts forward a more differentiated view.

24. Cf. Blum, *Pentateuch*, 131ff.

25. Ibid., 134, 152, 155, where he refers to influences from early post-exilic prophecy and a changed situation of discussion in relationship to prophecy.

26. Thus Ex.15.15b-16; 16.4f., 28; Blum, *Pentateuch*, adopting the findings of Rupprecht, 'Mannawunder'.

27. Thus Num.32; 33.50-56; Blum, *Pentateuch*, 378f.

28. Cf. Ex.3.16,18; 4.29; 12.21; 24.1,9,14 and especially Num.11.16ff.; see below 478f.

29. The royal officials (e.g. the Shaphanids) and the Jewish aristocracy ('am hā-'āreṣ) played an important role in the broad reform coalition, see above, 201ff.; however, parts of the Jerusalem priesthood were also involved in it (cf. Hilkiah, II Kings 22.4ff.); I would like to maintain this despite the doubts expressed by Blum (*Pentateuch*, 342 n.31). But the majority probably went over to the nationalist religious camp after the collapse of the reform coalition, see above, 237.

30. The Jeremiah narratives suggest that the descendants of the reform officials' party (Shaphanids) are probably to be regarded as tradents of the Deuteronomistic Jeremiah tradition, see above, 382f.

31. On p.388 above the DtrG group were defined as descendants of the former nationalistic religious party, which probably consisted of leading laymen ('elders') and former priests and temple prophets. We may conjecture that this group dissolved with the rebuilding of the temple and that its priestly members reorientated themselves by the newly created priestly college. However, here the tone was evidently set by a group of reform priests who came from among Ezekiel's pupils and had returned from Babylon. The Nehemiah memorandum also shows that we should not imagine the early priesthood of the second temple as a unitary block (cf. Neh.3.1,22,28; 13.4,28f.).

32. See below, 473, 477f.

33. For the reform priesthood which set the tone here see below, 481f.

34. The Chronistic history from the third century presupposes the Pentateuch as a normative entity (cf. only Ezra 3.2ff.; Neh.10; 13.1f.) and the Samaritans, who separated from the Jews in the fourth century, adopted it as their (only) holy scripture. The translation of the Pentateuch into Greek which took place in the middle of the third century also already presupposes its completion and canonical status, cf. Crüsemann, 'Pentateuch', 254f.

35. Nehemiah 13.25-27 refers to the Deuteronomic/Deuteronomistic prohibition of mixed marriages and the Deuteronomistic picture of Solomon; the measures indicated in Neh.13.4-13 are based on the relationship of priests and Levites which is typical of K^P.

36. I.e. under Artaxerxes II in 398/7 or at least towards the end of the fifth century; Ezra still cannot be dated with any certainty.

37. The later Jewish tradition which celebrates Ezra as the 'second Moses' and sees him behind Nehemiah and the eighty-five men of the Great Assembly (Neh.8-10) as the founder of the canon thus has a basis in historical reality. The Chronistic picture of this assembly (Neh.10) also reflects the juxtaposition of leading laity and priests.

38. See above, 454.

39. In what follows I am indebted for many essential insights to Blum, *Pentateuch*, who with his traditio-historical approach also has a deeper grasp of the theological dimension of the pre-priestly Pentateuch than was possible under the aegis of the source theory. Here I must largely presuppose the way in which he assigns the texts.

40. See above, 398f.

41. Cf. Deut.4-11 or Deut.1-3.

42. Cf. Blum, *Komposition*, 396ff.; id., *Pentateuch*, 107f.

43. Cf. Crüsemann, 'Urgeschichte'.

44. For the proximity of Gen.24 to the D composition see Blum, *Komposition*, 383; the thesis put forward in *Pentateuch*, 67ff., 369ff., that Ex.34.11-27 is a later insertion into the D composition is at least worth considering.

45. Cf. Deut.31.7f.,14-15,23; 34.9f., taking up the threads of DtrG (Deut.3.28) and leading to it (Josh.1), and Blum, *Pentateuch*, 109ff.

46. Cf. Deut.34.10 with its summary verdict and Blum, *Pentateuch*, 110f., 207; possibly this section was orientated on the Deuteronomic Torah of Moses.

47. See above, 386.

48. Cf. the experiment already attempted once with Gedaliah, above 241f.; for further connections with JerD see below, 475f., 477f.

49. Cf. Blum, *Pentateuch*, 363f., correcting earlier views.

50. The unfinished character of the narrative span in the Pentateuch is thus given an illuminating political explanation in terms of the Persian period. Precisely because the realization of the renewed 'settlement' was left for the future, the ideas of the extent of the land in K^D could take on utopian features (Gen.15.18, from the Nile to the Euphrates).

51. If the king was originally mentioned in the Book of the Covenant (Ex.22.27), as can be assumed on the basis of I Kings 21.10,13, his appointment by the *nāśî* 'prince, sheikh' goes back to an anti-monarchical (priestly?) revision.

52. For the probable place of the Balaam pericope in K^D cf. Blum, *Pentateuch*, 116f. The anti-monarchical tendency is also taken over by K^D, see below, 480f.

53. The preceding Deuteronomic/Deuteronomistic tradition had still included Moses *in* the prophetic tradition as the model of the true prophet, cf. Deut.18.14-22; Jer.1.7,9; 28.9; cf. already Hos.12.14.

54. This above all inevitably caused a conflict with the reform priesthood, which otherwise was agreed on many points, see below, 482ff.

55. Cf. Gen.22.15-18; 24.7; 26.3bβ-5; Ex.13.5,11; 32.13; 33.1; Num.11.12; (Deut.31.23;) cf. Num.14.16,23.

56. As still the earlier Moses narratives... Ex.1.9-12, 15-2.22... 4.19,20a...5.3f.*, 6-19; for their conception in the revolt of Jeroboam see above, 141ff.

57. Cf. the great significance of signs ('*ōt*), Ex.3.12; 4.8,8,9; 13.9,16; Num.14.11, 22 (*niplā'ōt*), Ex.3.20; 34.10.

58. Cf. the emphasis on religious experience ('see', *rā'ā*), Ex.14.13,31: 19.4; 20.22; (24.10;) 34.35; Num.14.22f. and Blum, *Pentateuch*, 16f.

59. See above, 228ff.

60. Thus for the first time Ruprecht, 'Exodus 24', 166f., with reference to Ex.29.20f.; Lev.8.24,30; taken up affirmatively by Blum, *Pentateuch*, 52.

61. It is widely accepted that it represents an insertion into the theophany narrative Ex.19.1-19 + 20.18-21; for a discussion cf. Blum, *Pentateuch*, 97ff.; 19.20-25 is an even later insertion with priestly interests.

62. Cf. Blum, *Pentateuch*, 91ff.; he thinks that the introductory verse 20.22 and 20.23(b) have been revised by K^D.

63. Cf. above on Hezekiah's reform, 180ff.

64. Thus clearly tangible in DtrG, which uses exclusively religious and cultic commandments of Deuteronomy as criteria for the course of the history of Israel, see above, 390f. The binding nature of the Deuteronomic social legislation had been an important point of dispute on which the Deuteronomistic reform coalition had split, see above, 233ff.

65. Cf. especially the section Ex.22.20-23.9 of the Book of the Covenant, which, with its special concern for the alien, surely became topical again in the early post-exilic period (the integration of those who had returned); it must be pointed out that the Book of the Covenant also contains religious cultic commandments (for its structure see above, 183ff.), but the 'civic'-social regulations stand in the foreground. If this interpretation is correct, then at this point, too, K^D is moving along the lines of JerD, see above, 385.

66. Even if it can no longer be ascertained with any certainty whether Ex.24.1,9-11 was once the focus of the earlier theophany tradition before the incorporation of the Book of the Covenant (according to Ruprecht, 'Exodus 24', 150, the text is only exilic), the cultic elements of the theophany narrative itself (Ex.19.12f., holy place; vv.10,14f., holy time; 20.21, mediator of the holy) and general considerations from the history of religion (cf. e.g. Gen.28.10-19) make it probable that theophany and cult were also originally connected in the Sinai tradition, see also above, 56ff.

67. Significantly K^D is especially interested in such cultic rites which had already been connected with the history of deliverance since the time of Deuteronomy (passover, Ex.12.21-27a; mazzoth, Ex.13.3-10) or can again refer to it (offering of firstfruits, Ex.13.11-16; for the firstfruits of plants cf. already Deut.26.1-11); for the lay theologians of K^D the cult has primarily a didactic function, more one of

recollection; it is to keep alive remembrance of the history of deliverance and see that it is handed on.

68. Cf. the postponement of the judgment in Ex.32.34, which connects the foundation history with the present situation of those addressed.

69. On its probable origination in the northern kingdom see above, 145ff.

70. See below, 484f.; the starting point must be that the authors of K^D already knew the most important theological positions of the priests before these were worked into the writing.

71. This becomes even more striking if we reflect that K^D gives the council of elders such a markedly theological legitimation, cf. Num.11.16ff.

72. They limited themselves to the more indirect statements which Deuteronomy had already made on the central place of worship (Deut.12) and the priesthood (18.1-8).

73. See above, 373f.

74. Cf. the remarkable way in which in Gen.15.1f. the oracle of salvation precedes the lament. As the introduction to the former is still in the style of the prophetic word and in form recalls Deutero-Isaiah, it is probably meant as a stylization of the exilic/post-exilic prophecy of salvation which is already a thing of the past for those who are now lamenting, something by which they feel they have been deceived.

75. The connection of the two themes of Gen.15, increase and land, is provided by the keyword *yāraš*, 'inherit, take possession of' (vv.3,4a,4b,7,8). The tribal ancestor Abraham does not lament in general about his lack of children but specifically that he has no heirs, so that an alien will inherit from him; the same combination of lack of population and loss of land also has a role in other exilic and post-exilic texts: Jer.49.1ff.; Obad.17,19f.; Isa.65.9-10). The 'synoecism' (Neh.11.1-2) is evidence that in fact the Jewish community still suffered from a lack of population in the time of Nehemiah.

76. The utopian description of the extent of the land 'from the river of Egypt (the Nile) to the great river (Euphrates)' in Gen.15.18 probably has the function of stirring the imagination of the faint-hearted.

77. Cf. the intensification of the punishment in comparison with the Deutero-nomistic version of the material in Deut.1.35.

78. Thus in K^D faith also assumes the character of offering obedience, cf. Gen.15.6 and also the promised 'reward' in Gen.15.1.

79. At any rate in the case of the D composition it cannot be claimed that the Pentateuch is 'unprophetic' or even 'anti-prophetic', as Crüsemann, *Israel in der Perserzeit* (5.5.1), 216; *Pentateuch*, 265, states, following Blenkinsopp. The former is perhaps the case for P. Schmitt can even speak of a redaction 'in the spirit of prophecy'.

80. Cf. the formula of the utterance of the word in Gen.15.1, the structure of the prophetic call account in Ex.3f., etc.

81. Cf. Jer.1.; Ezek.2f.; according to Blum, *Pentateuch*, 20ff., the call of Moses was first created by K^D and was inserted into the older narrative thread Ex.2.23a + 4,19,20a.

82. This applies especially to Jeremiah, but also to Amos, etc.

83. Cf. the particularly close connection between the call of Moses in Ex.4.10 and Jer.1.6; the anti-monarchical and social tendency characteristic of K^D and JerD

(see above, 385f.) and the positive assessment of collaboration with foreign rule which can be recognized in both (cf. Gedaliah, Jer.40f.).

84. See above, 451ff.

85. This tendency, which puts a critical limit on prophecy, is overlooked by Schmitt, 'Redaktion'.

86. See below, 479f.

87. The number is possibly taken from the existing tradition Ex.24.1,9-11, to which there is an explicit allusion in vv.16, 25 (cf. the word-play *'āṣal – 'āṣil*); i.e. the group which represents Israel cultically is to be identified with the leading political and theological body.

88. *ziqnē hā'am wᵉsōṭᵉraw*; *šōṭēr*, which as an Akkadian loanword literally means 'scribe', is used in the Old Testament for various political and military functions (cf. Ex.5.6; Josh.1.10; Deut.20.5). The fact that here it is put alongside 'elder' means that the term is probably being distinguished from elders in the customary sense as officially appointed functionaries. This would correspond well to the character of the post-exilic council of elders as the official body responsible for Jewish self-administration.

89. Instead of MT v. 25 'and did not lead forth' (*yāsᵉpū*) read 'and did not obey' (*yāsūpū*), thus also Noth, *Numbers*, ad loc. We have permanent divine inspiration here. The notion of perpetually 'enthusiastic' elders was evidently uncanny to the Masoretes.

90. Exodus 18 is probably not part of the D composition, see Blum, *Pentateuch*, 153ff.

91. Cf. Noth, *Numbers*, 89f.

92. See above, 468.

93. Cf. e.g. the striking parallelism of the two compositions in Ex.1-6 and Blum, *Pentateuch*, 357 n.87.

94. Cf. the priestly account of the making of the ark in Ex.25.10-22; 37.1-9 in a prominent position, and the bracketting with K^D in Ex.32.15f.; because of the important function which the ark had acquired in the Deuteronomic/Deuteronomistic tradition as the container for the tables of the Decalogue (Deut.10.1-5; I Kings 8.6f.), it must be assumed that a similar account of its manufacture in K^D has been omitted in favour of K^P.

95. Cf. the 'covenant-makings' in Gen.9.8ff.; 17.1ff. and the covenant formula in Gen.17.7; Ex.6.7; 29.45; Lev.26.12; for their Deuteronomic origin see above, 228ff. It can be said that P repudiated the Deuteronomic covenant theology, as Lohfink, 'Priesterschrift', 217, claims, only if like him one constructs a basic document concerned purely with the theology of salvation and puts this at a considerable distance from the priestly traditions which grew up later, see Lohfink, 'Abänderung', 130ff. Westermann, 'Genesis 17', 76ff., already showed that for P, too, the covenant is two-sided.

96. The supplements Ex.4.13-16 (along with the introduction of Aaron in 4.27-30) and 19.20-25 (access to the holy of holies) can also be understood as such concessions to the lay theologians.

97. Cf. Gen.17.8; 23; 28.4; 35.12; 48.3f.; 49.29f; 50.12f.; Ex.6.4; Num.10.29; 13ff.; 27.12; Deut.34.1.7-9. It is probably wrong to suppose that the land of Canaan was the original goal of the priestly historical narrative, as Elliger, 'Sinn und Ursprung', 182, claims. The only explanation of this is an aversion (a Protestant

aversion) to the cult; but cf. also the Catholic assent by Lohfink, 'Priesterschrift', 194ff.; cf. the justified critical reflection by Saebø, 'Priestertheologie', 366f. In the light of the history of the canon the theme of the 'land' proves to be a consensus with the existing tradition; the emphasis does not lie on it, whether or not one reckons with a continuation of P in the book of Joshua.

98. Koch, 'Eigenart', 40f., and 'Priesterschrift', 98f., 108, is already beginning to recognize the anti-monarchical thrust of the 'Priestly Writing'; cf. also Fritz, *Tempel*, 153, and already Kuschke, 'Lagervorstellung', 89, 98. The promise that kings will come forth from Abraham's loins (Gen.35.11; cf. 17.6) is only taken up in the framework of K^P by the line of Esau, and may be meant for Israel only as a cautious hint at a distant horizon of hope which plays no role in the present: cf. the reflections by Blum, *Komposition*, 457f.

99. Cf. Lev.19.9-18,33-36 and 25.8-55. The institution of the year of jubilee can be understood as a compromise to restore to the sabbath year its old significance of leaving fields fallow (Ex.23.10f.) in accordance with the priestly interest and nevertheless to retain the social reinterpretation made by Deuteronomic legislation (Deut.15.1-11). Kippenberg, *Religion und Klassenbildung* (see 5.4), 62ff., and Crüsemann, 'Israel in der Perserzeit' (see 5.0), 215f., had already demonstrated the solidarity of the priests with the underprivileged small farmers.

100. Whether and to what extent the so-called 'Holiness Code' in Lev.17-26 can be separated from P as a distinct complex of tradition is again an open question today, cf. already Wagner, 'Existenz', 315, and now Blum, *Pentateuch*, 318ff.; cf. simply the compositional relations between Lev.11.43-45 and 20.25f.; Ex.6.2ff. and Lev.26.9-13. The elements of Ezekelian and Deuteronomistic language accumulated in Lev.18ff. can be explained without any problem by saying that here we have the work of members of the group of reform priests who derived from the disciples of the prophets or the priests orientated on the Deuteronomists.

101. That the social stimulus of the Pentateuch continued to be effective in post-exilic society is evident from the document of commitment in Neh.10 which extracted, combined and developed important commandments from it, cf. Clines, 'Nehemiah 10', 111f.: in Neh.10.32b the commandment to let the fields lie fallow was taken up from Ex.23.10f. and the remission of debts from Deut.15.1-8. That means that while it proved impossible to implement the new priestly institution of the year of jubilee, a compromise in accord with it was achieved, which combined the leaving of fields fallow and the remission of debts in a seven-year cycle.

102. So it was also a combination of interests within Israel and not just the external pressure of the Persian imperial authorization that made possible the compromise work of the Pentateuch.

103. Cf. Neh.13.4ff.,28.

104. The agreement with the group of reform priests in succession to Ezekiel which stands behind Ezek.40-48 related above all to the self-administration of the temple cult, the separation of priests and Levites and the general orientation on the social conditions of the pre-state period, see above, 427f.; the most important differences related to architectural details of the temple complex, provisions for priests or Levites and the office of high priest. A more precise connection between the two groups, which would also have to explain why parts of K^P stand closer to the ideas and language of the book of Ezekiel (e.g. Lev.18-26) than others, certainly needs more thorough investigation.

105. This circumstance at least partially explains the 'utopian' elements of 'P' which have been noted time and again (cf. Noth, *Pentateuchal Traditions*, 246f.; Fritz, *Tempel*, 149ff.; Blum, *Pentateuch*, 303f., etc.). The widespread assumption that the text would have had to have been composed before the rebuilding of the temple thus becomes superfluous.

106. Cf. simply the quite different ways in which a distinction is made between P^g and P^s e.g. by Noth, *Pentateuchal Traditions*, 16ff.; Elliger, 'Sinn und Ursprung', 174f.; Koch, *Priesterschrift*, 98; Fritz, *Tempel*, 122f., or Lohfink, *Priesterschrift*, 198. Blum, *Pentateuch*, 293ff., shows how quite essential compositional brackets are ignored by such a division.

107. There should no longer be any dispute that the main emphasis of 'P' lies on the foundation of the cult and ordinances and legal regulations which result from it, as Wellhausen, *Prolegomena*, 8f., etc., already recognized – though he made a false theological assesment of this (cf. e.g. 423f.), despite the continual challenges raised in the wake of Noth, *Pentateuchal Traditions*, 8ff.; 242 (but cf. 244ff.), and Elliger, 'Sinn und Ursprung', 182; cf. the justified criticism by Saebø, 'Priestertheologie', 364ff.

108. Cf. the deliberate parallelism between Ex.24.16a par 40.34f. and Ex.24.16b par Lev.1.1.

109. Koch, *Priesterschrift*, 99, recognized that the manifestations of the *k^{e}bōd yhwh* structured the whole legend of the foundation of the cult in Ex.24.15b-Lev.9.(10), and this was worked out theologically by Westermann, 'Herrlichkeit', 123ff.

110. See above, 474f.

111. The tent of meeting now no longer appeared in it, as in K^D, only after the apostasy and more by chance (Ex.33.7-11), but was commanded by God himself even before the apostasy (Ex.26ff., with its full name first in 27.21).

112. That is the reason why in Ex.24.15b-18 the priests created a parallel to the theophany narrative in Ex.19f.

113. Cf. Lev.4f.; 16; Num.17.9ff., and above 462ff.

114. Thus, following von Rad, 'Priesterschrift', 191ff.; Noth, *Pentateuchal Traditions*, 244-7; Fritz, *Tempel*, 151, 159, etc.; cf. the critical working out of the discussion in Schmitt, *Zelt und Lade*, 219-28, and Mettinger, *Dethronement*, 83-5. Fretheim's conclusion from this that P wanted to sketch out an 'anti-temple' to the Jerusalem temple tends more to meet the modern prejudices against the cult which underlie this whole line of argument than what the biblical text says ('Priestly Document', 315f.).

115. Cf. the same formulations with *petaḥ*, 'in front', Ex.29.4, 32 etc.; *lipnē*, 'before', Ex.29.10,42 etc.; *ḥāṣer*, 'forecourt', Lev.6.19; *'abōdā*, 'work', Ex.30.16; or the combinations with *miškān* in Ex.39.32; 40.2,6,29 or in parallel Ex.40.34f.

116. Cf. with *petaḥ*, Ex.35.15; with *lipnē*, Lev.17.4; with *ḥ^{a}ṣer*, Ex.27.9; with *'abōdā*, 39.32,40. It cannot be maintained that *miškān* originally denoted only a wooden insertion (Ex.26.15ff.) and denotes the whole sanctuary only in secondary strata of 'P', as Fritz, *Tempel*, 163, claims; cf. just Ex.40.34f., a text which represents a necessary junction in the priestly cult legend. Probably with *miškān*

the priests are taking up a term from the earlier Zion theology, cf. Ps.26.8; 74.7; cf. 76.3; 132.13f.; in the plural Ps.43.3; 46.5; 84.2; 132.5,7.

117. Ex.25.22; 29.42f.; 30.6,36; Num.17.19; the use of this term is best explained as a learned interpretation of the term *'ōhel mō'ēd*.

118. Ex.24.16; 25.8; 29.45; 40.35; Num.5.3; cf. Lev.26.11. So it cannot be said, as Fritz, *Tempel*, claims, that 'the conception of dwelling associated with the verb *šākan* is alien to the Priestly Writing'. But the priest-theologians differed from the earlier Zion theology in relating the dwelling of Yahweh not so much to the holy place (Isa.8.18; I Kings 8.12f.; Ps.68.17; 74.2; 135.21; Zech.2.14f.; 8.3; Joel 4.17) as primarily to the people, following the Ezekiel school (Ezek.43.7,9; cf.37.27). However, this was not meant to do away with the bond of Yahweh with Zion (thus Mettinger, *Dethronement*, 96f.), but only to emphasize the people's connection with the cult, see below, 485f.

119. Cf. Ex.26.33; 27.9ff.; Lev.16.2, etc.; there is explicit mention of the sanctification of the tent and the altar in Ex.29.44. Cf. also the use of the term *miqdāš*, 'sanctuary', in Ex.25.8; Lev.12.4; 16.33; Num.18.1, etc., i.e. not just in passages which according to Fritz, *Tempel*, 159f., can be said to be 'secondary'.

120. Cf. Ex.25.22; 30.6,36; Lev.16.2; Num.7.89; the fact that the priestly theologians speak here of a meeting (*yā'ad*, niphal) or appearance (*rā'ā*, niphal) of Yahweh in the holy of holies without adopting the lay theological notion of the descent (*yārad*) of Yahweh (cf. Ex.33.9; 34.5; Num.11.17, 25), and instead of this presuppose the constant presence of Yahweh in the sanctuary, as is shown by the natural use of *lipnē yhwh*, 'before Yahweh' (Ex.29.10f.; Lev.9.5; 16.12; Num.16.16f., etc.), can only mean that for them Yahweh is invisibly present in the holy of holies, there on occasion to meet with Moses or the high priest; Schmitt, 'Zelt und Lade', 222, and Blum, *Pentateuch*, 297ff., arrive at a similar conclusion.

121. Cf. Ex.16.10f.; Num.14.10,14; 16.19f.; 17.7-9; 20.6f.; the difference between the two sets of ideas has been worked out by Westermann, 'Herrlichkeit', 128ff. According to him (130), among other things these public appearances of the *kᵉbōd yhwh* are also related to the founding of occasional cultic functions (Ex.16, oracle of salvation; Num.14, decision on an oath; Num.16, ordeal; Num.17, lamentation of the oppressed; Num.20, asylum). The two sets of notions come into contact only in Ex.29.42, which is a general description of the function of the sanctuary; but here too the encounter with the people before the sanctuary is distinguished from the revelatory discourse which is granted only to Moses. In turn, the ascent and descent of the cloud to lead the people (Ex.40.36-38; Num.9.15ff.) is to be kept quite separate from these two sets of ideas; in contrast to Ex.16.10f.; 24.15bf.; 40.34; Lev.16.2; Num.17.7 it has no quality of revelation (no *kᵉbōd yhwh*, no encounter or appearance of God).

122. Yahweh's presence in the holy of holies remains completely invisible, in contrast to e.g. Isa.6.1ff. or Ezek.43.4f. The disciples of Ezekiel were much more firmly rooted in the traditional world of ideas of the Jerusalem sanctuary, cf. also the broad visionary description of the *kᵉbōd yhwh* in Ezek.1.26ff. with the restrained allusion in Ex.24.17.

123. The fundamental continuity between 'P' and the earlier Jerusalem cult theology is rightly emphasized by Schmitt, 'Zelt und Lade', 225ff.; Mettinger, *Dethronement*, 87ff.; Blum, *Pentateuch*, 298.

124. Cf. Mettinger, *Dethronement*, 96f., 114f.

125. The *kᵉbōd*, which had been an attribute of the god-king in the earlier Jerusalem theology (Ps.29.9; 24.7-10; cf. Ps.96.7f.; 97.6), was stripped even more markedly of its royal connotations by the priestly theologians and made the identity of the God appearing in power; for details see Mettinger, *Dethronement*, 116f.; cf. also Westermann, 'Herrlichkeit', 134ff.

126. The notion that Yahweh dwells in the midst of his people as one who is present in the temple was probably taken over from the Ezekiel tradition by the priest theologians (Ezek.37.16,28; 43.7); elsewhere it occurs only once in the Deuteronomic tradition (I Kings 6.13).

127. Cf. I Kings 6-8; II Kings 22f. and above, 398f.

128. The group of tradents of DtrG probably also included priests, see above, 388.

129. It should no longer be disputed that in the layout and equipment of the tent sanctuary the priestly theologians in principle went by the Jerusalem sanctuary (thus Fretheim, 'Priestly Document', 315, and the literature referred to there). As Fritz, *Tempel*, rightly states, 'the form of construction as a tent is an adaptation to the conditions of the wilderness period which are presupposed, and does not go back to the traditional construction of a tent sanctuary'. There are agreements with the long-house type in the two rooms of increasing holiness (Ex.26.31-37, see above, 130), the altar in front (27.1-8), and the equipment including table (25.23-30; cf. I Kings 7.48), lampstands (Ex.25.31-40; I Kings 7.49, where there are still ten), altar of incense (Ex.30.1-10; cf. I Kings 7.48) and lavers (Ex.30.17-21; cf.I Kings 7.38). There are differences especially in respect of the cherubic throne with the ark (see below) and the forecourt: in Ex.27.9-19 only one is to be created, whereas the Jerusalem temple had two forecourts (II Kings 21.5; 23.12). But it may be that in the ideal conception of the reform priests in the early period the pure camp (Num.) took the place of the second forecourt. However, the lack of pillars in the entrance hall, the bronze sea and the basins is probably intentional, see n.131.

130. See below, 476.

131. This insight of Fritz, *Tempel*, 148, is true, with some uncertain points, even if one does not adopt his literary-critical divisions of the text. At least the ark, the table of showbread and the altar are certainly attested as cultic objects for the period before the state (I Sam.4; 21.7; Judg.6.24); this is uncertain for lampstand, altar of incense and lavers, which Fritz wants to attribute to a secondary expansion, ibid., 160ff. By contrast, the typical innovations of the Jerualem state cult (cherubic throne, pillars, brazen sea, basins) have not been taken over.

132. A deliberate modelling on the cult of the pre-state period may also be the explanation why the priestly theologians accord such a prominent place to the ark, although it was probably not replaced in the second temple (cf. Jer.3.16). But it remained important to them as a symbol of the 'enthronement' (Mettinger).

133. The derivation and understanding of the word are disputed: cf. Janowski, *Sühne* (5.2), 271ff.; if like him one thinks of an abstract formation from *kipper*, 'atone', in the sense of a 'sign of atonement', then the purely symbolic character of this 'cultic object' already appears in the designation.

134. Cf. Ex.25.10-22; as the *kapporet* is said to be only 2.5 x 1.5 ells, the cherubs to be attached to its ends (v.18) can hardly be bigger than 50cm.; that means a reduction to about a tenth of the cherubs on the throne in the temple of Solomon;

moreover the cherubs were turned round ninety degrees so that they faced each other and any association with the old throne (I Kings 6.23-28) of which they formed the armrests was lost; cf. Mettinger, *Dethronement*, 87f. The miniaturization of the cherubs to about ten per cent of their former size can be understood as a symbol of the corresponding reduction of the state cult theology of Jerusalem; for the elements of Zion theology that have been taken over see below, 489f.

135. See above, 389f.

136. See above, 459f.

137. Cf. e.g. II Sam.6.6f.

138. Cf. the technical use of *zār*, properly 'alien', in Ex.29.33; 30.33; Lev.22.10,12,13; Num.1.51; 3.10,38; 17.5; 18.4,7.

139. Here the priests again occupied a special position on the 'holy' east side (Num.3.38); for the whole question see still Kuschke, 'Lagervorstellung', 90ff.; Kuschke already clearly recognized the anti-monarchical focus of this social model.

140. Cf. *qeşep*, 'anger', Num.1.53; 17.11; 18.5 in a distinctively absolute use and *negep*, 'blow, plague', Ex.12.13; 30.12; Num.8.19; 17.11f. or *maggepā*, Num.17.13,14,15; cf. Magonet, 'Korah Rebellion', 10f.

141. See above, 428f.

142. Usually only chs.16-17 are regarded as belonging together, but that ch.18 is meant to be understood as the conclusion to the whole is evident not only from the transitional verse 17.27f. but also from the references back to these chapters in Num.18.5,(4,7,)22.

143. Still perceptible in Num.16.12-15,25-26,27b-32a,33-34; cf. Deut.11.6. For the literary-critical discussion cf. the list in Ahuis, *Authorität*, 72f.; Blum, *Pentateuch*, 263ff. A consensus seems to be developing that three strata are to be distinguished in Num.16: the pre-priestly Dathan and Abiram story, only fragments of which have been preserved (see above, 486); a priestly narrative about the 250 nobles (Num.16.2abβ-7,17*,35); and the priestly Korah stratum which binds the two together as a composition (Num.16.1-2aα,5*,6*,7*, 8-11,16-25,27a,32b), which also includes 17.6-15,27-28; 18.1ff. and is to be assigned to K^P. The combination of the latter into a Deuteronomistic Tetrateuch redaction by Ahuis is a misconception. Num.17.1-5,16-26 are further priestly supplements.

144. It has already often been observed that these chapters are an argument of the priestly theologians against positions of Deuteronomic/Deuteronomistic theology (cf. the authors mentioned by Blum, *Pentateuch*, 270f. n.156); that the reference is in particular to the views of the lay theological tradents of the pre-Pentateuch is a thesis of Blum, *Pentateuch*, 271, 334f. exp.39, which I accept in what follows.

145. Similarly also Num.14.4f.; cf. Magonet, 'Korah Rebellion', 16. There is no reason to change the text (cf. BHS).

146. Cf. Num.11.29 and Deut.7.6; 14.2.

147. Cf. the deliberate parallel between Num.17.11 and 16.6f., 17, 18.

148. For the view that the tradition of primal times was only integrated into the Pentateuch at the stage of the priestly composition cf. Blum, *Komposition*, 428ff.; id., *Pentateuch*, 107f.

149. See above, 471f.

150. Cf. simply the emergence of the structure of divine command and human execution (Gen.6.-9*; Ex.14*; cf. Gen.1, etc.) and the fact that according to K^P –

in contrast to K^D in Ex.4.1ff., 31 – Yahweh goes on with the exodus from Egypt although the people does not believe (Ex.6.9,12). But it is probably going too far to speak, as Lohfink, 'Priesterschrift', 202ff., does, of a remythicizing of history.

151. See above, 136f.

152. See above, 133f.

153. Crüsemann, 'Urgeschichte', has demonstrated that the 'Yahwistic creation stories' are an independent unit. For these analogies cf. Zenger, *Gottes Bogen*, 173f.; for Enuma Elish cf. especially Beyerlin, *RT*, 106ff.

154. The battle of Marduk against Tiamat in I.107-IV.134 is followed in IV.135-V.66 by the creation of the world; both issue in the distribution of booty and homage to Marduk as king (V, 67-88). After this Marduk takes up his rule, the most important features of which are the planning (V, 117-48) and building (VI, 45-81) of Esangila (the creation of human beings is connected with this, VI, 37).

155. Cf. the reconstruction of the Baal cycle in Kinet, *Ugarit*, 68-82: unfortunately it is impossible to reconstruct the whole chain of action precisely, see Beyerlin, *RT*, 210ff.

156. Cf. especially the shaping of the conclusion of the creation (Gen.1.31; 2.2,3) and of the building of the temple (Ex.39.32-43), which are parallel even down to formulae. The seven-day scheme of the creation of the world (Gen.1.1-2.3) is matched by Moses' seven days of waiting on the mountain (Ex.24.16-18) and the seven divine discourses in which God commands the building of the temple (25.1; 30.11,17,22; 31.1,12), in which again the hallowing of the seventh day (Gen.2.2f.) finds a parallelism in the sabbath commandment of Ex.31.12-17. Further echoes are mentioned by Zenger, *Gottes Bogen*, 170-5, and *Blum, Pentateuch*, 306f.

157. Here mention need only be made of the striking parallels between the chronological details in the flood narrative and those in the Sinai pericope: according to Gen.8.13 the waters of chaos had dried up on New Year's Day, and according to Ex.40.17 it was again a New Year's Day on which the sanctuary was built, cf. Weimar, 'Struktur', 111ff.

158. So the increase (and settlement) of Israel cannot be understood directly as 'fulfilment' of the command at creation, as Lohfink, 'Priesterschrift', 218f., proposes; cf. the justified objections by Blum, *Pentateuch,*, 295f. n.28.

159. Ex.1.7 or Josh.18.1 are at most meant as a partial realization of Gen.1.28 (pace Lohfink, 'Priesterschrift', 218f.).

160. The positioning of the sabbath commandment Ex.31.12-17 between the orders for building the temple and their execution puts the latter in the rhythm of work set by creation.

161. For what follows see again Blum, *Pentateuch*, 287ff., who has defined 'the longing of the creator for community or "nearness to God" as a leading theme of the priestly composition'.

162. In the view of the priest theologians, even Abraham no longer walked 'with' God but only 'before' God (*hithallek lipnē*, Gen.17.1). And they stressed that God by no means conversed directly with the patriarchs, as one might suppose from the earlier tradition, but appeared to them in an extraordinary way in theophanies (Gen.17.1; 35.9) and then went away again (17.22; 35.13).

163. In speaking in this connection of the 'completion' of creation, Zenger,

'Gottes Bogen', 172, overplays somewhat the lasting disruption and danger presupposed in the atoning cult.

164. As attested by the many quotations from the promises in the book of Ezekiel (cf. Ezek.34.25ff.; 36.9ff.), the priest theologians at this point also want to integrate the prophecy of salvation into their theology of the sanctuary. In particular in view of Gen.7 and Lev.11 one cannot say that their work as a whole should be understood along the lines of an eschatology projected backwards, as Lohfink, 'Priesterschrift', 219, 224 thinks.

165. Thus at least the beginnings of an aspect which had accrued to Yahweh religion in the exilic period (see above on the prophecy of Deutero-Isaiah, 419ff.) are taken up into the official foundation document.

166. See above, 445ff.

5.4 The social and religious split in the community

1. Isaiah 58 has grown successively: vv.1-4,5-9a,9b-12,13f.; the earliest part, vv.1-4, already presupposes the rebuilding of the temple; for details see Albertz, ' "Antrittspredigt" Jesu', 192-6.

2. Read with LXX, Σ, Θ, 'obṭ'kem, 'your pledges'; MT, 'your workers' is less specific.

3. Cf. also Mal.3.5 for the time around 480; this usual dating has once again been confirmed on a linguistic basis by Hill, 'Dating', 86. The cultic transgressions which Malachi attacks (blemishes in the sacrificial animals [Mal.1.6ff.; 3.3]and in the delivery of the tithes [3.8ff.]) indicate a rough business climate.

4. See above, 481.

5. Thus also Schottroff, 'Arbeit', 104.

6. ḥōrīm and sᵉgānīm, cf. 2.16; 4.8,13; 5.17; 6.17; 7.5; 12.40; 13.11,17.

7. Read 'ōrᵉbīm with BHS.

8. Schottroff, 'Arbeit', 109ff.; Kreissig, Sozial-ökonomische Situation, 78f.; and Gunneweg, Nehemia, 86, envisage different groups, Kippenberg, Klassenbildung, 55f., thinks in terms of three stages of social decline (1. mortgaging the workforce; 2. mortgaging the means of production; 3. selling children into slavery abroad).

9. If this interpretation of v.5 by Kippenberg, Klassenbildung, 57f., is correct; Joel 4.6 is evidence for a rather later time that Jews were sold to Greeks as slaves through Phoenician middlemen.

10. Cf. Herodotus, Histories III, 89. Kippenberg, Klassenbildung, 49ff., emphasizes very strongly that the transition to coinage was the decisive difference from former kinds of tribute; however, the archaeological evidence points more to a slow establishment of coinage in Palestine in the Persian period (cf. H.Weippert, Palästina, 696), and passages like Neh.5.15 seem rather to attest that the silver was still counted traditionally by weight. The decisive innovation in Persian taxation policy was the transformation of tributes in kind into a fixed amount of money. According to Herodotus, for the fifth district ('Abar-Nahara), in which Judah lay, this amounted to 350 talents of silver.

11. Apart from the governor's tax, which in the time of Nehemiah amounted to forty silver shekels a day, and the various cultic offerings, see above, 460ff.

12. The Hebrew text as handed down seems to be thinking of a reduction to one

per cent, but instead of *ūmᵉ'at* we should probably read *umašša't*, cf. Schottroff, 'Arbeit', 147f. Here legally he moved in the tradition of extraordinary royal remissions of debt (*dᵉrōr*), cf. Jer.34.8ff., which indeed was in line with his function as Persian governor; an attempt was made to establish the remission of debts every seven years (*shemitta* or 'sabbath year', Lev.25.2-7) as laid down in Deut.15.1ff. only when Nehemiah was succeeded by self-administration in Judah (Neh.10.32).

13. Unfortunately it is impossible to give an exact date to the texts mentioned in what follows (Job, some psalms and late prophetic passages). But in any case it should be pointed out that Beyerlin (*Der 52.Psalm*, 138) would date Ps.52 and Irsigler (*Ps.73*, 351) Ps.73 in this particular period.

14. Isaiah 58.1-4 in the years after 515; Malachi around 480, see n.3 above.

15. The book of Job is usually put in the wide span between the fifth and the third centuries. That it belongs late in the Persian period and reflects the social crisis on which Neh.5 puts a spotlight is a theory which I advanced in 1981 (Albertz, 'Hiobbuch', 366ff.).

16. Cf. Job 24.3f.,9; 29.12f.; 31.16f.,19,21.

17. Cf. Albertz, 'Hiobbuch', 364 and already Schwantes, *Arme*, 269, 275.

18. Cf. Job 4.11; 29.13; 31.19; cf. Prov.31.6 and the expression *rᵉṣūṣīm*, 'broken', Isa.58.6 for those enslaved for debt. In describing the poor man (*'ebyōn*) as one whose 'day was hard', Job 30.25 is giving a vivid illustration of the structural violence to which the small farmer was exposed.

19. Of course given the nature of this literature, one must suppose this to be a general theme. However, it is by no means timeless or even 'universally human', as is often assumed, but has grown out of a long-drawn-out social crisis as a result of concrete experiences.

20. Thus also Kippenberg, *Klassenbildung*, 65ff., for whom Neh.5 etc. is evidence of the rise of a class society in Judah which lasts until the Greek and Roman period; similarly also Schottroff, 'Arbeit', 116f. The exegesis of Rudolph, *Esra*, 128ff. is a prime example of how one can even play down the conflict of Neh.5 if one overlooks the background of the other texts; Gunneweg, *Nehemia*, 85ff., is now more accurate.

21. For the thesis that the 'prominent men' (*ḥōrīm*) were partly active in the council of elders and the 'counsellors' (*sᵉgānīm*) were in the service of the Persian governors, see above, 445f.

22. Cf. the way in which Nehemiah describes the members of the Jewish people demonstratively as 'brothers' (Neh.5.1,8) in order to appeal to a sense of solidarity, or the admonition in Isa.58.7 'not to hide yourself from your own flesh'; similar appeals to the lower class can be found in Neh.5.5. For the literary context of Isa.58.6-9a see below, 501.

23. The same question had already led to the break-up of the Deuteronomic coalition after the death of Josiah, see above, 233f.

24. See above, 235.

25. See above, 234.

26. Cf. Westermann, 'Struktur', 285-90; Schwarzwäller, *Feinde*; Keel, *Feinde*, esp. 109ff.; Ruppert, *Gerechte*, 4-16; Ruppert, *Feinde*; Beyerlin, *Der 52. Psalm*, 87ff.; Irsigler, *Psalm 73*, 258-62.

27. Cf. the surveys of the literature in Keel, *Feinde*, 11f.; Rupert, *Gerechte*, 4-

16. It is impossible here to enter into a thorough discussion of the theories presented.

28. Thus above all Keel, *Feinde*, 19ff.; 124ff., and following him e.g. Beyerlin, *Der 52.Psalm*, 87-90. The flaws in Keel's investigation are, first, that he regards the pious-wicked sayings as old and therefore makes this type the starting point of his conceptual history (110ff.), and secondly, that while he recognizes the concrete social significance (lack of solidarity from the upper class) which the term *rāšāʿ* takes on in Jeremiah (114f.), he does not go on to ask why this has been 'introduced' into certain psalms (he mentions Pss.10; 12; 36; 73; 94) (127f.). As for the social reasons, he contents himself with a vague conjecture by Westermann ('Struktur', 290), 130f. I think that his thesis that distinctions must be made between individual strata of 'hostile stereotypes' is basically right. Unfortunately he does not investigate further the interesting question how it could come about that the picture of the enemies of the person lamenting came to be overpainted in some of the psalms by the 'rāšāʿ image'.

29. Cf. above all the occurrences in late prophecy: Mal.3.13-21; Isa.56.9-57.21; 59.5-8, 13-15a, etc.

30. Thus already rightly Ruppert, *Gerechte*, 15; Golka's extensive researches into the proverbs in 'primitive' cultures have indicated that there is virtually no proverb which can be compared with the many wicked-pious proverbs in Israelite proverbial material ('Flecken', 162f.).

31. Cf. Pss.37.16f.; 49.7; 52.9; 73.12; Job 20.15,17-22; 21.9ff.; 22.8; see also Albertz, *Hiobbuch*, 362ff.

32. Cf. Ps.73.4,7; Job 8.16; 15.27.

33. Cf. Pss.37.7; 49.17; Job 21.7; cf. Ps.62.11.

34. Cf. Pss.49.7; 52.9; and further Ps.62.11; Job 31.24f.; Prov.11.28.

35. Cf. Pss.37.12,13,32f.; 94.5f.; Job 20.19; 24.4,9; Isa.29.21; 57.1; 59.6-8; cf. Prov.1.10-13.

36. Cf. Job 22.7-9.

37. Cf. Ps.73.10; Job 21.31ff.

38. Cf. Pss.73.11; 94.7; Job 15.25f.; 21.14f.; Mal.3.14f.

39. Hence the general talk of evil, lying and deception.

40. Thus above all in the book of Job, but also largely in Ps.49; 52; 69; 73, where those who are speaking are not victims of the wicked but merely suffering at the good fortune of the wicked, against Irsigler's conjecture, *Psalm 73*, 370.

41. Thus e.g. Ps.37.12, 14, 16, 32f.; 94.21; Isa.29.19, 21; 57.21.

42. For more detail see Albertz, *Hiobbuch*, 358-62.

43. See above, n.41.

44. This largely applies to the so-called 'wisdom psalms' (Pss.37; 49; 52; 61; 73; 94; 112). The 'theologized wisdom' that they represent will prove to be the theologized piety of the upper class, see below, 512f.

45. For the latter see below, 503ff.; in addition there also seems to have been a theological dispute between the lower class and the pious upper class, see below, 506f.

46. The quotations which are put on the lips of the wicked (e.g. Ps.73.11; 94.7; Job.21.14f.) are made up; they are meant to show up the misconduct of the opponent.

47. Cf. above nn.31, 33, 37.

48. Westermann, 'Weisheit', 160f. has argued against Skladny and others that for the most part the wicked-pious language belongs to the late stage of Proverbs; his thesis was confirmed by the wide-ranging investigation into cultural history by Golka, 'Flecken', 162f.: this group of proverbs has no parallel among the many thousand proverbs of 'primitive' cultures. Scott, 'Wise', 160f., now arrives at a similar view to that of Westermann. This totally undermines the 'transactional' theory of Keller ('Vergeltungsglauben', 225ff.) which sought to prove the great antiquity of the wicked-pious proverbs. The accumulation of them at the beginning of the collections of proverbs (Prov.10-15) can simply be explained from the fact that they did not get anywhere with this material in teaching. By contrast, the 'Hezekian collection' standing at the end (Prov.25-29) represents an older stage of the tradition (late monarchy) in which *rāšāʿ* is a concrete designation of the guilty person (Prov.28.1), the unjust judge (Prov.29.7, 27), unjust official or king (Prov.25.5; 28.12, 15, 28; 29.2, 12). Here only Prov.28.3; 29.16 are on the way towards being the type of the heedless rich. That the bulk of the wicked-pious proverbs are to be put in the late, post-exilic stage of the tradition is also suggested by the fact that this antithesis has become established in a series of proverbs with older contrasts (the diligent – the lazy; the wise – the fool), Prov.13.25; 10.21,31.

49. Prov.10.11,16,32; 11.18f.; 12.5,6; 13.5; 15.9,26,29; cf. Prov.1.16-19.

50. Prov.10.3,6,30; 11.10,28; 13.22,25; 15.6,8; cf. the wisdom admonitions in Prov.1-9, which were similarly used in the education of children: Prov.1.16-19; 2.21f.; 3.25, 31-35; 4.14-19; 5.22f.; and Lang, *Lehrrede*, esp.81f. The proximity to the piety and ethos of the Book of Job (cf. simply the admonition to give alms in 3.27ff.) suggests that the admonitions, too, only took on their present form in the post-exilic period; Lang, *Lehrrede*, 46ff., differs.

51. Cf. Keel, *Feinde*, 113; Westermann, 'Weisheit', 158, 160, emphasizes that these proverbs no longer draw on experience but develop a pre-existing thematic statement.

52. In ' "Antrittspredigt" Jesu', 192-5, I attempted to demonstrate that Isa.58.5-9a is a late interpretation of vv.1-4, which come from the circles of the pious upper class. Verses 9b-12 further tie this individual admonition and promise into the horizon of the community as a whole.

53. Isa.58.8a refers to Isa.60.1; 8b to Isa.52.12; so the aim is to reinterpret the unfulfilled great eschatological promise of the Deutero-Isaiah group and its successors in individual terms, in order to utilize it to support the social appeal to the rich and at the same time to neutralize it politically.

54. The texts mentioned are usually included in the so-called 'wisdom psalms' (for the problem of this classification and the demarcation of the text see Murphey, 'Consideration', 159ff.). However, in recent times scholars have seen increasingly clearly that they may in no means be attributed to 'wisdom schools' remote from the cult (cf. generally, Perdue, *Wisdom*, 261ff., and specifically Beyerlin, *Der 52. Psalm*, 101f.; Irsigler, *Psalm 73*, 368ff., and already Mowinckel, 'Psalms and Wisdom', 210ff.; Murphey, 'Considerations', 161). That is indicated not only by explicit allusions to the temple (Ps.52.10; 73.17) but also by the situation of public utterance presupposed in the liturgical community (Ps.62.9; 52.3ff.,8; 73.1 and therefore probably also by Ps.37.1; 49.2-5). The much-discussed question of the influence of wisdom is solved relatively simply when it is recognized that 'pious wisdom' was none other than the special personal piety of the educated pious upper

class, to which laity as well as priests and Levites belonged, very much in line with the reform coalition (see below, 517ff.).

55. Beyerlin, *Der 52.Psalm*, 102, thinks in terms of a stylized disputation in the forecourts of the temple.

56. By his confession to the contrary in Job 31.24f., Job thus wants to assert that he does not belong among the wicked.

57. While v.8 acknowledges that even the wicked in fact are part of Israel, in vv.5,14f. the concept of the people of God is deliberately limited to the righteous. These still include the poor victims of the wicked (vv.5,21) and all those 'who are upright in heart' (vv.14f.), i.e. the pious part of the upper class.

58. For details see Albertz, 'Hiobbuch', 357f.; a similar social crisis can probably be inferred as the background to the so-called 'Babylonian Theodicy', ibid., 351ff.

59. That the book of Job is addressed to educated circles is already evident from its markedly metaphorical language, cf. Albertz, 'Hiobbuch', 368f.

60. See below, 513ff.

61. Cf. the individualizing reinterpretation of the nationalistic eschatological promise in Isa.58.8 and above, n.53.

62. See above, 477ff.

63. This has been brought out in particular by Crüsemann, 'Hiob', 391f.; but in concluding from this that the aristocracy which depicts itself in this book had 'detached itself from the interests and the faith of the rest of the people' (392) and accusing it of having developed an 'ethic bypassing the Torah' (id., 'Israel in der Perserzeit', 221), he is describing more those opponents who are not in solidarity with it than the group itself. In my view the canonization of the Torah was supported by the same circles as those from which the poets who wrote Job emerged, namely the upper class who bore the burden of the whole situation; however, in the Pentateuch they were formulating the foundations for an official Yahweh religion which applied to everyone, while in the texts of theologized wisdom they were expressing their own special personal piety.

64. The elliptical phrase *nᵉśūʾpānīm*, 'the one whose face is raised', is focussed on the favour with the (Persian) rulers (II Kings 5.1; Isa.3.3; 9.14) which the wicked, the 'men of the elbow', enjoy.

65. Cf. the model of the post-exilic historical development of religion created by Plöger, Steck and Crüsemann, and reported above, 437ff.

66. The dating of Malachi in the period around 480 is relatively certain, cf. Hill, 'Dating', 86; it is difficult to date Isa.29.17-24, which scholars put anywhere between the fifth and the second centuries; it is certain that the text presupposes Deutero-Isaiah (cf. Isa.43.8; 42.18 on v.18) and probably also already Isa.32.15 (cf.v.17); so a dating in the late Persian period (first half of the fourth century) is quite possible (so also Barth, 'Assurredaktion' [3.9], 292f.). Isa.56.9-57.12 is certainly later than Isa.60-62 (cf. only the reference of 57.14 to 62.10), but I see no reason to follow Steck, *Heimkehr*, 80, in dating it in the early-Hellenistic period. The fronts, which are by no means rigid, point rather to an earlier phase of the crisis (second half of the fifth century). Koenen, *Ethik*, 58, 222f., assigns the composition, which he even extends to Isa.56.2-57.21, to a redactor in the second half of the fifth century. However, it remains to be seen whether his thesis of a single-stage redaction can be substantiated over the whole book.

67. Steck, 'Beobachtungen', 234, has recently argued that Isa.56.9-57.21 is to be regarded as a literary unity.

68. However, in a unique prophetic cipher which consists of allusions to earlier prophetic texts (cf. the reference of 56.9 back to 55.3 and the quotations of pre-exilic accusations in 57.3,5,6-11 or of early post-exilic prophecy of salvation in 57.15-19). This scribal form of prophecy burdens any attempt at exegesis in terms of a particular period with additional uncertainties.

69. Cf.Jer.2.19ff.; 3.1ff.; Ezek.16; 23.

70. Cf. the process of canonization (above, 467), which extends to the period of social crisis.

71. The promise that the righteous will possess the land runs through a large number of texts of the period, cf. Pss.37.9,11,22,27,29,34; Prov.2.21; Pss.25.13; 69.36f. It can be seen only against the background of the creeping eviction of the small farmers by the great landowners (cf. Job.22.8; Prov.10.30).

72. Thus probably rightly Steck, 'Beobachtungen', 233.

73. Certainly v.22 begins anew with a messenger formula, but the subsequent divine speech in vv.22-24 is simply an extension of the previous description of salvation (vv.17-21); moreover, as v.24 takes the span back to v.18, the text can be regarded as a unit.

74. Cf. Isa.32.15 and the metaphor of the forest in the book of Isaiah (Isa.2.13f.; 10.33f.), which expresses the hybris of political power that is laid low by God.

75. Cf. the use of the term *'ārîṣ*, 'tyrant, man of violence', which also denotes external enemies (Isa.13.11; 25.3-5). Nevertheless, as v.21 indicates, the reference is clearly to political enemies at home, as also in Isa.29.5: in particular *'ārîṣ* denotes the wicked upper class in Ps.37.35; Job 6.23; 15.20; 27.13; the parallel term *leṣ*, 'good for nothing, mocker', denotes the wicked in Ps.1.1; Prov.3.34; 9.7.

76. For the religious connotation of *'ānāw*, 'poor', see below, 518f.; already in the late monarchy Zephaniah could see the simple population of the land rather than the city aristocracy as those who were handing down true faith in Yahweh, see above, 195, and Zeph.2.1-3.

77. Cf. Isa.42.18; 43.8, which describe the Israelites who did not want to perceive Yahweh's promise.

78. See above, 502f.

79. There we have mention of 'your brothers who hate you and want to cast you out' for God's sake. In the present context, the wicked are meant (cf. v.6), but 'your brothers' also indicates a degree of solidarity. Unfortunately it is uncertain how Isa.66.5 is to be dated; if it belongs in the time of social crisis it could be evidence that the demarcation of the lower-class groups orientated on prophecy also emanated from the official community.

80. See above, 477, 492.

81. See above, 478ff.

82. 'Jacob' or 'house of Jacob' in v.22 probably already means the whole community united with the poor through the conversion of the upper class. The idea of the hallowing of God's name which is given a new stamp here is that God will only be truly honoured when he visibly dissociates himself from being compromised by unjust social and economic structures. Therefore true worship of God must aim at the demolition of such structures. This insight of the prophetic

theologies of the lowest stratum of the people was taken up by Jesus in the first petition of the Our Father (Matt.6.9).

83. Cf.e.g. TestJob IXf. from the time between the first century BCE and the second century CE, where Job practises a well-organized diaconia, and Bolkestein, *Wohltätigkeit*, 213f., 418ff. In ' "Antrittspredigt" Jesu' I have described how Luke attempts to rescue this Jewish heritage for his Hellenistic-Christian community.

84. Thus above all in the later apocalyptic tradition, cf. e.g. the messianic interpretation of the 'year of grace' (Isa.61.1f.) in 11QMelch, see Albertz, ' "Antrittspredigt" Jesu', 189f.

5.5 The convergence of the religious strata and the split in personal piety

1. Cf. Gunkel and Begrich, *Einleitung*, 397-404; Becker, *Psalmen*; Albertz, *Frömmigkeit*.

2. Pss.3.9; 25.22; 28.8f.; 51.20; 53.6 = 124.7; it is impossible to determine whether the petitions for the king in Ps.61.7f.; 63.12 still belong in the pre-exilic period or have to be referred to the Hasmonaean kings.

3. Pss.22.5-6; 102.13-23; 143.5; Ps.77 is probably already exilic.

4. Pss.22.23-32; 69.31, 33-36.

5. Pss.62.2f., 6-8; 94.17, 22; 130.7f.; 131; cf. 33.20-22; 90.1f.; Lam.3.22-33; Isa.63.15; 64.7 are already exilic.

6. Cf. Pss.7.7-10; 9; 54.5; 56.8; 59.6,9,12,14.

7. Pss.30.5f.; 66; 107.

8. Ps.69.7 and see n.2 above.

9. Or pious groups in it, cf. Ps.22.23ff.; 69.7, 33; 107.42; 140.14; 142.8 and below, 520f.

10. Cf. Becker, *Psalmen*, 22ff. etc.

11. Clearly where the enemies of the suppliant are related to the enemies of Israel, see n.6 above.

12. See above, 399ff.

13. Pss. 90; 123; 125; 126.

14. Ps.8; 103: 107; 124; 145; 146.

15. There is a generalized reference to Israelite history only in Ps.103.7.

16. Cf. also the sometimes word-for-word allusions to the book of Job in vv.40, 41f. (Job 12.21a, 24b; 5.11, 16b); the didactic tendency which is evident in v.43 has been brought out particularly by Beyerlin, *Werden*, 11, 66f., etc.; it is quite probable that the poet of this community psalm comes from the same pious upper-class circles as the poet of Job. Even according to Beyerlin's investigation a dating at the end of the fifth century is quite possible (83ff.).

17. Verse 9 refers to Isa.57.16 and thus presupposes the 'eschatological' continuation of the Deutero-Isaiah prophecy; thus the psalm equally belongs well on into the early post-exilic period. The reference to the liturgical confessional formula in v.8 (Ex.34.6 etc.) shows how much the poet is concerned to put personal piety in line with the offical cultic traditions of Israel.

18. It is generally recognized that Ps.90 differs markedly from a traditional lament of the people with its reflective introduction (vv.1-12) which generalizes the confession of confidence and the lament over transitoriness from the lament of

the individual, see Kraus, *Psalms 60-150*, 796f.; there are no external criteria for dating.

19. Cf. Pss.90.8; 103.3,10; 107.11,17 (sin); Pss.90.7,9,11; 103.9 (anger); only rarely is there mention of God's anger in the thirty-nine individual laments (Ps.88.8,17; Ps.6.2 = 38.2; 38.4; 102.11); and there are only five texts (Pss.25; 38; 51; 130; 32) in which the theme of sin is central, see Albertz, *Frömmigkeit*, 39, 70f.

20. Cf. Pss.125.1,5; 145.19f.; 146.9.

21. Cf. Pss.25.7; 32.2; 51.5-7; 130.3; 143.2.

22. Cf. Pss.32.2-6; 51.9-11; 86.5; 130.4; a formation with the verb *sālaḥ*, 'forgive', first emerges in the personal names at Elephantine.

23. Cf. Pss.62.9ff.; 118.8f.; 115.9-11; 146.3; in Ps.125.1 the phrase 'who trust in Yahweh' is a designation for the pious.

24. For the basis of this theory see Albertz, *Frömmigkeit*, 44-8.

25. Cf. Pss.3.7f.; 11.2; 17.9; 140.5f. etc., and e.g. the desires for retribution on the wicked, Pss.28.4f.; 58.11; 139.19-22.

26. Thus e.g. von Rad, *Old Testament Theology* I, 441ff.

27. Thus e.g. the young von Rad, see above; McKane, *Proverbs*, 11; Wittenberg, 'Context', 8ff.; Albertz, 'Sage'; the old von Rad, *Wisdom*, blurs these traditio-historical distinctions again.

28. Gordis, 'Background', 101ff. id., *Poets*, 169; Pleins, 'Poverty', 62ff,; for the book of Job see especially Albertz, 'Hintergrund' (5.4), 366f.

29. Thus very emphatically Crüsemann, 'Israel' (5.0), 220, see above, 438f.

30. Cf. the difficulties which e.g. Preuss (171) gets into: on the one hand he works out very sharply a 'class-specific YHWH faith' in wisdom the deviation of which from the salvation-historical traditions of Israel he even interprets as a form of poly-Yahwism or syncretism (60), but on the other hand he has to concede wisdom influences in all the great lines of tradition, prophecy, law and the psalms (154ff.). Unless we want to accept that all the 'educated' who concerned themselves over centuries (!) with prophetic, legal and psalm traditions were schizophrenic, Preuss's assumption that the 'wise men' sought to converge with the rest of Yahweh religion only at the time of Jesus Sirach (137) is quite absurd. What Sirach attests is the fusion of a wisdom which had hitherto moved on the level of personal piety with official Yahweh religion.

31. See above, 95ff.

32. E.g. Prov.14.35; 16.14; 23.1; 29.6; the limited extent of the proverbs concerned with the king or conduct at court make it impossible to understand Proverbs as a special class ethic of officials; in contrast, say, to wisdom in Egypt, Israelite wisdom always stayed very close to the people.

33. E.g. Prov.10.22; 16.3,9,33; 9.21; 20.24; 21.31, etc.

34. Reference was made to it only above, 162f., in connection with the legitimation of well-to-do groups against which the social accusation of the prophets was directed.

35. Cf. Prov.18.11 with 10.15; 22.2 with 29.13; also 11.28; 15.16; 16.8; 19.1, 22; 28.6.

36. Cf. Prov.14.21,31; 19.17; 21.13; 22.2,9,22f.; 28.8, 27. Prov.22.22f., an admonition, is particularly interesting: on the one hand it is derived from Egyptian wisdom (cf. Amenemope IV.4-7); on the other it has a similar theological motivation

to Ex.22.20-23.9. That could indicate that in view of the social crisis of the eighth century the reform group behind the Book of the Covenant (see above, 104f.) also had recourse to Egyptian wisdom because here there were already existing maxims of conduct for a society with marked social distinctions. Pleins probably tends to underestimate the change taking place here in the wisdom attitude to riches (69f.). However, I can agree with his verdict that the book of Job goes a whole step further in social commitment than the 'caritative Proverbs' (70, differing from Malchow, 'Justice', 122).

37. E.g. Prov.18.23; 22.7,16,26f.

38. For more detail see Albertz, 'Sage'. However, with the theologizing a speculative reshaping of wisdom also took place (Prov.3.13-20; 8; Job 28) which is to be regarded as an early form of philosophy and has nothing to do with personal piety. The fact that this goes back to an official Yahweh tradition, the creation of the world, does not put in question the general sociological setting of theologized wisdom.

39. Delete the copula with BHS.

40. Cf. the religious conceptuality of the confession of confidence: *mibṭaḥ*, *kesel*, 'trust', Job 8.14; 31.24; 4.6; *tiqwā*, 'hope', Job 4.6; 8.13; 11.18,20; *mānōs*, 'refuge', Job 11.20 with corresponding psalm texts, e.g. Pss.71.6; 59.17. There is already similar borrowing from the language of private prayer in Proverbs: 2.7; 14.26; 22.19; 23.17; 30.5.

41. For this sociological setting for the book of Job cf. Albertz, 'Hintergrund' (5.4).

42. The wisdom instruction in the book of Job itself already has a pastoral function (Job 4.3-5; 13.4; 16.2; 26.2f.; 29.24; 30.25).

43. The original form can probably no longer be discovered with any certainty; possibly the dialogue has suppressed a narrative part in which the friends appeared as tempters (see Müller, *Hiob*, 20ff.); the concluding part shows signs of revision. That the present Job narrative is post-exilic, although it uses old material (cf. the still-nomadic Chaldaeans in Job 1.17), is already indicated by the person of 'Satan' in the heavenly court (1.6ff.), who is attested for the first time in Zech.3.1f.

44. The Hebrew word for shameful, *tiplā*, which Job refrains from using, echoes the word for 'prayer', *tᵉpillā* (Job 1.22).

45. However, this praise presupposes the experience of happiness and prosperity in former life, which is usually overlooked in pious Christian adaptation of this verse.

46. Job 4.7-11; 5.3-5, 12-14; 8.12-15; 15.20-35; 18.5-21; 20.4-29.

47. Job 5.17; 22.22; cf. Prov.3.11f. This interpretation becomes a regular theme in the Elihu speeches: in Job 33.16-20; 36.7-12, 15; 36.22 God is regularly termed *mōrē*, 'teacher'.

48. Job 5.17f.; 22.21.

49. Cf. the conditional promises in Job 5.19-26; 8.6bf.,21f.; 11.15-19; 22.21,26-28.

50. Cf. in detail Job 35.9-16; here Elihu can even compare the cries of the crowd at the violence of the oppressors (v.9) with the foolish behaviour of animals. Against such an arrogant lament he sets the positive possibility of turning in trust to the creator, who himself makes possible songs of praise in distress (v.10).

51. Job 5.17f.; 22.21f.; 35.10.

52. Job 4.17-21; 15.14-16; 25.2-6.

53. In Job 4.12-16 the age-old insight which already occurs in the 'Sumerian Job' (c. 2000 BCE, *ANET*³ 590, lines 101f.) is therefore also introduced with extra emphasis as a divine revelation. The recourse to such religious sources of truth (cf. 33.14-18; 36.7-12) points to the loss of plausibility of experience as a source of wisdom; this probably spoke more for the successful upper class who showed no solidarity.

54. A similarly transcendent statement of trust is made in Ps.73.26-28; the psalm probably comes from the same milieu as the Job poem (see above, 501ff.).

55. See above, 195.

56. Lohfink, 'Von der "Anawim Partei" zur "Kirche der Armen"'.

57. Gerstenberger, 'Psalm 12', 95f.

58. Stolz, *Psalmen*, 29.

59. Ps.86.1; cf. the parallel confession of confidence in Ps.40.18 = 7.6 and with the plural Pss.9.10f.; 12.2,26; 22.27; 40.17 = 70.5; 69.33,37.

60. Thus emphatically van der Ploeg, 'Pauvres', 267; more cautiously Kraus, *Psalms 1-59*, ad loc.; Botterweck, *"ebyōn"*, 38ff. Gerstenberger already wants to see these statements as being anchored in petitionary ritual ('Bittende Mensch', 140; *'ānāh*, 263) and to distinguish them clearly from the plural statements. He understands the former as a 'general signal for personal "misery"' which expresses 'a claim' to the fulfilment of the petition (263); behind the latter he sees groups of the persecuted and exploited (264f.). However, the question is whether this sharp differentiation makes sense. – The attempts to differentiate semantically between *'ānī* and *'ānāw* in a social and a religious sense (cf. Rahlfs, *'ānī*, 73ff., etc.) have largely been abandoned, cf. Gerstenberger, *"ānāh"*, 259; *KBL*³, 809.

61. Cf. Birkeland, *"ānī"*, 93f.; but he also includes the designations in the third person and occurrences in the plural in his verdict; this is questionable, cf. already the retort by Munch, 'Bemerkungen', 21ff.

62. Thus already Munch, 'Bemerkungen', 21ff., and again Michel, 'Armut', 75; Gerstenberger, 'Psalm 12', 92; id., *"ānāh"*, 260ff.

63. Certainly the statement in v.27, 'the poor may come and be satisfied', could refer to an occasional Toda community; but because the suppliant expressly proclaims his praise in a 'great community' (vv.23, 26), which in v.24 he calls seed of Jacob or Israel, the demarcation remains uncertain. So despite the worthwhile suggestion by Stolz, *Psalmen*, that Ps.22 should be assigned to the group of the *'anāwīm*, I am leaving it on one side.

64. They occur in 42 of the 150 psalms.

65. van der Ploeg, 'Pauvres'.

66. Lamentation, Pss.10; 25; 35; 40.14ff. = 70; 69; 109; 140; cf. 102; 88; thanksgiving, Pss.9; 34; cf. Ps.22.23ff.

67. Ps.35.10; 69.34; Jer.20.13; cf. Ps.22.25.

68. Ps.12; 14; 82; certainly the term for poor does not occur in Ps.75, but when the *ṣaddīq* (v.11) is depicted as the victim of the wicked man the same group is meant, cf. Ps.69.29; 140.14.

69. The wisdom psalms Pss.37.11,14; 112.9 probably refer to the same group of people, but are probably formulated from the perspective of the upper class, see above, 501ff.; the royal psalm 72.4,12,13 can be left out of account.

70. For the eschatological-prophetic orientation of these groups see above, 503ff.

71. Jeremias has taught us to understand these texts as cult-prophetic liturgies from the social conflict of the late post-exilic period, parallel to the prophecy of Habakkuk (*Kultprophetie*, 110ff.); but he himself already drew attention to some indications of late language (111 n.1). In my view this post-exilic dating is supported by the customary talk of the wicked (12.9; 75.5,9,11; 82.2) and the circumstance that the liturgical setting of the oracle points more to those concerned worshipping in small groups than to the whole community (cf.12.8; 75.10f.; so also Gerstenberger, 'Psalm 12', 94). Psalm 82 seems to presuppose the judgment speeches of the book of Deutero-Isaiah, see Jüngling, *Tod*, 79f.

72. For the personal theology of the pious upper class see above 511ff.

73. Pss.10.12; 69.30; 70.6; 19.22; cf. 86.1.

74. Pss.9.13,19; 10.17f.; 35.9f.; 69.33f.; Jer.20.13; cf. the certainty of being heard in Ps.140.13.

75. Pss.9.6,18; 35.25f.; 69.23-29; 70.3-5; 109.6-16,17-20; 140.9-12; 14.5f.; 75.9,11.

76. Thus Gerstenberger, 'Psalm 12', 88f., who for the first time has worked out the liturgical context of the 'prophetic' oracle (Ps.12.6; cf. Isa.33.10) in sociological terms.

77. See above, 504; there I had to attribute the text Isa.56.9-57.21 to groups of the lower class with an eschatological orientation.

78. Read first person plural suffixes in v.8 with some MSS and LXX; thus also Gunkel, *Psalmen*, 45.

79. Read *tōbīšū* with Jeremias, *Kultprophetie*, 115: 'By the blow of the poor you "will be" put to shame'; the reference to the poor has fallen out from Ps.53.

80. In Ps.14.1-4 a lament over the godless comes first; Ps.75.2 begins with a plural invitation by the community to give praise and ends with a generalized vow of praise in the singular (vv.10f.). Ps.82.8 follows a petition for God's judgment.

81. Gerstenberger, too, thinks of 'other places of worship' than the temple, 'possibly also early synagogues in the interior of the land, in which liturgical actions would be performed and prayer said and promises made for the poor' ('Psalm 12', 96). Stolz thinks, in the post-exilic period, in terms of the assurance and representation of distant salvation in 'small religious communities'. 'One could describe their worship, in which assurance and instruction are basic processes, as a "school of worship" of a kind which had its place not only in Palestine but also in the Diaspora' (*Psalmen*, 29).

82. Pss.9.18; 10.15; 35.4-8,25f.; 69.23-29; 70.3f.; 109.6-20,28f.; 140.9-12.

83. Cf. especially the curse in Ps.109.6-16; it is hardly possible to follow a conjecture by Schmidt and understand it as a quotation from the adversary (thus also Kraus, *Psalms 60-150*, 340), since the 'wretched and poor' in v.16 who is attacked is identical with the suppliant (v.22); possibly the desperate rage of the oppressed poor is also expressed in the drastic desire for vengeance in Ps.58, even if the term does not occur.

84. Pss.9.5, 8f.,17,20; 75.3,8; 82.8.

85. In Pss.9.6, 16f.,18,20; 10.15f., the people and the wicked are put in parallel, although, as 10.3-15 shows, in the case of the latter we clearly have an opponent within politics. The acrostic prevents any literary-critical division.

86. See above, 504f.

87. For the notion cf. also Ex.32.32f.; Isa.4.3; Ps.139.16; it is taken up in the apocalyptic conception of an individual resurrection to judgment in Dan.12.1f.

88. In Ps.9.8-11 the expressions of trust in the confession of confidence are made consequences of the future divine judgment.

89. Cf. Pss.9.10f.; 12.2,6; 69.33, 37; 70.6; and 22.27; 86.1.

90. Thus rightly van der Ploeg, 'Pauvres', 270, against Causse, *Pauvres*, 104ff.

91. Cf. the striking negative formulations of divine concern: he has not forgotten (Ps.9.13,19); he has not despised (Ps.69.34; cf. 22.25), which have an undertone of challenge.

92. Pss.69.30; 70.6; 109.22; cf. 25.16; 86.1.

93. Ps.12.2; cf. Ps.86.2.

94. Pss.14.5; 69.29; 75.11; 140.14.

95. Ps.12.2, and cf. the similar circumlocutions Pss.9.11; 22.27; 69.7,33,37; 70.5.

96. Cf. Pss.74.19, 21; 147.6; 149.4 and the rest of the broad distribution in the Psalter.

97. For example the Qumran sect understood itself as the 'community of the poor' (4QpPs.37.8f.) in its fight against 'godless' Jerusalem, cf. 1QH 2.32, 34; 3.25; 5.13-15 etc.; cf. Maier, *Texte* II, 83-7.

5.6 The Samaritans: a political and cultic split

1. Cf. e.g. Talmon, 'Jüdische Sektenbildung' (5.1), 255f.; in addition to the Samaritans he cites only the Qumran community as an example.

2. The following passages will be discussed: II Kings 17.24-41; Ezra 4.1-5.9f.; Neh.2.10-20; 3.33; 4.1ff.; 6.1ff;. 13.28; II Chron.11.14f.; 13.4-12; 30.11,18; 34.6,9; 35.18; Zech 11.14; however, the reference becomes clear only in the apocryphal literature of the second and first centuries BCE: II Macc.5.23; 6.2; Sirach 50.15f.; Judith 5.16; Jub.30.5ff.; TestLev.5-7.

3. Cf. e.g. Talmon, 'Überlieferungen', 138ff.; Würthwein, *Könige* II, 400ff.; Gunneweg, *Esra*, 78ff., is more cautious.

4. Alt, 'Rolle Samarias', 337; 'Grenze', 358ff.

5. Cross, 'Aspects', 208; Purvis, *Samaritan Pentaeuch*, 118; Kippenberg, *Garizim*, 143; Dexinger, 'Limits', 107; Mor, 'History', 18.

6. Coggins, *Samaritans*, 114f.; Pummer, 'Polemic', 241f.; Egger, *Josephus*, 106, 310.

7. Thus e.g. Talmon, 'Überlieferungen', 150.

8. They called themselves *šamᵉrīn*, 'preservers, guardians' instead of *šōmᵉrōnīm*, 'Samarians, Samaritans' denoting aliens,which developed from II Kings 17.29 (wrongly) (LXX = *Samareitai*).

9. In the time of Antiochus IV there seem to have been Hellenistic groups among the Samaritans (cf. Josephus, *Antt.*XII, 257-64). But if the 'Sidonians' are not foreign colonists (cf. Egger, *Josephus*, 267ff.), the Hellenistic influence was no stronger than in Jerusalem.

10. Cf. Rowley, 'Samaritan Schism', 208f.; Cross, 'Aspects', 205f. Würthwein , *Könige* II, 402, also notes the discrepancy but without drawing the consequences.

11. Thus Josephus, *Antt.* IX, 288-91 and then the rabbis, cf. Talmon, 'Überlieferungen', 134f.

12. Thus rightly Dexinger, 'Limits', 91.

13. Thus still Coggins, *Samaritans*, 15.

14. Thus rightly Dexinger, 'Limits', 91, with reference to Rashi and Kimchi.

15. Cf. Kippenberg, *Garizim*, 37, etc.

16. Cf. Würthwein, *Könige* II, 403; Talmon, 'Überlieferungen', 138ff.; Dexinger, 'Limits', 91ff., as an intepretation of the Chronicler; Dexinger regards vv.34a, 41 as a Chronistic insertion (90), but then brings the whole text very close to the Chronistic historical perspective in Ezra 4.1-5 (93).

17. In terminology and content no clear references can be recognized in Ezra 4.2, 9f. to II Kings 17.24, and II Kings 17.24-41 clearly points to a Deuteronomistic and not a Chronistic terminology.

18. There is evidence of continuous settlement in Bethel beyond the destruction of Jerusalem in 587 right through the exilic period, cf. EAE I, 1975, 192f.; as is well known, the sanctuary has not yet been found.

19. Cf. the allusions in II Kings 17.29, 32 to I Kings 12.31f.; 13.33f.

20. Cf. also the break between vv.33 and 34b; similarly also Würthwein, *Könige* II, 410; by contrast the division by Dexinger, 'Limits', 90 (I: vv.25-28; II vv. 29-31; 34b-40; III, 34a, 41) is questionable.

21. Against Würthwein, *Könige* II, 401.

22. Verse 41 is a redactional bracket which is meant to connect the addition to vv.24-33.

23. The term *'am hā'āreṣ* in v.4 probably also has the same meaning as the plural usage which is customary for Chronicles elsewhere (Dexinger, 'Limits', 93, differs, supposing collaborating Israelites). Ezra 6.21 shows that even Chronicles still knows Israelites among these foreign peoples.

24. Alt, 'Rolle Samarias', 37; similarly Rowley, 'Samaritan Schism', 216ff.; Kippenberg, *Garizim*, 39f.

25. Sanballat, from Sinuballiṭ, 'Sin has kept alive', is a Babylonian name, but such names also occur among Jews (Sheshbazzar, Zerubbabel, Mordechai, etc.); the names of Sanballat's children in the Elephantine letters (AP 3.30; 32.1), Shemariah and Delaiah, indicate that Sanballat was a worshipper of Yahweh – at least in his personal piety. The Samaria papyri 8 and 14 from Wadi ed-Daliye attest two other names containing Yahweh from the later family dynasty, probably Hananiah and Joshua; cf. Cross, 'Papyri', 42f.

26. Cf. the lists Ezra 2 and Neh.7 and the pressure towards registration in Neh.7.5; cf. above, 446f.

27. In this rendering I largely follow the 'Sanballat narrative' which Büchler, 'La relation', 4-8, has reconstructed as Josephus' source (302f., 306, 317a, 321-325a, 345); he dates it to the second century in Alexandria and regards it as being of Samaritan origin. The Samaritan origin has been disputed, probably rightly, by Kippenberg, *Garizim*, 52: the bias is Jewish. It can be left open whether it contains an older proto-Samaritan stratum, as Dexinger, 'Limits', 96f., conjectures for 321, 324, following Jewish authors. However, Kippenberg's reconstruction of a 'Shechemite stratum' which gives chronological priority to the section 340-44 (53ff.) is unconvincing, as this presupposes the legendary report of the meeting

between Alexander and the high priest Jaddua (317b-320, 325b-339), which is certainly later (according to Dexinger from the time of Caesar).

28. Montgomery, *Samaritans*, 67-9; Rowley, 'Sanballat', 249f., 265; but cf. Mor, 'History', 4.

29. Cf. the inscriptions from a Samaritan Diaspora community found on the island of Delos which seem to presuppose the practice of taking sacrificial offerings to the temple on Gerizim. Unfortunately at the present time it is impossible to date them precisely (between 250 and 50 BCE); cf. Pummer, 'Material Remains', 150f., 172.

30. The investigations on Tell er-Rās carried out in 1984 had indicated that the podium under the Roman temple which since the excavations of J.Bull in (1964-1968) had been claimed as the Samaritan temple did not come from Hellenistic times but was part of the Roman site; cf. Pummer, 'Material Remains', 165ff.; on the basis of oral information from Magen, Pummer still believed in the article mentioned that the temple had not been found.

31. Cf. the provisional report of the excavator, Magen, 'Town', 97ff.; the site is part of a Hellenistic city (Hirbet Louza), the burnt stratum of which is very probably to be connected with its destruction by John Hyrcanus in 127 BCE (*Antt.*, XIII, 255f.).

32. Cf. Wright, *Shechem*, 170-81.

33. For this new assessment, which has been accepted by many scholars, see basically Cross, 'Aspects', 203. Beforehand it was thought that Josephus had spun his account in legendary fashion from Neh.13.28, see above, n.28.

34. Especially between Alexander's positive attitude to Sanballat (XI, 323f.) and his negative attitude to the Shechemites (340-344).

35. Cf. the reflections by Dexinger, 'Limits', 97f.

36. Thus Mor, 'History', 6f., who wonders whether Alexander's approval was not gained subsequently.

37. Cf. the coalition of interests in the building of the Jerusalem temple in Ezra 5.1f., see above 450f., and the cult-political functions which the governor Nehemiah claimed for himself (Neh.13.4-14).

38. The Samaritan sources can hardly be traced back to the early period, but we may see the way in which the Samaritans later orientate their history on a genealogy of the high priests as indirect confirmation of Josephus' view that the separation began with the expulsion of a member of the high-priestly family, cf. Kippenberg, *Garizim*, 61.

39. Cf. II Chron.11.6; 13.4-12; 15.9; 30.1ff; 34.6f.,9; 35.18.

40. Cf. Mor, 'History', 11-14.

41. Thus the majority of scholars, see above, n.5. The hostile attitudes to the Samaritans in Sirach 50.25f. (probably secondary in the context), Jub.30.5ff. and TestLev 5-7 probably reflect this break.

42. Similarly already Alt, 'Rolle Samarias', 322f.

43. See above, 446.

44. Bethel seems to have been added to Judah in the post-exilic period, Ezra 2.28; Neh.7.32; cf. II Chron.13.19; I Macc.9.50.

45. Cf. AP 32; the governors of Judah, Bagohi, and Samaria, Sanballat I, certainly did not act without the approval of the imperial government. Here the exclusion of animal sacrifices in line 9 need not be a measure against Jerusalem, but can

express Persian reservations about bloody sacrifices. If Sanballat, unlike the leaders of the community of Judah, who had probably ignored an earlier enquiry from the Jews of Elephantine (AP 30.18f.), agreed to allow Yahweh worshippers a temple outside Jerusalem, then we already have here the indication of a more open understanding of the Deuteronomic law of centralization than prevailed in Judah.

46. To this degree the view of Mor, 'History', 6, that the Persian policy had prohibited the further building of a temple has to be modified.

47. For the shifting of the Deuteronomic synthesis by DtrG to the saving elements of the state, 'the Davidic kingship' and 'Jerusalem temple', see above, 392ff.

48. See above, 226f.

49. The relatively late references to Jerusalem in Gen.14.18 ('Salem') and 22.2 ('Moria', cf. II Chron.3.1) are not explicit.

50. Significantly this too was turned into Gerizim in the Samaritan Pentateuch.

51. But it is surely going too far to limit the new community of Samaria to those who had gone over from Judah, as Montgomery, *Samaritans*, 69; Kippenberg, *Garizim*, 56ff.; Egger, *Josephus*, 68ff., want to do. The report of Josephus that many other countrymen (*homoethneis*) wanted to join with Manasseh in building a temple (*Antt*.XI, 322) already tells against this. This must at least also mean the Samarian adherents of Yahweh. The people of Judah whom Manasseh brought in were only the focal point around which things crystallized.

52. Thus polemically the later stratum of the Josephus account in *Antt*. XI, 345.

53. Cf. the dispute between the Samaritans and Jews in Alexandria as to which of the two temples was holier, handed down by Josephus, *Antt*. XII, 74-9; cf. also the dispute over the temple offerings, *Antt*. XII, 10.

54. Thus especially in the Diaspora, as the example of Delos shows, see Pummer, 'Material Remains', 150f. Crown calculates two million Samaritans in the Hellenistic-Roman period, one and a half million of them in the Diaspora, compared with eight million Jews, six million of them in the Diaspora ('Diaspora', 201).

55. The foundations of temples in Leontopolis (Egypt) and 'Araq el-'Emir (Transjordan) shows that this cultic split could have continued further.

6.1 The sociological developments

1. Ptolemy I conquered Palestine four times between 320 and 301; once Jerusalem was occupied violently on the sabbath, cf. *Antt*. XII, 5f.; *Contra Apionem* I, 205-211, probably in the year 302 BCE; cf. Tcherikover, *Civilization*, 55-9; Stern, *Authors*, 108. In this connection, according to Letter of Aristeas 12, a large number of Jews were deported to Egypt and, together with voluntary emigrants, became the basic stock of the Alexandrian Diaspora which was later to become so flourishing.

2. While there is evidence for this first in the decgree of the Seleucid ruler Antiochus III from 197 BCE (*Antt*. XII, 142; cf. *TGI*², 89f.), we may conclude simply from the fact that the Ptolemies left the organs of self-administration from Persian period untouched that they, too, already accorded Judaea a comparable status, cf. Tcherikover, *Civilization*, 83, against Hengel, *Judaism*, 22f. Administratively Judaea formed a hyparchy or an ethnos.

3. See above, 446f.

4. Or *presbyteroi*, 'elders', in II Macc.14.37; I Macc.11.23; 12.35; 13.36; 14.20. The *gerousia* appears as an organ of leadership in many official documents, cf. e.g. *Antt.* XII, 138, 142; II Macc.11.27; I Macc.12.6, par. *Antt.* XIII, 166; II Macc.1.10; 4.44; Sirach 33 (36).27. Hengel thinks that in analogy to the later Sanhedrin, 'prominent members of the priesthood' belonged to the *gerousia* (*Judaism*, 25f.; similarly Stern, 'Zeit', 239), but a purely lay body is suggested not only by the continuity of the Persian conditions but also by the fact that in some evidence the priests are mentioned as a separate group alongside the *gerousia* (*Antt.* XII, 142; I Macc.12.6; *Antt.* XIII, 166; I Macc.14.20), thus also Kippenberg, *Klassenbildung*, 83 n.30. Hengel's view that the *gerousia* was only constituted in the Ptolemaean period under the possible influence of Greek models (*Judaism*, 27) is less probable if one evaluates the sources of the Persian period correctly.

5. Thus the interesting reading *Antt.* XIII, 166, which is to be preferred to the variant *to koinon ton Ioudaion* as the *lectio difficilior; to koinon* then does not mean 'totality', but 'community, council'. Normally only *hoi hiereis*, 'the priests', are mentioned in the document (*Antt.* XII, 142; I Macc.12.6; 14.20).

6. Cf. I Macc.12.6; 14.20; 15.17; cf. II Macc.11.27.

7. For example the assembly of the people is not mentioned in the decree of Antiochus III; for its new sigificance at the time of the Maccabaean fight for freedom cf. I Macc.4.59; 5.16; 13.2,8; 14.28. Alongside the popular assembly of Judaea there also seems to have been one for Jerusalem (*Antt.* XII, 164; I Macc.14.19). Sirach 4.7; 7.7; 38.33 can also be connected with the popular assembly.

8. Thus resolutely Tcherikover, *Civilization*, 59. The appointment of an 'overseer' (*epistates*) in Jerusalem and on Gerizim, II Macc.5.22f., was a penal measure taken by Antiochus IV.

9. The official function (*prostasia*) of the high priest in leadership is already attested by Hecataeus of Abdera for the period around 300 (Diodorus Siculus, *Bibliotheca Historica* XL, 3, 5, in Stern, *Authors*, 26); cf. later *Antt.* XII, 162; Sirach 45,24 (LXX). Thus we can conjecture that the growth in high-priestly power was already prepared for in the late Persian period.

10. Whether the high priest had fiscal autonomy (thus e.g. Stern, 'Zeit', 239) or not (thus e.g. Gunneweg, *Geschichte*, 146; Hengel, *Judaism*, 24ff.) is a matter of dispute. *Antt.* XII, 158, where under the impact of the third Syrian war Onias refuses to take the tribute for the Ptolemaeans from the temple treasure, seems to presuppose this, and the same goes for Jason's payment to the Seleucids in II Macc.4.7f. We cannot conclude from the fact that in II Macc.3.4 we hear of a separate temple administrator (*prostates tou hierou*) that this man was active only in the service of the foreign power and was not also subject to the supervision of the high priest (thus Hengel, 24f.), but at any rate Simon was a Jew and probably even came from a priestly family (Bilga, cf. the Latin and Armenian versions of II Macc.3.4 and the rabbinic tradition). But of course the taxes were strictly controlled by the foreign power; according to II Macc.4.28 this was the task of the commander of the Acra.

11. With this qualification one can agree with Tcherikover's assessment: 'the High Priest at the head of the people assumed the aspect of a petty monarch' (*Civilization*, 59).

12. Cf. *Antt.* XII, 164, 167.

13. Cf. Kippenberg, *Klassenbildung*, 82ff.

14. Diodorus Siculus, *Bibliotheca Historica*, XL, 3, 7, in Stern, *Authors*, 27; Stern points out (33) that Hecataeus was particularly interested in this theme because of similar social abuses in Greece.

15. Cf. simply Koheleth 4.1-3; 5.7f.; Sirach 13.2f, 4-13, 16-18,19,20,21-23. Whereas Koheleth merely notes these abuses and does not criticize them, Sirach never tires of warning against the danger of riches (5.1-8; 26.29-27.3; 31.1-11) and calling for support for the poor (4.1-10; 7.32; 22.23; 29.1-2,8-13,14). In the face of the former he threatens the rich with eschatological judgment, taking up an argument from the piety of the poor (35.13-17); in the latter he explicitly goes beyond pious wisdom theology in referring to the Torah of Moses (29.9,11).

16. Cf. the decree of Ptolemy II, Papyrus Rainer recto 16-22 in Kippenberg, *Klassenbildung*, 79f.; there is also a release of slaves in the decree of Antiochus III (*Antt.* XII, 143), but this probably refers to prisoners of war. II Macc.8.10 makes blindingly clear that even tributes were financed by the sale of prisoners of war into slavery.

17. Cf. Hengel, *Judaism*, 40f.

18. Tcherikover, *Civilization*, 60-73; Hengel, *Judaism*, 39-47.

19. Cf. the calculation made by Hengel, *Judaism*, 27f.

20. Cf. Stern, 'Zeit', 246-8.

21. See Kippenberg, *Klassenbildung*, 78ff.

22. In taking the statement as referring to cash coinage, Hengel, *Judaism*, 27, is overlooking the partisan standpoint of the Tobiad romance, which probably comes from the circle of the family of Joseph's son Hyrcanus, cf. Tcherikover, *Civilization*, 141. Schäfer, 'Periods', 574, is similarly critical of Hengel's estimate.

23. Thus in a letter from Joseph's father, Tobias, to the 'economics minister' Apollonius: *polle charis tois theois*, 'many thanks to the gods' (Tcherikover and Fuks, *Corpus*, no.4). But Tobias, who installed a military colony of mixed nationality on his land in Transjordan, was perhaps an extreme case. Tcherikover, *Civilization*, 71; Goldstein, 'Acceptance', 72-3; Feldman, 'Hellenism', 86ff., stress that for a long time 'Hellenization' only related to external features. There is no clear evidence of a far-reaching 'Hellenization' as early as the third century, as Hengel, *Judaism*, 101f. also assumes for Judaea.

24. Tcherikover, *Civilization*, 114; Goldstein, 'Acceptance', 74f., and Feldman, 'Hellenism', rightly point out that there is no evidence of Greek settlements in Judaea before 175 BCE. Jerusalem itself had only a small foreign garrison.

25. Cf. his admonitions to solidarity with the poor in n.15 and the 'Praise of the Fathers', Sirach 44-49. The deliberate synthesis which Sirach makes between wisdom speculation and official Israelite Yahweh religion (Sirach 1; 24) is to be understood in terms of this concern. Probably he was not originally a member of the upper class, but had gone up in society.

26. The passage in the book of Daniel usually described as an 'obscure saying' (cf. Hengel, *Judaism*, 9; Tcherikover, *Civilization*, 77-9) is not so obscure if we note the difference between a political (Aramaic book of Daniel) and a quietistic

(Hebrew book of Daniel) apocalyptic, see below 581ff. Täubler, 'Jerusalem', 23ff., already pointed out the right direction for exegesis.

27. Jason's official initiative in II Macc.4.7ff. is hardly conceivable without the involvement of the council of elders; a majority must have agreed to it before the constitution of the polis provided for the domination of the Hellenists in the *gerousia*. Only after the radicalization under Menelaus did the *gerousia* split; the 'pious' minority which had previously thought a compromise possible went into open opposition and had to repent of it bitterly (II Macc.4.43-49).

28. See the survey in Kampen, *Hasideans*, 1-43.

29. Plöger, *Theocracy*, 7f.

30. Hengel, *Judaism*, 175ff.

31. Ibid., 176.

32. Tcherikover, *Civilization*, 125f.; 196-7.

33. Kampen, *Hasideans*, 214ff.; unlike earlier scholars, who saw the Hasidim as forerunners of both the Pharisees and the Essenes, Kampen distinguishes them from the latter (151ff.). However, his etymological considerations here are more than suspect.

34. This is usually interpreted in a military sense as 'brave men from Israel', but the Hebrew equivalent *gibbōrē hāḥayil* by no means has only a military connotation (Josh.1.14; I Chron.12.9, etc.); it also means landowners (capable of bearing arms, II Kings 15.20), and especially in the terminiology of Chronicles the influential heads of clans (I Chron.5.24; 7.2, 4,7,9,11,40; 26.6) and various leadership functions (I Chron.9.13; 26.6,31; II Chron.26.12; Neh.11.14).

35. The word is usually understood as a temporal adverb ('the Hasidim were the first to seek'); but it is the predicate of an independent sentence: 'But the Hasidim were the first (= leaders) among the Israelites, and they sought...'

36. Kampen, *Hasideans*, 107, 113f., 120, 149.

37. Cf. the corresponding characterization as a group (*synagoge*) in I Macc.2.42 and 7.12 and the parallel verbs in 7.12 and 7.13 (*ek-/epzeteo*, 'they sought just things', i.e. conditions of peace, 'they sought peace with them'), Kampen, *Hasideans*, 121f., against Plöger, *Theocracy*, 7f., who here assumes two different factors.

38. Kampen, *Hasideans*, 135ff.

39. Ibid., 219.

40. The scribal features (cf. e.g. the presentation of Enoch as *ho grammateus tes dikaiosynes* in I Enoch 12.4 and Dan.9) and the wisdom features of apocalyptic (cf. e.g. the great significance of the 'teachers' [*maskīlīm*] in Dan.11.33, 35; 12.3, 10) which do not seem to match a location of them in lower-class circles already led Steck and others to see the Hasidim as a broad anti-Hellenistic collective movement of quite different groups ('Strömungen' [5.0], 313f.). However, this watering down of Plöger's theory shows that his simple contrast between a 'theocratic' upper class and an 'apocalyptic' lower class does not work, see below, 565ff.

41. It mentions the council of elders, priests, temple scribes (*grammateis tou hierou*) and temple singers as the leading groups who are to be exempt from certain taxes (*Antt.* XII, 142).

42. See above, 468ff.

43. See above, 465f.

44. The beginnings of the oral Torah may go back to these early scribes, cf. Mantel, 'Development', 52ff.

45. For details see the extensive account by Schäfer, 'Periods', 560-604; he discusses in detail the differences between Bickermann and Hengel on the one hand and Tcherikover on the other.

46. Thus Tcherikover, *Civilization*, 160ff.

47. Maier, *Geschichte*, 11, has emphasized this objective compulsion towards stronger integration.

48. There has been much argument among scholars past and present over the background to this religious edict of Antiochus IV, transmitted in a somewhat divergent form in I Macc.1.44-50 and II Macc.6.1-11. It is quite unprecedented for a Hellenistic ruler. However, it is impossible to go into the matter here, cf. the discussion in Schäfer, 'Periods', 562-4. I tend towards the view of Bickermann, *Gott*, 128ff., to the extent that the decree can hardly be explained without the collaboration of the radical Hellenists. But whether there was still any positive notion of reform behind such radical measures as prohibition of the sabbath and circumcision, the compulsory sacrifice pigs and burning the scrolls of the Torah, as he and Hengel, *Judaism*, 292f., suppose, seems to me improbable; they all too clearly bear the mark of punitive actions.

49. The erection on top of the altar of burnt offering, which is polemically called 'abomination of desolation' (*šiqqūṣ [meʲ]šōmem*, Dan.11.31; 12.11; I Macc.1.54), which was probably dedicated to Baal Šamem, and the naming of the temple after Zeus Olympios (II Macc.6.2) are meant to make Yahweh a form of this supreme Phoenician and Greek god of heaven and are understandable on the basis of a Hellenistic theology of identification.

50. Certainly according to the account in Maccabees this initiative by the Hasidim failed, and in its view these were trustful martyrs (I Macc.7.14-18), but the crisis in which the Maccabean struggle was now involved (9.6f.) shows that it had lost its broad support among the population (cf. 7.22,24,33).

51. Cf. the estimation of Tcherikover, *Civilization*, 258: 'The foundation of the Jewish state brought about a very important change in the political position of the Jewish nation, but from the social point of view nothing had changed; or, if there was a change, it was for the worse.'

52. The Sadducees as members of the lay and priestly aristocracy who supported the formation of a Hellenistic state on a national Jewish foundation challenged the right of the Pharisees to be leaders in the interpretation of the Torah (*Antt.* XII, 296) and instead retreated to the written Mosaic law, cf. Tcherikover, *Civilization*, 263-5.

53. Thus Diodorus Siculus, *Bibliotheca Historica* XL.2, see Stern, *Authors*, 185; cf. *Antt.* XIV, 41.

6.2 *The scribal ideal of a theocracy (Chronicles)*

1. Joel 4.4ff.; Zech.9.1ff., 13ff.: 11.15; clearly first in Dan.8.21; 10.20; 11.2ff.

2. Cf. the surveys in Williamson, *Israel*, 83-6, and Oeming, *Israel*, 44f.; the *terminus ad quem* is the fact that the Jewish historiographer Eupolemus already quotes from Chronicles in the Septuagint translation around 158 BCE.

3. The list of Davidides in I Chron.3.17ff. goes down at least six generations below Sheshbazzar – depending on what one decides about v.21, the text of which is difficult. The early dating of Chronicles in the time of Zerubbabel, which has become customary in the Cross school (cf. e.g. Newsome, 'New Understanding'), would certainly fit quite well theologically (royalist option, rebuilding of the temple) but necessitates such airy literary-critical operations that it is not convincing; cf. the repudiation by Williamson, 'Eschatology', 120-30.

4. E.g. Rudolph, *Chronikbücher*, X; Myers, *Chronicles* I, LXXXVIIff.; Oeming, *Israel*, 444.

5. The thesis that Chronicles and Ezra-Nehemiah belong together, which was first presented by Zunz in 1832, was for the first time put in question by Japhet, 'Authorship', 1968; since then the discussion has swayed to and fro, cf. the detailed discussion in Williamson, *Israel*, 5-82, who supports Japhet with qualifications; similarly also Braun, 'Chronicles', 52ff. Talshir, 'Reinvestigation', 193, and Gunneweg, *Esra*, 21-8, are critical.

6. The dependence of the list in I Chron.9.2-17 on Neh.11.3-19 above all supports the priority of Ezra/Nehemiah, cf. Johnstone, 'Guilt', 114.

7. Cf. the similarities in ways of working (use of sources), interests (temple, Levites) and style (cf. e.g. Ezra 6.19f. with II Chron.35) which have often been noted. Welten, *Geschichte*, 199; Willi, *Chronik*, 181f.; Smend, 'Entstehung', 228; Oeming, *Israel*, 44, think in terms of different works by the same author. I think it more appropriate to begin from the continuity of a circle of tradents.

8. Cf. simply the confusion in the chronological sequence of Ezra 4 and Noth, *Chronicler*, 70ff.

9. Granted, scholars have not yet arrived at a convincing solution to the literary growth of Chronicles (cf. simply the various analyses by Noth, *Chronicler*, 30ff.; Rudolph, *Chronik*, 93, etc.; Willi, *Chronik*, 194ff.; Williamson, 'Origins', 252ff.), but the shifts in the organization of temple personnel which can be recognized in it (cf. Gese, 'Kultsänger', 148ff.) already suggest a phase of origin lasting some decades. In my view the literary evidence is best explained by the assumption of several authors in a closed group of tradents who were active over a lengthy period, so too Ackroyd, *History*, 502.

10. Thus e.g. Noth, *Chronicler*, 70-3, etc. Welten, *Geschichte*, 110-13, 119f., has presented new arguments for a dating in the Hellenistic period; he points to reflections of the Greek army system in Chronicles, especially the use of catapults also for defending the city (II Chron.26.15).

11. See below, 566ff.

12. See above, 522ff.

13. See above, 529ff.

14. Cf. Ezra 2.2ff., 59ff.; 6.21; 10, etc.

15. See above, 531f.

16. See above, 472f.; but cf. the references to kingship and temple which the authors of Chronicles already incorporated into their 'tribal history' of Israel (I Chron.1-9: 1.43; 2.15; 3.1ff.; 4.31,41; 5.2, 36; 6.16f.; 7.2; 9.3ff.).

17. These are twenty-nine out of sixty-five chapters! By contrast, the early history of Israel is reduced to a genealogical skeleton (I Chron.1-9) with which the post-exilic Judaeans safeguard their legitimate descent and their claim to leadership within Israel; cf. now Oeming, *Israel*, 206ff. The central period of salvation in the

early monarchy is followed in II Chron.10-36 by the further period of the monarchy as a period of proving. The tripartite division of I Chron.10-II Chron.9 going by types, proposed by Mosis, *Untersuchungen*, 164ff. (Saul, period of disaster; David, intermediate period between disaster and salvation; Solomon, time of salvation), does not work. The downfall of Saul is simply the dark background for the splendid period of salvation, and the time of David and Solomon is a unity.

18. Cf. I Chron.16.39f.; 21.29; 23.32; II Chron.1.3,6,13; cf. I Chron.6.17; 23.26. After the ark is moved, the Jerusalem temple can consistently be called the 'tent of meeting' (I Chron.9.21) or 'tent of witness' (II Chron.24.5; cf. Num.9.15 etc.).

19. Cf. I Chron.28.11ff. with Ex.25.9; the expression *bēt hakkappōret* for the holy of holies recalls Ex.25.17.

20. Cf. I Chron.23-27; the extensive complex certainly shows clear traces of growth, but as a whole it is hardly an insertion (thus Noth, *Chronicler*, 31ff.,etc.), since it is presupposed too often in the sequel (I Chron.28.21; 29.8; II Chron.8.15; 35.4,15); cf. the more cautious solution of Williamson, 'Origins'. The parallelism in the references to Moses and David in II Chron.35 demonstrates particularly vividly the Chronistic conception of a continuation of the cultic ordinances of the Torah by David.

21. Jerusalem: II Chron.6.5f.,34; 12.13; temple: II Chron.7.12,16; 33.7; Levites, priests: I Chron.15.2; II Chron.29.11 (following Deut.18.5). The election of David, Jerusalem and the Temple can already be found in DtrG. What is new is the election of the Jerusalem cult personnel, a special election of Solomon and the inclusion of the election of David in the election of Judah; cf. the placing of the Davidides (I Chron.3) in the middle of the Judah genealogy (I Chron 2 and 4).

22. See above, 472f.

23. Cf. I Chron.16.40; 22.12; II Chron.12.1; 31.3f; 'book of the law of Yahweh', II Chron.17.9; 34.14 and *mišmeret yhwh*, 'ordinance of Yahweh', II Chron.13.11; *debar yhwh*, 'word of Yahweh', II Chron 30.12; 35.6.

24. Cf. II Chron.23.18; 30.16; 'book of Moses', II Chron.35.12; *miṣwat mōše*, 'commandment of Moses', II Chron.8.13; verb form I Chron.6.34. Moses' function as mediator is already expressed technically by the phrase *beyad mōše* 'by Moses', II Chron.33.8; 34.14; 35.6.

25. Cf. II Chron.23.18; 25.4; 35.12, 26, or in the negative 30.5,18; also Ezra 3.2,4; Neh.8.15; 10.35,37.

26. Cf. e.g. I Chron.21.6 (Num.1.49); 21.23 (Num.15.1ff.); II Chron.33.3 (Deut.12.3); 33.6 (Deut.18.20).

27. According to the Deuteronomic theory all priests were Levites, see above, 219ff.; consequently while DtrG also knew 'levitical priests', it had virtually no knowledge of Levites as an independent group alongside the priests (only Deut.27.14; I Sam.6.15; by contrast Josh.3.3; II Sam.15.24; I Kings 8.4 are corrections of the text in line with Chronicles). The constant insistence of the Chronistic historians on the important role of the Levites is at least partially to be understood from the fact that it had to anchor this group, which was a projection of the exilic/post-exilic reform priesthood (Ezek.44.9ff.; Num.3f.), in the pre-exilic historical tradition, cf. e.g. I Chron.15; II Chron.5.4,12; 23.7; 34.12f. with the

passages underlying them. Alongside this they also still use the comprehensive Deuteronomic/Deuteronomistic terminology, thus e.g. II Chron.29.5ff.; 30.22.

28. Cf. the double Tamid sacrifice in I Chron.16.40; II Chron.2.3; 13.11; 31.3, following Ex.29.38-41; Num.28.3-8; the pre-exilic period and even still DtrG knew only a burnt offering in the morning – alongside a simple *minḥā* in the evening (II Kings 16.15; cf. Ezek.46.13-15); as in P, the burnt offering also includes a food offering (*minḥā*) as an additional sacrifice (I Chron.21.23; Num.15.1ff.; 29.28ff.). The dedication of the temple in II Chron.29.20-24 is orientated on the sin offering (*ḥaṭṭā't*) ritual (Lev.4; 16.11ff.) of the Day of Atonement, even if the number and nature of the sacrificial animals differ, see above, 462f.

29. Cf. the dating of the passover in II Chron.35.1 with Ex.12.6; the later celebration of the passover in II Chron.30.2ff. is orientated on Num.9.1-14.

30. von Rad, *Geschichtsbild*, 53, can sometimes also bring out this Chronistic exegesis aimed at a compromise. But in stressing for much of the time how markedly Chronicles differs from P and how much it is influenced by Deuteronomy (55ff.), he allows himself to be too influenced by polemic against the earlier view which put Chronicles in a direct line with P. He fails to recognize that – even more in the time of Chronicles – there never was an independent Priestly Writing. The juxtaposition and interweaving of Deuteronomic and Priestly notions in Chronicles is the most telling indication that it had in front of it the finished Pentateuch, which combined the two in a tense structure, and that compelled a compromise.

31. That is how, for example, the divergences over the table of the showbread and the lampstands emphasized by von Rad, *Geschichtsbild*, 48ff., are to be interpreted.

32. Thus e.g. II Chron.29.34; 30.17; 35.11 against Num.18.2f.; however, the Chronistic historians could refer e.g. to Ezek.46.24 for their participation in the sacrificial cult.

33. See above, 460.

34. The exodus motif is mentioned only six times and even then emphatically in passing (I Chron.17.5,21; II Chron.5.10; 6.5; 7.22; 20.10), cf. Kegler, 'Exodustradition', 64: 'The exodus event is certainly mentioned as an inherited tradition, but it is stripped of its dynamic – and the experience of liberation which it contains. Its significance is transcended by that of the temple and its (fictitious) origin.'

35. See above, 398f., 472f.

36. See above, 428f., 484.

37. See above, 478ff.

38. Cf. I Chron.13; 15f.; 21-29; II Chron.3-7, i.e. almost two-thirds of the content of the text dealing with the central period of salvation is about cult-political measures of David and Solomon; in DtrG this was less than a tenth – related to the same period of time (I Sam.31 – II Kings 11).

39. Cf. I Chron.13.1f.,4; II Chron.30.2,4,23.

40. The information from the list of officials in DtrG II Sam.8.17 = I Chron.18.16 is commented on in I Chron.29.22 in a way which suggests that the whole community anoints Zadok priest; the information in II Sam.8.18b that even David's sons were priests is deleted by Chronicles.

41. II Chron.13.5,8; cf. I Chron.5.2.

42. II Chron.6.16; 7.18; 21.7; we should probably answer the quite difficult question whether the Chronistic historians understood the promise of Nathan

unconditionally (the limited threat of punishment in II Sam.7.14 is absent from I Chron.17.13f.) or conditionally (I Chron.22.10-13; 28.7,9f.) along the line taken by Williamson, 'Dynastic Oracle', 9ff.; 'Eschatology', 140ff. According to him, the loyal fulfilment of the will of God which Solomon achieved in the building of the temple brought him a promise of eternal duration and unconditional validity which at first applied only to him (II Chron.6.16; 7.18; 13.5,8). To excise the conditions (I Chron.22.12f.; 28.7b-10) as Mosis, *Untersuchungen*, 90-2, proposes, is no solution.

43. Thus explicitly qualified in I Chron.28.5 along the lines of the title of God as king reinterpreted in Deutero-Isaiah in terms critical of rule (cf. Isa.41.21; 43.15; 44.6, see above, 424f.). However, in contrast to the Deutero-Isaiah group, for the Chronistic historians the kingship of Yahweh over Israel did not completely exclude human kingship but merely limited it. In addition they also knew a universal kingship of Yahweh (I Chron.29.11); however, this is not given to the Davidides to exercise, in order to rule out from the start all the claims of the old kingship theology to world power.

44. Japhet, *Ideology*, 417ff., has demonstrated impressively that the Chronistic theologoumenon of theocracy does not represent a divinization but a 'democratization' of Israelite kingship. Cf. I Chron.11.1ff.; 12.39f.; 15.3,11,25; 23.2; 28.1; II Chron.5.2ff.; 15.9f.; 20.4; 23.20; 29,20; 30.1ff.; 34.29ff.

45. II Chron.20.21; 32.3.

46. Cf. the instruction of the people in the Torah by officials, Levites and priests ordained by Jehoshaphat, II Chron.17.7-9, and the covenant-makings introduced by the kings, II Chron.15.8-15; 29.5-11; 34.29-32.

47. Cf., quite apart from the foundation of the temple by David and Solomon, the constant concern of kings for the temple, II Chron.24.4ff.; 20; 31.2ff.; 34.8ff. and their generous gifts of sacrifices, II Chron.30.24; 35.7.

48. Cf. Jehoshaphat's judicial reform, II Chron.19.4b-11.

49. Here mention should be made above all of the fortresses built to provide security for the people: II Chron.11.5-12; 14.5f.; 17.2,12f.; 26.9f.; 27.3f.; 32.5f.; 33.14; cf. Welten, *Geschichte*, 9ff.

50. Cf. the complete silence over Solomon's murder (I Kings 2) in I Chron.29.23ff.; in II Chron.2.16f. his forced labour is restricted to foreigners, with I Kings 9.20-22 and against I Kings 5.27-30. Only very occasionally is there any mention of royal oppressive measures, II Chron.16.10; 24.22.

51. Cf. II Chron.11.2f.; 12.5,7; 15.1-7; 16.7-9; 19.2f.; (20.14-17;) 20.37; 21.12-15; 25.15f.; 28.9-11; 34.22-28; 36.12,15f.

52. Cf. II Chron.20.34 and in this sense I Chron.29.29; II Chron.9.29; 12.15; 13.22; 26.22; 32.32; 33.19. This introduces the development of understanding the historical books as 'Former Prophets'.

53. I Chron.28.18 cf. Ezek.1; 10; II Chron.15.2 cf. Jer.29.13f.; 15.5 cf. Amos 3.9; 15.7 cf. Jer.31.16; 16.9 cf. Zech. 4.10; 19.7 cf. Zeph.3.5 alongside Deut.10.17; 20.7 cf. Isa.41.8; 20.20 cf. Isa.7.9; 36.12 cf. Jer.29.10 and Lev.26.34.

54. See above, 478f.

55. Of the prophets of judgment, only Isaiah and Jeremiah appear in Chronicles; here as already in DtrG Isaiah is a prophet of salvation (in II Chron.32.30 an intercessor) and as in JerD Jeremiah warns and admonishes (36.12ff.); his message of judgment is *a priori* terminated (36.21) along the lines of Jer.29.10 and Lev.26.34.

56. There is no reference to the prophecy of salvation in the book of Deutero-Isaiah.

57. Cf. Deut.4.29; Isa.55.6; Zeph.1.6; Ps.105.4.

58. For saving trust in God cf. II Chron.13.18; 14.10; 16.7f.; 20.9, 17, 20ff.; II Chron.28,16,20f.,23 (negative); 32.7f.; for the successful seeking of God see II Chron.14.6; 15.15; 17.3-6; 20.3f.; 41.21; cf. II Chron.12.5-8; 33.12f.

59. Cf. I Chron.17; 25; II Chron.5.12ff.; 7.6; 29.25-30; 30.21; 35.15, and Gese, 'Kultsänger'.

60. Pss.105.1-15; 96.1-11; 106.1, 47f. are quoted. In addition Ps.105.4, 'Seek Yahweh and his strength, seek constantly his face', is quoted in I Chron.16.11, again in line with a prophetic quotation from Jer.29.13f.

61. Cf. I Chron.16.34,41; II Chron.5.13; 7.3,6; Ezra 3.11.

62. Thus impressively worked out by Welten, 'Lade', 181: 'One can get the impression that all these stories about David and Solomon are no more than a tremendous extension of the first verses of Ps.132.'

63. *'elōhīm*, 'God', with suffix occurs seventy-seven times, an increase of more than a third over the corresponding section of DtrG (I Sam.31-II Kings 25).

64. Thirty-two times in all; but of these only four are in the singular (I Chron.28.9; II Chron.17.4; 21.12; 34.3, dynastic God), twenty-six in the plural and twice as the God of tribal ancestors or a named ancestor (I Chron.29.10; II Chron.30.6); in the parallel section of DtrG 'designations of patriarchal gods' occur only three times.

65. See above, 29ff.

66. Cf. I Chron.4.10; 11.9; 22.11,16,18; 28.20; II Chron.13.12; 15.2,9; 17.3; 19.6,11; 20.17; 25.7; 32.7; 35.21; however, it is typical of Chronicles that this personal support of God is also extended to the political and military sphere.

67. The verb is used in Chronicles as a theological term; it occurs forty times. The starting passage is probably Jer.29.13f.

68. The verb is used loosely in later times for *dāraš*, cf. Westermann, 'Suchen', 165; in Chronicles it occurs nine times, perhaps deliberately taking up Ps.105.4 = I Chron.16.11.

69. See Westermann, 'Suchen', 177, thus also still in some passages in Chronicles: I Chron.10.13f.; II Chron.18.4,6,7; 34.21,26.

70. Cf. Ps.22.27; 34.5, etc.; I Chron.21.30.

71. Thus explicitly I Chron.22.19; cf.13.3; 15.13; II Chron.31.21.

72. II Chron.17.3f.; 19.3; 34.3; cf. II Chron.12.14; 25.15.

73. II Chron.14.3,6; 15.2,4,12,15.

74. I Chron.21.30; 28.9; II Chron.11.6; 20.3f.; 30.19; cf. II Chron.16.12.

74. I Chron.28.8; II Chron.22.9; 26.5.

76. Thus II Chron.15.15, taking up the Deuteronomic phrase and considerably changing it, cf.II Chron.11.6; 15.12; 22.9, etc, see also Japhet, *Ideology*, 250ff.

77. Cf. the verb *šā'an*, niphal, 'support oneself on', II Chron.13.18.14.10; 16.7,8, and *bāṭaḥ*, 'trust', I Chron.5.20; II Chron.32.10.

78. Cf. the verb *kāna'*, niphal, 'humble oneself', II Chron.7.14; 12.6f.,12; 30.11; 32.26; 33.12,19,23; 34.27; negatively 33.23; 36.12; it occurs fourteen times in all. The starting point is possible the exemplary behaviour of Josiah, II Kings 22.19.

79. See above, 513ff.

80. See above, 514f.

81. Cf. the often-noted Chronistic reinterpretations and periodizations which are meant to make the conduct and fate of each king match: e.g. the deletion of all rebellions and failures from the reigns of David and Solomon, the favoured builders of the temple (cf. e.g. I Chron.29.20ff. with I Kings 1f.), the division of the rule of Asa into a happy (II Chron.14; 15.1-19) and an unhappy period (16) in order to be able to evaluate both his reform of the cult (I Kings 15.12-15) and the wars with Baasha and his illness (II Kings 15.16, 23), or the introduction of a conversion of Manasseh (II Chron.33.10-13) to give an explanation for his long and quite successful reign (cf. the building work in v.14). It is not the concept of retribution as such which is a special feature of Chronicles – this can already be found in DtrG – but the way in which it is focussed on the individual, thus already, rightly, von Rad, *Geschichtsbild*, 11-13 (with pertinent references to Job) and Noth, *Chronicler*, 98f.

82. Thus for example for the history of the northern kingdom the 'sin of Jeroboam', which, according to the Deuteronomistic conception, brought the downfall of the rump state over a period of two hundred years (I Kings 14.14-16; II Kings 17.22f.) and could not even be done away with by Jehu's revolution (II Kings 10.30f); and for the history of the southern kingdom the fearful 'sin of Manasseh' which dragged Judah into the abyss after around 100 years – despite Josiah's reform of the cult.

83. II Chron.14.2f.; 17.3f.; 33.15; 34.3-7,33, etc.

84. Thus the most comprehensive Chronistic term for sin (*mā'al*, I Chron.5.25; 9.1; 10.13; II Chron.12.2; 26.16,18; 28.22; 29.6,19; 30.7; 36.14), which here has both a sacral legal and a personal aspect, cf. Johnstone, 'Guilt', 116ff.

85. Thus as an innovation compared with DtrG, II Chron.12.1; 18.1; 25.19; 26.16; 32.25f. in contrast to a humble and pious attitude. According to Isaiah (30.1ff.; 31.1ff.) relying on foreign covenant partners (II Chron.16.7; 19.2; 20.37; 28.16; 32.31) is also hybris.

86. This is also the reason why the Chronistic historians disputed the derivation of the exile from the sins of Manasseh in DtrG; in their view it was only the punishment for the sins of the generation living directly before it (II Chron.36.11ff.). And this is the reason why – in contrast to DtrG – they differentiate between a terse condemnation of the state and cultic independence of the northern kingdom (cf. II Chron.13.4-12 and their passing over of the state [!] history of the northern kingdom) and a conditionally positive, welcoming attitude towards its population (II Chron.11.13-17; 15.9; 19.4; 28.9ff.,30; 34.6,9,21; 35.18).

87. See above, 538f.; interestingly, Oeming describes I Chron.1-9 as 'literature by scribes for scribes' (*Israel*, 206), but does not put this insight to sociological use, seeking rather to locate the author(s) of Chronicles traditionally among the circle of levitical Jerusalem temple singers (ibid., 46).

88. Thus Willi, *Chronik*, 177, following Rosenzweig. Willi has impressively worked out the interpretetative character of Chronicles; but he is wrong to conclude (293) that it therefore has no reference to the present. Then as now exegesis is always concerned with present interests!

89. According to Oeming, *Israel*, 46 n.46, scholars are still not agreed.

90. Cf. only II Chron.29.34; 30.22.

91. Thus clearly II Chron.29.34; 30.17; 35.3-6,11ff.

92. Cf. I Chron.13.1,4; 28.1ff; II Chron.30.2,4,23.

93. Cf. II Chron.29.34; 30.3,15 (read 'levitical priests').

94. The only social conflict which is taken over from DtrG is the revolt of the north against Rehoboam in II Chron.10.1-19; however, there is no justification at all for it in Chronicles since there is no previous mention of Israelite forced labour under Solomon (II Chron.2.16f. knows only foreigners as forced labourers, as opposed to I Kings 5.27-30) and it is therefore commented on in II Chron.13.7 as a malicious quarrel. Accordingly, in II Chron.33 the social sin of Manasseh in II Kings 21.16 is also omitted.

95. There is emphasis on it in I Chron.12.41; 15.25; 29.9,17,22; II Chron.15.15; 20.27; 29.30,36; 30.21-26.

96. Cf. II Chron.30.24; 35.7-9.

97. Thus rightly already Noth, *Chronicler*, 99ff., and again Oeming, *Israel*, 45.

98. Thus e.g. by Mosis, *Untersuchungen*, 15, etc.; Williamson, *Israel*, 24, 87ff.; Braun, 'Reconsideration', 87ff.; Japhet, *Ideology*, 325ff. Welten, *Geschichte*, 172f., is restrained.

99. Cf. I Chron.5.1ff.,7; the authors mentioned in n.98 have shown this clearly enough.

100. II Chron.12.6; 15.9; 19.4; 28.9-15; 30.25.

101. II Chron.30.1ff.

102. II Chron.31.1ff.; 34.6,9,21; 35.18.

103. II Chron.7.1ff.; 30.25f.

104. I Chron.22.9,18; 23.25; II Chron.14.5,6; 15.15; 17.7-11; 20.29f.

105. Thus rightly Williamson, 'Eschatology', and Japhet, *Ideology*, 493ff., esp.499, against von Rad et al. (*Geschichtsbild*, 135). The attitude of the Chroniclers to the Davidides is 'royalistic' (Williamson, 'Eschatology', 154), not messianic.

106. See above, 535f.

107. Cf. Welten, *Geschichte*, 110-13.

108. This contribution of the Chronistic historians has been evaluated above all by Ackroyd, 'Theology', 108ff.; cf. also Johnstone, 'Chronicles', 13f.

6.3 Torah piety

1. Deissler, *Psalm*, 288-91.

2. E.g. by Wolff, 'Psalm 1', 387f.; Meinhold, 'Überlegungen', 123.

3. For 19.1-7 cf. 119.89-91; for 19.8bβ cf. 119.130; for 19.9aα cf. 119.137; for 19.10aα cf. 119.140; for 19.10aβ cf. 119.89 etc.; for 19.10bα cf. 119.142 etc.; for 19.11a cf. 119.127; for 19.11b cf. 119.103; for *'eqeb* 19.12 cf. 119.37, 112; for *š*e*gi'ā* 19.13 cf. 119.67, 118: for the designation of the wicked as *zēdīm* 19.14 cf. 11.21, etc.; for dedication 19.15 cf. 119.108; in addition, if one allows the conjecture *'imrā* in v.10, Ps.19 uses almost the same synonyms for Torah as Ps.119. Probably the old theory of Müller (1898) that Ps.119 is a worked-out version of Ps.19 is no longer tenable, cf. the discussion in Levenson, 'Source', 561f., but the two psalms doubtless come from the same milieu. By contrast the distance of both Psalms from Ps.1 is greater.

4. Cf. Sarna, 'Psalm XIX'; Fishbane, 'Text', 85f.; if Ps.19 is a literary unity,

which has much to be said for it (cf. Fishbane, 'Psalm'; Gese, 'Einheit'; Fischer, 'Psalm'; Meinhold, 'Überlegungen', etc.), then the quotation of earlier material in vv.1-8 is to be assessed in the same way as the inclusion of Aramaic sources or the Nehemiah memoirs in Ezra/Nehemiah.

5. See above, 553; the term was introduced by Willi; Deissler coined the term 'anthological method' for the same thing, *Psalm*, 281, etc.

6. See above, 538ff. and 579f.

7. Thus recently again Levenson, 'Sources', 563ff.

8. Thus the terms *dābār* and *'imrā*, 'word, saying'; in addition to laws the term *mišpāṭ* can also denote the judgment of God, thus certainly Ps.119.84.

9. Ps.119.6(,15),18; Levenson's argument, 'Sources', 375 n.35, that the verb is to be understood in a visionary sense fails to understand the connection between scriptural exegesis and revelation which Ps.119 means (v.8).

10. Ps.119.117.

11. Ps.119.15,23,27,48,78,148; noun vv.97,99.

12. See above, 548ff.

13. Cf. the complicated reflections by Deissler, *Psalm*, 294ff.; Kraus, *Psalms 60-150*, 412ff.; id., 'Gesetzesverständnis', 184ff. Does the hesitation over a clear identification with the Pentateuch derive from a Christian prejudice against 'law' and 'faith in the letter'? Gunkel, *Psalmen*, 2, and many earlier scholars already criticized this.

14. Cf. the priestly category of sins committed unwittingly (*šagi'ā*, *šāgag*, *šāgā*), Ps.19.13; 119.67, 118 and Lev.4.13; 5.18; Num.15.22,28; Ezek.45.20; however, P uses the noun formation *šᵉgāgā* more frequently.

15. See above, 470.

16. Thus a typically Christian prejudice leads Noth, *Laws*, 102ff. astray; however, even the corrective retort by Kraus, 'Freude', 340ff., cannot explain why the concept of covenant is absent from Pss.1; 19; 119; Amir, 'Psalm', 1ff., has demonstrated impressively how strongly dogmatic interests govern the Christian exegesis of the Torah psalms.

17. The explanation of Amir, 'Psalm', 33, that the author of Ps.119 'put aside the national-historical dimension of the Torah to celebrate the eternal character of the Torah' is hardly enough. In vv.89-91 the author virtually attempts to mediate between the pre-existent eternal word of God and the dispositions of God in history.

18. This is impressively worked out by Amir, 'Psalm', 5-10, taking up Gunkel, *Psalmen*; his list can be extended if we note not only the conceptual but also the form-critical reinterpretations.

19. Cf. vv.25,93,154,156 (*ḥāyā* piel + *kᵉ*); with *hiṣṣīl* + *kᵉ* ('save according to' v.17); *qūm* hiphil + *kᵉ* ('raise up according to'), v.28; *sāmak* + *kᵉ* ('support according to'), v.116; *ḥānan* + *kᵉ* ('be gracious according to'); v.58 with a double accusative, 'with', v.29); *zākar* + *kᵉ* ('remember according to'), v.49, also the predicative phrases *yešū'a* + *kᵉ* ('salvation according to'), v.41 and *'āśā ṭōb kᵉ* ('do good according to'), v.65. That means that the whole spectrum of God's caring and saving action is related to the Torah. The thought here is probably of the promises contained in it.

20. So this not just 'external legalism', which is what is always imputed by Christians.

21. At no point in the Torah psalms is it made clear that 'joy in the law' is the expression of an anticipated eschatological reality, as Kraus, 'Freude', 347ff.; id., 'Gesetzesverständnis', 187ff., asserts; moreover the reference to Jer.31.33; Ezek.26.26f. which Krauss brings out in no way runs through it but through Ps.40.8f. and in linguistic terms is markedly thin; there is nothing of a joy in the law in the prophetic passages. This again is a construction governed by Christian interests.

22. Thus taking up the differentiation made by Urbach in the understanding of the Torah among the early Tannaites, cf. Amir, 'Psalm', 15ff.

23. See above, 212f.; cf. the inclusion of Deuteronomic/Deuteronomistic phrases like *bᵉkol lēb*, 'with all the heart', Ps.119.2,10,34,58,69,145; *dābaq*, 'adhere', v.31, cf. Deut.4.4; *'āhab*, 'love', Ps.119.47,97,113,119,127,132,140,163,165,167; cf. Deut.6.5 etc.

24. See above, 513f.

25. Cf. *nāṣar*, 'observe', Ps.119.2,22,(33,)34,56,69,100,115,129,145; *šāmar*, 'follow', vv.4f.,8f.,17,34,44,55,57,63,67,88,101,134,(136,)146,(158,)167,168; *'āśā*, 'do', vv.112,121,166; *yāšar*, piel, 'observe carefully', v.128.

26. Thus rightly Amir, 'Psalm', 16ff.; cf. the new coinages 'way of the commandments', etc., which in Ps.119.27,32,33,35 take the place of the 'way of the pious' in theologized wisdom (cf. e.g. Prov.2.8,20; Ps.101.2 and even in Ps.1.6). The distinction between the ways of life take on a new sharpness by reference to a divine norm instead of being characterized by types of people: the 'false' way and the 'true' way which the individual can choose are abruptly contrasted (Ps.119.29f.).

27. That in v.155 it is said of the wicked that they do not seek God's laws in no way limits the term *dāraš* to a nomistic significance; it can certainly – at least also – be that the wicked do not even care intellectually about the law, thus Amir, 'Psalm', 22, 25ff., against a remark by Heinemann to this effect.

28. See the lists made by Deissler, *Psalm*, passim.

29. See above, 513f.

30. Cf. Ps.119.71 with Prov.3.12; Job 5.17; 22.2; 36.10ff.

31. Cf. Ps.119.21,78,84,121,155, etc., say, with the speeches by the friends in the book of Job.

32. Cf. Ps.119.71,75,176 with Job 5.1f.,8,17; 22.29; here the Torah piety also corresponds to the ideal of piety in the books of Chronicles, cf.Ps.119.19 with I Chron.29.15, and above, 514ff.

33. Thus wrongly Amir, 'Psalm', 3; nor does *ḥāsīd*, 'pious', occur, so it is inaccurate to call the poet of Ps.119 a 'spokesman of the pious', as Gunkel, *Psalmen*, 515, does. The neutral self-designation 'your servant' predominates, Ps.19.12; 119.23,38,49,65,84,122,176.

34. The scribe Jesus Sirach seems to have had such an experience, see Sirach 33.16f., but the verbose praise of his profession (38.24-39.11) shows that its recognition was still not undisputed at the beginning of the second century and its success consisted more in ideal values, cf.also Ps.119.36,72,127.

35. See above, 521f. and Ps.119.43, and often, 126,132,141,151.

36. Cf. the designations of the wicked as *śārīm* ('official, leader'), Ps.119.23,161, and *'šq* ('oppressor'), vv.121f., 134; for the confrontation in the fifth and fourth centuries see above, 499ff.

37. Cf. the new characterization of the wicked as *zēdīm*, 'insolent', which apart from Ps.86.14 occurs only in the Torah psalms: Ps.19.14; 119.21,31,69,78,85,122.

38. They expect an improvement – like the lower-class circles – only from Yahweh's judgment on the wicked (Ps.119.126).

39. See above, 501ff.

6.4 The late prophetic and apocalyptic theology of resistance

1. Thus forthrightly, sparking off more recent discussion, von Rad, *Theology* II (1965), 301ff.; otherwise, von der Osten-Sacken, *Apokalyptik*, 634; cf. the account of the literature in Schreiner, 'Bewegung', 234ff.; Koch, *Daniel*, 171-6.

2. Cf. Ezek.1-3; 8-11; 40ff.; Zech.1.7-15; 2.1-4,5-9; 4.1-6, 10-14; 5.1-4,5-11; 6.1-4 with Dan.7; 8; 10-12; I Enoch 14-16; 17-19; 21ff.; 85.2ff.; cf. the careful investigation by Koch, 'Visionsbericht', 414ff.

3. Cf. Ezek.8.2ff.; 40.3ff; Zech.1.8ff.; 2.7f.; 4.4f.; 5.1of.; 6.4ff.; with Dan.7.16ff.; 8.15ff.; 9.21ff.; 10.5ff.; I Enoch 14.25ff.; 21.5ff.

4. Zech.11.4-16 with Dan.8; I Enoch 85-90.

5. Cf. Ezek.38f.; Joel 4.1ff.; Zech.14.2f.,12; with I Enoch 90.17-19; Dan.12.1.

6. Cf. e.g. Micah 1.2-9 with I Enoch 1.3-9, where Micah 3 is explicitly cited.

7. Cf. Isa.52.7; Zech.9.9f.; 14.5b,9; Isa.24.23; with Dan.2.44f.; 7.14; I Enoch 25.3; 90.29f.; 91.13.

8. Here mention should be made above all with Lebram, 'Apokalyptik', 520f., of the technical method of revelation consisting of 'synchronization', which in an indirect coded way demonstrates pseudonymous regularities in the course of the world on the basis of which readers can determine through their own reflection their position in the course of world history as being shortly before the dawn of the end-time.

9. Thus above all by Hanson, *Dawn*, and – in a more differentiated way – Gese, 'Anfang'; Stegemann, 'Bedeutung', 498ff. rightly attacks this, making a sharp – perhaps too sharp (cf. e.g. 507) distinction between eschatology, i.e. the expectation of a future 'turn for the better' and apocalyptic, i.e. the literary communication of 'heavenly revealed knowledge'.

10. Cf. Stegemann, 'Bedeutung', 502ff., and the editions of Milik, *Enoch*, and Beyer, *Texte*, 223-71; according to Milik, the earliest manuscript 4QEnª which already contains the complicated formation of tradition from the 'Book of Watchers' (fragments preserved from chs.1-11), comes from the first half of the second century; according to Beyer from the years around 170 BCE.

11. Nickelsburg, 'Apocalyptic', 391, conjectures the time of the Diadochi for the earliest part, I Enoch 6.10, etc.; Kvanvig, *Roots*, 97, also advances the same argument; Milik, *Enoch*, 27, wants to see the whole 'Book of Watchers' (1-36) completed in the middle of the third century.

12. Thus e.g. Gese, 'Anfang', 220.

13. It is certainly no solution of the problem for Hanson to seek to bring the whole of eschatological prophecy into the fifth and beginning of the fourth centuries so as to make the apocalyptic tradition beginning with I Enoch 6-11 appear at the end of the third century as its continuation (*Dawn*, 440f.).

14. Plöger, *Theocracy*, 108ff.; Hanson, *Dawn*, 427ff.; cf. also Hengel, *Judaism* (6.1), 175ff.

15. See above, 437f.

16. See above, 454f.; Gese, 'Anfang', 221, attacks Plöger's theory, pointing out that Zechariah was a member of the 'priestly aristocracy': 'Apocalyptic is first put forward by a personality than whom it is hard to imagine anyone so to speak more official'; but he is then not only illegitimately broadening the term apocalyptic, but also failing to recognize that it was the failure of the officially acknowledged proclamation of Haggai and Zechariah which ushered in the eschatologizing of prophecy and again forced it to the margins of society.

17. See above, 454ff., and the poverty of the poor that goes with it, 517ff.

18. Cf. Mal.2.17; 3.5; 3.13-21; Isa.29.17-24; 56.9-57.21; also, probably from a rather later time, Isa.59; 65f.

19. Not clearly for Zech.9-11, 12-14, where the social terminology is absent; nevertheless an oppositional attitude to leading political circles can be recognized, see below, 570ff.

20. Cf. Nickelsburg, 'Social Aspects', 650, and below, 594ff.

21. A priestly origin has been assumed especially for the 'astronomical book' of the Enoch cycle (I Enoch 72-82), but in Qumran it is a scroll of its own (4QEnAstr) – much longer than the Ethiopic text, cf. Stegemann, 'Bedeutung', 504. Hultgaard sees apocalyptic literature from circles of the Zadokide priests in the Apocrypha of Levi and Amram, the Book of Jubilees and the Book of Noah ('Judentum', 548ff.); Lebram, 'Apokalyptik', 523f., etc., would also want to claim a priestly origin for the Hebrew book of Daniel, and Lampe, 'Apokalyptiker', 91, also for the 'Animal Apocalypse' of the book of Enoch (I Enoch 90-95), but the arguments are not compelling, see below, 590f. The arguments of Kvanvig, *Roots*, 330ff., for a levitical origin of the Enoch literature are even more fanciful. Koch contemplates a 'class of itinerant preachers' comparable to the Iranian magi 'with apocalyptic scribal learning and their own experiences of revelation' (*Daniel*, 178) as tradents of the book of Daniel, but no priestly interests are to be discerned at least in its Aramaic part. Thus there is something to be said for differentiating between lay and priestly scribal groups of tradents, even if the demarcation is not yet completely clear.

22. Here we may well think of the Hasidim, but, as will emerge, in a more differentiated way than usually happens; except that against Plöger, Hengel, Hanson and others, these are not to be defined as a 'conventicle' but as an influential group of pious scribes, see above, 538ff.

23. But this first happened after the failure of the Jewish revolt in 70 CE, so that the apocalyptic literature was able to develop a broad influence over 300 years.

24. There are no reasons for deleting 'your sons, Yawan' as a dittography, as Hanson, *Dawn*, 298, does, to maintain its early dating, cf. Saebø, *Sacharja*, 57f., 193f.; Willi-Plein, *Prophetie*, 11.

25. Elliger, 'Zeugnis', 107f.; cf. in 11.14 the allusion to the cultic separation of the Samarians, see above, 523.

26. Cf. Willi-Plein, *Prophetie*, 105ff., between 332 and 320; similarly Gese, 'Anfang', 224f. and others; for the discussion of research, cf. Hanson, *Dawn*, 281ff.

27. Cf. Zech.12.8 – 9.8; 12.6, 7 – 9.7; 12.8 – 9.15 and Willi-Plein, *Prophetie*,

95ff.; his somewhat hesitant decision, 103f., on the basis of this and other references back, that 9-11 and 12-14 go together, is not at all convincing.

28. Cf. the new heading in 12.1 and the explanatory statement of what will happen 'on this day' of the eschatological turning-point envisaged in ch.9 (12.3,4,6,8,9,11; 13.1,2,4,8; 14.1,6,8,9,12,13,15,16,17,20,21). Here in keeping with the heading ('on Israel') 12.9-13.9 develops the inner purification (cf.10.1f.), and ch.14 the outer purification on the breakthrough of Yahweh's kingly rule (cf.9.7f.).

29. The earliest parts of the chapter are the poem about the subjection and the future bringing of the rest of the nations to Yahweh in 9.18 and the word of salvation about the establishment of Messianic rule on Zion in 9.9f. This nucleus has been expanded several times by explanations: 9.11f. adds the aspect of the liberation of the captives of Zion; 9.13f. the conquering of the world power which Yahweh had used formerly; 9.14-17 rounds the whole passage off by taking up the two aspects of 9.1-10, the conquering of the powers and the preservation of their victims.

30. See above, 419f., 424f.

31. Thus in the LXX reading in v.10; in making Yahweh himself the subject, MT is merely showing that the king of v.9 only represents Yahweh's coming kingdom.

32. Thus Dan.7.13f., see below, 586f.

33. Zech.10.3 leaves it vague whether foreign or native rulers are meant; the verse quotes Jer.23.2, which is directed against its own kings, but opposes these to 'his flock'. 11.1-3 puts in a sequence the judgment on the mighty cedars of Lebanon (= world rulers) and the lament of the shepherds/lions (= potentates dependent on them). In 11.4-16 the rulers of the world are again meant by the shepherds, and in 11.17 the 'worthless shepherd who abandons his flock' is probably again a reference to the ruling class of Judah.

34. Similarly already the lower-class prophecy of the fifth century, see above, 502f. and the piety of the poor, see above, 518ff.

35. See below, 581f., 591.

36. The annihilation of three shepherds in a month and the melting of the thirty pieces of silver in the temple (v.13) remain particularly obscure; cf. e.g. the divergent interpretations by Willi-Plein, *Prophetie*, 52-6, 113-16, and Gese, 'Nachtrag'.

37. Cf. then generally in apocalyptic, Dan.2.31ff.; 7.2ff.; I Enoch 90.1ff., see below, 586.

38. One could interpret the three shepherds (v.8) in this way: their annihilation 'in one month' need not tell against this, cf. the notion of the destruction of all the eastern empires at the same time in Dan.2.44; 7.11f.

39. Read $k^e na^{'a} niyy\bar{e}\ ha\d{s}\d{s}\bar{o}'n$ with LXX instead of MT 'most wretched of the sheep', despite the objections by Willi-Plein, *Prophetie*, 21f.; 'Canaanites' in the sense of traders, cf. Isa.23.8 etc. She is right that an Israelite group must be meant in v.11 (ibid., 54f.); however, this is not the lower class ('poorest'), in connection with which the criticism of vv.12f. would be incomprehensible, but the upper class, 'for whom' Yahweh sees to the delegation of rule (v.7); for the juxtaposition of traders and shepherds see also v.5.

40. $d^e bar\ yhwh$ in 11.11, as in 9.1, denotes the word of God of eschatological

prophecy which bring about the historical upheaval. Therefore Yahweh and the prophetic group can be identified in the symbolic action in vv.12ff.

41. See above, 546f.

42. See above, 550.

43. Cf. Dan.2.31ff.; 7.2ff. and even, with a similar metaphor, Dan.8 and I Enoch 85-90. Both times the concealment has a pedagogical function, but the aims differ: if in Zech.11.4f. it is meant to serve to move the readers to an insight into their guilt, in apocalyptic it is meant to define their position in a course of history which is necessarily moving towards a goal.

44. Unfortunately we do not know what concrete conflicts are referred to in 12.9-14; 13.2-6; cf. the markedly different interpretations in the literature.

45. Zech 13.1,2.

46. Zech.14.1-3 deliberately plays on the contrasting meaning of the 'day of Yahweh' as a day of victory (Isa.9.3; 28.21) and a day of God's devastating judgment (Amos 5.18-20; Lam.1.12; 2.1, 21f.; Ezek.30.3; Joel 1.15; 2.1,11 etc.); in the background are both the tradition of the Yahweh war and notions of theophany (Zeph.1.7,14), cf. von Rad, *Theology* II, 119-25.

47. See above, 136f.

48. See above, 537f.; a relationship of rivalry between Judah and Jerusalem can also be recognized in 12.2-7.

49. Cf. I Enoch 6-11; 90; Dan.7.7f.; 8.19ff.; 9.25ff.; 11.21ff.; 12.1 and Mark 13.

50. Plöger, *Theocracy*, 56.

51. Kaiser, *Isaiah*, 182f.

52. For the 'fall of the angels' in Isa.24.21f. cf. I Enoch 10.12f.; 19.1 etc.; for the resurrection Isa.26.19; (25.8,) cf. I Enoch 22.12f.; Dan.12.2; I Enoch 92.3; 103.4; cf. 91.10.

53. Cf. the surveys of research in Kaiser, *Isaiah*, 173-9, and Wildberger, *Jesaja*, 893-6.

54. Plöger, *Theocracy*, 59ff.; Kaiser, *Isaiah*, 192f., and Wildberger, *Jesaja*, 904, all assign 24.21-23 and 25.6-10a to a secondary stratum. Plöger, *Theocracy*, 73f., emphasizes the special position of Isa.27; it is distinguished in form from chs.24-26 by the introductory formulae 'on that day' etc. (vv.1,2,12,13) and in content by the lack of social terminology; instead of this the social conflict is again turned back to the controversy between Israel and the nations. It seems to be an extension of Isa.24-26.

55. This is true above all of the updating of the controversy on Moab, 25.10bf., bracketed through v.12 with 26.5, which is difficult to interpret.

56. The secondary stratum 24.21-23; 25.6-8 is expressly tied in through 25.9f. in the style of 26.7-18; the hymns of 25.1-5, 26.1-8 breathe the same spirit, regardless of what literary context one may give them.

57. Thus the reading of LXX; the reading of MT, *zārīm*, foreigners, may be connected with ch.27 through reinterpretation in national terms.

58. See above, 505f., 521f.

59. Verse 14a, which is difficult to understand in the context, is possibly a quotation of the 'lords' who mock the eschatological expectations of the pious – very much in line with the tradition.

60. Verse 18bβ need not be understood purely metaphorically (in the sense of a

meaningless birth), as Plöger, *Theocracy*, 67, and Wildberger, *Jesaja*, 994, understand it, but is a specific reference to the fall of the opponents mentioned in v.9 (for *nāpal* in this sense cf. 24.18,20); in that case *yᵉšūʿōt* in v.18aβ does not mean 'salvation' but specifically the 'victories' which the impotent pious cannot achieve despite all their prayers.

61. See above, 521.

62. It only comes into view again in ch.27; in chs.24-26 of the Israelite traditions of salvation only Jerusalem plays a role, but that is already transcended in the direction of the heavenly Jerusalem (24.23; 25.6,7,10a; 26.1-3).

63. Cf. I Enoch 5; 10.16ff.; 19; 22; 93.1-10 + 91.11-17; Dan.7.13f.; and even more strongly Dan.11f.

64. Cf. the eschatological songs of praise in 24.14-15aα; 25.1-5; 26.1-6; the lamentations, 24.16aβ; 26.7-18 and the confessions of confidence in 25.9-10a; 26.19.

65. Those who especially in the so-called 'city songs' consistently and misleadingly encouraged the expectation of a real event are no more to be referred to the past than are the perfects in the hymns of praise in the book of Deutero-Isaiah.

66. Thus explicitly in the eschatological interpretation of Gen.6-9.

67. MT reads *mᵉrom ʿam-hāʾāreṣ*; there is no occasion to amend the text ('the heights with the earth', thus Kaiser, Wildberger), as is often done.

68. See above, 536.

69. See above, 537f.

70. Cf. Deut.32.8; Dan.8.13ff.; 10.13, 20f., and probably also the seventy shepherds of I Enoch 89.55ff.

71. Thus especially in the Enoch tradition, starting from Gen.6.1-4.

72. The liberation of Israel from its ruling class is hinted at in the fact that in Isa.24.23 the revelation of the glory of Yahweh is to take place before the elders as in the early, pre-state, period (Ex.24.1,9f.).

73. This is what is meant by the 'veiled face ' in v.7; cf. II Sam.15.30; 19.5; Jer.14.3f.; Esther 6.12; cf. Kaiser, *Isaiah*, 201.

74. Verse 8aα is clearly secondary in the context, cf. Kaiser, *Isaiah*, 201, etc.

75. Cf. vv.20f., 9; as such it cannot be an element of the text (against Kaiser, *Isaiah*, 201). In that case 'my bodies' alongside 'your dead' means that the dead are not only related to God but at the same time are also members of the community.

76. The notion that God's dew makes the earth fertile, so that it gives birth to the spirits of the dead as new people, recalls Sumero-Babylonian notions of the creation of human beings; cf. e,g, the 'Praise of the Mattock', RT 101f., and the 'KAR 4 Myth', Pettinato, *Menschenbild*, 74-82.

77. See above, 564f.

78. I Enoch 19.3 has clear characteristics of a conclusion, cf. Nickelsburg, 'Apocalyptic', 390; Milik, *Enoch*, 25f.; Uhlig, 'Henochbuch', 506.

79. Kvanvig, *Roots*, 279.

80. Nickelsburg, 'Apocalyptic', 391.

81. Ibid., 384ff.; Nickelsburg also adds 10.9f., but there is no real doublet to v.15.

82. The thought is usually of the reign of Alexander Jannaeus, 103-76 BCE; cf. Nickelsburg, 'Social Aspects', 651.

83. It includes Dan.2.1-7abα, 9f.,11*,13-19,22a,23,26abα,27f.; the other verses

of ch.7 belong to an updating revision of the Maccabean crisis. It is uncertain whether 2.1 forms the beginning or was preceded by an introduction which was suppressed when ch.1 was put in front of it; probably 2.14a was later translated into Hebrew to smoothe over the linguistic transition, see Albertz, *Gott des Daniel*, 170ff.

84. Ibid., 155ff.

85. Others of the texts which stand close to the apocalypses belong between the second main phase and the subsequent phase – the book of Jubilees, the Testament of Levi, the Amram Apocryphon (4QAmram) and the first column of the War Scroll (1QM 1), and perhaps the Testament of Moses, which can only be mentioned in passing here.

86. See Albertz, *Gott des Daniel*, 165-7.

87. Ibid., 168f.

88. Cf. Isa.44.5; 45.18-25; 55.5; 56.3,6; 66.18,20; Zech.2.15; 8.20-22; 14.16-21.

89. Cf. the similarly optimistic perspective in Tobit 14.6f. and Aristeas 172ff.; the conception of the future in the book of Tobit, which moves very much along the lines of eschatological prophecy, makes improbable the assumption that apocalyptic (with all the Iranian influences) began from the Babylonian Diaspora, cf. Hultgaard, 'Judentum', 555, against Kvanvig, *Roots*, 154ff.

90. Cf. the names (Epiphanes, Soter, etc.) with which they adorned themselves; for the claim to divine descent cf. Nickelsburg, 'Apocalyptic', 396f.; Bartelmus, *Heroentum*, 175f., and the literature given there.

91. Cf. Bartelmus, *Heroentum*, 60-78, 175ff.

92. Cf. I Enoch 93.2,10; as the basic prophetic passage proves (*ṣaddīqīm, ṣedeq*), the Aramaic *qōšeṭ*, 'truth', in the book of Enoch also has the sound of 'righteousness' and is therefore quite appropriately rendered *dikaiosune* in the Greek edition.

93. Probably resorting to the Greek tradition of the battle of the Titans or giants, cf. especially the theme that the divine fathers had to watch the annihilation of their semi-divine children, cf. Nickelsburg, 'Apocalyptic', 395f.

94. I Enoch 10.2,14; 22.4; 91.15; cf. Dan.8.17,19; 11.27,35,40.

95. Here the text envisages two stages of judgment: 1. the self-annihilation of the giants and binding of the fallen angels (10.12); 2. the final condemnation and punishment in the fiery abyss (10.13f.).

96. For this apocalyptic method of revelation see Lebram, 'Apocalyptic', 520f.

97. Cf. the localizing of the fall of the angels on Hermon (6.6), and in addition that of the vision of Enoch in Abel-main (Abel-beth-Maacah), 13.7.9.

98. See Nickelsburg, 'Apocalyptic', 399f.

99. Cf. the extensive reflections which Kvanvig, *Roots*, has offered here.

100. Cf. Num.23f.; Deut.33; Ezek.1-3; 8-11; 37; 40ff.; Zech.1-6.

101. Wacker, *Weltordnung*, 144-75, notes an interweaving of Israelite, Babylonian and Greek notions and in particular draws attention to the close connections with the Greek notions of Hades.

102. This is identified with the Ben-Hinnom valley (27.1f.).

103. For the interesting phenomenon that it is the anti-Hellenistic apocalyptic battle literature that makes use of Greek notions see Wacker, *Weltordnung*, 211-18, 308-15.

104. Cf. I Enoch 20.8; 91.10; 92.3; 103.4 and Isa.26.19.

105. For the difficulties of text and interpretation caused by the division into groups in I Enoch 22 cf. Wacker, *Weltordnung*, 178ff.

106. See above, 552.

107. For detail see Albertz, *Gott des Daniel*, 178-82, etc.

108. Only in Dan.3.28f does he leave a remnant.

109. Cf. also the detailed demonstration in Albertz, *Gott des Daniel*, 59ff. etc.

110. Thus also in Ps.145, a psalm which probably comes from a community of the pious (*hᵃsîdîm*, v.10) and on the theology of which the author demonstrably draws (Ps.145.13a = Dan.3.33b), see Albertz, *Gott des Daniel*, 187f.

111. Cf. Hultgaard, 'Judentum', 524.

112. Ibid., 525.

113. Kvanvig, *Roots*, 345-53, lists no less than eighteen different theories put forward by scholars.

114. Thus in I Enoch 37-71; IV Ezra 13 and the New Testament.

115. Cf. the discussion in Kvanvig, *Roots*, 571-93; Albertz, *Gott des Daniel*, 192f.

116. There is no reason to treat *'am*, 'people', as an addition.

117. Cf. Dan.4.14, where their heavenly counterpart is also envisaged.

118. Thus the characterization of the kingly rule of God in the 'basic text' Ps.145.13; cf. also Zech 9.9f.

119. For details see above, 540ff.

120. Leaving aside the scatterings in related genres of literature like Jub.23, TestLevi, TestMose, 4QAmram, 1QM1.

121. See above, 542f.; there could be a reflection of this distancing in Jub.23.21, cf. Hengel, *Judaism* (6.1), 226. The battle theology of the Hasidim is probably also reflected in Ps.149, see Nickelsburg, 'Social Aspects', 648.

122. See above, 538f., 565f.

123. Cf. already the hints in Hengel, *Judaism*, 327; it is then clearly worked out by Collins, 'Apocalyptic Vision', 205-18; Lampe, 'Apokalyptiker', 75-93; Nickelsburg, 'Social Aspects', 645-8. But Lampe's conjecture that the Animal Apocalypse and the book of Daniel should be assigned to completely different circles of tradents (see below, n.133) is not convincing.

124. For the need to distinguish between the Hasidaeans of I Macc.2.42 and the groups mentioned in 2.29-38, see above, 538f.

125. For the symbolism cf. Zech.11.4-17; the coded account has a pedagogical function in compelling readers as they decipher it to reflect on history and their situation in it and to adopt the interpretation of history offered as 'illumination'.

126. See above, 580ff.; such an interpretation of I Enoch 90.6-8 in terms of the first main phase of apocalyptic ('Book of Watchers') makes the synchronization of the 'Animal Apocalypse' considerably easier.

127. Cf. I. Macc.3.18-22; 4.8-11, etc.

128. See below, 590ff.

129. The 'Animal Apocalypse' in 85.2-90.41 has been incorporated into the 'Dream Book'(I Enoch 83-90) by compositional brackets at 85.1 and 90.42.

130. Thus in the adoption of the early apocalyptic political protest, I Enoch 6-11.

131. Cf. Uhlig, 'Henochbuch', 693.

132. We are to understand from this military interest that the 'Animal Apocalypse'

emphasizes the early monarchy (alongside the exodus) as the time of salvation (I Enoch 89.41-50); if we leave aside the amazingly positive evaluation of Saul (v.43), the Hasidic evaluation corresponded completely with that of DtrG (see above, 392ff.) and Chronicles (see above, 548ff.).

133. This tells against the assumption of Lampe, 'Apokalyptiker', 90ff., that the Animal Apocalypse comes from (lowly) priestly circles. His attempt to attribute the non-violent resistance to the scribes (Hebrew book of Daniel, Apocalypse of Weeks) but the armed resistance to the country priests (Animal Apocalypse, 1QM1), 'learned exegetes are men of the pen... the cudgel lies better in the hands of the country priests' (92) is too schematic. The latter is perhaps true of 1QM1, but not of the learned Enoch apocalypse.

134. Thus for example the rather late book of Jubilees, cf. Jub.1.10,17,27,29; 23.21.

135. The remarkable description of Dan.11.33f., which gives the *maśkīlīm* such a prominent place in the religious political controversy, can only be explained from an internal dispute of the scribes over the right option.

136. For this meaning of *kāšal* see Lebram, 'Piety', 182.

137. Cf. e.g. the intervention in the calendar (Dan.7.25; 8.10), the abolition of the Tamid sacrifice (8.11f.; 9.27; 11.31), the desecration of the sanctuary (9.26; 11.31) and the deposition of the legitimate high priest (9.26; 11.22). Here it is interesting that the Daniel apocalyptists by no means see Antiochus IV's blasphemy as being only against their own religion; for them it is also against other Near Eastern Hellenistic cults (11.36-39).

138. But this would mean that we cannot infer, as Lebram, 'Apocalyptic', 523f., does, a priestly origin. Texts like 4QAmram, 1QM 1, Jubilees show what priestly apocalypses look like.

139. See above, 585f.

140. Cf. the seventy shepherds of the foreign rule (I Enoch 89.5ff.), which are divided by periods into groups of 2 x 23 (89.65-70: Assyrian/Babylonian rule; 90.1-5, Greek/Ptolemaean rule) and 2 x 12 (89.71-77, Persian rule; 90.6ff., Seleucid rule): the background is probably Jeremiah's announcement of the seventy years of slavery (Jer.25.11).

141. See the discussion in Koch, *Daniel*, 149-57.

142. See the connection between *qēṣ*, end, and *mōʿēd*, 'point of time, date', in Dan.8.19 and 11.27, 35.

143. The calculations vary a little: 8.14, 1150 days; 12.11, 1290 days; 12.12, 1335 days.

144. Cf. 8.17, 19; 11.27,35,49.

145. Cf. historical interpretations of priestly origin like Jubilees, Testament literature like TestLevi, 4QAmram, TestMoses; conventicle instructions like 1QM and CD.

146. See above, 542.

147. See above, 570ff.

148. Against the current dating in the early Maccabean period (cf. e.g. Hengel, *Judaism*, 176), Koch, 'Sabbatstruktur', has proposed a date in the time of John Hyrcanus (134-104 BCE) on the basis of his demonstration that 'weeks' of 490 years (7 x 70) are envisaged. Such a late dating is also suggested by the fact that the

'Apocalypse of Weeks' already depicts an extension of the calculation of world ages in Dan.9.

149. The *terminus ad quem* through 4QEn^g is the middle of the first century BCE; Nickelsburg dates it more closely to the reign of Alexander Jannaeus, 102-76 BCE ('Social Aspects', 651), cf. also Uhlig, 'Henochbuch', 709.

150. Cf. Nickelsburg, 'Message', 326f.

151. Cf. I Enoch 94.6-9; 95.5-7; 96.6-8; 97.8-10; 98.2; 99.12; 100.7; 102.9. etc.

152. Koch, 'Sabbatstruktur', 414ff., 420f.

153. Cf. 94.7,8,9: 95.4,5,7; 96.4,5,6,7,8: 97.7,8; 98.9,11,12,13,14,15; 99.1,2,11,12,13,14,15; 100.7,8,9: cf. Nickelsburg, 'Message', 310f.

154. Cf. just Luke 6.20-26 and Nickelsburg, 'Riches'.

Abbreviations

Abbreviations for journals, series and other scholarly publications are now too numerous to list. For details the reader is referred to the lists in *Theologische Realenzyklopädie*, or S.Schwerter, *Internationales Abkürzungsverzeichnis für Theologie und Grenzgebiete*, 1974. The following list indicates some other relevant abbreviations.

AHw   W.von Soden, *Akkadisches Handwörterbuch* (3 vols.), 1965–81

AOB[2]   H.Gressmann, *Altorientalische Bilder zum Alten Testament*, [2]1927

ANEP   J.B.Pritchard, *Ancient Near Eastern Pictures Relating to the Old Testament*, 1969

ANET   J.B.Pritchard, *Ancient Near Eastern Texts Relating to the Old Testament*, [3]1969

AP   A.E.Cowley, *Aramaic Papyri of the Fifth Century BC*, 1923

ARAB   D.Luckenbill, *Ancient Records of Assyria and Babylonia* (2 vols), 1927

ARM   *Archives royales de Mari*

BATAJ   Beiträge zur Erforschung des Alten Testaments und des antiken Judentums

BHK   *Biblia Hebraica*, ed. R.Kittel, [3]1937 = 1951

BHS   *Biblia Hebraica Stuttgartensia*, [3]1987

BRL[2]   K.Galling (ed.), *Biblische Reallexikon*, HAT I.1, [2]1977

BWL   W.G.Lambert, *Babylonian Wisdom Literature*, 1960 = 1975

CAD   I.J.Gelb, A.Landsberger and L.Oppenheimer (eds.), *The Assyrian Dictionary of the University of Chicago*, 1964ff.

cj   conjectured text

CTA   A.Herdner, *Corpus des tablettes en cunéiform alphabétiques. Découvertes à Ras-Shamra-Ugarit de 1929–1939* (2 vols), 1963

Dtr   Deuteronomists

DtrG   Deuteronomistic history

EAE   M.Avi-Yona and E.Stern, *Encyclopedia of Archaeological Excavations in the Holy Land* (4 vols), 1975–8

EdF   Erträge der Forschung

FS   Festschrift

Gadd   C.J.Gadd, 'Tablets from Kirkuk', *RA* 23, 1926, 49–161

HSS	Harvard Semitic Series
JEN	*Joint Expedition with the Iraq Museum at Nuzi*, American Schools of Oriental Research. Publications of the Baghdad School, Texts (6 vols.), 1927–1939
JerD	Deuteronomistic revision of the book of Jeremiah
KAI	H.Donner and W.Röllig, *Kanaanäische und aramäische Inschriften* (3 vols), I, ⁴1979; II, ³1973; III, ³1976
K^D	Pre-priestly composition of the Pentateuch
K^P	Priestly composition of the Pentateuch
KTU	M.Dietrich, O.Loretz and J.Samartín, *Die Keilalphabetischen Texte aus Ugarit*, I, AOAT 24, 1976
LA	W.Helck and W.Westendorf, *Lexikon für Ägyptologie*, 1975ff.
LXX	Septuagint
MT	Massoretic text (Codex Leningradiensis)
NTOA	Novum Testamentum et Orbis Antiquus
P	'Priestly Writing'
par	parallel
r.	reverse
RLA	E.Ebeling et al. (eds.), *Reallexikon für Assyriologie und vorderasiatische Archäologie*, 1932ff.
SAHG	A.Falkenstein and W.von Soden, *Sumerische und akkadische Hymnen und Gebete*, 1953
Sam.	Sameritanus
SBA	Stuttgarter Biblische Aufsatzbände
sing.	singular
Syr	Peshitta (Syriac translation)
Targ	Targum
TGI²	K.Galling (ed.), *Texte zur Geschichte Israels*, ²1968
TUAT	O.Kaiser et al. (eds.), *Texte aus der Umwelt des Alten Testaments*, 1982ff.
TWAT	G.J.Botterweck and H.Ringgren et al. (eds.), *Theologisches Wörterbuch zum Alten Testament*, 1970ff. (translated as *Theological Dictionary of the Old Testament*)
UBL	Ugaritisch-Biblische Literatur
VAB	Vorderasiatische Bibliotek
Vulg.	Vulgate
YBC	Yale Babylonian Collection, New Haven

Index of Biblical References

(Old Testament references are given in the numbering of the Hebrew Bible, which in some cases differs slightly from that of the English translations)

Genesis					
1–11	490	11.9	571, 573	15.1	249, 477, 627
1	633	12–50	27, 28, 29, 35, 39, 42, 250	15.2f.	477
1.1–2.3	634			15.3	627
1.2	416	12	472, 489	15.4a	627
1.26	491	12.1ff.	35, 70	15.4b	627
1.28	491, 634	12.1–4	250	15.5	474
1.31	491, 634	12.1–3	406	15.6	474, 627
2.2f.	410, 634	12.1	406	15.7ff.	474
2.2	634	12.2	406, 607	15.7	473, 627
2.3	634	12.2b	406	15.8	627
2.5–11.9	287	12.3	406	15.9–12	477
2.7	606	12.3b	607	15.15	255
2.24	558	12.6	36, 332, 532	15.17–21	477
4.1ff.	491	12.7	473	15.18	364, 474, 625, 627
4.1–8	474	12.8	36		
4.15	52	12.10–20	34, 36	16.1–6	33
4.25	289	12.16	35	16.5f.	277
5	491	13.4	36	16.7ff.	34
5.1ff.	491	13.5ff.	35	16.7	33
5.22	491	13.5–13	250	16.11	33
5.24	491, 581	13.5	35	16.13	30
6–9	667	13.14–16	405	17	407, 489, 490, 628
6.1–4	578, 667	13.15	365		
6.3	30	13.17	365	17.1	27, 30, 490, 634
6.4	578	13.18	30, 36, 250		
6.9	491, 633	13.53b	251	17.2f.	407
6.12	491	14	253	17.2	491
6.13	492, 579	14.1–11	304	17.6	491, 629
6.17	492	14.12–17	304	17.7	492, 628
7	635	14.17–20	308	17.8	491, 628
7.11	571, 573	14.18–20	295, 300	17.10f.	407
8.13	634	14.18	292, 300, 649	17.12	407
8.21f.	573			17.15ff.	252
8.22	357	14.19	30, 135, 300	17.16	491
9.1	491	14.20	300, 304, 357	17.22	634
9.6	491			17.25	407
9.7	491	14.21–24	304	18	405
9.8ff.	492, 628	14.22	30	18.1–16	250
9.21ff.	287	15	624, 627	18.1–16a	252
10f.	491	15.1–6	252	18.2	491
10	491	15.1f.	627	18.7	35

18.9f.	33	28.11ff.	30	35.20	255
18.10	252	28.13f.	405	35.29	38
18.14	252	28.13	30, 365	37	277
18.20–22a	250	28.15	35, 36, 473	37.12ff.	29, 35
20.7	315	28.16f.	36	36.10	260
21.4	407	28.18	36, 64, 332	36.13	260
21.8ff.	33	28.20ff.	36	38	73, 277
21.13	406	28.20–22	282	38.15	276
21.16ff.	34	28.22	274, 286,	42	30
21.18	406		332	42.26	608
21.20	34, 35	29	30	45.4–11	120
21.32	250	29.31ff.	33	46.1–3	406
21.33	30, 36	30f.	36	46.2f.	35
21.34	250	30.33	277	46.3	406
22	34, 37, 123,	31	37, 39, 251	46.13	30
	255, 282,	31.3	35, 36, 253	46.31–34	258
	406	31.5	30, 405	47.27	491
22.2	649	31.11	406	47.30	255
22.3	608	31.13	30, 144,	48.3f.	491, 628
22.15–18	626		282, 406	48.3	30
22.18b	607	31.16	37	48.4	491
23	628	31.19	37	48.20	607
24	472, 625	31.25–42	277	48.21	35
24.7	626	31.30	38	48.22	253
25–33	251	31.32	37, 38	49	124
25	250	31.34f.	37	49.5–7	58
25.8f.	38	31.42	30, 251, 405	49.8–12	292
25.17	38	31.44	364	49.22–26	292
25.21ff.	250	31.45	36	49.24f.	271
25.22	101	31.51–53	250	49.24	249, 309
26	36	31.53	30, 36, 38,	49.25	30, 31
26.1ff.	250		250, 251	49.29f.	628
26.2f.	35, 406	31.53a	250, 251	49.29	38
26.3	36	32.2f.	36	49.32	249
26.3bb–5	626	32.10	30	49.33	38
26.4	607	32.23–33	35	50.1–14	255
26.8	311	32.25–32	143	50.17	30
26.11	277	32.29	270	50.20	120
26.12f.	29, 35	33.11	324	50.24	472
26.12	324	33.18ff.	532	50.25	473
26.14	35	33.18	143, 270	50.26b	473
26.19ff.	29, 35, 36	33.19	473		
26.22	36	33.20	36, 76, 143,	*Exodus*	
26.24f.	36		270, 271	1–15	258
26.24	30, 35	34	58, 253, 407	1–14	43
26.28	36, 364	34.7	91	1–12	45, 52
26.33	250	34.30	253	1–6	628
27–33	250, 308	35.2ff.	32	1f.	46, 256
27	250, 405	35.4	532	1.1–5	43
27.28	324	35.5	253	1.6	43, 472
28.3	30	35.6f.	270	1.7	491, 634
28.4	491, 628	35.7	30, 144	1.8	472
28.10–22	36	35.9	634	1.9–12	43, 307, 626
28.10–20	532	35.11	30, 491, 629	1.9–11	308
28.10–19	78, 308, 626	35.12	491, 628	1.11–14	44
28.10	33	35.13	634	1.11	44, 256

1.15–2.23	43, 307	3.18	44, 45, 52, 53, 256, 257, 624	5.10	256
1.15f.	45			5.12	46
1.15	258			5.13–19	256
1.16–2.23	43	3.18b	47	5.13–16	256
1.16	258	3.20	626	5.14ff.	45
1.19	45, 258	4.1ff.	49, 256, 634	5.19	142
2.1–3	491	4.1–8.31	474	5.20	43
2.1	258	4.1	47	5.20–21	43, 45
2.6f.	45	4.8	626	6	26, 46, 489
2.6	258	4.9	626	6.1ff.	260
2.7	258	4.10	627	6.1–17	43
2.11–15	142	4.13–16	43, 628	6.2ff.	629
2.11–14	46	4.13	259	6.2f.	490
2.11–13	45	4.18	51	6.2	27, 49
2.11f.	46	4.19–20a	43, 46, 307	6.3	492
2.11	43, 45	4.19	142, 256, 626, 627	6.4	491, 628
2.13	45, 258			6.7	492, 628
2.15ff.	51	4.20a	142, 256, 626, 627	6.9	45, 634
2.15–22	46			6.12	634
2.15	142	4.21	43	6.16	263
2.16	51	4.22f.	606	6.19	263
2.18	51, 257	4.23	53	6.20	263, 278
2.19	45	4.24–26	35, 307, 607	7–14	43
2.22	59	4.25	407	7	43
2.23	43	4.27–30	628	7.1	315
2.23	46, 142, 256	4.27	54	7.13f.	43
2.23a	627	4.29–31	43	7.14–12.39	43
3ff.	489	4.29	44, 253, 624	7.14–16	256
3f.	26, 46, 307, 627	4.31	49, 634	7.15	43
		5	46, 47, 142, 307	7.16	45, 52, 53, 256
3	311				
3.1ff.	53, 54, 256	5.1–2	307	7.17	43, 256, 258, 472
3.1–4.18	43, 142, 256	5.2	258		
3.1–6	51, 54, 257	5.3–19	307	7.20	43
3.1–4	43, 478, 624	5.3f.	626	7.26	53, 256
3.1	51, 52, 54	5.3	256, 257, 258	8	43, 47
3.2	257			8.4	256
3.4	257	5.4	308	8.6	256, 258, 472
3.6	26, 472	5.5	308		
3.6aa	258	5.6	256, 628	8.16	53, 256
3.6ab	258	5.8	256, 307	8.18	256, 258, 472
3.7f.	47, 256	5.15	307		
3.9f.	256	5.17	256	8.21	256
3.10–17	47	5.20–21	307	8.23	256
3.10	47	5.22–6.1	43	9	47
3.12	50, 53, 261, 478, 626	5.1–21	256	9.1	45, 52, 53, 256
		5.1–2	43, 256		
3.13f.	49	5.1	43, 257	9.13	45, 52, 53, 256
3.13	258	5.2	256		
3.14	50, 51, 259	5.3–19	43, 142, 257	9.14	256, 258, 472
3.15f.	472	5.3	45, 52, 53, 142, 256		
3.15	49, 258			9.26	45
3.16–18a	47	5.4	43, 142, 256	9.27	258
3.16	44, 253, 258, 478, 624	5.5	256	9.29	256, 258, 472
		5.6–19	142		
		5.6	256	10.2	256, 258

10.3	45, 52	14.13f.	43	19ff.	42, 43, 53, 54, 60, 356
10.7f.	256	14.13	626	19f.	55, 214, 630
10.11	256	14.14	47	19	33, 53
10.12	256	14.23	253	19.1–19	626
10.31	256	14.25	47	19.1–9	356
11.1–3	43	14.27	47	19.1	55
11.7	258	14.31	49, 474, 626	19.2f.	61
12	35, 43, 410, 548	15–17	66	19.2	55
12.1–14	410	15	26, 43, 299	19.2b	55
12.3–11	253	15.1–8	226	19.3–9	624
12.3f.	410	15.1	299	19.3a	55
12.3	410, 472, 618	15.1a	43	19.3b–8	55, 66
		15.2	30, 50	19.4	474, 626
12.3b	253	15.3	47	19.5f.	487
12.6	410, 656	15.5	363	19.5	365, 472, 474
12.6b	253	15.8	363	19.6	472, 474, 475, 480
12.7a	253	15.13	295		
12.8ff.	410	15.15b–16	624	19.7ba	336
12.8	548	15.17	299, 363	19.8	474
12.8a	253	15.18	298, 363	19.9	55
12.11	426	15.19	43	19.10–19	60
12.11b	253	15.20	315	19.10f.	57
12.12	253	15.21–22	43	19.10	55, 626
12.13	633	15.21	46, 80, 256	19.11a	55
12.15–19	410	15.22–27	66	19.11b	55
12.21–27	253	16f.	55	19.12–13a	55
12.21–27a	626	16	66, 631	19.12f.	626
12.21–23	43	16.4f.	624	19.13b	55
12.21–22	253	16.10f.	631	19.14f.	626
12.21	44, 253, 624	16.25f.	491	19.15	57
12.24–27	253	17f.	43	19.17a	55
12.33f.	253	17	54	19.17b	55
12.38	44	17.1–7	66	19.18	54, 261
12.43ff.	410	17.6	54	19.18–19	55
12.43–50	410	17.8–16	66	19.19	263
13	26, 61, 624	17.8–13	310	19.20–25	55, 356, 626, 628
13.3–16	43	17.15	270		
13.3–10	213, 626	17.16	80	19.20–24	460
13.3	356	18–22.16	183	19.25	263
13.5	626	18	51, 55, 256, 260, 628	20–23	64
13.9	626			20	336
13.11–16	626	18.1ff.	51, 52	20.1–17	55, 60, 214, 356, 475
13.11	626	18.1–12	56, 611		
13.12f.	193	18.1	51	20.1	263, 356
13.14	356	18.3	59	20.2–23.19	182
13.16	626	18.4	30	20.2–17	214
13.17–19	43	18.5	54	20.3	61
13.19	473	18.6–8	346	20.4–6	64
13.21–22	43	18.10f.	260	20.4a	65
13.21	66	18.12	51, 54, 55, 57	20.4b–6	65
14f.	47			20.5	264
14	43, 633	18.13–27	205, 336, 350	20.8–11	409, 410, 608
14.5	46				
14.5a	142, 307	18.27	261	20.8	608
14.11ff.	49	19–24	478		

20.10	282, 608	21.30	184, 326	23.14–19	183, 277,
20.11	410, 491,	22	336		336
	608	22.6f.	88	23.14–17	607
20.12	92	22.7	92	23.14	90, 214
20.18ff.	261, 263	22.8	92	23.15	89, 410
20.18–21	55, 60, 356,	22.10–23.9	626	23.16	89
	626	22.10	88, 92	23.17	89, 91
20.18	263	22.17–19	183	23.19	103, 354
20.21	626	22.17	184	23.19b	184
20.22–		22.18	184	23.20–33	55
23.29	60	22.19	61, 263, 264	23.24	264, 274
20.22–	61, 257,	22.20–26	183	23.29	55
23.19	269, 475	22.20f.	183, 185	24–27	43
20.22f.	55	22.20	183, 185,	24–26	43
20.22	346, 626		257, 277	24	626
20.23–		22.22	185	24.1	55, 56, 475,
23.13	183	22.24	183, 185,		624, 626,
20.23–			358		628, 667
23.19	182	22.25f.	183	24.1b–2	55
20.23–26	183	22.26	185	24.3ff.	66
20.23	335, 626	22.27–30	183	24.3–8	55, 66, 346,
20.23a	184, 336	22.27	78, 183,		474
20.23b	64, 65, 265,		269, 317,	24.3–7	475
	336, 626		625	24.3	55, 474
20.24–26	336, 337	22.28–		24.4	262
20.24	184, 335,	23.12	182	24.5	57, 475
	337	22.28f.	103, 191	24.7f.	365
20.24a	265	22.28	103, 193	24.7	346, 474
20.24b	362	22.28b	103, 192	24.8	55, 261
20.25	193	22.30	182, 183,	24.9–11	55, 56, 261,
20.26	184		184, 335		475, 626,
20.40	283	22.31	184		628
21.1–22.16	92	23.1–9	183	24.9f.	667
21.1	336	23.1–8	184	24.9	624
21.2–22	182	23.1	366	24.10	626
21.2–11	183	23.2bb	358	24.11	57
21.2–6	218, 338	23.3	183, 338	24.12–15a	55
21.2	185	23.4f.	92	24.13	54
21.5f.	161	23.7	183	24.14	624
21.5	359	23.9	183, 185,	24.15b–	
21.6f.	100		257	Lev. 9	630
21.6	92, 161	23.10–19	89, 183	24.15b–18	630
21.7–11	185	23.10–13	182, 183	24.15bf.	631
21.12–17	183	23.10f.	102, 186,	24.16	57, 628, 631
21.13f.	93		629	24.16a	630
21.13	92	23.10f.	185, 217,	24.16b	482, 630
21.14	185		629	24.18b	55
21.20f.	183, 338	23.11	183	24.15b–18	482
21.20	185	23.12	102, 186,	24.15b–18a	55, 56
21.21	185		282, 409,	24.16–18	634
21.23b–25	185		410, 607,	24.17	631
21.23b	338		608	24.25	628
21.24f.	338	23.13	182, 183,	25ff.	132, 483
21.26f.	185, 338		264, 335,	25–Lev. 9	484
21.26	182		336	25–31	55
21.28	326	23.13b	184, 335	25.1ff.	484, 490

25.1–31.17	482
25.1	634
25.3–8	549
25.8ff.	56
25.8	484, 487, 492, 631
25.9	290, 655
25.10–22	621, 628, 632
25.17	655
25.18	632
25.22	484, 631
25.23–30	458, 632
25.25	185
25.30	462
25.31–40	632
26ff.	630
26f.	183
26.15ff.	630
26.31–37	632
26.31	458
26.33	631
27–30	43
27	52
27.1–8	632
27.9–19	632
27.9	630
27.20f.	458, 462
27.21	630
28	485
28.1ff.	485
28.4	622
28.15ff.	622
28.25f.	485
28.39	622
29–31	47
29	563, 482, 485
29.4	630
29.10f.	631
29.10	630
29.20f.	626
29.22–23.19	475
29.32	630
29.33	633
29.38–42	462
29.38–41	656
29.42–46	483
29.42f.	631
29.42	630, 631
29.44	485, 631
29.45f.	492
29.45	484, 487, 628, 631
30f.	43

30.1–10	458, 632
30.6	484, 631
30.7–8	458, 462
30.11–17	634
30.11–16	461, 485
30.12ff.	549
30.12	633
30.16	630
30.17–21	632
30.17	634
30.22	634
30.33	633
30.36	484, 631
31.1–11	485
31.1	634
31.2–11	185
31.12–17	491, 634
31.12	634
31.13	408, 410, 489
31.15	608
31.17	408, 410
32	55, 145, 183, 261, 265, 308, 310, 336
32.1–10	475
32.1–6	55, 65, 310, 311
32.1	66, 338
32.2ff.	263
32.2f.	311
32.4–6	311
32.4	309, 338
32.6	311
32.7–14	55, 261, 311, 624
32.7–13	476, 478
32.8	145, 309
32.9	476
32.13	476, 477, 626
32.15–34	55
32.15f.	628
32.18	311
32.21–29	263
32.21–24	476
32.22	311
32.23	66
32.24	263
32.25–29	58, 59, 263, 431
32.25	311
32.25b	263
32.26–29	476
32.26	476

32.27	263
32.28–34	475
32.29	58, 262
32.30–32	476
32.30f.	261
32.30	263, 476
32.32f.	646
32.33	55
32.34	477, 627
32.34b	261
32.35	55
33	55
33.1	55, 475, 476, 477, 626
33.2	55
33.3	474, 476, 477
33.3a	55
33.3b	55
33.4	55
33.5–34.10	55
33.5f.	475
33.5	476
33.7–11	57, 476, 478, 630
33.7	476
33.7a	476
33.9	631
33.16	472
33.12–17	475
33.17	476
33.18ff.	320
33.21f.	320
33.28	55
33.29ff.	55
34	55, 66, 624
34.1–10	476
34.2	54
34.4	54
34.5	631
34.6	338, 641
34.6–7	476
34.9	476
34.10	472, 474, 626
34.11–27	625
34.11–26	60, 61
34.11–17	55
34.11–14	209
34.11b–26	257
34.14	61, 263, 264, 357, 410
34.15	472

34.17	64, 265, 309	3	464	16.14f.	463
34.18–26	89, 183, 277	4f.	630	16.16	462, 463
		4	656	16.17	463
34.18–20	89	4.1–12	463	16.18f.	462
34.18	90, 607	4.3	622	16.18	463
34.19f.	103, 282	4.5	622	16.20–22	463
34.19	103	4.8ff.	463	16.24f.	463
34.20	193, 282	4.13–21	463	16.26	463
34.21	409	4.13	661	16.33	462, 463, 631
34.22	89, 103, 607	4.16	622		
		4.27–35	463, 622	17–26	60, 489, 629
34.23	89	5	622	17.1–4	352
34.26	103, 354	5.14	461	17.4	630
34.27f.	365	5.18	661	17.7	344
34.28	476	5.23	316	17.11	463
34.29ff.	55	6	464	18ff.	629
34.29f.	191	6.12–16	462	18–26	629
34.29	478	6.15	622	18	60
34.35	626	6.18f.	461	18.1–5	493
35ff.	55, 56	6.19	463, 622	18.5	463
35.2f.	608	6.23	463	18.21	192, 193, 342, 602
35.3	608	7.6f.	461		
35.4ff.	311	7.8	461	18.21a	341
35.4–29	485, 549	7.9	461	18.24–30	493
35.15	630	7.11–21	464	19ff.	489
35.25–27	261	7.18	330	19f.	489
35.30–36.7	485	7.28–34	464	19	439
36.2f.	485	7.30–34	622	19.2	489
36.3–6	485	8	463, 482	19.3	92
37.1–9	621, 628	8.12	622	19.4	64, 264
37.10–16	458	8.24	626	19.4a	216
37.25–29	458	8.30	626	19.5–8	489
38.21ff.	485	9	56, 482, 483	19.7	330
39.32–43	634			19.9–18	629
39.32	630	9.5	631	19.9f.	102, 222
39.40	630	9.23f.	482	19.13	323
39.42	485	10	486	19.19	360
40.1–33	485	10.1–3	310, 486	19.22	360
40.2	630	10.2	487	19.23–25	103
40.6	630	10.14f.	622	19.28	332
40.17	634	11ff.	60	19.31	38, 255
40.29	630	11–26	483	19.33–36	629
40.33	484	11	353, 408, 635	20.1–5	602
40.34f.	482, 630			20.2–5	341
40.34	631	11.43–45	629	20.2–4	342
40.35	631	11.44f.	489	20.2	192
40.36–38	631	12	464	20.3ff.	193
		12.3	407	20.3	192
Leviticus		12.4	631	20.4	192
1ff.	486	15.14	464	20.5	191
1–13	612	16	459, 460, 630	20.6	38, 255
1–8	56			20.7f.	489
1–7	459	16.2	484, 631	20.22–27	493
1.1	630	16.7–9	463	20.25f.	629
2.3	461	16.11ff.	656	20.26	489
		16.12	631		

20.27	254, 255	1.53	633	12.1	260
21.1–23	489	2	485, 486	12.2	478
21.1–22	489	3f.	655	12.4ff.	57
21.5	332	3.1–3	486	12.4–10	476
21.10–13	460	3.9	485, 613	12.6–8	478
21.10	612	3.10	633	12.6	478
21.12	622	3.12	485	12.7	479
21.16	489	3.38	486, 613,	13ff.	628
22.1–16	489		633	13f.	66
22.9	489	3.40–49	485	13.26	54
22.10	633	4.1–33	486	14	631
22.12	633	4.5ff.	431, 613	14.4f.	633
22.13	633	5.3	631	14.10	631
22.17–25	489	7.1ff.	485	14.11–24	477
22.31f.	489	7.2	618	14.11–23	477, 624
23.3	409, 607,	7.8–9	631	14.11	474, 477,
	608	8	463		626
23.23–25	462	8.1–4	458	14.12	477
23.26–32	462	8.5–22	486	14.13–19	478
23.42f.	90	8.16	485	14.14	66, 472,
24.1–4	458, 462	8.19	485, 613,		631
24.5–9	458, 461,		633	14.15	477
	462	9.1–14	411, 656	14.16	476, 477,
24.17–22	338	9.15ff.	631		626
25	439, 614	9.15	655	14.18	476, 609
25.2–7	636	10	53	14.22	626
25.2	271	10.29–32	45	14.23	476, 477,
25.8ff.	481	10.29	51, 628		626
25.8–55	629	10.30	261	14.25b	477
25.13	614	10.33	54, 66	14.44	57
25.23	79, 268	10.35f.	57	15.1ff.	655, 656
25.25ff.	73	11f.	615	15.1–16	462, 622
25.25	323	11	66	15.17–21	461
25.39–43	359	11.4–35	66	15.22	661
25.47ff.	7, 498	11.4	44	15.28	661
25.49	323	11.9	478	15.30	623
26.1	64, 216,	11.11f.	479	15.32–36	608
	264, 332	11.12	626	15.32	608
26.3–10	492	11.14–17	479	16ff.	431, 459
26.9–13	629	11.16ff.	624	16–18	486, 488
26.11	487, 631	11.16f.	57, 257	16	631, 633
26.12	492, 628	11.16–17	476	16.1–2aa	633
26.14ff.	381	11.16	627	16.2abb–7	633
26.27	463	11.17ff.	478	16.3	487
26.34	657	11.17	479, 631	16.4	487
		11.24–29	476	16.5	364, 487,
Numbers		11.24b–30	479		633
1	485	11.24	57	16.6f.	633
1.3f.	485	11.25f.	479	16.6	633
1.4	618	11.25	479, 628,	16.7	364, 487,
1.5–16	252		631		633
1.5–15	97	11.26	479	16.8–11	633
1.48–54	485	11.27–29	479	16.9	487
1.49	655	11.28	479	16.10	487
1.50–53	486	11.29	478, 479,	16.12–15	633
1.51	633		480, 633	16.16–25	633

16.16f.	631	21.4b–9	66	1.13–17	205
16.17	633	21.14	79	1.19	54
16.18	633	21.29	312	1.35	627
16.19–24	487	21.34	82	1.46	54
16.19f.	631	23.18–24	299	3.2	53
16.22	488	23.19	464	3.28	625
16.25–26	633	23.21	298	4–11	625
16.27–34	487	23.22	271, 309,	4.1	349, 355
16.27a	633		310	4.4	662
16.27b–32a	633	24f.	668	4.5	349, 354
16.32b	488, 633	24.4	252	4.6	349
16.33–34	633	24.7	271	4.10	200, 349,
16.35	487, 633	24.8	309, 310		350
17	631	24.16	252	4.12ff.	65
17.1–15	488	24.17ff.	473, 616	4.13	365
17.1–5	633	26	485	4.14	349
17.5	633	26.2	618	4.15–20	357
17.6	488	26.31	270	4.15–17	65
17.7–9	631	27.1	251	4.23	365
17.7	631	27.12	628	4.24	264, 357
17.7b–10	488	28.3–8	462, 656	4.29	658
17.9ff.	630	28.9f.	462	4.35	319, 610
17.11f.	633	28.9	409	4.37f.	364
17.11	633	28.11–15	462	4.37	228, 354
17.13	633	28.15	464	4.39	228, 319,
17.14	633	28.16–25	462		610
17.15	633	28.22	464	4.40	229, 355,
17.16–26	633	28.26–31	462		356
17.16–17	633	28.26	90	4.44ff.	601
17.17	618	29.5	464	4.44f.	205
17.18	633	29.11	464	4.44	346
17.19	631	29.12–34	462	5	60, 214,
17.27f.	488, 633	29.12	89		261, 356,
17.20	364	29.16ff.	464		475
17.21	618	29.28ff.	656	5.1	349, 350
18.1	486, 631	32	624	5.2ff.	66
18.1ff.	488	33.50–56	624	5.2f.	230, 231
18.2f.	656	34	614	5.4f.	356
18.4f.	488	34.14	618	5.6–21	214
18.4	633	35.19	93	5.6–10	215, 356,
18.5	613, 633	35.21ff.	93		390
18.6f.	485	35.25ff.	612	5.6–8a	356
18.7	633	35.31	326	5.6	215, 226,
18.8–9	614	35.33	93		230, 338,
18.9	461	35.34	93		356, 364
18.12f.	283	36.1ff.	316	5.7	61, 356
18.12	461	36.10	251	5.7–9a	215
18.13	461	36.33	251	5.8–10	64
18.14	461			5.8f.	395
18.20–22	461	*Deuteronomy*		5.8	209
18.22	633	1–II Kings		5.9f.	230, 356
18.25–32	614	25	387, 389	5.9	356, 609
20f.	66	1–3	625	5.9b–10	215
20	54, 631	1.2	54	5.9b	215, 356
20.6f.	631	1.8	365	5.10	354
21.4–9	180	1.9–18	336	5.10a	356

5.12–15	214, 409, 608	7.6f.	228, 364, 607	10.17	228, 657
5.12	409	7.6	209, 223, 226, 229, 474, 633	10.18f.	338
5.14	282			10.20	350
5.15	608			11.1	354
5.15b	409	7.7	228	11.6	633
5.16–20	214	7.8–11	357	11.8ff.	607
5.16	92, 212, 213	7.8f.	230, 365	11.9	355, 365
		7.8	228, 354, 356, 364	11.13	354
5.17–21	356			11.18	213
5.17–18	357	7.8b–11	356	11.19	213, 349
5.22	311, 356	7.9	218, 228, 354	11.20	213
5.23–31	230			11.21	355, 365
5.23	263	7.9b	218	11.22	354
5.29	264, 355, 356	7.10f.	220	11.32	349
		7.10	218	12ff.	60, 356, 475
5.31	349	7.11	218		
5.32	349, 340	7.12ff.	230, 607	12–26	199
5.33	355, 356	7.12–16	225	12	199, 206, 352, 390, 397, 532, 627
6.1	349	7.12f.	355		
6.2	355	7.12	349		
6.3	349	7.12b	230		
6.5	662	7.13	354, 365	12.2–13.1	351
6.10	365	7.14	362	12.2–7	351
6.15	264	7.15–17	353	12.2f.	206
6.18	365	7.15	256	12.3	274, 655
6.23	365	8.1	355, 365	12.5	277, 364
6–28	201, 214	8.6	350	12.7ff.	411
6–11	224	8.8	103	12.7	212, 324, 363
6.1ff.	60, 261	8.11ff.	230		
6.2	350, 355	8.13	364	12.8ff.	394
6.3	355	8.14	356, 357	12.8–12	226, 351, 361
6.4f.	212	8.18	230		
6.4	206	8.19	357	12.9	393
6.5	208	9f.	311	12.10	277, 393
6.8f.	213	9.5	365	12.11f.	222, 359
6.12ff.	391	9.7–10.11	61	12.11	363
6.12–15	356, 357	9.9	365	12.12ff.	411
6.12	356, 364	9.10ff.	311	12.12	220, 221, 363
6.13	350	9.11	365		
6.18	355, 356	9.12	309	12.13–19	351
6.20	213	9.15	365	12.13–18	352
6.21–24	213	9.16	309	12.13f.	206
6.21	364	9.27	365	12.14	362
6.24	350	10.1–5	57, 628	12.15f.	208
6.28	356	10.2	297	12.15	121, 352
7	353	10.8	220, 360, 365, 548	12.17f.	206
7.1ff.	391			12.17	286, 351, 411
7.1f.	209	10.11f.	226		
7.1–2	353	10.11	365	12.18f.	359
7.2f.	390, 391, 472	10.12f.	229	12.18	220, 221, 222, 303, 362, 363
		10.12	350, 354		
7.2	390, 391	10.13	355	12.20–28	351
7.4	357	10.14f.	364	12.20–27	351, 352
7.5	274	10.14	228	12.21	227
		10.15	228, 354	12.23–25	208

12.23f.	408	15.1f.	358	16.10	212, 218, 608
12.25	212	15.2	361		
12.26	362	15.2b	358	16.11	91, 220, 221, 222, 363
12.28	212	15.2ab	358		
12.29–13.1	351	15.3	218, 358, 360	16.12	219, 349, 364, 410
12.31	191, 341, 342, 390	15.4–6	358		
		15.4	358	16.13	89, 90
12.43–50	411	15.7–11	218, 358, 359	16.14	91, 220, 221, 222
13	209				
13.1	349	15.7	358, 360, 361	16.15	212, 218, 362, 608
13.2ff.	353				
13.2–6	210	15.9	218, 358, 360	16.16	362
13.3f.	357			16.17	212
13.4	354	15.10	212, 218	16.18–	200, 347, 350
13.5	350	15.11	358, 361	18.22	
13.6	349, 356, 364	15.12ff.	358	16.18	199, 204, 225, 347, 349, 362
		15.12–18	601		
13.7–12	59, 210, 352	15.12	324, 361		
		15.13f.	218	16.20	212
13.7	352	15.13	324	16.21f.	65, 206, 209, 274
13.10f.	210	15.14	212, 324		
13.11	356, 364	15.14b	218	16.21	199
13.12	350, 352	15.15	218, 219, 338, 355, 364, 410	16.22	332
13.13–19	209			17.2–7	59, 210, 211, 352
13.16	353				
13.18f.	352	15.16	218, 359	17.3	199, 209
14	363, 408	15.18	212, 218, 219, 323, 359	17.4	91
14.1f.	210, 228			17.7	349
14.1	332			17.8ff.	362
14.2	209, 223, 226, 229, 474, 633	15.19–22	208	17.8–13	203, 220, 225, 336
		15.19f.	103		
		15.20	222, 362, 363	17.8–11	204
14.3–21a	210			17.8	362
14.21	209, 229, 474	15.21	358	17.9	204, 220, 613
		15.23	408		
14.21b	210	16	35	17.10–13	350
14.22–27	286	16.1–8	90, 208, 213, 222, 352, 353, 548	17.10f.	349
14.22–29	208, 622			17.10	349, 362
14.23	216, 350, 363			17.11	349
		16.1–7	607	17.12	204, 220, 349, 360
14.24	212, 218, 227, 324	16.1	363, 364, 608		
				17.12cj	360
14.25	362	16.1aab	352	17.13	350
14.26f.	221, 222	16.2	352, 363	17.14ff.	199, 362
14.26	216, 363	16.3ab–4a	352	17.14–20	201, 225
14.27	220	16.3	355, 364, 426	17.14–17	473
14.28f.	216, 223, 286			17.14f.	199, 362
		16.3ab	352	17.15	225, 226
14.29	212, 218, 220, 324	16.6	363, 364	17.16f.	217, 362
		16.7	352, 362, 548	17.16	353, 357
14.23	350			17.16aa	225
15.1ff.	385, 636	16.7b	352	17.16b	362
15.1–11	217, 481, 601, 629	16.8	352	17.16ab	225
				17.17	209
15.1–8	629			17.17a	225
15.1–3	358				

17.17b	225	20.1	364	24.17	217, 219,
17.18f.	225, 362	20.2	206, 220		338
17.18	362, 613	20.5–7	216	24.18	219, 338,
17.19	350	20.5	628		355, 364
17.20	226, 349,	20.7	657	24.19–22	222
	355, 362	20.8	217	24.19	212, 218,
18	220	20.11–26	361		324, 355
18.1ff.	433	20.15–18	209	24.22	219, 338,
18.1–8	627	20.15–17	353, 390,		364
18.1–5	220		391	25.1–3	349
18.1–3	207	20.18	349	25.1	366
18.1	58, 219,	20.24–26	361	25.3	361
	220, 461,	20.27	208	25.4	607
	613	21.1–19	93	25.5–10	73, 349
18.3	220, 622	21.1–9	349	25.15	212, 213
18.4	283	21.2	349	25.19	277, 393
18.5	220, 360,	21.5	220, 360,	26f.	384
	364, 655		364	26	361
18.6–8	220, 222,	21.10–14	359	26.1–11	103, 213,
	360, 613	21.18–21	349		355, 626
18.6f.	430, 604	21.21	349, 350	26.1	359
18.6	220, 362	22.1	361	26.2	283, 363
18.7	360	22.2	361	26.3f.	220
18.7b	220, 360	22.3	361	26.3	36
18.8b	360	22.4	361	26.5–10	53, 213
18.9–20	615	22.7	212, 355	26.5	365
18.9–14	209	22.10	607, 608	26.5abb	355
18.9	350	22.13–21	349	26.8	364
18.10	199, 341,	22.21f.	349	26.10	283
	342, 390	22.21	91	26.11	103, 220,
18.10a	210	23.2ff.	600		222
18.10b–14	210	23.5	364	26.12–15	208, 286
18.11f.	101	23.6	354	26.12–14	216, 223
18.11	38, 255	23.16	219	26.12f.	223
18.14–22	626	23.18f.	87, 397	26.12	220, 357
18.14	390	23.18a	343	26.13	220
18.16	354	23.18b	194	26.14	38, 354
18.18b	384	23.19	87	26.16–19	229
18.20	384, 644	23.20	217, 361	26.16	349, 365
19	350	23.21	212, 213,	26.18	223
19	208		218, 324,	26.19	209, 228,
19.1–13	349		361		229, 474
19.8	365	23.22–24	354	27	361
19.9	354	24.6	217	27.1a	361
19.12	93	24.7	349	27.1–3	361
19.13	212, 277,	24.8f.	205	27.2–3a	361
	349	24.8	220, 613	27.3b	361
19.17f.	349	24.9	364	27.4	361, 532
19.17	220	24.10f.	217	27.5–7	361
19.18	361	24.12f.	217	27.5a	361
19.19	338, 361	24.12	358	27.7	361
19.20	350	24.14f.	219	27.8	361
20	350, 353	24.14	323, 358	27.9f.	603
20.1ff.	362	24.15	356, 358	27.9	613
20.1–13	66	24.16	609	27.11f.	532
20.1–9	225			27.14	603, 655

27.15	64, 65, 265	31.25	365	6.17f.	603
28	225, 229,	31.26	346, 365	6.18f.	391
	361, 390,	32	228	6.19	602
	391, 606	32.6b	403, 404	6.21	391, 603
28.1	361	32.8f.	271, 272	7	391
28.3ff.	355	32.8b	271	7.6–9	600
28.3–5	324	32.17	31	7.10ff.	603
28.9	209, 223,	32.18	404	7.11	365
	229, 361,	32.37	667	7.13	93
	474	33	124, 668	7.14–18	268
28.11	361, 365	33.2–5	299	7.15	277, 365
28.14	349	33.2	51, 52, 53,	8	267
28.16ff.	381		54	8.1	82
28.20	365	33.4	346	8.26f.	603
28.32	356	33.5	298	8.26	391
28.58	350	33.8–11	58, 59	8.30–35	390
28.60	256	33.8	58	8.30–33	361
28.61	346	33.8b	59	8.31	346, 466
28.69	230	33.9	262	8.33	603
28.69b	365	33.9a	58	8.34	346
29	230	33.10a	59	9	391
29.8	365	33.10b	58	9.3ff.	603
29.11	229, 230,	33.11	58	9.6ff.	603
	365	33.13–17	324	9.15	364
29.12	365	33.19	83	9.23	613
29.13	365	33.26–29	299	9.27	362, 602
29.15–27	603	34.1–9	628	10.8	82
29.20	346, 365	34.4	365	10.28ff.	603
29.24	319, 365,	34.9f.	625	10.28–33	391
	601	34.10f.	615	10.39f.	391
30.1–10	603	34.10	315, 478,	11.16	82
30.6	354, 355		625	13.1–6	391
30.10	346			14.4	614
30.16	354	*Joshua*		14.7	54
30.18	355	1–12	70	15.21–62	285
30.19	355	1	531, 625	17.2	270
30.20	354, 355,	1.7	349	17.3	251
	365	1.8	346	17.14ff.	614
31ff.	199	1.10	628	18.1	634
31.7f.	625	1.13	393	18.21–28	285
31.7	365	1.14	652	21	263
31.9ff.	390	1.15	393	21.2	614
31.9–13	231, 350	3f.	394	21.44	393
31.9	346, 365,	3	390	21.45	391, 393
	603	3.3	603, 655	22.10–34	83
31.11	362	3.6ff.	603	22.19	271
31.12f.	350	3.11	391	22.21	273
31.14f.	57	3.13	391	22.22	273
31.14–15	625	4.3ff.	603	22.24–26a	273
31.16ff.	603	4.19f.	361	22.24	273
31.16	365	4.24	391	22.27	273
31.19	349, 603	5.2–9	407	23	391, 395,
31.20	365	5.3–9	604		604
31.22	349	5.10–12	410, 604	23.4f.	391
31.23	625, 626	5.13–15	132	23.6	346, 349,
31.24	346	6	267		466

23.7f.	603	5.1	257	9.6	84
23.7	391, 603	5.2f.	78	9.11–15	123
23.8	391	5.2	80, 81	9.27	84, 276
23.12ff.	391	5.3	76, 77	9.37	332
23.12f.	313	5.4f.	51, 52, 82,	9.46	84, 604
23.12	603		89	10.1–5	91
23.14	391, 393	5.4	53, 82	10.3f.	269
23.21	393	5.5	51, 53, 76,	10.4	276
24	53, 71, 473		77	10.6ff.	389
24.2	27	5.6–8	79	10.6	86, 312,
24.15	392	5.6	97		322, 392
24.17	356	5.7	81	10.10	322, 392
24.19	264, 357	5.9	80, 81	10.13	392
24.26	84	5.11	81	10.16	392
24.33	310	5.12	81	11f.	79, 392
		5.13	81	11.1ff.	74, 81
Judges		5.20	80, 82	11.1	74, 75
1	391	5.21	82	11.3	75
1.12ff.	271	5.23	80	11.5ff.	73, 74
1.16	51	6.2b–5	79	11.6	74
1.27ff.	70	6.7–10	602	11.9	74
2–I Sam.		6.8	356	11.11	74, 88
12	391	6.10	392	11.16–26	53
2.2f.	391	6.12	75	11.24	228
2.2	391, 603	6.13	600	11.29	81
2.3	392	6.24	73, 270,	11.30ff.	191
2.10ff.	389		632	11.30f.	282
2.10–16f.	392	6.25–32	604	12.1–7	74
2.10	391	6.25–31	392	12.1	269
2.11	322, 392	6.25f.	274	12.4ff.	73
2.12	391, 392	6.25	392	12.7	93
2.13	86, 604	6.28	392	12.8ff.	269
2.16	392, 605	6.30–32	392	12.8–14	91
2.17	392	6.30	392	12.11	603
2.18	88	6.32	97	13	33
2.19	391, 392	6.34	80, 81	13.3f.	33
2.21–23	391	7	392	13.3	33
2.27	88	7.2–8	80	15.10ff.	74, 269
3.1–6	313	7.8	123	17–18	58
3.1–4	391	7.9	82	17.1–5	265
3.3	391	7.14	82	17f.	38, 58, 65,
3.6	31, 392,	7.16	272		83, 85, 100,
	603	7.18	80		305
3.7	274, 312,	7.19ff.	82	17	251
	322, 392	7.22	82	17.2–4	305, 308
3.10	81	7.24	269	17.5f.	59
3.12ff.	79	8.1–3	74	17.5	37, 100,
3.31	97	8.1	269		251, 332
4.3	82	8.22–28	65	17.6	305
4.4f.	93	8.22f.	78, 123	17.7–12	58
4.4	81, 315	8.23	299	17.7	58, 262,
4.6	83, 88	8.27	88		263
4.11	51	8.33	322, 392,	17.10	39, 251
4.13	82		604	17.13	58
4.17ff.	52, 271	8.34f.	391	18.1a	305
5	80, 272	9.4	75, 84, 604	18.5	100

18.14	37
18.17f.	37, 221
18.17	305
18.18ff.	58
18.29	37
18.29a	305
18.30	221, 308
18.30a	305
18.30b	58, 59, 262
18.31b	305, 308
19f.	58, 74
19.1ff.	58
19.22	74
19.29	272
20f.	93
20	58
20.1–10	269
20.1	269
20.6	91
20.10	91
20.12	91
20.26–28	310
20.26f.	89
20.41	269
21.5	277
21.19ff.	91

Ruth

1–4	73
2.1	75
2.20	323
3.12	323
4	73
4.1–9	323
4.13	253

I Samuel

1–3	83
1	33, 101, 193
1.1ff.	278
1.2–8	33
1.2	123
1.3	88, 132
1.9	88
1.11	88, 282, 289
1.14	91
1.16	52
1.21	101
1.24	364
2.4–8	415
2.19	101
2.27–36	394
2.27	58
2.28	364
2.35	291, 603

3.3	88
3.20	315
4–6	394
4	108, 632
4.1ff.	88
4.3ff.	57
4.3	269
4.4	88, 132, 298
4.10	123
4.19–22	96
4.39	284
6.15	603, 655
7.3f.	389, 392
7.3	392
7.4	322, 392
7.6	93
7.7	392
8–12	393
8.1–13	330
8.2	98
8.3	287
8.4f.	330
8.5	393
8.7	123, 298, 393, 425
8.8	283, 392, 393
8.9	393
8.11ff.	603
8.11–17	113, 123
8.14	112
8.15	111, 357
8.17	111, 299, 357
8.19f.	330
8.19	393
9f.	84, 85, 294
9	282
9.1	75, 98
9.4	73, 268
9.7	75
9.12ff.	101
9.16	294, 612
9.22	84
10.1	125, 294
10.5f.	315
10.5	108
10.10–12	315, 479
10.17–27	283
10.19	393
10.19b	268
10.24	362, 393
10.26	110
10.27	110

11	79, 108, 132
11.1–15	283
11.1	364
11.4	110
11.5	74
11.6	81
11.7	272
11.10	73, 74
11.13	73
11.15	269, 330
12.3	326
12.10	322, 392
12.12	123, 298, 299, 393, 425
12.13	393
12.17	393
12.19	605
12.20ff.	393
12.21	393
13.1	392
13.2	109
13.3f.	108
13.6	269
13.7b–15a	294
13.14	294
14.3	129, 295
14.22	269
14.24	269
14.32–34	408
14.38	269
14.41	88
14.50f.	110
14.52	110
15.6f.	52
15.9ff.	603
15.23	603
15.27f.	307
16.3	621
16.4	74
16.6	98
16.8–10	364
16.8	294, 362
16.9	294, 362
16.13f.	125
16.13	121
16.14	124
16.18	293
16.20f.	110
16.20	110
17.2ff.	269
17.25	284
17.37	293
18.8	294
18.12	293

18.13	290	26.6	98	5.9	285
18.14	293	26.9	288	5.10	293
18.17	79, 115	26.11	289	5.12	124, 273
18.25	407	26.16	288	5.15	294, 364
18.28	293	26.19	228, 276,	5.17–25	111, 304
19–21	108		293, 377	5.19	293
19	39	26.23	288	5.23	293
19.4	255	26.25	293	6	57, 289,
19.13	37, 332,	27.3f.	293		290, 291,
	603	27.6–12	286		394
19.16	37, 603	27.6	284, 286	6.2	88, 132,
19.18–24	315, 479	27.11f.	293		298
20.6	101	28	38, 101,	6.5	311
20.13	293		604	6.6	633
20.16	293	28.3ff.	603	6.11	548
20.20	101	28.3	38	6.14ff.	121
20.22	293	28.3b	604	6.17f.	121
20.25	295	28.9	604	6.17	130, 295,
20.31	294	28.13	38		296
20.46	293	28.15	38	6.18	121
21.7	632	28.15f.	290	6.19	173
21.10	332	29.7ff.	293	6.21	273, 294,
21.12	294	29.19	271		311, 362,
22	129	29.30	293		364, 612
22.2	75, 108,	30.7	129, 293,	7	117, 118,
	110		332		119, 287,
22.3	293	30.26	73		290, 292,
22.5	293, 315	31	656, 658		484
22.6	110			7.1–4a	296
22.7	112, 284	**II Samuel**		7.1	393
22.9	284, 295	1.11ff.	293	7.1a	118, 289
22.10	293	1.12	81	7.1b	119, 289,
22.13	293	1.14	289		291
22.15	293	1.16	289	7.2–7	289
22.20	295	2.1	293	7.2–5	289
22.23	259	2.4b–7	293	7.2–4a	118
23.1–12	293	2.4	110, 284	7.2f.	289
23.6	88, 332	2.6	129	7.2	130, 290,
23.9	129, 332	2.18ff.	278		295
23.10–11a	600	3.3	202	7.3	289
23.14	293	3.9f.	294	7.4–16	315
23.17	293, 294	3.12f.	364	7.4–8	604
24.7	289	3.17	269, 294	7.4b–7	131, 290,
24.11	289	3.18	294		292
24.21	294	3.21	294	7.5	290
24.22	293	3.22–39	392	7.6	290, 307
25	284	3.27	93	7.8–11a	290
25.2	269	3.39	293	7.8–9	118, 289,
25.26	293	4.4	293		362
25.27	291	4.9ff.	293	7.8f.	292
25.28b–31a	291	4.9	293	7.8	290, 294
25.28	79, 115,	5.2	125, 273,	7.8a	289
	294		294	7.9	607
25.30	294	5.3	110, 269,	7.9a	289
25.31	293		284, 364	7.10–11a	292
25.33f.	293	5.6–9	110	7.10	119

7.11	393	8.18	129, 278,	16.18	269, 294,
7.11a	119, 289		285		362
7.11b–13	291	8.18b	656	17.4	122, 123,
7.11b	117, 118,	9	124, 287,		269, 284,
	289, 290,		293		285
	296, 307	9.4	98	17.11	123
7.12–15	289	9.7ff.	112	17.14	122, 123,
7.12–14a	289	10.1–19	116, 285		184, 285,
7.12	117, 118,	11.1	285		293
	289, 290,	11.7	277	17.15	269
	362	11.11	57	18	123
7.12b	290, 291	11.27b–		18.7	110
7.13	119, 289,	12.15a	604	18.18	337
	290, 291	12–15	117	18.19	293
7.13a	289	12	602, 604,	18.31	293
7.13b	290		605	19.5	667
7.14–17	290	12.5–14	315	19.9bff.	110
7.14–16	393	12.5	277	19.10	113
7.14b–16	289	12.15bff.	302	19.12	284
7.14–15	118, 362	12.15	293	19.15	269, 284
7.14f.	289	12.16–31	285	19.25–31	293
7.14	117, 119,	12.23	255	19.30	112
	290, 291,	12.26–31	116	19.33	269
	606, 657	12.30	312	19.42ff.	284
7.14a	289	12.31	112	19.43f.	269
7.14bf.	118	13.12	91	20	122
7.14b	290	14.4–12	120	20.1	123, 306
7.15	290	14.5ff.	93	20.4f.	269
7.16	117, 118,	14.7	73	20.6f.	285
	289, 291,	14.16	271, 276	20.21	305
	296, 298,	14.17	293	20.23–26	285
	362	15–19	122, 287	20.23	285
7.17	289	15ff.	113	20.24	112
7.18–22a	289	15.1ff.	120	20.25	129
7.18–21	289	15.1–6	285	20.26	294
7.21	289	15.7	282	21	93
7.22–24	289	15.12	98	21.6	84, 88, 289
7.22	610	15.13	122, 269	21.9	84, 88
7.22b–26	119, 292	15.17	83	21.17	603
7.24	119, 291	15.18f.	285	23.1–7	621
7.25–29	289	15.19ff.	111, 285	23.1	117
7.26	119, 291	15.20	259	23.2	121
7.27	289	15.23	37	23.3f.	121
7.29	291	15.24ff.	57	23.5	118
8	111	15.24–29	295	23.6	365
8.1–15	285	15.24	603, 655	23.10f.	621
8.1–5	116	15.25	295	23.13ff.	285
8.6	120	15.30	667	23.24–39	111
8.11f.	602, 604	15.31	293	23.31	98
8.11	119	15.32ff.	293	24	285
8.13	607	16.3	293	24.2	285
8.14	120	16.4	112	24.9	285
8.15–18	285	16.12	293	24.11–13	315
8.16	285	16.15	269	24.11	315
8.17	129, 294,	16.17	283	24.16ff.	130
	295, 656				

24.18	315	5.5	113, 120	8.12	131, 363,
28.3–25	293	5.7	111		631
		5.8	111	8.14	121
I Kings		5.9–13	113	8.16–21	393
1f.	659	5.15ff.	112, 148	8.16f.	604
1	110	5.18	393	8.16	303, 362,
1.7	287	5.19	290		363, 393,
1.9	335	5.26	364		394, 397,
1.11–13	118	5.27–30	287, 657,		351, 602,
1.12	293		660		604
1.29	293	5.27f.	287	8.18f.	394
1.32ff.	295	6–8	388, 484,	8.19	290
1.35	125		632	8.21	226, 601
1.37	118, 293	6–7	394	8.25	290, 393
1.38f.	295	6f.	112, 129	8.27	363, 394
1.39	130, 295	6	130, 296	8.29ff.	395
1.46	607	6.1ff.	131	8.29	394
1.47	294	6.1–9a	296	8.31f.	366
1.50–53	293	6.1	296	8.43	227, 602
1.50–53	296	6.2f.	296	8.44	303, 363,
2	124, 287,	6.4	296		602
	293, 657	6.5–8	296	8.46ff.	395
2.1–4	393	6.7	296	8.46–51	377
2.1b–9	293	6.9a	296	8.47	605
2.3	346	6.9b–10	296	8.48	363, 394
2.4	119, 290,	6.13	632	8.55	121
	393	6.14	296	8.56	393
2.11	293	6.16	130	8.60	610
2.15	287, 293	6.20	298	8.62f.	121, 128
2.24aa	294	6.23–28	130, 363,	9.1–9	383, 394
2.24ab	290, 291		633	9.3	364, 395
2.24abb	293	6.23f.	298	9.4f.	393
2.26–27a	293	6.31f.	130	9.5	119, 290,
2.26	129	6.33–35	130		393
2.27b	293	6.37f.	296	9.6	603, 604
2.28f.	295, 296	7.12	129	9.9	394, 603,
2.28	130	7.13–47	602, 604		604
2.31b–33	293	7.13–22	298	9.10–14	286
2.32–34	293	7.21	298	9.11f.	153
2.35	291, 394	7.38	632	9.11	148
2.44–45	293	7.48–50	602, 604	9.15ff.	112
2.44	291	7.48	298, 632	9.15	285
2.45	118, 291	7.49	632	9.16	112, 148,
2.46	293	7.51	602, 604		285
3.1f.	112	8	375, 394	9.17–19	285
3.1	112, 148	8.1ff.	130	9.20–22	287, 657
3.2	130, 397	8.1	390, 603	9.24	112
3.4–15	292	8.3ff.	603	9.25	276
3.4	84, 130	8.4	390, 603,	9.26–28	112
4.1–6.7ff.	285		655	10	112
4.2	129	8.6ff.	57, 394	10.12–16	321
4.4	285	8.6f.	298, 628	10.14f.	111
4.7–19	111	8.7f.	297	10.15–16	321
4.10	113	8.7	394	10.16	321
4.20	120	8.9	226, 297,	10.25	111
5.2f.	111		390	10.26	285

10.28f.	112, 285		139, 140,	13.2	396
10.33	112		142, 287,	13.3–32a	344
11f.	307, 308		307, 395,	13.11ff.	316
11	139, 140,		604	13.22	274
	604	12.1	139	13.25	139
11.1ff.	393	12.1a	141	13.26–32	139
11.1–13	392, 395	12.2	206	13.32	396
11.1–4	148	12.2	139, 142,	13.33f.	139, 647
11.2	604		307	13.33	604
11.3f.	603	12.3a	306	13.34	304
11.4	604	12.3bff.	141	14	101, 316
11.5–7	606	12.3b–15	142	14.1–18	307, 602
11.5	148, 312	12.3b–11	139	14.1–16	316
11.7f.	603	12.4ff.	287	14.2	280
11.7	148, 312,	12.10f.	142	14.7	125, 143,
	341, 603	12.12	139, 306		294
11.10	604	12.13f.	139	14.8–16	396
11.12f.	393	12.16	139, 141,	14.8f.	395, 603,
11.13	363, 394,		142, 306		604, 605
	602	12.17ff.	388	14.8	393
11.18	53	12.18f.	139	14.9	304, 309
11.14–25	304	12.18	46, 141,	14.10	605
11.22–27	118		307	14.14–16	659
11.26–28	140, 142,	12.19	142	14.15f.	604
	287, 293	12.20	130, 141,	14.16	304
11.26f.	305		142, 305,	14.17	306, 310
11.26	139, 307		306	14.21	363, 364,
11.27ff.	123	12.20a	139, 307		394, 397,
11.27f.	139, 140	12.22–24	602		602
11.27	46	12.22	307	14.22	397
11.28	287	12.21–24	139 306	14.23	274, 334,
11.29ff.	316	12.21	603		603
11.29–39	139, 140,	12.24	305, 395	14.24	603, 605
	141, 142,	12.25–32	139	14.25ff.	397
	395, 602	12.25	143, 306	14.25–38	604
11.29–31	141	12.26–32	140, 305,	14.25–28	602
11.30f.	141, 307		310, 395	14.25–27	306
11.32	363, 388,	12.26f.	140, 305	14.31	280
	394, 602	12.28–32	304	15.4f.	397
11.33	148, 312	12.28f.	143, 305	15.4	119, 291,
11.34	388	12.28	140, 143,		393, 394,
11.34a	141		144, 145,		395, 603
11.35aba	141		257, 338,	15.5	393, 604
11.36	119, 291,		364, 605	15.12–15	659
	363, 364,	12.29–31	307	15.12f.	397
	388, 394,	12.30	305	15.12	603, 605
	395, 602,	12.31f.	603, 647	15.13	85, 87, 135,
	603	12.31	143, 274,		188
11.36a	141		308, 603,	15.14	603
11.37	141		604, 605	15.15	604
11.38	291, 388,	12.32	143, 144,	15.18f.	602
	393		605	15.19	364
11.38bab	141, 307	12.40	140	15.26	304
11.40	139, 142,	13	316, 602,	15.27	310
	287, 307		605	15.29	605
12	112, 123,	13.1–2ba	344	15.30	304

15.33	306	18.40	319	22.19ff.	132
16.1ff.	605	18.41–46	152, 318	22.19b	329
16.1–10	296	18.41–45	153	22.38	317
16.2	294	19	51, 154	22.40	317
16.4	313	19.1–19	319	22.44	603
16.8	306	19.1–18	321	22.47	397, 603,
16.12	605	19.1–2	319		605
16.13	605	19.2	154, 314	22.53	304
16.19	304	19.9	320	22.54	605
16.24	149	19.10	154, 299,		
16.26	304, 605		319, 320	**II Kings**	
16.30f.	603	19.11f.	320	1	101, 188,
16.31ff.	396	19.11ab–12	320		602
16.31	149, 304,	19.12	320	1.4ff.	202
	603, 605	19.14	299, 320	1.6–17	605
16.32	149	19.15–18	321	2.4ff.	203
16.33	605	19.16	151	2.6	602
16.34	98	19.17ff.	257	2.25	199
17–21	602	19.19–21	151, 319	2.19–25	316
17–18	318	19.19	151	3	152
17.1ff.	153	20	313	3.2ff.	604
17.1	151, 318	20.13ff.	327	3.2f.	396
17.7	319	20.42	364	3.2	154
17.11	290	20.35–42	316	3.3	304
17.12	152	21	605	3.11ff.	327
17.14	290	21.1–20a	152	3.13	151
18	153, 154,	21.1	317	3.14	299, 300
	313	21.2f.	79, 268	3.26	282
18.4	154, 314	21.3f.	152	3.27	191
18.8	163	21.3	316	4	152
18.13	154, 314	21.4	316	4.1	151, 160
18.15	299, 300	21.7	152	4.1–7	316
18.17–18a	318	21.8ff.	323	4.8–17	316
18.17	153	21.8	317	4.16	33, 252
18.18	153, 172,	21.9ff.	93	4.23	408
	322	21.10	152, 269,	4.38ff.	151
18.18b	153		625	4.38–44	316
18.19ff.	154	21.11	317	4.38	151
18.19–40	318	21.13	269, 625	4.42	269
18.19	319	21.15	112, 317	5	316, 611
18.21ff.	154	21.16	317	5.1	639
18.21–40	153, 154	21.17–20a	152, 317	5.17	377
18.21–20	318	21.18	317	6.1ff.	151
18.21	319	21.19a	317	6.1–7	151, 152,
18.21b	319	21.19b	317		316
18.22	154	21.20a	316	6.8–7.20	313
18.24	319	21.20b–29	316	6.26ff.	120
18.27	153	21.20ba	316	7.13	601
18.29	462	21.21f.	605	8	121
18.30a	319	21.26	605	8.1–6	112, 317
18.30b	154	21.27–29	605	8.1	259
18.31	319	22	151, 313,	8.3ff.	120
18.36	319, 462		316, 602	8.7–15	602
18.37	153	22.5ff.	273	8.18	150, 397,
18.38	154	22.6ff.	327		603
18.39	153, 319	22.17	82	8.18ab	314

8.19	119, 291, 388, 393, 395, 603	11	603, 656	17.1–6	163
8.20ff.	605	11.2	129	17.6	524, 526
8.23f.	320	11.4ff.	118	17.7ff.	605
8.26	314	11.4	364	17.7–23	396, 399
8.27	150	11.8	277	17.7	604, 605
8.28f.	155, 320	11.12	288	17.9–11	605
8.28	154	11.15	277	17.9	525
9	602	11.17f.	397	17.10	33
9.1–10.27	155, 321	11.18	397	17.12	604, 605
9.1–13	154, 155, 320	11.18a	150, 314	17.13–15	396
		12	602	17.13f.	602
9.1–6	320	12.4	398, 603	17.13	605
9.3	321	12.5ff.	129	17.15	604, 605
9.6	321	12.18f.	604	17.16	309, 318, 605
9.7–10a	320	13.4	389, 396		
9.10b	320	13.6	304, 604, 605	17.17	341, 342, 603, 605
9.11–13	320				
9.14–15a	320	13.7	155	17.19	605
9.14a	320	13.11	304	17.21–23	304, 396
9.14bf.	155	13.14–21	602	17.21f.	388
9.14b	154	13.14–19	156	17.21	261
9.16–24	155	14.4	398	17.22f.	659
9.19b	317	14.6	346, 466	17.22	605
9.22	155, 603	14.24	304	17.23f.	526
9.22ab	321	14.25–28	602	17.23	154, 524
9.25f.	317, 320	14.25–27	389, 396	17.24ff.	524, 525, 526
9.26	317	15.4	398, 603		
9.29	320	15.9	304	17.24–41	396, 524, 646, 647
9.30–35	155	15.16	659		
9.36f.	320	15.18	304	17.24–34a	524, 525, 529
10	318	15.19f.	162		
10.1–9	155	15.20	652	17.24–33	647
10.8ff.	149	15.23	659	17.24	647
10.9	321	15.24	304	17.25–28	188, 647
10.10	320, 602	15.28	304	17.28	525
10.15f.	321	15.29	162	17.29–31	188, 274, 647
10.15	154	15.30	162		
10.16	155, 320	15.35	398, 603	17.29	524, 646, 647
10.17	313	16.3f.	398, 605		
10.17abb	320	16.3	282, 341, 342, 603, 605	17.30–33	525
10.18ff.	121, 149, 396			17.31	191, 192, 193, 341, 342, 603
		16.4	603		
10.18–27	155	16.5–8	162	17.32	188, 274, 525, 604, 647
10.19	277	16.5	398		
10.23	320, 321	16.6	398		
10.24	277	16.7f.	167	17.33	647
10.25	313	16.8	602, 604	17.34–41	604
10.25b–28	321	16.10ff.	398, 463	17.34a	525, 647
10.29	304, 309, 396, 605	16.10–18	181	17.34b–40	525, 529, 647
		16.10–16	188, 340		
10.30f.	659	16.15	339, 462	17.34b–36	525
10.30	396	16.16ff.	602	17.34b	647
10.31	396	16.17f.	408	17.37–39	525
10.32f.	155	16.22f.	602	17.40	525, 526
		17	525	17.41	647

18–20	389, 601, 605	21.10–16	398		340, 344, 345, 605
18f.	367	21.10–15	602	23.6f.	198, 211
18.4	65, 180, 337, 397, 398, 603	21.16	604, 660	23.6	605
		21.21	604	23.7	135, 209, 276, 343, 345, 603, 605
		21.23f.	201		
		21.23	602		
18.6–8	207	21.27	602		
18.7	163	22–25	279	23.7a	345
18.8	280	22–23	196, 197, 198, 199, 200, 345, 348, 389, 632	23.8f.	604
18.9ff.	398			23.8	198, 397, 603
18.13–16	163				
18.18	285				
18.20	239			23.8a	344, 345
18.22	240, 334, 366	22	200, 202, 390, 603	23.8b	344, 345
				23.9	221, 222, 346, 360, 430, 431, 613
18.24f.	239	22.1–23.24	398		
18.26f.	240	22.1	345		
18.27	313	22.2–11	345		
18.33–35	240	22.3–23.3	345	23.10	193, 198, 341, 342, 344, 603, 605
18.36	240	22.3–5	345		
19f.	602	22.3	345		
19.3f.	240	22.4ff.	624		
19.3	241	22.4	345	23.10b	345
19.4	240	22.6	245	23.11f.	606
19.6	240	22.7–23	345	23.11	135, 190, 198, 199, 209, 302, 344, 345
19.7ff.	325	22.8	199		
19.7	240	22.10f.	345		
19.8f.	239	22.11	199		
19.13	351	22.12–23	345	23.12ff.	148
19.15	298	22.12	345, 366	23.12	189, 198, 344, 345, 632
19.16	240	22.13–20	345		
19.32–34a	325	22.14–20	602		
19.32ab–34	240	22.14f.	202	23.13f.	198, 344, 606
19.34	241	22.16–18	345		
19.35	325	22.18–20	398	23.13	148, 312
20.5	30, 187, 294	22.19	658	23.14	334
		22.20–24	345	23.15–20	198
20.12ff.	163	22.20b–23	345	23.15–18	146, 344
20.17– 24.13	605	22.21–23	345	23.15	345, 605
		23	337, 484	23.16–18	344, 605
21	335	23.1–13	623	23.19f.	345
21.2–9	398	23.1–3	205, 229, 230, 345, 350, 362	23.19	274, 345
21.3–7	603			23.21–23	353
21.3f.	605			23.21	199, 345, 548
21.3	133, 334, 335, 603, 605	23.1	345		
		23.2	199, 229	23.24	37, 345, 603, 604, 605
		23.3	345, 350		
21.4f.	606	23.4–14	345		
21.4	364, 602	23.4	38, 87, 198, 334, 343, 344, 605	23.25	198, 388, 602
21.5	190, 335, 632			23.26	398
21.6	341, 342, 603, 605	23.4b	345	23.27	363, 602
		23.5–6	345	23.29f.	345, 353
21.7	85, 363, 364, 602	23.5	133, 190, 198, 209,	23.29	232
21.10ff.	605			23.31– 25.26	399

23.34–37	233	9.1	659	20.25	295
24.4ff.	129	9.2–17	654	21–29	656
24.8–17	252	9.3ff.	654	21.6	655
24.12	242	9.13	652	21.23	655, 656
24.13f.	388, 602,	9.21	655	21.26ff.	547
	604	10–II		21.29	655
24.14	598	Chron. 9	655	21.30	658
24.16	598	10.13	659	22.9	660
24.34a	525	11–II		22.10–13	657
25	658	Chron. 9	546	22.10	550, 606
25.12	371	11.1f.	657	22.11	658
25.13–17	388, 602,	11.9	658	22.12f.	657
	604	11.32	280	22.12	655
25.15–20	396	12.6	280	22.16	658
25.16f.	298, 367	12.9	652	22.18	658, 660
25.18–21	241	12.17–29	295	22.19	658
25.18	366, 460	12.29	295	23–27	655
25.19	366	12.39f.	657	23.2	657
25.27–30	386, 598,	12.41	660	23.3	622
	602, 619	13	547, 656	23.25	660
25.27	388	13.1f.	656	23.26	655
28.8f.	207	13.1	659	23.32	654
		13.3	658	24.7–18	460
I Chronicles		13.4	656, 659	25	658
1–9	654, 659	13.6	298	26.6	652
1.9	654	15f.	547, 656	26.31	652
1.43	654	15	655	27.25–31	286
2	655	15.1b	296	28.1ff.	659
2.15	654	15.2ff.	548	28.1	549, 657
3	655	15.2	655	28.2	298, 551,
3.1ff.	654	15.3	657		552
3.17ff.	654	15.11	657	28.4–6	547
3.18	616	15.13	548, 658	28.4	547
3.24	278	15.15	548	28.5	550, 657
4	655	15.25	660	28.6	550, 606
4.10	658	15.26	548, 657	28.7	657
4.31	654	16.7–36	551	28.7b–10	657
4.41	654	16.11	658	28.8	557, 658
5.1ff.	660	16.15	656	28.9f.	657
5.2	547, 654,	16.34	658	28.9	30, 658
	656	16.41	658	28.10	547
5.7	660	16.39f.	655	28.11ff.	655
5.20	658	16.40	462, 655,	28.20	658
5.24	652		656	28.21	655
5.25	659	17	550, 658	29.1ff.	549
5.27–41	295	17.5	656	29.1–9	549
5.36	654	17.10b	289	29.5ff.	311
5.39f.	366	17.11ff.	550	29.8	655
6	623	17.11	255	29.9	660
6.16f.	654	17.13f.	657	29.10	658
6.17	655	17.13	606	29.11	657
6.34	655	17.14	550	29.14	549
6.35–38	295	17.15	289	29.15	662
7.2	652, 654	18.14–17	285	29.17	549, 660
7.14	270	18.16	656	29.18	657
7.37	73,269	18.21	656	29.20ff.	550, 659

29.22	656, 660	11.15	344	17.3–6	658
29.23ff.	657	11.16	305	17.3f.	658, 659
29.23	550	11.22f.	550	17.3	658
29.29	657	12	658	17.4	30, 658
		12.1	655, 659	17.7–9	657
II Chronicles		12.2	659	17.7–11	660
1.3	655	12.5–8	658	17.9	655
1.6	655	12.5	657	17.12f.	657
1.13	655	12.6f.	658	18.1	659
1.14f.	308	12.6	660	18.4	658
1.16f.	287, 660	12.7	657	18.6	658
2.3	656	12.13	655	18.7	658
2.16f.	657	12.14	658	18.8	349
3–7	656	12.15	657	18.17	294
3.1	296, 308, 649	13.4–12	646, 648, 659	19.2f.	657
				19.2	659
3.8	459	13.5	50, 656, 657	19.3	658
3.10–14	130			19.4	659, 660
3.12	298	13.7	660	19.4b–11	657
3.14	458	13.8	550, 656, 657	19.6	658
4.1	459			19.8ff.	203
5.2ff.	657	13.11	458, 655, 656	19.8–11	184
5.4	655			19.11	658
5.5	547	13.12	658	20	80, 657
5.10	656	13.18	658	20.3f.	658
5.12ff.	658	13.19	648	20.4	657
5.12	655	13.22	657	20.9	658
5.13	658	14	659	20.10	656
6.5f.	604, 655	14.2f.	659	20.14–17	657
6.5	656	14.3	658	20.17	658
6.16	550, 656, 657	14.5f.	657	20.20ff.	658
		14.5	660	20.20	550, 551
6.34	655	14.6	657, 658, 660	20.21	551, 657
6.41	551			20.27	660
7.1ff.	660	14.10	658	20.29	660
7.1–3	547	15.1–9	659	20.34	657
7.3	658	15.1–7	657	20.37	657, 659
7.6	658	15.2	551, 657, 658	21.7	550, 656
7.12	655			21.12–15	657
7.14	658	15.3–6	549	21.12	658
7.16	655	15.4	658	22.9	658
7.17f.	550	15.8–15	657	23.3	550
7.18	656, 657	15.9f.	657	23.6	549
7.22	656	15.9	648, 658, 659, 660	23.7	655
8.13	655			23.18	655
8.15	655	15.12	658	23.20	657
9.8	550	15.15	657, 658, 660	24.4ff.	657
9.29	657			24.4	322
10–36	655	16.7–9	657	24.5	655
10.1–19	660	16.7f.	658	24.6f.	549
10.13f.	658	16.7	658, 659	24.7	322
11.2f.	657	16.8	658	24.22	657
11.5–12	657	16.10	657	25.4	655
11.6	648, 658	16.11	658	25.7	658
11.14f.	646	16.12	658	25.15f.	657
11.13–17	659	17.2	657	25.15	658

25.19	659	30.25	660	35.7	657
26.5	658	31.1ff.	659, 660	35.11	656, 659
26.9f.	657	31.2ff.	657	35.12	548, 655
26.12	652	31.3f.	655	35.15	655, 658
26.15	654	31.3	656	35.18	646, 648,
26.16	659	31.4ff.	549		659, 660
26.18	549, 659	31.21	658	35.21	658
26.22	657	32.3	657	35.26	655
27.3f.	657	32.5f.	657	36.11ff.	659
28	322	32.7	658	36.12ff.	657
28.2	322	32.10	658	36.12	657, 658
28.9ff.	659	32.17	30	36.14	659
28.9–15	660	32.25f.	659	36.15f.	657
28.9–11	657	32.26	658	36.21	371, 657
28.16	658, 659	32.30	657	41.21	658
28.20f.	658	32.31	659		
28.22	659	32.32	657	*Ezra*	
28.23	658	33	660	1.1ff.	569
28.30	659	33.3	322, 655	1–6	450
29.5ff.	656	33.6	655	1.2–4	546
29.5–11	657	33.7	655	1.3	546
29.6	659	33.8	655	1.6	623
29.11	655	33.10–13	659	1.7–11	444
29.19	659	33.11–13	659	1.7	546
29.29–30	658	33.12f.	658	1.17	621
29–31	334	33.12	658	2	616, 619,
29.20–24	656	33.14	657, 659		647
29.20	657	33.15	659	2.2ff.	654
29.30	660	33.19	657, 658	2.2	280, 617
29.34	659, 660	33.23	658	2.6	280
29.36	660	34.3–7	659	2.21–35	619
29.44	656	34.3	30, 658	2.28	648
30.1ff.	648, 657,	34.6f.	648	2.36ff.	373, 447
	659, 660	34.6	646, 659,	2.41ff.	460
30.2ff.	656		660	2.43–58	613
30.2	656, 659	34.8ff.	657	2.59ff.	654
30.3	660	34.8	280	2.59	446, 599
30.4	656, 659	34.9	646, 648,	2.61f.	447
30.5	655		659, 660	2.64	619
30.6	658	34.12f.	655	2.68f.	446, 623
30.7	659	34.14	655	2.69	373
30.9	338	34.21	658, 659,	3.2ff.	625
30.11	646, 658		660	3.2	655
30.12	655	34.22–28	657	3.4	655
30.15	660	34.26	658	3.11	658
30.16	655	34.27	658	4	546, 654
30.17	656, 659	34.29ff.	657	4.1–5.9	646
30.18	646, 655	34.29–32	657	4.1–5.7	524
30.19	658	34.33	659	4.1–5	525, 526,
30.21–26	660	35	654, 655		647
30.21	658	35.1–19	548	4.1f.	526
30.22	656, 659	35.1	656	4.1	328
30.23	656, 659	35.3–6	659	4.2	446, 546,
30.24	549, 657,	35.4	548, 655		647
	660	35.6	655	4.3	446, 526,
30.25f.	660	35.7–9	549, 660		546

4.4	616	8.21	599	5.8	323, 498,
4.6	445, 526,	8.23	599		636
	529	8.30	373	5.9	498
4.7–22	526, 529	8.33	277, 623	5.10–12	496
4.7–16	372	8.36	446	5.12f.	498
4.7	445	9.29	446	5.12	616
4.8–23	445	10	472, 541	5.13	447, 616
4.9f.	647	10.1	447	5.14	446, 616
4.10	546	10.8	449, 619	5.15	498, 617,
4.12f.	445	10.12	447		635
4.15	445			5.17	446, 617,
4.17	446	*Nehemiah*			619, 635
5.1	648	1	623	5.18	446
5.3ff.	616	1.5–11	438	5.19	616
5.3–17	445	1.9	363	5.22	616
5.5	446	2.7	446	5.31	616
5.9	446	2.8	622	6	546
5.13	546, 620	2.9	446	6.1ff.	646
5.14f.	546	2.10–20	646	6.2	526
5.14	616	2.10	372, 526	6.5	526
5.17	616	2.13	335	6.6–14	446
6.1–15	445	2.16	446, 447,	6.7	439
6.1–5	444		635	6.10	621
6.4	459	2.19	372, 526	6.12	526
6.5	546	3ff.	546	6.14	277, 439,
6.7	446, 617	3	495, 546		526
6.8–10	459	3.1	447, 624	6.16–18	530
6.8	446, 620	3.2–32	619	6.17	446, 635
6.10	459, 654	3.9ff.	446	7	460, 616,
6.14	446	3.22	624		619, 647
6.16–18	620	3.28	624	7.2	446, 622
6.21	449, 529,	3.29	96	7.5	446, 447,
	647, 654	3.33	526, 646		635, 647
7.1–8	466	4–6	529	7.25–38	619
7.1	366, 557	4.1ff.	646	7.32	648
7.8	617	4.1	526	7.61	446, 599
7.11–26	466, 468	4.7	618	7.66	619
7.11f.	466	4.8	446, 635	8–10	546, 625
7.12	446, 466	4.13	446, 635	8	347, 601
7.14	466	5	217, 439,	8.13	446
7.15f.	623		497, 498,	8.14ff.	90
7.21–23	459		503, 618,	8.15	655
7.23	459		636	8.17	619
7.24	459, 460,	5.1–5	160, 161,	9	53, 606
	613		495	9.6	608
7.25f.	466	5.1	494, 496,	9.18	144, 145,
7.25	446, 466,		636		309
	619	5.2	495	10	625, 629
7.26	466, 467,	5.3–5	495	10.1	617
	470, 623	5.3	495	10.3–9	460
8.1	446	5.4–5	495	10.18	208
8.15–20	600	5.4	496	10.27	280
8.17	373, 599	5.5	496, 636	10.29ff.	447
8.18f.	622	5.6f.	496	10.29	449
8.20–23	621	5.7	446, 447,	10.32	410, 498,
8.20	613		495, 497		608, 636

10.32b	629	1.6ff.	133, 643	15.18	133
10.33f.	461	1.9	515	15.20–35	643
10.33	549	1.17	643	15.20	640
10.35	461, 655	1.21	515	15.25f.	637
10.36	461	1.22	516, 643	15.27	637
10.37	655	2.10	515	16.2	643
10.38	283, 461	3–27	515	16.8–21	517
11.1–2	627	3	216	16.19	517
11.3–19	654	4.3–5	502, 643	16.21	517
11.4–22	619	4.6	561, 643	18.5–21	643
11.13	446	4.7–11	643	19.23–27a	517
11.14	652	4.11	636	19.26	517
11.18	622	4.12–16	644	20.4–29	643
11.25–35	619	4.17–21	644	20.15	637
12.1–7	447, 460	4.17	516	20.17–22	637
12.4	280	5.1f.	662	20.19f.	514
12.17	280	5.2–5	516	20.19	496, 637
12.28f.	619	5.3–5	643	21	515
12.40	635	5.8ff.	616	21.7	637
13.1ff.	459	5.8	662	21.9ff.	637
13.1f.	625	5.11	641	21.14f.	637
13.4ff.	278, 629	5.12–14	643	21.28	499
13.4–14	648	5.16b	641	21.31ff.	637
13.4–13	625	5.17f.	643, 662	22.2	662
13.4	447, 530, 62	5.17	643, 662	22.3f.	515
		5.19–26	643	22.6f.	497
13.10ff.	439	6.22f.	498	22.6	496
13.10–13	461	6.23	323, 640	22.7–9	637
13.1	635	7.2–3	496	22.8	499, 503, 637, 640
13.15ff.	608	7.11ff.	516		
13.15–22	541, 602	8.5f.	513	22.21ff.	616
13.17	446, 608, 635	8.6bf.	643	22.21f.	643
		8.12–15	643	22.21	643
13.22	608	8.13–15	513, 514	22.22	643
13.23ff.	472	8.13	643	22.26–28	643
13.25–27	625	8.14	643	22.30	513
13.26	438	8.16	637	23	669
13.28f.	624	8.21f.	643	23.21	669
13.28	447, 449, 460, 526, 530, 531, 629, 646, 648	10.3	278	24.3f.	636
		10.8–12	278	24.4	637
		10.13	502	24.9	636, 637
		10.15	502	25.2–6	644
		11.15–19	643	26.2f.	643
13.30	527	11.18	643	26.12f.	133
13.31	461	11.20	643	27.13	640
		12.21a	641	28	643
Esther		12.24b	641	29–31	515
1.19	623	13	516, 517	29.2ff.	516
2.5	280	13.4	643	29.6ff.	500
2.18	358	14.6	496	29.12ff.	439
6.12	667	14.13–17	517	29.12f.	636
8.17	408	14.15	278, 517	29.13	636
		14.19	606	29.14–17	498
Job		15.4	516	29.16f.	514
1.1–2.13	514	15.5f.	516	29.16	500
1.4	282	15.14–16	644	29.17	496, 499

29.18–20	517	2.7	116, 117,	10.15	645
29.18f.	616		119, 290,	10.16–18	520
29.24	643		291, 339,	10.16f.	520
30.1f.	502		606	10.16	520, 521,
30.1	514	2.8–12	425		522
30.5ff.	646, 648	2.8	119	10.17f.	645
30.15	499, 514	2.9	119	10.17	519
30.25	636, 643	2.10ff.	333	10.18–20	520
31	516	2.10	119	10.18	522
31.5ff.	513	2.12a	119	11.1	606
31.13ff.	439	3.4	249	11.2	642
31.13–34	498	3.7f.	642	11.21	660
31.13–15	500	3.8	354	12	443, 519,
31.16ff.	500, 514	3.9	641		520, 637,
31.16f.	636	5.3	354		644
31.19	636	6.2	642	12.2–5	519
31.21	636	7.2	354, 606	12.2–3	520
31.24–28	513	7.4	354	12.2	519, 644,
31.24f.	637, 639	7.6	644		646
31.24	643	7.7–10	641	12.4f.	520
31.35–37	516, 517	7.11	249	12.5	520
31.38–40	498	8	641	12.6	519, 521,
33.14–30	281	9f.	443, 521		645, 646
33.14–18	644	9	520, 641,	12.6b	520
33.16–20	643		644	12.7–9	521
35.9–16	643	9.5	645	12.8	645
35.9	643	9.6	572, 645	12.9	520, 645
35.10	278,643	9.8–11	646	12.26	644
36.7–12	643, 644	9.8f.	520, 521,	13	510
36.10ff.	662		645	13.3–5	510
36.15	643	9.10f.	644, 646	13.4	354
36.18	326	9.11	519, 646	14	519, 644
36.22	643	9.13	645, 646	14.1–4	645
38–42.6	515	9.16f.	645	14.1	519
40.8–14	517	9.17	645	14.4	519, 522
40.17	251	9.18	645	14.5f.	521, 645
40.42	251	9.19	645, 646	14.5	521, 646
41.6	559	9.20	521, 645	14.16	519
42.1–6	517	10	520, 637,	16.1	606
42.7–17	514		644	16.8	558
42.12–17	515	10.2–11	519	17.1	135
		10.2	250	17.9	642
Psalms		10.3–15	645	18	287
1–59	126	10.4	519	18.3	249
1ff.	661	10.5	520	18.12	519
1	556, 557,	10.6	519, 520	18.16	519
	562, 660,	10.7–15	529	18.40	120
	661	10.9	519	18.44	120
1.1	640	10.10	520	19	556, 557,
1.2	558, 559	10.11	519, 520		560, 660,
1.6	662	10.12	518, 519,		661
2	119, 273,		645	19.1–8	557, 661
	287, 301,	10.13	519	19.1–7	660
	424	10.14f.	520	19.1–5	561
2.1–3	119	10.14	522	19.4f.	118
2.6	288	10.15f.	645	19.5–7	135

19.8–12	558	28.8f.	641	38.4	642
19.8	558	29	133, 301	38.16	334
19.8bb	660	29.1f.	133	40.2	334
19.9	558, 559	29.5–9a	301	40.5ff.	606
19.9aa	660	29.9	133, 632	40.7–9	521
19.10aa	660	29.10	299, 300	40.8f.	662
19.10ab	660	29.11	134	40.14ff.	644
19.10ba	660	29.41ff.	301	40.15	518
19.11a	660	30.5f.	641	40.17	644
19.11b	660	31.2	606	40.18	518, 644
19.12	660, 662	32	642	43.3	631
19.13	660, 661	32.2–6	642	44	378, 600
19.14	560, 660, 663	32.2	642	45	287
		32.8ff.	606	45.7f.	120
19.15	660	33	661	45.7	117, 118, 327
19.22	645	33.20–22	641		
19.29	119	33.20	616	45.18	337
19.35	119	33.22	616	46	302
19.40	119	34	644	46.2–4	136
20	129, 287	34.3	518	46.5f.	136, 363
21.2	298	34.5ff.	606	46.5	136, 363, 614, 631
21.7	120, 121	34.5	568		
22	443	35	520, 644	46.6	136
22.2	354	34.4–8	645	46.7	136
22.3	354	34.25f.	645	46.8	299
22.5–6	96, 641	35.9f.	520, 645	46.9–11	136, 292
22.10f.	100	35.10	519, 522, 644	46.9f.	137
22.10	278, 339			46.10f.	292
22.11	354	35.20	519	46.10	304, 333
22.23–32	509, 641	35.25f.	645	46.12	299
22.23ff.	641	36	637	47	273, 299, 301, 425
22.23	644	37	497, 502, 637		
22.24	644			47.3–6	134
22.25	644, 646	37.1	502	47.3	299
22.26	644	37.7	497, 637	47.4f.	292
22.27	518, 644, 646, 658	37.8f.	646	47.4	301, 422
		37.9	502, 640	47.5	362, 603
24.7ff.	299	37.10	502	47.6	125, 134, 300, 301, 303
24.7–10	134, 632	37.11	640, 644		
24.7	299	37.12	497, 637		
24.8	299	37.13	637	47.7	299
24.9	299	37.14	497, 637, 644	47.8	134
24.10	299, 300			47.9f.	333
25	642, 644	37.15	502	47.9	134, 299, 300, 301, 425
25.5f.	509	37.16f.	637		
25.5	334	37.16	637		
25.7	642	37.21	502	47.10	119, 134, 228, 422
25.13	640	37.22	640		
25.16	518, 646	37.27f.	520	48	302
25.20	606	37.27	640	48.2f.	363
25.21	334	37.32f.	497, 637	48.3	136, 137, 299, 301, 600
25.22	606, 641	37.32	497		
26.8	631	37.35	640		
27.9	558	37.24	640	48.4ff.	367
27.10	100, 606	38	642	48.4	136
28.4f.	642	38.2	642	48.5–8	136

48.8	304	68.8–11	82	73	502, 633,
48.9	136, 299	68.8f.	51, 52		637
48.13–15	136, 137	68.9	53	73.1	638
48.14f.	363	68.10	271	73.2ff.	502
48.14	600	68.17	631	73.4	637
49	502, 637	69	520, 637,	73.7	637
49.6f.	502		644	73.10	637
49.7	502, 637	69.7	520, 641,	73.11	637
49.14ff.	502		646	73.12	637
49.17	637	69.23–29	645	73.13	515
51	642	69.27	518	73.17	638
51.5–7	642	69.29	521, 644,	73.18ff.	502
51.9–11	642		646	73.26–28	644
51.20	606, 641	69.30	518, 645,	74	378, 600
52	502, 633,		646	74.2	96, 631
	637	69.31	509, 641	74.7f.	600
52.3ff.	638	69.32	521	74.7	631
52.3–7	502	69.33–37	520	74.9	316
52.8	638	69.33–36	509, 641	74.13f.	133
52.9	502, 637	69.33f.	519, 645	74.19	518, 519,
52.10	638	69.33	518, 641,		646
53	645		644, 646	74.21	518, 519,
53.6	641	69.34	644, 646		646
54.5	641	69.35–37	606	75	519, 644
56.2f.	282	69.36f.	640	75.2	645
56.6b	606	69.37	519, 522,	75.3–9	521
56.8	641		644, 646	75.3	520, 645
56.9b	606	70	644	75.5	519, 645
56.12	606	70.2	518	75.8	521, 645
56.14	606	70.3–5	645	75.9	645
57.2	606	70.3f.	645	75.10f.	645
58	6745	70.5	520, 644,	75.11	519, 521,
58.11	642		646		644, 645,
59.6	641	70.6	518, 519,		646
59.9	641		645, 646	76	302
59.12	641	71.1	100, 606	76.3	136, 300,
59.14	641	71.5	278, 334		363, 603,
59.17	643	71.6	643		631
60–150	126	71.10f.	100	76.4	137, 304
60	378, 600,	72	120, 129,	76.6f.	333
	609		287, 457	76.10	519
61	637	72.2	120, 327,	76.13	333
61.7f.	641		518, 644	77	96, 641
62	502	72.4	120, 327,	77.7–11	400
62.2f.	641		518, 644	77.8–11	425
62.4f.	402	72.5	120	77.8–10	402
62.6–8	616, 641	72.6f.	120	77.9	377
62.9ff.	642	72.7	120	78.35	301
62.9–11	502	72.8–11	292	78.68f.	363, 364
62.9	638	72.9	120	78.68	303
62.11	637	72.12f.	120, 327	79	378, 600
63.12	641	72.12	518	79.6f.	381, 600
66	641	72.13	518, 644	80	96, 299
66.13ff.	101	72.16	120	80.2	298
68.5	52	72.17	120, 406,	80.9–12	401
68.6	606		607	80.18	117

81.10	264	89.27	290, 291,	101	120, 297,
82	133, 519,		339, 606		327
	644, 645	89.27b	339	101.2	662
82.1–7	521	89.28	117, 292,	102	644
82.1	132, 520		339	102.4	378, 606
82.2–7	522	89.29	119, 365	102.11	642
82.2	645	89.31–33	119, 290	102.13–23	509, 641
82.3	519	89.34–38	292	102.14–23	606
82.8	521, 645	89.34	291	103	641
84	302	89.35	365	103.3	642
84.2	299, 363,	89.37f.	118	103.7	641
	631	89.37	118, 291	103.8–10	511
84.4	299, 300	89.40	365	103.9	642
84.12	135	89.50	119, 377	103.10	642
84.13	299	90	510, 641	103.11–12	511
84.14	518	90.1f.	510, 641	103.11	511
85	609	90.7	642	103.13	511, 606
85.11	135	90.8	642	103.18	511
85.12	135	90.9	642	103.19–21	300, 510
84.14	135	90.11	642	103.13	510
86.1	518, 644,	93	133, 299	103.21	132
	645, 646	93.1–4	133	105.1–15	658
86.2	646	93.1	299	105.4	658
86.5	642	93.2	134, 299	106.1	658
86.14	663	94	497, 502,	106.19	309
87–90	637		616, 637	106.37	31, 341
87.1f.	136	94.5–6	502	106.38	342
87.3	136	94.5	497, 502,	106.47f.	658
87.5	136		637, 639	107	510, 641
88	644	94.7	637	107.2f.	510
88.8	642	94.8–11	502	107.4–32	510
88.17	642	94.8	639	107.11	642
89	119, 287,	94.14f.	502, 639	107.17	642
	290, 378,	94.15ff.	502	107.33–42	510
	600	94.16ff.	502	107.41	519
89.4f.	365	94.17	641	107.42	641
89.4	362, 603,	94.20f.	502	109	497, 520,
	612	94.21	497, 637,		644
80.6–19	291, 300		639	109.2–5	261
89.6–13	133	94.22	641	109.2f.	497
89.6–8	133	95.3	133, 299,	109.6–20	645
89.8	133		425	109.6–16	645
89.9	299	96.1–11	658	109.16	518, 645
89.10–13	292	96.6ff.	502	109.17–20	645
89.10f.	133	96.7f.	632	109.20f.	519
89.15	291, 299	96.10	299	109.22	518, 645,
89.16	135	97.1	299		646
89.18	612	97.2	135	109.28f.	645
89.20–38	117, 118	97.6	632	109.30f.	520
89.20–30	292	97.7	133	110	287
89.20–28	133	98.6	299	110.1f.	120
89.20	362, 603	99.1	298, 299	110.1	117, 600
89.22	612	99.4	299	110.3	116, 117
89.25	291	99.5	57, 298,	110.4	292, 295
89.26	291, 292		600	112	502, 637
				112.2f.	502

112.4	502		119.32	559, 561, 662		119.89	660
112.5	502					119.90f.	561
112.7	502		119.33	559, 561, 662		119.90	560
112.9	502, 518, 644		119.34	559, 662		119.92	558
			119.35	558, 559, 561, 662		119.93	661
113.7	518, 519					119.94-155	557
115.9-11	642		119.36	662		119.94	558, 559
115.9	616		119.37	559, 660		119.95	560, 562
115.15	135		119.38	662		119.56	559
116.14	101		119.40	558		119.97	558, 559, 661, 662
116.17-19	282		119.41	661			
116.18	101		119.42	558		119.98	558
117ff.	364		119.43	558, 662		119.99	559, 661
118.8f.	642		119.44	662		119.100	562, 662
119	441, 556, 557, 558, 560, 562, 660, 661, 662		119.45	557, 559		119.101	662
			119.47	558, 662		119.103	660
			119.48	558, 559, 661		119.105	558, 559, 561
119.2	662		119.49	661, 662		119.108	559, 560, 660
119.3	559		119.50	560			
119.4f.	662		119.51ff.	562		119.110	559
119.5	559		119.53	562		119.111	558
119.6	558, 559, 661		119.55	662		119.112	660, 662
			119.56	662		119.113	558, 562, 662
119.7	559		119.57	662			
119.8f.	662		119.58	661, 662		119.114	558
119.8	661		119.61	562		119.115	662
119.10	662		119.63	561, 662		119.116	661
119.12	559		119.65	661, 662		119.117	558, 559, 661
119.14	559		119.66	558, 559			
119.15	559, 661		119.67	558, 660, 661, 662		119.118	562, 660, 661
119.16	558					119.119	558, 662
119.17	558, 661, 662		119.68	559		119.120	558
			119.69f.	562		119.121f.	560
119.18	559, 661		119.69	662, 663		119.121	662
119.19	558, 662		119.70	558		119.122	662, 663
119.20	558		119.71	559, 662		119.123	558
119.21	562, 662, 663		119.72	662		119.124	559
			119.73	278, 559		119.125	558, 559
119.22	662		119.74	558, 561		119.126	560, 562, 663
119.23	559, 661, 662		119.75	560, 662			
			119.77	558		119.127	558, 660, 662
119.24	558		119.78	559, 560, 562, 662, 663			
119.25ff.	662					119.128	662
119.25	661					119.129	559, 662
119.26	559		119.79	559		119.130	559, 660
119.27	559, 561, 662		119.81	558		119.131	558
			119.82	558		119.132	662
119.28	661		119.84	560, 661, 662		119.134	558, 560, 662
119.29f.	562, 662						
119.29	661		119.85	562, 663		119.135	559
119.30	558, 559		119.87	560, 562		119.136	562, 563, 662
119.31	558, 662, 663		119.88	558, 662			
			119.89-91	561, 660, 661		119.137	558, 660
						119.139	562, 563

119.140	558, 559, 660, 662	132.5	249, 296, 309, 631	1.7	561
119.141	662	132.6–8	118	1.10–13	637
119.142	559, 660	132.7	57, 298,	1.16–19	638
119.143	558		363, 600,	2.7	643
119.144	558, 559, 560		631	2.8	662
119.145	558, 662	132.11ff.	117	2.20	662
119.146	558, 662	132.11a	119, 363	2.21f.	638
119.147f.	559	132.11b–13	290, 363	2.21	640
119.147	559	132.11b–12	119	3.9f.	283
119.148	559, 661	132.13f.	364, 361	3.11f.	643
119.149	558	132.13	303, 603	3.12	662
119.150	562	132.14–18	118	3.13–20	643
119.151	559, 662	132.15	519	3.16	4324
119.152	559	132.17f.	292	3.25	638
119.154	661	132.17	291, 603	3.27	638
119.155	559, 562, 662	132.18	622	3.31	638
		134.3	135	3.34	640
119.156	661	135.21	631	4.11	561
119.158	562, 662	137	374, 412	4.14–19	638
119.160	559	137.1–6	412	5.22f.	638
119.161	558, 662	137.4	377	6.23	561
119.162	558	137.7–9	413	6.35	326
119.163	558, 662	138.8	278	8	561, 643
119.164	559	139.16	646	9.7	640
119.165	558	139.19–22	642	9.21	642
119.166	662	140	520, 644	10–15	638
119.167	558, 662	140.5	642	10.2	324
119.168	662	140.9–12	645	10.3	638
119.169	559	140.13	519, 520,	10.4	324
119.171	558, 559		522, 645	10.6	638
119.172	560	140.14	518, 519,	10.11	638
119.174	558		641, 644,	10.15	32, 642
119.175	558		646	10.16	638
119.176	662	141.8	606	10.21	638
121.2	135	142.8	641	10.22	642
123	641	143.2	642	10.30	638, 640
124	641	143.5	96, 641	10.31	638
124.7	641	144.1–11	287	10.32	638
124.8	135	145	641, 669	11.4	324
125	641	145.10	669	11.10	638
125.1	642	145.13	669	11.16b	324
125.5	642	145.13a	669	11.18f.	638
126	641	145.19f.	642	11.20	561
130f.	334	146	641	11.26	324
130	606, 642	146.3	642	11.28	637, 638,
130.3	642	146.9	642		642
130.5	642	147.6	518, 519,	12.5	638
130.7f.	641		646	12.6	638
131	641	148.2	132	12.27	324
132	118, 287,	149	519, 669	13.5	638
	290, 363,	149.4	518, 646	13.8	324, 326
	551, 658			13.22	638
		Proverbs		13.25	638
132.2	249, 309	1–9	441, 512,	14.13	512
			513, 638	14.20	324
				14.21	324, 642

14.26	643	29.2	638	6.1ff.	303, 429,
14.31f.	327	29.7	638		484, 631
14.31	324, 642	29.12	638	6.1–8.18	177, 328
14.35	642	29.13	324, 642	6.1–8	300
15.6	638	29.14	327	6.1	131, 132,
15.8	638	29.16	638		299, 325
15.9	638	29.27	638	6.3	132, 135,
15.15	324	30.5	643		299
15.16	642	31.6	636	6.5	132, 299
15.26	638	31.8f.	326	6.9f.	179
15.29	638			6.11	168, 179,
16.3	642	*Isaiah*			415
16.8	324, 642	1.2	606	6.14	168
16.9	642	1.2–20	600	7.1–17	329
16.10	121	1.5–8	324	7.3ff.	325
16.14	642	1.10–17	171	7.3	178, 334
16.19	324	1.11	330	7.4–9a	327
16.33	642	1.13	408	7.4	82, 167,
17.5	324	1.16f.	171		327, 328
18.11	324, 642	1.17	171	7.5–9a	327
18.23	324, 643	1.23	160, 165,	7.5f.	167
19.1	324, 642		324, 338	7.7–9	167, 169
19.4	324	1.24	309	7.7b–8a	327
19.7	324	1.26	166, 302	7.7b	329
19.17	324, 327,	2.2–4	567	7.8b	328
	642	2.4	304	7.9	551, 657
19.22	324, 642	2.6aa	600	7.9b	167, 177,
20.22	92	2.10	169		328
20.24	642	2.12–17	169	7.11f.	167
21.3	208	2.13f.	640	7.13	170
21.13	324, 642	3.1ff.	329	7.14	278
21.31	642	3.3	639	7.16	167
22f.	324	3.12	160	7.17	167, 169
22.2	324, 642	3.14f.	322	8.1–6	177
22.7	324, 643	3.14	160, 323,	8.1–4	334
22.9	324, 642		324	8.2	325
22.16	324, 643	4.3	646	8.3	177
22.19	643	4.10	354	8.5–7	167
22.22f.	642	4.13	354	8.7f.	167
22.22	327	5.1–7	166, 177	8.7	169
22.26f.	643	5.1–4	166	8.8b	600
23.1	642	5.5f.	167	8.9f.	303
23.17	643	5.7	166, 269,	8.10	328, 329,
25–28	638		323		415, 600
25.5	638	5.8–10	158	8.11ff.	164
25.21	92	5.8	165	8.11–15	168, 177
26.6	642	5.11f.	165	8.11f.	178
28.1	638	5.12	329	8.12f.	328
28.3	638	5.19	329, 415	8.12	325
28.6	324, 642	5.20	165	8.13	299
28.8	324, 642	5.23	165, 184	8.16ff.	164
28.12	638	5.24	612	8.17f.	178, 415
28.15	638	5.25ff.	415	8.17	179
28.20	324	5.26ff.	167, 169	8.18	131, 178,
28.27	324, 642	5.26f.	176		179, 299,
28.28	638	6	334		

	303, 363, 631	24.2	571, 573, 666	26.10a	571
8.23ab–9.6	203	24.4	571, 573	26.10bf.	571
8.24–26	600	24.5	572, 573	26.13	337, 571
9.1–8	570	24.7–12	573	26.14a	666
9.1–6	240	24.10–12	570	26.16–18	571
9.3	666	24.12	666	26.17f.	334
9.5	288	24.13	666	26.18	572
9.7–20	169	24.14–15aa	667	26.18ab	667
9.14	639	24.16	571, 572	26.18bb	666
10	415, 461	24.16ab	667	26.19	574, 596, 666, 667, 668
10.1–4	169	24.18	667		
10.1f.	165, 324, 326, 338	24.18b	571, 573, 579	26.20f.	575, 667
10.1	121	24.19f.	573	26.21	581
10.2	322	24.20	572, 667	27	571, 666, 667
10.5ff.	176	24.21–23	571, 573, 585, 666		
10.5–15	169			27.1	133
10.33f.	640	24.21	578, 666	27.7–18	571
11	567	24.22	579	28.7b–13	171
11.1–5	240	24.23	663, 667	27.10	570
11.2	121	24.24	415	28.12	168
11.4	291	24.26	415, 571	28.14ff.	163
11.35	121	24.27	415	28.14–19	168
12f.	325	25.1–5	667	28.14	170
13.11	640	25.2	570, 571, 573	28.15	364
13.21	344			28.16f.	168, 240
14.2	271	25.3–5	640	28.16	328
14.9	255	25.4f.	571	28.17	166
14.13f.	301	25.4	571, 573	28.18	328, 364
14.24–27	103	25.5	571, 573	28.21	329, 666
14.26	329	25.6–10a	571	28.29	329
14.32	168	25.6–8	666	29.5	640
15.6–8	574	25.6	666, 667	29.14	329
16.12–14	303	25.7	667	29.15	329, 415
17.12–14	303	25.8	666	29.17–24	49, 504, 505, 639, 664
18.19f.	38	25.8aa	574, 667		
19.1	52	25.9–10a	667		
19.13	38	25.9f.	572, 666	29.17–21	640
20.20	657	25.10a	667	29.17	506
22.2–23	347	25.10bf.	666	29.18–24	506
22.12	353	25.12	570, 573, 666	29.18	506, 640
22.15ff.	325			29.19	505, 506, 637
22.21	622	26.1–8	666		
23	323	26.1–6	667	29.20f.	506
24ff.	572, 575	26.1–3	574, 667	29.20	497
24–27	438, 565, 566, 570, 572, 573, 615	26.2	667	29.21	497, 498, 637, 640
26.5	570, 573, 666				
24–26	571, 666, 667	26.6	571, 573	29.22–24	640
26.7–18	572, 667	29.22	506, 640		
24	571	26.7	571	29.23	507
24.1	571, 572, 666	26.8	571	29.24	506, 640
		26.9f.	572	30.1ff.	240, 357, 362
		26.9	667	30.1–5	168
		26.10	571	30.1	329, 415
				30.8ff.	164

30.9	162	41.2	414, 415, 421	43.3	354
30.15	168	41.4	418, 610	43.3b	421
30.18–26	600	41.5	421	43.5–7	403
30.33	192, 341, 342	41.6f.	610	43.5	403
31.1ff.	357, 362	41.8–13	403	43.8–13	418, 611
31.1–3	168, 424	41.8f.	610	43.8	415, 417, 639 640
31.1	240	41.8	405, 657	43.9	418
31.5	240, 367	41.9	403, 405	43.10–12	421, 423, 610
32.15	639, 640	41.10	403	43.10	418, 423, 611
32.17	639	41.11f.	421		
33	600	41.13	403	43.11	418
33.10	645	41.14–16	403	43.12	418, 611
33.21ff.	136	41.14	403	43.14f.	415
34.14	344	41.15f.	421	43.15	292, 425, 657
35.1f.	497	41.17	426		
36.12	657	41.18	510	43.16f.	610
37.16	298	41.21–29	418, 611	43.18f.	417
38.21	100	41.21f.	418	43.26–28	416
40–55	414	41.21	292, 319, 425, 657	43.27	610
40–52	424			44.1–5	403
40.1ff.	505	41.22a	418	44.2	403
40.1–52.12	609	41.22b	418	44.5f.	421
40.1–8	415	41.23a	418	44.5	292, 422, 668
40.1–5	611	41.24	418		
40.2–9	610	41.25	415, 417, 418, 421	44.6–8	418, 611
40.2	415, 611	41.26	418	44.6	418, 425, 610, 657
40.3–5	609	41.27	418, 610		
40.4–9	11	41.28	418	44.7	418
40.5	421, 611	41.29	418	44.8	418, 421, 423, 610
40.9–11	424, 609, 611	42.1–4	423, 426, 567, 611		
				44.9–20	318, 610
40.11	611	42.1	121, 610	44.17	354
40.12–17	416	42.3	426	44.21f.	610
40.14	421	42.4	421	44.21	403, 418
40.15–17	421	42.5–8	423	44.22–24	611
40.18–24	416	42.5	610, 611	44.22	415
40.18	611	42.6	421	44.24– 48.22	420
40.19	610	42.7	415	44.24–28	416, 611
40.20	421	42.8	611	44.24	403
40.22b	610	42.9	417	44.24b	610
40.23f.	421	42.12	611	44.25	419, 610, 611
40.23	415	42.13	421, 422		
40.23b–24	421	42.15	510	44.26	610
40.25–26	416	42.16	415	44.27	510
40.26	610	42.18–20	415	44.28	414, 424, 610
40.27	374, 377, 402, 413	42.18	639, 640		
		42.20–25	422	45.1–7	414, 424
40.28	610	42.20–22	417	45.1–4	424
40.29–31	426	42.20	422	45.1–3	421
40.29	415	42.22	426	45.1	416
40.55	451	42.23	415	45.2f.	424
41.1–5	418, 611	42.24	416, 611	45.3	420
41.1	418	43.1–4	403	45.4f.	415
41.2f.	418	43.1	403, 610		

45.4	415, 417, 420	48.15	415	52.12	426, 610, 638
45.5f.	420	48.20–21	610	52.13–	423, 416,
45.5	416, 420, 611	48.20	420, 421	53.12	611
		48.22	582	53.1ff.	421
45.6f.	610	48.28	415	53.1–3	402
45.6	420, 421	49.1–13	611	53.9	611
45.7	418, 610	49.1–6	423, 611	54.4–6	403
45.8	416, 610	49.5	403, 423, 610	54.5	403
45.9	416			54.9	610
45.11–13	420	49.6	421, 423	55–56	456
45.12	610	49.7	421	55.3ff.	426
45.13	414, 415, 421, 610	49.8	421, 610	55.3–5	610
		49.9f.	417	55.3f.	118, 119
45.14	420, 421, 611	49.13	457	55.3	119, 365, 640
		49.14ff.	610		
45.18–25	419, 422, 610, 668	49.14– 52.12	611	55.4	421, 423
		49.14	402, 413	55.5	421, 422, 668
45.18	420	49.15	403		
45.20ff.	421, 449	49.21	402	55.6	658
45.20–25	420, 421, 611	49.22–26	422	55.8–13	610
		49.22	421	56–66	615, 621
45.20–21	422	49.22b–23	421	56.2–57.21	639
45.20	418	49.23	421	56.3–8	449
45.20b	610	49.25	421	56.3	668
45.21	418, 420, 610, 611	49.26	249, 309, 421	56.6	668
				56.7f.	255
45.22ff.	422	50–66	618	56.7	600
45.22f.	426	50.1f.	374	56.9–57.21	504, 637, 640, 645, 664
45.22	420, 422, 610	50.1	413		
		50.2	377, 413, 510	56.9–57.12	639
45.23–24	422			56.9ff.	505, 521
45.25	423	50.4–9	423, 611	56.9–12	504, 505
46.1f.	413, 420	50.40–42	510	56.9	504, 640
46.1	415	51.1f.	405, 610	56.10f.	446, 504
46.3f.	403	51.4–6	421	56.12	504
46.6f.	610	51.4f.	423	57.1f.	504, 520
46.9f.	610	51.9f.	96, 133, 378, 610	57.1	504, 505, 637
46.9	419, 420, 611				
		51.13	610	57.3–13	599
46.11	414, 421	51.15	610	57.3–11	504
46.13	610	51.22f.	421	57.3–5	504, 505
46.14	421	52f.	611	57.3	640
47	204	52.7ff.	200	57.4	505
47.8	420, 424	52.7–12	424	57.5	341, 342, 640
47.10	420, 424	52.7–10	456, 609, 611		
47.12f.	419			57.6–11	505, 640
48.3	417	52.7f.	610	57.12–21	505
48.5f.	417	52.7	567, 574, 585, 611, 663, 667	57.12f.	505
48.6b–8	417			57.13b	504, 505
48.12f.	610			57.14ff.	504
48.12	418, 419, 420	52.9	665	57.14	505, 639
		52.10–12	611	57.15–19	504, 640
48.14f.	424	52.10	421, 665	57.15	505
48.14	414, 421, 424	52.11–12	610	57.16–19	505

57.16	641	62.1–7	457	2.7b	601
57.20f.	505	62.3	457	2.11	602
57.21	582, 637	62.8f.	457, 610	2.13	602
58	621,635	62.10–12	610	2.14	349
58.1–4	494, 618,	62.10	505, 639	2.17	602
	635, 636,	62.12	457, 478	2.18	600
	638	63f.	96	2.19ff.	640
58.2	49	63.7–64.11	378, 401,	2.19–4.2	348
58.3	494		600	2.19	602
58.4	496	63.7–10	606	2.20	602
58.5	501	63.10	606	2.20b	384
58.5–9a	497, 635,	63.11–14	401	2.21	452
	638	63.11	606	2.23f.	602
58.6–9a	636	63.16	401, 403,	2.23	322
58.6–7	498		405, 606	2.26	349
58.6f.	501	64.4b–6	401	2.26b	385
58.6	497, 636	64.7	339, 401,	2.27f.	602
58.7	497, 636		403, 404	2.27	32, 188,
58.8	401, 639	64.8	401		278, 404,
58.8a	538	65	664		606
58.9a	501	63.3–5	599	2.28a	188
58.9b–12	635, 638	65.9–10	627	2.31	349
58.13f.	635	65.11	279, 599	2.32	602
58.13	410	65.14	255	2.34	322
59	664	66.1f.	290	2.36f.	203, 600
59.1–21	497	66.1	131	3.1ff.	640
59.5–8	637	66.5	506, 640	3.1	602
59.6–8	637	66.6	640	3.2	602
50.13–15a	497, 637	66.13	403	3.4f.	403, 606
60–62	456, 457,	66.17	599	3.5–7	349
	621, 639	66.18	668	3.6–11	389
60	621	66.20	478, 668	3.12–15	349
60.1–3	457	66.23	608	3.12	601
60.1	638			3.16	458, 632
60.4–9	457	*Jeremiah*		3.18–20	349
60.5–6	457	1	334, 627	3.19	403, 606
60.6	457	1.4–10	334	3.20f.	349
60.7–9	621	1.6	627	3.22ff.	20
60.7	457	1.7	626	3.22	349, 354,
60.8b	638	1.7b	384		601
60.9	457	1.9	384, 626	3.22a	349
60.10	457	1.10	384	4.1	349, 601
60.11b	457	1.14f.	235	4.3ff.	366
60.13	457	1.16b	384	4.3–6	200
60.14	457	1.17	384	4.3	601
60.16	309, 457	1.18	366, 385,	4.5–31	235
60.16b	249		601	4.7	367
60.21	578	2–6	339, 349,	4.8	235, 241
61.1f.	641		366, 600	4.10	200, 232
61.1	121, 457	2.4–4.2	203, 366	4.14	235, 601
61.3	457, 578	2.4	349	4.22	235
61.5f.	621	2.5–4.2	339	4.30	237, 346
61.6	457, 478	2.5–8	602	5.1–6	327, 348
61.7f.	457, 621	2.6–9	452	5.1–3	601
61.9	457	2.6	346, 348	5.1	235
62	621	2.7	271	5.2	235

5.4f.	200, 235	7.18f.	385	10.19–21	380
5.4	236, 348	7.18	193, 194,	10.23–25	380, 381
5.5	202, 236		339, 343	10.23	381
5.8	233	7.21f.	386	10.24f.	381
5.15–17	235	7.22f.	383	10.25	600
5.19	377, 383,	7.22	57	11.1–14	601
	384	7.23	387, 601	11.1–3	665
5.26–29	361	7.25	384	11.3f.	383
5.26–28	233	7.28	601	11.4–16	665
5.26	234, 500	7.30	227, 385,	11.4	291, 383,
5.27f.	323		386		387, 601
5.27	165	7.31	192, 341,	11.6f.	383
5.28	234, 322		342, 343,	11.7	383, 601
5.30f.	235		385, 599	11.8	384
6.1–8	235	7.32	227, 386	11.9	384
6.6f.	233	7.34	227, 386	11.10	384, 385
6.6b	361	8.3	385	11.13	65
6.8–27	601	8.4ff.	200	11.17	385, 601,
6.8	235	8.4–10.25	378, 379,		665
6.9–15	327		600	11.19	179
6.13–15	600	8.4–23	381	11.20	179
6.13f.	233	8.4–6	381, 601	11.21	384
6.13	233	8.5–18	366	12.1–6	334
6.14	166, 233,	8.5a	380	12.1	24
	234	8.7–9	381	12.3b	179
6.16	236	8.7	200, 380	12.6	178
6.17	236	8.8f.	202, 348	13–17	225
6.19–20	330	8.8	200, 236	13.13	385
6.20	235	8.9	236	13.18f.	237
6.22–26	235	8.10–12	381	13.20–22	237
6.27–30	327	8.10ab–12	600	13.27	346
6.30	236	8.13f.	361	14	609
7	233	8.13	380, 381	14.1–10	316
7.1–15	235, 240,	8.14	381	14.3f.	667
	383, 385,	8.15	381	14.8	338
	452	8.16–17	381	14.12	330
7.3	385, 386,	8.18–23	380, 381	15.5	385, 657
	387	8.19	299	15.10–20	334
7.4	137, 172,	8.19ab	380	15.10f.	179
	233, 248,	8.21–23	179	15.19f.	178
	386	9.1–10	381	16	164
7.5ff.	387	9.1–5	233, 381	16.5–7	255
7.5	385, 286	9.6	381	16.6	332, 353
7.6	338, 385	9.7	381	16.9	657
7.7	386	9.9	380	16.10–13	383
7.8	385	9.11–15	383, 600	16.11	384, 601
7.9	171, 233,	9.12	318, 601	16.18	271, 385
	357	9.13	322, 384	16.29	178
7.10	227, 386	9.16–21	380	17.14–18	334
7.11	234, 386	9.19–21	381	17.15	179
7.12	108, 172,	9.22–25	600	17.16	179
	363	9.22	381	17.18	179
7.13	383	9.24	407	17.19–27	383, 602,
7.14	172, 227,	9.27	602		619
	386	10.1–16	600	17.21ff.	608
7.17	86	10.18–22	381	17.22	608

17.23	601	22.24–30	386	29.13	387, 554
17.25	386, 287, 602	22.24–26	452	29.16–19	601
		23.1–6	619	29.16–18	602
17.26	386	23.2	665	29.19	384, 601
18.7–10	384	23.4	386, 387	27.20	387
18.11	384, 385	23.11	315	29.21f.	237
18.13–15	346, 602	23.14	24	29.24–29	238
18.15	346	23.18	133	29.25	366
18.18	384	24.6	386	29.26	238, 315
18.19–23	334	24.7	387	29.31	237
18.19	318	24.7b	387	30f.	348
18.20	179	24.8	374, 387, 601, 602	30.3	386
18.21	318			31.2–6	200, 349
18.22–24	318	24.9	607	31.4–6	2–3
18.22	318	25.4	383	31.15–17	203, 349
18.22b	179	25.5b	386	31.16	554, 657
18.23	179	25.11f.	593	31.18–20	203, 349
18.25–28	318	25.11	620, 670	31.21f.	349
18.39	318	25.30	295	31.21	349
19.1ff.	192	26	315, 366	31.29f.	609
19.5–9	602	26.3	384	31.31	387
19.5	191, 341, 342, 343, 385	26.4	384, 601	31.32	383
		26.5	383	31.33	387, 662
		26.13	384, 385	31.34	387, 601
19.12f.	385	26.16	384	32.6ff.	73
19.13	189, 385, 599	26.18	325, 384	32.6–9	323
		26.19	334, 384	32.15ff.	601
19.32	191	26.20–24	234	32.15	241
19.35	191	26.22	366	32.20–36	389
20.1ff.	315	26.24	234, 347, 366	32.23	601
20.1–6	234			32.25	193
20.1	367	26.25	202	32.29	189, 387
20.7–10	334	27.1–3	237	32.32	385
20.7a	179	27.5ff.	601	32.33	601
20.7b	179	27.5f.	387	32.34	385
20.8	179	27.6	416	32.35	341, 342, 343, 385
20.9	178	27.7	387, 601		
20.10	179	27.11	237	32.36–44	619
20.13	519, 644, 645	27.19	239	32.37	386
		28	233, 237	32.38	387
20.14–18	334	28.1–4	237	32.40	387
21.1	237, 366	28.9	626	32.41	386
21.8f.	383	28.10f.	237	32.42–44	386
21.15ff.	235	28.14	601	32.44	372
22.1–5	383, 385, 286	29	373	33.11	620
		29.1–7	238	33.13	620
22.2	286, 602	29.1	373	33.14	620
22.3	338	29.3	366, 367	33.17f.	620
22.4	386, 602	29.7	240, 241	33.21	365
22.6	322	29.10–15	386	33.22	620
22.9	319	29.10–14	619	34	217, 358, 385, 601
22.13–17	322, 361	29.10	387, 593, 601, 620, 657		
22.13	233			34.8ff.	350, 367, 636
22.15ff.	121				
22.15	200	29.13f.	551, 657, 658	34.12f.	384
22.16	332			34.13f.	383

34.13	356	42–44	387	2.1	376, 378,
34.14–17	385	42f.	374		600
34.15	227, 386	42.6	601	2.2	378, 600
34.18f.	477	42.10–17	383	2.6f.	378, 600
34.19ff.	385	42.10–12	386, 601	2.12	371
34.19	366, 385,	42.11	601	2.13	408
	601	43.10	387, 601	2.14	379, 600
35.1–11	320	44	374	2.15	378, 600
35.6	320	44.1	374	2.17	379, 600
35.13	601	44.4	384	2.18–22	378
35.15	384, 385,	44.15ff.	385, 398,	2.20	315, 371,
	386		599		600
36	177, 178,	44.15–19	52, 193,	3	378, 599
	379, 413,		194, 339,	3.1–21	606
	601		366	3.22–38	402
36.1	234	44.15f.	311	3.22–24	402
36.3	384, 601	44.17ff.	189	3.22–23	606
36.7	384, 601	44.17–19	86, 377	3.24	334, 402
36.9ff.	202	44.18	200, 211	3.26	402
36.10	234, 366	44.19	194	3.27–30	402
36.11	366	44.21	385, 601	3.31–33	402
36.12	366	44.23	601	3.34–39	402
36.21–36	234	45	177	3.40–47	606
36.23f.	345	45.5	178	3.48–51	606
36.25	366	46.15	300	3.52–54	606
36.26	234, 366	48.15	300	3.54	606
36.31	601	48.46	312	3.55ff.	402
37	413	49.1f.	627	3.55–63	606
37.3ff.	367	49.1	312, 372	3.57	281, 403
37.3–43.7	379	49.3	312	3.64–66	606
37.3–40.6	376	50.11	271	4	378, 599
37.3–9	240	51.23	617	4.1–11	378
37.3–8	239	51.57	300	4.4	371
37.3	239, 366	51.59	367	4.10	371, 376
37.5	239	52.13	600	4.11–16	378
37.7f.	240	52.16	371	4.12	367, 372,
37.9	239	52.30	598		376, 378,
37.11	239	53.28–30	598		600
37.13	239			4.13	379
38.1	237, 367	*Lamentations*		4.17	378
38.2	240	1–5	599	4.20ff.	379
38.4	239	1–4	599	4.20	372, 378,
38.6	237	1	378		600
38.17f.	240	1.1	378, 600	5.1–16a	378
38.29f.	239	1.5	378	5.2	371, 372
39.3	241	1.8	378	5.6f.	378
39.10	242, 371	1.9	379	5.11–13	371
39.14	241	1.10	376, 600	5.12f.	372
40f.	628	1.11	371	5.12	372
40.4–6	241	1.12	666	5.13	373
40.7ff.	202	1.18	378	5.16b	378
40.7	241, 242	1.21f.	379	5.19	379, 600
40.10	242, 371	1.22	378		
41.1f.	242	2	378, 599		
41.5ff.	349	2.1–10	378		
41.5	361, 377				

Ezekiel

1–39	428, 612	18.31–32	240	34.16	568
1–3	334, 663, 668	20	389	34.23f.	428
		20.1	373	34.25ff.	635
1	657	20.5	258	35.12	372
1.3	334, 427, 428	20.12	408	36f.	619
		20.13	608	36.5	372
1.26ff.	631	20.16	608	36.9ff.	635
2f.	627	20.20	408, 608	37	402, 668
3.15	599	20.21	608	37.11	377, 402, 403
4	238	20.24	608		
4.13	408	20.31	341, 342	37.15ff.	569
5.12	238	20.32	598	37.15–28	612
7.1	373	21.26	37, 341	37.16	632
8–11	429, 591, 663, 668	21.30–32	614	37.22–25	428, 614
		21.30	428	37.24f.	434
8.2ff.	663	21.31	612	37.26–28	429
8.5–18	200	22.6	428	37.27	614, 631
8.11	348, 367	22.7	338	37.28	632
8.14ff.	599	22.8–11	428	38f.	663
8.16ff.	135	22.8	608	38.12	136
9.6f.	238	22.12	323	40ff.	132, 199, 200., 317, 442, 445, 612, 663, 668
10	657	22.25f.	428		
11	238	22.26	428, 429		
11.11	665	22.27	428		
11.14–21	367, 607	22.29f.	428		
11.15	372, 373, 413, 609	22.29	165, 322, 338, 366	40–48	427, 428, 440, 451, 471, 612, 614, 629
11.16–20	413	23	389, 640		
11.16b	600	23.6	617	40.1–43	429, 612
11.20	291	23.18–27	463	40.1–37	612
12.22	609	23.37	341	40.1f.	428
13.17–23	599	23.39	341, 342	40.2	427
14.1–11	599	25.25	372	40.3ff.	663
14.1	373	26.2	372	40.6–27	429
14.7	338	26.26f.	662	40.11	613
15.13	600	26.26	37	40.12	612
15.20f.	341	28.10	408	40.13	613
16	389, 640	28.13	117	40.15bf.	613
16.20	342	29.6	239	40.22	429
16.21	342	30f.	622	40.31	429
16.23	342	30.3	666	40.34	429
16.29	322	31.18	408	40.37	429
16.37	342	32.19ff.	408	40.45	430, 612, 613
16.49	322	33.10ff.	221		
17.4–21	238	33.10	413	40.46a	430, 612
17.15	238	33.23–29	367	40.46b	430, 612
17.20	238	33.24	372, 373, 413, 609	40.47–49	612
18	413, 609			40.48–41.4	429
18.2	413, 609	34	619	40.49	429
18.5–19	609	34.2ff.	428	41.1–4	612
18.12	322	34.3f.	568	41.5–15a	612
18.19	413, 609	34.5	665	41.12–15	429
18.22	322	34.7	665	42.6	434
18.25	239	34.8	665	42.13	612
18.29	322	34.11	665	42.15–20	612
		34.12f.	665		

42.20	429	45.13–17	461	2–7	576, 581,
43.1–12	121, 429,	45.13–15	435		584, 587
	612	45.16–17	432	2	585, 593
43.1–11	612	45.16	608	2.1–7aba	667
43.1–5	432	45.17–		2.1	668
43.4f.	631	46.15	432	2.9f.	667
43.7	429, 614,	45.18–25	464	2.11	667
	631, 632	45.18–20	463	2.13–19	667
43.7b	432	45.20	661	2.14a	668
43.8	129, 432	46	121	2.22a	667
43.9	429, 614,	46.1	409, 608	2.23	667
	631	46.2	434	2.26aba	667
43.10ff.	432	46.4	609	2.27	667
43.13–17	612	46.8f.	430	2.28	457, 586
43.13–15	432, 612	46.8	434	2.31ff.	586, 665,
43.16–17	612	46.9	409		666
43.19	220, 430,	46.10	434	2.34	586
	431, 604,	46.12	608, 614	2.40	586
	612, 613	46.13–15	656	2.44	586, 663,
44	430, 431,	46.16	434		665
	613	46.16–18	112, 434,	3	584, 592
44.1–46.24	612		435	3.6	587
44.1–5	612	46.16f.	286	3.28f.	669
44.1–2	612	46.17	614	3.31–33	585
44.3	434	46.18	286	4–6	576, 577
44.5	612	46.19–24	430	4	577
44.6–16	431	46.24	656	4.14	669
44.6–9	432	47	615	4.27	585
44.8a	613	47.1–12	136	4.31f.	585
44.8b	613	47.1–11	612	4.31bf.	585
44.9–16	220, 612	47.13ff.	614	4.37a	477
44.9f.	655	47.13–48	35, 612	4.37b	577
44.10–12	261	47.13–		5	577
44.10	263, 431,	48.29	435	5.21	585
	613	47.13ff.	612	6	577, 584,
44.11	430	47.13f.	435		592
44.12	222, 431,	47.13b	614	6.8	578
	613	47.15–20	614	6.9	623
44.13f.	613	47.16	342	6.15f.	623
44.13	430, 431	47.22f.	435	6.26–28	577, 585
44.14	613	47.22	338	7	585, 586,
44.15f.	430, 612	48	614		663, 668
44.15	220, 431,	48.3–34	435	7.2ff.	665, 666
	604, 613	48.8–14	433	7.7f.	666
44.28–31	433	48.10	612	7.7aba	586
44.28–30	461	48.11	430, 612	7.11f.	665
44.28	433	48.15–18	435	7.13f.	586, 665
45.1–8	433, 461	48.18	435	7.16ff.	663
45.3f.	612	48.21f.	286	7.18	584, 586
45.4	433, 614	48.21	434	7.22	584
45.5	433	48.35	435, 614	7.25	594, 670
45.6	435			7.26	593
45.7f.	434	*Daniel*		7.27	584
45.8a	434	1	587, 592,	7.28	586
45.8b	434		668	8	592, 663
45.9	434	1.8–16	408	8.2ff.	593

8.10	670	12.1	591, 592, 663, 666	4.13b	331
8.11f.	593, 670			4.14	87, 276, 334
8.12	587	12.2f.	592		
8.13ff.	667	12.2	575, 593, 666	4.14abb	171
8.13	594			4.14ab	331
8.15ff.	663	12.3	566, 591, 592, 652	4.14b	173
8.17	457, 668, 670			4.17	65, 173
		12.6f.	594	4.18	354
8.19ff.	666	12.7	594	5.6	17, 331
8.19	457, 593, 668, 670	12.10	566, 591, 592, 652	5.11	169, 329
				5.12–14	169, 600
8.21	653	12.11	653, 670	5.15	176
8.25	592, 593	12.12	594, 670	6.1	331
9	652, 671			6.1–13	173
9.21ff.	663	*Hosea*		6.3	333
9.24–27	593	1–3	329	6.5	330
9.24	594	1.2	173, 354	6.6	330, 333
9.25ff.	666	1.3–9	178	7.3–7	170
9.26f.	594	1.4	170, 171	7.7	170, 329
9.26	594, 670	1.5	309	7.8f.	169
9.27	594, 670	1.9	176, 259, 291	7.11f.	169, 600
10–12	592, 663			7.11	329
10.5ff.	663	2	174	7.13–16	87, 173
10.13	592, 667	2.1	606	7.14	171, 172, 173, 331
10.20f.	592, 667	2.2	330		
10.20	653	2.7	173, 174, 329, 331, 354	7.16	329
10.21	593			8.1–13	156, 157
11f.	667			8.1	271
11.2ff.	653	2.8f.	169	8.2	331
11.2bff.	593	2.10	173, 174	8.4–6	171
11.3a	591	2.13	331, 408	8.4f.	65
11.14	576, 580, 587, 594	2.14	173, 329	8.4	170
		2.15	172, 173, 174, 322, 331	8.4b	173
11.21ff.	666			8.5f.	173, 305, 309
11.22	670	2.16f.	24, 330		
11.27	668, 670	2.17	174	8.5	309
11.28	593	2.18	173	8.6	65, 146, 309
11.31	593, 653, 670	2.19	173, 322	8.9	169, 329
		3.1–4	178, 354	8.10	169
11.32	591	3.1	172, 173	8.11	173
11.33f.	670	3.4	37, 169, 173, 332	8.13	174, 329, 330
11.33	591, 652				
11.34	592	3.5	330	9.1	171, 172, 354
11.34a	591	4.1	333		
11.34b	591	4.2	357	9.3	271, 329, 408
11.35	591, 592, 652, 668, 670	4.3	571	9.5	89, 331
		4.6	173, 174, 331	9.6	329
11.36–39	591, 670	4.7f.	173	9.7–14	179
11.36	594	4.11–14	87, 173	9.7–9	164
11.40–45	591, 692	4.11	171, 173	9.8	178, 330
11.40	668	4.12	172	9.10	173, 174, 329, 354, 601
11.45	457	4.13ff.	173		
11.49	670	4.13f.	172, 276	9.14	178
12.1f.	646	4.13bf.	171	9.15	170, 176

10.1f.	173, 174, 329	14.5	174, 349, 354	5.10	165, 323
10.3f.	169	14.6ff.	173	5.11	165, 322
10.3–8	146	14.9	65	5.12	165, 166, 185, 322, 323, 326
10.4	364	16.2	309		
10.5f.	173				
10.5	65, 145, 173, 305	*Joel*		5.18–20	666
		1.15	666	5.21–24	330
10.6	174	2.1	666	5.22	330
10.8	173	2.11	666	5.24	166, 171
10.12cj	333	2.13	338	5.25	330, 386
10.13b	169	3f.	438	5.26	193, 194, 330, 342, 343
11–13	174	3.1f.	478		
11	174	4.1ff.	663	6.1–7	161, 165
11.1ff.	354	4.4ff.	653	6.6	166
11.1–4	329	4.6	372, 635	6.12	166
11.1	174, 606	4.17	631	7.1–9	334
11.2	65, 173, 322	4.18	136	7.9	329
				7.10–17	333
11.5	24, 174, 329	*Amos*		7.11	320
		1	176	7.13	128
11.8–11	174, 330	1.1	325	7.14	163, 325
12.1	169	1.2	381	7.17	166, 408
12.2	364	1.9	372	7.25	179
12.3ff.	607	1.11f.	372	8.1–3	334
12.6	299	1.17	171	8.4–6	161, 323
12.9	24	2.6ff.	166	8.4	165, 322, 335
12.10f.	320	2.6	161, 165, 166, 184, 322, 323		
12.10	169, 174, 258, 329			8.5	408
				8.6	165, 322
12.11	330	2.7	165, 185, 322	8.14	305
12.13	408	2.8f.	171	9.1–4	172, 334
12.14	174, 320, 330, 350, 626	2.8	165, 185	9.7	70
		3.9–12	609	9.11–15	619
13.1	173	3.9f.	161, 165		
13.2	65, 145, 173, 309	3.9	657	*Obadiah*	
		3.10	165	17	627
13.4–6	169	3.14	172	19f.	627
13.4f.	175	3.15	165, 326	19	372
13.4	24, 62, 169, 171, 174, 258	4.1–5	609		
		4.1	161, 165, 322	*Jonah*	
				4.2	338
13.5f.	174	4.4f.	171, 330, 600		
13.5	174			*Micah*	
13.6	174, 601	4.4	286	1–3	325
13.10	24, 170, 171	4.6–13	380, 381, 600	1.1	325
				1.2–9	663
13.10b	330	4.6–11	381	1.2–7	325
13.11	170	4.12a	381	1.3	581
13.12	309	4.12b	381	1.6	325
13.15f.	173	4.13	381, 600	1.8–16	324
14.2–4	329	5.1f.	327	1.10ff.	325
14.2	349	5.1–17	600	2.1f.	160, 165, 166
14.4	65	5.5	335		
14.5–9	330	5.7	166	2.2	75, 79, 165
				2.4	166

2.6ff.	164	3.3	324	2.14f.	631
2.8ff.	219	3.5	657	2.15	449, 453,
2.9f.	165	3.11ff.	195		668
2.9	165			2.15b	454
3.1–9	160	*Haggai*		2.16	53
3.1–3	165, 324	1.13–15	455	3.1–7	454
3.1	166	1.1–3	455	3.1f.	643
3.2f.	165	1.1	451, 460,	3.1	460, 612
3.5	164, 171		617	3.8	612
3.8	166	1.2–9	452	3.8b	454
3.9	165, 166,	1.2–11	452	4.1–6	617, 663
	324	1.2	452, 619	4.1–6aa	453
3.10f.	303	1.3–11	386	4.4f.	663
3.10	172, 322	1.4	455	4.6	620
3.11	137, 165,	1.6	444, 451	4.6ab–10	452
	171, 172,	1.9–11	444	4.9b	454
	324	1.9	451	4.10b–14	617
3.13–21	637	1.10f.	451, 620	4.10	657
3.12	172	1.13–15	455	4.14	453
4.5	600	2.1–2	455	5–11	663
4.7b	600	2.2a	455	5–9	663
4.11	303	2.3–9	452	5.1–4	451, 453,
5.1ff.	619	2.4	445, 620		663
5.9–13	304	2.5a	455	5.5–11	453
7.10–20	401	2.6–9	457	5.10f.	663
7.7	401, 600	2.10–14	525	6.1–8	453
7.8–10	600	2.10	455	6.1–4	663
7.8bb	401	2.15–19	386, 452	6.4ff.	663
7.9bf.	401	2.15–17	455	6.5	453
		2.16	451	6.8	453
Nahum		2.18f.	620	6.9ff.	453
1.2	264	2.20–23	617, 620	6.9–14	453, 620
1.12	357	2.20	455	6.10–15	617
3.4	321	2.23	452	6.10	628
				6.11	454
Habakkuk		*Zechariah*		6.15ab	454
2.1	179	1–8	300, 615,	6.15b	455
2.3	179		617	7.1–8	455
2.12	322	1–6	668	7.1–3	620
3.3	51, 52, 53,	1.3	455	7.2ff.	377
	257	1.6	189	7.3	315
3.7	53, 260	1.1–6	455, 616,	7.4–14	455, 616,
			620		620
Zephaniah		1.7–17	453	7.5	242
1.4–6	340	1.7–15	663	7.19	455
1.4	190	1.7	620, 666	8–11	566
1.5	189, 342	1.8ff.	663	8.3	631
1.6	189, 340,	1.12	620	8.9–13	455, 456
	658	1.14	666	8.9	452, 455
1.8	189	2.1–4	453, 663	8.10	444, 451
1.9	344	2.4	452	8.12	452, 455
2.1–3	195, 348,	2.4b	452	8.13	455, 607
	640	2.5–9	453	8.14–18	616
2.1f.	344	2.5b	452	8.14–	
2.2b–3	344	2.7f.	663	17.19b	620
2.5	312	2.13b	454	8.16f.	456

8.18ff.	377
8.18	620
8.19	242
8.19a	620
8.19b	456
8.20–22	453, 668
8.23	453
9ff.	566, 570
9–14	565, 566, 571, 577, 615
9–11	566, 567, 664, 665
9	567, 585, 665
9.1ff.	567, 653
9.1–10	585, 665
9.1–8	566
9.1	569
9.3f.	567
9.5f.	567
9.7	567, 664, 665
9.8	567, 664
9.9f.	663, 665, 669
9.9	567, 669
9.10	304, 567
9.11f.	665
9.12	567
9.13ff.	653
9.13f.	665
9.13	566, 567, 569
9.14–17	665
9.14f.	567
9.15	664
9.17	567
9.18	665
10–14	663
10	568
10.1f.	665
10.1–2	568
10.2	37, 568
10.3–5	453, 568
10.3	568, 585, 665
10.6f.	569
10.11	566, 568
11	568
11.1	568
11.3	568
11.4–17	669
11.4–16	568, 569, 570, 663
11.4–14	568

11.4f.	666
11.4	568
11.5	665
11.6	568
11.7	568, 665
11.8–10	569
11.10	568
11.11	569, 665
11.12ff.	666
11.12f.	665
11.12	569
11.14	569, 646
11.15f.	568
11.15	566, 653
11.17	568, 570
12–14	438, 566, 665
12.1	665
12.2–4	303
12.2–7	666
12.3	665
12.4	665
12.6	664
12.7	664
12.8	664, 665
12.9–14	666
12.9–13.9	665
12.9	665
12.11	665
12.14	664
13.1–3	666
13.1	665, 666
13.2–6	666
13.2	665, 666
13.4	665
13.7–9	570
13.7f.	570
13.8	665
14	665
14.1	570, 665
14.2f.	663
14.2	570
14.3	585
14.5b	570
14.6	665
14.8	136, 665
14.9	570, 665
14.12	663, 665
14.13	665
14.14	570
14.15	665
14.16–21	668
14.16f.	300
14.16	665
14.17	665

14.20	665
14.21	665
Malachi	
1.6ff.	635
1.8	617
1.10	330
2.10	404, 606
2.17	504, 664
3.3	635
3.5	323, 496, 504, 635, 664
3.8ff.	635
3.13–21	504, 664
3.14f.	504, 515, 637
3.16–21	504
3.16	521
3.19	504
3.20	504
3.21	504
3.22	257
Sirach	
1	651
4–13	651
4.7	650
4.1–10	651
5.1–8	651
7.7	650
7.32	651
13.2f.	651
16.18	651
16.19	651
16.20	651
16.21–23	651
22.23	651
24	651
26.19	326
26.29–27.3	651
29.1–2	651
29.8–13	651
29.9	651
29.11	651
29.14	651
31.1–11	651
33	650
33.13–17	651
33.16f.	662
34.21–24	208
35.1–5	208, 650
36.27	
36	650
38.24–39.11	662

38.33	650	14.20	650	5.5f.	582
44–49	651	14.41	543	5.7–9	582
45.24	650	14.47	543	5.7	581, 584
50.1–4	535	15.17	650	5.9	584
50.5	458			6–11	575, 576,
50.15f.	646	**II Maccabees**			578, 579,
50.25f.	648	1.23	549		580, 581,
		3.4	650		582, 586,
Tobit		4.6f.	536		663, 666,
14.6f.	668	4.7ff.	652		669
		4.7–10	540	6.1f.	578
Judith		4.7f.	536, 650	6.3–6	578
5.16	646	4.23–25	541	6.6	668
14.10	408	4.24	536	6.10	663
		4.28	650	7.1	580
I Maccabees		4.30–39	542	7.1b	576
1.10	650	4.39–42	542	7.2	578
1.21	621	4.43–49	542, 652	7.3–5	578
1.22	621	4.44	650	7.3	576, 578
1.44–50	543	4.59	650	7.6	578
1.54	653	5.1–7	542	8.1–3	576, 580
2.27	542	5.16	650	8.4	578
2.29–43	542	5.22f.	650	9.1–10	578
2.29–41	539	5.23	528, 646	9.1	578
2.29–38	588, 669	5.27	542	9.2	596
2.42	438, 538,	6.1–11	653	9.6f.	576, 580
	539, 587,	6.2	52, 646,	9.6	580
	652, 669		653	9.8b	576
3f.	542	8.10	651	9.9	578
3.8	542	11.22–26	543	10.2	579, 668
3.18–22	69	11.27–33	542	10.2b	578
3.21	542	11.27	650	10.4–8	576
4.8–11	669	13.2	650	10.9f.	667
4.24	542	13.8	650	10.9	578, 579
4.36–61	542	14.6	438, 538	10.12f.	666
4.49	621	14.16	539	10.12	578, 579,
5f.	543	14.19	650		668
6.24	542	14.28	650	10.13f.	668
7.3	539	14.37	650	10.14	578, 579,
7.12ff.	543				668
7.12	539, 587,	**I Enoch**		10.15	578, 667
	652	1–36	575, 576,	10.16ff.	667
7.13	652		581, 584,	10.16b–	
7.14–18	653		587	11.2	579, 584
7.22	653	1–19	576, 581	10.18	576
7.24	653	1–10	581	10.21	579
7.33	653	1–5	576	12–19	576
9.6f.	653	1.1	581	12–16	582
9.50	648	1.2	581	12.3	566
9.54	621	1.3ff.	581	12.4	566, 652
10.15–21	543	1.3–9	663	13.8	581
11.23	650	1.8	582, 584	14–16	633
12.6	650	1.9	581	14.1ff.	581
12.35	650	2.5	582	14.25ff.	663
13.36–41	543	5	667	15.1	566
13.36	650	5.4	581, 582	15.8ff.	582

15.11	582	89.51	590	91.18f.	595
16.1	582	89.54ff.	590	92–105	565, 595
16.3	581	89.54	590	92.1–5	595
17–19	583, 633	89.55–		92.1	595
17.1ff.	581	90.17	589	92.3	666, 668
19	576, 667	89.55ff.	667	93.1–10	595, 596,
19.1f.	583	89.56	591		667
19.1	582, 666	89.62f.	590	93.2	668
19.3	581, 667	89.65–70	670	93.4	596
19.22	583	89.69	590	93.6f.	596
20–36	576, 583	89.71–77	670	93.9f.	596
20.8	668	89.73	591	93.10	596, 668
21ff.	663	89.74	590	93.11–14	595
21.1ff.	581	90–95	664	94.6–9	671
21.5ff.	663	90	666	94.7	671
22	667, 669	90.2	590	94.8	671
22.4	669	90.4	590	94.9	671
22.9	583	90.6–19	589	95.3	597
22.10f.	583	90.6–8	669	95.4	671
22.12f.	583, 596,	90.6f.	588, 592	95.5–7	671
	666	90.6	590	95.5	671
25	583	90.7	590	95.7	671
25.3	663	90.8	588, 590	96.1	597
25.4–7	584	90.9f.	590	96.3	597
26f.	583	90.9bf.	588	96.4	671
27.1f.	668	90.11	590	96.5f.	595
37–71	576, 669	90.11a	589	96.5	671
72–82	576, 664	90.11b	588	96.6–8	671
83–90	575, 669	90.12	589, 590	96.6	671
85–90	577, 587,	90.13f.	590	96.7	671
	588, 594,	90.14	589	96.8	671
	663, 666	90.15f.	589	97.1	597
85.1	669	90.17–19	591, 663	97.7f.	595
85.2ff.	663	90.17	589, 590	97.7	671
85.2–90.41	669	90.18f.	589, 594	97.8–10	671
85.2–3a	589	90.20–37	589	97.8	671
85.3–89.9	589	90.20–26	591	98.2f.	595
85.4ff.	589	90.22	590	98.2	671
86–88	575	90.25	590	98.9	671
86.5	589	90.27–29	591	98.11	671
89f.	593	90.29f.	663	98.12	597, 671
89.1	590	90.39–41	589	98.13	671
89.3	590	90.42	669	98.14	671
89.4	590	90.91	588	98.15	671
89.5ff.	670	91–105	577	99.1	595, 671
89.10–		91.1–10	595	99.2	671
90.19	589	91.10	596, 666,	99.7	595
89.13–27	590		668	99.11	671
89.15ff.	589	91.11–17	576, 596,	99.12	671
89.31–33	590		667	99.13	671
89.32	590	91.11	596	99.14	595, 671
89.41–50	670	91.12	596, 597	99.15	671
89.41	590	91.13	596, 663	100.7	671
89.43	670	91.14	596	100.8	671
89.48	590	91.15	596, 668	100.9	671
89.51–54	590	91.17	596		

102.4–		
103.4	597	
102.4	597	
102.5	597	
102.9	671	
103.4	596, 666, 668	
103.14f.	595	
104.2	597	
104.3	597	
104.4	597	
104.6	597	
104.9	595	
104.10	595	
105	595	
105.2	597	

Test Lev.

5–7	648
5.7	646

Jubilees

1.10	670
1.17	670
1.27	670
1.29	670
23.21	670

Matthew

6.9	641
16.21	618
17.24	461

Mark

13	666

Luke

4.16	600
6.20–26	671

Acts

2.24f.	46
13.15	600

Galatians

3.24	250

Index of Subjects

Aaron, 59, 476, 480, 485–8
Aaronides, *see also* Zadokides, 59,
  145, 221
Abiathar, 129
Abraham, 405–7
  covenant with, 407, 480, 490–2
Absalom rebellion, 110
Adad-Milki, 192–4
Adonis, 97
Adoption, 117
Adrammelek, 193
Aetiology, cultic, 143, 153–4, 549
Ahab, 149
Ahijah of Shiloh, 141, 151
Ahura Mazda, 417–18
Alcimus, 543
Alexander the Great, 527–8, 532,
  566–7, 570
Alien gods,
  polemic against, 148, 392
  prohibition against, 61–4, 184,
    214–15, 384, 390
Aliens, 58, 183, 185, 219–20, 222,
  315, 407, 409, 435–6, 492
Alliances, policy of, 162–3, 169, 201,
  203, 209, 217, 225, 235–9, 378,
  391, 445–6, 505, 540, 543–4, 552
  prohibition of, 209, 390–1
Alms, 498–500, 502, 514, 536
Altar, 36–7, 84, 85, 131, 180–1, 430
  of burnt offering, 188, 458–9, 463,
    484
  horned, 99
  law of, 183–4, 225
Amalekites, 109
'am hā-āreṣ, 198, 201, 204, 222, 232,
  234, 383
Ammonites, 79, 109, 148, 407
Amos, 159, 163, 173, 185, 381
  book of, 382
  disciples of, 177
'Amphictyony', 83
Amram apocryphon, 565, 576,
  587–8, 593–4
Anammelek, 193
Anath, 85, 97, 144, 172
Anath-Bethel, 211

Anath-Yaho, 211, 385
Ancestor worship, 26–7, 36–9, 97
Ancestral possession, *see also* Land,
  possession of, 73, 79, 152, 435
Angels, 33, 578, 586, 589
  fall of, 578, 583
  interpreting, 565
  of the nations, 574, 590, 592
Angra Mainyu, 418
Anointed of Yahweh, 117, 415, 424,
  453
Anshar, 136
Anti-Judaism, 4, 6, 11, 12
Antiochus III, 535, 539–40, 580, 587,
  592
Antiochus IV Epiphanes, 528, 536,
  541, 591, 593–4
  religious edict of, 542, 587, 590–1
Apocalypse, 581, 587
Apocalyptic, 437–9, 441, 456–7, 521,
  538, 545, 564–6, 568, 570–1, 572,
  574–97, 663, 668–70
  as scriptural exegesis, 579, 593–4
  as theology of social resistance,
    594–7
  its place in the history of tradition,
    564–5
  political, 538, 586–9
  pseudeponymity of, 565, 580–1, 585
  quietistic, 538, 587–8, 590–3
  'synchronization', 565, 569–70,
    579–80, 593–4
  theology, 594
  tradition history of, 566, 575–7, 641
'Apodeictic law', 92–3, 183
Arabia, 50, 57, 112, 372–3, 407
Arad, 65, 83–5, 87–8, 96, 180–1
Aram, 149, 155, 169, 172, 190–3,
  396, 399
Aristocracy (*see also* Upper class),
  499–500, 530–8, 540–3
Ark, 57, 66, 88, 118, 128–30, 136,
  227, 388, 390, 394, 432, 458,
  484–5, 518, 628
Army,
  leader of, 74, 80, 81
  levy, 80, 110, 111, 117

nature of, 79–83, 111–12, 216–17,
  225, 535, 545, 555
professional, 109, 116
Ash cakes, 194
Ashera (goddess), 85–7, 135, 172,
  187, 193–4, 198, 211, 392, 396,
  399
Ashera (cultic pole), 85, 180, 188,
  199, 206, 209, 392
Ashtar, 191
Ashtar-Chemosh, 148
Assur, 155–6, 198, 229
Assyria, 28, 30, 79–81, 151, 155,
  159, 162, 168–9, 176, 188, 190–3,
  195, 198, 209–10, 217, 229,
  239–40, 329, 340, 378, 399, 444,
  529, 588, 593
  religious policy of, 188–9
Astart, 87
Astarte, 148, 172, 193, 198
Astarte-name-of-Baal, 148
'Astarte' plaquettes, 86–7, 216
Astral religion, 189, 194, 233
Astrology, 574, 580
Astronomical omens, 190, 198, 399
Asylum, 93–4, 208, 483
  law of, 204, 208
Aten, 121–2
Atonement, 94, 426–4, 488
Authorization,
  Mosaic, 9, 205, 580
  pseudeponymous, 580–3, 585

Baal, 7, 38, 52, 62, 89–90, 96–9,
  133–4, 136, 144, 149, 153–4,
  172–3, 198, 264, 301, 331–2, 392,
  399, 414
  as hostile image, 155–6, 172–4
  Berit, 83–4, 89, 392
  Carmel, 153–4
  cult of, 395–7
    in northern kingdom, 62, 84–5,
      149–50, 153–6, 170, 172–4
    in southern kingdom, 99, 150
  -El syncretism, 137
  Hammon, 191
  Hermon, 83, 153–4
  Lebanon, 153–4
  of Ekron, 101, 188
  'of the hill country', 153
  of Sidon, 149
  of Tyre, 149, 153–4
  Shamem, 135, 149, 153–4, 542
  temple of in Samaria, 149, 155
  -Yahweh syncretism, 133–4, 144–5

-Yam cycle, 136, 425, 490
Zaphon, 136
'Baalized' Yahweh cult, 145, 172, 209
Baals, 153, 173, 391–2
  sanctuaries of, 150, 153
Babylonia, 24–5, 29, 32, 38, 56,
  62–4, 79, 87, 98, 101, 116–17,
  129, 134–5, 137, 140, 144, 151,
  159, 172, 188–90, 193–4, 207,
  217, 235–9, 241, 371–4, 385, 387,
  400, 407–8, 412–13, 414, 416–18,
  419, 424, 444, 453, 458, 515, 568,
  570, 574, 577, 585, 593
  provincial administration of, 371–2
Ban, 184
Baruch, 177
Beersheba, 181
Bel, 420
Belet Seri, 193
bēt 'ābōt, 443, 529, 546, 619
Bethel, 59, 77, 88, 140, 143–6, 172,
  188, 198, 200–3, 207, 221, 226,
  388, 395–6, 525, 530–2
'Bible piety', 588
Birth, 100, 194, 407, 464
Birth ritual, 87
Blessing, 89, 96, 102, 120, 162, 173,
  212–13, 218, 242, 390, 401, 416,
  457, 490, 492, 501, 522, 567, 579
  promise of, 212
  conditional, 218, 225, 238, 404–5,
    502
  unconditional, 406
Blood
  guilt, 93
  rite, 463, 474–5
  vengeance, 73, 80, 88, 93, 185
'Book, finding of', 198, 205, 390
Book, religion of, 231, 460
Brazen sea, 484
'Brotherhood ethic', 218, 223, 495,
  498, 503
Bull image, 65, 77, 84, 144–6, 173–4,
  308–11, 395
'Bull site', 84, 143–4
Byblos, 151, 172

Canaanite(s), 111, 209, 331
  city culture, 69, 76, 82, 111
  city states, 69, 72, 75, 77, 79, 110
  religion, 7, 10, 77, 87, 105, 137,
    172–4, 191, 209, 331, 557
Cannibalism, 371
Canon,
  commission on, 478–80

revision of, 547
Canonization, 639
Carmel, 150, 153–4, 318–19
Casuistic law, 92, 183
Central sanctuary, 82, 392, 436
Centralization,
law of, 532
of cult, 128, 207, 436, 485
political, 207, 434
Chaos, 573
fight with, 119, 133–4, 136, 226, 425, 490
Charismatics, 47, 81, 110, 115, 120
charismatic law, 93
Chemosh, 148–9
Cherub, 117, 130, 227
Cherubic throne, 64, 88, 130, 132, 144, 227, 458, 484
Chiefdom, 109, 141
Child mortality, 34, 36
Child sacrifice, 34, 37, 103, 190–3, 199, 210, 385, 505
Children, dedication of, 192–3, 199, 210, 385, 398
Christianity, 523, 566, 597
Chronicles, 438, 528, 546–7, 560, 563–4, 569, 580–1, 583, 590, 653–4, 656
its a-Hellenistic tendency, 555
its anti-Samarian aim, 545–6, 553–4
its unescatological tendency, 550–1
tradents of, 553
tradition of, 545, 554
Chronistic history, 371, 440, 445, 470, 526, 545, 557, 613, 647
Chthonic deity, 180
Circumcision, 407–8
'Citizen-temple community', 448
Clan, 29, 73–5, 92, 95, 109, 219, 546
Cleanness, *see* Purity
Clergy, minor, 220, 431, 461
Coinage, 496
Collared rim jars, 70
Colonization, 70, 76–7, 109
Commandments,
cultic, 183, 483
obedience to, 212–13, 229–30, 393, 395, 474–5, 472, 492, 533, 546, 552, 559, 561, 592
proclamation on Sinai, 54–5, 227
social, 92, 183, 214–15, 483
Confession, 407, 410, 510, 562
Conflict, social, 112, 159–62, 165–7, 184–5, 233, 486, 494–7, 503–4, 510, 512–14, 532–8, 553, 562, 565, 571, 574, 595

Conversion of pagan rulers, 577, 584–5
Coronation ritual, 117–18, 454–4
Court, divine, 117, 133, 227, 484, 514–15
Covenant, 410, 601
Book of, 55, 60, 92, 166, 182–6, 199, 203–4, 214, 235, 261, 409, 475, 512, 643
breach of, 383–4
eternal, 410
formula, 118, 247
making of, 526, 559
new, 387
political, 229
religious, 65–6, 119, 154, 225, 228–31, 480, 557
renewal of, 475–6
renewal festival, 230–1
sign of, 407
with peoples, 568
Creation,
of human beings, 96, 134, 162, 212, 401, 403, 517, 520, 575
of the world, 134, 228, 410, 415–17, 561
theology, 415–17, 489
Credit, law of, 151, 160–1, 165, 216–17, 495–6, 498
Crown property, 110, 112, 129, 152, 159, 373
Cult,
centralization of, 83, 127–8, 139, 181, 183, 198–9, 202, 206–28, 233, 390, 394, 395–7, 399, 409, 428, 430–1, 531–3
criticism of, 60, 170–2, 206–8, 417–17, 466, 474, 476, 483
democratization of main cult, 485, 487
didactic function of main cult, 381, 475, 501
foundation of, 54–5, 451–3, 475, 482–3, 485, 492, 546–7
historicization of main cult, 90–1
main cult, 56–60, 82–91, 100, 102, 127–8, 139, 171, 184, 305, 377, 386, 402, 409–11, 462, 476, 482–3, 492, 509, 529–30, 532–3
on high places, 82–3, 181, 392, 395–8, 505
prostitution in, 87, 171–3, 193–4, 209, 276, 390, 397, 399
reform of, 181, 184, 198, 203, 233–4, 240–1, 376–7, 390–1, 397–9, 428–34

separation from state, 377–9, 431–2, 445, 459–60, 484–6, 549
state cult, 86–9, 105, 121, 127–32, 140, 143–6, 148, 150, 152–3, 173, 188, 226, 428–34, 452, 459, 462, 484, 548, 597
subsidiary cult, 29, 36–7, 39, 65, 88–9, 99–103, 178, 210, 377–8, 401, 408, 410, 508–9, 520–1, 571
Cultic decalogue, 60
Cultic kiss, 145–6
Cyrus, 413, 415, 418, 424, 444, 528, 570

Damascus, *see* Aram
Dan, 82–3, 140, 143, 198, 221, 395
Dance, 91
Daniel, 576–7
Daniel, Book of, 539, 565
David, 110, 111, 115–16, 124–5, 128, 280, 392–4, 424, 531–2, 547, 548, 552, 590
as servant of Yahweh, 388
covenant with, 105, 119
democratization of, 119, 426
history of the rise of, 117–18, 124–5
merits of, 393
promise to, 75–119, 121–2, 125, 130, 225, 386, 389–97, 549–50, 552
Davidides, 426, 444, 452
rehabilitation of, 554
Day of Atonement, 459, 462–3
Death, 403, 583
penalty, 93, 165, 204
Debir, 130, 458
Debts, remission of (*see also* Shemitta), 358–9
Debt, 323
Decalogue, 55, 60, 204, 213–16, 226, 230, 383, 390, 394, 409, 464, 475, 480
dating and origin of, 214
Decentralization,
cultic, 82–3, 143, 411, 435, 528, 531–2
political, 74–6, 424–5, 434–5, 436
legal, 91, 93–4
Deir 'Alla, 132, 151
Delos, 527
Demons, 27, 35, 100, 511, 582
belief in, 578
Deportation, 162–3, 169, 188, 237, 570, 589
Deurbanization, 70, 72

Deutero-Isaiah, 119, 153, 200, 402–4, 414–23, 437–8, 449, 451, 472–3, 477, 493, 505, 550, 567, 609
book of, 414
group, 414–15, 423, 433–4, 444, 453, 456, 509, 510, 577
Deuteronomic Reform, *see* 'Josiah, reform of', 344–6
law of, 199, 204–23, 234–6, 349–51, 362–3, 383–4, 388, 393, 397
theology of, 60, 65, 82, 105, 133, 161–2, 223–31, 240, 369, 376, 382, 383, 388, 398, 465, 471, 475, 486–8, 633
tradition, 626
formation of, 200–201, 225
understanding of priests, 220–2, 431, 548
Deuteronomistic history, 117–19, 139, 143, 148, 180, 184, 198–201, 225–7, 379, 382, 385–6, 387–99, 424, 469, 471, 525, 531, 548–50, 552, 590
canonization of, 547–51, 555
Chronistic interpretation of, 546–52
dating of, 387–7
literary-critical hypotheses on, 387–8, 389, 395
localization of, 388
tradents of, 388, 390
Deuteronomists, 19–20, 85, 201–5, 224–34, 418
Deuteronomy, 182, 195–231, 241–2, 387, 469, 531, 647–8
as state law, 204–5, 226, 229, 465
dating of, 199–201
disintegration of its group of tradents, 233, 428
introductory speeches in, 214, 224
origin of, 200–1, 225
pedagogical purpose of, 205, 215
tradents of, 201–5, 210, 224
wisdom elements in, 202, 205, 513
Deutero-Zechariah, Book of, 566, 569
Diaspora, *see also* Gola, 424, 444–5, 458, 465, 473, 477, 508, 530, 534, 541, 623
Alexandrian, 535–6, 577, 584
Bablylonian, 577
community, 509
Samaritan, 527
theology of, 577
Diplomacy, 112, 149, 155–6

Discourse model, 72
Disintegration,
  religious, 440–3, 448–50, 495, 534,
    542, 543
  social, 447, 450
Ditheism, 32, 150, 154, 252
Dome of the Rock, 130
Dreams,
  interpretation of, 210, 577
Dynastic god, 28, 30, 552
Dynasty, promise of, 118, 395
  conditional, 119

Ebal, 224, 390, 532
Ebla, 28, 31, 50, 191
Edom, 54, 97, 372, 397, 407, 413
Egypt, 44–6, 49, 51–2, 57, 64, 70,
    108, 117, 118, 120, 121, 135, 142,
    162–3, 168, 169, 180, 201, 209,
    225, 232–3, 237, 238–9, 241, 374,
    407, 435, 444–5, 467, 535, 557
El, 27, 30–1, 49, 76–9, 85, 89, 97–9,
    133–4, 136–7, 144–5, 149
El-Bethel, 30, 83, 144
El-Elyon, 30, 134, 136
El, God of Israel, 30, 76
El-Olam, 30, 83
El Roeh, 30
El Shaddai, 31, 37, 97, 490, 492
Eol-Yahweh syncretism, 78, 134–5,
    138, 145–6, 150
Eldad and Medad, 479
Elders, 44, 92–3, 152, 163, 177, 184,
    204, 224, 372, 373, 375, 388, 390,
    445–6, 469, 479, 527, 535, 549,
    574
  council of, 73–4, 78, 109, 110, 113,
    122, 373, 440, 446–9, 453, 455,
    468–70, 473, 481–2, 487–8,
    497–8, 532, 536–9, 542
Election,
  of Abraham, 406
  of Israel, 226, 228, 405–6
  of Jerusalem, 135–6, 226, 389, 394,
    397, 531, 546
  of Judah, 547
  of the king, 125, 225, 228–9, 386,
    389, 395, 547
  of the priest, 228, 388, 394, 547
Elephantine, 85, 211, 374, 385,
    467–8, 511, 531
Eli, sons of, 98, 129, 221
Elijah, 62, 64, 89, 150–4, 172
  tradition, 152–3
Elisha, 150–1, 154–5

Elyon, 74, 134, 135
End time, 591, 594
Enoch, 419, 581–2, 589, 595–6
  book of, 539, 565, 574–85, 587–90,
    595–7, 664
Enuma elish, 134, 490
Ephebeion, 600
Ephod, 37, 88
Epiphany, 52, 82, 96, 457, 567
Esangila, 24, 490
Eschatological hymns of praise, 519,
    572
Eschatologizing, 456–8, 478
Eschatology, 438–9, 443, 456, 566
Essenes, 539
Eternal damnation, 592
Eternal life, 592
'Ethical monotheism', 176–7
Ethics, 162, 177, 212–16, 513–15,
    562, 597
  eschatologically orientated, 596–7
Exile, 98, 154, 180, 199, 202,
    369–75, 390, 408, 412, 422, 426,
    476, 509–10, 525, 530, 552, 589,
    590–1
Exodus, 42–9, 56, 90, 95–6, 99, 122,
    143, 145, 213–14, 218, 226, 228,
    410, 489, 492
  covenant, 229–30, 383
  group, 44–5, 54, 62, 69, 77, 80, 91,
    95, 175, 213
  new, 426
  theology, 226, 369, 393
    crisis of, 405
  tradition, 35, 44, 124, 142, 174,
    213, 227, 415, 549
Exorcism, 100
Exorcist, 151, 189, 190
Ezekiel, 200, 233, 237–40, 389,
    402–3, 405, 407, 427–9, 505
  school of, 200, 379, 427, 453, 458,
    460–1, 463, 471, 485
    critical wing of, 428, 433
Ezra, 446, 466, 468, 470, 539
  decree, 466, 470
  book of, 545–6, 554, 557

Faith
  community, 375, 448–9
  in God, 47, 49, 167–8, 474, 477,
    597
  in the Torah, 558
'Fall', 475, 491, 606
Family, 29–30, 33, 72–5, 92, 95–6,

109, 198, 219, 222–3, 373, 375,
  400, 404–5, 509, 548
Fast liturgy, 89, 499–500
Fertility, 85, 89–90, 102, 120, 144–6,
  172–3, 193
  cult, 145–6, 211
  religion, 87
Festivals, 607
  calendar of, 89, 409
  date of, 143, 410, 548
  joy at, 90, 91, 102, 146, 211, 222,
    464, 554
Firstfruit sacrifice, 102, 213, 409, 475
  animal, 102–3, 208, 222
  human, 102–3, 190, 193–4, 461,
    485
  plant, 90, 99, 213, 222, 433, 461
Flood, 492, 572–3, 578–80, 582, 589,
  634
Forced labour, 44–6, 112, 122,
  141–2, 160, 216, 225, 233, 306,
  550
Freedom, ideal of, 75–8, 82, 108–9,
  113, 435, 447, 550

Gad, 97, 111
Gedaliah, 202, 237, 241, 371, 377,
  383, 386, 445
Genealogy, 28–9, 405, 546
Gerizim, 224, 525, 527, 532
Gezer, 429
Gibeon, 130
Gilgal, 224
God,
  as father, 19, 97, 100, 401, 403, 510
  as male-female duality, 85–7, 184,
    188, 193, 211, 385, 392, 403–4
  as mother, 19, 97, 100, 403, 514
  as teacher, 515–16
  cultic, 381–2, 483–4, 551, 614
  denationalization of, 420–4
  encounter with, 492
  enquiring of, 88, 100, 125, 171, 552
  experience of,
    cultic, 173
    from scripture, 559
    historical, 47, 55–6, 79–80, 89,
      174–5, 404, 471, 474, 510, 551,
      567
    personal, 174, 178, 212, 400–3,
      441–2, 513, 517, 556–8, 560
  fear of, 205, 513, 559, 561
  glory of, 56, 96, 133, 238, 425, 429,
    432, 453, 456–7, 482, 483–4,
    487, 490

image of, 9, 36–8, 64–5, 100, 131,
  144, 146, 173, 181, 184, 188,
  208, 216, 384, 396–7
  feminine, 100, 393
  jealous, 61, 215
  kingship of, 116–17
  name of, 133, 226, 251, 386, 394–5,
    490, 492
  nationalizing of, 79, 228
  of the Hebrews, 44, 49, 52, 63
  of humankind, 49
  of Israel, 117–18, 120–2, 167, 171,
    212, 215, 226, 228–9, 231, 387,
    400, 403, 474–7, 483, 489–90,
    492
  of the king, 116–17, 121–2, 125,
    225, 404
  pedagogy of, 383, 515
  people of, 81, 164
    eschatological, 578
    unity of, 205, 223, 435, 553
  personal, 30, 62, 100, 179, 187,
    212, 215, 401, 403, 522, 552
  presence of,
    in the people, 428–9, 435, 483,
      487, 497
    in the Torah, 558
  relationship with, 32, 39, 49, 59, 61,
    64, 98, 150, 155, 169–70, 174,
    206, 209, 210, 212, 215, 228
    disruption of, 49
    ethical permeation of, 211–16, 369,
      511, 513–15, 536, 556–60
    interiorization of, 4–5, 211, 215,
      551
    legal structuring of, 231
    royal monopolizing of, 122, 124–6,
      170–1, 222–6, 228
    unconditional nature of, 36, 39, 48,
      212, 404–5, 511
  repentance of, 384
  seeking, 552, 555, 557
  word of, 383, 561, 567–8
  worship of,
    cultic, 171–2, 385, 475, 482–3, 552
    ethical, 171–2, 208, 212, 240, 385,
      471, 475, 482, 552
Goddess, 85–8, 97, 184, 193–4, 211,
  343, 374, 385, 392, 403–4
Godlessness, 168, 173, 501, 505, 519
Gola, *see also* Diaspora, 439, 598
  Babylonian, 237–8, 242, 371, 373,
    382, 386, 406–8, 412–13, 415,
    422, 445–6, 449, 453, 546
  Egyptian, 371–2, 374, 387, 444–5
Golden calf, 143–6

Grace,
  of God, 185, 402, 476, 510–11,
    513, 520, 551–2, 562, 568, 583
Gratitude, 167, 215, 410
Greece, 226, 446–7, 527, 534, 536,
  586
Groups, Formation of Religious, 177,
  370, 439, 449–50, 456–7, 503–7,
  520, 522, 538–40, 588
Guilt, 165–6
Gymnasium, 540

ḥabiru, 45, 47
Hadad/Adad, 144, 189, 193, 210
Hadad-Yahweh syncretism, 193, 194
Hades, 583
Haggai, 440, 451–2, 455–6, 565
Hallowing, 489, 493
  of divine name, 507
Haruspication, 151, 190, 198
Hasidim, 438, 538–43, 566, 587, 652
  militant, 588–92, 595
  quietistic, 590–4
  split among, 587–8
Hasmonaeans, 528–9, 543, 555, 565,
  595
Hazor, 65, 84, 99, 429
Healing, 37, 39, 403, 510
Heaven, host of, 190
  queen of, 86, 188, 193, 374, 377,
    385
Hell, 583
Hellenization, 528, 534, 537–8, 564,
  580, 653
Hellenistic city culture, 570, 573
Hezekiah, 163–4, 180–2, 207, 240,
  554
  narrative, 239–40
  reform of, 61, 121, 180–6, 198, 200,
    207, 216, 397
hieros gamos, see also Sacred
  marriage
High places, see also Sanctuaries, 59,
  84–8, 101, 173, 180, 198, 211,
  234, 390, 397
  priests on, 222, 395–6, 430
High priest, 427, 446, 453, 455–6,
  458, 460, 482, 485, 488–9,
  522–32, 535–6, 538–42, 545, 593
  as messiah, 493
  as representative of the messiah, 454
  associated with royal office, 543
  fiscal autonomy of, 535
Hilkiah, sons of, 201–2
Hill sanctuary, 54, 57

Hirbet el Qom, 50, 86
History, interpretation of, 370, 376,
  378, 380, 384, 387, 395–9, 419,
  426, 585
  apocalyptic, 588–91, 592–4
  dispute over, 241, 568–70
Hittites, 229
Holiness Code, 60, 385, 481, 489,
  602
Holy, separation of from profane,
  429, 459, 485–9
Holy place, see Sanctuary and Temple
Holy war, see Yahweh, War of
Hope, 390, 394, 491, 506
  eschatological, 571, 597
  in God, 179, 379, 384, 402, 513,
    517, 575
  in the Torah, 558
Horeb, see also Sinai, 54, 226, 230
Hosea, 23–4, 61–5, 75, 87, 89, 146,
  154–5, 159, 163–4, 178, 184, 203,
  205, 206, 209, 213, 215
  disciples of, 177, 180–1, 203, 224
Hostile stereotype, religious, 237–8
House gods, 36–8
Household cult, 37–8, 84–5, 99–101,
  187–9, 210–11
Human dignity, 505–6, 521
Human sacrifice, 103, 194
Hymn, 415–16, 452

Identity,
  ethnic, 206, 526–7, 529–30
  family and ritual, 408
  loss of, 169
  religious, 19–20, 173, 181, 206,
    209, 375, 424, 440, 467, 472–3,
    505, 540, 555, 563
  safeguarding of, 206
Ideology, 122–3, 168, 550
  critique of, 176
Idols, 216, 610
Idolatry, 171, 265–6, 395–7, 431, 552
  of pagan rulers, 577
  polemic against, 153, 418
ikribu prayers, 191
Images, cult of, 59, 61, 64–6, 173
  prohibition of, 184, 214–15, 390,
    395
Imperialism, 80
Incense, altar of, 99, 189, 458, 484
Individualism, 6, 162, 413, 552, 559
Inferiority, sense of, 51, 53–5, 57,
  59–80
Infiltration model, 70

Initiation rites, 172
Integration,
  cultic, 56, 101–2, 222–3, 465
  economic, 373, 412–13
  political, 448
  religious, 36–7, 221, 224, 410,
    440–3, 448, 465, 494, 529,
    541–2, 547, 550–4, 562–3
  social, 374
Integrity,
  ethnic, 450
  loss of territorial, 373–5, 449, 466,
    562
  safeguarding of ethnic and religious,
    410, 449
Intercession,
  for enemies, 237–8
  for Israel, 509
  for the king, 129
  for the Persian king, 459
  of angels, 587
  of the king, 120–1, 509
  of Moses, 475, 478
  of the pious, 582
  prophetic, 239, 393, 478
Interest, 185
  prohibition of, 217
Invocatory prayer, 194
Isaiah, 163, 178–9, 215, 240–1,
  415–16, 551, 567
  apocalypse, 570–5
  disciples of, 177, 203, 240, 415
  'memorandum', 167, 177
Ishtar, 86, 193, 211
Israel,
  as people of God, 81, 201, 223,
    228–9, 435, 554
  as priest, 457, 474, 480
  as prophet, 480
  as son of God, 174, 404
  as spouse of God, 174
  eschatological, 578
  foundation history of, 225, 230,
    476, 479, 482, 488, 547, 555
  conception of, 206, 227, 466
  'true', 450, 502, 505, 522, 584

Jachin and Boaz, 131
Jason, 536, 538, 540–1
Jehoiachin, 237, 373, 386, 445, 452
Jehu, revolution of, 60, 155–6, 170,
  172–3, 396
Jeremiah, 89, 178–80, 200, 202–3,
  232–7, 239–42, 339, 373, 377–8,
  380–4, 452, 505, 593

Deuteronomistic book of, 382–7,
  478
disciples of, 177, 380
Jeroboam, 140–3, 148, 395
  revolt of, 43, 112, 123, 140–3, 150,
    213, 227, 395, 540, 550, 553
Jerusalem, 110, 183, 226, 531–2,
  535, 570, 604
  as city of God, 132, 135, 226, 240,
    436, 453, 457
  as 'federal district', 435
  as polis, 540
  heavenly, 573
  miraculous escape of in 701, 163,
    240, 398
  prayer towards, 377, 394
  supreme court of, 120, 182, 184–5,
    203–6, 225
  temple theology, 133–4, 143–8,
    162–3, 224, 226–7, 233, 269,
    388–9, 393–5, 398, 415, 422,
    427–8, 466, 483–4, 531, 547
Jesus movement, 597
Jesus Sirach, 536, 662
Jewish self-administration, 445–8,
  470, 473, 478, 497–8, 509, 535–6,
  538, 554
Jezebel, 149, 154–5
Job, Book of, 96, 494, 496, 500,
  502–3, 511–17, 636
John Hyrcanus, 525, 528
Joseph story, 120
Josephus, 524, 527–8
Josiah, 98, 148, 198, 200–1, 232–3,
  240, 366, 388, 398, 525, 548, 554
  reform of, 121, 139, 180–1, 184,
    194, 198–206, 214, 225–6,
    240–1, 243, 334–5, 336, 377,
    378, 385, 397–401, 409, 430–2,
    531
  failure of, 200, 202–3, 223, 232–3
Jubilee, year of, 434, 481, 629
Jubilees, Book of, 566
Judah, 372, 391, 400, 528, 535, 536,
  541, 593
  community of, 445–50, 458, 481,
    509, 526, 528, 535–8, 543–5,
    554, 588
  political independence of, 445, 529
Judahites, 372, 383, 386, 388, 445,
  449, 452
Judas Maccabaeus, 588
Judaism, 245, 566, 597, 598
  personal theology of, 562–3
Judges, 203

Judgment of God, 376, 378, 381,
384, 389, 488, 546, 590, 665
Justice, local, 92, 161, 166, 183,
203–4, 393, 498
Justice in the gate, 92, 161, 183

Kapporet, 458, 463, 484–5
Kenite hypothesis, 52
King,
as elect of God, 125, 225, 386,
415–16
as helper of the weak, 119–21, 225,
556
as image of God, 116–17
as mediator of blessing, 119–21,
170–1, 377, 406
as son of God, 116–17, 119, 122,
125, 225, 434, 550
criticism of, 122–4, 152–3, 170,
225–6, 393, 424–5, 427–8, 473,
484–6, 543–4
his bond with the law, 225–6, 393
priesthood of, 119, 128–9, 434, 460,
549
rule over the world, 119, 132, 137,
161, 378, 406, 425
Kingdom of God, *see also* Rule of
God, 123–4, 132–3, 162, 379,
393, 484, 550
as criticism of domination, 122–3,
176, 420, 424, 567–8, 574, 585
as legitimation of rule, 119, 133–4,
424
establishment of, 424–5, 456–7,
510, 520, 522, 565, 567, 569–70,
573–4, 585–7, 592
Kingship, Monarchy, 7, 24, 63, 78,
108–29, 140–3, 148–52, 242, 436,
546, 549–51, 590
as saving gift, 393–5, 471, 548
charismatic, 116
desacralization of, 434
dispute over, 105, 113, 122–4,
170–1, 393
downfall of, 170, 370, 372, 374–5,
378
dynastic, 116
establishment of, 63–4, 105,
108–13, 140–1, 138, 170
restoration of, 170–1, 386, 424–5,
429, 440, 446, 451, 453, 457,
536, 543, 555
sacral, 116–18, 121, 123–4, 129,
225–6, 434, 543, 549
theology, 20, 81, 113–24, 168, 276,

224–9, 287–8, 369, 378, 382,
388, 389, 393, 398, 404, 406,
415, 420, 424–8, 441, 471, 552
Kittu and Misaru, 135
Korahites, 487
Kuntillet 'Ajrud, 50, 84, 86, 101

Laity, 488–9, 541, 563, 572
Lament of the individual, 100, 212,
218, 402, 510, 513, 515–17, 519
Lament of the people, 96, 173, 378–9,
401–2, 414, 510
Lamentations, 377–9, 600
Land, 79, 474, 477, 480–1
levitical, 432–3
priestly, 432–4, 462
return to, 374, 386, 405–6, 444,
466–7, 477, 481, 491, 504
royal, 110, 112, 129, 152, 159, 341
Landowners, great, 162, 216, 496,
574
Last Judgment, 579, 581–4, 588–92,
596–73
place of, 582–3
Law, 40–6, 60–6, 91–4, 182–6,
205–24, 225–6, 337, 369, 389,
393–4, 407–8, 440, 449, 455, 483,
557–3, 623
exposition of, 536, 539
Mosaic authorization of, 91, 205,
466
of Moses, 199, 205, 390, 466, 470,
480, 539, 541, 546–7
prophetic authorization of, 428–9
reform of, 184–6, 203–24, 465–93
religious authorization of, 60, 91,
183
religious reading aloud of, 183–4,
204, 230–1
sacral, 166, 238–9, 552
state, 204–5, 226, 229
theologizing of, 60, 92–3, 177, 183,
204
tradition of, 230, 561
understanding of, 557
unification of, 183, 204
Lay theologians, 469–71, 478, 485–7
Leprosy, 464
Levirate marriage, 73
Levites, 55–60, 84–5, 100, 143,
201–2, 208, 219–23, 373, 388,
430–2, 433, 436, 447, 460, 470,
476, 485–6, 545, 548, 553, 655
Libation, 100, 189, 462
Liberation, 19, 24, 35, 44–9, 52–3,

55–6, 63, 66, 72, 95–6, 105, 142, 166, 213, 218, 223–4, 410, 415–16, 418–20, 426, 436, 457, 472, 504, 519–20, 522, 543–4, 563–8, 597
tradition, 94, 129–30, 218–19, 471, 474, 544
war of, 46, 52, 78–83, 95–6, 108, 115, 120, 134, 391–2, 420–1, 424, 540, 542–3, 589–92
Liturgy, *see* Cult
Love,
of God, 167, 174, 211, 228–9
of Israel, 174, 206, 211–12, 229–30
of the Torah, 558, 562–3
Lower class, 216, 223, 371, 439, 441, 458, 500, 505–7, 518–19, 538–9, 554, 560, 566
country, 195, 540, 542, 566, 573, 580
pious, 505, 518–22, 560, 571
urban, 541, 542, 566, 580

Ma'at, 135
Maccabees, 542, 589
wars of, 536, 540, 542–3, 556, 573, 587–95
Magic, Magicians, 37, 46, 81, 151–3, 173–4, 189, 463, 580
Malik, 97, 191
Malta, 191
Manasseh, 188, 190, 398
Marduk, 56, 98, 134, 136, 419, 490
Mari, 34, 80, 151, 191
Martyrs, 542, 585, 587–9, 592
Masseboth, 36, 64, 84, 85, 88, 173, 180, 187–8, 189, 206, 209
Mazzoth, feast of, 35, 98, 90, 102, 208, 213, 410, 475
Meditation, 557, 559, 562
Megiddo, 84, 100, 429
Melchizedek, 135
Menelaus, 536, 538, 541
Menorah, 458, 462, 484, 548
Menstruation, 464
menuha, 393, 554
Messiah, 117, 121, 240, 415–16, 424, 445, 453–5, 554, 567
Micaiah ben Imlah, 151
Micah, book of, 382
Micah, prophet, 159, 163
Middle class, 165, 201, 224, 235, 242, 553
Milkom, 149, 231
'Mission', 422–8, 449, 472–3

Mixed marriages, 391–2, 449, 470, 472, 522, 529–32, 541, 576–7
Moab, 79, 148, 407
Moloch cult, 190–4
Moon cult, 190–1
Monarchy, *see* Kingship
Monarchy, constitutional, 110–11, 122, 201, 226, 386, 447, 550
Monolatry, 32, 59, 61–4, 150, 153, 175, 184, 206, 215, 417–18
Monotheism, 32, 61–4, 153, 216, 240, 252, 417–20, 425–6, 472–3
Monoyahwism, 206
Moriah, 532
Mosaic succession, 205, 478–80
Moses, 4–5, 23, 45–9, 51–5, 59, 91, 141–3, 154, 198–9, 205, 221, 263, 388, 428, 476, 480, 482, 486
Moses-David analogy, 547
Moses-Elijah analogy, 154
Moses-Ezra analogy, 420
Moses-Jeremiah analogy, 384
Mot, 97
Mount of Olives, 148
Music, 91
Myth, 117, 121–2, 134
Myth and Ritual school, 9, 116–17
Mythology, 583–5
Greek, 576, 578–80, 583

Nabataeans, 64
Nabu, 417
nāgīd, 125, 426
Names, personal
theophorous, 30–32, 39, 95–9, 373, 511
with Baal, 149
with El, 97
with Yahweh, 96–8, 150, 187
nasi, 74, 78, 152, 432–5, 473, 486
Nathan, 132, 151
promise of, 117–19, 121–2, 125, 130, 225, 386, 393–5, 549–50
National god, 83, 96–9, 187–8, 420
National religion, 64, 160, 155, 203, 240, 420–7
Nationalistic religious party, 201–2, 237–42, 373–4, 378, 388–90, 398, 414–15, 420, 428, 440–6, 453, 469
Nations,
as God's instrument, 176, 239, 415, 418, 424, 568, 577
as witnesses to Yahweh's action, 421
conversion of, 422, 453, 457, 577, 585

judgment on, 521, 589
pilgrimage of, 420 457, 574
subjection of, 119, 134, 420, 425,
    453
Nebi Samwil, 94
Nebo, 420
Necromancy, 38, 191, 381
Nehemiah, 438-9, 446-7, 459-60,
    468, 470, 495, 498, 520-2, 557,
    648
  book of, 545-6, 554, 557
  memorandum, 438
Nehushtan, 65, 180, 398
Nergal, 148
New moon festival, 462
New Year, 490
nīr promise, 118-19, 389, 395, 397
Noah, 491, 589
  covenant with, 490, 492, 573
Nomads, 34-6, 45, 71-2, 258, 267
Nomadic religion, 27-8, 34-7, 45,
    52, 62, 89, 97, 105, 154-5, 172
Nomenclature, 95-6 (*see also* Names)
Northern kingdom, 125-6, 139-46,
    170-1, 187-8, 198, 200-2, 388,
    394-7, 398-400, 524-5, 550
  downfall of, 179-80, 181-2,
    229-30, 237
  monarchy of, 116, 140-1, 148-9,
    152-3
  traditions of, 224
Nuzi, 36-8, 152, 217-8

Officials, reform, 202-4, 208, 216,
    221-2, 233-4, 241, 377, 379-80,
    382-3, 386, 445, 447, 469, 478,
    512-13
Oligarchy, 448
Onias III, 536, 540, 588, 594
Opposition groups, 66, 113-14
  apocalyptic, 534
  political, 19, 122-4, 227, 234, 241,
    393
  prophetic, 150, 159, 164, 177-80,
    224, 370, 457, 566
  religious, 19-20, 60, 63-4, 587
  religious literature of, 164, 575
  theology, 224, 457
Oppression, 122, 134, 522, 536, 550,
    573, 590, 593
Ordeal, 173
Outlaws, 72, 75

Pacifism, 36, 167-8
pāḥad yizḥaq, 36

Pantheon, 52, 63, 78, 133, 206
Paraenesis, 183, 204-5, 409, 594-5
Parent-child relationship, 19, 100,
    401, 403
Parents, command about, 94, 214
Passover, 35, 90, 208, 213, 222-3,
    253, 390, 407, 410, 467, 475, 548
  and mazzoth, 208, 213, 410, 462
paterfamilias, 92-3, 204, 403-4, 408,
    411
'Patriarchal religion', 28-39, 44
Patriarchs,
  as figures for families to identify
    with, 404
  as models for the return, 406, 473
  covenant with, 404-6
  gods of, 27-32, 44, 76
  promise of increase to, 27, 406, 471,
    491
  promise of land to, 27, 228, 394,
    405, 473, 477
Peace, 36, 80, 92-3, 120, 137, 167-8,
    492, 505, 567, 582
Pentateuch, 23, 438-9, 445-6,
    466-93, 499, 503, 531, 536, 541,
    546-8, 557, 561-2, 580-2, 590
  canonization of, 440, 466-70, 494,
    506, 531, 539, 557
  dating of, 470, 548
  end of, 473
  interpretation of, 547-9, 578
  origin of, 20-1, 455-6
  pre-priestly compositon of, 469,
    471-82, 487-90, 492-3, 557
  priestly composition of, 427, 430-4,
    470, 480-93, 547-8, 557
  redaction of, 468
  Samarian adoption of, 470, 531
Penuel, 141, 143
Persia, 417, 439, 443-7, 451, 452-3,
    456, 473, 478, 493, 521, 531, 534,
    565-8, 577, 585, 592-3, 616-19
  economic policy of, 446, 496-7, 504
  imperial authorization by, 466-8,
    470, 473, 539
  provincial administration, 446, 449
  religious policy of, 443-4, 447, 451,
    466-8
Pharisees, 534, 539, 543
Philistines, 70, 74, 108-9, 112-13,
    115, 251-2, 403, 567
Phoenicia, 97-8, 131, 148-9, 153-4,
    191, 392, 567
Piety, personal, 19, 21, 149, 177-80,
    187-9, 211, 215, 233, 235, 277,

353, 374, 398, 404–5, 439, 463,
  502, 513, 522, 533, 559
ethical permeation of, 212–16, 511,
  513–14, 516, 560
link with official religion, 210–16,
  400–1
orientation on Torah, 558, 562
split in, 441–508
theologizing, 441–2, 508, 510, 513,
  520, 557
universality, 20, 32, 98, 408, 511
Pilgrimage, 101, 203, 207, 216, 465
festival, 208, 410, 548
Pious, 195, 506, 509, 511, 517–21,
  539–40, 553, 560–3, 569, 573,
  584, 593, 596–7
community of the, 585–6, 596–7
Pledge, 160, 165, 184, 216, 494
Pluralism, internal religious, 19, 28,
  39, 95–9, 114, 150, 178, 187–9,
  194, 210, 215, 246, 369, 439, 507,
  512, 557
Polygamy, 33
Polytheism, 37, 61–4, 78, 133, 135,
  144, 148, 171, 417, 538
Polyyahwism, 83, 206–7
Poor, 160, 171, 183, 195, 200,
  216–17, 261, 494, 500, 505–6,
  518–19, 521, 536, 567–8, 571,
  595–7
care of, 216, 218–24
piety of, 441–2, 505–6, 508,
  511–12, 517–22, 536, 560–2,
  572, 587
tithe for, 216, 222, 461
welfare of, 91, 185, 176
Popular assembly, 73–5, 93, 447, 496
Population,
growth, 108, 160, 183, 537, 541
lack of, 477–91
Post-exilic period, assessment of, 3–4,
  6, 9–13, 257, 437, 615–16
Poverty, 161–2, 512, 519–20
religious compensation for, 522
Powers, division of, 201, 435–6
Priestly tradition, 438, 548
Priests, 39, 57–60, 85–100, 101, 121,
  128–9, 143, 171–4, 184, 193, 204,
  210, 219–22, 224–5, 233–4, 240,
  348, 360, 373, 375–7, 379, 436,
  438–9, 447, 448–9, 456, 460,
  474–6, 481–2, 485, 488–9, 536,
  540–2, 548, 603, 622, 650
college of, 440, 446–7, 455, 468,
  481, 487, 535, 539
consecration of, 463, 474, 482

Jerusalem, 202–4, 207, 220–2, 234,
  237, 388, 391, 395
provincial, 202, 207–8, 220–3, 428,
  430, 461, 591
provision for, 433, 461, 482, 549
reform, 132, 202, 426–9, 445, 461,
  481, 512, 548
theology of, 133, 382, 410, 440,
  480–96
subdivision of, 429–32, 436, 460,
  470, 481–2, 488, 548
Promise, 466, 477, 546
conditional, 386, 395, 405, 455,
  501, 551
fulfilment of, 391, 419
non-fulfilment of, 454, 462–3
unconditional, 34, 405, 452
Prophecy, Prophets, 4, 6, 19, 93, 100,
  125, 141, 150–6, 159–80, 202,
  224, 238–41, 326, 379–87, 397,
  402, 414–26, 428–36, 451–8, 478,
  503–7, 550, 566–75, 590
calling of, 478
court, 151, 167, 452
cultic, 151, 171–2, 233, 379, 388,
  414, 520
disciples of, 164, 169, 177, 370
ecstatic, 151, 177, 479
eschatological, 445, 456–8, 478,
  503–7, 554, 565–75, 577, 579,
  581, 585, 641, 663
'false', 237–42, 454
groups of, 151, 163, 177
interpretation of, 383, 415, 440,
  506, 558
of judgment, 159, 163–77, 203, 370,
  379–80, 382–3, 388, 416, 504,
  550, 568
of salvation, 167, 238, 240, 402,
  405, 414–15, 440, 451, 457, 471,
  478, 504, 550, 565
reception of, 379, 412, 414, 550
Prophetic books, redaction of,
  379–80, 382–7, 478
Prophetic opposition theology,
  163–80, 441, 566–70
Protest, religious, 402, 441
Psalms, 95–7, 117–22, 131–8, 377–8,
  501, 509–23, 661–2
canonization of, 443
cult-prophetic, 519
genres, mixed, 177–8, 401–3,
  509–11, 572–3
royal, 116–22
wisdom, 500–2, 519
Zion, 136–7

Ptolemies, 535–6, 540, 580, 586
  economic policy of, 536
  religious policy of, 576
Purity,
  cultic, 377–8
  ritual, 408
    commands for, 408, 489
    rites of, 192–3, 464

Qumran, 543, 565, 575

Rebellion, 43, 110, 112–13, 122–3,
    140–3, 166, 455, 566
  inspired by apocalyptic, 538, 580–1,
    587, 588–91, 553
Rechabites, 154
Reeds, Sea of, 46–7, 80
Reform, social, 185, 203, 233, 235,
    379, 382, 400, 409, 434–6, 475,
    494–5, 543
Release, year of, *see* Shemitta
Resident alien, 75, 151 (*see also*
    Aliens)
Rest, day of, 102, 409
Resurrection, 571, 574
  general, 575, 592
  of Israel, 403
  of the just, 513, 575, 583–4, 592,
    596–7
  to judgment, 521, 596–7
Reunion of Israel and Judah, 554, 569
Revelation, 7–8, 227–8, 483, 490,
    516, 547, 559, 565, 579, 582, 588,
    590
Revolution, 55–6, 506, 556
Retribution, *see* Reward
Reward, 92, 501, 560, 596–7
Riches, 595, 599
  as god, 499, 502, 514
  as God's blessing, 161–2, 218
Righteous, the, 448, 499–502, 504,
    571, 578, 581, 583, 596
Righteousness, 93, 166, 171, 195,
    236, 492, 504, 517, 571–2, 578
  of God, 514, 517, 520
Rome, 173, 527, 543
Rule,
  absolute, 420, 424, 426, 589, 593
  alien, 444, 447, 456, 481, 503, 584,
    590
  'democratic', 473, 549
  religious destabilization of, 169,
    176, 420, 543, 567–8, 585
  religious legitimation of, 78, 115–17

religious legitimation of alien, 569,
    578, 590
  totalitarian, 420, 584, 593
Rule of God, *see also* Kingdom of
    God
  destabilizing, 76, 378, 391, 414, 416
  establishment of, 122–3, 169, 176,
    420, 424–6, 550, 567–8, 571
  non-violent, 568
  strengthening the weak, 426
Ruler cult, Hellenistic, 578, 584

Sabbath, 102, 386, 408–10, 462, 491,
    535, 541, 607
  as family festival, 408–9
  as full moon festival, 408
  commandment, 214, 408–10, 490
Sabbatical year, 217–18, 481, 486
Sacral law, 93, 152
'Sacred marriage', *see also hieros
    gamos*, 331
Sacrifice, 57, 121, 207, 282, 341–2,
    386, 410, 433, 460, 463–4, 489,
    548, 549, 560
  animal, 37, 84, 100, 369
  laws of, 482, 486
  priestly portions of, 433, 461, 488–9
Sacrificial cult, 28–9, 171–4, 462,
    471, 476, 482–3
Sacrificial meal, 85, 89–91, 90–2,
    208, 211, 221–2, 430, 461, 463,
    475, 548
  eschatological, 574
  polemic against, 171, 173, 521
Sadducees, 543
Salvation,
  announcement of, *see also* Promise,
    151, 379, 414, 504–6
  oracle of, 96–7, 101, 178, 212, 414,
    477
  unconditional, 550
Salvation history, 23, 95–7, 231, 525,
    551, 562, 593
  collapse of, 376, 387, 401, 405
  conception of, 166–7, 169, 174,
    213, 227–8, 555, 589–91
  dispute over, 546
  formulation of, 471–3
  limitation of to Judah, 528–9
  relationship of individual to, 95,
    213, 215, 512
Samaria, 88, 149, 529, 570
Samarians, 306, 399, 445, 449, 524,
    526, 531–2
Samaritans, 523–5, 529, 646

Samaritan schism, 470, 523–32, 546, 569

Sanballat, 527–8, 530–2

Sanctuary, *see also* Temple
  as place of asylum, 93, 130, 184, 208
  as temple, 88
  national, 127–32, 140, 143, 171, 198
  on high places, 59, 84–8, 101, 128, 180–1, 209, 390, 395, 397
  royal, 88, 127–8, 140, 143, 171–2, 198, 207, 395–6

Sanhedrin, 535

Sardinia, 191–2

Saturn, 193

Saul, 98, 108–10, 124–5, 141, 170, 590

Scapegoat, 463

Sects, formation of, 448–50, 453

Seleucids, 535, 540, 542–3, 580–1, 586, 588, 593–4

Settlement, 23, 69–72, 95, 105, 108, 173–4, 213, 228, 384, 391, 473

Shaddai, 27, 30

Shamash, 98, 135, 189, 198, 233

Shaphan, 201–2

Shaphanids, 201, 234, 236, 241, 383, 469, 624

Sheba revolt, 110, 123

Shechem, 76, 84–5, 89, 143, 224, 525, 527, 532

Shema yiśrā'ēl, 462

Shemitta, 217–18, 231, 385, 481, 496, 545

Showbread, 461
  table of, 131, 458, 484

Sicily, 191–2

Sidon, 148–9

Shiloh, 57, 83–4, 88, 90, 101, 108, 132, 141, 221

Simon II, 538–40, 587

Sin, 166, 235, 378, 389, 401, 416, 424, 463, 511, 553, 557
  confession of, 511
  forgiveness of, 415, 463, 511
  of Jeroboam, 139, 396–7, 525

Sinai, *see also* Horeb, 51–5, 90, 96, 136, 154, 474, 482, 543

Sinai covenant, 65, 105, 230, 474

Sinai tradition, 52–3, 227

Slaves, 15, 161, 323, 359, 409–10, 493–8, 500, 573
  liberation of, 501
  trade, 373

Slavery, 219

for debt, 160, 165, 185, 218–19, 385, 495–6, 498, 501, 536

Society
  acephalous, 75, 79, 95
  egalitarian, 71, 74–5, 79, 93, 159–60, 166, 435–6, 446
  politically split, 162, 170, 236–41, 540
  pre-state, 72–6, 166–7, 435, 443–4, 447, 472
  religious integration of, 15, 236, 447–8, 499–501, 543, 562
  religious split in, 450, 507, 541, 553
  retribalized, 435–6, 447, 485
  segmentary, 75, 109, 113
  social split in, 160–2, 166, 186, 223, 233, 496–501, 505–6, 508–11, 518, 535–6, 543, 553–6, 541, 573
  tribal, 28–9, 73–6, 109–11, 124, 374–5

Sociology of religion, 18–19, 99, 105, 512, 557, 649–53

Solidarity, 72, 78, 80–1, 91, 164–5, 218–19, 222–3, 233–4, 373, 391, 447, 481, 498, 501–2, 508, 538, 566, 572, 574, 580, 637

Solomon, 44–5, 110–12, 116, 128, 140–2, 148, 225, 291, 392, 531, 543–8, 550

Son of man, 586

Southern kingdom, 187–8, 200, 387
  downfall of, 232–42, 376, 398, 476, 492

Spain, 191–2

Spirit of God, 81, 121, 125, 453, 457, 479–80

Star cult, 189–90, 199, 209, 210, 233, 385, 396

Stars, 82, 133, 189–90, 194

State,
  formation of, 105, 108–14, 159, 506, 595
  restoration of, 445, 451–4, 532–4, 541–4, 554, 569, 595

Statehood, loss of, 241, 369, 374, 389–90, 400, 406, 424, 430, 439, 449

Storm god, 50, 52, 82, 89, 144

Suicide, 517

Sumer, 24, 29, 38, 79, 87, 121–2

Sun cult, 135

Synagogue, 508
  community, 381–2, 464, 521, 533

Syncretism, 20, 59, 63–4, 78, 85, 87, 97, 138, 146, 172–3, 175, 200, 207, 228, 233, 304, 374, 387,

390–3, 396–7, 512, 524, 532, 557, 642
diplomatic, 62, 148, 154–5, 194, 209, 225, 392, 395
imperial, 133
official, 148, 206–9, 312–22, 392
political, 181, 184, 188, 398
pre-state, 76–8, 145
private, 188–95, 210–11, 216, 374
state, 129, 132–8, 144, 153–4, 394
unconscious, 99, 373
Syria, 130–1, 190, 192
'Syro-Ephraimite war', 162, 167, 168, 177, 398

Taanach, 99
Tabernacles, feast of, 88–91, 143, 462
Tabor, 83
Tabu, 102, 185, 222, 408
Tāmīd sacrifice, 128, 408, 462, 548, 593
Tax, exemption from, 216
Taxes, 110–12, 128, 160, 162, 216, 225, 372, 446, 448, 495, 537, 543, 580, 685
Tell er-ras, 527
Temple, 297–8, 435, 455–6, 482, 490, 492
architecture, 130–2
at Elephantine, 374
dedication of, 462, 482, 491, 548, 594–5
destruction of Jerusalem, 241, 376–8, 591
economy, 448, 460–2
First Jerusalem, 64, 87–8, 128–32, 172, 188, 198, 206, 238, 388, 302, 429, 458, 546, 549
Jerusalem, 56–7, 377, 427, 428, 431, 528, 431, 602
police, 460
Samarian, 155
Second Jerusalem, 458–64, 526, 546, 591
singers, 380, 415, 460, 551, 553
Solomonic, 120, 392, 394, 484, 546, 548, 552
tax, 357, 432, 435, 460, 549
treasure, 535, 542
Tent of meeting, 57, 476, 483–4, 630
Tent sanctuary, 57
Teraphim, 37, 381
Tetragrammaton, 49–51
Thanksgiving, celebration, 101, 211, 402, 509

of individual, 96, 402, 441, 514, 519
Theodicy, 166–7, 412, 502–3, 514–15, 517
Theocracy, 4–5, 438, 539, 550, 553–4
Theology, personal, 441–2, 508, 511–23, 556–63
Tiamat, 134
Tithe, 111, 216, 223, 357, 435, 461
Tobiads, 530, 536, 537, 580, 651
Tophet, 190, 385
Torah piety, 443, 484–91, 492, 660–3
Trade, 74–5, 109, 112, 447, 536–7, 541
ban on, 408, 541
Transhumance, 35
Transportation, Rapture, 533
Tribal alliance, 73–4, 78, 81, 83, 109–10, 124, 270, 435
Tribal leaders, 74, 92–3, 434
Tribe, 29, 44, 60, 73–4, 83, 270
Tribute, 111, 162–3, 169, 174, 233, 421, 536, 537
Trito-Isaiah, 438, 456–7, 566, 577
Trito-Zechariah, 570
Tyre, 112, 148–9

Ugarit, 10, 30, 38, 85–6, 133–4, 136, 144, 172, 191, 255, 490
Underworld, 38, 583
Universalism, 4, 6, 134, 136, 176, 228, 238, 375, 406, 420–4, 439, 453, 472–3, 490–3, 522, 572, 577–9, 589
Upper class, 159–60, 161–7, 195, 200, 217–17, 223, 233, 235, 242, 324, 371, 374, 385, 428–39, 441, 447–8, 505, 511–12, 521, 536–9, 561, 569, 578–80, 584
anti-social, 499, 501, 505, 509–10, 553–4, 561–2, 595
city, 647
conflict of loyalty in, 447–8, 497–8
Hellenized, 538, 540–2, 572–3, 581–5, 587
Jerusalem, 202
loyal to the Torah, 538, 540–2, 583–4
socially commited, 498, 500–7, 510, 519, 553, 560–3
split in, 185, 202, 234–5, 241, 439, 489, 538–40, 543
Urbanization, 112
Urim and Thummim, 59, 88
Utopia, 47, 199, 223, 625

Vassal treaties, 205, 229
Violence, monopoly of, 160
structural, 161, 495–7, 503
Vision, 427, 429, 453, 571, 582, 586, 592

War, 36, 47, 49–81, 136, 162–3, 209, 378, 535, 540, 579
civil, 487, 497, 542, 570, 594
of conquest, 111, 120, 122–3, 134, 393, 406, 420, 424–5, 542
of religion, 154–6, 538, 541–3, 587
pre-state, 79–82, 115–16, 225
state, 79–80, 111, 115–16, 120, 134, 167–9, 393, 421, 424
Wealth, *see* Riches
Weeks, Feast of, 89–90, 102, 462
Weeks of years, 593, 596
Wicked, *see also* Upper class, Antisocial, Hellenized
Widows and orphans, 165, 185, 219, 222, 497
Wilderness, 23, 62, 64, 66, 90, 169, 174, 256
Wisdom,
court, 165, 512
mediation of in revelation, 561
speculative, 561
theologized, 438, 441, 507–8, 512–13, 559–62
literature, 113, 557
tradition, 202, 208, 433, 499, 512–13, 560, 595
Woman, 33–4, 81, 91, 185, 252–3, 275, 402–4, 534
Wrath of God, 66, 170, 235, 568

Yahweh, 49–52, 260, 301, 419–20, 490, 658
as leader of a tribe, 63, 66
as liberator, 52, 62–3, 76, 82, 122, 143, 145–6, 185, 213–15, 404, 410, 520, 522
as owner of the land, 79, 89
as personal God, 215
as warrior, 47, 82, 420–1
cherubic throne of, 130, 132
cult of,
at Bethel, 143–6, 198, 525, 530
ethical permeation of, 226, 395
exclusiveness of, 181, 184, 188, 198, 207, 233, 235, 399, 533
in Jerusalem, 128–38, 180–4, 198–209, 526, 529–30, 549, 554
split in, 143, 532

day of, 570
distanced from the cult, 168, 172, 176, 227, 370, 378, 591
distanced from political power, 168, 176, 227, 370, 378, 419–46, 568
God of Israel, 62–3, 77, 83, 215, 228, 403–4, 420
Hadad type, 50, 52, 62, 78
his tie with a group of people, 483
his tie with a place, 60, 79, 89, 131, 226, 228, 240
judge of the world, 520
king of gods, 63, 77–8, 133, 228, 425
king of Israel, 124, 393–4, 404, 425, 550, 657
king of nations, 119, 124, 134, 145, 176, 228, 425, 550
of Bethel, 206
of Hebron, 83, 101, 206
of Samaria, 83, 98, 100, 206
of Teman, 51, 86, 101
on the side of the weak, 166, 176–7, 567
only God, 418–20, 425–6, 472–3
ruler of the world, 119, 132, 138, 168, 176, 228, 377, 384, 415, 421, 424, 426, 453
universality of, 134, 138, 176, 228, 391
Yahweh religion, 47–9, 264, 606–8
crisis of, 369–70, 400
definition of, 471–4, 482–4, 489, 547
during the state, 105, 224, 227–8, 389, 435–6, 471, 555
ethical claim of, 167, 177, 186, 206, 369, 501
exclusivist tendency of, 49, 59, 64, 98, 155, 169, 174
exclusivity of, 168, 171, 174, 194, 209–10, 215, 228, 235
integration of, 440–4, 534
legal formulation of, 176–7, 183–6
openness to Hellenization, 540–2
pre-state, 46–66, 75–94, 105, 121–2, 124, 134, 143, 146, 150, 154, 156, 174, 205, 224, 230, 389, 435, 471, 484, 549, 555, 574
renewal of, 159, 176–8, 181–6, 223–31, 397, 531
social potential of, 48, 94, 166, 185–6, 218–19, 223–4, 390, 410, 426, 436, 455, 507, 597
split in, 370, 439–44, 449, 539

tie to history, 56, 89, 134, 174–5, 213, 215
Yam, 97, 136

Zadok, 129, 132, 135, 295
Zadokides, 59, 129, 220–1, 394, 427–9, 430–1, 460, 528, 532, 536, 543
Zaphon, 136
Zarathustra, 417
Zechariah, 440, 452, 455–6, 558
 redaction of, 441, 445, 455, 468
Zephaniah, 202
Zerubbabel, 444–5, 451, 452, 459–55

Zion, 145, 179, 240, 402, 456, 579, 585
 as guarantee of salvation, 136, 168, 233, 240, 376, 394, 552
 as centre of the world, 136, 453
 as God's dwelling, 131, 136, 156–8, 226, 376, 378, 429, 483, 574
 peaceful kingdom of, 137, 567
 Yahweh's rule from, 136
 battle of nations against, 136, 590
Zion theology, 135–7, 168, 224, 226–8, 233, 240, 376, 378, 394, 415, 421, 425, 435, 471, 484, 531, 551